Issues for Debate in
American Public Policy

Issues for Debate in American Public Policy

ELEVENTH EDITION

CQ PRESS

A Division of SAGE
Washington, D.C.

SELECTIONS FROM CQ RESEARCHER

CQ Press
2300 N Street, NW, Suite 800
Washington, DC 20037

Phone: 202–729–1900; toll-free, 1–866–4CQ-PRESS (1–866–427–7737)

Web: www.cqpress.com

Cover design: www.RichdesignStudio.com
Cover photos: Getty Images
Composition: C&M Digitals (P) Ltd.

☺ The paper used in this publication exceeds the requirements of the American National Standard for Information Sciences—Permanence of Paper for Printed Library Materials, ANSI Z39.48–1992.

Printed and bound in the United States of America

14   13   12   11   10   1   2   3   4   5

A CQ Press College Division Publication

Director	Brenda Carter
Acquisitions editor	Charisse Kiino
Marketing manager	Christopher O'Brien
Managing editor	Stephen Pazdan
Production editor	Allyson Rudolph
Electronic production manager	Paul Pressau

ISSN: 1543–3889
ISBN: 978–1–60426–729–7

Contents

BUSINESS AND THE ECONOMY

HOMELAND SECURITY AND FOREIGN POLICY

Annotated Contents

The sixteen *CQ Researcher* reports reprinted in this book have been reproduced essentially as they appeared when first published. In the few cases in which important developments have since occurred, updates are provided in the overviews highlighting the principal issues examined.

EDUCATION

Revising No Child Left Behind

President Obama is proposing a substantial overhaul of the No Child Left Behind act, the controversial centerpiece of George W. Bush's educational policy. Both liberal and conservative critics say the eight-year-old law has hurt education by overemphasizing standardized tests and unfairly labeling schools as underperforming without providing help to improve. Obama wants to focus federal enforcement on the lowest-performing schools, which could be required to fire staff, convert to charter schools or close altogether. He also wants to hold teachers more accountable for student performance. State policymakers and many experts are welcoming the proposed changes, but the powerful teachers' unions say firing teachers is unfair and ineffective in raising student achievement. Obama also wants states to adopt national "core standards" developed by the states' governors and education chiefs.

The Value of a College Education

President Obama's $12 billion American Graduation Initiative—announced in July 2009—aims to help millions more Americans earn degrees and certificates from community colleges. The president wants the United States to have, once again, the highest proportion of college graduates in the world. Along with the administration, economists and many students and parents embrace the notion that higher education offers the most promising ticket to financial security and upward mobility. However, some argue that many young people are ill-prepared or unmotivated to get a four-year degree and should pursue apprenticeships or job-related technical training instead. The debate is casting a spotlight on trends in high-school career and technical education—long known as vocational education—and raising questions about the ability of the nation's 1,200 community colleges to meet exploding enrollment demand.

Bilingual Education vs. English Immersion

More than 5 million public school students have limited English proficiency, and the number is growing. Most English learners enter school behind fluent English speakers, and many never catch up either in language or other academic areas. In the 1960s and '70s, the federal government supported bilingual education: teaching English learners in both their native language and in English. A backlash developed in the 1980s and '90s among critics who attacked bilingual education as academically ineffective and politically divisive. They favored instead some form of "English immersion." Educators and policy makers continue to wage bitter debates on the issue, with each of the opposing camps claiming that research studies support its position. Some experts say the debate should focus instead on providing more resources, including more and better-trained teachers.

THE ENVIRONMENT

Climate Change

Delegates from around the globe arrived in Copenhagen, Denmark, for the U.N. Climate Change Conference in December 2009 hoping to forge a significant agreement to reduce greenhouse gas emissions and temper climate change. But despite years of diplomatic preparation, two weeks of intense negotiations and the clamor for action from thousands of protesters outside the meeting, the conferees adopted no official treaty. Instead, a three-page accord—cobbled together on the final night by President Barack Obama and the leaders of China, India, Brazil and South Africa—established only broad, nonbinding goals and postponed tough decisions. Yet defenders of the accord praised it for requiring greater accountability from emerging economies such as China, protecting forests and committing billions in aid to help poorer nations. But the key question remains: Will the accord help U.N. efforts to forge a legally binding climate change treaty for the world's nations?

CIVIL LIBERTIES AND CIVIL RIGHTS

Gays in the Military

Political passions over the ban on open homosexuality in the U.S. military are stirring again. A new legislative fight on the issue has headed for House and Senate hearings, as Iraq War veteran Rep. Patrick J. Murphy, D-Pa., proposed legislation to end sexuality-based discrimination in the armed forces. Under the "don't ask, don't tell" policy, gays and lesbians are barred from military service unless their orientation stays hidden. The policy was designed as a compromise to a 1993 call to lift the ban. Supporters of the policy say dropping it would degrade the "unit cohesion" that is critical to battlefield effectiveness. But Murphy and some other recent vets argue that most of today's warriors don't care about their comrades' sexuality. In another element of political drama, some gay political activists are questioning President Barack Obama's level of commitment to pushing for repeal, as he has promised to do.

Government and Religion

A decades-long culture war over the relationship between government and religion and the role of faith in civil society shows no sign of abating. New cases are coming before the Supreme Court, and fresh conflicts are arising over the placement of religious displays on public property and the use of government money to support faith-based social-service programs. At the heart of the battle lies the question of whether the United States was formed as a "Christian nation"—as many conservatives contend—or whether the Founding

Fathers meant to build a high wall of separation between church and state. President Obama outraged conservatives when he declared, "we do not consider ourselves a Christian nation or a Jewish nation or Muslim nation" but a "nation of citizens who are bound by ideals and a set of values." Still, the share of Americans who profess to be Christians has been shrinking, while the percentage who claim no religious preference has nearly doubled since 1990.

SOCIAL POLICY AND SOCIAL MOVEMENTS

Gun Rights Debates

The Supreme Court gave gun rights advocates a major victory in June 2008, recognizing for the first time an individual right under the Second Amendment to own and possess firearms. The 5-4 decision struck down a handgun ban adopted by the District of Columbia in 1976. Gun rights advocates the very same day began challenging similar bans in Chicago and elsewhere. In his majority opinion, Justice Antonin Scalia said the decision did not invalidate laws establishing qualifications to buy weapons, limiting the carrying of weapons in "sensitive" places or barring possession by felons or the mentally ill. Dissenting justices argued the ruling misinterpreted the history of the Second Amendment and would lead the court into striking down many gun laws. Gun control groups hope the ruling sets the stage for more reasoned debate over gun regulations by removing the specter of confiscation of weapons. But gun owners plan to use the ruling to challenge licensing schemes and to urge state legislators to ease restrictions on carrying weapons in public.

Housing the Homeless

The face of homelessness is changing in the United States. In the past, the homeless typically were single men and women who lived on the street or in shelters; many were mentally ill or drug addicts, or both. But today's homeless may well be a suburban couple with children who lost their home to foreclosure and are staying with relatives or living at a shelter. As the recession continues to ravage the middle class and the working poor, job losses and medical emergencies add to the number of homeless Americans. Advocates for the homeless also cite a shortage of affordable housing. A 2008 federal government survey showed a one-year 9 percent increase in families relying on homeless shelters. Local governments and school districts have reported homelessness cases more than doubling in 2009. But funding shortages may force agencies that help the homeless to curtail services.

Prisoner Reentry

Nearly three-quarters of a million prisoners were released from state and federal prisons in 2009—an unprecedented number—and about half of them will be returned to prison over the next three years after committing new crimes or violating parole. As the recession makes it harder for ex-prisoners to find jobs and limits states' ability to house rising numbers of inmates, worries about revolving-door incarceration are escalating. Many experts see an answer to the problem in so-called reentry programs, which are designed to lower recidivism by helping soon-to-be-released or newly released prisoners land on their feet, sometimes assisting them in getting jobs before leaving prison. But even after enactment of former President George W. Bush's Second Chance Act, which supports reentry programs, they remain relatively scarce. In fact, in many states, funding for prison needs has overtaken proposals to pay for reentry.

Tea Party Movement

The Tea Party movement seemed to come out of nowhere. Suddenly, citizens angry over the multi-billion-dollar economic stimulus and the Obama administration's health-care plan were leading rallies, confronting lawmakers and holding forth on radio and TV. Closely tied to the Republican Party—though also critical of the GOP—the movement proved essential to the surprise victory of Republican Sen. Scott Brown in Massachusetts. Tea partiers say Brown's election proves the movement runs strong outside of "red states." But some political experts voice skepticism, arguing that the Tea Party's fiscal hawkishness won't appeal to most Democrats and many independents. Meanwhile, some dissension has appeared among tea partiers, with many preferring to sidestep social issues, such as immigration, and others emphasizing them. Still, the movement exerts strong appeal for citizens fearful of growing government debt and distrustful of the administration.

BUSINESS AND THE ECONOMY

Financial Bailout

Bowing to doomsday warnings that the U.S. and global financial systems could collapse, Congress passed a $700 billion rescue bill in October 2008. Part of a sweeping $1 trillion government plan to calm the stock market and unfreeze credit—the unprecedented rescue came amid mounting fears of a deep recession and the collapse of such major financial institutions as Lehman Brothers and Washington Mutual. The government's efforts included the federal takeover of mortgage giants Fannie Mae and Freddie Mac, which together hold or guarantee $5.4 trillion in mortgage loans—45 percent of the national total. The quasi-governmental firms were dragged down by investments in subprime mortgages and other "toxic" financial instruments. Meanwhile, even as the Bush administration and congressional leaders were calling the bailout plan vital, fundamental questions were being raised, including: Is the bailout big enough? And did risky lending by Fannie and Freddie and poor regulatory oversight fuel the crisis?

HOMELAND SECURITY AND FOREIGN POLICY

Interrogating the CIA

Attorney General Eric H. Holder Jr. has asked a career federal prosecutor to reexamine evidence of possible abuses by Central Intelligence Agency operatives years ago in the questioning of "high-value" terrorism suspects. The CIA's role in interrogating detainees has been controversial because the agency used so-called "enhanced" techniques, including waterboarding. Under President George W. Bush, the Justice Department approved the harsh measures even though many critics said some amount to torture. President Obama has now barred the use of the techniques, but former Vice President Dick Cheney is among those who say the practices yielded valuable intelligence that helped keep the country safe after the Sept. 11 terrorist attacks in 2001. A newly released internal CIA report documents several apparent abuses during the interrogation program. The release of the report is said to be hurting morale at the CIA even as it prompts renewed calls for a broad investigation of the Bush administration's policies in the war on terror.

Prosecuting Terrorists

President Obama is under fierce political attack for the administration's decision to try Khalid Sheikh Mohammed, the alleged mastermind of the Sept. 11 attacks, and Umar Farouk Abdulmutallab, the so-called Christmas Day bomber, in civilian courts instead of military tribunals. Republican lawmakers argue the defendants in both cases should be treated as "enemy combatants" and tried in the military commissions established during the Bush administration. Administration officials and Democratic lawmakers say criminal prosecutions are more effective, having produced hundreds of convictions since 9/11 compared to only three in the military system. And they insist that Abdulmutallab is providing useful information under interrogation by FBI agents. But the administration is reconsidering Attorney General Eric Holder's original decision to hold Mohammed's trial in New York City and considering making greater use of military commissions with other terrorism cases.

U.S.-China Relations

Disputes that have bedeviled relations between the United States and China for decades flared up again following President Obama's decision to sell weapons to Taiwan and receive Tibet's revered Dalai Lama. From the U.S. perspective, China's refusal to raise the value of its currency is undermining America's—and Europe's—economic recovery. Beijing also rebuffed Obama's proposal of "a partnership on the big global issues of our time." In addition, the Chinese insist on tackling their pollution problems in their own way, and have been reluctant to support U.S. diplomatic efforts to impose tough sanctions on nuclear-minded Iran. With the central bank of China holding more than $800 billion of the U.S. national debt in the form of Treasury notes, and their economy speeding along at a 9 percent growth rate, the Chinese are in no mood to be accommodating.

Afghanistan Dilemma

More than eight years ago, U.S. forces first entered Afghanistan to pursue the al Qaeda terrorists who plotted the Sept. 11 terror attacks. American troops are still there today, along with thousands of NATO forces. Under a new strategy crafted by the Obama administration, military leaders are trying to deny terrorists a permanent foothold in the impoverished Central Asian country and in neighboring, nuclear-armed Pakistan, whose western border region has become a sanctuary for Taliban and al Qaeda forces. The Afghanistan-Pakistan conflict— "Af-Pak" in diplomatic parlance—poses huge challenges ranging from rampant corruption within Afghanistan's police forces to a multibillion-dollar opium economy that funds the insurgency. But those problems pale in comparison with the ultimate nightmare scenario: Pakistan's nuclear weapons falling into the hands of terrorists, which foreign-policy experts say has become a real possibility.

HEALTH CARE

Health-Care Reform

The health-care reform legislation signed into law by President Obama in March 2010 marked the biggest attempt to expand access to health care since Medicare and Medicaid were launched in the 1960s. The massive legislation will help 32 million Americans get health insurance coverage and bans insurers from denying coverage to those with preexisting illnesses. It also expands Medicaid to all poor people—except illegal immigrants— and gives subsidies to low- and low-middle-income people to buy insurance. But opponents, including every Republican member of Congress, say the coverage expansion is simply too expensive, at a price tag of about $1 trillion over 10 years. They also say new fees and taxes to help pay for the coverage place too big a burden on currently insured people. Meanwhile, a group of state attorneys general is challenging the constitutionality of the law's requirement that everyone buy health insurance.

Preface

Should suspected terrorists be given military or civil trials? Should teachers be held more accountable for students' performance? Will health-care reform make care more affordable? These questions—and many more—are at the heart of American public policy. How can instructors best engage students with these crucial issues? Students need objective, yet provocative, examinations of these issues to understand how they affect citizens today and will for years to come. This annual collection aims to promote in-depth discussion, facilitate further research and help readers formulate their own positions on crucial issues. Get your students talking both inside and outside the classroom about *Issues for Debate in American Public Policy*.

This eleventh edition includes sixteen up-to-date reports by *CQ Researcher*, an award-winning weekly policy brief that brings complicated issues down to earth. Each report chronicles and analyzes executive, legislative and judicial activities at all levels of government. This collection is divided into six diverse policy areas: education; health care; the environment; civil liberties and civil rights; social policy and social movements; business and the economy; and homeland security and foreign policy—to cover a range of issues found in most American government and public policy courses.

CQ RESEARCHER

CQ Researcher was founded in 1923 as *Editorial Research Reports* and was sold primarily to newspapers as a research tool. The magazine was renamed and redesigned in 1991 as *CQ Researcher*. Today, students are its primary audience. While still used by hundreds of journalists and newspapers, many of which reprint portions of the reports, the *Researcher*'s main subscribers are now high school, college and public libraries. In 2002, *Researcher* won the American Bar Association's coveted Silver Gavel award for magazine excellence for a series of nine reports on civil liberties and other legal issues.

Researcher staff writers—all highly experienced journalists—sometimes compare the experience of writing a Researcher report to drafting a college term paper. Indeed, there are many similarities. Each report is as long as many term papers—about 11,000 words—and is written by one person without any significant outside help. One of the key differences is that writers interview leading experts, scholars and government officials for each issue.

Like students, staff writers begin the creative process by choosing a topic. Working with the *Researcher*'s editors, the writer identifies a controversial subject that has important public policy implications. After a topic is selected, the writer embarks on one to two weeks of intense research. Newspaper and magazine articles are clipped or downloaded, books are ordered and information is gathered from a wide variety of sources, including interest groups, universities and the government. Once the writers are well informed, they develop a detailed outline, and begin the interview process. Each report requires a minimum of ten to fifteen interviews with academics, officials, lobbyists and people working in the field. Only after all interviews are completed does the writing begin.

CHAPTER FORMAT

Each issue of *CQ Researcher*, and therefore each selection in this book, is structured in the same way. Each begins with an overview, which briefly summarizes the areas that will be explored in greater detail in the rest of the chapter. The next section chronicles important and current debates on the topic under discussion and is structured around a number of key questions, such as "Can aid to ex-inmates significantly reduce recidivism?" and "Should laws restricting ownership of firearms be relaxed?" These questions are usually the subject of much

debate among practitioners and scholars in the field. Hence, the answers presented are never conclusive but detail the range of opinion on the topic.

Next, the "Background" section provides a history of the issue being examined. This retrospective covers important legislative measures, executive actions and court decisions that illustrate how current policy has evolved. Then the "Current Situation" section examines contemporary policy issues, legislation under consideration and legal action being taken. Each selection concludes with an "Outlook" section, which addresses possible regulation, court rulings and initiatives from Capitol Hill and the White House over the next five to ten years.

Each report contains features that augment the main text: two to three sidebars that examine issues related to the topic at hand, a pro versus con debate between two experts, a chronology of key dates and events and an annotated bibliography detailing major sources used by the writer.

CUSTOM OPTIONS

Interested in building your ideal CQ Press Issues book, customized to your personal teaching needs and interests? Browse by course or date, or search for specific topics or issues from our online catalog of *CQ Researcher* issues at http://custom.cqpress.com.

ACKNOWLEDGMENTS

We wish to thank many people for helping to make this collection a reality. Tom Colin, managing editor of *CQ Researcher*, gave us his enthusiastic support and cooperation as we developed this eleventh edition. He and his talented staff of editors and writers have amassed a first-class library of *Researcher* reports, and we are fortunate to have access to that rich cache. We also thankfully acknowledge the advice and feedback from current readers and are gratified by their satisfaction with the book.

Some readers may be learning about *CQ Researcher* for the first time. We expect that many readers will want regular access to this excellent weekly research tool. For subscription information or a no-obligation

free trial of *Researcher*, please contact CQ Press at www
.cqpress.com or toll-free at 1-866-4CQ-PRESS (1-866-
427-7737).

We hope that you will be pleased by the eleventh edition of *Issues for Debate in American Public Policy*. We
welcome your feedback and suggestions for future

editions. Please direct comments to Charisse Kiino,
Editorial Director, College Publishing Group, CQ Press,
2300 N Street, NW, Suite 800, Washington, D.C.
20037, or *ckiino@cqpress.com*.

—*The Editors of CQ Press*

Contributors

Thomas J. Colin, managing editor of *CQ Researcher*, has been a magazine and newspaper journalist for more than 30 years. Before joining Congressional Quarterly in 1991, he was a reporter and editor at the *Miami Herald* and *National Geographic* and editor in chief of *Historic Preservation*. He holds a bachelor's degree in English from the College of William and Mary and in journalism from the University of Missouri.

Thomas J. Billitteri is a *CQ Researcher* staff writer based in Fairfield, Pa., who has more than 30 years' experience covering business, nonprofit institutions and public policy for newspapers and other publications. His recent *CQ Researcher* reports include "Youth Violence," "Afghanistan's Future" and "Financial Literacy." He holds a BA in English and an MA in journalism from Indiana University.

Marcia Clemmitt is a *CQ Researcher* staff writer and a veteran social-policy reporter who previously served as editor in chief of *Medicine & Health* and staff writer for *The Scientist*. She has also been a high school math and physics teacher. She holds a liberal arts and sciences degree from St. John's College, Annapolis, and a master's degree in English from Georgetown University. Her recent reports include "Preventing Cancer," "Reproductive Ethics" and "Teen Pregnancy."

Roland Flamini is a Washington-based correspondent who writes on foreign affairs for *CQ Weekly*, *The New Republic* and other publications. Fluent in six languages, he served as *Time* bureau chief in Rome, Bonn, Beirut, Jerusalem and the European Common Market and later served as international editor at United Press International. His previous reports for *CQ Researcher* were on Afghanistan, NATO, Latin America, Nuclear Proliferation and U.S.-Russia Relations. His most recent reporting trip to China was in November–December 2009.

Kenneth Jost, associate editor of *CQ Researcher*, graduated from Harvard College and Georgetown University Law Center. He is the author of the *Supreme Court Yearbook* and editor of *The Supreme Court from A to Z* (both *CQ Press*). He was a member of the *CQ Researcher* team that won the American Bar Association's 2002 Silver Gavel Award. His previous reports include "Bilingual Education vs. English Immersion" and "Testing in Schools." He is also author of the blog *Jost on Justice* (http://jostonjustice.blogspot.com).

Reed Karaim, a freelance writer living in Tucson, Arizona, has written for *The Washington Post*, *U.S. News & World Report*, *Smithsonian*, *American Scholar*, *USA Weekend* and other publications. He is the author of the novel, *If Men Were Angels*, which was selected for the Barnes & Noble Discover Great New Writers series. He is also the winner of the Robin Goldstein Award for Outstanding Regional Reporting and other journalism awards. Karaim is a graduate of North Dakota State University in Fargo.

Peter Katel is a *CQ Researcher* staff writer who previously reported on Haiti and Latin America for *Time* and *Newsweek* and covered the Southwest for newspapers in New Mexico. He has received several journalism awards, including the Bartolomé Mitre Award for coverage of drug trafficking, from the Inter-American Press Association. He holds an A.B. in university studies from the University of New Mexico. His recent reports include "New Strategy in Iraq," "Rise in Counterinsurgency" and "Wounded Veterans."

Issues for Debate in
American Public Policy

1

Revising No Child Left Behind

Kenneth Jost

President-elect Barack Obama and newly nominated Secretary of Education Arne Duncan visit with students at the Dodge Renaissance Academy, a public charter school in Chicago, on Dec. 16, 2008. Former Chicago school system chief Duncan is leading the administration's effort to overhaul the unpopular No Child Left Behind law, which calls for regular testing to increase schools' accountability and penalties on underperforming schools.

From *CQ Researcher*,
April 16, 2010.

Getty Images/Ralf-Finn Hestoft-Pool

I n his first year as superintendent of Chicago's schools, Arne Duncan heartily embraced No Child Left Behind, President George W. Bush's signature education initiative. As the bill cleared Congress in December 2001, Duncan applauded the law's emphasis on holding schools accountable and welcomed its promise of additional funds for struggling school districts.

Over the years, however, Duncan chafed under some of the requirements and restrictions imposed by the act — commonly cited as NCLB in educational circles. Late in 2004, Duncan went so far as to threaten to sue the U.S. Department of Education over its insistence that a private company instead of the school system run a tutoring program for struggling students. Education Secretary Margaret Spellings later relented.[1]

Today, as secretary of Education himself under President Barack Obama, Duncan is leading the administration's effort to overhaul the increasingly unpopular eight-year-old law, which requires regular testing to increase schools' accountability and prescribes penalties to discipline underperforming schools. Echoing many complaints from educators and education policy experts, Duncan says the law creates "perverse incentives" for school districts, sometimes encouraging them to lower instead of raise their standards, and fails to measure growth for individual students or to reward schools that raised scores.

"We all recognize that NCLB had its flaws," Duncan told the House Education and Labor Committee on March 17. "The time to fix those problems is now."[2]

The administration described its proposed fixes in a 41-page "Blueprint for Reform" sent to Congress two days earlier.

Few Gains Seen From No Child Left Behind

Students' reading and math scores have improved only minimally since passage of the No Child Left Behind law in 2002. Reading scores for fourth- and eighth-graders have remained stagnant the last two decades, according to the National Assessment of Education Progress, known as "the nation's report card." Math scores for both age groups have risen steadily since the 1990s — at about the same rate both before and after the law was enacted.

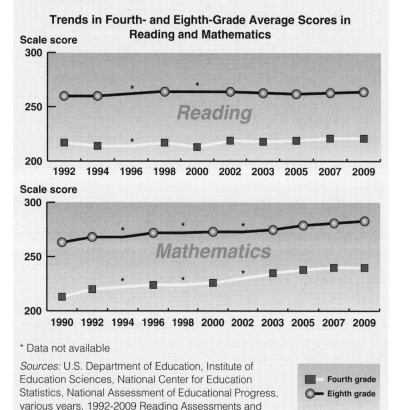

Trends in Fourth- and Eighth-Grade Average Scores in Reading and Mathematics

* Data not available

Sources: U.S. Department of Education, Institute of Education Sciences, National Center for Education Statistics, National Assessment of Educational Progress, various years, 1992-2009 Reading Assessments and 1990-2009 Mathematics Assessments

Fourth grade
Eighth grade

high-school graduates by 2020 college- or career-ready. Toward that end, the blueprint endorses the recent initiative by the states' governors and education chiefs to develop common curriculum standards in English language arts and mathematics.[4] (*See boxes, pp. 7-8; sidebar, p. 15.*)

The blueprint appears to deemphasize test scores somewhat by calling for broader assessments of schools and students, including such measures as graduation rates. But instead of rating all schools, Obama's plan calls for focusing enforcement on the worst-performing schools. They would face the possibility of stringent "restructuring" remedies that range from firing the principal and at least half the teaching staff to turning the school over to new management or closing it altogether.

The administration is drawing praise from a wide range of groups and experts for proposing to dismantle some of the most contentious features of No Child Left Behind. "They've removed a number of the problems with NCLB and have set out a vision of where they want to take schools in the next four to five years," says Jack Jennings, president of the Center for Education Policy, a Washington think tank, and a former staffer for House Education Committee Democrats.

"The general thrust of the Obama proposal strikes me as sensible, given where we stand in the aftermath of NCLB," says Frederick Hess, director of education policy studies at the American Enterprise Institute (AEI), a conservative think tank in Washington. The advocates of No Child Left Behind, Hess says, "allowed their eyes to be bigger than their stomachs."

The Obama proposal is "pretty good," says Patrick McGuinn, an associate professor of political science at

In a two-page introduction, Obama said the proposal is "not only a plan to renovate a flawed law but also an outline for a re-envisioned federal role in education."[3] (*Major provisions, p. 3.*)

The Obama plan calls for several significant changes to No Child Left Behind. First and foremost, perhaps, Obama would replace Bush's call for all students to be proficient in reading and math by 2014 with the goal of having all

Obama Seeks Major Changes in No Child Left Behind

The Obama administration's "Blueprint for Reform" calls for significant changes to No Child Left Behind (NCLB), President George W. Bush signature education initiative.* The widely criticized eight-year-old law calls for regular testing to increase schools' accountability and penalties to impose discipline on underperforming schools. The administration has yet to prepare formal legislation, but here are some of the highlights of the plan:

Blueprint for Reform	No Child Left Behind
Goals	
All students by 2020 to be college- or career-ready when they graduate from high school.	All students must be proficient in reading and math by 2014.
Standards	
States to upgrade existing standards in conjunction with state public university or consider state-developed common standards, geared to college- or career-readiness; must also adopt English language proficiency standards for English language learners.	Each state permitted to adopt its own standards.
Testing	
"New generation of assessments" to be developed to "better capture higher-order skills, provide more accurate measures of student growth and better inform classroom instruction to respond to academic needs."	Standardized testing in reading and math required annually for students in grades 3 through 8 and at least once during high school.
Charter Schools	
Education Department to support expansion of "high-performing" public charter schools and other autonomous public schools.	Authorized funds to aid states and localities in establishing charter schools.
Coverage	
Focus on bottom 5% of schools.	"Adequate yearly progress" applied to all schools.
Penalties	
Four "restructuring" options are to be adopted for the lowest-performing schools: **Transformation model:** Replace principal, strengthen staffing, implement research-based instructional program, extend learning time and implement new governance. **Turnaround model:** Replace principal and rehire no more than 50 percent of school staff; implement research-based instructional program; extend learning time; implement new governance. **Restart model:** Convert or close and reopen school under management of effective charter operator, charter management organization or education management organization. **School-closure model:** Close school; enroll students in higher-performing schools in district.	Provides technical assistance for schools that fail to make "adequate yearly progress" two years in a row; after third year, schools required to offer students supplemental tutoring or allow transfer to higher-performing schools; after fifth year, school must be identified for "reconstitution." Obama blueprint drops tutoring, transfers.

* No Child Left Behind is an amendment to the 1965 Elementary and Secondary Education Act (ESEA), which has been up for renewal since 2007. Obama's blueprint calls for reauthorizing ESEA with amendments to NCLB provisions. Title I of ESEA provides aid to school districts based on their population of "educationally deprived children."

Source: "A Blueprint for Reform: The Reauthorization of the Elementary and Secondary Education Act," U.S. Department of Education, March 2010, www2.ed.gov/policy/elsec/leg/blueprint/blueprint.pdf

AP Photo/Michael Dwyer

Former students mount a silent vigil on March 9, 2010, in support of teachers at chronically underperforming Central Falls High School in Rhode Island after the school board voted to fire most of the staff. President Obama endorsed the move, which is now on hold. "If a school continues to fail its students year after year after year . . . there's got to be a sense of accountability," he said.

Drew University in Madison, N.J., and author of a book tracing the evolution of federal education policy from enactment of the first broad federal aid to education act in 1965 through No Child Left Behind. "It does address a number of the major problems and takes a number of steps in the right direction."[5]

Major education groups, however, quickly move from praise for Obama's proposed NCLB modifications to criticisms of some of the plan's specifics and its lack of detail in several major areas. Anne Bryant, executive director of the National School Boards Association, describes Obama's plan as "a vast improvement" over NCLB but calls for more information about the proposed use of multiple assessments to measure student achievement.

In a prepared statement issued as Obama's plan was being released, Bryant also questioned conditioning federal aid funds on the use of common standards and flatly opposed the automatic replacement of principals at the lowest-performing schools. She closed the statement by saying that the group's decision whether to support the plan would depend on "details yet to be developed."

Meanwhile, the National Education Association (NEA) and American Federation of Teachers (AFT), the two major national teachers' unions, are sharply

denouncing provisions in the plan that judge teacher effectiveness on student assessment scores and include replacement of at least half of the teaching staff as one of the proposed restructuring remedies for failing schools. Citing those provisions, the NEA urges members on its Web site to call on Congress "to rip out the pages of the blueprint that don't work for kids and replace them with better solutions."

No Child Left Behind "created an accountability strategy and didn't focus on instruction," says AFT President Randi Weingarten, "The reason you don't have this huge cheerleading for the blueprint is there's an absence of instructional strategies. What we're saying is that you have to focus on both."

The Obama plan also has been sharply criticized — somewhat surprisingly — by one of the country's leading education scholars: Diane Ravitch, a research professor in education at New York University and author, co-author or editor of two dozen books over the past 35 years. Ravitch, who served as assistant secretary of education under President George H. W. Bush, was a prominent supporter in the 1980s and '90s of such conservative policies as school choice and charter schools.[6]

In her new book, *The Death and Life of the Great American School System*, Ravitch disavows those positions, saying choice and charter schools have undermined the public school system. Ravitch harshly criticizes No Child Left Behind in the book and is now almost equally critical of Obama's plan. She says Obama's plan could result in even greater emphasis on standardized testing than under No Child Left Behind.[7] She also says it threatens underperforming schools with "draconian" restructuring remedies instead of providing constructive assistance to improve. (*See "At Issue," p. 17.*)

Even before proposing a rewrite of No Child Left Behind, the administration began promoting education reform by getting Congress to approve $4.35 billion of stimulus money for competitive grants to states. The "Race to the Top" program called for states to submit proposals to improve standards and assessments, upgrade data systems, strengthen recruitment and training of teachers and turn around lowest-achieving schools. Tennessee and Delaware were announced on March 31 as the first states to receive grants — as much as $502 million and $107 million respectively; a second round of grants is to be announced in September.[8] (*See "Current Situation," p. 16.*)

Duncan made a round of appearances to congressional committees as the education blueprint was released, but no legislation has been introduced yet. With the congressional calendar moving quickly to campaign season, Capitol Hill watchers generally doubt the likelihood of action this year. No Child Left Behind — enacted as an amendment to the 1965 Elementary and Secondary Education Act — has been due for reauthorization since 2007. The law includes language keeping its provisions in force pending reauthorization.

Supporters of NCLB give the law credit for the slight gains registered in test scores since it was enacted. Even so, a wide range of education groups, advocates and experts are voicing a measure of frustration about the lack of broader progress.

"We have an educational system that is stubbornly resistant to providing anything approaching a quality education to minority kids," McGuinn says. "We're now more than 25 years into the reform era. We've had a lot of money poured into the system, and we haven't seen much change."[9]

As Congress and others consider the Obama administration's education blueprint, here are some of the major questions being addressed:

Should states adopt the proposed "common core standards" for English and math?

When Virginia adopted its Standards of Learning in 1995, the state's school superintendent described them as "the most rigorous" educational guidelines ever adopted in the state. For math and science, the standards prescribed algebra and two lab courses for graduation; in English, the standards called for greater emphasis on reading, writing, research and speaking skills.

In 2009, when the nation's governors and state education chiefs began a movement to develop "common core standards" for all states to consider adopting, Virginia joined the effort. When the draft standards were released in March, however, Virginia Gov. Bob McDonnell demurred. "We do not have a desire to substitute the common core standards for our Standards of Learning," McDonnell said.[10]

Virginia's reaction exemplifies one side of the difficulties anticipated in trying to develop common standards, according to Gene Wilhoit, executive director of the Council of Chief State School Officers. "Some states don't want to back away from the commitments they've made," Wilhoit explains.

Overall, however, Wilhoit says the proposed standards are more rigorous than those adopted in most states since the standards movement emerged in the early and mid-'90s. States with less rigorous guidelines, he says, want to be sure that the standards in their final form are "clear and straightforward" to aid their presentation to legislators or school boards for possible adoption.

Education groups and experts are generally praising the proposed standards even as some caution that adoption would be only the first step in actually introducing and teaching them in the classroom. "Our members are very aware that it doesn't make much sense for states to have different standards," says NEA President Dennis Van Roekel.

Chester Finn, a former assistant secretary of education under President Ronald Reagan and a longtime advocate of national standards, calls the proposals "one of the most important events" in public education in recent years. "If this is done well, it's a huge gain for the country to have expectations in common against which results can be measured and made public," says Finn, who is now president of the Washington-based Thomas B. Fordham Institute, an education think tank.

One state, Kentucky, acted quickly to adopt the standards in February on the basis of the then-existing draft and plans to begin using them in the classroom in the fall. At least five other states are actively considering adopting them, according to Dane Linn, education division director at the National Governors Association.[11]

Some other states are balking, however. Karen Klinzing, Minnesota's assistant education commissioner, applauds the proposed English standards but told *Education Week* that the math standards were inadequate. "We would have to go backwards to implement the standards as they are now," Klinzing said of the math draft.[12]

The standards "should be voluntary, not mandated," says Reginald Felton, director of federal relations for the National School Boards Association. "States that want to adopt their own standards ought to be able to do that."

Wilhoit acknowledges the risk that different actions in different states could result in a "patchwork" of standards comparable to the existing pattern. "One of the central purposes was to bring greater coherence and commonality," he says. "If we don't do that, this effort is going to fall short."

Adoption of the standards, however, is only the first step in a process, Wilhoit stresses. "These documents are incomplete of themselves," he says. "We'll need to translate them into curricular development and into a scope and sequence so that teachers can see their particular responsibilities."

Teachers' unions agree. "You need an engaging curriculum," says AFT President Weingarten. "You need to give teachers the education and professional development around that curriculum. And you need to make sure that teachers and kids have the tools to work with that curriculum."

The Obama administration is giving the standards a boost by including in its education blueprint a call for states to adopt "rigorous" standards in English language arts and math and "high-quality statewide assessments" aligned with the standards. The administration stresses that the standards should be "state-developed" and acknowledges "following the lead" of the states' governors and education chiefs. But the administration also is proposing to put some teeth into the push by requiring adoption of adequate standards for receipt of so-called Title I funds, the federal assistance provided under the Elementary and Secondary Assistance Act to schools with high percentages of low-income students.

Despite the many steps needed to adopt and implement the proposed standards, political scientist McGuinn says they are an essential part of the administration's education policies. The administration is "trying to drive states to something substantive that they will feel some pressure to sign on to," he says. "The standards are the crucial piece."

Should the Education Department focus remedial efforts on the worst-performing schools?

About one-third of the nation's public schools — nearly 32,000 out of the total of 94,170 — were listed in the 2008-2009 school year as failing to make "adequate yearly progress," the benchmark established by No Child Left Behind. As enacted, the law sets a goal of 100 percent of students "proficient" in reading and math by 2014 and calls for schools to show "adequate yearly progress" in students' reading and math test scores to reach that goal.

Eight years later, the so-called AYP requirement appears to be the most unpopular of any of the provisions of No Child Left Behind. Education groups and experts across the ideological spectrum say the 100 percent proficiency goal is itself completely unrealistic and the labeling of so many schools as failing is both inherently imprecise and vastly overinclusive.

In fact, the Center on Education Policy, a Washington think tank, forecasts that unless the law is changed, some states would show nearly all of their schools as failing by the 2012-2013 school year. That result, the group warned in a report in March, would render the concept "meaningless" and would "overburden" state departments of education, which are required to provide special assistance to failing schools.[13]

The Obama administration's blueprint would drop the AYP requirement and reporting on failing schools and replace the 100 percent proficiency goal with another ambitious target. By 2020, all students should graduate or be on track to graduate ready for college or a career.

To reach that goal, however, the administration proposes to focus "the most rigorous support and interventions" only on "the very lowest-performing schools and districts" — specifically, the worst-performing 5 percent of schools as well as those with especially high disparities between the highest- and lowest-performing students. The top 10 percent of schools would be eligible for unspecified rewards.

"Tight on goals, loose on means" is the administration's catchphrase to describe the policy. "We don't think we should micromanage schools from Washington," Duncan told reporters in a March 12 conference call as the blueprint was about to be released.[14]

Many experts applaud the decision to focus on the worst-performing schools. "Targeting the worst schools for radical intervention is a better idea than targeting an unmanageable number of schools for unworkable intervention," says the Fordham Institute's Finn.

Political scientist McGuinn agrees. "The Education Department has nothing like the needed administrative capacity to enforce federal requirements," he says.

Some education advocates, however, disagree. "An accountability proposal that doesn't put much pressure on 85 percent of the schools is not going to get there," says Kati Haycock, president of the Education Trust, a Washington-based advocacy group for minorities and low-income families. "It's hugely important that we have a sense of urgency about changing [the worst-performing] schools," Haycock says, "but that doesn't mean that the other 85 percent of schools shouldn't do better."

Under No Child Left Behind, schools that fail to make adequate yearly progress on test scores must provide special tutoring to students or allow students to transfer to other, better-performing schools. The provisions are widely seen as less effective than supporters had hoped. Fewer students took advantage of tutoring than had been expected, and many students at "failing" schools were unable to transfer to a better-performing school within the same district.

The Obama plan drops those provisions altogether. Finn, a supporter of the law, has no objections. "The cascade of sanctions was not working," he says.

But fellow conservative Terry Moe, a senior fellow at the Hoover Institution at Stanford University and a leading advocate of market-based approaches to education reform, disagrees. "In my view they should have been kept," Moe says.

The restructuring remedies proposed in their place for the lowest-performing schools would have significantly more bite. Finn applauds that approach. "A school that manages to get itself in the bottom 5 percent needs radical surgery if anything is to be changed," he says.

Several other experts, however, question the approach. "We don't believe the research is there to support those reform strategies," says Jennings with the Center on Education Policy. "We believe the administration is acting on belief, not on research." Ravitch says the options for new management or closure amount to threatening "death sentences" for 5,000 schools.

Essential Math Skills

To ensure that students are college- and career-ready by the time they graduate from high school, mathematics curricula should encourage the development of the following "common core" skills, according to newly released standards developed by the nation's governors and state education chiefs:

- ***Make sense of problems and persevere in solving them.*** Explain meaning of problem and look for entry points to solution.

- ***Reason abstractly and quantitatively.*** Make sense of quantities and their relationships in problem situations.

- ***Construct viable arguments and critique the reasoning of others.*** Understand stated assumptions and definitions; make conjectures and build logical progression to explore truth of conjectures.

- ***Model with mathematics.*** Apply mathematics to solve problems in everyday life.

- ***Use appropriate tools strategically.*** Use technological tools to deepen understanding of concepts.

- ***Attend to precision.*** Communicate precisely to others.

- ***Look for and make use of structure.*** Look closely to discern pattern or structure.

- ***Look for and express regularity in repeated reasoning.***

Source: "Common Core State Standards for Mathematics," National Governors Association and the Council of Chief State School Officers, March 2010, pp. 5-6, www.corestandards.org/Files/K12MathStandards.pdf

---

"There's nothing in this turnaround model to encourage people to think creatively," says the American Enterprise Institute's Hess, citing as an example the use of distance teaching to strengthen instruction. "I worry that the administration in its desire to offer a model is teeing this up in a way that may lead to a great deal of disappointment."

Should teachers be held more accountable for students' performance?

When teachers at chronically underperforming Central Falls High School in Rhode Island balked at agreeing to extend the school day by 25 minutes without any additional pay, the school board and school superintendent decided on Feb. 23 to fire the entire staff. Termination notices were read aloud at a contentious school board meeting for 93 people altogether, from the principal and

Essential English Skills

To ensure that students are college- and career-ready by the time they graduate from high school, English curricula should stress the following "common core" skills, according to newly released standards developed by the nation's governors and state education chiefs.

- *Demonstrate independence.* Comprehend and evaluate complex tests; construct effective arguments and convey intricate information; ask relevant questions, build on others' ideas and articulate their own.

- *Build strong content knowledge.* Establish base of knowledge across wide range of subject matter; become proficient in new areas through research and study.

- *Respond to varying demands of audience, task, purpose and discipline.*

- *Comprehend as well as critique.* Work to understand author or speaker, but also question assumptions and assess veracity of claims.

- *Use technology and digital media strategically and capably.* Tailor searches online to acquire information efficiently and integrate information with what they learn offline.

- *Come to understand other perspectives and cultures.* Actively seek to understand perspectives and cultures through reading and listening; communicate effectively with people of other backgrounds.

Source: "Common Core State Standards for English Language Arts and Literacy in History/Social Studies and Science," National Governors Association and the Council of Chief State School Officers, March 2010, p. 4, www.corestandards.org/Files/K12ELAStandards.pdf

assistant principal down through 74 classroom teachers and other educational or administrative aides.

The episode gained national attention when President Obama — echoing earlier favorable comments from Education Secretary Duncan — endorsed the board's action. "If a school continues to fail its students year after year after year, if it doesn't show signs of improvement, then there's got to be a sense of accountability," Obama said on March 1. "And that's what happened in Rhode Island last week."[15]

The mass firings are now on hold, pending mediation between the school board and the local teachers' union. But the cooling-off came only after heated comment from NEA and AFT leaders and many individual teachers. Anthony J. Mullen, a Greenwich, Conn., teacher and the current teacher of the year, said the call for firing teachers to improve schools reflects an "off-with-their-heads mentality."[16]

The focus on tenure for individual teachers represents a significant policy change from No Child Left Behind in its present form. "Teachers were not really accountable under No Child Left Behind; schools were," says McGuinn, the Drew University political scientist. "There were no consequences for teachers if students didn't perform."

Conservative education experts are applauding the administration's approach. Increasing teacher accountability is "a good thing," says the Fordham Institute's Finn. "While any given teacher may not have huge control over a kid, the cumulative effect of teachers is the single most important influence on what a kid learns — or maybe the second most important after home and neighborhood."

Leaders of the two national teachers' unions sharply disagree with the administration's approach. They say firing teachers is a punitive approach with no sound basis that ignores other factors in student performance and in the end does little if anything to help students improve.

"The idea that you can measure a teacher's work or a student's work on the basis of a test on a single day is absurd," says the NEA's Van Roekel. "There's no test that you can give that can evaluate what I've taught over the year."

Obama's plan "seems to be holding teachers 100 percent responsible for students' success," says the AFT's Weingarten, "without giving teachers any authority or leverage to get the tools they need to do their jobs and any countervailing responsibility on anyone else."

School management groups also view the administration's approach as too severe. "I would like to see more latitude in terms of model intervention," says Wilhoit of the state education chiefs' group, specifically referring to teacher dismissals. But, he adds, "we need to get serious as a country to turn around these chronically underperforming schools."

"We don't think there are any data out there that show that those remedies will help," says Felton of the school boards association. Some principals or teachers may need to be reassigned, Felton says, but the administration's blueprint "doesn't focus on the skill sets that you need to really turn around any program."

Criticism also has come from Ravitch, the supporter-turned-critic of conservative versions of school choice and accountability. "Wouldn't it make more sense to send in help instead of an execution squad?" Ravitch writes on an *Education Week* blog.[17]

The administration's blueprint ties the firing of teaching staffs with the implementation of "a research-based instructional program" along with a "new governance structure" and "extended learning time." Interestingly, Obama strikes a more supportive tone in the two-page introduction to the blueprint. "We must do better to recruit, develop, support, retain, and reward outstanding teachers in America's classroom," the president writes.

"Some of these schools have real numbers of teachers who either are ineffective or have become discouraged," says American Enterprise Institute expert Hess. "Replacing teachers can bring in more effective teachers and create a necessary sense of urgency. What bothers me is that there's some stock playbook and that somehow this is going to take a consistently underperforming school and put it on a better trajectory."

BACKGROUND

Limited Federal Role

The federal government played only a limited role in public education from the nation's founding until the mid-twentieth century. In the 1950s, however, the Supreme Court's ruling to outlaw racial segregation and the Soviet Union's launching of the first man-made Earth satellite forced the federal government to take on roles to promote equal opportunity and improve math and science education. Congress followed in the 1960s by passing the first broad program for federal aid to education, an anti-poverty measure renewed repeatedly over the

years and later given a broader mandate as the foundation of President Bush's No Child Left Behind Act.[18]

Public education was itself in an embryonic stage through much of the 19th century. Two early laws, the Lands Ordinance Act of 1785 and the Northwest Ordinance of 1787, helped spur school construction by setting aside funds from the sale of unsettled lands to fund public education. During the Civil War, Congress passed the Morrill Act, which similarly devoted proceeds from the sale of public lands to support land-grant colleges in the states.

After the Civil War, Congress went further by requiring newly admitted states to establish systems of free, non-sectarian public education. Only in 1917, however, did Congress approve direct aid to public education. With wartime manpower shortages in mind, Congress passed the Smith-Hughes Act to provide matching funds to states for vocational education.

Education assumed a greater importance after World War II, according to political scientist McGuinn, as high school graduation became a norm and many returning veterans enrolled in college under the GI Bill of Rights. Meanwhile, the decades-long litigation strategy aimed at desegregating public education culminated with the Supreme Court's 1954 decision in *Brown v. Board of Education* outlawing racial segregation in elementary and secondary schools. Over time, the ruling broke down explicit racial barriers in public schools, but in the short term it reinforced strongly held views in the South and elsewhere against federal intrusion in educational policy.

Cold War imperatives helped to overcome that opposition with passage of the National Defense Education Act of 1958. Enacted less than a year after the Soviet Union's launch of the first *Sputnik*, the law provided aid to the states to support math, science and foreign language instruction in public schools. Still, as McGuinn points out, federal aid to education in 1960 totaled less than $1 billion, including assistance dating from the New Deal to communities impacted by the presence of federal facilities, such as military bases. In the early 1960s, President John F. Kennedy called for broadening federal aid, but he could not overcome opposition from Republicans and Southern Democrats in Congress based on states' rights, resistance to desegregation and conflicts over aid to parochial schools.

CHRONOLOGY

Before 1950 *Federal government plays limited role in public education.*

1950s-1970s *Federal government approves first broad aid programs for elementary, secondary education.*

1954 U.S. Supreme Court rules racial segregation in public schools is unconstitutional.

1958 National Defense Education Act provides federal aid to states for teaching math, science and foreign languages; act responds to Soviet Union's launch of first man-made Earth satellite.

1965 Congress passes and President Lyndon B. Johnson signs Elementary and Secondary Education Assistance Act, first broad federal aid for public schools; Title I allocates funds to schools with high proportion of "educationally deprived" students.

1979 Congress passes and President Jimmy Carter signs law creating U.S. Department of Education; Republican Party platform adopted in July 1980 calls for abolishing department.

1980s-1990s *Federal role in education increases under Republican and Democratic presidents.*

1981 Republican President Ronald Reagan cuts federal spending on education by 20 percent in first year in office.

1983 A Nation at Risk depicts U.S. education system as failing and students lagging behind those in other industrialized countries.

Mid-1980s *Republicans drop calls to abolish Education Department.*

1988 Republican George H. W. Bush elected after campaigning on pledge to be "education president."

1989 Congress kills Bush education initiative; president hosts "education summit," but session produces few concrete results.

1991 Bush proposes "America 2000" legislation calling for national standards and student assessments; Republicans kill bill after Democrats strip out assessments piece.

1992 Democrat Bill Clinton elected president; stresses education in platform.

1994 Clinton wins enactment of two education initiatives: Goals 2000 calls for states to develop education standards; Improving America's Schools Act ties Title I funds to adoption of standards; both laws are weakly enforced.

2000-Present *No Child Left Behind (NCLB) mandates testing, accountability for elementary, secondary schools; broad support for law fades over time.*

2000 Republican George W. Bush elected president after competing with Democrat Al Gore on which candidate will do more for education.

2001-2002 Bush makes No Child Left Behind Act his first major domestic initiative; bill calls for annual testing of students in reading and math, reporting of results and penalties for schools that fail to make "adequate yearly progress" toward goal of 100 percent proficiency for students by 2014; bills approved with bipartisan majorities in House, Senate late in 2001; Bush signs law on Jan. 8, 2002.

Mid-2000s *Resistance to, complaints about NCLB grow in states.*

2007 Democratic-controlled Congress shuns Bush's call to reauthorize NCLB.

2008 Democrat Barack Obama elected president with detailed education platform.

2009 Congress approves $4.35 billion in economic stimulus bill for Race to the Top grants for states with education reform plans; 41 states join competition for grants.

2010 Governors, education chiefs propose "common core standards" in English, math (March 10). . . . Administration's "Blueprint for Reform" calls for revising NCLB; plan provides stringent restructuring remedies for lowest-performing schools (March 13). . . . Delaware and Tennessee chosen as first two states for grants (March 29); winners in second round to be announced in September.

After Kennedy's assassination, President Lyndon B. Johnson capitalized on the widely felt desire to vindicate the slain president's legacy and his own landslide election to win congressional approval in 1965 of the first broad federal aid program for elementary and secondary education. A former schoolteacher himself, Johnson accepted the recommendation of his commissioner of education, Francis Keppel, to structure the Elementary and Secondary Education Act (ESEA) as an anti-poverty program. The heart of the bill, Title I, provided aid to school districts based on their population of "educationally deprived children." Opposition to federal control of education was circumvented by giving school districts broad discretion on how to use the funds. By the end of Johnson's presidency, federal aid to education totaled $4 billion, but the money was being spent not as the federal government specified but as local school boards saw fit.

Democratic-controlled Congresses extended and expanded the law through the 1960s and '70s — for example, in 1975, by requiring equal access for children with disabilities. Under President Jimmy Carter, education gained its own seat at the Cabinet table with the creation of a Department of Education; previously, the Office of Education had been housed in the Department of Health, Education and Welfare. Creation of the new department was in part a payoff to the NEA, which had become a major constituent group within the Democratic Party.

The close ties fed a critique from Republicans and conservatives that the department had been captured by the teachers' unions. The critics also complained that there was little to show from a decade-plus of growing federal aid to and involvement with local education. The 1980 Republican platform called for "deregulation by the federal government of public education … and elimination of the federal Department of Education." The election of the staunchly conservative Ronald Reagan in November appeared to set the stage for the federal government to retreat from the educational policy scene.

Schools Seen 'At Risk'

The federal role in education did not shrink but instead grew over the last decades of the 20th century against the backdrop of increasing public concern about the performance of U.S. public schools. The Reagan administration initially cut federal aid to education but later increased funding and abandoned plans to abolish the

Department of Education. The next two presidents — Republican George H. W. Bush and Democrat Bill Clinton — set out ambitious goals for public schools to raise student achievement without strong federal enforcement to translate goals into action. In No Child Left Behind, however, President George W. Bush and bipartisan majorities in Congress created a regime that uses regular testing to increase schools' accountability and penalties to impose discipline on underperforming schools.

Fresh from his election victory, Reagan cut education spending by 20 percent in his first year in office. Two years later, however, a presidential commission convened by his secretary of education, Terrell Bell, produced a scathing report, "A Nation at Risk," which depicted U.S. schools failing and students lagging behind those in other industrialized countries. Political scientist Guinn notes that in receiving the report, Reagan mischaracterized it as endorsing his policy prescriptions for private-school vouchers and tuition tax credits. As time went on, Reagan and his second education secretary, William Bennett, adopted as their own the report's harsh attack on public schools. That stance, Guinn says, served only to increase political pressure for the federal government to act to strengthen the public education system.[19]

George H. W. Bush promised in his 1988 campaign to be "an education president," but he left office after four years with no major legislative accomplishments on the issue. Bush called in 1989 for reallocating federal funds to support such programs as rewards for excellent teachers, public school choice and teacher certification programs; the Democratic-controlled Congress killed the bill as inadequate on funding and policy alike.

That fall, Bush convened an "education summit" in Charlottesville, Va., which garnered headlines but generated no concrete results. In 1991, Bush introduced legislation, "America 2000," that combined national standards with national student assessments. When Democrats stripped out the assessments, Senate Republicans filibustered the measure to spare the president from having to veto an education bill markedly different from his own.

Clinton similarly emphasized education in his 1992 campaign, but unlike Bush achieved two significant victories in his first years in office. Goals 2000, signed into law in March 1994, called for states to develop educational standards, but gave the states leeway on the content and

Obama Gives Boost to Charter Schools

With charters in 40 states, movement is at a crossroads.

Charter schools have received strong support — both symbolically and substantively — from President Barack Obama's administration.

One of Obama's first forays as president to a public school of any kind was to the Capital City Public Charter School in Washington, just days after his inauguration. "[T]his kind of innovative school . . . is an example of how all our schools should be," the president told students at the school on Feb. 3, 2009, as he promoted the then-pending economic stimulus plan. The plan, which Congress adopted, included millions of dollars for K-12 education, including the Race to the Top grants competition designed to prod the states on key education issues.[1]

In January, in a visit to a regular public school in Falls Church, Va., the president noted that many states were adopting reforms to better position themselves for a grant. "In Illinois, Louisiana, Tennessee, California, we've seen changes in laws or policies to let public charter schools expand and succeed," Obama said. "These are public schools with more independence that are formed by teachers, parents and community members."[2]

Now nearly two decades old, charter schools are widely considered to be at a crossroads. Since the first one opened in St. Paul, Minn., in 1992, 40 states and the District of Columbia have enacted laws authorizing charters, which operate with public funds but largely free of the bureaucracy surrounding traditional public schools. Some 1.4 million children attend nearly 4,700 U.S. charter schools, according to the National Charter School Research Project at the University of Washington at Bothell.

While charter enrollment growth has increased about 9 percent annually over the last five years, charter enrollment represents just 3 percent of the public school population.

But President Obama and Education Secretary Arne Duncan have been working to get charters into the mainstream mix. As part of Race to the Top, Duncan encouraged states with caps on the number of charter schools to increase those caps. States that did not act would be last in line to receive grants from the $4.35 billion fund, the secretary made clear. (The two states receiving the first grants this spring, Delaware and Tennessee, both acted to permit more charter schools.)

In March, the Obama administration released its plan for reauthorizing the Elementary and Secondary Education Act (ESEA) of 1965 (of which the No Child Left Behind Act of 2001 is the latest version), and the plan includes significant proposals on charter schools. One would make "school turnaround grants" available to states and school districts to help them impose "rigorous interventions" in their lowest-performing schools. Under the "restart" model, a low-performing school would be closed and reopened under the direction of a charter board or charter management organization.

The second major charter piece of the ESEA plan comes under the rubric of "expanding educational options." The proposal would provide competitive grants to states, charter school authorizers, charter management organizations, school districts and other groups to start or expand "high-performing" charter schools. The plan stresses that grant recipients would have to show progress with all subgroups of students, as the No Child Left Behind law outlined, such as English-language learners and students with disabilities.

The administration's proposals have mostly won praise in the charter school world.

"We are really excited about the strong support from this administration," said Brooks Garber, vice president for

dropped an initial proposal to condition funding on federal approval of standards. Later that year, Clinton signed the Improving America's Schools Act, which reauthorized the Elementary and Secondary Education Act and required states to adopt standards in order to receive Title I funds. The act also required assessments of students at some

point between grades 3 and 5 and again in high school.

The two laws put the federal government behind standards, ostensibly with real teeth to make schools put them into effect in classrooms, but they proved to be ineffectual in operation. The Clinton administration had

federal advocacy at the National Alliance for Public Charter Schools. "These proposals will help grow our best models."

But not every advocate for charter schools is enamored by the growing federal role in the sector. Jeanne Allen, president of the Center for Education Reform, which has long advocated for more choice in education, is troubled by the conditions the administration's plan would impose on charter schools.

"There is a memory loss about why we have public charter schools in the first place," Allen says. "The notion of the autonomous public school that we call a charter that comes from the ground up and can break the rules is getting lost."

The growing federal role has focused attention on whether charter schools are living up to their promise. An analysis of charter school performance in 15 states and the District of Columbia, conducted by the Center for Research on Educational Outcomes at Stanford University, showed mixed results for charters. While 17 percent of charter schools reported academic gains that were significantly better than traditional public schools, 37 percent showed gains that were worse than traditional schools, with 46 percent demonstrating no significant difference.

"In some ways, charter schools are just beginning to come into their own," said the study. "And yet, this study reveals in unmistakable terms that, in the aggregate, charter students are not faring as well as their [traditional public school] counterparts."

Such studies play a part in a new critique of the charter movement by the education researcher Diane Ravitch. In a new book, Ravitch reexamines her longtime support for

Capital City Public Charter School

Students at Capital City Public Charter School in Washington visit Ben's Chili Bowl, one of the few U Street businesses to survive the 1968 riots, as part of their study of the Civil Rights movement.

choice and competition in public education.

"Charters are supposed to disseminate the free-market model of competition and choice," writes Ravitch, who was an assistant secretary of education under President George H. W. Bush. "Now charters compete for the most successful students in the poorest communities, or they accept all applicants and push the low performers back into the public school system." [3]

Allen of the Center for Education Reform takes issue with she calls Ravitch's "ivory tower" critique.

"What have charter schools done after all these years?" Allen said. "You not only have 1.5 million children who were not served well by the public school system being served by them. But they have helped spark this debate we're having on standards and performance pay — all as a result of having 5,000 schools challenging the status quo."

— Mark Walsh, Washington freelancer and contributing writer, Education Week

---

[1] For background, see Charles S. Clark, "Charter Schools," *CQ Researcher*, Dec. 20, 2002, pp. 1033-1056, and "Hopes, Fears, and Reality: A Balanced Look at American Charter Schools in 2009," National Charter School Research Project, Center on Reinventing Public Education, University of Washington, Bothell.

[2] "Multiple Choice: Charter School Performance in 16 States," Center for Research on Education Outcomes, Stanford University, 2009.

[3] Diane Ravitch, *The Death and Life of the Great American School System: How Testing and Choice Are Undermining Education* (2010).

no stomach for taking money away from states that did not comply with the standards and testing requirements, so it never did. Meanwhile, the standards-writing process hit a major political snag in 1995 with the release of proposed national history standards that were widely criticized by conservatives as multicultural political correctness. The history standards were shelved, and the bruising battle reinforced state capitals' inclinations to write their own standards and steer clear of anything that might be labeled national. [20]

Education moved to the forefront of presidential politics in the 2000 campaign between Republican George

AP Photo

With his first-grade teacher at his side, President Lyndon B. Johnson signs the landmark Elementary and Secondary Education Act on April 11, 1965, beside his childhood school near Stonewall, Texas. The act was the first broad federal aid program for public education and provided aid to school districts based on their population of "educationally deprived children."

W. Bush and Democrat Al Gore. Bush blamed what he called the nation's "education recession" on the Clinton-Gore administration's failure to hold schools and teachers accountable; Gore called for more money for education and criticized school choice and charter schools. Despite those differences, the two candidates both called for reform and accountability measures that Drew University political scientist McGuinn calls "remarkably similar." Most important, McGuinn adds, the campaign "continued — and expanded — the trend of nationalizing the rhetoric and politics of education reform."[21]

In office, Bush made education his first domestic initiative. Working with the senior Democrats on congressional education committees, Rep. George Miller of California in the House and Sen. Edward M. Kennedy

of Massachusetts in the Senate, Bush secured bipartisan support early in 2001 for measures combining annual testing in reading and math with penalties for schools that failed to achieve "adequate yearly progress." The House and Senate approved separate versions in May and June, respectively; the two chambers approved the final version in the fall, following the Sept. 11 terrorist attacks.

In signing the bill, Bush stressed the goal of education for all. "We know that every child can learn," Bush said in a ceremony at Hamilton High School in Hamilton, Ohio, on Jan. 2, 2002. "Now is the time to ensure that every child does learn." Writing shortly afterward, Richard Elmore, a professor at Harvard's Graduate School of Education in Cambridge, Mass., called the bill "the single largest expansion of federal power over the nation's education system in history."[22]

'No Child' Loses Support

The broad support for No Child Left Behind faded over time. Democrats on Capitol Hill and a wide range of state officials and educators complained that the Bush administration was underfunding the law and micromanaging its implementation. By the 2008 presidential campaign, both Obama and Sen. John McCain of Arizona, the Republican nominee, were promising to change the law but offering only a few specifics. After his election, Obama signaled his support for school reform by picking Duncan, an aggressive reform advocate, as secretary of education. Duncan then emphasized the need for thoroughgoing changes in schools as he presided over Race to the Top, the $4.35 billion competitive grant program aimed at stimulating innovation by the states.

From the outset, the act's central requirement for schools to move toward the 100 percent proficiency goal fell victim to what many observers called the school districts' decisions to "dumb down" the standards for measuring proficiency. "It's a lot easier to push down your standards than to push your students up," says political scientist McGuinn. Many states also set modest steps toward the 100 percent goal in the first few years only to realize the need for unrealistically rapid progress in later years. "They delayed the day of reckoning," Jennings explained when his Center for Education Policy issued a report on the practice in May 2008.[23]

Standards Stress Skills, Not Memorization

"Students are asked to do progressively more challenging things."

The "common core standards" for English language arts and mathematics proposed by the states' governors and education chiefs do not set out names, dates and places for students to memorize. Instead, they look to students to master concepts and develop skills necessary to be ready for college or career by the time they graduate from high school.

By omitting specific curriculum content, the standards released in draft form on March 10 by the National Governors Association and the Council of Chief State School Officers seek to allay any concern about establishing a national curriculum.

The omission does mean, however, that the standards represent only the first step in an ambitious effort to establish and raise minimum, uniform expectations for schools throughout the United States. Even if states adopt the standards — some have started, but some are balking — textbook publishers, curriculum materials suppliers and testing services will need to adapt their products to the new standards for teachers actually to apply them in the classroom.

The standards "will not stand alone," says Gene Wilhoit, executive director of the state school superintendents' group. Chester Finn, a longtime advocate of standards, agrees. The standards "are only the tip of the iceberg," says Finn, assistant secretary of education under President Ronald Reagan and now president of the Thomas B. Fordham Institute in Washington, an education think tank. [1]

Forty-eight states — all but Alaska and Texas — and the District of Columbia joined in supporting the drafting of the standards, which began in 2009. The standards were released on March 10 for a public comment period that closed on April 2. A revised version is expected this spring.

Despite the nearly unanimous support from states at the outset, officials in some states are now voicing opposition or reservations. In Virginia, Republican Gov. Bob McDonnell says the state will stick with its own "Standards of Learning." In Minnesota, Karen Klinzing, assistant education commissioner, says the math standards would be a step backward for the state.

The standards are set out in a 70-page draft for mathematics and a 36-page draft for English language arts and literacy in history/social studies and science. Each document proposes grade-by-grade mastery of "rigorous content and application of knowledge through high-order skills."

"Students are asked to do progressively more challenging things," said Michael Cohen, an Education Department official in the Clinton administration who is now president of Achieve, a Washington-based group working to improve standards and assessments. "Although that may sound obvious," Cohen continued, "it's a real breakthrough." [2]

The writing standards, for example, place increasing emphasis on persuasion, beginning in the 4th grade. Reading standards call for increased mastery of informational text in higher grades. By graduation, a student should be able to read a text closely, analyze structure, synthesize and apply the information presented and evaluate the reasoning and rhetoric.

Math standards start in 1st grade with addition and subtraction, whole number relationships, linear measurements and geometric shapes. By 12th grade, students are expected to link mathematics and statistics to everyday life and decision-making. As an example, students might be asked to estimate how much food and water is needed for emergency relief in a devastated city of 3 million people and how the supplies might be distributed.

Wilhoit says the adoption of assessments may prove to be more difficult than approval of the standards themselves. "Each state has different assessments," he says. "Each state has different ideas about what constitutes a good assessment."

Finn says the proposed standards are "better than what a lot of the states are doing." But he also cautions that adoption of the standards does not ensure good instruction. "Many states have pretty good standards, but pretty miserable performance," he says.

"Standards give you a destination," Finn adds, "but they don't get you there."

— Kenneth Jost

---

[1] For text of standards, see www.corestandards.org/Files/K12ELAStandards.pdf (English language arts); www.corestandards.org/Files/K12Math-Standards.pdf (mathematics). For coverage, see Catherine Gewertz, "Draft Common Standards Elicit Kudos and Criticism," *Education Week*, March 17, 2010, p. 1; Sam Dillon, "Panel Proposes Single Standard for All Schools," *The New York Times*, March 11, 2010, p. A1; Nick Anderson, "Common set of school standards to be proposed," *The Washington Post*, March 10, 2010, p. A1.

[2] Quoted in Dillon, *op. cit.*

Along with efforts to skirt or soften NCLB's requirements, state and local officials from both parties were complaining about the act's restrictions, even to the point of directly challenging the law. In 2005, Utah passed a law, signed by the state's Republican governor, declaring that the state's education policies took precedence over any conflicting requirements in NCLB. Officials in the states were also complaining that the federal government was not providing sufficient funds to meet the act's goals. The NEA filed a federal court suit along with eight school districts claiming that — contrary to a provision in the law — local school boards were being forced to spend their own funds to comply with the act.

Meanwhile, many critics were complaining that the law was encouraging educators to "teach to the test" — emphasizing test-taking skills in reading and math at the expense of broader learning and teaching in other subjects. Nearly half of school districts surveyed in 2007 — 44 percent — said they had reduced the time in elementary grades for science, social studies and the arts, according to a Center on Education Policy report. "There are just so many minutes and hours in the day," Ravitch writes in a critical assessment of NCLB in her new book.[24]

The law came up for reauthorization in a Democratic-controlled Congress in 2007 against the backdrop of still intense criticism, despite some efforts by Education Secretary Spellings to respond to state and local officials' complaints. Twice in the fall, Bush publicly urged Congress to consider the administration's proposed rewrite of the act. Democrats had a draft of their own, but the session ended with no action. "No Child Left Behind may be the most negative brand in America," House Education Committee Chairman Miller remarked.[25]

As the presidential campaign got under way, Democrats sought to recapture the partisan advantage they had historically enjoyed on education. By the fall, Obama was presenting a detailed education platform that included promises of new spending and new help for low-performing schools. Despite endorsements by both major teachers' unions, Obama also promised to increase spending on charter schools and to support pay-for-performance plans — steps opposed by both the NEA and AFT. By contrast, GOP nominee McCain gave little attention to education in his campaign. Both candidates said they supported the goals of No Child Left Behind but were largely silent about broad questions such as how to raise state standards or boost achievement at underperforming schools.[26]

For his secretary of Education, Obama in mid-December selected Chicago schools chief Duncan, a friend and basketball buddy with a reputation as a school reformer who also maintained good ties with teachers' unions. In accepting the appointment during a Dec. 16 visit to a Chicago school, Duncan said schools should "focus on basics like reading and math … embrace innovative new approaches" and "create a professional climate to attract great teachers." The selection drew approving comments from advocates and experts across a wide spectrum of opinion. Observers noted that Duncan had previously called for more funding for NCLB as well as more flexibility.[27]

The administration backed up the promise of more money by getting Congress to approve more than $4 billion in the economic stimulus bill approved in February for the Race to the Top competitive schools grant program. But Duncan raised eyebrows in the spring among teachers' unions and other public education advocates by warning that states that limited the number of charter schools were unlikely to receive money. Final regulations approved in November said states also had to devise systems for evaluating principals and teachers in part based on student achievement. AFT president Weingarten said the regulations appeared to "strike a balance," but the NEA's Van Roekel said he was "disappointed" over the emphasis on tying teacher evaluation to student test scores.[28]

CURRENT SITUATION

Racing to the Top

Officials in Delaware and Tennessee are celebrating their selection as the first two states to win funds from the Education Department's $4.35 billion Race to the Top competition, while losing states are either reworking their proposals or considering dropping out of the program.

The two states are to begin receiving installments in July from the awards they won on the strength of proposals that promised to improve principal and teacher evaluation, use student performance data to improve instruction and turn around their lowest-performing schools. Tennessee, with about 930,000 school children, ranked first and

AT ISSUE

Should Congress adopt President Obama's approach in rewriting No Child Left Behind?

YES
Michael J. Petrilli
Vice President, National Programs and Policy, Thomas B. Fordham Institute

Written for *CQ Researcher*, April 2010

The Obama administration's education blueprint is a serious proposal, and a very good starting point for congressional deliberations. It accomplishes two key goals that are often in tension with one another. First, it promotes bold education reform, especially in the areas of teacher quality, charter schools and school turnarounds. And second, it rests on a realistic view of what Washington can — and cannot — accomplish in education. This dose of "reform realism" is a steady foundation for the next iteration of No Child Left Behind.

On the reform front, the plan continues the momentum for the Race to the Top grant program. It would make competitive grants to the states and districts a key part of Uncle Sam's toolbox and would prod state and local education agencies to adopt changes in teacher evaluation, leadership development and other key areas. And it places a single-minded focus on the nation's lowest-performing public schools, calling for serious overhauls rather than tweaking around the edges.

But for the vast majority of America's schools, the blueprint would offer welcome breathing room. Gone would be a federally mandated definition of "Adequate Yearly Progress." No more would schools be labeled as "needing improvement" because a handful of special-needs students failed the state test. No longer would the typical school feel enormous pressure to narrow the curriculum, teach to the test or ignore the needs of its brightest students. These changes will occur because the federal role — for all but the worst schools in the country — would change from "accountability" to "transparency." School results would be made public. But most federally enforced sanctions would disappear.

For these reasons, the proposal has already elicited much pushback from NCLB's fiercest defenders. And their concerns are understandable. Without pressure from the federal government, won't many schools return to their old habits of ignoring achievement gaps, enabling mediocrity and holding certain kids to low standards? Perhaps.

This blueprint won't fix all that ails America's schools. But there's not much Uncle Sam can do anyway to transform all 100,000 schools in the country. Nor should it try. Handing responsibility back to the states for the vast majority of schools is the more appropriate — and pragmatic — approach.

And by pushing for the reform of America's most struggling schools, while easing up on federal intrusion for all of the rest, this plan is a winner politically, too. It's an awfully good package; now it's up to Congress to make it even better.

NO
Diane Ravitch
Education historian, New York University

Adapted from "Bridging Differences," March 23, 2010, http://blogs.edweek.org/edweek/Bridging-Differences/

The Obama administration has tried to distance itself from No Child Left Behind, but its proposal continues to be firmly rooted in NCLB's philosophy of "measure and punish."

NCLB's overemphasis on basic skills testing was harmful to schools across the nation, its results have been meager and its utopian goal of 100 percent proficiency unleashed unrealistic expectations. No school district or state could hope to meet the law's goal. But the failure to meet this goal has unfairly stigmatized public education in the United States, setting the stage for privatization.

Most educators hoped that the Obama administration would launch a fresh start and rethink the federal role in education. That has not happened. They have dropped the deadline of 2014. They have eliminated the complex calculation of AYP (adequate yearly progress), which put some very good schools on the "failing" list. Some of the micromanagement that characterizes NCLB will disappear.

But the federal role continues to be muscular, in fact, probably even more muscular than NCLB, for the 5,000 schools in the bottom 5 percent. Muscular, as in tough, mean-spirited and bullying.

All students in grades 3-8 across the United States will still be required by federal law to take annual tests in reading and math. The administration says it wants to reward "growth." But to reward "growth," there should be two tests a year for everyone, not just one. Since one of this administration's signal initiatives is to grade teachers by their students' test scores, students should be tested in September and again in May or June. So the proposal may bring more, not less, testing than is done now, with bigger stakes for teachers.

Most troublesome are the draconian "remedies" that will be imposed on the 5,000 schools at the bottom in test scores. These schools must be "transformed," "turned around" or closed. Their principals may be fired, their staffs may be fired and they may be turned over to state control or turned into privately operated charter schools. None of these remedies has proven successful on a large scale.

If this plan is enacted as proposed, it will eventually become just as toxic as NCLB. Only we won't know it for another five years or so after the evidence of devastated schools and communities has accumulated.

It's not too late to turn back and offer a helping hand, not a death sentence. Send help, not a firing squad.

was awarded $500 million; Delaware, with around 124,000 students, stands to receive $100 million. The money will be spread out over four years.

In announcing the selections on March 29, Education Secretary Duncan stressed that both states had passed new laws to support their policies and had secured broad support for the proposals, including from teachers' unions. Among the other finalists — 13 states and the District of Columbia — some lost points for lack of union support. States can resubmit proposals in a second round this summer, with up to 15 others to be selected for awards totaling $3.4 billion due to be announced in September.[29]

In Tennessee, Democratic Gov. Phil Bredesen called the Republican-controlled legislature into special session at the start of the year to consider a package of bills aimed at satisfying Race to the Top criteria. After a four-day session the legislature approved measures that would allow the state to intervene in failing schools and require student success to count for half of annual teacher evaluations.

Tennessee Education Commissioner Tim Webb says part of the money will be used to tie student data to individualized instructional strategies. As an example, Webb suggests a teacher who identifies a struggling student's specific weakness might use the state's database to locate a teacher elsewhere in the state who has successfully helped students struggling with those issues.[30]

In Delaware, a new law allows teachers rated as "ineffective" for three years to be removed from the classroom even if they have tenure. The state also gained authority to intervene in failing schools.[31]

The criteria listed for Race to the Top grants match major parts of the administration's education blueprint released in March. States were told they would be judged on adopting standards and assessments for students; building data systems tied to helping improve instruction; recruiting, training and retaining effective teachers and principals, "especially where they are needed most;" and turning around lowest-performing schools.

Among the disappointed states was Florida, which had asked for up to $1 billion and ranked fourth in the first round behind the two winners and Georgia. Despite proposing detailed reforms, the application lost points because only five local teachers' unions signed on, and the Florida Education Association, the largest statewide union, opposed the plan.[32]

Florida legislators are hoping to strengthen the state's position with a so-called merit pay plan that ties teacher salaries to their students' test scores instead of longevity. The bill has passed the state Senate and is pending in the state House. Teachers' unions had withheld support from the state's grant application because it linked principals' and teachers' pay to student performance.

On a 500-point scale, Delaware and Tennessee scored 454.6 and 444.2 points, respectively. The 14 other finalists all scored above 400, with the District of Columbia ranked 16th with 402.4 points.

Washington's application was closely watched because of D.C. Schools Chancellor Michelle Rhee's highly visible push for overhauling a school system widely regarded as badly failing. The Washington Teachers' Union refused to support the application, however, because reading and math teachers in grades 4 through 8 would have had half their evaluations based on growth in student test scores.

The Delaware and Tennessee grants are seen as likely to bring visible changes to the states' schools, according to Center on Education Policy President Jennings. He notes that Tennessee's outgoing governor, Bredesen, got commitments from gubernatorial candidates in both parties to stick with the policies outlined in the application.

"There will be changes in classrooms in the states that receive these grants — changes in the way teachers are evaluated and how students are tested," he says. "It's reasonable to expect there will be an increase in test scores in those states."

Jennings warns, however, about discouragement among states that lost out in the competition. "They've discouraged a large number of states that have already made changes in anticipation of getting grants," he says. In particular, Jennings says, large states may feel disadvantaged because of the comparatively greater difficulty of getting what Duncan calls "statewide buy-in" for reform plans.

Promoting the Blueprint

The administration's hopes for rewriting No Child Left Behind rest on alleviating concerns among some pivotal lawmakers, overcoming resistance from teachers' unions and school boards and getting time on an already crowded congressional agenda.

Duncan promoted the administration's blueprint in a round of Capitol Hill appearances in the week it was sent to Congress, with a generally favorable reception from the Senate and House education committees on March 17 and the House Education Committee's Appropriations Subcommittee the next day. Meanwhile, Education Department staffers are said to be meeting with Democratic and Republican congressional staffs alike to seek common ground and air potential differences.

"The administration is moving ahead," says Wilhoit of the state education chiefs' group. "The real issue is whether Congress is ready."

Inside the Beltway, education experts uniformly say Congress is not ready. "The likelihood of it moving this year is slim," says the American Enterprise Institute's Hess.

The Fordham Institute's Finn agrees. "I doubt that they're going to be able to pull off a full-fledged reauthorization this year," he says.

Jennings, the former House Education Committee staffer, also doubts that Congress will act this year: "It's possible but not probable to have a reauthorization." He credits the administration with seeking bipartisan support, but like others notes the number of issues competing for lawmakers' attention with only a few months left before the summer recess and fall campaign season. "There's not a lot of time," he says.

The chairs of the Democratic education committees both praised the administration's blueprint as a starting point for rewriting No Child Left Behind. Duncan traveled to Iowa on March 15 for public forums sponsored by Iowa's Sen. Tom Harkin, who chairs the Senate Health, Education, Labor and Pensions Committee. In a statement posted on his Web site, Harkin said the administration blueprint provides "an opportunity to fix the problems with the No Child Left Behind Act." In similar vein, House Education Committee chair Miller said in a Web site statement that the blueprint "puts our efforts to rewrite our education laws on a strong footing."[33]

On the Republican side, Tennessee Sen. Lamar Alexander, secretary of education under President George H. W. Bush, is urging a less than complete overhaul of NCLB. "Instead of getting bogged down in a comprehensive reauthorization of a 1,000-page bill, Congress needs to focus on an agreed set of problems with No Child Left Behind and fix what's wrong," Alexander said. "Secretary Duncan's blueprint is a good beginning."[34]

In hearings, GOP lawmakers pressed Duncan on some of the blueprint's omissions. Wyoming Sen. Michael Enzi,

the ranking GOP member on the education panel, voiced concern that the restructuring remedies proposed in the blueprint were not well suited to rural schools. Enzi's House counterpart, Minnesota's Rep. John Kline, criticized the administration's decision to drop school choice and tutoring services as penalties for underperforming schools.[35]

Despite the widespread doubts about congressional action, two major education groups with qualms about the blueprint are professing cautious optimism that Congress will get around to the issue. "All sides are working very hard to make that happen," says NEA President Van Roekel.

School boards lobbyist Felton strikes a similar tone. "The folks across the aisles from each other say they want to work on this," he says. "We're really in a short window here, but at this point we believe it's possible."

Both groups have an interest in some legislative action despite their reservations about details in the blueprint. "NCLB needs to be left behind," Van Roekel explains. "There's an overemphasis on testing, labeling and punishment."

For his part, Felton says school boards are hoping for "temporary relief" from some of NCLB's sanctions.

OUTLOOK

Catalysts for Change?

The federal government was drawn into education policy in the 1950s and '60s to meet a global challenge — the Soviet Union's early lead in the space race — and to try to reduce educational disparities between whites and blacks, rich and poor. The mechanism chosen was straightforward: federal aid, with relatively few strings attached.

A half-century later, the United States faces global academic competition probably more challenging than the Cold War contest with the Soviet Union. And the racial and income disparities in public education persist despite decades of desegregation suits and school financing litigation as well as compensatory federal aid under the Elementary and Secondary Education Act's Title I.

Over time, the federal role became more detailed — some would say intrusive. No Child Left Behind represents the culmination of that trend, with its detailed requirements for testing, reporting of results, labeling of schools and penalties for failing schools.

Eight years after enactment, NCLB's impact is disputed, but hardly anyone denies the need for significant changes in the law. "They took a good and useful opportunity to promote transparency and push accountability and turned it into a train wreck," says the American Enterprise Institute's Hess.

"We're essentially on the right track," says William Galston, an education policy adviser to President Clinton and now a senior fellow in governance studies at the liberal Brookings Institution. "We need to eliminate the flaws of NCLB," he continues, "but not throw the baby out with the bathwater."

Some other experts are more critical. In her new book, New York University's Ravitch calls NCLB "a punitive law based on erroneous assumptions about how to improve schools." She continues, "Good education cannot be achieved by a strategy of testing students, shaming educators and closing schools."[36]

Even without any changes in the law, two new developments may be catalysts for changes in U.S. public education. The "common core standards" proposed by the states' governors and education chiefs are viewed by supporters as a pathway not only for more useful comparisons between different schools and different states but also for better instruction in classrooms. "That direction is a strong one," says the Education Trust's Haycock. "It's got legs."

Meanwhile, the Obama administration's Race to the Top is putting real money — more than $4 billion — into its vision of school reform. "Money does buy change, especially if the political leadership, teachers' unions and school districts are willing to sign on," says Jennings with the Center on Education Policy. "This is something that the federal government has never done to this degree."

Whatever revisions are or are not made to No Child Left Behind, many education watchers are frustrated with the lack of progress — or limited progress — that public schools have made in a quarter-century or more of concentrated reform efforts. "Things have gotten a little better over time, but we are way below where we need to be," says Moe with the Hoover Institution. "We need a real transformation to push us ahead, and this kind of incrementalism is just not going to do it."

For her part, Ravitch sees no great progress in public education and blames many of the conservative reform ideas that she once supported. Charter schools siphon off the best students from public schools, she says, leaving the latter with the harder-to-teach special education students and English language learners. Choice turns what should be collaboration among schools into a struggle for survival. And testing engenders a "blind worship of data" and the erroneous equation of test scores with "achievement."

Some other experts are more sanguine but acknowledge the challenges that public schools are facing. "We are pretty much at the level we've always been," says Wilhoit with the state education chiefs group. "The problem is that people are expecting more out of the system.

"What was satisfactory in the past is no longer acceptable. We had in the past high numbers of dropouts; but we had ways in society for those dropouts to succeed. We have taken those away," he continues. "We have other nations in the world that are offering the same educational opportunities to their citizens that only we provided in the past, and we have the disappearance of routine kinds of manual labor jobs that are no longer available to large masses of people."

Public educators, however, are fond of pointing to polls that consistently find good-sized majorities of respondents voicing satisfaction with their own children's teachers. "If you ask people about their sons' or daughters' teachers, they get high marks," says NEA President Van Roekel. "We need to translate that into good public policy that helps teachers do better with students."

NOTES

1. See Stephanie Banchero, "Duncan may sue U.S. over tutoring," *Chicago Tribune*, Dec. 10, 2004, p. C1; Jill Zuckman, "Congress approves education overhaul," *Chicago Tribune*, Dec. 19, 2001, p. 1.

2. Quoted in "Obama Administration Looks to Overhaul No Child Left Behind," PBS "NewsHour," March 17, 2010, www.pbs.org/newshour/bb/north_america/jan-june10/nclb_03-17.html. For Duncan's prepared statement, "Education Act Reauthorization," CQ Transcriptions, www.cq.com/display.do?dockey=/cqonline/prod/data/docs/html/testimony/111/testimony111-000003569738.html@committees&metapub=CQ-TESTIMONY&searchIndex=0&seqNum=5.

3. U.S. Department of Education, "A Blueprint for Reform: The Reauthorization of the Elementary and Secondary Education Act," March 2010, www2.ed.gov/policy/elsec/leg/blueprint/blueprint.pdf. For coverage, see Sam Dillon, "Obama Proposes Sweeping Changes in Education Law," *The New York Times*, March 14, 2010, p. A1; Nick Anderson, "Obama calls for 'No Child' remake," *The Washington Post*, March 14, 2010, p. A1. For background see Barbara Mantel, "No Child Left Behind," *CQ Researcher*, May 27, 2005, pp. 469-492.

4. For background see Marcia Clemmitt, "Reading Crisis," *CQ Researcher*, Feb. 22, 2008, pp. 169-192. Kathy Koch, "National Education Standards," *CQ Researcher*, May 14, 1999, pp. 401-424.

5. Patrick J. McGuinn, *No Child Left Behind and the Transformation of Federal Education Policy, 1965-2005* (2006).

6. For background, see Charles S. Clark, "Charter Schools," *CQ Researcher*, Dec. 20, 2002, pp. 1033-1056.

7. For background see Kenneth Jost, "Testing in Schools," *CQ Researcher*, April 20, 2001, pp. 321-344.

8. U.S. Department of Education, "Race to the Top Fund," www2.ed.gov/programs/racetothetop/index.html.

9. For background see Marcia Clemmitt, "Fixing Urban Schools," *CQ Researcher*, April 27, 2007, pp. 361-384.

10. Quoted in Bob Stuart, "State: No-go on test drive," *The* (Waynesboro) *News Virginian*, March 12, 2010, www2.newsvirginian.com/wnv/news/state_regional/state_regional_govtpolitics/article/state_no-go_on_test_drive/53516/. For background, see Peter Baker, "Compromise reached on Va. school standards," *The Washington Post*, June 23, 1995, p. C1.

11. Quoted in Sam Dillon, "Panel Proposes Single Standard for All Schools," *The New York Times*, March 11, 2010, p. A1.

12. Catherine Gewertz, "Draft Common Standards Elicit Kudos and Criticism," *Education Week*, March 17, 2010, p. 1.

13. Shelby Dietz, "How Many Schools Have Not Made Adequate Yearly Progress Under the No Child Left Behind Act?" Center on Education Policy, March 11, 2010, www.cep-dc.org/indexcfm?fuseaction=Page.viewPage&pageId=495&parentID=481.

14. Quoted in Neil King Jr. and Barbara Martinez, "Squaring Off on U.S. Schools," *The Wall Street Journal*, March 15, 2010, p. A3.

15. See Steven Greenhouse and Sam Dillon, "A Wholesale School Shake-Up Is Embraced by the President, and Divisions Follow," *The New York Times*, March 7, 2010, p. A20. For local coverage of the school board action, see Jennifer D. Jordan, "Teachers fired, labor outraged," *Providence Journal-Bulletin*, Feb. 24, 2010, p. 1.

16. Quoted in Greenhouse and Dillon, *op. cit.*

17. Diane Ravitch, "Try Again, Secretary Duncan, It's Not Too Late," Bridging Differences, March 23, 2010, http://blogs.edweek.org/edweek/Bridging-Differences/.

18. Historical background drawn from McGuinn, *op. cit.*

19. *Ibid.*, pp. 42-43, 49.

20. For background on the history standards, see Kenneth Jost, "Teaching History," *CQ Researcher*, Sept. 29, 1995, pp. 849-872.

21. McGuinn, *op. cit.*, p. 163.

22. Richard Elmore, "Unwarranted Intrusion," *Education Next*, Vol. 2, No. 1 (spring 2002), cited in McGuinn, *op. cit.*, p. 179.

23. Quoted in David J. Hoff, "Steep Climb to NCLB for Many States," *Education Week*, June 4, 2008, p. 1.

24. Ravitch, *op. cit.*, p. 108. See Jennifer McMurrer, "Choices, Changes, and Challenges: Curriculum and Instruction in the NCLB Era," Center on Education Policy, 2007.

25. Quoted in Sam Dillon, "Democrats Make Bush School Act an Election Issue," *The New York Times*, Dec. 23, 2007, sec. 1, col. 1; see also Sheryl Gay Stolberg and Diana Jean Schemo, "Bush Prodding Congress to Reauthorize His Education Law," *ibid.*, Oct. 10, 2007, p. A16.

26. David J. Hoff, "NCLB Debate at the Sidelines," *Education Week*, Oct. 1, 2008, p. 1; Sam Dillon, "Obama Looks to Lessons From Chicago in His National Education Plan," *The New York Times*,

Sept. 10, 2008, p. A21; "McCain Calls for Limited U.S. Role in Schools," *ibid.*

27. See Maria Glod, "Education Pick Is Called 'Down-to-Earth' Leader," *The Washington Post*, Dec. 17, 2008, p. A3; Sam Dillon, "Schools Chief From Chicago Is Cabinet Pick," *The New York Times*, Dec. 16, 2008, p. A1.

28. See Michele McNeil, "Rules Set for $4 Billion Race to Top Contest," *Education Week*, Nov. 18, 2009, p. 1; Sam Dillon, "Dangling $4.3 Billion, Obama Pushes States to Shift on Education," *The New York Times*, Aug. 17, 2009, p. A1.

29. See "Delaware and Tennessee Win First Race to the Top Grants," U.S. Department of Education, March 29, 2010, www2.ed.gov/newspressreleases/2010/03/03292010.html. Some background drawn from Nick Anderson and Bill Turque, "Del., Tenn. Win education awards," *The Washington Post*, March 30, 2010, p. A3; Sam Dillon, "Delaware and Tennessee Win U.S. School Grants," *The New York Times*, March 30, 2010, p. A15.

30. See Jennifer Brooks, "Tennessee wins Race to the Top Funding," *The* (Nashville) *Tennessean*, March 30, 2010.

31. See "Delaware to get first round of 'Race to the Top' education grants," *The* (Wilmington) *News-Journal*, March 30, 2010.

32. See Hannah Simpson, "Florida loses contest for federal Race to the Top education grant," *The Miami Herald*, March 30, 2010, p. B3.

33. See "ESEA Blueprint a Step Forward for Public Education," http://harkin.senate.gov/blogitem.cfm?i=3cc8bf8b-d29f-42a9-b725-4fcc7469f983; "Chairman Miller Statement on Blueprint to Reform the Elementary and Secondary Education Act," http://georgemiller.house.gov/news/2010/03/chairman_miller_statement_on_b.html.

34. Quoted in Neil King Jr. and Barbara Martinez, "Squaring Off on U.S. Schools," *The Wall Street Journal*, March 15, 2010, p. A3.

35. See Alyson Klein, "Tests Loom for ESEA in Congress," *Education Week*, March 31, 2010.

36. Ravitch, *op. cit.*, pp. 110-111.

BIBLIOGRAPHY

Books

Hess, Frederick M., and Michael J. Petrilli, *No Child Left Behind Primer, Peter Lang*, 2006.
Two Washington experts on education policy provide a compact primer on the No Child Left Behind Act. Hess is director of education policy studies, the American Enterprise Institute; Petrilli is vice president for national programs and policy, Thomas B. Fordham Institute.

Irons, E. Jane, and Sandra Harris, *The Challenges of No Child Left Behind: Understanding the Issues of Excellence, Accountability, and Choice, Rowman & Littlefield*, 2007.
The book provides a basic overview of No Child Left Behind and its implementation in the first few years after enactment. Includes questions for discussion, 10-page list of references. Irons is professor of educational leadership at Lamar University, in Beaumont, Texas; Harris is director of Lamar's Center for Research and Doctoral Studies in Educational Leadership.

McGuinn, Patrick J., *No Child Left Behind and the Transformation of Federal Education Policy, 1965-2005, University Press of Kansas*, 2006.
An associate professor of political science at Drew University, in Madison, N.J., traces the evolution of federal education policy from the enactment of the first broad-scale aid program for elementary and secondary education through the first few years of No Child Left Behind. Includes detailed notes.

Ravitch, Diane, *The Death and Life of the Great American School System: How Testing and Choice Are Undermining Education, Basic Books*, 2010.
The well-known education historian and former assistant secretary of Education under President George H. W. Bush relates and explains her shift from supporter to opponent of such school policies as vouchers and charter schools. Includes detailed notes.

Reese, William J., *America's Public Schools: From the Common School to "No Child Left Behind," Johns Hopkins University Press*, 2005.
A historian at the University of Wisconsin provides a compact overview of the history of public education in the United States from the colonial era through the first

few years of No Child Left Behind. Includes 12-page essay on sources.

Articles

Anderson, Nick, "GOP Leaving 'No Child' Behind," *The Washington Post*, **July 13, 2009, p. A15.**
Dissent is growing among Republicans toward the No Child Left Behind initiatives enacted by former President George W. Bush.

Dillon, Sam, "Obama Proposes Sweeping Changes in Education Law," *The New York Times*, **March 14, 2010, p. A1.**
The article describes the Obama administration's approach to revising the No Child Left Behind Act.

Gewertz, Catherine, "Draft Common Standards Elicit Kudos, Criticism," *Education Week*, **March 17, 2010, p. 1.**
The draft "common core standards" proposed by the states' governors and education commissioners have drawn both positive and negative reactions.

Glod, Maria, " 'Nation's Report Card' Sees Gains in Elementary, Middle Schools," *The Washington Post*, **April 29, 2009, p. A16.**
Rising math and reading scores among 9- and 13-year olds provide momentum for those who want to renew No Child Left Behind.

McNeil, Michele, "Obama Seeks to Make Race to the Top Grants Permanent Program," *Education Week*, **Jan. 27, 2010, p. 16.**
The Obama administration wants to expand by $1.35 billion the 2011 federal budget for the Race to the Top competition.

Reports and Studies

"Common Core State Standards Initiative," *National Governors Association Center for Best Practices and Council of Chief State School Officers*, **March 2010, www.corestandards.org.**
The draft standards for English language arts and mathematics represent grade-by-grade expectations for student knowledge and skills needed for high school graduates to be prepared for success in college and careers. The standards were developed over the course of a year with consultation from a wide range of educators, content experts, researchers and others and were presented on behalf of 48 states (all but Alaska and Texas), two territories and the District of Columbia. A final version is to be published in spring 2010 following a public comment period that closed April 2.

On the Web

The Center on Education Policy prepared a compendium of more than 100 studies of No Child Left Behind published since 2005 by education scholars, government agencies, universities, research organizations or national organizations with research divisions. The compendium includes brief summaries of and links to each of the reports; they are organized according to nine subject-matter categories. The compendium can be found at www.cep-dc.org/index.cfm?fuseaction=Page.viewPage&pageId=558&parentID=481.

For More Information

Alliance for Excellent Education, 1201 Connecticut Ave., N.W., Suite 901, Washington, DC 20036; (202) 828-0828; www.all4ed.org. Promotes high-school transformation to ensure preparedness of students for postsecondary education and success in life.

American Enterprise Institute, 1150 17th St., N.W., Washington, DC 20036; (202) 862-5800; www.aei.org. Conservative think tank promoting school choice and accountability in education.

American Federation of Teachers, 555 New Jersey Ave., N.W., Washington, DC 20001; (202) 879-4400; www.aft.org. Labor union and affiliate of AFL-CIO working to improve the teaching profession to the benefit of teachers.

Center on Education Policy, 1001 Connecticut Ave., N.W., Suite 522, Washington, DC 20036; (202) 822-8065; www.cep-dc.org. National advocate for public education and more effective public schools.

Council of Chief State School Officers, 1 Massachusetts Ave., N.W., Suite 700, Washington, DC 20001; (202) 336-7000; www.ccsso.org. Provides leadership, advocacy and technical assistance for local education officials.

Council of the Great City Schools, 1301 Pennsylvania Ave., N.W., Suite 702, Washington, DC 20004; (202) 393-2427; www.cgcs.org. Works for higher standards of academic excellence for inner-city schools.

Education Trust, 1250 H St., N.W., Suite 700, Washington, DC 20005; (202) 293-1217; www.edtrust.org. Works to close the achievement gap among minorities and low-income families.

National Education Association, 1201 16th St., N.W., Washington, DC 20036; (202) 833-4000; www.nea.org. Labor union representing education personnel working to advance the cause of public education.

National School Boards Association, 1680 Duke St., Alexandria, VA 22314; (703) 838-6722; www.nsba.org. Promotes excellence and equity in public education through school board leadership.

Thomas B. Fordham Institute, 1016 16th St., N.W., 8th Floor, Washington, DC 20036; (202) 223-5452; www.edexcellence.net. Promotes policies that strengthen accountability and expand education options for families.

2

The Value of a College Education

Thomas J. Billitteri

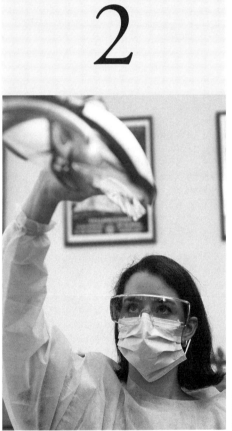

Courses in dental hygiene are popular at many of the nation's 1,200 community colleges. Today's "career and technical education" (CTE) programs integrate core academic training into job-specific courses like computer programming, medical technology, restaurant and hotel management and construction.

From *CQ Researcher*, November 20, 2009.

Mike Rowe, host of the cable-TV show "Dirty Jobs," has a thing or two to say about work and education.

For 30 years, writes Rowe, whose show profiles some of the more challenging sides of blue-collar work, "we've convinced ourselves that 'good jobs' are the result of a four-year degree. That's bunk. Not all knowledge comes from college."[1]

Rowe's plainspoken view contradicts the lofty advice routinely dispensed to young people, that a bachelor's degree is a fundamental requirement for achieving the American Dream.

But with college costs soaring, skilled jobs such as welders and medical technicians in demand and millions of young adults ill-prepared for the rigors of a university education, some policy experts argue that while post-high-school education is vital in today's global economy, a four-year degree may be unnecessary for economic security — and perhaps even ill-advised.

"In many cases, young people think they are going to make substantial income just by having a college degree," says Edwin L. Herr, a professor emeritus of education at Pennsylvania State University and co-author of *Other Ways to Win*, a book that analyzes alternatives to the traditional bachelor's degree. "There are a lot of people destined for unhappiness if we simply say that everybody ought to go to college. I don't think society in general requires everybody to go to college. It certainly requires people who have skills, and there certainly are ways to obtain those skills other than a four-year college."

The Obama administration seems to agree. Under his American Graduation Initiative, announced in July, President Barack Obama

Community Colleges at a Glance

More than 80 percent of the nation's approximately 1,200 community colleges are publicly supported. Of the 11.5 million students they serve, nearly 60 percent are enrolled part time, and 40 percent are among the first generation of their families to attend college.

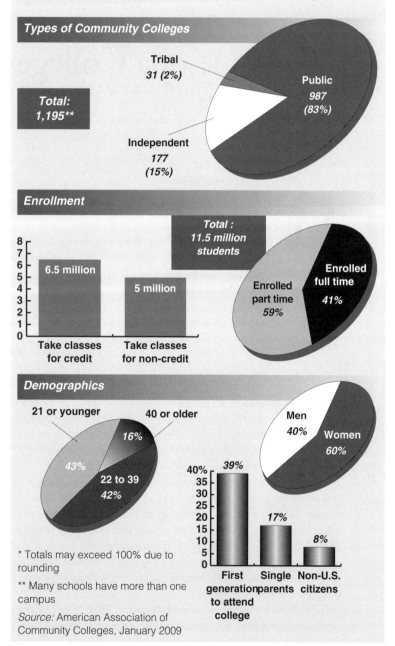

Types of Community Colleges

Total: 1,195**

Public 987 (83%)

Independent 177 (15%)

Tribal 31 (2%)

Enrollment

6.5 million — Take classes for credit

5 million — Take classes for non-credit

Total: 11.5 million students

Enrolled full time 41%

Enrolled part time 59%

Demographics

21 or younger 43%

22 to 39 42%

40 or older 16%

Men 40%

Women 60%

First generation to attend college 39%

Single parents 17%

Non-U.S. citizens 8%

* Totals may exceed 100% due to rounding

** Many schools have more than one campus

Source: American Association of Community Colleges, January 2009

is calling for an additional 5 million community college graduates by 2020, including those who earn associate degrees or certificates or who go on to graduate from four-year institutions. Beyond that, he wants every American to commit to at least a year of higher education or career training, whether at a community college or a four-year school, or through a vocational program or apprenticeship.[2]

The United States had the highest percentages of college graduates in the world for most of the post-World War II era, but now the rates remain stagnant, according to the Indianapolis-based Lumina Foundation for Education. About 39 percent of U.S. adults hold a two- or four-year degree, but in some countries, including Japan and South Korea, more than half of young adults ages 25 to 34 hold degrees, a foundation report said. "Even more disturbing for the U.S.," it added, "rates in these other countries continue to climb while ours remain stagnant."

Lumina estimated that at current college-graduation rates, "there will be a shortage of 16 million college-educated adults in the American workforce by 2025."[3]

Obama proposes to spend a record $12 billion over the next decade to strengthen the nation's system of 1,200 community colleges, part of a larger goal to restore the United States as the leader in college graduates by 2020.

"[F]or a long time there have been politicians who have spoken of training as a silver bullet and college as a cure-all," Obama said. "It's not, and we know that." But, he added, "We know that in the coming years, jobs requiring at least an associate degree are projected to grow twice as fast as jobs requiring no college experience. We will not fill those jobs — or even keep those jobs here in America — without the training offered by community colleges."[4]

To be sure, a bachelor's degree is a laudable goal for many young adults, one that can pay big dividends in personal satisfaction, career opportunities and earnings. In 2007 people with a bachelor's degree earned an average $57,181, or 63 percent more than those with some college or an associate's degree and 83 percent more than those with only a high-school diploma.[5] (*See graph, p. 31.*) And the seasonally adjusted unemployment rate was 4.9 percent in September for adults 25 and older with a bachelor's degree or higher, compared with 8.5 percent for those with less college and 10.8 percent for those with only a high-school education.[6]

Still, a four-year degree is not always the best option, workforce and public-policy experts argue.

For one thing, many students simply aren't cut out for college. "No one wants to really talk about this, but a lot of [teens] come out of high school unprepared to do legitimate college-level work," says Kenneth C. Gray, a Pennsylvania State emeritus professor of education and coauthor with Herr of *Other Ways to Win.*

At the same time, four years of college demands a steep investment that may take years to recoup. In-state tuition, fees and room and board at a public four-year college now average $15,213 per year, up 5.9 percent in a year, though student aid often lowers the tab. At private schools, the bill — not counting any aid — runs $35,636 per year, up 4.3 percent in a year.[7] (*See graph, p. 30.*)

And a bachelor's degree is no guarantee of career success or upward mobility. Much may depend on the field of study. For instance, degrees in health care, computer

Canada Leads World in Young College Graduates

Canada has the highest percentage in the world of young adults with two- and four-year college degrees. The United States is tied for sixth place, with Australia, Spain and Sweden.

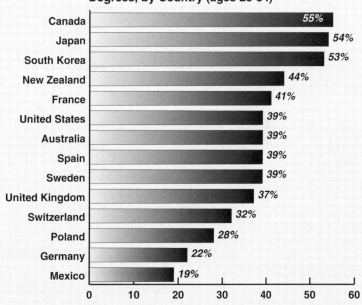

Percentage of Young Adults With Two- or Four-Year College Degrees, by Country (ages 25-34)

Country	Percentage
Canada	55%
Japan	54%
South Korea	53%
New Zealand	44%
France	41%
United States	39%
Australia	39%
Spain	39%
Sweden	39%
United Kingdom	37%
Switzerland	32%
Poland	28%
Germany	22%
Mexico	19%

Source: "A Stronger Nation Through Higher Education," Lumina Foundation for Education, February 2009

science or engineering may offer far better prospects than those in the humanities.

Meanwhile, many good jobs simply don't require a bachelor's degree. About half of all employment is in so-called middle-skill occupations — jobs that require more than a high-school diploma but less than a four-year degree, according to a 2007 study by Robert Lerman, an economics professor at American University, and Harry J. Holzer, a professor at Georgetown University's Public Policy Institute. Demand for such workers will likely remain strong compared to the supply, they said.[8]

"Real pay for radiological technicians increased 23 percent between 1997 and 2005, speech/respiratory therapists saw real increases of 10 to 14 percent and real pay for electricians rose by 18 percent," they found.

"These increases compare very favorably with the overall 5 percent increase for the average American worker."[9]

In June, in the depths of the current economic downturn, *The New York Times* noted that "employers are begging for qualified applicants for certain occupations, even in hard times."[10] Most of the jobs take years of experience, the newspaper noted. But some jobs in high demand, such as those in welding, don't require four years of college.

"Not everyone needs a degree, and not every job requires a four-year degree," says Tony Zeiss, president of Central Piedmont Community College, a six-campus institution in and around Charlotte, N.C., with more than 70,000 part- and full-time students. "For decades, only about 22 percent of jobs have required a baccalaureate degree or higher, and yet 75 percent of the jobs consistently require training beyond high school but below a baccalaureate. That's community college."

Still, whether community colleges, which get most of their money from recession-battered state and local governments, can keep up with demand remains an open question, especially as the Obama administration puts them at the center of his postsecondary education policy.[11]

Nearly 40 percent of 18- to 24-year-olds were enrolled in college last year, a record number that was propelled by swelling community college attendance, according to Pew Research Center data reported by *The New York Times*.[12]

"At the same time that we have tremendous increases in enrollment, states are cutting budgets like crazy," says Norma G. Kent, vice president for communications at the American Association of Community Colleges. "Our tradition has been to do more with less, but there gets to be a stretching point beyond which you cannot go. Our credo is open access and open doors, and whether consciously or de facto, we are turning away students."

In California, community colleges lost $840 million in state funding in the combined fiscal 2008-2009 and 2009-2010 budgets, according to Scott Lay, president and CEO of the Community College League of California. Institutions face eliminating course offerings and turning away students, he says. "We believe when this all shakes out, total enrollment will drop by about 250,000 students," or 8.6 percent, by the 2010-2011 academic year, Lay says.

High-school vocational education programs have long offered the potential for non-college-bound students to learn the fundamentals of a marketable trade or craft, and then move directly into the job market or on to further training at a community college, technical school or even a four-year institution. Yet for decades "vo-ed" programs — typically wood shop or auto repair — carried a stigma, often unfairly, as a dumping ground for low achievers. In recent years, however, many vocational education programs have been transformed into progressive "career and technical education" (CTE) programs that integrate core academic training in math, reading and other essentials into job-specific courses like computer programming, medical technology, restaurant and hotel management and construction.

"Historically, there's been a real divide between the academic and vocational side," says Julian Alssid, executive director of the Workforce Strategy Center in New York, a national nonprofit group that focuses on making education and workforce development more responsive to the economy. But, he adds, "we're seeing much more melding" of academic and technical training in career and technical programs.

As policy experts and educators debate the merits of a four-year college degree versus other options, here are some of the questions being raised:

Is a four-year college degree necessary for financial security?

In a report last year, the American Youth Policy Forum, a nonprofit group in Washington, said that "while the benefits of college in terms of lifetime earnings, health and civic participation are known, success in our economy and society isn't limited to the attainment of a four-year college degree."[13]

Many well-paying fields don't require a bachelor's degree, the group noted. "All you have to do," says Betsy Brand, the report's author and the policy forum's executive director, "is look at [Labor Department] numbers to realize that yes, indeed, we need people with associate degrees and industry certificates in order to keep our economy running."

That is not to say that postsecondary education is unimportant or that a four-year degree isn't a worthy objective for many students. "I spent 40 years teaching in graduate schools and colleges," points out Herr, the Pennsylvania State emeritus professor and *Other Ways to Win* coauthor. "That's not the issue." The issue, he says, is having realistic expectations about a college degree and a clear-eyed understanding of the options.

In their book, Gray and Herr argue that "the current enthusiasm for a four-year college degree is excessive and unreasonable." Not all teenagers "are blessed with the academic talent to do college-level work or mature enough to pursue college at age 18," they write, and "many just plain do not like school." What's more, they assert, while most teens say they want to go to college to get a good-paying job, few consider "that the economy will not generate enough jobs that pay them a college-level wage" even if they get a degree.[14]

Studies are mixed on the issue of job demand. Some point to a rising need for workers with bachelor's degrees, and others to a shortfall in the number of people qualified for "middle-skill" jobs, which don't require four years of college.

For example, the Public Policy Institute of California said the supply of college-educated workers won't meet projected demand, in part because of impending retirements. In 2025, 41 percent of workers in the state will need a bachelor's degree if recent trends persist, the institute projected. That compares with 34 percent who had bachelor's degrees in 2006 and 28 percent in 1990. During that 16-year period, the institute noted, "The wages of college-educated workers grew substantially, whereas the wages of less-educated workers were relatively stagnant."[15]

But a separate study by the Workforce Alliance and two other groups that advocate for workforce-training education projected more than 2.7 million middle-skill job openings by 2016 in California. Such jobs would account for 43 percent of all openings in the state between 2006 and 2016, it said.[16] Studies in Rhode Island, Connecticut and elsewhere came to similar conclusions.[17]

Meanwhile, middle-class jobs requiring no college-level knowledge or skills are quickly vanishing, primarily because of global competition, the Lumina foundation said. And Americans who hold lower-skills jobs that do exist "are less likely to have access to quality health care, save for retirement or assure their children access to higher education." Getting a middle-class job these days

"is now mostly dependent on completing some form of postsecondary education."[18]

Still, experts in labor-force trends say the value of a degree depends in significant part on what academic field the degree is in, the quality of instruction and what job opportunities await the graduate.

"On average, people do better getting a four-year degree," says Lerman of American University, "but some [degrees] are better to begin with.... There is a lot of variability, and also a considerable amount of frustration" because many students aren't finding good jobs after graduation. "You're hearing that a fair number of them are going to community college later" to obtain a marketable skill, he says.

Alssid, of the Workforce Strategy Center, says that to achieve economic self-sufficiency "one really does need to have some form of postsecondary credentialing," but "the paper really has to have some value." And that, he argues, means that colleges and other training institutions should have a "much closer alignment" and a "strong partnership" with workforce and economic-development officials and industry.

Asked on the National Public Radio show "Tell Me More" whether a high-school graduate heading to a four-year college amid today's economic downturn is making an investment or a mistake, Syracuse University finance professor Boyce Watkins answered that "it's certainly an investment," but added: "The question is whether or not you get your return on that investment in actual financial capital or some sort of human capital or emotional capital or social capital.

"This blanket notion that going to college will guarantee you a better economic future is not always true," he continued. "When you have students who are going to college for economic advancement, and they choose majors that don't fit that particular objective and then take a lot of debt on in the process, then ... you have to ask them, well, did you plan it all the way through when you ended up with an outcome that you didn't quite expect?"

Going to college is important, Watkins said, but "we have to be very intelligent about what we expect to get out of our education."

Another guest on the show, Ohio University economics professor Richard Vedder, said 45 percent of people who go to four-year colleges don't get a bachelor's degree within six years. Another group of people, he said,

Two-Year Colleges Cost the Least

Publicly supported community colleges have the lowest average tuition rates and usually no room and board fees, while private not-for-profit four-year colleges have the highest average tuition and room and board fees.

Type	Average Tuition and Fees, 2009-10	Average Room and Board, 2009-10	Average Total Charges 2009-10
Public two-year	$2,544	N/A	N/A
Public four-year in-state	$7,020	$8,193	$15,213
Public four-year out-of-state	$18,548	$8,193	$26,741
Private not-for-profit four-year	$26,273	$9,363	$35,636
Private, for-profit*	$14,174	N/A	N/A

* Subsidiaries of larger parent companies, such as DeVry or the Apollo Group, that offer degree and non-degree programs and compete with community colleges to teach students specific workforce skills.

Sources: "Tuition and Fee and Room and Board Charges, 2009-10," The College Board, Annual Survey of Colleges, 2009, www.trends-collegeboard.com /college_pricing /pdf/2009_Trends_College_Pricing.pdf; Francesca Levy, "For-Profit Colleges Improve Their Financial Grades," BusinessWeek, August 12, 2008, www.businessweek.com/bschools/content/aug2008/ bs20080812_253727. htm?chan=bschools_bschool+index+page_top+stories

graduate but have trouble finding work and wind up taking jobs for which a college education isn't required.[19]

At the U.S. Chamber of Commerce, Arthur Rothkopf, a senior vice president in charge of the business group's Education and Workforce Initiative, says the Chamber "comes down very strongly" in favor of those "for whom a four-year degree is important and useful and is part of what they want to do with their lives," professionally or otherwise. But, he adds, "there needs to be far more emphasis on middle-skill jobs," whose requirements, he says, include both a rigorous high-school education and some form of postsecondary schooling such as a two-year degree or certificate.

"A lot of these middle-skill jobs are not going to get outsourced," whether the jobs entail working in factories, being welders, physician's assistants, technicians at nuclear power plants, or working for Intel, Cisco or Microsoft, Rothkopf says. "There are lots of jobs that don't require a four-year degree."

Are high-school career and technical-education programs adequately preparing students for upward mobility?

At Sussex Technical High School in Georgetown, Del., mathematics and English are incorporated into lessons in auto-body repair, cosmetology and computers, an approach that Patrick Savini, superintendent of the Sussex Technical School District, calls "techademics."

Technical instructors must know math and grammar, and academic teachers must be able to demonstrate how algebra and English apply to reading repair manuals and programming computers. "It's a dual expectation," Savini says. "It's the technical teacher understanding state standards [for] teaching math, science" and other core subjects, "and it's the academic teachers checking their ego at the door."

Sussex Technical has won recognition from the U.S. Department of Education and others, and not just for its integrated classroom approach. Ninth-graders get to explore six career majors for about a month each before choosing one for the rest of the year — and perhaps their entire time at the school. Classes last 90 minutes, allowing for deeper engagement with lessons and minimizing discipline problems. And Sussex offers extracurricular activities common at traditional high schools: athletic teams, a band program and a prom.

"It's about options," says Savini. "If you do career tech right, you prepare [students] for immediate employment but also take their aspirations and have them reach beyond."

Such an approach defies the negative images that have long dogged high-school career-training programs, which over the decades have been accused of "tracking" minorities and others into academic dead-ends.

"The public and many policy makers tend to have a negative and/or outdated image of CTE, believing that CTE lacks academic rigor, leads to antiquated, undesirable or low-paying jobs, limits access to college and serves only low-performing students," Brand noted in the American Youth Policy Forum report.[20] "But this is not today's reality," she added. CTE can increase student engagement, improve attendance and graduation, enhance academic learning and allow students to earn college credit while in high school, among other things, Brand wrote.

Still, CTE programs remain in flux. "High-quality CTE programs are not accessible to every student that wants to pursue such studies, and there are still outdated CTE programs that lack academic rigor and relevance to the labor market," Brand wrote.

Lerman of American University questions whether the types of course requirements being pushed for high-school diplomas "crowd out types of learning that could be more directly linked to careers." Lerman, who supports "work-based" learning or "apprentice-type activities," says that while "many [CTE] programs are pretty good," he would like to see more that link "much more directly" to careers and allow "people a chance to try things out. There's a lot about careers that you can only learn by doing," he says.

Measuring the success of CTE programs can be difficult. The Carl D. Perkins Career and Technical Education Act of 2006, or "Perkins IV" — the main federal law governing CTE programs — mandates that core academic subjects be integrated into career and technical programs and that schools assess results.

But a U.S. Government Accountability Office report this year said states say their biggest challenge is gathering data on students' attainment of technical skills and

College Graduates Earn the Most

Workers with bachelor's degrees earned an average of $57,181 in 2007 — or 63 percent more than those with some college or an associate's degree and 83 percent more than those with only a high-school diploma.

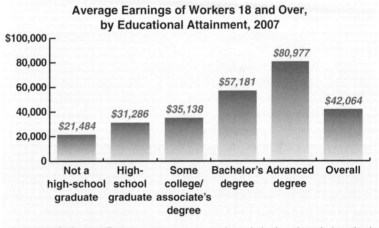

Average Earnings of Workers 18 and Over, by Educational Attainment, 2007

Source: U.S. Census Bureau, www.census.gov/population/socdemo/education/cps2008/tabA-3.xls, Table A-3.

student placement in jobs or further education after completion of CTE programs.[21]

"There's a real debate about what constitutes an accurate assessment of student performance," says Richard Walter, a Penn State education professor who directs the university's Workforce Education and Development Program. "Are we talking industry credential? Test assessment?"

A related problem, he and others say, is that CTE students seeking to gain industry certification sometimes have to pay for their own qualification tests, which may discourage low-income students from receiving credentials for skilled jobs.

Still, CTE programs are making strides. "States have been working to increase the rigor and effectiveness" of CTE education, noted a September report by the Education Commission of the States that highlights noteworthy state policy efforts at accountability, dropout prevention, preparation for high-demand occupations and other categories.[22]

In an interview, Brand says high-performing CTE programs work closely with employers and have employer advisory boards that guide administrators on economic and employment trends and industry needs. Such programs "really see themselves as contributing to the economic-development and labor-market needs of the community or the state or region," she said. At the same time, she said, many high schools link their CTE programs with local community colleges, enabling high-school students to become certified for jobs in health care, computer programming and other fields.

"This is what career and tech education should look like," Brand says. "If it's not connected to business and industry and postsecondary education, if it doesn't lead to some of these skill certificates, it shouldn't be here." Still, while many CTE programs are putting all the pieces together, some are behind. "It's hard to get educators to change rapidly."

James Kemple, executive director of the Research Alliance for New York City Schools at New York University, led a study of one kind of CTE program —"career academies" — which are schools within high schools that combine rigorous academics and training in such fields as travel and tourism, video technology, health care and finance. The academies establish close ties with local employers, raising students' familiarity with career options and providing opportunities for on-the-job experience.

Kemple says his study found that such programs produced a "substantial impact" on the long-term earnings and employment of participating students without decreasing the likelihood that the students would go on to college.[23]

Can community colleges meet rising demand for their programs?

At North Carolina's Central Piedmont Community College, Zeiss says he's never had to turn away students in the 42 years he's been in the higher education field — until last year.

"We turned away 5,000 students [who applied for at least one class] because we didn't have the money," he says. "We're up 35 percent in college-credit enrollment in the past two and half years, and we're down about 9 percent in budgets. You can increase your class sizes and number of students you counsel [only] so much, and we're bending at the limit. I've been spending my time raising private money so we can hire part-time teachers."

Central Piedmont's instructors each have 28 students per class on average this year, instead of the traditional 20, Zeiss says, and the counselor-to-student ratio is one-to-1,900. Meanwhile, applications for financial aid have doubled over the past year.

"We can't keep this up," Zeiss says. "Everybody loves us, and they're starting to put grants out there — Obama now and Bush before him. But we've got to shore up the revenue base of these colleges."

It's a message echoing throughout the nation's community college system, which educates nearly 12 million students, or 44 percent of the nation's undergraduates. Public community colleges depend on state and local revenues for about 60 percent of their funding — a source hit hard by the economic crisis.

What's more, community colleges typically lag four-year institutions in government support. "The country spends about three times more to educate students at four-year universities than to educate community college students," *USA Today* stated last year, citing Education Department data.[24]

In a survey this year, state directors of community college systems predicted that despite surging enrollment, state operating budgets for community colleges would decline an average of 1 percent while tuition is expected to rise at twice the inflation rate. Among 43 responding states, nine predicted cuts next year in their state student aid programs, and 21 forecast no increase. Many respondents expressed concern about what will happen as federal stimulus money — used by states to support education budgets — runs out.[25]

As states slash education budgets, the economic downturn has propelled huge numbers of unemployed adults into community colleges. "We've got a lot of adult learners who are out of a job or in a field that's going extinct, and they're coming back to community college for a lifeline," says Kent of the American Association of Community Colleges.

While Obama's proposed $12 billion community college plan would give the institutions a major boost, the money may not go as far as some would hope. It would be spread over a decade among 1,200 institutions, and $9 billion would be in the form of competitive grants requiring community colleges to improve student educational and employment outcomes.

Meeting such benchmarks could be a challenge for community colleges. Typically, they not only grant

Ph.D. Mechanic Celebrates Challenge of Manual Labor

Matthew B. Crawford straddles two worlds: He has a Ph.D. in political philosophy from the University of Chicago and is a fellow at the Institute for Advanced Studies in Culture at the University of Virginia. He also operates a motorcycle repair shop in Richmond and is author of the best-selling 2009 book *Shop Class as Soulcraft: An Inquiry into the Value of Work*, in which he argues that too often students are forced into a college track when manual trades offer a viable and rewarding alternative. Here are excerpts from the book:

Matthew B. Crawford, motorcycle mechanic and philosopher.

www.matthewbcrawford.com/Robert Adamo

"Today, in our schools, the manual trades are given little honor. The egalitarian worry that has always attended tracking students into 'college prep' and 'vocational ed' is overlaid with another: the fear that acquiring a specific skill set means that one's life is determined. In college, by contrast, many students don't learn anything of particular application; college is the ticket to an open future."

"The trades are then a natural home for anyone who would live by his own powers, free not only of deadening abstraction but also of the insidious hopes and rising insecurities that seem to be endemic in our current economic life."

"Piston slap may indeed sound like loose tappets, so to be a good mechanic you have to be constantly attentive to the possibility that you may be mistaken. This is an ethical virtue."

"I landed the job at the think tank because I had a prestigious education in the liberal arts, yet the job itself felt illiberal: coming up with the best arguments money could buy. This wasn't work befitting a free man, and the tie I wore started to feel like the mark of the slave."

"At issue in the contrast between office work and the manual trades is the idea of individual responsibility, tied to the presence or absence of objective standards."

two-year degrees but also do workforce training in areas such as health and computer science, provide English-as-a-second-language classes for non-native students, prepare some students for transfer to four-year schools and perhaps offer on-site training tailored to the specific needs of employers. Community colleges also often work with small businesses to provide training for entrepreneurs.

"Community colleges mean many different things," says Alssid of the Workforce Strategy Center. "A big part of the challenge for community colleges is that almost all of them are being called upon to fulfill this multiplicity of missions."

What's more, community colleges must provide remedial classes to a significant portion of incoming students — a problem that four-year institutions also face but is most pronounced at community colleges.

A study on college readiness by Strong American Schools, a project of Rockefeller Philanthropy Advisors, concluded that well over a third of all college students need remedial coursework to acquire basic academic skills and that 43 percent of students at public two-year institutions have enrolled in a remedial course.

"In many ways, the problem is the American high school," the study concluded. It noted that nearly 80 percent of students needing remedial work had a high-school grade-point average of 3.0 or higher, suggesting that many teens finish high school ill-prepared for college-level study.[26]

"Community colleges have huge amounts of energy siphoned away by providing remediation to students who aren't yet ready to do college-level work," says Alssid. "The country is going to have to figure out how to fix that problem."

Meanwhile, enrollment continues to grow at community colleges, fueled by people looking to acquire marketable skills. And many of those people are ones who already have four-year degrees. Gray, the Pennsylvania State University emeritus professor, sees something of an irony in the trend.

"Community college enrollment is way up," he says, while most "non-competitive" four-year colleges — those with easy admission standards — "are looking for students."

The noncompetitive colleges "attribute this to the fact that there's less money for financial aid, and therefore students are seeking less-expensive alternatives," Gray says, but "I'm not convinced of that. I suspect people are starting to sense that maybe they should go" to a community college to gain an industry credential "and get a four-year degree later."

BACKGROUND

Rise of Community Colleges

From the Republic's earliest days, leaders stressed that education is important for the well-being of the nation and its citizens. "Knowledge, being necessary to good government and the happiness of mankind, schools and the means of education shall forever be encouraged," the Continental Congress wrote in the Northwest Ordinance in 1787.[27]

Yet questions arose in the new nation over how widespread higher education should be. In 1862 Congress passed the Morrill Act, also known as the Land Grant Act, which called for public land to be donated for colleges emphasizing agricultural and mechanical-arts training. The law was the cornerstone for a system of state colleges and universities that made higher education available to millions of students.[28] Still, not all Americans benefited. A second Morrill Act, in 1890, sought to expand college opportunities for African-Americans.

As the economy evolved from rural and agricultural to urban and industrial, education evolved, too. In 1901, Joliet Junior College, in Illinois, became the nation's first public community college, formed as an experimental program for high-school graduates.

College enrollment was still a rarity among young people in the early 20th century — Joliet Junior College started with just six students — and educational and political leaders debated how best to prepare for what they saw as increasingly competitive global economy.

"[T]he great battles of the world in the future are to be commercial rather than military," the educational historian Ellwood P. Cubberley wrote in 1909. He added: "Whether we like it or not, we are beginning to see that we are pitted against the world in a gigantic battle of brains and skill, with the markets of the world, work for our people and internal peace and contentment as the prizes at stake."[29]

A key way to win those prizes, it was widely viewed, was to promote job-specific vocational education.

Educational theorist Charles Prosser, a steelworker's son, was critical of a single-minded focus on academics and scholarship. He argued that high schools should offer separate skills training to meet the interests, capabilities and job prospects of a significant portion of students. Traditionalists such as the philosopher and educational reformer John Dewey vehemently disagreed. In the end, Prosser's theories prevailed.

"World economic competition was viewed as the best strategy for national economic growth," Gray, the co-author of *Other Ways to Win*, wrote in a 1996 journal article, and "the schools were accused of doing little to help the cause, particularly with regard to the education of children from working-class families who were beginning to go to high school in large numbers." The solution, he added, was to develop a separate curriculum in high schools tailored to training students for jobs in commerce, industry, agriculture and home economics.[30]

In 1914, a commission appointed by President Woodrow Wilson cited census data showing that more than 12 million Americans worked in agriculture and 14 million in manufacturing, mechanical and allied pursuits. But the commission concluded that probably fewer than 1 percent were adequately prepared for their jobs.[31]

Three years later, Congress passed the landmark Smith-Hughes Act, which became known as the Magna Carta

CHRONOLOGY

1860s-1930s *As U.S. economy industrializes, country focuses more on higher education and vocational training for potential workforce.*

1862 Congress passes Morrill Act, known as the Land Grant Act, which calls for public land to be donated for colleges that emphasize agricultural and mechanical-arts training.

1890 Second Morrill Act seeks to expand college opportunities for African-Americans.

1901 Nation's first public community college, Joliet (Illinois) Junior College, opens with six students.

1917 Congress passes landmark Smith-Hughes Act, which provides money to states for high-school vocational education.

1920 Only 3 percent of Americans 25 and older hold bachelor's degrees.

1940s-1970s *World War II baby boom and GI Bill trigger huge wave of college enrollment.*

1944 GI Bill of Rights provides financial help for World War II veterans seeking to attend college.

1947 Truman Commission on Higher Education calls for a network of public community colleges.... College enrollment stands at 2.3 million.

1952 Veterans Readjustment Assistance Act of 1952 — the Korean War GI Bill — is passed, eventually helping 2.4 million vets attend college or receive on-the-job or other training.

1965 Congress passes Higher Education Act to provide financial aid to students pursuing higher education; college enrollment climbs to 5.6 million.

1975 Community colleges number more than 1,200; college enrollment nationwide grows to 10.9 million.

1980s-1990s *Vocational-education enrollment begins to decline sharply as more and more students pursue four-year college degrees.*

1983 In "A Nation at Risk," U.S. Education Department warns of a "rising tide of mediocrity" in education and says the United States is falling behind in global economic competition.

1984 Congress passes Carl D. Perkins Vocational Education Act to help improve labor-force skills and provide broader job training for adults, disabled people and others.

1990 Tech-Prep program helps students begin learning a technical field in high school, then a certificate or two-year degree in that field at a community college.... Twenty percent of Americans 25 and older have at least a bachelor's degree, up from 7.7 percent in 1960 and 16.2 percent in 1980.

1991 College enrollment continues to climb; 63 percent of high-school graduates go directly to college, compared with 46 percent in 1973.

2000-Present *President Obama calls for higher graduation rates and more money for community colleges.*

2000 Republican-dominated Congress does not renew School to Work Opportunities Act, passed during the Bill Clinton administration, which allows some students to earn academic credit for work experience.

2002 President George W. Bush signs No Child Left Behind Act, which holds schools accountable for student achievement.

2006 Perkins Act amendments mandate closer integration of skills training and core academic subjects in high-school vocational courses; the law replaces the term "vocational education" with "career and technical education," or "CTE." ... Bush seeks to eliminate funding for vocational education, but funding is retained after protests.

2009 President Obama proposes to spend $12 billion over the next decade to strengthen the community college system and calls on every American to commit to at least a year of higher education or career training.... Obama eases Pell Grant restrictions for unemployed adults.... Unemployment rate exceeds 10 percent, sending many laid-off adults to community colleges in search of new skills.

Community Colleges Welcome Night Owls

But please take the bus, busy schools ask students.

Community colleges are getting so many applicants that sometimes they can't admit everybody, as they once did. Or they are turning to unorthodox approaches.

When a flood of new students descended on Bunker Hill Community College in Boston, the school inaugurated what has been dubbed the "Burning the Midnight Oil" schedule. It offers several popular introductory courses from 11:45 p.m. until 2:30 a.m. And the school pushed the first class of the day up to 7 a.m. Makeshift parking lots were created to accommodate the overload.

At Holyoke Community College, also in Massachusetts, parking was so strained by rising enrollment that the school sent postcards to all 7,500 students urging them to take public transportation.

Clackamas Community College in Oregon City, Ore., has been offering a late-night welding course since last spring.

Northern Virginia Community College (NVCC) added 20 popular lower-level classes, such as English, biology, psychology and accounting, this semester that begin before 7 a.m.; other classes run late into the evening.

"Over the last two years, our annual student enrollment has jumped over 8,000 students while our physical capacity has grown only modestly," says NVCC President Robert G. Templin, Jr. "To respond to the dramatic increase in student demand, we've stretched our class schedule by offering classes as early as 6 a.m., and pushed night classes past 10 p.m. Nearly everything we've offered has been snapped up regardless of the time or format."

But some schools control the overflow by closing their doors when they fill up. The six community colleges that are part of the City University of New York (CUNY) traditionally have accepted applications up to a week before classes start — enough time for students to apply for financial aid and receive the required immunizations. This fall, however, all but one of the campuses had to stop accepting applications a month before the semester began because it didn't have enough teachers and other resources to support the flood of new students.

"Enrollment has been growing steadily, but this was a tidal wave for us this fall," said Gail O. Mellow, president of LaGuardia Community College, in Long Island City. The school's student body has risen by almost 50 percent over the past decade.[1]

Virtually every state has had to deal with rising enrollments at public community colleges, according to the American Association of Community Colleges. Some in California have reported increases of 35 percent just since 2008.[2]

At Sinclair Community College in economically suffering Dayton, Ohio, enrollment has jumped 25 percent over the past year alone as laid-off General Motors employees and other auto industry workers seek new skills in the evolving labor market. Recent high-school graduates are also finding two-year institutions more preferable to pricier

---

of vocational education.[32] Under Smith-Hughes, federal money was distributed to the states for vocational education in high schools, but unlike today's integrated approach for blending academics and skills training, the 1917 act drew a clear distinction. The law stipulated that vocational-education money could not be used to pay salaries of academic teachers, and it limited the amount of academic instruction a vocational student could receive.[33]

"By explicitly defining vocational education as preparation for occupations that did not require a bachelor's or advanced degree, the Smith-Hughes Act affirmed that vocational education was not intended to prepare high-school students for college," wrote David Stern, an education professor at the University of California-Berkeley.

Still, college was less of an issue back then than it is today. As Stern noted, in 1920 a mere 3 percent of Americans age 25 and older held bachelor's degrees.[34]

Over the decades, vocational education served a variety of purposes — to strengthen national defense in the 1920s, ease unemployment in the 1930s, address wartime

four-year colleges, as many parents struggle to make ends meet. School officials say they are trying to keep Sinclair affordable as many Dayton residents become financially challenged.

Sinclair currently offers high-school students in the area who take technical courses and maintain a C-plus average in their junior and senior years an automatic $3,000 scholarship, enough to cover tuition for three semesters. Courses range from radiology to traditional information technology disciplines.

The community college also has helped 53 area high schools upgrade their technical courses and make it easier for students to transition to college. It recently made a $4 million grant to a local school district to create a "career technology" high school that offers advanced science courses and will serve as a feeder school for the college.

Such initiatives support President Obama's American Graduation Initiative — a 10-year, $12 billion plan to invest in community colleges and add 5 million new graduates by 2020. Obama has embraced the nation's community colleges, calling them "vital bulwarks" against the decline of the American middle class and, hence, the nation's competitiveness.

"Jobs requiring at least an associate degree are projected to grow twice as fast as jobs requiring no college experience," he

The first session of Kathleen O'Neill's evening class in psychology draws a crowd at Bunker Hill Community College in Boston.

said during a speech about vanishing jobs this July in Warren, Mich., among the recession's hardest-hit areas. "We will not fill those jobs — or even keep those jobs here in America — without the training offered by community colleges."[3]

Meanwhile, some educators worry that community colleges may not have enough resources to meet the growing current demand.

"The community college is a second-chance institution for the country," said Patrick M. Callan, president of the National Center for Public Policy and Higher Education. "Most people would agree that this is not a good time in terms of the economic competitiveness of the country to be turning people away."[4]

— Darrell Dela Rosa

[1] Lisa W. Foderaro, "Two-Year Colleges, Swamped, No Longer Welcome All," *The New York Times*, Nov. 12, 2009, www.nytimes.com/2009/11/12/education/12community.html.

[2] Abby Goodnough, "New Meaning for Night Class at 2-Year Colleges," *The New York Times*, Oct. 28, 2009, www.nytimes.com/2009/10/28/education/28community.html.

[3] "Remarks by the President on the American Graduation Initiative," Office of the Press Secretary, The White House, July 14, 2009, www.whitehouse.gov/the_press_office/Remarks-by-the-President-on-the-American-Graduation-Initiative-in-Warren-MI.

[4] Foderaro, *op. cit.*

industrial needs in the 1940s and smooth the transition to peacetime after World War II.[35] But vocational education sometimes faced accusations that it provided an inferior education and was used to channel students into economic blind alleys.

James Fraser, former dean of the School of Education at Northeastern University in Boston, told *The Christian Science Monitor* that in the 1940s and '50s some groups began to see vocational education as problematic. "It was popular in working-class white communities," Fraser said,

"but among immigrants and in communities of color it was mistrusted. They feared that [vocational education] was being used to steer their kids into second-class citizenship."[36]

College Degree Beckons

Meanwhile, a college degree beckoned more and more young people. Policy changes spurred the trend. The 1944 GI Bill of Rights provided financial help for World War II veterans seeking to attend college. After the war, a report by the President's Commission on Higher Education, known as the Truman Commission Report, called for a network of public community colleges that would charge little if anything in tuition, offer a comprehensive program emphasizing civic responsibility and serve their local areas.[37] The report also called for a doubling of college attendance by 1960.[38]

"[W]e shall aim at making higher education equally available to all young people … to the extent that their capacity warrants a further social investment in their training," the commission wrote.[39]

Later, Congress passed various financial-aid bills, notably the Higher Education Act of 1965.

Meanwhile, demographic, economic and geopolitical developments were fueling college enrollment. The postwar baby boom created a huge bubble of college-age young adults. The Cold War space race sparked enrollment in university science and technology programs. And in the 1960s and early '70s, the Vietnam War led millions of young men to seek college deferments from the military draft.

College enrollment exploded from about 2.3 million students in 1947 to 10.9 million in 1975, according to the U.S. Census Bureau.[40] It kept climbing as recession and global competition for manufactured goods fueled a perception in the 1980s that blue-collar work was no longer secure and a college education — preferably a four-year degree — was a ticket to economic success.

By 1990, 20 percent of the American population age 25 and older had at least a bachelor's degree, up from 7.7 percent in 1960 and 16.2 percent in 1980. By 2000, the figure stood at more than 24 percent.[41]

As four-year-college enrollments rose, community colleges also were booming. The number of institutions and their branch campuses exploded from roughly 600 in 1955 to more than 1,200 in 1975 and about 1,600 (including multiple campuses) by the end of the 1990s.[42]

During this period, enrollment in high-school vocational programs fell sharply, beginning in the early 1980s, Gray wrote. Spurring the decline was not only a worry that secure, well-paid industry jobs were disappearing but also the notion that "in the eyes of the public the only thing that seemed to be at all certain was the increasingly publicized idea that college graduates made more money than high-school graduates," he wrote.[43]

"Faced with uncertainty about economic opportunities in the future and misinformation about career opportunities for future college graduates, and aided by an oversupply of college seats and thus open admissions at many colleges, students … [rejected] traditional vocational education offerings and [enrolled] in college preparatory programs. The nation concluded that there is only 'one way to win' … — to get a four-year baccalaureate degree."[44]

As a result, Gray argued, many "academically average" students who in the past would have taken vocational-education courses were instead on the college track and finished high school "prepared neither for college nor work."

In 1973, 46 percent of high-school graduates went directly on to college, Gray noted, citing Education Department data. By 1991, the proportion had risen to 63 percent. And the proportion continues to grow.[45]

"A new vocationalism" had emerged, Gray wrote, "manifested in the form of growing percentages of academically average students enrolling in traditional college preparatory programs." Motivating their enrollment, he wrote, was not "some newly found thirst for knowledge" but rather "vocational reasons."

Meanwhile, as economic and social conditions changed in the 1980s and '90s, American education came under severe scrutiny. In 1983, the Education Department's "A Nation at Risk" report warned of a "rising tide of mediocrity" in schools and colleges and said the United States was falling behind in global economic competition. The report spurred deep soul-searching among reformers and government officials about how to improve the educational system — introspection that continues today as high-school and college dropout rates soar, and even elite universities have high numbers of students who need remedial coursework.[46]

Education Reforms

In the wake of the report, policy officials began to look for ways to reform the educational system, and some of those efforts centered on vocational education. In 1984 Congress passed the Carl D. Perkins Vocational Education Act with a goal of improving the nation's labor-force skills and providing broader job-training opportunities for adults, disabled people and so-called at-risk populations. Since then, the Perkins Act has gone through a series of reauthorizations and reforms aimed at strengthening the link between academic and vocational training.

In 1990, for example, more emphasis was placed on developing career prospects for all students, rather than just those who were not college-bound. Under a program called Tech-Prep, students could begin learning a technical field in high school and then earn a certificate or two-year degree in that field at a community college.

In a 2006 revision of the Perkins law, the term "career and technical education," or CTE, was officially adopted in place of "vocational education," and schools were required to more closely integrate core academic coursework into job-skills training.

At the same time, Washington was placing more and more emphasis on the ability of schools to meet academic benchmarks. That approach became enshrined in 2002 in the George W. Bush administration's No Child Left Behind Act, which holds schools accepting federal funds accountable for student achievement.[47]

By then, however, vocational education was under fire. In 2000 the Republican-dominated Congress did not renew the School to Work Opportunities Act, a Clinton-era law that in some cases allowed students to earn academic credit for job internships or other work experience. Conservatives argued that School to Work shifted the educational focus away from core academics. Others said it sought to replicate the German apprenticeship model and steered students too early onto a career path.

Then, in 2006, Bush sought to completely eliminate federal funding for vocational education, arguing that it had "produced little or no evidence of improved outcomes for students despite decades of federal investment."

"Bush wasn't impressed with CTE," says Walter of Pennsylvania State University. "He tried to zero out Perkins — tried to remove every cent, [in part because] that [was] the largest chunk of money that would have been available to him to work on high-school reforms" under No Child Left Behind.

Bush didn't succeed. Advocates, including community colleges, argued that vocational education enhanced student achievement and increased postsecondary enrollment. Still, while vocational funding survived, the federal outlay

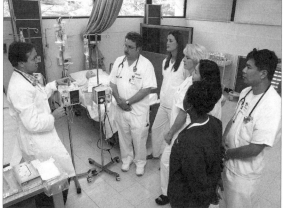

Central Piedmont Community College (both)

Training for the Workforce

A student (top left) in the sustainability technology program at Central Piedmont Community College in Charlotte, N.C., reviews a rooftop photovoltaic installation with his instructor. Two-year degrees offered at the school prepare students to work in the alternative energy, green construction and sustainable manufacturing fields. Nursing students (bottom) at the school can earn a two-year associate's degree and take the national test for licensing as a registered nurse.

devoted to career and technical education has declined in recent years. Obama proposed keeping it flat at $1.3 billion in fiscal 2010, but CTE and community college advocates want it raised to at least $1.4 billion.[48]

At the same time, Obama has proposed expanding the overall 2010 education budget by $1.3 billion, including increasing spending on postsecondary education by 6 percent — or $200 million — to $3.6 billion. His budget would expand student financial aid, elevate the role of community colleges and support innovative state efforts to help low-income students complete their college education.[49]

Even so, students face skyrocketing college costs at a time when family incomes remain stagnant and state education budgets are getting pounded. In a *Newsweek* article in October, Sen. Lamar Alexander, R-Tenn., former education secretary in the George H. W. Bush administration, said state higher-education funding rose 17.6 percent from 2000 to 2006 but that average tuition at public four-year institutions shot up 63 percent, with state support for education hit hardest by "runaway" Medicaid costs.[50]

A big worry for many state officials is the looming termination of federal stimulus spending. Alexander cited a comment made by Tennessee Gov. Phil Bredesen in March, that "when this money ends 21 months from now, our campuses will suddenly need to begin operating with about $180 million less in state funding than they had this year."

Among the possible ways to cut college costs, Alexander advocates having students finish a bachelor's degree in three years. Schools could make year-round use of academic facilities, and students could reduce their college expenses, he argued.

But speeding up graduation is no small feat. A study this year by the American Enterprise Institute, a conservative Washington think tank, found that on average, four-year colleges graduate fewer than 60 percent of their freshmen within six years."[51] Another study, published in the new book *Crossing the Finish Line*, found that only 65 percent of students at highly selective flagship public universities graduated in four years. At several less selective state systems, only about 26 percent finished in four years.[52]

Coauthor William G. Bowen, president emeritus of both the Andrew W. Mellon Foundation and Princeton University, told the online publication *Inside Higher Ed* of an atmosphere at many schools that suggests it is normal to take six years to graduate.

"At a very highly regarded flagship university," Bowen said, "when you talk there to students about graduation rates, you can be told, as we were told by one person, 'graduating in four years is like leaving the party at 10 o'clock.'"[53]

CURRENT SITUATION

Obama's Initiative

In a speech to a joint congressional session in February, Obama declared that "a good education is no longer just a pathway to opportunity — it is a pre-requisite." But he noted that while three-quarters of the fastest-growing occupations require education beyond high school, just over half of Americans have that much schooling.

What's more, Obama said, the United States has "one of the highest high-school dropout rates of any industrialized nation," and "half of the students who begin college never finish," which he called "a prescription for economic decline."

The centerpiece of Obama's effort to boost postsecondary education and college completion is the American Graduation Initiative, which he announced at Macomb Community College in Warren, Mich., the state's largest grantor of associate degrees. The aim of the record $12-billion, 10-year plan, Obama said, is to help an additional 5 million Americans earn degrees and certificates in the next decade. The money would be used to improve community college programs, buildings and classrooms and academic courses.[54]

"Community colleges are an undervalued asset in our country," Obama said. "Not only is that not right, it's not smart."

The administration's plan for community colleges makes up part of a much broader bill, called the Student Aid and Fiscal Responsibility Act, introduced in July in the House Education and Labor Committee and passed in the House in September.[55] The House bill would invest $10 billion in community colleges, $7 billion of it through competitive grants, according to the committee. The measure includes $40 billion to incrementally raise the maximum annual Pell Grant scholarship over the next decade, $3 billion to help improve college access and completion and $2.55 billion for historically black colleges and other institutions that serve minorities.

Notably, the bill would replace guaranteed student loans administered by private lenders with direct government loans, a controversial idea that the administration says would save billions of dollars but that opponents argue would lead to inefficiencies.[56]

Separately, the $787 billion economic-stimulus bill passed this year expanded the Pell Grant student-aid

Should college-preparatory and career-training programs get equal priority?

YES Sen. Roderick D. Wright *(D-Los Angeles)*
California State Senate

NO Arun Ramanathan
Executive Director The Education Trust-West

Written for *CQ Researcher*, November 2009

Written for *CQ Researcher*, November 2009

Recently, I attended a Senate committee hearing where someone quoted from a new report that stated 35 percent of all jobs would require a four-year college degree by 2020. The members of the committee responded by drafting legislation to increase college-preparatory requirements in California schools.

I looked at that same report, from The Workforce Alliance, and thought: What about the other 65 percent that won't require a bachelor's degree?

College was never intended for everyone. It used to be assumed that some kids would become plumbers and some would become doctors. Some would become police officers and some would become accountants.

But today's high-school students are told if they don't go to college they are failures who will never amount to anything. So kids with an aptitude for auto mechanics instead try to become lawyers or financial managers and end up with no job and no marketable skills.

This quest to send everyone to college has had disastrous consequences: High-school dropout rates are at all-time highs. The percentage of kids entering and not finishing college is at an all-time high. The percentage of kids with four-year degrees enrolled at vocational programs at community colleges, or dubious private postsecondary institutions, is at an all-time high. The number of high-school graduates with no job skills is at an all-time high. Here in California, the number of prison inmates is at an all-time high.

If we are going to rebuild our economy, we will need skilled workers more than ever. It is estimated that openings for middle-skill jobs such as electrical linemen, respiratory therapists and computer technicians will surge by 20 percent in the next decade.

As baby boomers retire, this lack of trained workers could stall our nation's economic recovery. Meanwhile, kids are being pushed into college, becoming disillusioned and dropping out of both high school and college. So society loses all the way around.

Clearly, we need to maintain our development of professional careers for kids with that aptitude. There will always be a need for engineers and doctors. I believe our educational system can and must prepare for both career and college tracks. One without the other is a complete failure.

We are long past the time when young people could graduate from high school and go directly into careers that guaranteed lifetime employment and a living wage. Now, the annual wage difference between a four-year college degree and a high-school diploma is $25,895. And, for African-Americans and Latinos, wage differences between high-school and college completion are striking.

An African-American woman with a college degree earns $16,836 more than an African-American woman without one. And a Latino male with some college earns almost $5,000 more than a Latino male with a high-school diploma. Times have changed, and there is no debating the link between educational opportunity and economic success.

What has not changed is the lack of educational opportunities for many low-income students and students of color. While it is true that not all students will go to college, far too often our most vulnerable students are tracked into low-level career-tech classes and end up prepared for neither college nor career. These students, if they graduate from high school, do so with the empty promise of a bright future in a trade, only to find they are missing the critical skills necessary for success. This matters, because even skilled trades — plumbing, auto technicians and manufacturing — all require intensive academic preparation.

Rigorous career technical education (CTE) classes integrated into a college-prep curriculum can enhance the students' academic experience and allow them to explore real-world applications in areas such as mathematics or physics. In some districts, innovative high schools, like Kearny Construction Tech School in San Diego, are doing just that.

Construction Tech aligns its classes with the graduation requirements of the University of California and California State University systems. As a result, its graduates have a true choice between college and career, and the skills to succeed in either.

The question is not whether school districts should give equal priority to college-prep and career-training programs. High schools must provide all students with a rigorous curriculum that prepares them for the challenges of college, career and civic participation so that young people can explore a wide range of options for work and higher education. If not, they may suffer crippling limitations that do a tragic disservice to them, their communities and our nation.

The Institute of Culinary Education in New York City offers six- to 11-month career-training programs in culinary arts, pastry and baking and culinary management. The school holds night classes because of the increasing demand for cooking classes from both amateurs and aspiring professionals.

program and raised the maximum annual award by $500 in the first year — to $5,350 — and more in the second.

And in May the administration made it easier for some unemployed adults to receive Pell Grants, a move advocates hail as an important step in linking jobs and education. Pell Grants cover tuition at most community colleges.

"The Pell move is pivotal because it shows that the president understands that postsecondary education is the workforce development system and a key piece of the workforce adjustment system in response to trade and technology change," wrote Anthony Carnevale, director of the Georgetown University Center on Education and the Workforce. Obama's remarks on education and jobs and his action on Pell Grants "is clearly more than another love note to community colleges, gushing over how they do so much with so little, or another boutique program funded with departmental transfers," he added.[57]

Not that Pell Grants are immune to criticism. Florida's *St. Petersburg Times* reported in October that more than $2.3 million in Pell Grants funded by the economic stimulus had gone to Tampa-area cosmetology and massage schools "to pay tuition for the hairdressers, masseuses and nail technicians of tomorrow" despite limited job opportunities.[58]

"It would raise the eyebrows of many Americans to know that is where their Pell Grant and stimulus money

is going," Steve Ellis, vice president of Taxpayers for Common Sense, a watchdog group in Washington, told the newspaper.[59]

Overall, the president's education plans have been viewed with a mix of praise and skepticism.

"He is the first president I have ever heard … actually address" the need for postsecondary education without simply prescribing a four-year degree, says Walter, the Penn State workforce-education director.

Likewise, Nancy Cauthen, director of the Economic Opportunity Program at Demos, a liberal think tank in New York, said the proposed increase in community college funding "will increase postsecondary success and improve economic opportunity and mobility for young adults." It recognizes that "low graduation rates at these institutions will not increase if community colleges are forced to cut back their spending" and if students, particularly low-income and first-generation college students, can't afford to stay enrolled, she said.[60]

But Neal McCluskey, associate director of the Center for Educational Freedom at the Cato Institute, a libertarian think tank, termed Obama's call for a year of postsecondary education for everyone "essentially a 'consume-more-education' policy. We're encouraging people to consume education that they're either not prepared for or aren't really interested in by subsidizing it and having our leaders tell us it's the ticket to the middle class and the American dream."[61]

Evolving Labor Market

The full Congress has yet to digest the Obama plan — a companion Senate bill hadn't been filed as of mid-November. Meanwhile, some education experts are focusing on the 2010 budget and their concerns about career and technical-education funding under the Perkins Act.

"It is refreshing that this administration recognizes the need for an investment in career technical education," said Kimberly A. Green, executive director of the National Association of State Directors of Career Technical Education Consortium. "However, I am disappointed that the president's budget proposes flat funding for Perkins. Level-funding this program is like putting a temporary patch on a hole in a dam that is ready to burst. Demand for these programs is up. The pace of technological change is increasing. Equipment needs are growing.

To be able to support our country properly, CTE needs a significant new infusion of funding."[62]

Still, observers are hopeful that Obama will put more money into CTE after the nation's current budget woes ease. A positive sign, they say, is the appointment of Brenda Dann-Messier as assistant secretary for vocational and adult education. A former Clinton-era Education Department official, Dann-Messier most recently was president of Dorcas Place Adult and Family Learning Center, an educational facility for low-income residents in Providence, R.I.

"We're waiting to see how things play out with the new assistant secretary," Walter says. "She has a real background in adult education."

However things play out for CTE and the administration's broader education policy, the labor market will continue to evolve in ways that make some form of postsecondary education necessary for economic security, many experts say — but not without challenges for both employers and students.

For employers, one of the biggest challenges is finding workers with adequate skills. Nearly half of respondents to a 2008 survey of more than 200 employers said they provide remedial-training programs for newly hired graduates at three educational levels: high school, two-year college and four-year college. The programs are designed to remove deficiencies among new hires in skills the employers expected them to have when hired. But most companies said their training programs were only moderately or somewhat successful at best.[63]

"U.S. business is increasingly outspoken about the competitiveness threat posed by an ill-prepared workforce — but employers must do a better job of quantifying this threat and communicating it to key stakeholders," said Mary Wright, program director of the Workforce Readiness Initiative at The Conference Board, a business membership organization that participated in the survey.[64]

For students, figuring out a career path can pose daunting challenges. A 2008 study by researchers at MPR Associates, a research and consulting firm specializing in education, and the National Center for Education Statistics compared employment experiences of 1992-1993 bachelor's degree recipients 10 years after college. The study found that compared with graduates with academic undergraduate majors — such as social sciences,

arts and math — those with career-oriented majors such as business, health and engineering "appeared to establish themselves in the labor force earlier, and relatively fewer obtained additional education."[65]

Some adults who already hold four-year degrees are finding themselves without the necessary skills to find work. In growing numbers, white-collar college graduates are turning to community colleges to upgrade their skills or learn new ones that might land them a second career.[66]

"Continuing education used to be personal enrichment, primarily, but it has moved steadily toward workforce development," James B. Jacobs, president of Macomb Community College, told *The New York Times.* "People would go to classes to learn to cook Chinese food to impress their friends and relatives or to learn interior decorating.

"Those courses have been transformed and have become areas for a lot of people coming out of white-collar jobs," he continued. "They now take culinary programs to help open a restaurant. They learn not just how to cook, but how to buy and how to run a restaurant."[67]

OUTLOOK
Many Challenges

The issues surrounding educational pathways for young adults will no doubt become more complex in coming years.

Career and technical-education programs will have to satisfy the needs of college- and career-bound students seeking training in fields such as computers and health care while also making the vocational-education programs worthwhile for students who may not be cut out for postsecondary education or middle-skill jobs.

"A huge issue" for schools offering a CTE program is "who is it serving?" says Walter of Penn State. "There are two sides of the argument. How does CTE fulfill its mission?"

CTE programs also must figure out how to measure success as high-school career training, postsecondary education and industry certification become more integrated, Walter says. In the past, programs "were assessed by how many students graduated [from high-school CTE classes] and were placed in employment." Now, he says, success is often measured by whether students complete a CTE program in high school, advance to other training and then gain a good job.

Community colleges must absorb a growing enrollment load despite severe budget limitations. Zeiss, of Central Piedmont Community College, points out that money designated in the House education bill for improving community college facilities is in the form of loans for shovel-ready projects. Zeiss says he doesn't know of many states that allow community colleges to borrow money. He says he hopes the Senate version of the bill will call for grants — at least matching grants — instead of loans.

For students, perhaps the biggest hurdle to overcome is the rising cost of education. Many students receive financial aid, of course. Full-time students at private not-for-profit four-year institutions get an estimated average of $14,400 in grant aid and federal tax benefits, according to the College Board, cutting tuition and fees to about $11,900 on average. At public four-year institutions, the aid and benefits average about $5,400, reducing the tab to $1,600.[68]

Still, many students finish college in debt — a problem made worse when no job is waiting after graduation. In 2007-2008, 38 percent of bachelor's degree recipients from public four-year institutions had no school debts, but 6 percent owed at least $40,000, according to the College Board.

The debt load was lighter for community college students. Sixty-two percent of those graduating with associate degrees from two-year public institutions had no debt, and less than 1 percent owed $40,000 or more.[69]

NOTES

1. Mike Rowe, "Work Is Not the Enemy," www.mike-roweworks.com.

2. "Remarks of President Barack Obama, Address to Joint Session of Congress," The White House, Feb. 24, 2009, www.whitehouse.gov/the_press_office/Remarks-of-President-Barack-Obama-Address-to-Joint-Session-of-Congress.

3. "A Stronger Nation through Higher Education," Lumina Foundation for Education, February 2009, www.luminafoundation.org/publications/A_stronger_nation_through_higher_education.pdf. The Lumina Foundation said its data source is the Organisation for Economic Co-operation and Development, "Education at a Glance 2008."

4. "Remarks of President Barack Obama," op. cit. For background, see Scott W. Wright, "Community Colleges," CQ Researcher, April 21, 2000, pp. 329-352.

5. U.S. Census Bureau, www.census.gov/population/socdemo/education/cps2008/tabA-3.xls.

6. Bureau of Labor Statistics, Oct. 2, 2009, www.bls.gov/news.release/empsit.t04.htm.

7. "Trends in College Pricing 2009," College Board, www.trends-collegeboard.com/college_pricing/pdf/2009_Trends_College_Pricing.pdf.

8. Harry J. Holzer and Robert Lerman, "America's Forgotten Middle-Skill Jobs," Workforce Alliance, November 2007, www.urban.org/UploadedPDF/411633_forgottenjobs.pdf. Holzer and Lerman are both scholars at the Urban Institute.

9. *Ibid.*

10. Louis Uchitelle, "Despite Recession, High Demand for Skilled Labor," *The New York Times*, June 24, 2009, www.nytimes.com/2009/06/24/business/24jobs.html?scp=1&sq=despite%20recession,%20high%20demand%20for%20skilled%20labor&st=cse.

11. For background on jobs and the economy, see the following *CQ Researcher* reports: Alan Greenblatt, "State Budget Crisis," Sept. 11, 2009, pp. 741-764; Peter Katel, "Vanishing Jobs," March 13, 2009, pp. 225-248; Marcia Clemmitt, "Public-Works Projects," Feb. 20, 2009, pp. 153-176; Kenneth Jost, *et al.*, "The Obama Presidency," Jan. 30, 2009, pp. 73-104; Peter Katel, "Straining the Safety Net," July 31, 2009, pp. 645-668.

12. Tamar Lewin, "College Enrollment Set Record in 2008," *The New York Times*, Oct. 30, 2009, www.nytimes.com/2009/10/30/education/30college.html?scp=1&sq=college%20enrollment%20set%20record%20in%202008&st=cse.

13. Betsy Brand, "Supporting High Quality Career and Technical Education through Federal and State Policy," American Youth Policy Forum, May 2008,

www.aypf.org/documents/SupportingHighQuality
CTE.pdf.

14. Kenneth C. Gray and Edwin L. Herr, *Other Ways to Win* (2006), p. 8.

15. Deborah Reed, "California's Future Workforce: Will There Be Enough College Graduates?" Public Policy Institute of California, December 2008, www.ppic.org/content/pubs/report/R_1208DRR.pdf.

16. "New Report: More than 2.7 Million 'Middle-Skill' Job Openings Projected for California by 2016," press release, The Workforce Alliance, Skills2Compete and California EDGE Campaign, Oct. 19, 2009, accessed at www.reuters.com/article/pressRelease/idUS86731+19-Oct-2009+PRN20091019.

17. Press releases accessed at www.skills2compete.org/site/c.fhLIKYPLLuF/b.3356267/k.89B1/Media_Center.htm.

18. Lumina Foundation, *op. cit.*

19. "Is a College Education Worth the Debt?" "Tell Me More," National Public Radio, Sept. 1, 2009, www.npr.org/templates/story/storyphp?storyId=112432364.

20. Brand, *op. cit.*

21. "Career and Technical Education: States Have Broad Flexibility in Implementing Perkins IV," U.S. Government Accountability Office, July 2009, www.gao.gov/new.items/d09683.pdf. For a discussion of this issue, see Demenic Giandomenico, "Career Technical Education Success Difficult to Measure," *The Chamber Post*, July 31, 2009, www.chamber-post.com/2009/07/career-technical-education-success-difficult-to-measure.html.

22. "Noteworthy State Legislation for Improving Career and Technical Education," Education Commission of the States, September 2009, www.ecs.org/clearinghouse/82/07/8207.pdf.

23. See James J. Kemple with Cynthia J. Willner, "Career Academies: Long-Term Impacts on Labor Market Outcomes, Educational Attainment and Transitions to Adulthood," MDRC, June 2008, www.mdrc.org/publications/482/overview.html.

24. Mary Beth Marklein, "Four-year schools get bigger share of revenue pie," *USA Today*, July 22, 2008, www.usatoday.com/news/education/2008-07-22-comcol-funding_N.htm.

25. Stephen G. Katsinas and Terrence A. Tollefson, "Funding and Access Issues in Public Higher Education: A Community College Perspective," University of Alabama Education Policy Center, 2009, http://education.ua.edu/edpolicycenter/documents/fundingandaccess2009.pdf.

26. "Diploma to Nowhere," Strong American Schools, 2008, www.deltacostproject.org/resources/pdf/DiplomaToNowhere.pdf. The group analyzed 2004 data.

27. "The People's Vote: 100 Documents that Shaped America, Morrill Act (1862)," *U.S. News & World Report*, www.usnews.com/usnews/documents/docpages/document_page33.htm.

28. *Ibid.*

29. Ellwood P. Cubberley, *Changing Conceptions of Education* (1909), pp. 49-50, accessed at http://books.google.com.

30. Kenneth Gray, "Vocationalism and the American High School: Past, Present and Future?" *Journal of Industrial Teacher Education*, vol. 33, no. 2, winter 1996, http://scholar.lib.vt.edu/ejournals/JITE/v33n2/gray.html.

31. Neville B. Smith, "A Tribute to the Visionaries, Prime Movers and Pioneers of Vocational Education, 1892 to 1917," *Journal of Vocational and Technical Education*, vol. 16, no. 1, fall 1999, http://scholar.lib.vt.edu/ejournals/JVTE/v16n1/smith.html.

32. *Ibid.*

33. "Smith-Hughes Act of 1917," Prentice Hall Documents Library, http://cwx.prenhall.com/bookbind/pubbooks/dye4/medialib/docs/smith917.htm.

34. David Stern, "Expanding Policy Options for Educating Teenagers," *The Future of Children*, vol. 19, no. 1, spring 2009, pp. 211-239, http://futureofchildren.org/futureofchildren/publications/docs/19_01_10.pdf. The journal is a collaboration of the Woodrow Wilson School of Public and International Affairs at Princeton University and The Brookings Institution.

35. Prentice Hall Documents Library, *op. cit.*

36. Marjorie Coeyman, "Practical skills vs. three R's: A debate revives," *The Christian Science Monitor*, July 8, 2003, www.csmonitor.com/2003/0708/p13s02-lepr.html.

37. "Significant Events," American Association of Community Colleges, www.aacc.nche.edu/AboutCC/history/Pages/significantevents.aspx.

38. "Statement by the President Making Public a Report of the Commission on Higher Education," Public Papers, No. 235, Harry S. Truman Library and Museum, Dec. 15, 1947, http://trumanlibrary.org/publicpapers/index.php?pid=1852.

39. *Ibid.*

40. U.S. Census Bureau, www.census.gov/population/socdemo/school/TableA-6.xls.

41. U.S. Census Bureau, "Decennial Census of Population," 1940 to 2000, www.census.gov/population/socdemo/education/phct41/table2.xls.

42. American Association of Community Colleges, www.aacc.nche.edu/AboutCC/history/Documents/np10.pdf.

43. Gray, *op. cit.*

44. *Ibid.*

45. Of the 3.2 million young people who graduated from high school from October 2007 to October 2008, 2.2 million — about 69 percent — were attending college in October 2008, according to the U.S. Labor Department. About 60 percent of those who enrolled in college attended four-year institutions. See "College Enrollment and Work Activity of 2008 High-school Graduates," April 28, 2009, www.bls.gov/news.release/pdf/hsgec.pdf.

46. For background, see R. Thompson, "Teachers: The Push for Excellence," *Editorial Research Reports*, April 20, 1984, available at *CQ Researcher Plus Archive.*

47. For background, see Barbara Mantel, "No Child Left Behind," *CQ Researcher*, May 27, 2005, pp. 469-492.

48. An April 3, 2009, letter to Obama from officials of the Association for Career and Technical Education, the National Association of State Directors of Career Technical Education Consortium and the American Association of Community Colleges sought at least $1.4 billion in funding under the Perkins Career and Technical Education Act and said federal investment in the act had decreased by $42 million since fiscal 2002 while enrollments have soared to record highs. See www.acteonline.org/uploadedFiles/Issues_and_Advocacy/files/FY10_President_Signon.doc.

49. Office of Management and Budget, www.whitehouse.gov/omb/fy2010_department_education.

50. Lamar Alexander, "The Three-Year Solution," *Newsweek*, Oct. 26, 2009, www.newsweek.com/id/218183.

51. Frederick M. Hess, Mark Schneider, Kevin Carey and Andrew P. Kelly, "Diplomas and Dropouts," American Enterprise Institute, June 2009, www.aei.org/docLib/Diplomas%20and%20Dropouts%20final.pdf.

52. William G. Bowen, Matthew M. Chingos and Michael S. McPherson, *Crossing the Finish Line* (2009).

53. Quoted in Scott Jaschik, "(Not) Crossing the Finish Line," *Inside Higher Ed*, Sept. 9, 2009, www.insidehighered.com/news/2009/09/09/finish.

54. "Remarks by the President on the American Graduation Initiative," The White House, July 14, 2009, www.whitehouse.gov/the_press_office/Remarks-by-the-President-on-the-American-Graduation-Initiative-in-Warren-MI/.

55. The bill is HR 3221.

56. See Michael A. Fletcher, "Obama Spotlights Student Loan Reform," *The Washington Post*, April 24, 2009, http://voices.washingtonpost.com/44/2009/04/24/obama_spotlights_student_loan.html. For an analysis of the bill, see "Congressional Budget Office Cost Estimate," July 24, 2009, www.cbo.gov/ftpdocs/104xx/doc10479/hr3221.pdf.

57. Anthony Carnevale, "Postsecondary Education Goes to Work," *Inside Higher Ed*, May 15, 2009, www.insidehighered.com/views/2009/05/15/carnevale. Obama spoke on "job creation and job training" on May 9, 2009; see www.whitehouse.gov/the_press_office/Remarks-by-the-President-on-Job-Creation-and-Job-Training-5/8/09/.

58. Will Van Sant, "$2.3 million in federal stimulus money is going to pay for Tampa Bay area beauty school tuition," *St. Petersburg Times*, Oct. 17, 2009, www.tampabay.com/news/education/23-million-in-federal-stimulus-money-is-going-to-pay-for-tampa-bay-area/1044637.

59. Quoted in *ibid.*

60. "President Obama's Plan to Invest in Community Colleges Could Vastly Improve Young People's Ability to Achieve Economic Security," *Demos*, July 22, 2009, http://demos.org/press.cfm?currentarticle ID=BE413099%2D3FF4%2D6C82%2D5592F9B 4EF236F90.

61. Quoted in Kelly Field, "A Year of College for All: What the President's Plan Would Mean for the Country," *Chronicle of Higher Education*, May 22, 2009, accessed at http://cew.georgetown.edu/media/news/. McCluskey made his comments at a forum, according to the *Chronicle* article.

62. "Obama Budget Level Funds Career Technical Education," press release, National Association of State Directors of Career Technical Education Consortium, May 7, 2009, www.careertech.org/press_releases/show/28.

63. Jill Casner-Lotto, Elyse Rosenblum and Mary Wright, "The Ill-Prepared U.S. Workforce," Corporate Voices for Working Families, American Society for Training & Development, Conference Board and Society for Human Resource Management, July 2009, www.astd.org/NR/rdonlyres/A7A0ECFF-333E-445C-BAA5-99486742F7F0/22788/Workforcekeyfindings0709final.pdf.

64. "New Report Shows Employers Struggle with Ill-Prepared Workforce," The Conference Board, press release, July 14, 2009, www.conference-board.org/utilities/pressDetail.cfm?press_id=3693.

65. Susan P. Choy, Ellen M. Bradburn and C. Dennis Carroll, "Ten Years After College: Comparing the Employment Experiences of 1992-93 Bachelor's Degree Recipients With Academic and Career-Oriented Majors," National Center for Education Statistics, February 2008, http://nces.ed.gov/pubs2008/2008155.pdf.

66. Steven Greenhouse, "More White-Collar Workers Turn to Community Colleges," *The New York Times*, Aug. 19, 2009, www.nytimes.com/2009/08/20/education/20COMMUN.html.

67. Quoted in *ibid.*

68. College Board, "Trends in College Pricing," *op. cit.*

69. "Trends in Student Aid 2009," College Board, p. 10, www.trends-collegeboard.com/student_aid/pdf/2009_Trends_Student_Aid.pdf.

BIBLIOGRAPHY

Books

Bowen, William G., Matthew M. Chingos and Michael S. McPherson, *Crossing the Finish Line*, Princeton University Press, 2009.
Public universities are crucial to the nation's future, yet fewer than 60 percent of students entering four-year colleges graduate, according to this scholarly examination of graduation rates at 21 flagship public universities and four statewide public higher-education systems.

Crawford, Matthew B., *Shop Class as Soulcraft: An Inquiry Into the Value of Work*, Penguin Press, 2009.
A think tank scholar turned motorcycle repair shop owner waxes philosophically about the satisfaction of working with one's hands and analyzes the unwillingness of American culture to recognize the merits of tradecraft and manual labor.

Gray, Kenneth C., and Edwin L. Herr, *Other Ways to Win*, Corwin Press, 2006.
Two Pennsylvania State University scholars focus on teens in the academic middle — those in the second and third quartiles of their high-school class — and question the premise that the only way to achieve economic security is by pursuing a four-year college degree.

Articles

Epstein, Jennifer, "Should Everyone Go to College?" *Inside Higher Ed*, Sept. 18, 2009, www.insidehighered.com/news/2009/09/18/college#.
In a panel discussion, four policy experts examine the question of whether everyone needs college — and how that postsecondary education should be defined.

Greenhouse, Steven, "At Sinclair Community College, Focus Is Jobs," *The New York Times*, Aug. 15, 2009, www.nytimes.com/2009/08/15/business/15college .html?scp=1&sq=sinclair%20community%20 college&st=cse.
The Dayton, Ohio, community college is in the fore-front of efforts to create a higher-skilled workforce — retraining thousands of laid-off autoworkers and helping local leaders foster growth industries and train workers for them.

Greenhouse, Steven, "More White-Collar Workers Turn to Community Colleges," *The New York Times*, Aug. 20, 2009, www.nytimes.com/2009/08/20/ education/20COMMUN.html?scp=1&sq=more%20 white-collar%20workers%20turn%20to%20com munity%20colleges&st=cse.
Many community college students are employed but want to increase their skills, while others have lost their jobs and are returning to school to obtain new skills.

Jan, Tracy, "These Bunker Hill Classes Make Late Arrival Mandatory," *The Boston Globe*, Sept. 11, 2009, www.boston.com/news/education/higher/ articles/2009/09/11/these_bunker_hill_classes_ make_late_arrival_mandatory/.
Several community colleges are working to accommo-date the needs of their students by offering midnight courses in psychology, writing and "graveyard" welding classes.

Lewin, Tamar, "College Costs Keep Rising, Report Says," *The New York Times*, Oct. 21, 2009, www .nytimes.com/2009/10/21/education/21costs .html?ref=us.
While overall consumer prices fell last year, the cost of a college education rose significantly, with tuition and fees at four-year public colleges up an average of 6.5 percent and those at private colleges up 4.4 percent, the College Board reported.

Uchitelle, Louis, "Despite Recession, High Demand for Skilled Labor," *The New York Times*, June 24, 2009, www.nytimes.com/2009/06/24/business/ 24jobs .html?scp=1&sq=despite%20recession,%20high%20 demand%20for%20skilled%20labor& st=cse.
Despite a national unemployment rate near 10 percent, some employers are seeking qualified applicants for skilled jobs in welding, critical-care nursing and other specialties.

Reports and Studies

"A Stronger Nation Through Higher Education," Lumina Foundation for Education, February 2009, www.luminafoundation.org/publications/A_stron ger_nation_through_higher_education.pdf.
College-attainment rates are climbing in nearly every industrialized or post-industrial country except the United States, where about 39 percent of adults hold a two- or four-year degree, according to this examination.

Casner-Lotto, Jill, Elyse Rosenblum and Mary Wright, "The Ill-Prepared U.S. Workforce," The Conference Board, Corporate Voices for Working Families, American Society for Training & Development and Society for Human Resource Management, July 2009, www.cvworkingfamilies. org/system/files/Ill_Prepared_Workforce_KF.pdf.
Employers are finding that many new hires lack impor-tant basic and applied skills, but company training pro-grams often are not correcting those deficiencies, the study concludes.

Holzer, Harry J., and Robert I. Lerman, "America's Forgotten Middle-Skill Jobs," Workforce Alliance, November 2007, www.urban.org/UploadedPDF/ 411633_forgottenjobs.pdf.
Researchers conclude that demand for workers to fill jobs that require more than a high-school diploma but less than a four-year degree will likely remain strong rela-tive to supply.

For More Information

American Association of Community Colleges, 1 Dupont Circle, Suite 410, Washington, DC 20036; (202) 728-0200; www2.aacc.nche.edu/research/index.htm. Represents nearly 1,200 two-year associate degree-granting institutions.

American Youth Policy Forum, 1836 Jefferson Pl., N.W., Washington, DC 20036; (202) 775-9731; www.aypf.org. Nonprofit professional-development organization engaged in youth and education issues at the national, state and local levels.

College Board, 45 Columbus Ave., New York, NY 10023; (212) 713-8000; www.collegeboard.com. Nonprofit membership organization that manages college admission tests and collects data on college costs and student debt, among other roles.

Community College League of California, 2017 O St., Sacramento, CA 95811-5211; (916) 444-8641; www.ccleague.org. Membership organization for 72 local community college districts in California.

Lumina Foundation for Education, 30 S. Meridian St., Suite 700, Indianapolis, IN 46204-3503; (317) 951-5300; www.luminafoundation.org. Provides grants, policy education and leadership development in education.

Workforce Strategy Center, 350 Fifth Ave., 59th Floor, New York, N.Y. 10118; (646) 205-3240; www.workforcestrategy.org. Works with education, workforce development and economic-development agencies to help students and workers succeed and to foster regional economic growth.

3

Bilingual Education vs. English Immersion

Kenneth Jost

Protesters at Arizona's capitol in Phoenix oppose Proposition 203 on Nov. 6, 2000. The next day voters decisively approved the ballot measure ending bilingual education in the state in favor of so-called sheltered English immersion. Similar measures in California and Massachusetts at about the same time reflected a popular backlash against bilingual education since the 1980s.

From *CQ Researcher*, December 11, 2009.

Miriam Flores remembers that her daughter Miriam was doing well in her first two years in school in the border town of Nogales, Ariz.

"She knew how to read and write in Spanish," Flores says of her daughter, now a college student. "She would even correct the teacher on accents and spelling."

In the third grade, however, Miriam began having difficulties. Her grades went down, and she began having nightmares.

Miriam's mother has a simple explanation for the change. In the early 1990s, Nogales provided bilingual education — teaching English learners in both their native language and English — but only through the first two grades. "It was the language," Flores says.

Miriam's new teacher did not speak Spanish, taught only in English and seemed uninterested in Miriam's language difficulties, Flores says. "Miriam is a very quiet child, and I thought it was strange that the teacher would say that she talked a lot," Flores recalls today. "Then Miriam told me, 'I ask the other kids what the teacher is saying.' She didn't understand."[1]

Flores' frustrations with her daughter's schooling led her to join with other Spanish-speaking Nogales families in 1992 in filing a federal suit aimed at improving educational opportunities for non-English-speaking students in the overwhelmingly Hispanic town. The class action suit claimed the school district was failing to comply with a federal law — the Equal Educational Opportunities Act of 1974 — which requires each state to take "appropriate action" to ensure that English-language learners (ELLs) enjoy "equal participation in its instructional programs."

English Learners Doing Poorly in Big States

More than 30 percent of the English-language learners are not making progress in 18 states, including those with big Hispanic populations, such as California, Florida, New York and Texas. Smaller states such as Connecticut, Delaware and Rhode Island have some of the best progress rates.

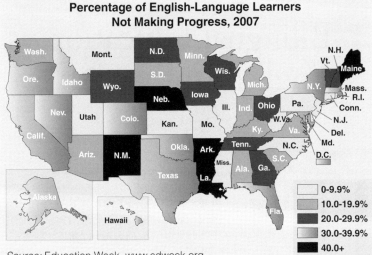

Percentage of English-Language Learners Not Making Progress, 2007

Legend:
- 0-9.9%
- 10.0-19.9%
- 20.0-29.9%
- 30.0-39.9%
- 40.0+

Source: Education Week, www.edweek.org

Seventeen years later, the case is still in federal court. The plaintiffs won a pivotal decision in 2001 requiring Arizona to boost funding for English-language learning in Nogales and the rest of the state. In a narrowly divided decision in June, however, the Supreme Court gave state officials an opportunity to set aside the lower court ruling.

Writing for the 5-4 majority, Justice Samuel A. Alito Jr. said the federal district judge had failed to adequately consider changed circumstances since 2001. Among other changes, Alito cited the state's decision to drop bilingual education in favor of so-called "sheltered English immersion" as the officially prescribed method of instruction for students with limited English proficiency.[2]

Arizona's voters had decisively rejected bilingual education in a 2000 ballot measure. Along with similar measures passed in California in 1998 and Massachusetts in 2002, Arizona's Proposition 203 embodied a popular backlash against bilingual education that had grown since the 1980s. Critics of bilingual teaching viewed it as a politically correct relic of the 1960s and '70s that had proven academically ineffective and politically divisive.

The debate between English-only instruction and bilingual education has been fierce for decades. "People get very hot under the collar," says Christine Rossell, a professor of political science at Boston University and critic of bilingual education.

Those who support a bilingual approach, says Arizona Superintendent of Instruction Thomas Horne, "aren't interested in teaching the kids English," but want to maintain "a separatist nationalism that they can take advantage of." Horne, a Republican, intervened with the state's GOP legislative leaders to try to undo the federal court injunction.

"When I tell people that the best way to learn English is to be taught in Spanish, they think I'm joking," says Rossell.

Supporters insist that bilingual education is the best way to ensure long-term educational achievement for English-language learners. "We have gone backwards on educating non-English speakers," says José Ruiz-Escalante, a professor of bilingual education at the University of Texas-Pan American in Edinburg and president of the National Association for Bilingual Education. English-only proponents, he says, are "in such a hurry for students to speak English that we're not paying attention to their cognitive development."

"The important thing that students need to learn is how to think," Ruiz-Escalante continues. "It doesn't matter whether you learn to think in Spanish or in English. Kids will learn to speak English, but they will be limited" in their academic learning.[3]

Out of nearly 50 million pupils in U.S. public elementary and secondary schools, about 5.1 million — more than one-tenth — are classified as having limited English proficiency. The number is growing because of increased immigration, both legal and illegal. The vast majority of English-language learners — nearly

80 percent — speak Spanish as their first language. But schools are also coping with rising numbers of students who speak a variety of other languages, almost all of which have far less similarity to English than Spanish has. *(See chart, p. 57.)*

"It's a growing challenge," says Patte Barth, director of the Center for Public Education at the National School Boards Association (NSBA). "We have many more children coming into our schools for whom their first language is not English. At the same time, the need to educate every child to a high level is much more important than it was even 20 years ago."

The imperative for results stems in part from enactment early in 2002 of the No Child Left Behind Act, the centerpiece of President George W. Bush's educational-accountability initiative. The act mandated annual testing of students in grades 3-8 and required that schools demonstrate "adequate yearly progress," including closing the achievement gap for English-language learners, at the risk of financial penalties for noncompliance.[4]

The act also withdrew the federal preference for bilingual education over English-only instruction. Even so, Latino advocacy groups that have long complained of inadequate attention to Spanish-speaking students applaud the law's emphasis on accountability. The act "changed the debate from what kind of education and curriculum to one of how do you best educate these kids," says Raul Gonzalez, director of legislative affairs for NCLR, formerly the National Council of La Raza. "That's where we think the debate should be."

The federal government has no official count on the number of English learners in each instructional method,

California Has Most English-Language Learners

More than 1.5 million English-language learners (ELLs) reside in California — one-quarter of the state's school-age population and by far the most in the nation (top graph). ELLs, however, are becoming more populous in Southern states such as South Carolina, Kentucky and Tennessee (middle graph). More than one in five students in California and New Mexico are ELL students (bottom graph).

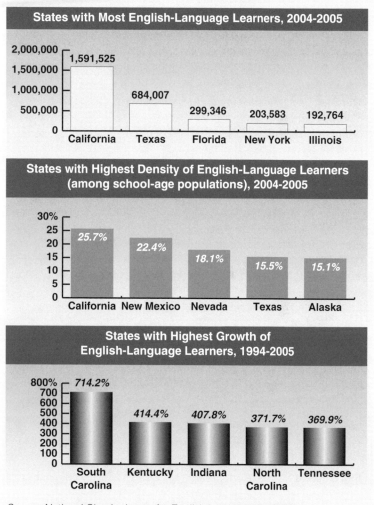

Source: National Clearinghouse for English Language Acquisition

but the most recent survey by researchers indicates that the majority — about 60 percent — are in all-English curricula. Of that number, 12 percent receive no special services at all to aid English proficiency.

A Bilingual/Immersion Glossary

The dizzying number of terms and acronyms in the teaching-English field reflects the intensity and complexity of the debate over which method works best. Here are some of the key terms:

Annual Measurable Achievement Objective (AMAO) — These are the criteria for the reports mandated by the No Child Left Behind Act (NCLB) on the progress of limited English proficiency (LEP) students in English-language acquisition and academic achievement.

Adequate Yearly Progress (AYP) — The accountability system mandated by NCLB requires each state to ensure all schools and districts meet set standards.

Bilingual Education — Teaching non-English-speaking people in both their native language and in English.

Dual Language — Programs that help students develop full literacy skills in English and another language.

Early Exit Transitional — Programs that help students develop English skills as quickly as possible, without delaying learning of academic core content. Instruction begins in native language and then moves rapidly to English, with students transitioning to mainstream classrooms as soon as possible.

Elementary and Secondary Education Act (ESEA) — Funds primary and secondary education, and forbids establishment of a national curriculum. Originally enacted in 1965, the act was reauthorized as the No Child Left Behind Act.

English Language Development (ELD) — Programs in which students leave mainstream classrooms to spend part of their day receiving ESL instruction focusing on grammar, vocabulary and communication skills, not academic content. Typically there is no support for students' native languages. Also known as ESL Pull-Out.

English Language Proficiency (ELP) Standards — Assist teachers in evaluating LEP students' progress in their acquisition of English and facilitate the alignment of curriculum between ESL services and general education programs.

English as a Second Language (ESL) — Refers to non-English speakers and programs designed to teach them English.

ESL Push-In — These are programs for ESL students who attend mainstream classrooms and receive instruction in English with native-language support as needed from ESL teachers.

Heritage Language Programs — These target non-English-speaking students or those who have weak literary skills in their native language, frequently American Indians. Also known as Indigenous Language Programs.

The remaining English learners — about 40 percent — receive some form of bilingual instruction using their native language and English. The length of time in the bilingual programs varies from as little as one year to several. And, as Stanford University education professor Claude Goldenberg notes, there is no way to know the amount of support the students receive or the quality of the instruction.[5]

In Arizona, state policy calls for English-language learners to receive four hours a day of intensive English instruction apart from their mainstream, English-only classes. Since the so-called "pullout" policy was implemented in 2008, the rate of reclassifying students from English-language learners to English-proficient has increased, Horne says. "Students need to learn English quickly to compete," he says.

Tim Hogan, executive director of the Arizona Center for Law in the Public Interest and the lead attorney in the *Flores* case, says it is "too early to tell" whether the four-hour pullout approach will be more effective than past policies that he describes as ineffective. But Hogan alleges that the policy segregates Spanish speakers from other students and risks delaying graduation by taking class time away from academic subjects.

Hogan stresses, however, that the lawsuit is aimed at ensuring adequate funding for English-language instruction, not at imposing a specific educational method. "We proved that the state funding [for English-language instruction] was totally arbitrary," he says.

Horne counters that the Supreme Court decision leaves funding decisions up to the state. "The district court judges are being told not to micromanage the finances of the state education system," he says.

Voluminous, statistics-heavy studies are cited by opposing advocacy groups as evidence to support their respective positions on the bilingual versus English-only debate. But Barth says language politics, not research, often determines school districts' choice of instructional method. "A lot of it is political," she says. "A lot of decisions about language instruction aren't really informed by the research about what works for children."

Whatever approach is used, many researchers say English-language learners' needs are not being met. In their new book, *Educating English Learners for a Transformed World*, former George Mason University professors Virginia Collier and Wayne Thomas — who strongly advocate bilingual education — cite statistics showing a big achievement gap at the high-school level between native English speakers and students who entered school as English learners. Native English speakers have average scores on standardized tests around the 50th percentile, Collier and Thomas say, while English learners average around the 10th to 12th percentile.[6]

Despite decades of attention and debate on the issue, "not much has happened," says Kenji Hakuta, a professor at Stanford University's School of Education in Palo Alto, Calif. "The problems of English-language learners persist whether it's English-only or bilingual education."

As educators look for ways to best teach students with limited English skills, here are some of the major questions being debated:

Immersion — Learning a language by spending all or part of the time speaking solely in the target language.

Late Exit Transitional — Instruction designed to help students develop some skills and proficiency in their native language, as well as strong skills and proficiency in English. Instruction in lower grades is in the native language, and in English in upper grades. Also known as Developmental Bilingual or Maintenance Education.

Limited English Proficiency (LEP) — Denotes individuals who cannot communicate effectively in English, such as those not born in the United States or whose native language is not English.

Local Education Agency (LEA) — A board of education or other public authority that has administrative control of, or performs a service for, publicly funded schools.

National Assessment of Educational Process (NAEP) — The continuing assessment of American students in targeted grades and various subject areas — known as the "Nation's Report Card" — is carried out by the U.S. Department of Education's National Center for Education Statistics.

National Clearinghouse for English Language Acquisition and Language Instruction Educational Programs (NCELA) — Supports the U.S. Department of Education's Office of English Language Acquisition in its mission to implement NCLB as it applies to English-language learners.

No Child Left Behind Act of 2001 (NCLB) — The most recent reauthorization of the ESEA calls for standards-based education reform and requires assessments of all students in certain grades before states can receive federal funding for schools.

Office of English Language Acquisition, Language Enhancement, and Academic Achievement for Limited English Proficient Students (OELA) — A U.S. Department of Education office that helps ensure English-language learners and immigrant students attain English proficiency and achieve academically.

Sheltered English Immersion — Classes specifically for ESL students aimed at improving their English-speaking, reading and writing skills. Prepares students for entry into mainstream classrooms.

Structured English Immersion (SEI) — Classes for LEP students only where the goal is fluency in English. All instruction is in English, adjusted to the proficiency of students so the subject matter is comprehensible.

Two-Way Immersion — Programs designed to develop proficiency in both native language and English through instruction in both languages. Also known as Two-Way Bilingual.

Source: "The Biennial Report to Congress on the Implementation of the Title III State Formula Grant Program," U.S. Department of Education, School Years 2004-2006, June 2008, www.ed.gov/about/offices/list/oela/title3biennial0406.pdf.

Is bilingual education effective for English-language learners?

Todd Butler teaches social studies and language arts to fourth-grade English learners in Mansfield, Texas, a rapidly growing exurb south of Fort Worth. Butler, an Anglo who began studying Spanish in fourth grade himself, uses only Spanish for social studies but alternates day by day between English and Spanish for language arts.

Butler, recipient of the National Association for Bilingual Education's teacher of the year award in 2009, is firmly convinced of the merits of bilingual education, especially in the so-called dual-language model now used in Mansfield and advancing in other school districts. By contrast, the older model — known as "transitional bilingual education" — focuses on using bilingual education only for a limited period.

"We don't do kids any favor by shoving them into English as fast as we can," says Butler, a teacher with more than a quarter-century of experience. "The research shows very clearly that the longer we can give them support in their language, the better they're going to do not just in elementary school but in secondary school as well."

The strongest supporting evidence comes from long-term research by George Mason scholars Collier and Thomas. The veteran researchers examined achievement levels through high school among English learners in 35 school districts who were taught using different instructional models. "Our research shows what works in the long term is different from what works in the short term," Thomas explains.

There is little difference in achievement levels between English learners in the elementary grades, the researchers found, regardless of whether the students were taught in dual-language, transitional-bilingual or English-as-a-Second-Language (ESL) models. (*See glossary, p. 54.*) By high school, however, the dual-language students come closer to narrowing the gap between them and the English-proficient students than those using the ESL approach. Students from transitional bilingual programs are in-between.

Students in English-only programs "look as though they're doing really well in early grades," Thomas explains, "but they've experienced a cognitive slowdown as they're learning English." As the two authors conclude in their book: "The more children develop their first language …, the more successful they will be in academic achievement in English by the end of their school years."[7]

The national school boards group agrees on the advantages of "first-language" instruction for English learners. "ELL students with formal schooling in their first language tend to acquire English proficiency faster than their peers without it," the NSBA's Center for Public Education concluded after reviewing the research. The center added that it takes four to seven years to become proficient in "academic English — the language needed to succeed in the classroom."[8]

Opponents of bilingual education say it fails because it does not completely close the gap between English learners and English-proficient students. "There is very little research to say that these programs are having good results," says Rosalie Pedalino Porter, a longtime critic of bilingual education who was ESL coordinator in Newton, Mass., in the 1980s. "It never proved itself effective, and all sorts of excuses are still being made." Porter now serves on the board of the pro-English advocacy group Center for Equal Opportunity.

To critics, bilingual education simply delays students' mastery of the new language: English. "If you don't pull them out [for English instruction], they're not going to learn English fast enough," says Arizona education chief Horne.

Supporters of bilingual education counter that the short-term perspective is ultimately detrimental for English learners. "Most districts are still in a hurry for them to learn English," says NABE president Ruiz-Escalante. They end up "learning English at the expense of an education."

"Schools are in a difficult position," says James Crawford, a bilingual-education advocate and author of a textbook on English learners now in its fifth edition. "Short-term pressures have determined how children are being taught." Crawford first developed an expertise in bilingual education as a writer and editor for *Education Week;* he also served as NABE's executive director until 2006.[9]

Some experts say the lines in the perennial and heated debate are beginning to blur. "The argument of bilingual education versus English immersion sounds like a fairly old way of characterizing the problem," says Stanford professor Hakuta.

Is "English immersion" effective for English learners?

As chief executive officer of the United Neighborhood Organization, Juan Rangel superintends a network of eight charter schools serving predominantly Hispanic communities in Chicago. UNO schools follow a philosophy of strong discipline, high expectations and English immersion — or teaching only using English — instead of bilingual education.

According to a study by the pro-English Lexington Institute, English learners from UNO schools score higher than their counterparts from other Chicago schools, who are subject to statewide bilingual-education requirements.[10] But Rangel says English immersion also promotes assimilation for Hispanic students. "What it means is having our families and children have an understanding of belonging," Rangel told *Education Week* reporter Mary Ann Zehr. "They have a role in developing this country."[11]

Rangel says bilingual education has not worked as intended. Some parents interviewed agreed. Guadalupe Garcia, an immigrant from Mexico with a fourth-grade education, told Zehr that the bilingual education one of her daughters received in a regular Chicago school was "pura español" — pure Spanish. Another of her daughters entered a UNO school in second grade speaking no English but could speak English well within a year and a half.

Advocates of English immersion emphasize assimilation as one of their reasons for favoring it over bilingual instruction. "I believe in the beauty of bilingualism," says Porter, of the pro-English advocacy group Center for Equal Opportunity, "but I have a very, very strong commitment to children like me who don't speak English at all." Porter was born in Italy and spoke no English when she immigrated with her family at age 6.

But the advocates of English immersion also claim that studies in two states that changed from bilingual to English instruction — Arizona and California — show that the change improved academic performance. Justice

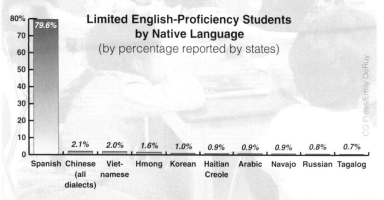

Most Student Native Speakers Are Hispanic

More than three-quarters of U.S. students with limited English proficiency (LEP) are native Spanish speakers. About 7 percent of LEPs are native speakers of Asian languages.

Limited English-Proficiency Students by Native Language
(by percentage reported by states)

Language	Percentage
Spanish	79.6%
Chinese (all dialects)	2.1%
Vietnamese	2.0%
Hmong	1.6%
Korean	1.0%
Haitian Creole	0.9%
Arabic	0.9%
Navajo	0.9%
Russian	0.8%
Tagalog	0.7%

Source: "The Biennial Report to Congress on The Implementation of the Title III State Formula Grant Program: School Years 2004-06," U.S. Department of Education, June 2008

Alito pointed to both studies in the Supreme Court's decision in the *Flores* case as evidence of "documented, academic support for the view that SEI [structured English immersion] is significantly more effective than bilingual education."[12] Critics, however, say both studies are flawed.

In one of the studies, Kelly Torrance, identified as an adjunct scholar with the Lexington Institute, a pro-English think tank based in Washington, D.C., cited statistics from California showing that the number of English learners who scored in the top two categories of proficiency on the state's English-language development test increased from 25 percent in 2001 to 47 percent in 2005. "This striking improvement is big news," wrote Torrance.[13]

Bilingual-education advocates dismiss the studies. Stephen Krashen, a linguistics professor at the University of Southern California in Los Angeles, says the state introduced the English test in 2001 and that improved scores are typical for the first few years after introduction of a new test. He points to several other studies by university academics that conclude dropping bilingual education did not accelerate English learners' development.[14]

The Arizona Department of Education similarly concluded in a report prepared in July 2004 that English learners in the state had benefited from the switch from bilingual education to English immersion following voters' decisive rejection of bilingual education in the 2000 ballot measure, Proposition 203. "Students in English immersion outperformed students in bilingual in all areas," Superintendent Horne says in describing the report.[15]

Jeff MacSwan, a professor of linguistics at Arizona State University in Tempe, says the state's report "has been completely discredited." In letters to the editor at the time and in comments since, MacSwan notes that the comparisons found in the study failed to control for other potential causes of the differences, including poverty, length of time in the United States or initial language proficiency. "That's a huge thing," he says.

In a more recent study he coauthored, MacSwan says it is impossible to determine whether English learners are doing better or worse since passage of Proposition 203, but that they continue to suffer "a persistent and dramatic achievement gap" in comparison to English-proficient students.[16]

Porter insists that English learners need only a little concentrated language instruction to become proficient. "They need two to three hours a day of intensive language instruction," she says. "These children within a year of this intensive instruction can make the transition from their native language to English."

Some supporters of bilingual education stop short of flatly dismissing English-only approaches. "You could find an elementary program that was English-only, and they did well," says Barth with the school boards' group. "But on average, that's an outlier."

"Any well-implemented program can work," says Stanford's Hakuta. "The issue is giving kids access to academic content that sparks their curiosity. The fundamental piece is that education isn't pouring knowledge into empty vessels. You have to get kids interested and excited in the content of what you're teaching."

Should funding for English-language learning be increased?

Twice in the past decade, federal district judges in Arizona have found that the state was not spending enough money to help English-language learners become proficient in English. State officials welcomed the first of the rulings, by Judge Alfred Marquez, in January 2000 as a useful spur to increase funding for English instruction.

In 2006, however, the state's Republican-controlled legislature approved only part of the funding increase proposed by then-Gov. Janet Napolitano, a Democrat, to satisfy the federal court. The new plan increased the special funding for English-language learners to $432 per student from the previous $358. Judge Raner Collins, who had taken over the *Flores* case after Marquez's retirement, found the new spending levels still inadequate.

In its ruling in June, the Supreme Court said that both Collins and the 9th U.S. Circuit Court of Appeals placed too much emphasis on funding levels in refusing the plea by the state's legislative leaders and Superintendent of Instruction Horne to reopen the case. Dissenting justices countered that the adequacy of the state's resources devoted to English-language instruction "has always been the basic contested issue" in the case.

Today, plaintiffs' attorney Hogan acknowledges that the Supreme Court's decision shifts the focus of the case away from funding and toward the effectiveness of the state's prescribed model of structured English immersion with English learners taken out of their mainstream English-only classes for four-hour "pull-out" sessions for intensive English instruction.

Nationwide, the question of funding for English-language instruction continues to be a point of discussion, but the lines are not as sharply drawn as they are on the instructional model used. "It's not about resources; it's about the quality of the program," says NABE president Ruiz-Escalante. "Whatever resources are available need to be devoted to appropriate programs that meet the educational needs of the students. Money alone is not the solution."

"The amount of money spent on a program is not a guarantee that a good education is produced," says English-immersion advocate Porter. "Certainly, there's a floor level. But to equate the amount of dollars with wonderful educational outcomes simply cannot be done. The real proof is not the amount of money but the evidence of student success."

Some bilingual-education advocates, in fact, minimize the need for additional resources for English-language learners. In their book, Collier and Thomas contend that bilingual (dual-language) instruction — that is, using a bilingual teacher to teach English learners in the same grade-level, mainstream curriculum as other students — is "the most cost-effective" educational model. The only additional cost, they say, is for materials. By contrast, they call ESL pullout "the least cost-effective model," because extra resource teachers are needed.

For her part, Barth, with the school boards' Center for Public Education, also says educational costs for English learners are not necessarily higher than for English-proficient students. But she does point to some needed additional resources that "could use funding," such as "more ESL teachers" and "broader access to good pre-K programs."

"We also know that students who come into school without English tend to be in communities that are poorer, and they tend to go to schools that have fewer resources," Barth says. But she adds, "That's not the same as saying it costs more to educate an ESL child."

In Arizona, Superintendent Horne says the state is meeting federal requirements for teaching English learners. "The law requires appropriate action to teach kids English," he says. "We're clearly doing that. I think we're one of the leaders in the nation."

Gonzalez of NCLR (La Raza), however, says Arizona is misusing funds provided under Title III of the No Child Left Behind Act, the language-acquisition section. "The federal law says you cannot use Title III to supplant your state funds or your Title I funds," Gonzalez says, referring to the major federal aid program for disadvantaged school districts. "Title III is complementary. Arizona was supplanting funds and using Title III funds for those purposes."

Veronica Rivera, a legislative staff attorney with the Mexican American Legal Defense and Education Fund (MALDEF) in Washington, says funding is partly to blame for "inadequate" programs for Spanish-speaking students in some states and school districts. But she also points to a need for consistent standards for bilingual teachers. "Some states and local education agencies require some type of bilingual certification," Rivera says. "Most of them do, but not all of them."

Whatever federal funding is provided, Gonzalez says No Child Left Behind helps English learners by holding school districts accountable for measurable results.

"Everyone knew that these kids weren't doing well in school for decades, but there was no accountability," he says. "No one suffered except the kids."

Julie Maxwell-Jolly, director of the Center for Applied Policy in Education at the University of California-Davis, agrees. "We have seen from No Child Left Behind that [English learners] are not achieving," she says. "That's been good. It's really shined a light."

BACKGROUND

American Languages

The American melting pot has always included many languages in addition to English — the dominant tongue since colonial times. Through much of the 19th century, non-English speakers commonly received some instruction in their native languages, whether in public or private schools. From the late 19th century on, however, opposition to rising immigration — along with anti-German sentiment during and after World War I — drove native-language instruction out of most public schools. The rise of bilingual education beginning in the 1960s was premised on a need to use native languages in some form for non-English speakers, but a backlash developed among critics who viewed the policy as failing either to educate or to assimilate youngsters with limited English proficiency.[17]

The European colonists encountered Native Americans who spoke a variety of mostly unwritten languages. Besides the British colonists, the early Americans included many Dutch and a lesser number of French, Germans and Swedes, who brought their native languages with them. African slaves, with limited if any formal schooling, learned English through their work, but not necessarily standard English. New waves of non-English speakers were added through the 19th and early 20th centuries with the conquests of the Mexican-American War (Spanish), the import of Chinese labor (Mandarin and Cantonese) and the immigration from southern and eastern Europe (Italian, Greek, Portuguese, Russian and Polish among many other European languages, along with Hebrew and Yiddish).

At first, the use of non-English languages was "supported, tolerated or sanctioned" by public and parochial schools, according to historian Guadalupe San Miguel Jr.,

C H R O N O L O G Y

1960s-1970s *Civil rights era sparks moves to improve language instruction for non-English-speaking students.*

1967 Bilingual Education Act is passed by Congress and signed by President Lyndon B. Johnson; law provides financial aid to school districts to help students with limited English.

1970 Regulations issued by Department of Health, Education and Welfare (HEW) instruct federally financed school districts to "rectify" language deficiencies of non-English-speaking students.

1971 Massachusetts law requires "transitional bilingual education" in all public schools.

1974 Supreme Court in *Lau v. Nichols* requires public school systems to provide non-English-speaking students with "basic English skills" needed to profit from attendance. . . . Congress codifies requirement later in year in Equal Educational Opportunities Act.

1975 HEW's Office of Civil Rights issues *Lau* regulations requiring use of non-English languages for language-minority students.

1978 Study by private research institute questions the benefits of bilingual education.

1980s-1990s *Opposition to bilingual education forms, grows.*

1980 Carter administration proposes regulations requiring bilingual education.

1981 Reagan administration cancels proposed bilingual-education regulation; begins reducing federal aid to English-language instruction.... Study by Education Department questions benefits of bilingual education.... Federal appeals court, in Texas case, says English-language instruction must be based on "sound educational theory," adequately resourced and proven to be effective (*Castañeda v. Pickard*).

1982 Federal appeals court lifts statewide injunction requiring Texas to improve English-language instruction after state legislature passes bilingual-education law.

1983 U.S. English organization founded to lobby for official English laws; many states pass such laws in 1980s, '90s.

1990 Veteran teacher Rosalie Pedalino Porter's book *Forked Tongue* sharply attacks bilingual education.

1991 Report prepared for U.S. Department of Education finds English-immersion and bilingual education both effective methods but says non-English-speaking students benefit from longer instruction in native language.

1992 Spanish-speaking families in Nogales, Ariz., file federal court suit saying school district fails to provide adequate language instruction.

1998 California voters approve Proposition 227 requiring English immersion for non-English-speaking students, with provision for parents to request waiver.

2000-Present *Support for bilingual education recedes further; plaintiffs in Arizona, Texas cases suffer setbacks.*

2000 Arizona held in contempt of court by federal judge for not providing adequate funding for language instruction. . . . State's voters approve Proposition 203, prescribing English-only for language instruction.

2002 President George W. Bush signs No Child Left Behind Act, repealing Bilingual Education Act but holding school districts accountable for non-English-speaking students to meet proficiency standards; English-language acquisition aid is revamped, reducing assistance to districts with large numbers of language-minority students.... Massachusetts voters approve English-only instruction.

2006 Arizona legislature approves modest increase in state aid for language instruction; federal judge deems funding inadequate, reaffirms statewide injunction; state education chief intervenes to undo injunction.

2008-2009 Federal judge in Texas says state not satisfying federal standards for English learners in secondary schools; federal appeals court issues stay in February 2009.... Supreme Court in June 2009 orders judge in Arizona case to reconsider effort to undo injunction; new hearing set for Dec. 14.

a professor at the University of Houston. Language-policy decisions were made at the state and local level. By mid-century, however, the federal government began discouraging the use of languages other than English in newly acquired territories. States followed. California prescribed English in schools in 1855, five years after statehood. As immigration increased, many other states passed similar laws in the late 19th century. World War I fueled anti-German sentiment that led to English-only laws in the Midwest in states with large German populations.

By the 1920s, most states had English-only laws for public school instruction. Teachers and administrators supported the policies, sometimes even with corporal punishment. President Lyndon B. Johnson's biographer Robert Caro writes that as a teacher in southwest Texas, Johnson sometimes spanked Mexican-American students if he heard them using Spanish on the playground. Three decades later, however, Johnson's fellow Texan and Democrat, Sen. Ralph Yarbrough, came to see the English-only policy as "the cruelest form of discrimination" against the state's large Mexican-American population and others with limited English proficiency. With Johnson in the White House, Yarbrough authored the Bilingual Education Act to encourage and provide financial assistance for programs to recognize the special needs of limited-English-speaking children. The act, attached as Title VII to the omnibus Elementary and Secondary Education Act, cleared Congress in December 1967; Johnson signed it into law the next month.

The new law authorized up to $85 million in federal aid for bilingual education, but only $7.5 million was appropriated the first year. The law did not specify any instructional method for English-language learners. In 1970, regulations issued by the old Department of Health, Education and Welfare (HEW) directed school districts receiving federal aid to "rectify" language deficiencies among non-English speakers but again did not specify a curriculum or instructional method. Meanwhile, however, states were beginning to enact their own initiatives. Massachusetts enacted a law in 1971 establishing what it called "transitional bilingual education." Texas followed suit two years later. Some other states passed laws authorizing but not mandating bilingual education.

The Supreme Court took on the issue in a case from San Francisco brought by Chinese-American students under Title VI of the Civil Rights Act of 1964, which prohibits discrimination in federally assisted services by state or local governments. The plaintiffs in *Lau v. Nichols* claimed that out of 2,856 Chinese-speaking students in the school system, only 1,000 received any supplemental instruction in English. Unanimously, the high court agreed that the school district was violating the Civil Rights Act.

"It seems obvious," Justice William O. Douglas wrote in the main opinion, "that the Chinese-speaking minority receive fewer benefits than the English-speaking majority from respondents' school system." Once again, the decision did not instruct local school systems on how to carry out the federal requirement. In a concurring opinion, Justice Harry A. Blackmun suggested that a school district with fewer non-English speakers might not be subject to the same requirement.[18]

Language Debates

With federal support, bilingualism advanced in the 1970s in schools as well as in society at large. With the election of Republican President Ronald Reagan, however, the federal government set itself against bilingual education and in support of "English-only" instruction. Opposition to bilingual education grew in the 1990s. Supporters of bilingual education succeeded in getting Congress to reauthorize the federal law, but California in 1998 became the first of three states to approve voter initiatives to limit the use of languages other than English in public schools.

Congress responded to the Supreme Court's decision later in 1974 with a law, the Equal Educational Opportunities Act, which codified the requirement that school districts take affirmative steps to deal with the needs of language-minority children. The next year, Congress recognized language minorities in a different context by amending the Voting Rights Act to require bilingual registration and voting materials in electoral districts with at least 5 percent language-minority population. For schools, HEW's Office of Civil Rights in 1975 issued the so-called *Lau* guidelines, which — for the first time — specifically required the use of non-English languages and cultures for language-minority students. The guidelines, however, stressed the goal of helping language-minority children gain proficiency in English.

The growing bilingual-education movement was challenged by several studies — including a major report

Native Americans Fight Language Extinction

"It is about losing history and identity."

Leaders from three Cherokee nations came together in October to mark the opening of the Eastern Band of Cherokee Indians' Kituwah Academy, a language-immersion school for kindergarteners to fifth-graders in Cherokee, N.C.

"It is a wonderful initiative for the Cherokee," says Ellen L. Lutz, executive director for Cultural Survival, a nonprofit advocacy group in Cambridge, Mass., which promotes the rights of indigenous communities. "Young, self-confident Cherokee kids will not forget who they are because of the education they receive at this school."

In 1838 members of the Ketoowah and Cherokee nations in Oklahoma were relocated from their homes by military force in direct violation of an 1832 Supreme Court ruling affirming their right to remain on their traditional territory. Some evaded relocation while others returned to tribal lands in North Carolina. In recent years, profits from several enterprises have encouraged the tribes to take on the multigenerational challenge of preserving their own language. The Cherokee Nation of Oklahoma opened its own immersion school in 2003, and its curriculum serves as the basis for the Eastern Band's.

Many such Indian schools have opened throughout the nation, but some Indian communities have opted for informal language instruction outside the classroom. The Hualapai Tribe in Arizona, for example, holds summer camps for younger generations.

Of the nation's 175 surviving Native American dialects, only 20 are expected to remain in 2050, according to the Indigenous Language Institute (ILI), a nonprofit advocacy group in Santa Fe, N.M. Fifty currently surviving languages have five or fewer speakers — all older than 70 — and face imminent extinction, according to Cultural Survival.

"This is a linguistic emergency," says Ineé Yang Slaughter, executive director of ILI. "It is about losing history and identity."

More than a century ago, during attempts to assimilate Native Americans into mainstream society, the federal government targeted Native American languages in a campaign termed by some linguists as "linguistic genocide."

In an 1887 report, Commissioner of Indian Affairs J.D.C. Atkins wrote, "In the difference of language today lies two-thirds of our trouble.... Schools should be established, which children should be required to attend; their barbarous dialects should be blotted out and the English language substituted."[1]

During the same period, boarding schools established by the Bureau of Indian Affairs tried to stamp out native languages. Under English-only rules students were punished and humiliated for speaking their native language.

The coercive assimilation policy met with limited success in eradicating Indian languages, but over time the policies took a toll on the identity of many Indians, alienating them from their cultural roots. Moreover, the policies left a

published in 1978 under the auspices of the American Institutes for Research — that showed no achievement gains from the use of native-language instruction for non-English speakers. Despite the controversies, the Department of Education — carved out of HEW under President Jimmy Carter — proposed regulations in August 1980 that tightened the requirement for bilingual education. The proposed guidelines, viewed by some as an appeal by Carter for Hispanic votes in the November election, called for bilingual education in any school with at least 25 limited-English-proficiency students in two consecutive grades.

The Reagan administration instituted what historian San Miguel calls a period of "retrenchment and redefinition" for bilingual education. On Feb. 2, 1981 — just two weeks after Reagan took office — Education Secretary Terrel Bell withdrew the proposed bilingual-education regulations from the Carter administration. Reagan himself told reporters he was opposed to bilingual education. He called it "absolutely wrong" to have a bilingual-education program "that is now openly, admittedly dedicated to preserving their native language and never getting them adequate in English."[19] Reagan's views helped encourage a growing English-only movement,

legacy of opposition toward bilingual and immersion education among Indians who remembered the pain they suffered in school and wanted to shield their children from similar experiences.

"The boarding schools turned to indoctrination. Native languages were burned out of their mouths," says Lutz. "Over time, the experience led grandparents to refuse to speak the native tongues to younger generations."

The eventual economic and social mobility of Native Americans aided in the beginning of several grassroots movements in the 1970s to bring back mother tongues.

"The next generation would say, 'It's my language. It's my people. America took it from me. I want it back,'" explains Lutz.

Prodded by language activists, Congress passed the Native American Languages Acts in 1990 and 1992 to facilitate efforts to preserve Native American languages. Among other things, the laws concluded that academic performance was directly tied to a respect for the first language of students.

While the U.S. Department of Education and the National Science Foundation already provided federal help for cultural preservation, the acts made tribes eligible for funding to carry out language conservation and renewal.

Eastern Band of the Cherokee Nation

Eastern Band Cherokee Indians attend the opening of Kituwah Academy, in Cherokee, N.C., in October. Housed in the renovated Boundary Tree Lodge, a historic visitors' lodge, the school teaches academic subjects and the Cherokee language (Kituwah).

Despite the recent surge in teaching Native Americans their native languages, several challenges still remain. Indian-language speakers often lack the academic credentials to teach, while outside teachers are not well-versed in the cultural and linguistic nuances of Native Americans.

"The key is teaching the language to communicate as opposed to more traditional textbook education," says Slaughter. Classroom teaching isn't always the best way to teach students to actually use the language in their communities."

But perhaps the biggest problem is the need to compete with other more pressing priorities such as health care, economic development, housing and general academic learning.

"These other issues are critical," Slaughter says. "But this is not just a language issue, it is an issue of cultural identity being lost. Once a language is gone, it is gone forever. We know that learning our languages strengthens us both as individuals and as a nation."

— *Darrell Dela Rosa*

[1] James Crawford, "Loose Ends in a Tattered Fabric," American Immigration Lawyers Association, www.ailadownloads.org/advo/Crawford-LanguageRights.pdf.

which succeeded over the course of the decade in enacting official-English measures in more than a dozen states.

For schools, the administration began cutting funding for bilingual education; from a high of $158 million in fiscal 1979, federal support fell to $133 million by 1984. A study by two Education Department researchers published in 1981 again questioned the effects of bilingual education. The department's inspector general published a harsh audit of bilingual programs in seven school districts in Texas, which required them to refund federal grants because of failing to meet stated goals. Enforcement actions

by the department's Office of Civil Rights to require bilingual programs, however, declined sharply.

The decline began and continued in the face of an influential ruling in 1981 by the federal appeals court for Texas that reinforced the federal requirement for bilingual instruction under the Equal Educational Opportunities Act. The ruling in *Castañeda v. Pickard* specified that bilingual-education programs must be "based on sound educational theory"; "implemented effectively with resources for personnel, instructional materials, and space"; and proven effective in overcoming language barriers and handicaps.[20]

As Reagan's Republican successor, President George H. W. Bush proved to be sympathetic to bilingual education. In a critical step, Bush allowed the publication in 1991 of an in-depth study of bilingual education commissioned under Reagan but withheld from publication. The Ramirez report — so-called after its principal investigator, J. David Ramirez — was summarized in a press release as affirming the effectiveness of the three most common language-instruction programs: immersion, early-exit bilingual or late-exit bilingual. As bilingual-education advocate Crawford notes, however, on closer examination the study supports longer bilingual instruction. The study found that students in late-exit programs had accelerated progress over time and that, regardless of instructional method, students generally needed five years or longer to achieve proficiency in English.[21]

The opposition to bilingual education continued to grow in the 1990s. After a decade of teaching English-language learners in bilingual Massachusetts, Porter harshly criticized the policy in her book, *Forked Tongue*, in 1990. Like other critics, Porter depicted bilingual instruction as ineffective educationally and politically and culturally divisive. Despite the criticism, the federal bilingual-education law was reenacted in 1994 under a Democratic-controlled Congress and a Democratic president, Bill Clinton.

Four years later, however, bilingual-education opponents won a major state-level victory with California's adoption of Proposition 227, a voter initiative that made so-called sheltered English-immersion the standard instructional method throughout the state for English-language learners. The initiative was bankrolled by Ron Unz, a millionaire businessman-turned-politician and political activist. Passed in 1998 with about 61 percent of the vote, the initiative requires sheltered English immersion for limited English proficiency (LEP) students during a transition not expected to last more than one year with transfer to mainstream classrooms after attaining "a good working knowledge" of English. Parents can waive the English-only rule if they show that native-language instruction would benefit their child. Two states followed California with stricter English-only initiatives: Arizona in 2000, Massachusetts in 2002.

Language Tests

Bilingual education had fallen so out of favor by the start of the 21st century that President George W. Bush and

Congress combined to repeal the federal Bilingual Education Act and expunge the term from federal law. Bush successfully pushed for a new federal law, the No Child Left Behind Act, which required standardized testing of all schools with penalties for those found to be "underperforming." Supporters said the law would hold schools accountable for teaching English learners, but bilingual-education advocates feared misleading results from testing English learners only in English. Meanwhile, the Arizona bilingual education suit moved up to an eventual Supreme Court decision that tilted in favor of English immersion and appeared to limit federal courts' authority to order extra funding for English-language learners.

Bush made the education reform bill his major social policy initiative, securing bipartisan support by appealing to Republicans with test-based standards to hold schools accountable and to Democrats with increased funding to help schools meet the standards. Largely unnoticed in the main debates, the act's Title III replaced the Bilingual Education Act with the English Acquisition Act. As Crawford explains in his historical account, the act increased the authorized funding for English-language instruction but allocated the moneys according to a population-based formula instead of through competitive grants. As a result, funding was no longer concentrated on proven programs, but spread widely. Average grants the first year amounted to only $150 per student, far less than the average grant under the old law.[22]

The act — passed by Congress in December 2001 and signed by Bush on Jan. 8, 2002 — pointedly makes no recommendation as to a particular method of instruction for English learners. As part of the change, the Office of Bilingual Education was renamed the Office of English Language Acquisition, Language Enhancement, and Academic Achievement for Limited English Proficient Students — OELA for short. As the Department of Education explained, the act required state and local education agencies to establish English-proficiency standards; provide quality language instruction based on scientific research; and place highly qualified teachers in English-language classes. All English-language learners were to be tested annually "so that their parents will know how they are progressing."[23]

Nearly five years later, guidebooks issued by the Education Department late in 2006 designed to provide scientifically based recommendations on teaching methods continued to give school districts no guidance on the bilingual versus English-only debate. "We intentionally avoided that," Russell Gersten, a bilingual-education critic who headed the panel of experts that reviewed the guidebooks, told *Education Week.* David Francis, a University of Houston professor and bilingual-education supporter who led the writing of the guidebooks, concurred with the decision. But bilingual-education supporter Krashen at the University of Southern California complained that the guidebooks were "omitting something that is important."[24]

The debate that policy makers tried to duck continued among researchers. A study of California schools published in March 2006 examining the impact of Proposition 227 concluded that no single instructional method for English learners was significantly better than another.

Unz, the English-only activist who had funded the initiative, criticized the study, insisting his analysis showed that the switch from bilingual to predominantly English-only had raised achievement levels. In any event, the study confirmed the drop in bilingual instruction from about 60 percent of English learners to only 8 percent. It also showed that only 40 percent of English learners were reclassified as proficient after 10 years of public schooling.[25]

Two years later, two University of California research centers found no gains in English proficiency in California or the two other states with similar measures, Arizona and Massachusetts. "There's no visual evidence that these three states are doing better than the national average or other states" in educating English learners, Russell Rumberger, director of the Linguistic Minority Research Institute at UC-Santa Barbara, told *Education Week.* The institute partnered with UCLA's Civil Rights Project on the study, which found a greater achievement gap for English learners in the three states than in two states, New Mexico and Texas, which continued to use native-language instruction for English learners. Gersten minimized the findings. He told the publication Proposition 227 had helped English learners by raising expectations and giving them the same curriculum as other students.[26]

Meanwhile, the Arizona suit had reached a critical stage with Judge Raner Collins' ruling in December 2005 that the state was in civil contempt for failing to

First lady Michelle Obama attends a Cinco de Mayo celebration at the Latin American Montessori Bilingual (LAMB) Public Charter School in Washington, on May 4, 2009. Bilingual-education advocates are hoping for support from the Obama administration, which backs "transitional bilingual education" and promises to help English learners by "holding schools accountable for making sure these students complete school."

"appropriately and constitutionally" fund English-language instruction. Collins' decision four months later to reject the legislature's funding increase and impose civil fines was set aside in August 2006 by the 9th U.S. Circuit Court of Appeals, which ordered a full hearing. After an eight-day hearing in January 2007, Collins reaffirmed his ruling, which the 9th Circuit upheld a year later.

On appeal by Superintendent Horne and the Republican legislative leaders, however, the Supreme Court in June 2009 ordered Collins to reconsider the motion to modify the injunction issued nine years earlier. For the majority, Justice Alito pointed to four changed circumstances warranting reconsideration, starting with the state's switch to English immersion. Research on English-language learning instruction, Alito wrote, "indicates there is documented, academic support for the view that SEI [sheltered English immersion] is significantly more effective than bilingual education." The other three factors cited were the federal No Child Left Behind Act; "structural and management reforms" in Nogales itself and the state's increased education funding.

Writing for the four dissenters, Justice Stephen G. Breyer said he would have upheld Judge Collins' order. The high court ruling, Breyer wrote, "will make it more difficult for federal courts to enforce … those federal standards."

CURRENT SITUATION

Lagging Indications

English-language learners (ELLs) are lagging behind other students on math and reading achievement tests, and one-fourth are failing to make progress toward language proficiency, according to state data collected by the federal Department of Education.

Opposing camps in the bilingual versus English-immersion debate predictably blame the achievement and language-proficiency gaps on school districts' failure to adopt their differing prescriptions on the best instructional model to use for English learners. Some experts with less partisan views, however, point to other factors, including the concentration of English learners in high-poverty, lower-resourced schools. English learners score far below the national average for fourth-graders in both reading and math on the National Assessment of Educational Progress (NAEP), often called the nation's report card. The gap widens in test scores for eighth-graders, according to a recent analysis by the Pew Hispanic Center.[27]

The center's analysis of the 2005 NAEP showed, for example, that nearly three-fourths of fourth-grade English learners (73 percent) scored below "basic" on reading — double the national average of 36 percent. For eighth-graders, the national average of below-basic scores fell to 27 percent, but the percentage of English learners scoring below basic remained almost unchanged at 71 percent.

A similar pattern was seen on math scores. Among English learners, 46 percent of fourth-graders scored below basic, compared to the national average of 20 percent. For eighth-graders, the gap widened markedly: 71 percent of English learners below basic compared to a national average of 31 percent.

On all four tests, only small fractions of English learners were rated as proficient or advanced, scores attained by roughly one-third of the students nationwide. The center's analysis, by senior researcher Richard Fry, found that English learners' scores were far below the average of white students and measurably below the averages for blacks and Hispanics.

Language-proficiency testing required of the states by the No Child Left Behind Act shows more directly the achievement gap for English learners. The federal law requires all public school students, including English learners, to meet reading and math proficiency standards by 2014. In tests administered in 2006 and 2007, however, only one-sixth of English learners nationwide were listed as having attained proficiency. One-fourth of the English learners were shown as not making progress.[28]

Both Fry and Barth at the school boards' Center for Public Education point to some precautions in interpreting the statistics. They both note, for example, that — in contrast to ethnic and racial groupings — students classified as English learners at one point can be reclassified as language-proficient later and no longer be included in the group.

Barth also stresses that English-language learners "are not a monolithic group." The vast majority are Spanish speakers, she says, but the others represent more than 400 different languages. Family backgrounds vary greatly as well: Some come from homes with well-educated parents, while others have parents with limited education and literacy. As a result, Barth says, "the range of performance between the high- and low-performing ELL students is greater than the gap between ELLs and their English-speaking peers."

Despite those precautions, bilingual-education advocates decry what they see as the lagging achievement scores for English learners. "Most U.S. schools are dramatically under-educating" English learners, Collier and Thomas write.[29] Both they and journalist-author Crawford blame in part the popularity of English-immersion programs. English-only programs "continue to spread," and enrollment in bilingual programs declines, Crawford says, despite what he calls "increasing" evidence that bilingual programs are more effective.

From the opposite perspective, author Porter of the Center for Equal Opportunity says English-immersion programs are best-suited to the English learners who present the biggest challenges for schools: students from immigrant families typically poor and often headed by parents with limited education. "These children have to be given a priority education," Porter says. "What is important? First, give them English-language skills."

The Pew Center's Fry suggests, however, that English-learners' gaps may be related to the characteristics of the schools that most attend. In a second, recent report, Fry found that in the states with the largest concentration of English learners, the ELL students were concentrated in

Is bilingual education best for English-language learners?

 James Crawford
President, Institute for Language and Education Policy; coauthor, English Learners in American Classrooms: 101 Questions, 101 Answers

Written for *CQ Researcher*, November 2009

 Rosalie Pedalino Porter
Board member, Center for Equal Opportunity

Written for *CQ Researcher*, December 2009

Bilingual education, perhaps the least understood program in our public schools, also turns out to be among the most beneficial. Its effectiveness — both in teaching English and in fostering academic learning in English — has been validated in study after study.

Yet U.S. media rarely report such findings. All too often, bilingualism is portrayed as a political controversy rather than a set of pedagogical challenges, a conflict over immigration instead of an effort to turn language "problems" into classroom resources.

In education, of course, there is no one-size-fits-all. What works for one student or group of students will not necessarily work for others. All things being equal, however, a large and consistent body of research shows that bilingual education is a superior way to teach English-language learners. Building on — rather than discarding — students' native-language skills creates a stronger foundation for success in English and academics.

This is a counterintuitive finding for many Americans, so it needs some explaining. Why does bilingual education work? Three reasons:

- When students receive some lessons in their native language, the teacher does not need to "dumb down" instruction in simplified English. So they have access to the same challenging curriculum as their English-speaking peers, rather than falling behind.
- The more these students progress in academic subjects, the more contextual knowledge they acquire to make sense of lessons in English. And the more "comprehensible input" they receive in English, the faster they acquire the language.
- Reading provides a foundation for all learning. It is much more efficiently mastered in a language that children understand. As they acquire English, these literacy skills are easily transferred to the new language. Once you can read, you can read!

Finally, let's consider the alternative: all-English "immersion." Independent studies have shown that after several years of such programs in California and Arizona, there has been no benefit for children learning English. In fact, the "achievement gap" between these students and fluent English speakers seems to be increasing.

Unfortunately, so is the gap between research and policy. Bilingual education has fallen out of favor politically for reasons that have nothing to do with its academic effectiveness. If we seriously hope to integrate immigrants as productive members of our society, that will have to change.

Bilingual education is the least effective method for teaching English-language learners. To meet the stated goals of federal and state laws of the past 40 years — that students would learn the English language rapidly and master school subjects taught in English — the experimental, theoretical model called bilingual education is a demonstrable, documented failure.

As a Spanish-English bilingual teacher in Massachusetts — the first state to mandate bilingual education — I saw firsthand the model's inadequacies. Our students were taught all subjects in Spanish most of the school day and provided brief English lessons. They were segregated by language and ethnicity in substantially separate classrooms for three to six years. The costs to school districts for this separate program are not as damaging as "the negative effect on English-language learner achievement," as documented in the 2009 study by the Texas Public Policy Foundation.

Reliable research was never the strong point in reporting on bilingual education in its first two decades. Valid studies of student achievement both in learning English and school subjects began to be published in the 1980s. Reliable studies must include two similar groups of students (socioeconomic status, level of English fluency), one enrolled in a bilingual program, one enrolled in an English-immersion program. At the end of two, three or four years, an objective assessment of which group of students showed measurable success in English language and academic learning can be determined.

From Dade County, Fla., in 1988, El Paso, Texas, in 1992, New York City in 1995, and numerous reports from California and Arizona over the past 10 years, English-immersion students outscored their counterparts in bilingual programs both in rapid acquisition of English language and literacy and on state tests of reading and math. The evidence for the superiority of English immersion surely influenced public opinion in the initiative referenda that legally threw out bilingual teaching by citizen vote in California (1998), Arizona (2000) and Massachusetts (2002). Of the 10 states that originally mandated native-language instruction bilingual programs, only four remain: Illinois, New Jersey, New York and Texas.

The debate is effectively over. A high accolade comes from the U. S. Supreme Court's recent ruling in the *Flores* case, which found "documented academic support for the view that structured English immersion is significantly more effective than bilingual education."

central city schools with higher average enrollment and higher student-to-teacher ratios than other public schools in the state. The schools with concentrated ELL populations also had a "substantially greater proportion" of students who qualified for free or reduced-price school lunches.[30]

Significantly, Fry found that the English learners' achievement gap was narrower in schools that had "at least a minimum threshold number of white students." Barth similarly sees what she calls "linguistically isolated" schools as a substantial cause of the achievement gap.

"We sometimes give the least to the kids and the schools that have the least to begin with," Barth says. "Those schools have greater challenges and aren't being given much to work with in terms of resources."

Fighting in Court

Civil rights lawyers in two states with substantial Latino populations are waging legal battles begun decades ago to improve English-language instruction for Spanish-speaking students.

Lower federal court judges issued broad rulings in both cases telling state officials in Arizona to increase spending on English learners and in Texas to improve services and monitoring for English learners in secondary schools. But plaintiffs in both cases suffered setbacks earlier this year.

The 5th U.S. Circuit Court of Appeals issued a stay of the lower court judge's January 2008 order in the Texas case in February pending its own review of the decision. A three-judge panel is currently deliberating on the case following oral arguments on June 2.[31]

The Supreme Court's June 26 decision in the Arizona case (*Horne v. Flores*) sent that 17-year-old lawsuit back to federal district court in Phoenix. The ruling requires Judge Collins to reconsider the effort by Superintendent of Instruction Horne either to modify or dissolve the injunction requiring more funding first issued by Judge Marquez in 2000 and reaffirmed by Collins in 2006.

Today, plaintiffs' lawyers in both cases say the state education systems are failing the public schools' English learners, who number more than 600,000 in Texas and nearly 170,000 in Arizona.

Roger Rice, an attorney who has worked on the Texas case since the early 1970s, blames poor performance and

Lourdes Carmona teaches Spanish pronunciation to first-graders at Birdwell Elementary School in Tyler, Texas. She was recruited from Spain, along with her husband, to teach Spanish-speaking youngsters in their native language.

Getty Images/Mario Villafuerte

high dropout rates for English learners in secondary schools in part on lack of monitoring by state officials. "The Texas language program, particularly at the secondary level, is failing," says Rice, founder of the Massachusetts-based advocacy group META (Multicultural Education Training and Advocacy). "And Texas has not evaluated the program to know why it's failing and has not made the changes to make it succeed."

In Arizona, plaintiffs' attorney Hogan says the state's model of four-hour pullouts for language instruction for English learners segregates them unnecessarily and unlawfully. "This is classic segregation," Hogan says. "Kids in these classes are regarded by others as dumb, as second-class citizens."

State officials are defending their programs in both cases. Lawyers for the Texas Education Agency told the appeals court in June that a computerized tracking system adequately monitors performance of English learners. They also urged the appeals court to dismiss the entire case, originally filed by the Justice Department as a desegregation suit in 1970 and expanded by Latino advocacy groups in 1975 to specifically address English-learners' rights under the federal Equal Educational Opportunities Act.

Lawyers representing Horne and state legislative leaders told Supreme Court justices that the mandate for increased funding originally issued in 2000 had been superseded by the voter-approved decision to shift from bilingual to English immersion and by the passage of the federal No Child Left Behind Act. Since the ruling, Horne has continued to defend the new system. "Kids who come to this country need to learn English quickly," he says.

The Texas case lay dormant for a quarter-century after the 5th Circuit appeals court in 1982 reversed a ruling by U.S. District Judge Wayne Justice two years earlier that the state was not providing equal opportunities to English learners as the federal law required. The appeals court noted that the Texas legislature had passed a bilingual-education law and held that the state was entitled to time to bring schools into compliance.

With assistance from MALDEF, Rice moved to reopen the Texas case in 2006 after education officials decided to drop active monitoring of classes and materials for English learners. Justice initially ruled in 2007 that state officials were complying with the ruling, but he reversed himself in 2008 in an 88-page decision sharply critical of poor performance and high dropout rates for English learners in secondary schools.

In the Arizona case, Collins ruled in 2007 that the changes in educational policy and the additional funding approved by the legislature in 2006 did not solve what he termed the "resource" problem. The 9th U.S. Circuit Court of Appeals upheld his decision to leave the injunction in place, but the Supreme Court's conservative majority said Collins had given inadequate consideration to the various changes.

Significantly for the plaintiffs in Arizona and in other cases, however, the justices rejected the state's argument that compliance with the No Child Left Behind Act was sufficient to establish compliance with the earlier law requiring equal opportunities for English learners. The act's funding and its reporting and assessment schemes could be relevant, Alito explained, but not necessarily determinative under the 1974 act.

Appeals court judges closed the hearing in the Texas case in June by cautioning lawyers not to expect a quick ruling. In Arizona, opposing lawyers submitted new filings to Collins earlier in the fall; Collins is to hold a hearing on Dec. 14 to determine whether to limit further proceedings to Nogales schools or to apply any ruling statewide.

OUTLOOK
Getting Results?

Two well-regarded school districts in the Washington, D.C., suburbs take different approaches to teaching English learners. Administrators in Montgomery County, Md., and Arlington, Va., both say they practice "immersion" as the best way to teach English to Latino students who enter their school systems more familiar with Spanish than with the nation's dominant tongue. But immersion has different meanings for the two systems.[32]

In Montgomery County, Spanish-speaking students at Sargent Shriver Elementary School — about half the student body — are immersed in English. ESL teachers "plug in" to mainstream classrooms to help English learners along or "pull out" students for individualized or group tutoring. Karen Woodson, the school district's head of ESL programs, says flexibility is important but stresses that the system strongly opposes use of native-language instruction to help students acquire English-language proficiency.

Across the Potomac River in Arlington, some Latino students are immersed in two languages: Spanish and English. At Francis Scott Key Elementary School ("Escuela Key"), each class is divided between Spanish and English speakers, and instruction is equally divided between the two languages. Principal Marjorie Myers says she favors dual-language immersion as the best long-term strategy for English learners even at the expense of short-term gains on language-proficiency tests.

In its influential *Castañeda* decision on the rights of English learners almost three decades ago, the federal appeals court in New Orleans said that courts ruling on such cases should examine three factors: whether a school system was using a program based on "sound educational theory," whether adequate resources were being provided and whether the program was proving to be effective.

In the intervening decades, many school systems picked one educational theory — bilingual education — or another — English immersion. The issue of adequate resources is muddy, with bilingual-education advocates claiming their approach is both better and cheaper. But the question of results appears less ambiguous. English learners lag in academic performance and in graduation rates, and the gaps do not appear to be narrowing.

With the number of English learners in public schools rapidly increasing — projected to be one-fourth of the school population by 2025 — the need to close that gap will only increase.[33] "It's going to be a long-term persistent problem," says Stanford professor Hakuta. "The number of English learners has increased to the point where it's no longer an issue like special education, a small subset. In many districts, it's a majority of the students."

Since the 1980s, teaching English learners has been an intensely political issue. English-immersion advocate Porter notes that former Boston University president John Silber, a critic of bilingualism and multiculturalism, once called English-language learning a "third-rail" issue — dangerous for politicians to touch.

In recent years, however, the politicization of the issue appears to be ebbing somewhat. "The black and white distinctions that existed before 1998 are no longer there," says Don Soifer, education analyst with the pro-English Lexington Institute.

In California, for example, the state's English-only initiative — Proposition 227 — remains on the books but has not stopped the Ventura County Unified School District from creating dual-language immersion programs at eight elementary- and middle-school campuses. "I think parents throughout the state recognize the value of having their kids be bilingual and biliterate," says associate superintendent Roger Rice.[34]

Bilingual-education advocates are hoping for support for their view from the Obama administration. The administration's stated agenda supports "transitional bilingual education" and promises to help English learners by "holding schools accountable for making sure these students complete school." The administration's education initiatives since January have given no emphasis to the issue, however, and the Education Department's Office of English Language Acquisition is operating with an interim director.

For educators, the next big event in Washington is the anticipated fight in Congress over reauthorizing the No Child Left Behind Act. Experts and advocates on both sides of the language-instruction issue applaud the act's goal — and 2014 deadline — of requiring language proficiency for English learners. But the National Education Association, the powerful teachers' union, wants more testing to be done in students' native language. Testing English learners in English "may be setting these students up for more failure," the NEA says in a policy brief.[35]

Despite the political controversies, some experts are predicting progress for English learners. "What we have now is good methodology about what works," says Barth with the school boards' Center for Public Education. "As we're collecting more data, we're seeing gains among English-language learners, and we're finding out more and more about what propels those gains. The more that information gets out, the politics will quiet down."

NOTES

1. Flores was interviewed in Spanish by *CQ Researcher* staff writer Peter Katel. See also Eddi Trevizo and Pat Kossan, "Mom at Head of Suit Still Worried About English Learners," *The Arizona Republic*, June 26, 2009, p. 15.

2. The decision is *Horne v. Flores*, 557 U.S. — (June 25, 2009). For coverage, see Pat Kossan, "A Win for State on English Learners," *The Arizona Republic*, June 26, 2009, p. 1.

3. For previous coverage, see these *CQ Researcher* reports: Craig Donegan, "Debate Over Bilingualism," Jan. 19, 1996, pp. 49-72; and Richard L. Worsnop, "Bilingual Education," Aug. 13, 1993, pp. 697-720; and these in *Editorial Research Reports*: Sarah Glazer, "Bilingual Education: Does It Work?," March 11, 1988; pp. 125-140, and Sandra Stencel, "Bilingual Education," Aug. 19, 1977, pp. 617-636.

4. For background, see Barbara Mantel, "No Child Left Behind," *CQ Researcher*, May 27, 2005, pp. 469-492.

5. Claude Goldenberg, "Teaching English Language Learners: What the Research Does — and Does Not — Show," *American Educator*, summer 2008, www.aft.org/pubs-reports/american_educator/issues/summer08/goldenberg.pdf. Goldenberg cited A. M. Zehler, *et al.*, "Descriptive Study of Services to LEP0 Students and LEP Students with Disabilities, Vol. 1, Research Report," Development Associates, Inc., 2003.

6. Virginia P. Collier and Wayne P. Thomas, *Educating English Learners for a Transformed World* (2009), pp. 3-4. The authors, professors emeriti at George Mason University, in Fairfax, Va., identify themselves as educational consultants on their Web site, www.thomasandcollier.com.

7. *Ibid.*, p. 48. Statistical chart appears at p. 55.

8. "What research shows about English language learners: At a glance," Center for Public Education undated, www.centerforpubliceducation.org/site/apps/nlnet/content3.aspx?c=lvIXIiN0JwE&b=5127 871&content_id={DE9F2763-8DA4-4C2A-B3D1-9AEF8B3AEDA1}&notoc=1.

9. James Crawford, *Educating English Learners: Language Diversity in the Classroom* (5th ed.), 2004.

10. Collin Hitt, "Charter Schools and Changing Neighborhoods: Hispanic Students and English Learners in Chicago," Lexington Institute/Illinois Policy Institute, Sept. 29, 2009, www.lexingtoninstitute.org/library/resources/documents/Education/FinalProof9.29.09.pdf.

11. See Mary Ann Zehr, "Nurturing 'School Minds': Through order and English immersion, a network of charter schools strives to turn Latino students into informed citizens and leaders inside and outside the community," *Education Week*, Oct. 7, 2009, p. 24.

12. *Horne v. Flores, op. cit.*, p. 24 of slip opinion and footnote 10.

13. Kelly Torrance, "Immersion Not Submersion: Converting English Learner Programs from Bilingual Education to Structured English Immersion in California and Elsewhere," October 2005; and "Immersion Not Submersion: Volume II: Lessons from Three California School Districts' Switch from Bilingual Education to Structured Immersion," March 2006, www.lexingtoninstitute.org/library/resources/documents/Education/immersion-not-submersion-converting-english.pdf.

14. Stephen Krashen, "Proposition 227 and Skyrocketing Test Scores in California: An Urban Legend," *Educational Leadership*, December 2004/January 2005, www.sdkrashen.com/articles/prop227/index.html.

15. See Arizona Department of Education, "The Effects of Bilingual Education Programs and Structured English Immersion Programs on Student Achievement: A Large-Scale Comparison," July 2004, http://epsl.asu.edu/epru/articles/EPRU-0408-66-OWI.pdf. The report is identified as a draft, but no later version was prepared.

16. Kate Mahoney, Jeff MacSwan, Tom Haladyna and David Garcia, "*Castañeda*'s Third Prong: Evaluating the Achievement of Arizona's English Learners Under Restrictive Language Policy," in Patricia Gandara and Megan Hopkins, *Forbidden Language: English Learners and Restrictive Language Policies* (forthcoming January 2010).

17. Background drawn from Guadalupe San Miguel Jr., *Contested Policy: The Rise and Fall of Federal Bilingual Education in the United States, 1960-2001* (2004). See also James Crawford, *Educating English Learners: Language Diversity in the Classroom* (5th ed.,), 2004; Rosalie Pedalino Porter, *Forked Tongue: The Politics of Bilingual Education* (2d ed.), 1996.

18. The decision is *Lau v. Nichols*, 414 U.S. 563 (1974). San Miguel writes erroneously at one point that the court decided the case on constitutional grounds.

19. Quoted in Crawford, *op. cit.*, p. 120.

20. The citation is 648 F.2d 989 (5th Cir. 1981). Despite the favorable legal standard, the defendant Raymondville Independent School District, in south Texas near the Mexican border, ultimately won a ruling that it was providing adequate bilingual education to the Mexican-American students in the system. See Richard R. Valencia, *Chicano Students and the Courts: The Mexican American Struggle for Educational Equality* (2008), pp. 187-191.

21. Crawford, *op. cit.*, pp. 148-152 in 4th ed.

22. Crawford, *op. cit.*, pp. 356-357.

23. Quoted in *ibid.*, p. 355.

24. All three quoted in Mary Ann Zehr, "Guides Avoid Bilingual versus English-Only Issue," *Education Week*, Nov. 8, 2006, p. 20.

25. Linda Jacobson, "Prop. 227 Seen as Focusing on 'Wrong Issue,' " *Education Week*, March 1, 2006, p. 18.

26. Mary Ann Zehr, "NAEP Scores in States That Cut Bilingual Ed Fuel Concerns on ELLs," *Education*

Week. May 14, 2008, p. 14. NAEP — commonly called the nation's report card — stands for National Assessment of Educational Progress.

27. Richard Fry, "How Far Behind in Math and Reading are English Language Learners?," Pew Hispanic Center, June 6, 2007, http://pewhispanic.org/files/reports/76.pdf. The report does not include national averages, which were supplied from the National Assessment of Educational Progress Web site: http://nationsreportcard.gov/reading_math_2005/.

28. Data from edweek.org, the Web site of *Education Week* and *Teachers Magazine*. See "English Language Learners" page on www.edcounts.org/createtable/viewtable.php.

29. Collier and Thomas, *op. cit.*, p. 3.

30. Richard Fry, "The Role of Schools in the English Language Learner Achievement Gap," Pew Hispanic Center, June 26, 2008, http://pewhispanic.org/reports/report.php?ReportID=89.

31. The case is *United States v. Texas*, 08-40858. The Latino advocacy groups GI Forum and League of United Latin American Citizens (LULAC) intervened in 1975 in what was originally a school desegregation case to raise English-language learning issues under the Equal Educational Opportunities Act of 1974.

32. Reporting by editorial intern Emily DeRuy, University of California, San Diego.

33. See Goldenberg, *op. cit.*, p. 10.

34. Quoted in Cheri Carlson, "Three more schools add bilingual immersion programs," *Ventura County Star*, July 15, 2009.

35. "English Language Learners Face Unique Challenges," National Education Association, fall 2008, www.nea.org/assets/docs/mf_PB05_ELL.pdf.

BIBLIOGRAPHY

Books

Collier, Virginia P., and Wayne P. Thomas, *Educating English Learners for a Transformed World,* **Fuente Press, 2009.**
Two former George Mason University professors specializing in research for "at-risk" students examine different methods for teaching English-language learners and repeat their research findings that English learners benefit from additional time in native-language instruction. The book closes with 11 recommendations for educators to follow in designing programs for English learners. Includes nine-page list of references.

Crawford, James, *Educating English Learners: Language Diversity in the Classroom* **(5th ed.), Bilingual Education Services, 2004.**
The longtime advocate for bilingual education provides a comprehensive history of language-education policies against the backdrop of growing language diversity due to increased immigration. Crawford, a former education reporter, served as executive director of the National Association for Bilingual Education and now writes and advocates on bilingual education as head of the Institute for Language Education and Policy. Includes chapter notes, 24-page compilation of sources and suggested readings.

Gandara, Patricia, and Megan Hopkins (eds.), *Forbidden Language: English Learners and Restrictive Language Policies,* **Teachers College Press, forthcoming (January 2010).**
The book examines the most up-to-date research on the impact of "restrictive language policies" adopted in three states by ballot measures: Arizona, California and Massachusetts. Gandara is professor of education at the University of California-Los Angeles; Hopkins is a doctoral student at UCLA's Graduate School of Education and Information Studies.

Porter, Rosalie Pedalino, *Forked Tongue: The Politics of Bilingual Education* **(2d ed.), Transaction, 1996.**
A prominent critic of bilingual education argues in favor of early and intensive instruction in English with no separation of language-minority children from fellow students. Porter served as director of language-instruction programs in Newton, Mass., in the 1980s and later as director of the READ Institute (Research in English Acquisition and Development), which has now been folded into the Center for Equal Opportunity. Includes chapter notes, four-page list of references. Porter is author most recently of the autobiographical *American Immigrant: My Life in Three Languages* (iUniverse, 2009).

San Miguel, Guadalupe Jr., *Contested Policy: The Rise and Fall of Federal Bilingual Education in the United States, 1960-2001,* University of North Texas Press, 2004.

The compact history traces the history of federal policy on education for English-language learners from the genesis of the Bilingual Education Act in the 1960s through its repeal with the No Child Left Behind Act in 2001. San Miguel is a professor of history at the University of Houston. Includes chapter notes, 45-page bibliographical essay organized by time period.

Schmid, Ronald Sr., *Language Policy and Identity in the United States,* Temple University Press, 2000.

A professor of political science at California State University-Long Beach examines the debate over bilingual education in the United States in the broader context of language policy with comparisons to policies in other multilingual countries. Includes chapter notes, 18-page list of references.

Valencia, Richard R., *Chicano Students and the Courts,* New York University Press, 2008.

A 46-page chapter sketches the history of bilingual education for Mexican-Americans since the Mexican-American War, discusses major bilingual-education suits in the 1970s and '80s and briefly treats the passage of state "English-only" initiatives and the repeal of the federal Bilingual Education Act. Valencia is a professor with the Center for Mexican American Studies at the University of Texas in Austin.

Articles

Goldenberg, Claude, "Teaching English Language Learners: What the Research Does — and Does Not — Show," American Educator, summer 2008, www.aft.org/pubs-reports/american_educator/issues/summer08/goldenberg.pdf.

A professor of education at Stanford University delineates three conclusions from the research on English learners, including the key finding that teaching students in their first language promotes higher levels of reading achievement in English. Adapted from "Improving Achievement for English Language Learners, in Susan B. Neuman (ed.), *Educating the Other America: Top Experts Tackle Poverty, Literacy, and Achievement in Our Schools* (Paul H. Brooke Publishing Co., 2008).

Reports and Studies

Rossell, Christine H., "Dismantling Bilingual Education, Implementing English Immersion: The California Initiative," Public Policy Institute of California, 2002, www.eric.ed.gov/ERICWebPortal/custom/portlets/recordDetails/detailmini.jsp?_nfpb=true&_&ERICExtSearch_SearchValue_0=ED467043&ERICExtSearch_SearchType_0=no&accno=ED467043.

The detailed report by the Boston University political scientist concludes that Proposition 227, the California initiative that restricted bilingual education in public schools, may have benefited English learners but cautions that English learners continued to suffer achievement gaps because of immigration status and family backgrounds.

For More Information

American Unity Legal Defense Fund, P.O. Box 420, Warrenton, VA 20187; www.americanunity.org. An educational organization that promotes conservative immigration reform in the legal arena.

Asian American Justice Center, 1140 Connecticut Ave., N.W., Suite 1200, Washington, DC 20036; (202) 296-2300; www.advancingequality.org. Works to advance human and civil rights for Asian Americans by providing them the tools and support needed to participate in the democratic process.

Asian American Legal Defense and Education Fund, 99 Hudson St., 12th Floor, New York, NY 10013; (212) 966-5932; www.aaldef.org. Promotes the civil rights of Asian Americans through litigation, advocacy, education and community organizing.

Center for Equal Opportunity, 7700 Leesburg Pike, Suite 231, Falls Church, VA 22043; (703) 442-0066; www.ceousa.org. Promotes color-blind public policies and seeks to block the expansion and use of racial preferences in employment, education and voting by promoting the assimilation of immigrants and opposing teaching in students' native languages.

Congressional Hispanic Caucus Institute, 911 2nd St., N.E., Washington, DC 20002; (202) 543-1771; www.chci.org. Helps increase opportunities for Hispanics to participate in the American policy-making process by offering educational and leadership-development programs.

English First, 666 Fu Zhou Rd., Shanghai, China 200001; +86 21 6133 6262; www.englishfirst.com. The world's largest private education company, specializing in language training, educational tours and cultural exchange.

Institute for Language and Education Policy, P.O. Box 5960, Takoma Park, MD 20913; www.elladvocates.org. Promoting research-based policies in serving English and heritage language learners to ensure that policies for serving children reflect the latest research about language and education.

Mexican American Legal Defense and Education Fund, 1016 16th St., N.W., Suite 100, Washington, DC 20036; (202) 293-2828; www.maldef.org. Promotes equality and justice through advocacy, litigation, public policy and education in the areas of employment, immigrants' rights, political access, voting rights and language rights.

National Association for Bilingual Education, 1313 L St., N.W., Suite 210, Washington, DC 20005; (202) 898-1829; www.nabe.org. Represents both English-language learners and bilingual education professionals through affiliate organizations in 23 states.

National Clearinghouse for English Language Acquisition, 2011 I St., N.W., Suite 300, Washington, DC 20036; (202) 467-0867; www.ncela.gwu.edu. Supports the U.S. Department of Education's Office of English Language Acquisition.

NCLR (National Council of La Raza), 1126 16th St., N.W., Washington, DC 20036; (202) 785-1670; www.nclr.org. The largest national Hispanic civil rights and advocacy organization in the U.S. works to improve opportunities for Hispanic Americans through applied research, policy analysis and advocacy.

National Education Association, 1201 16th St., N.W., Washington, DC 20036; (202) 833-4000; www.nea.org. An organization of 3.2 million members aimed at promoting the right of every child to quality public education, as well as advocating for education professionals.

National School Boards Association, 1680 Duke Street, Alexandria, VA 22314; (703) 838-6722; www.nsba.org. Seeks excellence and equity in public education through school board leadership in all communities.

Office of English Language Acquisition, Language Enhancement, and Academic Achievement for Limited English Proficient Students, 400 Maryland Ave., S.W., Washington, DC 20202; (202) 401-1423; www.ed.gov/about/offices/list/oela/index.html. Provides national leadership to help English-language learners and immigrant students attain English proficiency.

4

Climate Change

Reed Karaim

Reuters/Reinhard Krause

Erosion is washing away beachfront land in the Maldives. The island nation in the Indian Ocean faces possible submersion as early as 2100, according to some climate change predictions. President Mohamed Nasheed said the voluntary emission cuts goal reached in Copenhagen last December was a good step, but at that rate "my country would not survive."

From *CQ Researcher*, February, 2010

It was the global gathering many hoped would save the world. For two weeks in December, delegates from 194 nations came together in Copenhagen, Denmark, to hammer out an international agreement to limit global warming. Failure to do so, most scientists have concluded, threatens hundreds of millions of people and uncounted species of plants and animals.

Diplomatic preparations had been under way for years but intensified in the months leading up to the conference. Shortly before the sessions began, Yvo de Boer, executive secretary of the United Nations Framework Convention on Climate Change — the governing body for negotiations — promised they would "launch action, action and more action," and proclaimed, "I am more confident than ever before that [Copenhagen] will be the turning point in the fight to prevent climate disaster."[1]

But delegates found themselves bitterly divided. Developing nations demanded more financial aid for coping with climate change. Emerging economic powers like China balked at being asked to do more to limit their emissions of the greenhouse gases (GHGs) — created by burning carbon-based fuels — blamed for warming up the planet. The United States submitted proposed emissions cuts that many countries felt fell far short of its responsibility as the world's dominant economy. As negotiations stalled, frustration boiled over inside the hall and on the streets outside, where tens of thousands of activists had gathered to call world leaders to action. A historic opportunity — a chance to reach a global commitment to battle climate change — seemed to be slipping away.

Then, on Dec. 18 — the final night of the conference — leaders from China, India, Brazil, South Africa and the United States emerged

Major Flooding, Drought Predicted at Century's End

Significant increases in runoff — from rain or melting snow and ice — are projected with a high degree of confidence for vast areas of the Earth, mainly in northern regions. Up to 20 percent of the world's population lives in areas where river flood potential is likely to increase by the 2080s. Rainfall and runoff are expected to be very low in Europe, the Middle East, northern and southern Africa and the western United States.

Projected Changes in Annual Runoff (Water Availability), 2090-2099
(by percentage, relative to 1980-1999)

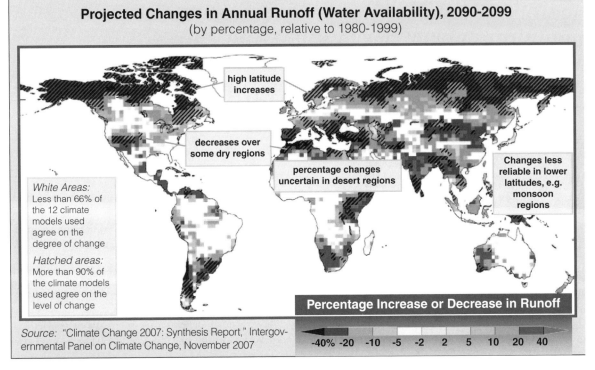

high latitude increases

decreases over some dry regions

percentage changes uncertain in desert regions

Changes less reliable in lower latitudes, e.g. monsoon regions

White Areas: Less than 66% of the 12 climate models used agree on the degree of change

Hatched areas: More than 90% of the climate models used agree on the level of change

Percentage Increase or Decrease in Runoff

-40% -20 -10 -5 -2 2 5 10 20 40

Source: "Climate Change 2007: Synthesis Report," Intergovernmental Panel on Climate Change, November 2007

from a private negotiating session with a three-page, non-binding accord that rescued the meeting from being judged an abject failure.

But the accord left as much confusion as clarity in its wake. It was a deal, yes, but one that fell far short of the hopes of those attending the conference, and one largely lacking in specifics. The accord vowed to limit global warming to 2 degrees Celsius (3.6 Fahrenheit) above pre-Industrial Revolution levels, provide $30 billion in short-term aid to help developing countries cope with the effects of climate change — with more promised longer-term — and included significant reporting and transparency standards for participants, including emerging economic powers such as China and India.

The accord did not, however:

- Include earlier language calling for halving global greenhouse gas emissions by 2050;
- Set a peak year by which greenhouse gases should begin to decline;
- Include country-specific targets for emission reductions (signatories began filling in the numbers by the end of January) (*See Current Situation, p. 90.*);
- Include a timetable for reaching a legally binding international treaty, or
- Specify where future financial help for the developing world to cope with climate change will come from.[2]

Called back into session in the early morning hours, delegates from much of the developing world reacted with dismay to a deal they felt left their countries vulnerable to catastrophic global warming.

"[This] is asking Africa to sign a suicide pact — an incineration pact — in order to maintain the economic dependence [on a high-carbon economy] of a few countries," said Lumumba Di-Aping, the Sudanese chair of the G77 group of 130 poor countries.[3]

British Prime Minister Gordon Brown, however, hailed the deal as a "vital first step" toward "a green and low-carbon future for the world."[4] A total of 55 countries, including the major developed nations, eventually signed onto the deal.

But at the Copenhagen conference, delegates agreed only to "take note" of the accord, without formally adopting it.

Since then, debate has raged over whether the accord represents a step backward or a realistic new beginning. "You had the U.S., China and India closing ranks and saying it's too hard right now to have a binding agreement," says Malini Mehra, an Indian political scientist with 20 years of involvement in the climate change debate. "It's really worse than where we started off."

Others are more upbeat. Michael Eckhart, president of the American Council on Renewable Energy, points out that the convention had revealed how unworkable the larger effort — with 194 participants — had become. "The accord actually sets things in motion in a direction that is realistic," he says. "To have these major nations signed up is fantastic."

Copenhagen clearly demonstrated how extremely difficult and complex global climate negotiations can be. Getting most of the world's nations to

Carbon Emissions Rising; Most Come from China

Global emissions of carbon dioxide (CO_2) — the most common greenhouse gas (GHG) blamed for raising the planet's temperature — have grown steadily for more than 150 years. Since 1950, however, the increases have accelerated and are projected to rise 44 percent between 2010 and 2030 (top graph). While China emits more CO_2 than any other country, Australians produce the most carbon emissions per person (bottom left). Most manmade GHG comes from energy production and transportation (pie chart).

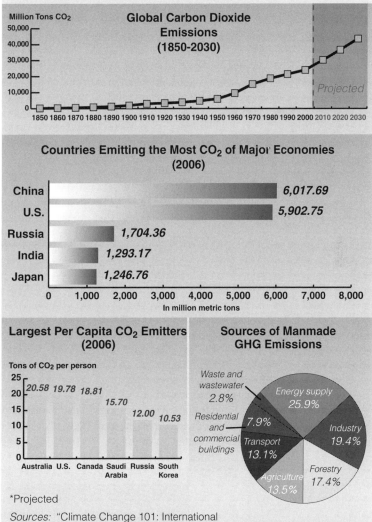

*Projected

Sources: "Climate Change 101: International Action," Pew Center on Global Climate Change, undated; "Climate Change 2007: Synthesis Report," Intergovernmental Panel on Climate Change, November 2007; Union of Concerned Scientists

Warming Trends Continue to Accelerate

During the last 25 years the Earth's average temperature steadily increased — and at increasingly higher increments — compared to the average temperature from 1880-1910. From 2004-2008, the increase was about 1.4 degrees F., or nearly double the increase from 1984 to 1988.

Average Temperature Increases in Five-year Periods, Relative to the Average Temperature in 1880-1910

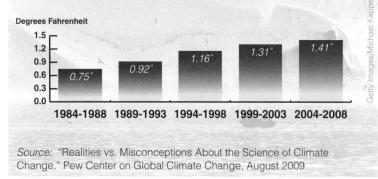

Degrees Fahrenheit

Source: "Realities vs. Misconceptions About the Science of Climate Change," Pew Center on Global Climate Change, August 2009

agree on anything is no easy task, but climate change straddles the biggest geopolitical fault lines of our age: the vast economic disparity between the developed and developing worlds, questions of national sovereignty versus global responsibility and differences in political process between democratic and nondemocratic societies.

Climate change also involves a classic example of displaced hardship — some of the worst effects of global warming are likely to be felt thousands of miles from those nations that are most responsible for the higher temperatures and rising seas, making it easier for responsible parties to delay action. Finally, tackling the problem is likely to take hundreds of billions of dollars.

None of this is comforting to those already suffering from climate change, such as Moses Mopel Kisosion, a Maasai herdsman who journeyed from Kenya to tell anyone who would listen how increasingly severe droughts are destroying his country's traditional way of life. (*See story on climate refugees, p. 84.*) But it does explain why reactions to the Copenhagen Accord — which even President Barack Obama acknowledged is simply a "beginning" — have varied so widely.[5]

For some U.S. environmental groups, the significance of the accord was in the commitment Obama secured from emerging economies to provide greater transparency

and accountability, addressing one of the U.S. Senate's objections to earlier climate change proposals. The Senate never ratified the previous international climate agreement, known as the Kyoto Protocol.

Carl Pope, executive director of the Sierra Club, called the accord "historic — if incomplete," but said, "Now that the rest of the world — including countries like China and India — has made it clear that it is willing to take action, the Senate must pass domestic legislation as soon as possible."[6]

But to nongovernmental organizations focused on global poverty and economic justice, the accord represented an abdication of responsibility by the United States and other developed countries. Tim Jones, chief climate officer for the United Kingdom-based anti-poverty group World Development Movement, called the accord "a shameful and monumental failure that has condemned millions of people around the world to untold suffering."[7]

Easily lost in the heated rhetoric, however, is another part of the Copenhagen story: The conference illustrated how a consensus now unites most of the globe about the threat climate change poses. And although skeptics continue to speak out (*see p. 85*), the scientific community has overwhelmingly concluded that average global temperatures are rising and that manmade emissions — particularly carbon dioxide from burning coal, oil and other fossil fuels — are largely to blame. According to a comprehensive assessment released in June 2009 by the U.S. Global Change Research Program, "Observations show that warming of the climate is unequivocal."[8] The conclusion echoes earlier findings by the U.N.'s Intergovernmental Panel on Climate Change (IPCC).[9]

The costs of climate change, both economic and in human lives, already appear significant. Disasters tied to climate change kill around 300,000 people a year and cause roughly $125 billion in economic losses, according to the Global Humanitarian Forum, a Geneva-based think tank led by former U.N. Secretary General Kofi Annan.[10] Evidence widely cited during the conference strengthens the conclusion the world is heating up. The World Meteorological Organization (WMO) reported that the last decade appeared to be the warmest on record, continuing a trend. The years 2000 through 2009 were "warmer than the 1990s, which were warmer than the 1980s, and so on," said Michel Jarraud, the secretary general of the WMO, as Copenhagen got under way.[11] Other reports noted that sea levels appeared likely to rise higher than previously estimated by 2100, with one estimating seas could rise more than six feet by then. The Antarctic ice shelves and the Greenland ice sheet are also melting faster than the U.N. scientific body previously found.[12]

Copenhagen also provided evidence of a growing international political consensus about climate change. About 120 heads of state attended the final days of the conference, hoping to sign their names to an agreement, an indication of the seriousness with which the global community now views the issue.

"It was remarkable the degree to which Copenhagen galvanized the public," says David Waskow, Oxfam America's climate change policy adviser, who attended the conference. "That's true with the literally millions who came out to show their support for strong action on climate change around the world. It's true with the number of heads of state who showed up, and even in terms of the number of developing countries making substantial offers to tackle their emissions."

As observers try to determine where the world is headed on climate change and how the Copenhagen Accord helps or hinders that effort, here are some of the questions they are considering:

Is the Copenhagen Accord a meaningful step forward in the fight against global warming?

No one claims that a three-page accord that leaves out hard emission-reduction targets or a firm timetable is the final answer to global climate change. But does it bring the world closer to adequately addressing the problem?

Accord supporters range from the dutiful to the enthusiastic. But the unifying thread is a feeling that the accord is better than no deal at all, which is where the conference seemed to be headed until the 11th-hour negotiations.

"If the standard is — were we going to get a blueprint to save the world? The fact is, we were never going to

Reuters/Christian Charisius

Protesters outside the U.N. Climate Change Conference in Copenhagen on Dec. 10, 2009, call for rich countries to take responsibility for their disproportionate share in global warming. Greenhouse gas emissions by industrial countries are causing climate changes in poor countries thousands of miles away. The nonbinding Copenhagen Accord calls for $10 billion a year for the next three years to help them deal with climate change.

meet it. None of the documents circulating were a feasible basis for agreement among the major players," says Michael A. Levi, director of the Program on Energy Security and Climate Change for the U.S. Council on Foreign Relations. "What we ended up with is something that can be useful if we use it the right way. It has pieces that empower all sorts of other efforts, like increased transparency, some measure of monitoring and reporting. It sets a political benchmark for financing. It can be a meaningful step forward."

Levi also notes that countries signing the accord agreed to fill in their targets for emissions cuts (as the major signatories and other nations did at the end of January), addressing one of the main criticisms of the deal.

But the Indian political scientist Mehra says even if countries abide by their commitments to cut emissions, the accord will not meet its target of holding global warming to 2 degrees Celsius (3.6-degrees Fahrenheit), which U.N. scientists consider the maximum increase that could avoid the worst effects of climate change, including a catastrophic rise in sea levels and severe damage to world food production.

She cites an IPCC conclusion that says in order to meet the 2-degree goal industrialized countries must reduce their emissions to 25-40 percent of 1990 levels by 2020 and by 50 percent by 2050. "What we actually got in the various announcements from the developed nations are far below that, coming in at around 18 percent," Mehra says.

Indeed, research by Climate Interactive — a joint effort by academic, nonprofit and business entities to assess climate policy options — found that the countries' commitments would allow temperatures to rise about 3.9 degrees Celsius (7 degrees Fahrenheit) by 2100 — nearly twice the stated goal.[13] "If you're looking at an average of 3 to 4 degrees, you're going to have much higher rises in significant parts of the world. That's why so many of the African negotiators were so alarmed by this," says Mehra. "It's worse than where we started because it effectively sets in stone the lowest possible expectations."

But other analysts point out that President Obama and other leaders who backed the accord have acknowledged more must be done.[14] They add that focusing on the initial emissions goals ignores the areas where the deal breaks important ground. "A much bigger part of the story, I think, is the actual money the developed world is putting on the table, funds for mitigation and adaptation," says Mike Hulme, a professor at the University of East Anglia in Great Britain who has been studying the intersection between climate and culture. "This is as much part of the game as nominal reduction targets."

The accord calls for $10 billion a year to help poorer, more vulnerable countries cope with climate change over the next three years, rising to $100 billion a year by 2020. The money will come from "a wide variety of sources, public and private, bilateral and multilateral, including alternative sources of finance," according to the agreement.[15]

Equally important, say analysts, is the fact that the agreement sets new standards of participation and accountability for developing economies in the global warming fight. "The developing countries, particularly China, made a step forward and agreed not only to undertake some actions to reduce emissions, but to monitor and report those. I think that's significant," says Stephen Eule, a U.S. Chamber of Commerce climate expert and former George W. Bush administration climate official.

However, to many of the accord's critics, the accord mostly represents a failure of political leadership. "It was

hugely disappointing. Watching world leaders lower expectations for three months coming into this, and then actually having them undershoot those expectations was unbelievable," says Jason Blackstock, a research scholar at the International Institute for Applied Systems Analysis in Austria, who studies the intersection of science and international affairs. He places some of the blame at the feet of President Obama: "This is clearly not one of his top issues, and that's disappointing."

But Thomas Homer-Dixon, who holds an international governance chair at the Balsillie School of International Affairs in Waterloo, Canada, and studies climate policy, believes critics are underestimating the importance of leaders from around the globe sitting down face-to-face to tackle the problem. "Symbolically, that photograph of the leaders of those countries sitting around the table with their sleeves rolled up was enormous," he says. "All of a sudden we're having a direct conversation among the actors that matter, both in the developed and developing world."

He also credits the conference for tackling difficult questions such as how much money developed countries need to transfer to the developing world to fight climate change and how much countries have to open themselves up to international inspection. "There's been sort of an agreement not to talk about the hard stuff," he says, "and now, at Copenhagen, it was finally front and center."

But to those who believe that the time for talk is running out, the dialogue meant nothing without concrete results. "This [deal], as they themselves say, will not avert catastrophic climate change," said Kumi Naidoo, Greenpeace International's executive director. "That's the only thing on which we agree with them. Everything else is a fudge; everything else is a fraud, and it must be called as such."[16]

Is the U.N.'s climate change negotiating framework outdated?

Although delegations from most of the world's nations came to Copenhagen, the final deal was hammered out by the leaders of only five countries. Those nations — the United States, China, India, Brazil and South Africa — provide a snapshot of the changing nature of geopolitical power.

Although they had been involved in larger group discussions of about 30 nations, the traditional European powers and Japan were not involved in the final deal. The five key players represented the world's largest economy (the United States), the largest emitter of greenhouse gases and second-biggest economy (China) and significant emerging economies in South America (Brazil), Africa (South Africa) and India, with the world's second-largest population.

The five-nation gathering could be seen as an effort to fashion a thin cross-section of the global community. But the U.N.-sponsored Copenhagen conference was supposed to embody the entire world community. To some observers, the fact that the accord was fashioned outside the official sessions appeared to be an attempt to undermine the U.N. effort.

Anne Petermann, co-director of the Global Justice Ecology Project, an international grassroots organization, notes the Bush administration also worked outside the U.N., setting up a smaller meeting of major economies to discuss climate change. "It wasn't particularly surprising the U.S. negotiated an accord that was completely outside the process," she says. "This wasn't the first time that the U.S. had come in with a strategy of undermining the U.N. Framework Convention."

To other analysts, however, the ability of the small group of leaders to come together where the larger conference had failed shows that the U.N. effort no longer fits the crisis. "The Framework Convention is actually now an obstacle to doing sensible things on climate change," says East Anglia's Hulme. "Climate change is such a multifaceted problem that we need to find sub-groups, multiple frameworks and initiatives to address it."

To others, the U.N. effort remains both the best chance for the world to reach a binding climate change agreement and essential to proceeding. "Because you've really got to have a global solution to this problem, it's essential that all the interested parties, including the most vulnerable countries, be around the table," says Oxfam's Waskow. "There's no question the U.N. Framework Convention, which has been working on this for many years, is the right place for that."

But Homer-Dixon, of the Balsillie School of International Affairs, believes the U.N. Framework process "has too many parties." He expects that on the negotiating side "we're going to migrate to something like the G-20 [economic forum], which includes all the major emitters. It would make sense to have the G-20 responsible."

However, Kassie Siegel, the climate law expert for the Center for Biological Diversity, a U.S. environmental group, thinks critics underestimate the U.N. effort. "Both the U.N. Framework Convention and the Intergovernmental Panel on Climate Change have been building capacity since 1992," she says. "There's not any other institution that came close to their experience on this issue. The U.N. Framework process is the best and fastest way forward."

Supporters also note that the United States and other signatories to the Copenhagen Accord have called for efforts to continue toward reaching a binding agreement at the next U.N. climate gathering in Mexico City at the end of this year. "I don't think the U.N. negotiations are irrelevant because the U.S. is still engaged in the Framework Convention," says Nicola Bullard, a climate change analyst and activist with Focus on the Global South, a nongovernmental group in Bangkok, Thailand.

But Eckhart believes the results in Copenhagen mean that key countries will now focus most of their efforts outside the U.N. framework. "I doubt Mexico City is still relevant," he says. "What can they get done in Mexico City that they couldn't get done in Copenhagen?"

The relationship between the Copenhagen Accord and the U.N. Framework Convention is somewhat ambiguous. Jacob Werksman, a lawyer specializing in international environmental and economics law at the World Resources Institute, concludes the conference's decision to only "take note" of the accord means that some provisions, including the call for setting up a Copenhagen Green Climate Fund to manage billions of dollars in aid through the U.N. mechanism, cannot occur without a conference decision to accept the accord.

U.N. Secretary General Ban Ki-moon has called on all U.N. countries to back the accord.[17] (*See "At Issue," p. 92.*) But some analysts believe the U.N. Framework Convention can't legally adopt it until the Mexico City conference, which would push the Climate Fund and possibly other accord provisions down the road another year — a delay climate change activists say the world can't afford.

Would a carbon tax reduce emissions more effectively?

Obscured by the immediate furor over Copenhagen is a longer-term debate over whether the developed world

Residents grin and bear flooding in Jakarta, Indonesia, in December 2007. Similar scenes would be played out in coastal cities and communities around the world if climate change causes glaciers and polar ice caps to melt, which many researchers predict. Analysts say the worst effects of climate change are expected to be felt in Asia.

is taking the right tack in its approach to reducing emissions.

The most popular approach so far has been the so-called cap-and-trade programs.[18] Progressively lower caps on overall emissions allow power companies and other entities to trade their emission quotas, creating a market-based approach to cutting greenhouse gases. Several European nations have embraced "cap-and-trade," and the climate change legislation that passed the U.S. House last June takes such an approach. But the system has been criticized for its complexity and susceptibility to manipulation and abuse.

Some analysts believe a carbon tax — a levy on carbon-emitting fuels, coupled with a system to rebate most of the tax back to consumers, is a more straightforward and effective way to control emissions. Robert Shapiro, former undersecretary of commerce during the Clinton administration and chair of the U.S. Climate Task Force, advocates such a program and works to educate the public on the need for action on climate change.

Shapiro's plan would use 90 percent of the carbon tax revenue to cut payroll taxes paid by workers and businesses, with the remaining 10 percent going to fund research and development of clean energy technology. The tax would provide a price incentive for discouraging the use of carbon emitting fuels and encouraging the use of green energy, while the tax cut would keep the

approach from unduly burdening lower-income Americans. "A carbon tax would both directly reduce greenhouse gas emissions and provide powerful incentives for technological progress in this area," Shapiro wrote. "It offers the best way forward in both the national and global debate over climate change."[19]

However, carbon tax opponents argue it would be no more effective than cap-and-trade and would lead to a huge expansion of government. Analysts at the Heritage Foundation, a conservative U.S. think tank, wrote that a carbon tax "would cause significant economic damage and would do very little to reduce global temperatures." Even coupling it with a payroll tax cut, they continue, "would do little to offset the high energy prices that fall particularly hard on low-income households." The real agenda of a carbon tax, they charge, is "about raising massive amounts of revenue to fund a huge expansion in government."[20]

Several Scandinavian countries have adopted carbon taxes, with mixed results. Norway has seen its per capita CO_2 emissions rise significantly. But Denmark's 2005 emissions were 15 percent below what they were in 1990, and the economy still remained strong.[21]

But to Bullard, at Focus on the Global South, a carbon tax is the approach most likely to spur changes in personal behavior. "Reducing consumption is really important, reducing our own dependence on fossil fuels," she says. "I think it's very important to have a redistributive element so that working people and elderly people don't end up with a huge heating bill. But it's really a simpler and more effective route than a complicated solution like cap-and-trade."

However, Bill McKibben — an American environmentalist and the founder of 350.org, an international campaign dedicated to scaling back GHG emissions — says a carbon tax faces an almost insurmountable political hurdle in the United States. "Even I can't convince myself that America is going to sit very long with something called a carbon tax," he says.

McKibben thinks "cap and rebate" legislation recently introduced by Sens. Maria Cantwell, D-Wash., and Susan Collins, R-Maine, would be more palatable to voters. It would cap total emissions — a limit that would be tightened over time — with the government auctioning off available carbon credits. The money raised would be rebated to consumers to offset any higher energy bills.[22]

Congressional efforts, however, have focused on cap-and-trade. But as wariness grows in the U.S. Senate toward the ramifications of cap-and-trade, Shapiro believes a carbon tax could prove a more appealing option. "A real public discussion and debate about a carbon tax tied to offsetting cuts in payroll or other taxes," he said, "could be the best news for the climate in a very long time."[23]

BACKGROUND
Road to Copenhagen

The road to Copenhagen was a long one. In one sense, it began with the Industrial Revolution in the 18th and 19th century, which brought with it the increased burning of coal and the beginning of large-scale carbon dioxide emissions in Europe and America. It also started with scientific speculation in the 1930s that manmade emissions could be changing the planet's climate.

Those first studies were widely discounted, a reflection of the difficulty humanity has had coming to grips with the idea it could be changing the global climate. But by the mid-1980s, thanks in large part to the work of David Keeling at the Mauna Loa Observatory in Hawaii, the world had a nearly three-decade record of rising carbon dioxide levels in the atmosphere.[24] Scientists were also reporting an overall warming trend in the atmosphere over the last 100 years, which they considered evidence of a "greenhouse effect" tied to CO_2 and other manmade emissions.

Humankind began a slow, often painful struggle to understand and deal with a global challenge. From the beginning, there were doubters, some well-intentioned, some with a vested interest in making sure that the world continued to burn fossil fuels. Even as the scientific consensus on climate change has grown stronger, and many nations have committed themselves to tackling global warming, the issue continues to provoke and perplex.

Climate and Culture

In her book *Field Notes from a Catastrophe, Man, Nature and Climate Change*, American writer Elizabeth Kolbert visits, among other spots, Greenland's ice fields, a native village in Alaska and the countryside in northern England, surveying how global warming is changing the Earth. In the opening section, she admits her choices

about where to go to find the impact of climate change were multitudinous.

"Such is the impact of global warming that I could have gone to hundreds if not thousands of other places," Kolbert writes, "From Siberia to the Austrian Alps to the Great Barrier Reef to the South African *fynbos* (shrub lands)."[25]

Despite mounting evidence, however, climate change remains more a concept than a reality for huge parts of the globe, where the visible impacts are still slight or nonexistent. Research scholar Blackstock, whose work focuses on the intersection between science and international affairs, points out that for many people this makes the issue as much a matter of belief as of fact.

"It really strikes to fundamental questions on how we see the human-nature interface," he says. "It has cultural undertones, religious undertones, political undertones." Blackstock thinks many climate scientists have missed this multifaceted dimension to the public dialogue. "Pretending this is just a scientific debate won't work," he says. "That's important, but we can't have that alone."

The heart of the matter, he suggests, is how willing we are to take responsibility for changes in the climate and how we balance that with other values. This helps to explain the varying reactions in the United States, which has been reluctant to embrace limits on carbon emissions, and Europe, which has been more willing to impose measures. "You're seeing the cultural difference between Europe and America," Blackstock says, "the American values of individualism and personal success versus the communal and collective good, which Europe has more of a sense of being important."

Other analysts see attitudes about climate deeply woven into human culture. The University of East Anglia's Hulme, author of *Why We Disagree About Climate Change*, notes that climate and weather have been critical to humanity for most of its history. The seasons, rains and hot or cold temperatures have been so essential to life — to the ability to obtain food and build stable communities — that they have been attributed to deities and formed the basis for religious ceremonies. Even in the modern age, Hulme says, "People have an instinctive sense that weather and climate are natural phenomena, that they work at such scales and complexity that humans could not possibly influence them."

He points out that weather was once the realm of prophets, "and part of our population is still resistant to the idea that science is able to predict what the weather

Climate Change Could Force Millions to Relocate

"Climate Refugees" from Africa to the Arctic could be affected.

Maasi herdsman Moses Mopel Kisosion had never been outside Kenya before. He'd never ridden on a plane. But he flew across parts of two continents to deliver a message to anyone who would listen at the Copenhagen climate conference in December.

Climate change, he believes, is destroying the ability of his people, the Kajiado Maasi, to make a living. "I am a pastoralist, looking after cattles, walking from one place to another looking for grass and pastures," Kisosion said. "And now, for four years, we have a lack of rain, so our animals have died because there's no water and no grass. . . . We are wondering how our life will be because we depend on them."[1]

The Maasi are hardly alone in worrying if they will be able to continue living where they are. From small South Pacific island nations to the Arctic, hundreds of millions of people might have to relocate to survive as a result of climate change. If global warming predictions prove accurate, some researchers believe the world could soon find itself dealing with a tidal wave of "climate refugees."

A study by the U.N. Office for the Coordination of Humanitarian Affairs and the Internal Displacement Monitoring Centre found that "climate-related disasters — that is, those resulting from hazards that are already being or are likely to be modified by the effects of climate change — were responsible for displacing approximately 20 million people in 2008."[2]

Norman Myers, a British environmentalist, sees the situation worsening as the effects of climate change grow. In a 2005 study, he concluded that up to 200 million people could become climate refugees.[3] But he recently revised his estimate significantly. "We looked at the best prognosis for the spread of desertification and sea level rise, including the associated tsunamis and hurricanes, and we meshed those figures with the number of people impoverished or inhabiting coastal zones," says Myers. "We believe we could see half a billion climate refugees in the second half of the century."

The human displacement is likely to take place over several decades, experts say, and determining who is a climate refugee and who is simply a political or economic refugee could be difficult. International organizations have just begun the discussion about their status and what kind of assistance they might require.

The European Commission is funding a two-year research project, "Environmental Change and Forced Migration Scenarios," based on case studies in 24 vulnerable countries.[4] An African Union Summit in Kampala, Uganda, also met last October to consider how it would address the growing number of displaced Africans.[5]

Wahu Kaara, a Kenyan political activist, says the need for action is pressing. Kenya has recorded four major droughts in the last decade, significantly higher than the average over the previous century. "Very many people are dislocated and have to move to where they can salvage their lives," she says. "We have seen people die as they walk from one place to another. It's not a hardship; it's a catastrophe. They not only have lost their animals, they have lost their lives, and the framework of their lives for those who survive."

While Africa already may be suffering population movement due to climate change, the worst consequences are will be. This deep cultural history makes climate change a categorically different phenomenon than other scientifically observed data."

Climate is also often confused with weather. England, for example, has a temperate, damp climate, but can have dry, hot years. The human inclination is to believe what's before our eyes, so every cold winter becomes a reason to discount global warming.

Sander van der Leeuw, director of the School of Human Evolution and Social Change at Arizona State University in Tempe, Ariz., notes that facing climate change also means contemplating the costs of consumerism. "Those of us in the developed world have the most invested in this particular lifestyle," he says. "If that lifestyle has to change, we'll be facing the most wrenching dislocations."

likely to be felt in Asia, analysts say. Rising sea levels threaten low-lying coastal areas, which constitute only 2 percent of the land surface of the Earth but shelter 10 percent of its population. About 75 percent of the people living in those areas are in Asia.[6]

The Maldives, a nation of low-lying islands in the Indian Ocean that could be submerged if predictions prove accurate, has taken the lead in trying to organize smaller island nations in the global warming debate. President Mohamed Nasheed initially supported the Copenhagen Accord and its 2-degree Celsius target for limiting global warming as a beginning. But before the deal was struck, he declared, "At 2 degrees, my country would not survive."[7]

Rising sea levels threaten every continent, including the Americas. Until recently, Kivalina Island, an eight-mile long barrier island in northern Alaska, had survived the punishing storms that blew in from the ocean because of ice that formed and piled up on the island.[8]

Inupiat hunters from the island's small village began noticing changes in the ice years ago, says the island's tribal administrator, Colleen Swan, but the change has accelerated in recent years. "In early September and October, the ice used to start forming, but now it doesn't form anymore until January and it's not building up," she says. "When that happened, we lost our barrier from fall sea storms, and our island just started falling apart. We started losing a lot of land beginning in 2004."

The U.S. Army Corps of Engineers is building a seawall to protect what's left of Kivalina, but Swan says it is expected to buy only 10 or 15 years. "People in the United States are still debating whether climate change is happening. The U.N. is focusing on the long-term problem of emissions," Swan says, "but we're in the 11th hour here. The bottom line is we need someplace to go."

— *Reed Karaim*

A house tumbles into the Chukchi Sea in Shishmaref, Alaska. Like other victims of climate change, residents may have to abandon the tiny community due to unprecedented erosion caused by intense storms.

[1] Moses Mopel Kisosion spoke in a video blog from Kilmaforum09, the "people's forum" on climate change held in Copenhagen during the official conference. It is available online at http://en.cop15.dk/blogs/view+blog?blogid=2929.

[2] "Monitoring disaster displacement in the context of climate change," the U.N. Office for the Coordination of Humanitarian Affairs and The Internal Displacement Monitoring Centre, September 2009, p. 12.

[3] Norman Myers, "Environmental Refugees, an Emergent Security Issue," presented at the 13th Economic Forum, Prague, May 2005.

[4] "GLOBAL: Nowhere to run from nature," IRIN, Nov. 9, 2009, www.irinnews.org/report.aspx?ReportId=78387.

[5] "AFRICA: Climate change could worsen displacement — UN," IRIN, Nov. 9, 2009, www.irinnews.org/report.aspx?ReportId=86716.

[6] Anthony Oliver-Smith, "Sea Level Rise and the Vulnerability of Coastal Peoples," U.N. University Institute for Environment and Human Security, 2009, p. 5, www.ehs.unu.edu/file.php?id=652.

[7] "Address by His Excellency Mohamed Nasheed, President of the Republic of Maldives, at the Climate Vulnerable Forum," Nov. 9, 2009, www.actforclimatejustice.org/2009/11/address-by-his-excellency-mohamed-nasheed-president-of-the-republic-of-maldives-at-the-climate-vulnerable-forum/.

[8] See John Schwartz, "Courts As Battlefields in Climate Fights," *The New York Times*, Jan. 26, 2010.

Van der Leeuw, who worked for the European Union on climate change issues in the 1990s, is actually optimistic about the progress the world has made on climate change in the face of these challenges. "It's a very long process," he says, "but I'm encouraged by my students. It's wonderful to see how engaged they are, how open to thinking differently on these issues. I know we have very little time, but history is full of moments where we've reacted in the nick of time."

However, there are still those who doubt the basic science of climate change.

The Doubters

To enter the world of the climate change skeptics is to enter a mirror reflection of the scientific consensus on the issue. Everything is backwards: The Earth isn't warming; it may be cooling. If it is warming, it's part of the

CHRONOLOGY

1900-1950s *Early research indicates the Earth is warming.*

1938 British engineer Guy Stewart Callendar concludes that higher global temperatures and rising carbon dioxide levels are probably related.

1938 Soviet researchers confirm that the planet is warming.

1957 U.S. oceanographer Roger Revelle and Austrian physicist Hans Suess find that the oceans cannot absorb carbon dioxide as easily as thought, indicating that manmade emissions could create a "greenhouse effect," trapping heat in the atmosphere.

1958 U.S. scientist David Keeling begins monitoring atmospheric carbon dioxide levels, creating a groundbreaking record of their increase.

1960s *Climate science raises the possibility of global disaster.*

1966 U.S. geologist Cesare Emiliani says ice ages were created by tiny shifts in Earth's orbit, backing earlier theories that climate reacts to small changes.

1967 Leading nations launch 15-year program to study the world's weather.

1968 Studies show Antarctica's huge ice sheets could melt, raising sea levels.

1970s-1980s *Research into climate change intensifies, and calls for action mount.*

1975 A National Aeronautics and Space Administration (NASA) researcher warns that fluorocarbons in aerosol sprays could help create a greenhouse effect.

1979 The National Academy of Sciences finds that burning fossil fuels could raise global temperatures 6 degrees Fahrenheit in 50 years.

1981 U.S. scientists report a warming trend since 1880, evidence of a greenhouse effect.

1985 Scientists from 29 nations urge governments to plan for warmer globe.

1988 NASA scientist James Hansen says global warming has begun; he's 99 percent sure it's manmade.

1988 Thirty-five nations form a global panel to evaluate climate change and develop a response.

1990s *As the world responds to global warming, industry groups fight back.*

1990 The carbon industry-supported Global Climate Coalition forms to argue that climate change science is too uncertain to take action.

1995 The year is the hottest since the mid-19th century, when records began being kept.

1997 More than 150 nations agree on the Kyoto Protocol, a landmark accord to reduce greenhouse gases. The U.S. signs but never ratifies it.

2000s *The political battle over climate change action escalates worldwide.*

2000 Organization of Petroleum Exporting Countries (OPEC) demands compensation if global warming remedies reduce oil consumption.

2006 National Academy of Sciences reports the Earth's temperature is the highest in 12,000 years, since the last Ice Age.

2007 A U.N. report concludes that global warming is "unequivocal" and human actions are primarily responsible.

2009 The 194 nations attending the Copenhagen Climate Change Conference cannot agree on a broad treaty to battle global warming. After two weeks of contentious discussion, five nations create a nonbinding climate change accord, which 55 nations eventually sign, but which falls far short of delegates' hopes.

2010 The U.N effort to get a global, legally binding climate change treaty is scheduled to continue in November-December in Mexico City.

planet's natural, long-term climate cycles. Manmade carbon dioxide isn't the heart of the problem; it's a relatively insignificant greenhouse gas. But even if carbon dioxide is increasing, it's beneficial for the planet.

And that scientific consensus? It doesn't exist. "What I see are a relatively small number, perhaps a few hundred at most, of extremely well-funded, well-connected evangelistic scientists doing most of the lobbying on this issue," says Bob Carter, a geologist who is one of Australia's more outspoken climate change skeptics.

Many scientists who take funds from grant agencies to investigate global warming, he says, "don't speak out with their true views because if they did so, they would lose their funding and be intimidated."

It's impossible to know if people are keeping views to themselves, of course. But professional science has a method of inquiry — the scientific method — and a system of peer review intended to lead to knowledge that, as much as possible, is untainted by prejudice, false comparison or cherry-picked data. The process isn't always perfect, but it provides our best look at the physical world around us.

In December 2004, Naomi Oreske, a science historian at the University of California, San Diego, published an analysis in *Science* in which she reviewed 928 peer-reviewed climate studies published between 1993 and 2003. She did not find one that disagreed with the general consensus on climate change.[26]

The U.S. National Academy of Sciences, the Royal Society of London, the Royal Society of Canada, the American Meteorological Society, the American Association for the Advancement of Science and 2,500 scientists participating in the IPCC also have concluded the evidence that humans are changing the climate is compelling. "Politicians, economists, journalists and others may have the impression of confusion, disagreement or discord among climate scientists, but that impression is incorrect," Oreske wrote, after reviewing the literature.[27]

The debate over climate change science heated up last fall, when, shortly before the Copenhagen conference, hackers broke into the University of East Anglia's computer network and made public hundreds of e-mails from scientists at the school's climate research center — some prominent in IPCC research circles. Climate change skeptics were quick to point to the "Climategate" e-mails as evidence researchers had been squelching contrary opinions and massaging data to bolster their claims.

Reviews by *Time*, *The New York Times* and the Pew Center on Climate Change, however, found the e-mails did not provide evidence to alter the scientific consensus on climate change. "Although a small percentage of the e-mails are impolite and some express animosity toward opponents, when placed into proper context they do not appear to reveal fraud or other scientific misconduct," the Pew Center concluded.[28]

Some skeptics are scientists, but none are climate researchers. Perhaps the most respected scientific skeptic is Freeman Dyson, a legendary 86-year-old physicist and mathematician. Dyson does not dispute that atmospheric carbon-dioxide levels are rapidly rising and humans are to blame. He disagrees with those who project severe consequences. He believes rising CO_2 levels could have some benefits, and if not, humanity could bioengineer trees that consume larger amounts of carbon dioxide or find some other technological solution. He is sanguine about the ability of the Earth to adapt to change and is suspicious of the validity of computer models.

"The climate-studies people who work with models always tend to overestimate their models," Dyson has said. "They come to believe models are real and forget they are only models."[29]

Unlike Dyson, many climate change skeptics are connected to groups backed by the oil, gas and coal industries, which have worked since at least 1990 to discredit global warming theories. A 2007 study by the Union of Concerned Scientists found that between 1998 and 2005 ExxonMobil had funneled about $16 million to 43 groups that sought to manufacture uncertainty about global warming with the public.[30]

The tactics appear to be patterned after those used by the tobacco industry to discredit evidence of the hazards of smoking. According to the study, ExxonMobil and others have used ostensibly independent front groups for "information laundering," as they sought to sow doubts about the conclusions of mainstream climate science.

Several prominent climate change skeptics — including physicist S. Fred Singer and astrophysicists Willie Soon and Sallie Baliunas — have had their work published by these organizations, some of which seem to have no other purpose than to proliferate the information. "By publishing and re-publishing the non-peer-reviewed works of a small group of scientific spokespeople, ExxonMobil-funded organizations have propped up and amplified work that

Climate Scientists Thinking Outside the Box

"Geoengineering" proposes futuristic solutions that sound like science fiction.

I magine: A massive squadron of aircraft spewing sulfur particles into the sky. An armada of oceangoing ships spraying sea mist into the air. A swarm of robotic mirrors a million miles out in space reflecting some of the sun's harmful rays away from the Earth. Thousands of giant, air-filtering towers girdling the globe.

The prospect of devastating global warming has led some scientists and policy analysts to consider the kind of planet-altering responses to climate change that were once the province of science fiction. The underlying concept, known as "geoengineering," holds that manmade changes in the climate can be offset by futuristic technological modifications.

That idea raises its own concerns, both about the possibility of unintended consequences and of technological dependence. But from an engineering perspective, analysts say the sulfur particle and sea vapor options — which would reflect sunlight away from the Earth, potentially cooling the planet — appear feasible and not even that expensive.

"Basically, any really rich guy on the planet could buy an ice age," says David Keith, a geoengineering expert at the University of Calgary, estimating that sulfur injection could cost as little as $1 billion or so a year. "Certainly, it's well within the capability of most nations."

"Technologically, it would be relatively easy to produce small particles in the atmosphere at the required rates," says Ken Caldiera, a climate scientist at the Carnegie Institution for Science's Department of Global Ecology in Stanford, Calif. "Every climate-model simulation performed so far indicates geoengineering would be able to diminish most climate change for most people most of the time."

To spread sulfur, planes, balloons or even missiles could be used.[1] For sea vapor, which would be effective at a lower altitude, special ships could vaporize seawater and shoot it skyward through a rotor system.[2]

A global program of launching reflective aerosols higher into the atmosphere would cost around $5 billion annually — still small change compared to the economic costs of significant global warming, says Caldiera. Other geoengineering options are considerably more expensive. The cost of launching the massive (60,000 miles by 4,500 miles) cloud of mirrors into space to block sunlight would cost about $5 trillion.[3] Building air-scrubbing towers would also be expensive and would require improved technology.[4]

has been discredited by reputable climate scientists," the study concludes.[31]

Is the world cooling? Is global warming a natural phenomenon? Is more CO_2 really good for the planet? Science and media watchdog groups have published detailed rebuttals to the claims of climate change skeptics.[32] To cite one example, assertions that the Earth is actually cooling often use 1998 as the base line — a year during the El Niño weather system, which typically produces warmer weather. The Associated Press gave temperature numbers to four statisticians without telling them what the numbers represented. The scientists found no true declines over the last 10 years. They also found a "distinct, decades-long" warming trend.[33]

James Hoggan, a Canadian public relations executive who founded DeSmogblog to take on the skeptics, feels climate scientists have done a poor job of responding to the skeptics, too often getting bogged down in the minutiae

of detail. "We need to start asking these so-called skeptics a number of basic questions," says Hoggan, the author of *Climate Cover-Up: The Crusade to Deny Global Warming*. "The first one is, 'Are you actually a climate scientist?' The second one is, 'Have you published peer-reviewed papers on whatever claims you're making?' And a third one is, 'Are you taking money directly or indirectly from industry?' "

Untangling the Threads

Since nations first began to seriously wrestle with climate change, most of the effort has gone into fashioning a legally binding international treaty to cut greenhouse gas emissions while helping poorer nations cope with the effects of global warming.

The approach has a powerful logic. Climate change is a worldwide problem and requires concerted action around the planet. Assisting those most likely to be affected — populations in Africa and Asia who are among the poorest

But cost is not what worries those studying geoengineering. "Everyone who's thinking about this has two concerns," says Thomas Homer-Dixon, a political scientist at Canada's Balsillie School of International Affairs in Waterloo, Ontario. "One is unintended consequences — because we don't understand climate systems perfectly — something bad could happen like damage to the ozone layer. The second is the moral-hazard problem: If we start to do this, are a lot of people going to think it means we can continue the carbon party?"

Keith thinks the consequences could be managed. "One of the advantages of using aerosols in the atmosphere is that you can modulate them," he says. "If you find it's not working, you can stop and turn the effect off." But he shares a concern with Caldiera and Homer-Dixon that geoengineering could be used as an excuse to avoid reducing carbon-dioxide emissions.

Geoengineering also raises geopolitical concerns, in part because it could be undertaken unilaterally. Unlike lowering greenhouse gas emissions, it doesn't require a global agreement, yet its effects would be felt around the planet — and not evenly.

That could aggravate international tensions: Any sustained bad weather in one nation could easily raise suspicion that it was the victim of climate modifications launched by another country. "If China, say, were to experience a deep drought after the deployment of a climate-intervention system," says Caldiera, "and people were starving as a result, this could cause them to lash out politically or even militarily at the country or countries that were engaged in the deployment."

Such scenarios, along with the fear of undercutting global negotiations to reduce emissions, make serious international consideration of geoengineering unlikely in the near term, says Homer-Dixon. But if the direst predictions about global warming prove accurate that could change. "You could see a political clamor worldwide to do something," he says.

Some scientists believe stepped-up geoengineering studies need to start soon. "We need a serious research program, and it needs to be international and transparent," says Keith. "It needs to start small. I don't think it needs to be a crash program, but I think there's an enormous value in doing the work. We've had enough hot air speculation. We need to do the work. If we find out it works pretty well, then we'll have a tool to help manage environmental risk."

— *Reed Karaim*

---

[1] Robert Kunzig, "A Sunshade for Planet Earth," *Scientific American*, November 2008.

[2] *Ibid.*

[3] *Ibid.*

[4] Seth Borenstein, "Wild ideas to combat global warming being seriously entertained," *The Seattle Times*, March 16, 2007, http://seattletimes.nwsource.com/html/nationworld/2003620631_warmtech16.html.

on the globe — is also a burden that is most equitably shared.

But the all-in-one-basket approach also comes with big problems. The first is the complexity of the negotiations themselves, which involve everything from intellectual-property rights to hundreds of billions of dollars in international finance to forest management. Global nations have been meeting on these issues for nearly two decades without a breakthrough deal.

Some observers believe the best chance for moving forward is untangling the threads of the problem. "We don't have to try to set the world to rights in one multilateral agreement," says East Anglia's Hulme. "It's not something we've ever achieved in human history, and I doubt we can. It seems more likely it's acting as an unrealistic, utopian distraction."

Analysts cite the 1987 Montreal Protocol, which phased out the use of chlorofluorocarbons that were damaging the ozone layer, as an example of a successful smaller-scale deal.

So far, the effort to control global warming has focused on limiting carbon-dioxide emissions from power plants and factories. But CO_2 accounts for only half of manmade greenhouse gas emissions.[34] The rest comes from a variety of sources, where they are often easier or cheaper to cut.

Black carbon, mainly produced by diesel engines and stoves that burn wood or cow dung, produces from one-eighth to a quarter of global warming.[35] Promoting cleaner engines and helping rural villagers move to cleaner-burning stoves would cut global warming gases, yet hardly requires the wrenching shift of moving from coal-fired electricity. Hydrofluorocarbons (HFCs) are more than a thousand times more potent as greenhouse gases than CO_2, but are used in comparably minuscule amounts and should be easier to limit.

Getty Images /Christopher Furlong

Ap Photo/John Stanmeyer

Hunger and Thirst

A young Turkana girl in drought-plagued northern Kenya digs for water in a dry river bed in November 2009 (top). Momina Mahammed's 8-month-old son Ali suffers from severe malnutrition in an Ethiopian refugee camp in December 2008 (bottom). Food and water shortages caused by climate changes are already affecting many countries in Africa. A sudanese delegate to the Copenhagen Climate Change Conference called the nonbinding accord reached at the convention "an incineration pact" for poor countries.

"Why are we putting all the greenhouse gases into one agreement? CO_2 is very different from black soot, or methane or HFCs," Hulme says. "Tropical forests, why do they have to be tied to the climate agenda? They sequester carbon, yes, but they're also valuable resources in other regards."

Those who support negotiating a sweeping climate change accord believe that untangling these threads could weaken the whole cloth, robbing initiative from critical parts of the deal, such as assistance to developing countries. But Hulme believes the poorer parts of the world could benefit.

"We can tend to the adaptation needs of the developing world without having them hitched to the much greater complexity of moving the economy in the developed world away from fossil fuels," he says.

Other analysts, however, are unconvinced that climate change would be easier to deal with if its constituent issues were broken out. "There are entrenched interests on each thread," says Blackstock, at Austria's International Institute in Applied Systems Analysis. "That's the real problem at the end of the day."

CURRENT SITUATION

Next Steps

The whole world may be warming, but as has been said, all politics is local — even climate change politics. "It's still the legislatures of the nation states that will really determine the pace at which climate policies are driven through," notes the University of East Anglia's Hulme. "In the end, that's where these deals have to make sense."

Nations around the globe are determining their next steps in the wake of Copenhagen. Most greenhouse gases, however, come from a relative handful of countries. The United States and China, together, account for slightly more than 40 percent of the world's manmade CO_2 emissions.[36] If India and the European Union are added, the total tops 60 percent.[37] The post-Copenhagen climate change status is different for each of these major players.

China — China presents perhaps the most complex case of any of the countries central to climate change. It was classified as a developing country in the Kyoto Protocol, so it was not required to reduce carbon emissions.[38] But as the country's economy continued to skyrocket, China became the world's largest carbon dioxide emitter in 2006, passing the United States.[39] (See graph, p. 77.)

But with roughly 700 million poorer rural citizens, promoting economic growth remains the Chinese government's essential priority. Nevertheless, shortly before Copenhagen, China announced it would vow to cut CO_2 emissions by 40 to 45 percent *per unit of gross domestic product* below 2005 levels by 2020. The complicated formula meant that emissions would still rise, but at a slower rate. China subsequently committed to this reduction when confirming its Copenhagen pledge at the end of January.

U.N. climate policy chief de Boer hailed the move as a critical step. But the United States — especially skeptical members of the U.S. Congress — had hoped to see more movement from China and wanted verification standards.

Some participants say China's recalcitrance is why Copenhagen fell short. The British seemed particularly incensed. Ed Miliband, Great Britain's climate secretary, blamed the Chinese leadership for the failure to get agreement on a 50-percent reduction in global emissions by 2050 or on 80-percent reductions by developed countries. "Both were vetoed by China," he wrote, "despite the support of a coalition of developed and the vast majority of developing countries."[40]

But the Global Justice Ecology Project's Petermann places the blame elsewhere. "Why should China get involved in reducing emissions if the U.S. is unwilling to really reduce its emissions?" she asks.

Jiang Lin, director of the China Sustainable Energy Program, a nongovernmental agency with offices in Beijing and San Francisco, thinks China's leaders take the threat of climate change seriously. "There's probably a greater consensus on this issue in China than the United States," says Jiang. "The Chinese leadership are trained engineers. They understand the data."

Jiang points out that China already is seeing the effects predicted by climate change models, including the weakening of the monsoon in the nation's agricultural northwest and the melting of the Himalayan glaciers. "The Yellow River is drying up," he adds. "This is very symbolic for the Chinese. They consider this the mother river, and now almost half the year it is dry."

More Countries Agree to Emissions Cuts

The nonbinding climate agreement reached in Copenhagen, Denmark, on Dec. 18 was originally joined by 28 countries, which were to send the United Nations by the end of January their individual goals for reducing carbon emissions by 2020. But other nations also were invited to sign on by submitting their own plans to cut emissions. On Feb. 1, the U.N. reported that a total of 55 nations had submitted targets for cutting greenhouse gases. Analysts say while these countries produce 78 percent of manmade carbon emissions, more cuts are needed. The U.N. will try to use the accord as a starting point for a binding treaty at the next international climate conference in Mexico City, Nov. 29-Dec. 10.

Key provisions in the Copenhagen Accord:

- Cut global greenhouse gas emissions so global temperatures won't rise more than 2 degrees Celsius above the pre-Industrial Revolution level.
- Cooperate in achieving a peak in emissions as soon as possible.
- Provide adequate, predictable and sustainable funds and technology to developing countries to help them adapt to climate change.
- Prioritize reducing deforestation and forest degradation, which eliminate carbon-consuming trees.
- Provide $30 billion in new and additional resources from 2010 to 2012 to help developing countries mitigate climate change and protect forests; and provide $100 billion a year by 2020.
- Assess implementation of the accord by 2015.

Sources: "Copenhagen Accord," U.N. Framework Convention on Climate Change, Dec. 18, 2009; "UNFCCC Receives list of government climate pledges," press release, United Nations Framework Convention on Climate Change, Feb. 1, 2010, http://unfccc.int/files/press/news_room/press_releases_and_advisories/application/pdf/pr_accord_100201.pdf

The Copenhagen Accord is not legally binding, but Jiang believes the Chinese will honors its provisions. "When they announce they're committed to something, that's almost as significant as U.S. law," he says, "because if they don't meet that commitment, losing facing is huge for them."

While attention has focused on international negotiations, China is targeting improved energy efficiency and renewable power. In 2005, China's National People's Congress set a goal of generating 20 gigawatts of power through wind energy by 2020. The goal seemed highly ambitious, but China expected to meet it by the end of 2009 and is now aiming for 150 gigawatts by 2020. The target for solar energy has been increased more than 10-fold over the same period.[41]

Is the Copenhagen Accord a meaningful step forward in halting climate change?

YES
Ban Ki-moon
Secretary-General, United Nations

NO
Nnimmo Bassey
Chair, Friends of the Earth International

From opening remarks at press conference, U.N. Climate Change Conference, Copenhagen, Dec. 19, 2009

Written for *CQ Global Researcher*, February 2010

The Copenhagen Accord may not be everything that everyone hoped for. But this decision of the Conference of Parties is a new beginning, an essential beginning.

At the summit I convened in September, I laid out four benchmarks for success for this conference. We have achieved results on each.

- All countries have agreed to work toward a common, long-term goal to limit global temperature rise to below 2 degrees Celsius.
- Many governments have made important commitments to reduce or limit emissions.
- Countries have achieved significant progress on preserving forests.
- Countries have agreed to provide comprehensive support to the most vulnerable to cope with climate change.

The deal is backed by money and the means to deliver it. Up to $30 billion has been pledged for adaptation and mitigation. Countries have backed the goal of mobilizing $100 billion a year by 2020 for developing countries. We have convergence on transparency and an equitable global governance structure that addresses the needs of developing countries. The countries that stayed on the periphery of the Kyoto process are now at the heart of global climate action.

We have the foundation for the first truly global agreement that will limit and reduce greenhouse gas emission, support adaptation for the most vulnerable and launch a new era of green growth.

Going forward, we have three tasks. First, we need to turn this agreement into a legally binding treaty. I will work with world leaders over the coming months to make this happen. Second, we must launch the Copenhagen Green Climate Fund. The U.N. system will work to ensure that it can immediately start to deliver immediate results to people in need and jump-start clean energy growth in developing countries. Third, we need to pursue the road of higher ambition. We must turn our back on the path of least resistance.

Current mitigation commitments fail to meet the scientific bottom line.

We still face serious consequences. So, while I am satisfied that we have a deal here in Copenhagen, I am aware that it is just the beginning. It will take more than this to definitively tackle climate change.

But it is a step in the right direction.

The Copenhagen Accord is not a step forward in the battle to halt climate change. Few people expected the Copenhagen climate talks to yield a strong outcome. But the talks ended with a major failure that was worse than predicted: a "Copenhagen Accord" in which individual countries make no new serious commitments whatsoever.

The accord sets a too-weak goal of limiting warming to 2 degrees Celsius, but provides no means of achieving this goal. Likewise, it suggests an insufficient sum for addressing international solutions but contains no path to produce the funding. Individual countries are required to do nothing.

The accord fails the poor and the vulnerable communities most impacted by climate change. This non-agreement (it was merely "noted," not adopted, by the conference) is weak, non-binding and allows false solutions such as carbon offsetting. It will prove completely ineffective. Providing some coins for developing countries to mitigate climate change and adapt to it does not help if the sources of the problem remain unchecked.

The peoples' demands for climate justice should be the starting point when addressing the climate crisis. Instead, in Copenhagen, voices of the people were shut out and peaceful protests met brutal suppression. Inside the Bella Center, where the conference took place, many of the poor countries were shut out of back-room negotiations. The accord is the result of this anti-democratic process.

The basic demands of the climate justice movement remain unmet. The U.N. climate process must resume, and it must accomplish these goals:

- Industrialized countries must commit to at least 40 percent cuts in emissions by 2020 by using clean energy, sustainable transport and farming and cutting energy demand.
- Emission cuts must be real. They cannot be "achieved" by carbon offsetting, such as buying carbon credits from developing countries or by buying up forests in developing countries so they won't be cut down.
- Rich countries must make concrete commitments to provide money for developing countries to grow in a clean way and to cope with the floods, droughts and famines caused by climate change. Funding must be adequate, not the minuscule amounts proposed in the accord.

Wealthy nations are most responsible for climate change. They have an obligation to lead the way in solving the problem. They have not done so with the Copenhagen Accord.

Coal still generates 80 percent of China's power, and the country continues to build coal-fired plants, but Chinese leaders clearly have their eyes on the green jobs that President Obama has promoted as key to America's future.[42] "Among the top 10 solar companies in the world, China already has three," says Jiang, "and China is now the largest wind market in the world. They see this as an industry in which China has a chance to be one of the leaders."

The United States — To much of the world, the refusal of the United States so far to embrace carbon emission limits is unconscionable. U.S. emissions are about twice Europe's levels per capita, and more than four times China's.

"The United States is the country that needs to lead on this issue," says Oxfam's Waskow. "It created a lot of problems that the U.S. wasn't able to come to Copenhagen with congressional legislation in hand."

In the Copenhagen Accord, President Obama committed the United States to reduce its carbon dioxide emissions to 17 percent below 2005 levels by 2020. That equates to about 4 percent below 1990 levels, far less stringent than the European and Japanese pledges of 20 percent and 25 percent below 1990 levels, respectively. However, Congress has not passed global warming legislation. Last year, the House of Representatives passed a bill that would establish a cap-and-trade system, which would limit greenhouse gases but let emitters trade emission allowances among themselves. The legislation faces stiff opposition in the Senate, however.

In 1997, after the Kyoto Protocol was adopted, the Senate voted 95-0 against signing any international accord unless it mandated GHG emission reductions by developing countries as well. Securing such commitments in Copenhagen — especially from China, along with improved verification — was considered critical to improving the chances a climate change bill would make it through the Senate.

Some analysts also blamed the lack of U.S. legislation for what was considered a relatively weak American proposal at Copenhagen. "Obama wasn't going to offer more than the U.S. Senate was willing to offer," says the International Institute for Applied System's Blackstock. "He could have done more and said, 'I cannot legally commit to this, but I'll go home and fight for it.' He didn't."

But Obama's negotiating effort in Copenhagen impressed some observers. "He could have stood back and worried about looking presidential," says the American Council on Renewable Energy's Eckhart. "He didn't. He rolled up his sleeves and got in there and tried to do good for the world."

Early reviews of the Copenhagen Accord were favorable among at least two key Republican senators, Lisa Murkowski of Alaska and Richard Lugar of Indiana. "Whenever you have developing countries, and certainly China and India stepping forward and indicating that they have a willingness to be a participant … I think that that is progress," said Murkowski.[43]

Still, analysts remain skeptical whether it will make a real difference on Capitol Hill. "I don't see Congress doing anything, even in line with the position in the Copenhagen Accord unless Obama makes it his 2010 priority," says 350.org's McKibben. "There's no question it's going to be hard because it's going to require real change."

The administration is planning to regulate some greenhouse gases through the Environmental Protection Agency (EPA). The Center for Biological Diversity has petitioned the EPA to make further use of regulation to reduce greenhouse emissions. "The president has the tools he needs. He has the Clean Air Act," says the center's Siegel. "All he has to do is use it."

However, some Senate Republicans are already calling for a resolution to undo the EPA's limited actions, and polls show a rising number of Americans skeptical about global warming, particularly Republicans.[44] Given the highly polarized nature of American politics, any significant move on climate change is likely to prove a bruising battle. President Obama has made promoting green energy jobs a priority, but with health care and joblessness still leading the administration's agenda, further action on climate change seems unlikely in the next year. Chances for major legislative action shrunk even further with the election of Republican Scott Brown, a climate change skeptic, to the Senate from Massachusetts. Brown's win ended the democrats' 60-vote, filibuster-proof majority.[45]

India — Although India's economy has grown almost as rapidly as China's in recent years, it remains a much poorer country. Moreover, its low coastline and dependence on seasonal monsoons for water also make it sensitive to the dangers of global warming. Jairam Ramesh, India's environment minister, said, "The most vulnerable country in the world to climate change is India."[46]

India's leaders announced recently they will pursue cleaner coal technology, higher emissions standards for automobiles and more energy-efficient building codes. Prior to Copenhagen, India also announced it would cut CO_2 emissions per unit of GDP from 2005 levels, but rejected legally binding targets.

After the negotiations on the accord, Ramesh told the *Hindustan Times* that India had "upheld the interest of developing nations."[47] But some analysts said India had largely followed China's lead, a position that could cost India some prestige with other developing nations, whose cause it had championed in the past.

"The worst thing India did was to align itself uncritically to China's yoke," says Indian political scientist Mehra, "because China acted purely in its own self interest."

The European Union — European leaders are calling for other countries to join them in backing the Copenhagen Accord, but they've hardly tried to hide their disappointment it wasn't more substantial. The European Union had staked out one of the stronger positions on emissions reductions beforehand, promising to cut emissions by 20 percent from 1990 levels to 2020, or 30 percent if other countries took similarly bold action. They also wanted rich nations to make 80 to 95 percent cuts in GHG emissions by 2050.[48]

Some national leaders also had expended political capital on global warming before the conference. French President Nicolas Sarkozy had announced a proposal to create a French "carbon tax" on businesses and households for use of oil, gas and coal. The proposal was blocked by the French Constitutional Council, but Sarkozy's party plans to reintroduce it this year.[49]

In the United Kingdom, Prime Minister Brown's government passed legislation committing to an 80 percent cut in U.K. greenhouse gas emissions by 2050.[50] Brown also pressed publicly for $100 billion a year in aid to the developing world to cope with climate change.

The European efforts were designed to lead by example. But analysts say the approach yielded little fruit in Copenhagen. "The European perspective that they could lead by example was the wrong strategy. This was a negotiation. Countries do not check their national interests at the door when they enter the U.N.," says the Chamber of Commerce's Eule, who worked on climate change in the Bush administration.

Although Europe's leaders finally backed the accord and formally pledged 20 percent emission reductions, they had only limited influence on the deal's final shape. "Europe finds itself now outside the driver's seat for how this is going to go forward," says Hulme at the University of East Anglia. "I think in Brussels [home of the E.U. headquarters], there must be a lot of conversations going on about where Europe goes from here." He believes Europe's stricter emissions regulations could now face a backlash.

Framework Conference chief de Boer, who is a citizen of the Netherlands, captured the resignation that seemed to envelope many European diplomats during his post-Copenhagen comments to the press. Before the climate conference kicked off, de Boer had predicted that Copenhagen would "launch action, action and more action" on climate change.

But in his December 19 press conference, when asked what he hoped could be accomplished in the year ahead, he responded, "Basically, the list I put under the Christmas tree two years ago, I can put under the Christmas tree again this year."

OUTLOOK
Too Late?

The world's long-term climate forecast can be summed up in a word: warmer. Even if the nations of the world were to miraculously agree tomorrow to reduce global greenhouse gas emissions, global warming could continue for some time because of the "lag" in how the climate system responds to GHG emission reductions.

In the last decade, researchers have poured a tremendous amount of effort into trying to foresee where climate change could take us. But the projections come with an element of uncertainty. Still, taken together, the most startling forecasts amount to an apocalyptic compendium of disaster. Climate change could:

- Lead to droughts, floods, heat waves and violent storms that displace tens of millions of people, particularly in Asia and sub-Saharan Africa (*see "Climate Refugees," p. 84*);
- Create a high risk of violent conflict in 46 countries, now home to 2.7 billion people, as the effects of

climate change exacerbate existing economic, social and political problems;[51]

- Cause the extinction of about a quarter of all land-based plant and animal species — more than a million — by 2050;[52]
- Effectively submerge some island nations by 2100,[53] and create widespread dislocation and damage to coastal areas, threatening more than $28 trillion worth of assets by 2050; and[54]
- Cause acidification of the oceans that renders them largely inhospitable to coral reefs by 2050, destroying a fragile underwater ecosystem important to the world's fisheries.[55]

If temperatures climb by an average of 3.5 to 4 degrees Celsius (6.3 to 7.2 Fahrenheit) by the end of the century, as some projections predict, it would mean "total devastation for man in parts of the world," says the Global Justice Ecology Project's Petermann. "You're talking about massive glaciers melting, the polar ice caps disappearing. It would make life on this planet completely unrecognizable."

But some analysts, while endorsing the potential dangers of climate change, still back away from the view that it's a catastrophe that trumps all others. "The prospective tipping points for the worst consequences are just that, prospective tipping points, and they're resting on the credibility of scientific models," says East Anglia University's Hulme. "We should take them seriously. But they're not the Nazis marching across Belgium. We need to weigh our response within the whole range of needs facing the human race."

The critical question likely to determine the shape of the planet's future for the rest of this century and beyond is when humans will stop pouring greenhouse gases into the atmosphere. If done soon enough, most scientists say, climate change will be serious but manageable on an international level, although billions of dollars will be needed to mitigate the effects in the most vulnerable parts of the globe.

But if emissions continue to rise, climate change could be far more catastrophic. "It is critically important that we bring about a commitment to reduce emissions effectively by 2020," said IPCC Chairman Rajendra Pachauri, shortly before Copenhagen.[56]

To accomplish Copenhagen's goal of holding warming to 2 degrees Celsius, Pachauri said emissions must peak

Causes of Climate Change

Rapidly industrializing China has surpassed the United States as the world's largest emitter of carbon dioxide—one of the greenhouse gases (GHG) responsible for rising world temperatures. Although most GHGs are invisible, air pollution like this in Wuhan, China, on Dec.3, 2009 (above) often includes trapped greenhouse gases. The destruction of tropical rainforests decreases the number of trees available to absorb carbon dioxide. Palm oil trees once grew on this 250-acre plot being cleared for farming in Aceh, Indonesia (below).

by 2015. The agreement, however, sets no peaking year, and the emission-reduction pledges by individual nations fall short of that goal, according to recent analysis by Climate Interactive, a collaborative research effort sponsored by the Sustainability Institute in Hartland, Vt.[57]

World leaders acknowledge they need to do more, and some observers remain hopeful the upcoming climate conference in Mexico City could provide a breakthrough that will avert the worst, especially if pressure to act continues to grow at the grassroots level. "Right now there is a massive gulf between where the public is and where the political process is," says India's Mehra. "But I think [in 2010] you will see government positions mature. And I think you will see more politicians who have the conviction to act."

Canadian political scientist Homer-Dixon considers bold action unlikely, however, unless the world's major emitting nations, including the United States and China, start suffering clearly visible, serious climate-change consequences.

"In the absence of those really big shocks, I'm afraid we're probably achieving about as much as possible," he says. "Because of the lag in the system, if you wait until the evidence is clear, it's too late."

NOTES

1. Yvo de Boer, the United Nation's Framework Convention on Climate Change video message before the opening of the Cop15 conference, Dec. 1, 2009, www.youtube.com/climateconference#p/u/11/xUTXsdkinq0.

2. The complete text of the accord is at http://unfccc .int/resource/docs/2009/cop15/eng/l07.pdf.

3. John Vidal and Jonathan Watts, "Copenhagen closes with weak deal that poor threaten to reject," *The Guardian*, Dec. 19, 2009, www.guardian.co.uk/environment/2009/dec/19/copenhagen-closes-weak-deal.

4. *Ibid.*

5. "Remarks by the President," The White House Office of the Press Secretary, Dec. 18, 2009, www .whitehouse.gov/the-press-office/remarks-president-during-press-availability-copenhagen.

6. http://action.sierraclub.org/site/MessageViewer?em_id=150181.0.

7. See Jones' complete comments at http://wdm .gn.apc.org/copenhagen-'deal'-'shameful-and-monumental-failure'.

8. Jerry Melillo, Karl Thomas and Thomas Peterson, editors-in-chief, "Global Climate Change Impacts in the United States," U.S. Global Change Research Program, executive summary, June 16, 2009, www .education-research-services.org/files/USGCRP_Impacts_US_executive-summary.pdf.

9. Intergovernmental Panel on Climate Change staff, "Climate Change 2007: Synthesis Report," The U.N. Intergovernmental Panel on Climate Change, Nov. 17 2007, www.ipcc.ch/pdf/assessment-report/ar4/syr/ar4_syr_spm.pdf.

10. "Climate Change responsible for 300,000 deaths a year," Global Humanitarian Forum, http://ghfgeneva.org/NewsViewer/tabid/383/vw/1/ItemID/6/Default.aspx.

11. Andrew C. Revkin and James Kanter, "No Slowdown of Global Warming, Agency Says," *The New York Times*, Dec. 8, 2009, www.nytimes.com/2009/12/09/science/earth/09climate.html.

12. "Key Scientific Developments Since the IPCC Fourth Assessment Report," in Key Scientific Developments Since the IPCC Fourth Assessment Report, Pew Center on Global Climate Change, June 2009.

13. "Final Copenhagen Accord Press Release," The Sustainability Institute, Dec. 19, 2009, http://climateinteractive.org/scoreboard/copenhagen-cop15-analysis-and-press-releases.

14. "Remarks by the President," *op. cit.*

15. "Copenhagen Accord," draft proposal, United Nations Framework Convention on Climate Change, Dec. 18, 2009, p. 3. http://unfccc.int/resource/docs/2009/cop15/eng/l07.pdf.

16. Kumi Naidoo, speaking at Copenhagen in a video blog posted by Greenpeace Australia, www.facebook.com/video/video.php?v=210068211237.

17. Ban Ki-moon, remarks to the General U.N. Assembly, Dec. 21, 2009, www.un.org/News/Press/docs/2009/sgsm12684.doc.htm.

18. Jennifer Weeks, "Carbon Trading, Will it Reduce Global Warming," *CQ Global Researcher*, November 2008.

19. Robert Shapiro, "Addressing the Risks of Climate Change: The Environmental Effectiveness and Economic Efficiency of Emissions Caps and Tradable Permits, Compared to Carbon Taxes," February 2007, p. 26, http://67.23.32.13/system/files/carbon-tax-cap.pdf.

20. Nicolas Loris and Ben Lieberman, "Capping Carbon Emissions Is Bad, No Matter How You Slice the Revenue," Heritage Foundation, May 14, 2009, www .heritage.org/Research/EnergyandEnvironment/wm2443.cfm.

21. Monica Prasad, "On Carbon, Tax and Don't Spend," *The New York Times*, March 25, 2008, www.nytimes.com/2008/03/25/opinion/25prasad.html.

22. "Cantwell, Collins Introduce 'Cap and Rebate' Bill," Clean Skies, Energy and Environment Network, Dec. 11, 2009, www.cleanskies.com/articles/cantwell-collins-introduce-cap-and-rebate-bill.

23. Robert J. Shapiro, "Carbon Tax More Likely," *National Journal* expert blog, Energy and the Environment, Jan. 4, 2010, http://energy.national-journal.com/2010/01/whats-next-in-the-senate.php-1403156.

24. A concise history of Keeling and his work is at "The Keeling Curve Turns 50," Scripps Institution of Oceanography, http://sio.ucsd.edu/special/Keeling_50th_Anniversary/.

25. Elizabeth Kolbert, *Field Notes from a Catastrophe: Man, Nature, and Climate Change* (2006), p. 2.

26. Naomi Oreskes, "Beyond the Ivory Tower: The Scientific Consensus on Climate Change," *Science*, Dec. 3, 2004, www.sciencemag.org/cgi/content/full/306/5702/1686.

27. *Ibid.*

28. "Analysis of the Emails from the University of East Anglia's Climatic Research Unit," Pew Center on Global Climate Change, December 2009, www.pewclimate.org/science/university-east-anglia-cru-hacked-emails-analysis.

29. Quoted by Nicholas Dawidoff, "The Civil Heretic," *The New York Times Magazine*, March 23, 2009, p. 2, www.nytimes.com/2009/03/29/magazine/29Dyson-t.html?pagewanted=1&_r=1.

30. "Smoke, Mirrors & Hot Air: How ExxonMobil Uses Big Tobacco's Tactics to Manufacture Uncertainty on Climate Science," Union of Concerned Scientists, January 2007, p. 1, www.ucsusa.org/assets/documents/global_warming/exxon_report.pdf.

31. *Ibid.*

32. Many are summarized in a policy brief by the non-profit Pew Center on Global Climate Change, "Realities vs. Misconceptions about the Science of Climate Change," August 2009, www.pewclimate.org/science-impacts/realities-vs-misconceptions.

33. Seth Borenstein, "AP IMPACT: Statisticians Reject Global Cooling," The Associated Press, Oct. 26, 2009, http://abcnews.go.com/Technology/wireStory?id=8917909.

34. Unpacking the problem," *The Economist*, Dec. 5-11, 2009, p. 21, www.economist.com/specialreports/displaystory.cfm?story_id=14994848.

35. *Ibid.*

36. It is important to note that if CO_2 emissions are calculated on a per capita basis, China still ranks far below most developed nations. The highest emitter on a per capita basis is Australia, according to the U.S. Energy Information Agency, with the United States second. See www.ucsusa.org/global_warming/science_and_impacts/science/each-countrys-share-of-co2.html.

37. A chart of the top 20 CO_2 emitting countries is at www.ucsusa.org/global_warming/science_and_impacts/science/graph-showing-each-countrys.html.

38. "China ratifies global warming treaty," CNN.com, Sept. 4, 2002, http://archives.cnn.com/2002/WORLD/africa/09/03/kyoto.china.glb/index.html.

39. "China overtakes U.S. in greenhouse gas emissions," *The New York Times*, June 20, 2007, www.nytimes.com/2007/06/20/business/worldbusiness/20iht-emit.1.6227564.html.

40. Ed Miliband, "The Road from Copenhagen," *The Guardian*, Dec. 20, 2009, www.guardian.co.uk/commentisfree/2009/dec/20/copenhagen-climate-change-accord.

41. "A Long Game," *The Economist*, Dec. 5-11, 2009, p. 18.

42. *Ibid.* Keith Bradsher, "China Leading Global Race to Make Clean Energy," *The New York Times*, Jan. 31, 2010, p. A1.

43. Darren Samuelsohn, "Obama Negotiates 'Copenhagen Accord' With Senate Climate Fight in Mind," *The New York Times*, Dec. 21, 2009, www.nytimes.com/cwire/2009/12/21/21climatewire-obama-negotiates-copenhagen-accord-with-senat-6121.html.

44. Juliet Elperin, "Fewer Americans Believe in Global Warming, Poll Shows," *The Washington Post*, Nov.

25, 2009, www.washingtonpost.com/wp-dyn/content/article/2009/11/24/AR2009112402989.html.

45. Suzanne Goldenberg, "Fate of US climate change bill in doubt after Scott Brown's Senate win," *The Guardian*, Jan. 20, 2010, www.guardian.co.uk/environment/2010/jan/20/scott-brown-climate-change-bill.

46. "India promises to slow carbon emissions rise," BBC News, Dec. 3, 2009, http://news.bbc.co.uk/2/hi/8393538.stm.

47. Rie Jerichow, "World Leaders Welcome the Copenhagen Accord," Denmark.dk, Dec. 21, 2009, www.denmark.dk/en/menu/Climate-Energy/COP15-Copenhagen-2009/Selected-COP15-news/World-leaders-welcome-the-Copenhagen-Accord.htm.

48. "Where countries stand on Copenhagen," BBC News, undated, http://news.bbc.co.uk/2/hi/science/nature/8345343.stm.

49. James Kantor, "Council in France Blocks Carbon Tax as Weak on Polluters," *The New York Times*, Dec. 31, 2009, www.nytimes.com/2009/12/31/business/energy-environment/31carbon.html.

50. Andrew Neather, "Climate Change could still be Gordon Brown's great legacy," *The London Evening Standard*, Dec. 15, 2009, www.thisislondon.co.uk/standard/article-23783937-climate-change-could-still-be-gordon-browns-great-legacy.do.

51. Dan Smith and Janini Vivekananda, "A Climate of Conflict, the links between climate change, peace and war," *International Alert*, November 2007, www.international-alert.org/pdf/A_Climate_Of_Conflict.pdf.

52. Alex Kirby, "Climate Risk to a Million Species," BBC Online, Jan. 7, 2004, http://news.bbc.co.uk/2/hi/science/nature/3375447.stm.

53. Adam Hadhazy, "The Maldives, threatened by drowning due to climate change, set to go carbon-neutral,"

Scientific American, March 16, 2009, www.scientificamerican.com/blog/post.cfm?id=maldives-drowning-carbon-neutral-by-2009-03-16.

54. Peter Wilkinson, "Sea level rise could cost port cities $28 trillion," CNN, Nov. 23, 2009, www.cnn.com/2009/TECH/science/11/23/climate.report.wwf.allianz/index.html.

55. "Key Scientific Developments Since the IPCC Fourth Assessment Report," *op. cit.*

56. Richard Ingham, "Carbon emissions must peak by 2015: U.N. climate scientist," Agence France-Presse, Oct. 15, 2009, www.google.com/hostednews/afp/article/ALeqM5izYrubhpeFvOKCRrZmWSYWCkPoRg.

57. "Final Copenhagen Accord Press Release," *op. cit.*

BIBLIOGRAPHY

Books

Hoggan, James, *Climate Cover-Up: The Crusade to Deny Global Warming*, Greystone Books, 2009.
A Canadian public relations executive who founded the anti-climate-skeptic Web site DeSmogblog takes on what he considers the oil and gas industry's organized campaign to spread disinformation and confuse the public about the science of climate change.

Hulme, Mike, *Why We Disagree About Climate Change: Understanding Controversy, Inaction and Opportunity*, Cambridge University Press, 2009.
A professor of climate change at East Anglia University in Great Britain looks at the cultural, political and scientific forces that come into play when we consider climate and what that interaction means for dealing with climate change today.

Kolbert, Elizabeth, *Field Notes from a Catastrophe: Man, Nature and Climate Change*, Bloomsbury, 2006.
A *New Yorker* writer summarizes the scientific evidence on behalf of climate change and looks at the consequences for some of the world's most vulnerable locations.

Michaels, Patrick J., and Robert C. Balling, *Climate of Extremes: Global Warming Science They Don't Want You to Know*, The Cato Institute, 2009.
Writing for a libertarian U.S. think tank, the authors argue that while global warming is real, its effects have been overstated and do not represent a crisis.

Articles

"Stopping Climate Change, A 14-Page Special Report," *The Economist*, Dec. 5, 2009.
The authors provide a comprehensive review of the state of global climate change efforts, including environmental, economic and political conditions.

Broder, John and Andrew Revkin, "A Grudging Accord in Climate Talks," *The New York Times*, Dec. 19, 2009.
The Times assesses the Copenhagen Accord and reports on the final hours of the climate change convention.

Kunzig, Robert, "A Sunshade for Planet Earth," *Scientific American*, November 2008.
An award-winning scientific journalist examines the various geoengineering options that might reduce global warming, their costs and possible consequences.

Schwartz, John, "Courts as Battlefields in Climate Fights," *The New York Times*, Jan. 26, 2009.
A reporter looks at environmental groups' and other plaintiffs' efforts to hold corporations that produce greenhouse gases legally liable for the effects of climate change on vulnerable areas, including Kivalina Island off the coast of Alaska.

Walsh, Bryan, "Lessons from the Copenhagen Climate Talks," *Time*, Dec. 21, 2009.
Time's environmental columnist provides predictions about the future of the climate change battle, based on the final Copenhagen Accord.

Walsh, Bryan, "The Stolen Emails: Has 'Climategate' been Overblown," *Time Magazine online*, Dec. 7, 2007.
The stolen East Anglia University e-mails, the author concludes, "while unseemly, do little to change the overwhelming scientific consensus on the reality of man-made climate change."

Reports and Studies

"Climate Change 101: Understanding and Responding to Global Climate Change," Pew Center on Global Climate Change, January 2009.
This series of reports aims to provide an introduction to climate change science and politics for the layman.

"World Development Report 2010: World Development and Climate Change," World Bank, November 2009, http://econ.worldbank.org/WBSITE/EXTERNAL/EXTDEC/EXTRESEARCH/EXTWDRS/EXTWDR2010/0,,contentMDK:21969137~menuPK:5287816~pagePK:64167689~piPK:64167673~theSitePK:5287741,00.html.
This exhaustive, 300-page study examines the consequences of climate change for the developing world and the need for developed nations to provide financial assistance to avert disaster.

Bernstein, Lenny, *et al.*, "Climate Change 2007: Synthesis Report," The Intergovernmental Panel of Climate Change, 2007, www.ipcc.ch/pdf/assessment-report/ar4/syr/ar4_syr_spm.pdf.
The international body tasked with assessing the risk of climate change caused by human activity gathered scientific research from around the world in this widely quoted report to conclude, "warming of the climate system is unequivocal."

Thomas, Karl, Jerry Melillo and Thomas Peterson, eds., "Global Climate Change Impacts in the United States," United States Global Change Research Program, June 2009, www.globalchange.gov/publications/reports/scientific-assessments/us-impacts.
U.S. government researchers across a wide range of federal agencies study how climate change is already affecting the United States.

For More Information

Cato Institute, 1000 Massachusetts Avenue, N.W., Washington, DC 20001; (202) 842-0200; www.cato.org/global-warming. A conservative U.S. think tank that maintains an extensive database of articles and papers challenging the scientific and political consensus on climate change.

Climate Justice Now; www.climate-justice-now.org. A network of organizations and movements from around the world committed to involving people in the fight against climate change and for social and economic justice at the grassroots level.

Climate Research Unit, University of East Anglia, Norwich, NR4 7TJ, United Kingdom; +44-1603-592722; www.cru.uea.ac.uk. Recently in the news when its e-mail accounts were hacked; dedicated to the study of natural and manmade climate change.

Greenpeace International, Ottho Heldringstraat 5, 1066 AZ Amsterdam, The Netherlands; +31 (0) 20 7182000; www.greenpeace.org/international. Has made climate change one of its global priorities; has offices around the world.

Intergovernmental Panel on Climate Change, c/o World Meteorological Organization, 7bis Avenue de la Paix, C.P. 2300 CH- 1211, Geneva 2, Switzerland; +41-22-730-8208; www.ipcc.ch. U.N. body made up of 2,500 global scientists; publishes periodic reports on various facets of climate change, including a synthesis report summarizing latest findings around the globe.

Pew Center on Global Climate Change, 2101 Wilson Blvd., Suite 550, Arlington, VA, 22201; (703) 516-4146; www.pewclimate.org. Nonprofit, nonpartisan organization established in 1998 to promote research, provide education and encourage innovative solutions to climate change.

United Nations Framework Convention on Climate Change, Haus Carstanjen, Martin-Luther-King-Strasse 853175 Bonn, Germany; +49-228-815-1000; http://unfccc .int/2860.php. An international treaty that governs climate change negotiations.

5

Gays in the Military

Peter Katel

Air Force Lt. Col. Victor Fehrenbach, a decorated Iraq War veteran with more than 80 combat missions, could be discharged over his homosexuality. Nearly 12,800 gay or lesbian service members were discharged from 1994-2008. The debate over gays in the military has intensified this year because President Barack Obama opposes the military's "don't ask, don't tell" policy and because gay service members are fighting and dying in Afghanistan and Iraq.

From *CQ Researcher*,
September 18, 2009.

Lt. Col. Victor Fehrenbach, an Air Force weapons control officer decorated for heroism in Iraq, was expecting to be deployed back to a war zone last year when his military career suddenly blew up.

A male civilian with whom Fehrenbach had had a sexual encounter at his Boise, Idaho, home falsely accused him of rape. Fehrenbach successfully rebutted the accusation, but to do so he had to acknowledge to police and Air Force investigators that he is gay. In the end, Fehrenbach was not charged with a crime, but his superiors at Mountain Home Air Force Base in Idaho began proceedings to honorably discharge the 18-year veteran.[1] Air Force Secretary Michael Donley is expected to make a final decision within a month.

The proposed discharge is based on Fehrenbach's alleged violation of the "don't ask, don't tell" regulations adopted by the Defense Department in 1993. They require anyone identified as gay or lesbian or who has engaged in homosexual activities to be expelled from the military. However, the rules do not require dismissal of homosexuals whose orientation remains secret.

"I kept my private life private for 18 years," Fehrenbach, the son of two Air Force officers, says in a telephone interview. "I didn't even tell my family; none of my coworkers knew. My dream for my whole life was to serve my country and be in the Air Force."

The "don't ask, don't tell" policy and a related law banning homosexual conduct by service members grew out of a 1993 political firestorm, sparked by newly elected President Bill Clinton's attempt to keep a campaign promise and lift the military's longtime ban on homosexuals. Instead, the Clinton administration crafted

Views Shift on Gays in the Military

About seven in 10 Americans favor allowing gays to openly serve in the military, an increase of 26 percentage points since 1993, when the "don't ask, don't tell" policy was created.

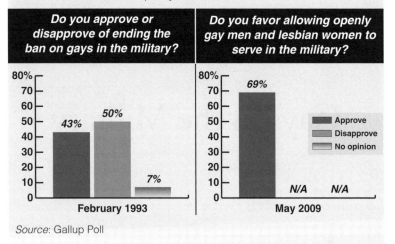

Do you approve or disapprove of ending the ban on gays in the military?	Do you favor allowing openly gay men and lesbian women to serve in the military?
February 1993	May 2009

Source: Gallup Poll

been discharged from the military on the basis of homosexuality between fiscal 1994 and 2008.[3] And the controversy has intensified this year, because President Barack Obama opposes the policy and because gay service members are fighting in Afghanistan and Iraq.

The Senate Armed Services Committee is expected to hold hearings on the policy this fall for the first time since 1993, and a House panel is tentatively planning its own hearing. Rep. Patrick J. Murphy, D-Pa., an Iraq combat veteran who served with the 82nd Airborne Division, has introduced a bill to repeal the 1993 law and prohibit sexuality-based discrimination in the military.

"It hurts our national security when we let go of 13,000 honorable troops, not for any misconduct but just because they happen to be gay," Murphy says.

For instance, opponents like Murphy note, at least 20 gay and lesbian Arabic and Farsi linguists were discharged between 1998 and 2004.[4] Army National Guard Lt. Daniel Choi, an Arabic specialist facing discharge after "coming out," has become the public face of that trend. The ban's supporters, however, say the dismissals prove the law prohibiting homosexuality should be better enforced so gays and lesbians don't enter the military in the first place.

Murphy's supporters say public opinion has changed dramatically since 1993, when opposition ran high. A Gallup Poll in June showed 69 percent of adults favor allowing open homosexuals in the military, up from 43 percent in 1993. Strikingly, 58 percent of self-identified conservatives support gays serving in the military — up from 46 percent four years ago.[5]

But Congress, not Gallup, must decide the fate of the bill. And Murphy and his cosponsors would have to overcome opposition from a phalanx of retired senior commanders.

"Team cohesion and concentration on missions would suffer if our troops had to live in close quarters with others who could be sexually attracted to them," four former

regulations that drew a line between sexual "orientation" and behavior and prohibited questioning service members and potential enlistees about their sexuality. The president also signed into law a bill that Congress passed in 1993 that doesn't mention orientation at all. Instead, it reinforces the military's ban on gays serving in the armed services:

"The presence in the armed forces of persons who demonstrate a propensity or intent to engage in homosexual acts, would create an unacceptable risk to the high standards of morale, good order and discipline, and unit cohesion that are the essence of military capability," the law says.[2]

Both sides dislike the "don't ask, don't tell" regulations, but they disagree over whether the law banning homosexuals from serving openly in the military should be repealed. Opponents of the law say current policies have made little change in the military's practice of weeding out gays and lesbians. Supporters of the ban say prohibiting homosexual conduct is impossible without asking service members or potential members if they are gay or lesbian.

In any case, the 1993 compromise didn't tamp down the controversy. Nearly 12,800 men and women have

high-level commanders said in a *Washington Post* op-ed last April. * "There is no compelling national security reason for running these risks to our armed forces." They and more than 1,000 other retired general and flag officers had signed a letter advocating retaining the ban, they said.[6]

The retired brass and their allies disdain the example of 25 other countries, including some key U.S. allies, which allow openly gay troops in their armed forces. "This is hardly convincing, to say, 'The others are doing it, so we should too,' " said Brian E. A. Maue, a professor of policy analysis at the U.S. Air Force Academy in Colorado Springs, speaking only for himself.[7]

Obama promised gay political activists who supported his presidential campaign that he will move to lift the prohibition — though he didn't say when. Some activists want Obama simply to halt homosexuality discharges by executive order.

Those favoring that approach argue that prospects for immediate congressional action are dim. Still, simply prohibiting discharges by presidential order would allow a successor president to restart discharges and would leave the homosexuality law on the books. A president can't repeal a law.

In any case, Obama has opted to toss the hot potato to Congress, asking lawmakers to discard the 1993 law, entitled, "Policy concerning homosexuality in the armed forces."

"My administration is already working with the Pentagon and members of the House and the Senate on … ending this policy, which will require an act of Congress," the president told gay and lesbian activists gathered at the White House on June 29 to mark the 40th anniversary of the "Stonewall Riots" in New York City, which launched the gay-rights movement.[8]

The U.S. Supreme Court could also strike down the policy as unconstitutional. In 2003 the court held that civilian laws prohibiting homosexual sex were unconstitutional. But in June, the court declined to hear a challenge to the military's "don't ask, don't tell" policy.[9]

The justices didn't explain their action. But it underlined a distinction between civilian and military codes of conduct. Indeed, advocates on both sides cite the importance of attitudes within the military. Those favoring a ban cite the most recent annual survey by the nongovernmental *Military Times* newspaper, which found that 58 percent of 1,900 active-duty respondents opposed lifting the ban.[10]

"In the field environment, you're in very close proximity to one another," Army Capt. Steven J. Lacy of the 71st Transportation Battalion at Fort Eustis, in Newport News, Va., told the paper. "The fact that someone could be openly gay could exacerbate stress on teams and small units when you're already at a high stress level."[11]

Ten percent of the respondents warned that they wouldn't re-enlist if the prohibition ended.[12] Elaine Donnelly, a key figure in efforts to retain the prohibition, cites that finding as evidence of disruptions that would occur if the ban were lifted. "With even just a few thousand departures in mid-level ranks you have crippled our all-volunteer force," she says. Donnelly is president of the

Discharges Number of Homosexuals Declined

The U.S. military discharged 634 homosexual personnel in 2008 — less than half the number discharged in 1980. Some say the decline reflects the effectiveness of the policy; others say the military knowingly retains homosexual personnel during times of crisis and conflict. Overall, 32,050 homosexuals have been discharged from the military during the 28-year period.

Fiscal year	Homosexual discharges	Percentage of total active force
1980	1,754	0.086
1985	1,660	0.077
1990	941	0.046
1995	757	0.050
2000	1,212	0.088
2005	726	0.052
2008	634	0.045

Source: David F. Burrelli, "Don't Ask, Don't Tell:" The Law and Military Policy on Same-Sex Behavior, Congressional Research Service, August 2009

Fierce Defender of the 'Culture of the Military'

Gays and lesbians don't belong, says Elaine Donnelly.

Among supporters of the military's ban on homosexuals, all roads lead to Elaine Donnelly, founder and president of the Center on Military Readiness in Livonia, Mich. Donnelly's steadfast defense of the ban runs through the nearly two decades that the issue has been on the public agenda.

"We defend the culture of the military," she says, a characterization that she prefers to "social conservative," though she doesn't reject the term. She does reject any suggestion that military culture is becoming any more open to its gay and lesbian members.

Donnelly says her omnipresence results from military strictures against senior active-duty personnel speaking out on political issues. "As a civilian woman, I am more free to address these controversial issues."

She's been doing so, under one organizational umbrella or another for decades. Her story began, she says, in the 1970s when she was a "young mother concerned about my family and the defense of this country." Feminist organizations were pushing for passage of an Equal Rights Amendment (ERA), with some supporters arguing that gender equality meant that women should be eligible for the draft. Donnelly, the mother of two young daughters, opposed the idea — which aroused considerable opposition among social conservatives, who blocked the measure by lobbying in state legislatures to prevent ratification by the required three-quarters of the states.

During the Reagan administration, involvement in Republican politics led to Donnelly's 1984 appointment to the Defense Advisory Committee on Women in the Services.

In 1992, President George H. W. Bush named her to the Presidential Commission on the Assignment of Women in the Services, where she helped engineer a narrow, 8-7 majority in favor of continuing to bar women from direct combat assignments. "Equal opportunity is not the primary goal of the military. Defending the country is," she said during earlier deliberations. [1]

The following year, as the fledgling Bill Clinton administration was attempting to overturn the military's ban on homosexuals, Donnelly founded the Center on Military Readiness, based in her hometown, to oppose Clinton's attempt.

Days before Christmas, when Defense Secretary Les Aspin issued the 1993 "don't ask, don't tell" regulations that represented the administration's compromise, Donnelly called them a "crowning insult in what has been a painful year for the military. President Clinton is playing Santa to homosexuals and liberals, while dropping lumps of coal into the stockings of the military." [2]

Since then, Donnelly seems to have lost nothing of her take-no-prisoners manner. Speaking at a House Armed Services Subcommittee on Military Personnel hearing last year, she painted a bleak picture of the military's future if the ban were repealed: "Inappropriate passive/aggressive actions common in the homosexual community, short of physical touching and assault, will be permitted in all military communities, to include Army and Marine infantry battalions, Special Operations Forces. Navy SEALS and cramped submarines that patrol the seas for months at a time." [3]

Rep. Vic Snyder, D-Ark., called the remark "just bonkers."

Donnelly offered an explanation: "What do I mean by passive/aggressive behavior? It means something of a sexualized [action] short of assault. It means the kind of thing like

Center on Military Readiness (CMR), an advocacy organization, in Livonia, Mich.

Some high-level military retirees discount the threat of departures. "I don't believe a large number would do that," says retired Brig. Gen. John Adams. "People who are unwilling to accommodate equal opportunity in the matter of open service — I would say the military is not for them."

Military Times says the survey results "are not representative of the military as a whole," because the Army is overrepresented and minorities, women and junior enlisted personnel are underrepresented. The newspaper's subscribers are generally older and more conservative. [13]

However, older personnel and retirees don't uniformly support the ban. "Within the military, the climate has changed dramatically since 1993," retired Gen. John M.

a woman who is stared at — her breasts are stared at. She is made to feel uncomfortable. She feels she has no recourse. She feels she cannot say anything, can't complain about it, because that would hurt her career. That's the kind of thing I'm talking about."

Rep. Ellen Tauscher, D-Calif. (now under secretary of state for arms control and disarmament), asked another witness, retired U.S. Navy Capt. Joan Darrah, who came out as a lesbian after leaving the military, "Do you think that because there are gay or lesbians in a work environment, that the work environment becomes sexualized, as Ms. Donnelly wants us to believe?"

"No," Darrah said. "When I was the deputy and chief of staff at the Naval Intelligence Command, I had about 400 military and about 1,100 civilians and contractors. I had several openly gay civilians. We all worked together. Everybody was judged on their performance and their ability, and there was no problem at all."

The answer didn't sway Donnelly. Nor did testimony from a gay Iraq War veteran, retired U.S. Marine Staff Sgt. Eric Alva, who lost his right leg to a land mine in Iraq. "I have proudly served a country that was not proud of me," Alva told the subcommittee.

Donnelly later said she respected the service of Alva, Darrah and "everybody who serves in the military."

Rep. Chris Shays, R-Conn., shot back, "How do you respect their service? You want them out."

"I'm standing for sound policy, congressman," Donnelly answered. "In the military we don't make policy based on individuals."

Donnelly laid out her views in some detail in 2007. In a 138-page article in the *Duke Journal of Gender Law and*

"Equal opportunity is not the primary goal of the military," says Elaine Donnelly, president of the Center for Military Readiness.

Policy, she made a detailed legal argument for maintaining the combat elements of the military as heterosexual male preserves. She also made clear that her technical arguments spring from a social doctrine.

"Many institutions in civilian life have been affected negatively by unsuccessful social experimentation," she wrote. "The baby boomer and 'Gen-X' generations, for example, have been subjected to 'look-say' reading, 'new math' and 'civics' courses that fail to teach students fundamentals.... In matters of urban policy, whole cities have been threatened by unrestrained crimes, ruinous taxes and crumbling neighborhoods." [4]

The military, by contrast, can't be subjected to social tinkering, Donnelly argued. "Americans have every right to question the flawed assumptions of social engineers who demand radical change in the culture of the military." [5]

---

[1] Quoted in Matt Yancey, "Panel Recommends Women Be Assigned Combat Positions Under Some Circumstances," The Associated Press, Nov. 3, 1992.

[2] Quoted in Bill Gertz, "Policy on gays detailed," *The Washington Times*, Dec. 23, 1993, p. A1.

[3] Unless otherwise noted, the following testimony comes from "House Armed Services Subcommittee on Military Personnel Holds Hearing on a Review of Don't Ask Don't Tell Policy," CQ Congressional Transcripts, July 23, 2008.

[4] Elaine Donnelly, "Constructing the Co-Ed Military," *Duke Journal of Gender Law & Policy*, June 18, 2007, p. 948, www.law.duke.edu/journals/cite.php?14+Duke+J.+Gender+L.+&+Pol%2527y+815.

[5] *Ibid.*, p. 818.

Shalikashvili, chairman of the Joint Chiefs of Staff in the Clinton administration, wrote in a *Washington Post* op-ed in June. "Conversations I've held with service members make clear that, while the military remains a traditional culture, that tradition no longer requires banning open service by gays." Last year, 104 retired generals and admirals signed a letter calling for an end to "don't ask, don't tell."[14]

Some outside experts share Shalikashvili's view. "There is a much clearer generation gap" on the issue than in the past, says David R. Segal, a professor of sociology at the University of Maryland and director of its Center for Research on Military Organization. "There are still senior people in the Army — the Army in particular — who do not want it to happen, but more junior people who, unlike their seniors, had gone to high school and college with people who were gay and 'out' were not as threatened."

Segal sees changed attitudes first-hand. "Talking to soldiers and sailors I'm finding more people who are gay and out than ever before," he says. "A lot of people are officially not out, but they're out to somebody, and usually the somebodies are buddies in their units, sometimes their platoon leaders or company commanders — more likely than to their first sergeants, because the first sergeants are from a different generation."

Fehrenbach, meanwhile, says he's suffered no problems with the men he serves with since he came out as gay, despite the macho culture of combat aviation. "From guys I've flown with in combat, I hear, 'I would go to war with you tomorrow.'"

As the conflict over allowing open homosexuals to serve in the military continues, these are among the key issues:

Can military units function effectively with openly homosexual members?

The debate over whether homosexuals belong in the military centers predominantly on the effect openly gay and lesbian service members would have on their units.

In the past, no doubts existed about the effect. As the United States geared up for the mass mobilization of World War II psychiatric consultants to the military developed a thesis based on the medical conclusion that homosexuality was a psychological disorder. "The reason for excluding them as psychopaths was that ... they were considered to be irresponsible troublemakers who were unable to control their desires or learn from their mistakes and thus threatened the other men," wrote historian Allan Bérubé in a groundbreaking account of gays and lesbians in the Second World War.[15]

The psychiatrists were also concerned about what would later be called "unit cohesion." Homosexuals would be unable to cope with regimentation and lack of privacy, so they would become magnets for aggression by their heterosexual comrades.

When the conflict over homosexuals in the military first became a nationwide issue in 1993, medical professionals no longer defined homosexuality as a malady, and stereotypes of all gays as effeminate and all lesbians as "mannish" were fading. Even so, debate still centered on the effect that openly declared homosexuals would have

on the morale and performance of the units to which they'd be assigned.

"At the very least, the lifting of the ban will create a controversy over the issue of privacy," Charles Moskos Jr., a leading sociologist of the military, wrote in 1993. "Just as most men and women dislike being stripped of all privacy before the opposite sex, so most heterosexual men and women dislike being exposed to homosexuals of their own sex."[16]

Moskos, who died in 2008 and frequently advised military leaders, lawmakers and executive branch officials, is credited with originating the "don't ask, don't tell" policy.[17] At the time, his views reflected majority sentiment from senior military leadership to the rank and file. Today, gay and straight opponents of the ban argue that military opinion has shifted.

"We knew of [gay] men in our unit, or kind of had suspicions," says Iraq veteran Rep. Murphy, who is sponsoring a bill to lift the ban on gays serving in the military. "But as long as they could do the job, fire their M-4 rifle, stand guard at 4 in the morning, lead a convoy at 2 in the afternoon in high heat and bring the guys home alive — that's what we cared about."

Murphy dismisses concerns about privacy in close quarters, in the presence of known homosexuals. "I happen to be heterosexual, but every woman that I come across, whether on a beach or in a supermarket, I'm not attacking her every time there's no one around," he says. "When people bring up these false arguments they're really questioning the professionalism of the best fighting force this Earth has ever seen."

But Maue of the Air Force Academy said in a recent debate at the McCormick Freedom Museum in Chicago that military life is filled with rules designed to minimize the risks associated with interactions between men and women thrown together in crowded facilities.

"We know that all human beings do not behave all of the time," said Maue. "This holds for both straight as well as homosexual people.... I'm 10 years married, faithful to my wife, no reason to stray. But the military is still not going to let me go into the female showers."[18]

Repealing the ban, Maue argues, would expand the kinds of interpersonal problems that arise. "The risk of demoralizing misconduct will escalate to include male-male and female-female issues in addition to those that already occur."

The gay ban generates its own problems, says Jon Soltz, chairman of VoteVets, which is campaigning to end the prohibition. For instance, while gay linguists were being discharged during the Iraq War, recruiting standards were being relaxed so that recruits like Steven D. Green — who was sentenced to life in prison earlier this year for raping and murdering a 14-year-old Iraqi girl and killing her family — were allowed to enlist. Green, who had a record of drug and alcohol abuse, had received a "morals waiver" to enter the Army.[19]

"The drama we have comes from a bunch of policies that are bad for unit cohesion — like allowing in Steven Green," says Soltz, who served as an Army captain in Iraq in 2003. "What's worse for unit cohesion, the interpreters you kicked out who helped me as a young officer, or someone who kills civilians?"

Yet Brian Jones, who retired from the Army as a master sergeant after a 21-year career in special operations, including Delta Force, testified that units working in rugged, dangerous conditions would be subjected to hazardous stresses if the ban were lifted. "As a U.S. Army Ranger, I performed long-range patrols in severe cold weather conditions — teams of 10 — with only mission-essential items in our backpacks — no comfort items," Jones told the House Armed Services Subcommittee on Personnel in 2008. "The only way to keep from freezing at night was to get as close as possible for body heat, which means skin to skin."[20]

In these circumstances, Jones testified, "Any attraction to the same-sex teammates, real or perceived, would be known and would be a problem. The presence of openly gay men in these situations would elevate tensions and disrupt unit cohesion and morale."

Is the "don't ask, don't tell" approach to differentiating sexual "orientation" from conduct a viable compromise?

"Don't ask, don't tell" grew out of political compromise, but it's under constant attack both from those who want to strengthen restrictions on homosexuals in the military and from those who advocate allowing gays and lesbians to serve openly.

The 1993 law on homosexuality in the military prohibits homosexual "behavior" and/or declarations of homosexuality or bisexuality.

The "don't ask, don't tell" regulations — which are distinct from the law — attempt to draw a more visible line between sexuality and conduct. "Applicants for enlistment, appointment, or induction shall not be asked or required to reveal their sexual orientation," the regulations say. Nevertheless, "Homosexual conduct is grounds for separation from the Military Services."[21]

Despite those differences the law and the regulations reflect a similar approach, a legal analyst at the nonpartisan Congressional Research Service (CRS) wrote recently. 'Both the law and the regulations ... are structured entirely around the concept of homosexual conduct as opposed to orientation."[22]

However, the regulations say conduct can include speech. "A statement by a member that demonstrates a propensity or intent to engage in homosexual acts" would be grounds for discharge. While the regulations acknowledge that speech isn't generally considered conduct, a discharge that resulted from a statement wouldn't be based on "orientation," the regulations say, but on an understanding that the "statement indicates a likelihood that the member engages in or will engage in homosexual acts."[23]

The legal arguments surrounding orientation, speech and conduct would seem to show that the practice of separating sexuality from sexual behavior is inherently complicated. "Attempts to implement the statute, or analyze and evaluate it, in terms of sexual orientation, have resulted in confusion and ambiguity, and are likely to continue to do so," the CRS analysis said.[24]

The Pentagon also worries about the ban as a tool of vengeance. Defense Secretary Robert M. Gates bemoaned to reporters on June 30 that the 1993 law "doesn't leave ... a lot of flexibility" and he is seeking a "more humane" way to apply it. "Do we need to ... take action ... if we get information from somebody who may have vengeance in mind or blackmail or somebody who has been jilted?" Gates asked. "I don't know the answer to that, and I don't ... pretend to."[25]

Donnelly responds: "If the secretary of Defense wants a more humane way to enforce the law, we wrote to him and said, 'The best thing you can do is explain what the law actually says, that everybody can serve the country in some way, but not everyone is eligible to serve in the armed forces.' "

Donnelly's group also cites Pentagon figures showing that homosexuality discharges account for far fewer expulsions than other violations of regulations. In fiscal 2008, drug violations accounted for nearly 29 percent

AFP/Getty Images/Timothy A. Clary

Members of ACT UP (AIDS Coalition to Unleash Power) at the military recruitment center in Times Square, New York City, protest on March 15, 2007, after then-chairman of the Joint Chiefs of Staff Peter Pace described homosexual acts as "immoral" and likened homosexuality to adultery.

and failure to meet weight standards, 23 percent. Only 3.2 percent of discharges were for homosexuality.[26]

Opponents of allowing homosexuals to serve in the military want to retain the law but scrap the "don't ask, don't tell" regulations. The Air Force Academy's Maue says that in his opinion, "It's a bad policy. People think, 'Oh, I can serve if I'm homosexual and it won't create any problems,' but it certainly has not been completely intelligible to the [service] members."

The main confusion, Maue argues, derives from the conflict between the law and the regulations. As he reads the law, "Congress directly and intelligibly … reaffirms the longstanding military judgment that homosexuality is incompatible with military service." But the regulations effectively allow homosexuals to serve if they keep their sexuality secret.

Those seeking to lift the ban on gays also attack the "don't ask, don't tell" regulations — though they also want the law authorizing discrimination based on sexual conduct discarded. "That policy says, 'Even though we know

there are gays in the military, we're going to institute a policy where no one talks about it,' as though soldiers are like children who, if they close their eyes, believe the problem will go away," argues Nathaniel Frank, who was Maue's opponent in the Chicago debate earlier this year. Frank, author of a book criticizing the prohibition, is a senior research fellow at Palm Center, a think tank at the University of California, Santa Barbara, that specializes in critical analysis of the military ban on homosexuality.[27]

As for the law under which the regulations exist, Frank and others question the basis for the statute. "The language of the law says openly gay service members would be an unacceptable risk," Frank says. "That was never rooted in anything…. It relied on this old stereotype that gays are somehow nonconformists, who are incapable of disciplined behavior and who are always engaging in something unusual or sexual."[28]

Donnelly of the Center for Military Readiness says the "don't ask, don't tell" regulations are "indefensible in court."

The regulations supposedly enforce a law that bars military service to people likely to engage in homosexual acts, Donnelly says, but the regulations effectively prohibit finding out who those people are. " 'Don't ask, don't tell,' if it applied to laws regarding use of alcohol, would say that you must be 21 to purchase or use alcohol, however the bartender is forbidden to ask about age and is not allowed to post a sign saying, 'We check ID.' "

David Hall, an Air Force staff sergeant who was honorably discharged after he was "outed," says "don't ask, don't tell" created more confusion than it resolved. "I believe the intent … was that the military was not going to ask, and you were not going to tell the military. That means, I'm not going to tell my commander, but the way it's been implemented, it means, 'Don't tell anybody ever.' "

Hall says young service members, raised in the increasingly open civilian culture, are especially vulnerable to that misreading. "There are 18- and 20-year-olds putting it on Facebook. If the military comes across that, that's [the same as] telling."

Should the United States follow other countries' examples and allow gays to serve openly in the military?

Countries that allow military service by openly gay service members have reported no difficulties because of the policy, according to the Government Accountability Office (GAO), which in 1993 studied foreign militaries that both banned and allowed homosexuals to serve.

"Military officials … [said] the presence of homosexuals in the military is not an issue and has not created problems in the functioning of military units,' " the GAO said of four countries it studied in depth — Canada, Israel, Germany and Sweden.[29]

But the report pointed out that homosexuals in foreign militaries are "reluctant to openly admit their sexual orientation for a variety of reasons" — creating a kind of informal version of "don't ask, don't tell." "Homosexuals fear discrimination or negative reactions from their peers or superiors if they reveal their sexual orientation, and homosexuals do not see any advantage to openly identifying their homosexuality," the report said.[30]

The GAO's findings closely tracked the conclusions of a similar but separate massive study for the Pentagon that same year by the RAND Corp., a Santa Monica, Calif., think tank. "Service members who acknowledged their homosexuality were appropriately circumspect in their behavior while in military situations," the RAND researchers reported. "Problems that did arise were generally resolved satisfactorily on a case-by-case basis."[31]

Since 1993, more than a dozen additional foreign militaries have lifted restrictions on service by homosexuals, bringing the total number to 25.[32] Of these, the most important, symbolically, is Great Britain, which has deep cultural and military ties to the United States. Britain's military began admitting openly homosexual recruits in 2000, and saw gay and lesbian service members march as a unit in the annual Pride London parade last July 4.[33]

Israel, an important ally whose military is among the world's most battle-hardened, has a longtime policy of open service. An Israeli military magazine this year featured a cover photo of two gay soldiers hugging each other. Editor Maj. Yoni Schonfeld, who was open about his homosexuality while commanding a paratrooper company, told The Associated Press, "If you're gay and live in the 'manly' world, there are no problems." He added, "Those who are more feminine in their speech and appearance have a harder time fitting in."[34]

Those who oppose the U.S. ban on gays in the military often cite the strength of Britain's and Israel's U.S. ties, the growth in the number of countries allowing gays

to serve and the reportedly trouble-free result. But advocates of maintaining the ban counter that the United States has no real counterparts, either in size, in the worldwide scope of its responsibilities nor in the intensity of its present commitments in Afghanistan and Iraq.

Donnelly of the Center on Military Readiness notes that Israel's small size and its defensive military mission mean its troops don't spend months and years overseas. "There are no long deployments," she says. "The defense perimeter is a few miles away, so people can live on bases close to home, or at home." Hence, in her view, the problem of living in close quarters — often cited by opponents of gays in the military — are minimal in the Israeli forces.[35]

She also points out that Israel is a socially conservative society. "There is a cultural prohibition that is very real," she says. "You don't have people walking around flaunting their homosexuality, which is the cultural demand for what is being asked in this country — the celebration of homosexuality as a normal alternative lifestyle."

But Segal of the University of Maryland's Center for Research on Military Organization says the differences in military culture between U.S., Israeli and British armed forces matter less than the similarities. "We have one of the few armies that expects to fight wars," he says. "The Brits are a war-fighting army; the Israelis are a war-fighting army. They don't deploy over the ocean, but they're highly cohesive."

These experiences are relevant to the United States, he says. The record shows that "there may be some resistance to gays in units at first, but once they show they can do the job there are few problems," he says.

Opponents of lifting the ban argue that those who cite other nations as examples have the U.S.-foreign military relationship backwards. "I've worked alongside a lot of them — Britain, France, Poland, the Italians," retired Master Sgt. Jones told the House Armed Services Subcommittee on Military Personnel last year. "The common thread between all of them is they want to be like us."

The feature of U.S. forces that inspires the most admiration from foreign militaries, Jones said, is the creation of highly disciplined and mutually supportive small units. "It's the way we train and mold teams," he said. "When you talk about cohesion, we have the best cohesive armed forces across the board of anybody in this world."

Rep. Murphy, the Iraq veteran pushing to lift the ban, counters that American forces have a long tradition of engaging in joint exercises and competitions with foreign militaries — including those of countries that allow open service by gays — and learning from them. "We always send our elite forces versus their elite forces," he says. "To make it sound like we have to ignore what they do — and I'm not saying we have to do exactly how they do — is frankly laughable."

When he served in the 1st Armored Division in Germany, he says, "I went through the requirements for the German Armed Forces proficiency badge. We do activities of that kind because it makes us more well-rounded; it's a staple of our training. That German proficiency badge is one that I proudly wore."

BACKGROUND

Practical Realities

The U.S. military explicitly prohibited homosexuality in 1916 through an anti-sodomy provision in the Articles of War. But homosexuality didn't emerge as a major military issue until decades later, as the military launched the largest mobilization in U.S. history for World War II. By the end of the war, 12 million people were serving.[36] Wartime eligibility standards excluded gay men, given what were considered their physical and moral weaknesses.[37]

But practical realities intervened. The military's immense manpower needs influenced draft board officials to accept as many men as possible. Most gay draftees were eager to do their duty — and in many cases to prove their bravery, then seen as synonymous with heterosexuality. Another powerful incentive to keep homosexual orientation secret: Potential civilian employers had access to draft records. Some military examiners preferred admitting homosexuals to burdening them with the stigma of being rejected because they were homosexual.

Enforcing a ban on lesbians proved even more difficult, as nearly 400,000 women enlisted in female military formations.[38] "Masculine" women were seen as potentially valuable to military performance, and questioning women about their sexuality violated the era's standards of decency.

For all the pragmatic realities that complicated the ban on homosexuals, the idea that gays and lesbians might demand the right to join the military without hiding their sexual orientation would have been unimaginable in the 1940s.

That trend didn't arise until after the gay liberation movement got started, following the 1969 "Stonewall Riots" in New York's Greenwich Village. New York City police raided a gay bar, the Stonewall Inn, provoking an explosion of outrage from homosexuals. The episode came to stand for the end of gay shame and the rise of gay pride.

But campaigning on behalf of gay soldiers wasn't a high priority in the early years of post-Stonewall activism. Homosexual militancy was politically on the left, which at that time was defined by opposition to the Vietnam War and, by extension, to the armed forces themselves. "Many liberal gay organizers still saw their struggle ... as a movement to allow every gay person the right to be a homosexual leftist," wrote Randy Shilts, a gay journalist and author.[39]

After the Vietnam War ended (in 1975), and the gay movement abandoned revolution for reform, an openly gay soldier took to the courts in the early 1980s to challenge attempts to throw him out of the military. Sgt. Perry J. Watkins had remained in the Army after he was drafted in 1968, at the height of the Vietnam War. Inducted even though he said he was gay, he openly moonlighted as a drag artist under the name Simone.

In 1975, Watkins' commanding officer concluded that Army regulations didn't allow an openly gay soldier to remain in the ranks. The commander began discharge proceedings — despite his high regard for Watkins' military performance. But an Army discharge board found no evidence of misconduct.

A subsequent attempt to deny Watkins a new security clearance on the grounds of his homosexuality led him in 1981 to sue the Army. The military initiated another discharge proceeding, this one successful.

Other legal challenges to the military on homosexuality were becoming troublesome as well. In 1982, the Defense Department enacted a new regulation designed to eliminate all ambiguities. "Homosexuality is incompatible with military service," the regulation said. No one who practiced homosexuality or demonstrated "a propensity to engage in homosexual conduct" would be allowed to enter or remain in the service. But an expulsion for homosexuality would not by itself be grounds for a less-than-honorable discharge.[40]

CHRONOLOGY

1940s *A World War II attempt to screen out homosexuals from the military faces practical complications, which resurface decades later in a legal challenge during the Vietnam War.*

1941 The Army, Navy and Selective Service System develop procedures for spotting and excluding homosexual draftees from military service.

1945 As World War II ended, only 4,000-5,000 men have been rejected from military service for being gay. Thousands of lesbians enlisted, largely because asking women about their sexuality violated the era's standards of behavior.

1960s-1980s *Modern gay-rights movement begins, encouraging gays and lesbians to stop hiding their sexuality — a development eventually leading to service members demanding to serve openly.*

1968 Perry J. Watkins is drafted as nation mobilizes for Vietnam War, despite his declaration that he's gay.

1969 Gay-rights movement is launched after police raid gay bar (Stonewall Inn) in New York, leading to days of street protests.

1981 Watkins, now a sergeant, is discharged from the Army. He files a lawsuit challenging the move.

1982 New Defense Department rule formalizes ban on gays in the military …. Demonstrators at Bolling Air Force Base near Washington, D.C., protest what they call efforts to discharge gay service members.

1990s *As gay-rights movement grows, military service becomes a major issue, leading Democratic presidential candidate Bill Clinton to promise to lift the ban.*

1990 Watkins wins his lawsuit because the Army had allowed him to serve for years with full knowledge of his homosexuality.

1992 Candidate Clinton calls for repealing the ban on gays in the military …. After the election, senior military and political figures protest the idea.

1993 President Clinton backs a compromise that allows homosexuals to serve if they don't disclose their sexuality …. Congress prohibits military service by anyone with a "propensity or intent to engage in homosexual acts." … Defense Department "don't ask, don't tell" regulations call sexual orientation "personal and private" but require discharge for "homosexual conduct."

1998 Pentagon acknowledges that gay discharges have risen since the new rules took effect.

2000s *With the military stretched thin by two wars, excluding homosexuals takes on new prominence. Barack Obama is elected president after vowing to push for lifting the ban.*

2003 Military discharges nine homosexual service members training as linguists, most of them in Arabic, leading opponents of the gay ban to argue that the prohibition endangers national security.

2005 Palm Center think tank says 20 gay Arabic and Farsi linguists have been discharged.

2008 In first congressional hearing on the issue since 1993, a gay Marine veteran who lost a leg in Iraq says his sexuality wasn't an issue in combat and a special operations veteran says unit cohesion would suffer if open homosexuals serve …. Subscriber survey by Military Times newspaper reports that strong support exists for maintaining the ban, but acknowledges that subscribers tend to be from the older, more conservative sector of the military and retiree population.

2009 Rep. Patrick J. Murphy, D-Pa., introduces bill to repeal ban on gays in the military …. More than 1,000 retired high-ranking officers call for retaining the ban …. Some gay-rights activists ask Obama to repeal the "don't ask, don't tell" rules, but he asks Congress to repeal the policy …. Obama acknowledges impatience of gay and lesbian supporters who perceive lack of White House urgency but vows continued support for lifting the ban …. Chairmen of House and Senate Armed Services committees say hearings on the issue may be held as early as the fall …. Air Force Lt. Col. Victor Fehrenbach and Army National Guard Lt. Daniel Choi challenge their discharges, publicizing opposition to ban.

President Obama Tries to Reassure LGBT Community

'This will buy him some time, but he'll have to deliver.'

President Barack Obama knew his star was fading a bit among a community with which he'd enjoyed the closest of ties. So, when he invited gay and lesbian political activists to the White House, he did so with great attention to positive symbolism.

For starters, the gathering was held on June 29, the official anniversary of the "Stonewall Riots" — the New York street protests that are considered the founding event of the modern lesbian, gay, bisexual and transgender (LGBT) movement.

And Obama made a point of connecting its struggles to those of the civil rights movement. "I know that many in this room don't believe that progress has come fast enough, and I understand that," the president told a crowd of about 250 gathered in the East Room. "It's not for me to tell you to be patient, any more than it was for others to counsel patience to African-Americans who were petitioning for equal rights a half-century ago."[1]

The president also acknowledged that the gay community's impatience wasn't a general sentiment, but one directed at him. "I want you to know that I expect and hope to be judged not by words, not by promises I've made, but by the promises that my administration keeps," the president said, to applause. "We've been in office six months now. I suspect that by the time this administration is over, I think you guys will have pretty good feelings about the Obama administration."[2]

For some of the invitees, Obama's message hit home. "He reminded us to continue to hold him accountable," Joe Solomonese, president of the Washington-based Human Rights Campaign, told *The Washington Post*.

"There certainly was the appropriate and inspiring acknowledgment that he made of what this community has been through. It's important for people to be reassured by the president."[3]

Others in homosexual political circles were more skeptical. Alan van Capelle, executive director of the Empire State Pride Agenda in New York, who said he hadn't gotten an invitation, likened the gathering to fashionable restaurant food — skimpy on the portions but expensive. "It costs a whole lot to get into the White House, but somehow, the meal feels unfulfilling," he said. "There are a lot of us who believe in change but do not believe it is a passive word. It is an active word. There is a level of disappointment that exists."[4]

Disillusionment had been building during the weeks leading up to the event. Some time before the gathering, Steve Hildebrand, a high-ranking Obama campaign operative who is gay, met privately with Obama to tell him that the president's gay supporters were feeling "hurt, anxiety and anger" over White House handling of matters on the gay-rights agenda.[5]

President Bill Clinton's adviser on gay issues, Richard Socarides, said the Obama team was "paralyzed" on gay-community issues.[6]

One of three big disappointments was the administration's legal defense of the federal anti-gay-marriage law, the Defense of Marriage Act (DOMA).[7] Obama told the Stonewall Day crowd that his administration was following longtime federal policy of defending statutes on the books. But he has called for repealing the law. (A bill to repeal DOMA, sponsored by Rep. Jerrold Nadler, D-N.Y., is

Another early sign of discontent over military policy on homosexuality came in the form of a small demonstration in 1983 at Bolling Air Force Base in Washington, D.C. About 50 people protested what one called "witch-hunt investigations of gay servicemen" at the base and other installations in the Washington area.[41]

Meanwhile, Watkins had continued his legal battle even after he was discharged. Eventually, the 9th U.S.

Circuit Court of Appeals ruled in 1989 that he should be reinstated, in part because the Army had failed to justify its ban on homosexuals.

Then, in November, 1990, the U.S. Supreme Court refused to consider the Army's challenge to the appeals court ruling — effectively approving the reinstatement order. After his victory, Watkins reached a settlement with the Army that included an honorable discharge, full

expected to be introduced in mid-September).[8]

The administration's perceived foot-dragging in pushing for a federal hate-crimes bill also has stirred criticism, along with its perceived slowness in tackling the ban on homosexuals in the armed forces. "Although candidate Obama had suggested that efforts to repeal the ban would begin when he became president, rhetoric shifted immediately after the inauguration," wrote Aaron Belkin, director of the Palm Center at the University of California, Santa Barbara, a think tank focusing on the military's ban on homosexuals.[9]

Belkin and his colleagues advocate presidential action to suspend discharges of gay and lesbian personnel as a way to jar Congress into repealing the military law on homosexuality. Gay activists and journalists share the blame with Obama, Belkin argued, for choosing to ask Congress to repeal the law rather than having Obama act by executive order.

"We had momentum, and then the gay community took its foot off the gas pedal," Belkin says. "The bottom line is that we're at the bottom of a very, very long list of crises and emergencies."

He adds, "Maybe I'll be wrong, and the White House will smile on our issue in the next three-and-a-half years."

At the White House, Obama reiterated his choice of the congressional repeal strategy, even while acknowledging that gays and lesbians are still being expelled from the military under his administration. "I know that every day that passes without a resolution is a deep disappointment to those men and women who continue to be discharged under this policy — patriots who often possess critical language skills and years of training and who've served this

President Barack Obama told gay activists he wants Congress to overturn the ban on gays and lesbians serving openly in the military.

Getty Images/Olivier Douliery

country well," he said. "But what I hope is that these cases underscore the urgency of reversing this policy not just because it's the right thing to do, but because it is essential for our national security."[10]

Socarides remained skeptical after the event, which he didn't attend. But he credited Obama with explaining the reasons for his decisions. "This will buy him some time," Socarides said, "but he'll have to deliver."[11]

[1] "Remarks by the President at LGBT Pride Month Reception," White House, June 29, 2009, www.whitehouse.gov/the_press_office/Remarks-by-the-President-at-LGBT-Pride-Month-Reception/.

[2] *Ibid.*

[3] Michael D. Shear, "At White House, Obama Aims to Reassure Gays," *The Washington Post*, June 30, 2009, p. A1.

[4] Quoted in *ibid.*

[5] Quoted in Adam Nagourney, "Political Shifts on Gay Rights Are Lagging Behind Culture," *The New York Times*, June 28, 2009, p. A1.

[6] Quoted in *ibid.*

[7] Linda Deutsch and Lisa Leff, "Obama Admin Moves to Dismiss Defense of Marriage Act Challenge," The Associated Press, June 12, 2009, ww.huffingtonpost.com/2009/06/12/obama-defends-antigay-def_n_214764.html.

[8] Kerry Eleveld, "DOMA Repeal Bill Coming Next Week," *The Advocate*, Sept. 10, 2009, www.advocate.com/News/Daily_News/2009/10/DOMA_Repeal_Bill_Coming_Next_Week/.

[9] Aaron Belkin, "Self-Inflicted Wound: How and Why Gays Give the White House a Free Pass on 'Don't Ask, Don't Tell,' " Palm Center, July 27, 2009, p.1, www.palmcenter.org/files/active/0/SelfInflictedWound.pdf.

[10] "Remarks by the President. . . ," *op. cit.*

[11] Quoted in Sheryl Gay Stolberg, "On Gay Issues, Obama Asks to Be Judged on Vows Kept," *The New York Times*, June 30, 2009, p. A14.

retirement benefits and retroactive promotion from staff sergeant to sergeant first class.

Transition

Watkins' unexpected legal victory boosted the morale of gay and lesbian service members and their allies. But the outcome reflected his unusual unbroken record of sexual candor. There seemed to be no other cases of service

members who had openly declared their homosexuality from the moment they were examined for fitness to serve in the military.

Underlining that difference, the Watkins ruling followed a U.S. Supreme Court decision earlier that year to let stand the expulsions of Army Reservist Miriam Ben-Shalom and former Navy Ensign James Woodward. Ben-Shalom had "come out" to her commander after graduating from an Army Reserve drill instructor's school. Woodward also acknowledged his homosexuality after joining the Navy.

Moreover, a 1986 Supreme Court decision had upheld state anti-sodomy laws against homosexuals — prohibitions then in effect in 24 states and in Washington, D.C. Sanctions against gay sex had "ancient roots" in English common law, the high court's majority opinion said. A concurring opinion by Chief Justice Warren E. Burger cited prohibitions on homosexuality "throughout the history of Western civilization."[42]

The decision didn't directly touch on the issue of gays in the military. But, taken together with the Ben-Shalom/Woodward ruling, the anti-sodomy ruling confirmed the wisdom of staying at least part-way in the closet while serving in the military. Meanwhile, the services' investigative agencies actively pursued cases of suspected homosexuals. In 1983, for instance, 1,815 service members were discharged for violating the gay ban. The following year, 1,822 were discharged.[43] Still, many more homosexuals remained, sometimes because they were valued by commanders who shielded them from discharge investigations.

In that uneasy and inconsistent state of affairs, the HIV-AIDS epidemic hit in the early 1980s. In the civilian world, the rapid advance of the disease, its inevitably fatal outcome and its predominant connection with gay sexual practices, focused new attention on the homosexual population. But the military still didn't see itself in the picture.

That response seemed to be confirmed by an early study by a military doctor, who found that about one-third of a small sample of AIDS sufferers in the armed forces reported contracting the infection from heterosexual sex. Later, those results were shown to be a result of the gay ban. Service members afraid of being thrown out of the military had refused to admit homosexual sexual contacts.

As the infection continued to spread, results of servicewide HIV tests that began in 1985 exploded like a bombshell. By late 1987, more than 3,300 military personnel tested positive. The infection rate was highest in the Navy at 2.4 per 1,000 members; in the Army the rate was 1.4 per 1,000, and the Air Force and Marine Corps were each at 1 per 1,000 members. By 1988, 6,000 personnel and recruits had tested positive.

To the shock of some in the military community, the infected included not only members of elite combat units, including the 82nd Airborne Division, but also high-ranking officers, including active-duty colonels and senior Pentagon staff officers.

Meanwhile, the armed forces continued to investigate suspected gays and lesbians. At Parris Island, S.C., the Marines' recruit training camp for the Eastern United States, 18 female drill instructors and other personnel were discharged by 1988. Three women were convicted at courts-martial of sodomy, obstruction of justice and other offenses and were sentenced to prison. Most officers caught up in the probe were allowed to resign, and other female Marines at the base quit rather than face investigators and discharges — as many as 65 women in all.

The Parris Island cases, taking place as the gay-rights movement grew in strength and as the AIDS epidemic gave new prominence to all issues involving homosexuals, helped build opposition to the military ban.

In late 1988, the National Gay and Lesbian Task Force, the National Organization for Women, Women's Equity Action League, the Lesbian-Gay Rights Project of the American Civil Liberties Union and the Military Law Project of the National Lawyers Guild joined forces to create the Gay and Lesbian Military Freedom Project. The organization was designed to stand behind gays in the military and to press for an end to the ban and associated rules.

'Don't Ask, Don't Tell'

Homosexual-rights organizations were also expanding their national political presence. During the 1992 presidential campaign, Democrat Clinton bid for gay support against incumbent President George H. W. Bush by promising repeatedly to lift the ban on gays and lesbians in the military.[44]

Following his victory, Clinton restated his commitment. "I don't think [sexual] status alone, in the absence of some destructive behavior, should disqualify people," he told reporters following a Veterans Day speech to active-duty and retired officers.[45]

Within days, military opposition began building. Gen. Colin Powell, chairman of the Joint Chiefs of Staff, told reporters: "The military leaders in the armed forces of the United States — the Joint Chiefs of Staff and the senior commanders — continue to believe strongly that the presence of homosexuals within the armed forces would be prejudicial to good order and discipline."[46]

Similar attitudes were heard lower in the ranks and in veterans' organizations. Politicians weighed in against using the military for what they termed social experimentation. Clinton — whose record of having avoided service in Vietnam was enough by itself to chill relations with the military and veterans' groups — showed himself open to compromise. In January 1993, he gave his newly appointed defense secretary, Les Aspin, until July 15 to draft an executive order ending "discrimination on the basis of sexual orientation in determining who may serve in the armed forces."[47]

As part of the same compromise, the Joint Chiefs agreed to stop asking about sexual orientation during the enlistment process. And Congress abstained from immediately passing legislation to retain the ban on enlisting homosexuals.

The Senate and House then launched four months of hearings. Midway through the process, Senate Armed Services Committee Chairman Sam Nunn, D-Ga., disclosed that lawmakers were leaning toward what he described as a "don't ask, don't tell" policy — an approach at which Clinton had hinted in his emphasis on ending discrimination based on "sexual orientation."

Essentially, the emerging congressional consensus would halt the questioning of potential enlistees about their sexual orientation. Gay and lesbian recruits could keep their homosexuality private. Those who didn't would be barred from service or discharged if already serving. The measure also would continue the ban on homosexual activity by anyone actively serving in the military, which covered behavior at any time, regardless of whether the service member was on base or on leave.

President Clinton accepted that approach. In a July 19, 1993, announcement he added that a declaration of homosexuality by a service member would create a presumption that he or she planned to "engage in prohibited conduct."[48] But the presumption would be "rebuttable." That is, the service member could present evidence that he or she had no intention of having sex.[49]

The power of sexual desire aside, the drawing of a line between orientation and conduct was more complicated than might have seemed at first. Under some definitions, "sexual orientation" includes behavior.

Regulations on discharge specify what a service member could show to fight a proposed discharge for homosexual conduct. He or she could try to prove that

the acts broke with customary behavior and are unlikely to recur; that no force or coercion was involved; that other circumstances make retaining the service member important to the military; or that the member doesn't have the "propensity or intent" to engage in homosexual acts.[50]

Wartime Controversies

Lulls in the debate over gays serving in the U.S. military have been only temporary. Confusion and complications have abounded within the military. On the one hand, regulations require respecting sexual privacy while homosexual conduct and declarations of homosexuality are grounds for discharge.

"The balance that the policy strikes … has posed a challenge to the Services," a Pentagon report said in 1998, using a classic bureaucratic code word ("challenge") for "major problem."[51]

The report also acknowledged that the number of discharges rose after the new law and policy took effect. After dropping sharply in the early 1980s, discharges of homosexuals rose from 597 in 1994 to 997 in 1997.[52]

Examining discharges closely, military researchers found that more than 80 percent followed declarations of homosexuality, rather than the discovery of sexual acts. Questions could still be raised about the circumstances in which service members declared their sexuality. But the report said the military services "believe" the statements were given voluntarily. Most of the declarations were given during the first years of service.[53]

In 1999, the murder of a gay soldier at Ft. Campbell, Ky., the home base of the 101st Airborne Division, raised questions about whether soldiers were being harassed due to sexual orientation. After the bludgeoning death of Pfc. Barry L. Winchell by a fellow soldier, investigators found that commanders had ignored reports that Winchell was being harassed over his presumed sexuality.[54]

Apparently prompted in part by Winchell's killing, discharges continued to increase. In June 2001, Pentagon figures showed the highest number of discharges since "don't ask, don't tell" took effect — 1,212 during the previous year.[55]

Three months later, when the military went on a war footing after the Sept. 11 terrorist attacks, the issue of gays and lesbians in the armed forces might have been expected to fade. Instead, a new element was added to the controversy. Opponents of the ban asked whether the armed forces could afford to shed personnel qualified in all respects except for sexual orientation. But supporters of prohibition said wartime was the worst time to tinker with social changes in the ranks.

Even before the war in Iraq began in 2003, the dismissal of nine service members training mostly as Arabic linguists — a language skill in short supply in the military — focused attention on whether the ban is practical in wartime.[56]

In 2005, the Center for the Study of Sexual Minorities in the Military (the Palm Center's earlier name) found that 20 Arabic and Farsi linguists or linguists in training had been discharged between 1998 and 2004.[57]

Supporters of the gay ban said the discharges showed the weakness of the "don't ask, don't tell" policy and its prohibition of any questions concerning a military volunteer's sexuality. "Resources unfortunately were used to train young people who were not eligible to be in the military," Donnelly, of the Center on Military Readiness, told The Associated Press.[58]

CURRENT SITUATION

Strategic Differences

Advocates of allowing gays to serve in the military may agree on the ultimate goal — but not on how to reach it. President Obama, for instance, wants Congress to repeal the 1993 law banning homosexuality in the armed forces. Congress passed the law, so Congress must undo it, he reasons.

But gay-ban opponents at the University of California's Palm Center say the congressional route is a dead end, at least for now.

"We don't think there is any chance of getting legislation through Congress any time soon," says Aaron Belkin, the center's director. "The issue in Congress is completely stalled."

Instead, he and five colleagues argued in a paper last May, the president should use authority granted him by the so-called "stop loss" law to halt sexuality-based discharges of military personnel. As the Palm Center team analyzes the law and related statutes, the president is authorized to prevent discharges during periods of national emergency if it is found that keeping personnel from leaving is essential to national security.[59] The liberal Center for American Progress advocates the same strategy.

Such a move, Belkin says, would show opponents that allowing gays and lesbians to remain in the ranks does no harm. With that result established, he says, "Politically and operationally, it would be extremely difficult to get this toothpaste back in the tube."

Remaking military policy by executive fiat would eventually make congressional action easier, not harder, he argues, although repealing the law would be necessary eventually. "It doesn't take any political capital to sign an order because the issue is polling at 75 percent in favor," he says, citing recent surveys.[60]

Ban supporter Donnelly at the Center on Military Readiness says bypassing the political process would be "outrageous," and an admission of desperation. "I don't think the president is politically unwise enough to do something like that."

The Palm Center also sees the proposed move as a way of short-circuiting Pentagon opposition, she notes. Indeed, a follow-up paper by the center said: "The legislative process would open a can of worms by allowing military leaders to testify at hearings and forge alliances with opponents on the Hill. A swift executive order would eliminate opportunities for them to resist."[61]

The Washington-based Servicemembers Legal Defense Network, however, views congressional action as the only practical approach — and one with excellent prospects. "We're looking at the next 12 months for repeal," says Kevin Nix, the network's communications director. That time frame would put the matter before the Democratic-controlled 111th Congress, which runs through 2010.

Congressional-strategy advocates say hearings expected later this year will create new legislative momentum by providing a national forum for evidence of the practical and moral benefits of opening the armed forces to gays.

By early September, however, no dates had been set for the hearings. On the House side, an aide to Armed Services Committee Chairman Ike Skelton, D-Mo., said the panel is unlikely to take up the issue until a new under secretary for personnel and readiness has been allowed to settle into the position. The Senate Armed Services Committee hasn't set a date either. Chairman Carl Levin, D-Mich., has said he would hold a hearing in the fall.

Should the U.S. follow the example of nations that allow gays to openly serve in the military?

YES

Rep. Patrick J. Murphy, D-Pa.
Veteran of Iraq War and sponsor of a bill to prohibit sexuality-based discrimination in the military

Written for *CQ Researcher*, September 2009

Our troops are currently fighting in two wars in Iraq and Afghanistan. These men and women in our military are stretched dangerously thin. Yet since "don't ask, don't tell" (DADT) took effect in 1993, more than 13,000 honorable men and women — the equivalent of over three and a half combat brigades — have been discharged from our armed forces.

They were removed not for any misconduct, but simply because they are gay.

I frequently hear the criticism about whether we should be using other countries' armed forces as an example for our military, but it rings false. Our heroes in uniform are the best fighting force in the world, plain and simple. Overturning DADT is about making decisions that allow our military to perform at its peak and keep our country safe.

Opponents of lifting the ban argue that allowing gays and lesbians to serve openly would be detrimental to unit cohesion and morale. As a former Army officer, that is an insult to me, and, more importantly, to my fellow soldiers still serving. In Iraq, my men and I didn't care whether a soldier was gay or straight or about their race, creed or color. We cared about completing our mission with honor and getting every member of our unit home alive.

More than 20 nations, including Great Britain and Israel, allow gays and lesbians to openly serve without any detrimental impact on unit cohesion. Believe me, our heroes in uniform are the best fighting force in the world, and just as professional as those of our strongest allies. What's more, we serve alongside these allies in numerous missions throughout the world every day.

The policy isn't working for our armed forces, it hurts our military readiness and it is making us less safe. Among the 13,000 service members who have been discharged are 800 "mission critical" individuals, including fighter pilots, battlefield medics and even Arabic and Farsi translators who are key to the success of our missions in Iraq and Afghanistan. Former senior military leaders agree that this policy is hurting our national security.

To remove honorable, talented and committed Americans from serving our country is contrary to the values that our military fights for and our nation holds dear. My time in Bosnia and Iraq taught me that our military needs and deserves the best and the brightest that are willing to serve. Overturning this wrongful policy is a long-overdue step toward this goal.

NO

Elaine Donnelly
President, Center on Military Readiness

Written for *CQ Researcher*, September 2009

The experiences of 25 countries without official restrictions on professed homosexuals in their militaries — out of 200 nations around the globe — do not justify repeal of the 1993 law that is usually mislabeled "don't ask, don't tell." With all due respect to Austria, Belgium, Czech Republic, Denmark, Estonia, Finland, France (excepting the elite Foreign Legion), Ireland, Italy, Lithuania, Luxembourg, New Zealand, Norway, Slovenia, South Africa, Spain, Sweden, Switzerland and Uruguay — none of these 19 nations' small militaries bear burdens and responsibilities comparable to ours. The U.S. Army, Navy, Air Force and Marines accept far-away, months-long deployments, and our direct ground combat battalions, special operations forces and submarines require living in conditions with little or no privacy.

Service in the Israeli Defense Force is mandatory, but deployments and housing conditions are not comparable to that of America's military. Germany has conscription for both civilian and military duties, but homosexuals serve primarily in civilian capacities. The Dutch, Australian and Canadian forces represent countries with social cultures far more liberal than ours. These forces primarily deploy for support or peacekeeping missions that depend on the nearby presence of U.S. forces. Most homosexuals are discrete, but American gay activists are demanding special status, mandatory "diversity" training and "zero tolerance" of dissent in order to enforce full acceptance.

That leaves the U.K., which demonstrated fundamental differences with American culture when it capitulated to a 1999 European Court of Human Rights order to accommodate homosexuals in the military. Not surprisingly, British activists claim success, since same-sex partners get to live in military family housing and march in gay pride parades. The Ministry of Defence meets regularly with lesbian, gay, bisexual and transgender (LGBT) activists to discuss further advances. Imagine the reaction of American military families — and our Muslim allies in Iraq and Afghanistan — if Pentagon leaders followed Britain's example in promoting the LGBT agenda.

Conspicuously missing from the list of 25 gay-friendly militaries are potential adversaries China, North Korea and Iran. Their 3.8 million combined forces (not counting reserves) represent more than twice as many active-duty personnel as the 25 foreign countries with gays in their militaries (1.7 million).

Congress is being asked to impose a risky military social experiment that has not been duplicated anywhere else in the world. Instead, Congress should focus on national security, putting the needs of our military first.

"We firmly believe that repeal can get done in this Congress," Nix says.

Fehrenbach's Case

Meanwhile, the case of Lt. Col. Fehrenbach is serving a strategic purpose for those on both sides of the conflict over gays in the military. His exemplary record and his ease in front of TV cameras made him a natural spokesman for gays and lesbians in the military facing exclusion.

"My initial reaction was, I just wanted … a quick, quiet, fair, honorable discharge," the officer told liberal TV commentator Rachel Maddow on May 19. "But the more I thought about it, about how wrong this policy is, I thought that I had to fight it and, perhaps with my unique perspective, I could speak out and help other people."[62]

Advocates of the ban don't challenge Fehrenbach's record, which includes an Air Medal for heroism during the invasion of Iraq in 2003. But the circumstances of his involuntary outing, they say, show that gays want better-than-equal treatment.

A heterosexual male in equivalent circumstances would have been discharged, argues gay-prohibition advocate Donnelly. "It [would have been] the end of his career," she said, based on her reading of the *Idaho Statesman* account of the circumstances that led to Fehrenbach's recommended discharge.

But Fehrenbach's lawyer, Emily Hecht of the Servicemembers Legal Defense Network, says, "If the same, exact allegation had been made against an Air Force officer by a woman and had been investigated in exactly the same manner with exactly the same findings and outcome — that officer would have gone back to work."

An expert with no connection to the case agrees. "A male officer, meeting a woman online, a meeting leading to non-adulterous, non-commercial fornication, would not be discharged," says Eugene R. Fidell, president of the National Institute of Military Justice and a senior research scholar and lecturer at Yale Law School. But that might not be the case, he adds, if nude pictures were an element of the case. The *Statesman* said Fehrenbach's one-time partner had seen nude photos of the officer, though the circumstances are unclear.

Fehrenbach's lawyer declines to discuss that issue. But the formal discharge notification cites only one justification for discharge: "I am taking this action because you did … engage in homosexual acts with another man," wrote U.S. Air Force Lt. Gen. Norman R. Seip, commander of the 12th Air Force.[63]

As Fehrenbach waits for Air Force Secretary Donley to decide his case, the Servicemembers Legal Defense Network notes that the Air Force discharge board found no "aggravating circumstances" that would trigger a less-than-honorable discharge.

Following Orders

On one point, everyone agrees: The U.S. military isn't a debating society. "The president has made his strategic intent very clear," Adm. Mike Mullen, chairman of the Joint Chiefs of Staff, said in August. "He wants to see this law changed.… When the law changes, if we get to that point, we'll carry out the law."[64]

"The units aren't going to collapse, and the mission will still get done," Maue said at the Chicago debate in June. "People can suck up an awful lot in the military and make sure the mission still gets done."[65] But, he adds, "That doesn't mean it's a good policy."

"The military is a culture of discipline, of obedience, of professional service members," said Nathaniel Frank, a senior research fellow at the Palm Center and Maue's debate opponent. "It is a real vote of no confidence in them to suggest that telling the truth, that allowing our law, our policy and our rhetoric to catch up with the reality on the ground is somehow going to … undermine cohesion."[66]

Throughout the debate, some advocates and experts have cited racial desegregation as a precedent for abolishing long-held traditions that seemed inviolable. Desegregation began with an executive order by President Harry S. Truman in 1948, according to the Army, though racially integrated units weren't formed until the Korean War in the early 1950s.[67]

"That experience shows that it is possible to change how troops behave toward previously excluded (and despised) minority groups, even if underlying attitudes toward those groups change very little," the RAND Corp. think tank said in a 2000 summary of a massive 1993 study that it performed for the Pentagon on the question of open homosexuals in the military. "When integration was mandated in the late 1940s, it was said to be inconsistent with prevailing societal norms and likely to create tensions and disruptions in military units and to impair combat effectiveness."[68]

RAND acknowledged that race and sexuality weren't directly analogous. That point was driven home in 1993 by then chairman of the Joint Chiefs of Staff Powell, who had experienced the gradual desegregation of the armed forces and was the highest-ranking African-American in the history of the American military.

"Open homosexuality in units is not to the benefit of our military force, and it is something quite different than the acceptance of benign characteristics such as color or race or background," Powell told the House Armed Services Committee in 1993, in remarks that were widely reported and influential.[69]

By 2008, Powell and former Georgia Sen. Nunn, who helped to devise the "don't ask, don't tell" system, had moderated their views. "I think it's appropriate to review it now," Nunn said at a conference in Aspen, Colo. "We certainly are having a lot of people who are getting out because of it. But on the other hand, there are an awful lot of people that may be affected the other way."[70]

"It's been 15 years, and attitudes have changed," Powell said during a television interview. "Let's review it, but I'm not going to make a judgment as to whether it should be overturned until I hear from the chairman of the Joint Chiefs of Staff … the commanders who are responsible for our armed forces in a time of war."[71]

Powell explained that the military has special characteristics. "It is not like any other institution in our system," Powell said. "You are told who you will live with. You are told who you will share your most intimate accommodations with. You are told whether you will live or die."

The Center on Military Readiness'Donnelly acknowledges that obedience is part of that culture. "Could we do it?" she asks. "Sure. Should we? Absolutely not. It would absolutely harm good order and morale. Military culture has to be taught, reinforced. Anybody who doesn't support a new policy — they're the ones who'd be out of bounds."

Opponents of the ban acknowledge that service members who oppose lifting the prohibition would have to adjust. "People come into the Army with values they learned in their own homes and communities, and we hope they hold onto those values," says retired Army Lt. Gen. Claudia Kennedy, who advocates training that would explain a new policy as a matter of extending

anti-discrimination regulations. "But there are Army values we teach them in the first eight weeks, and you are not allowed to ignore the lawful orders of those above you."

OUTLOOK
Question of Timing

Throughout American society — in the workplace, in movies, in television and in many families — homosexuality is being accepted to an extent that would have been hard to imagine when the Stonewall Riots exploded 40 years ago. But whether those societal changes make a similar transformation in the armed forces inevitable is by no means a decided issue.

Former Senate Armed Services Committee Chairman Nunn predicted last year that the prohibition would be lifted. "If you're going to have open service by gays and lesbians — and I think we will eventually have that — the question's timing."[72] What that timing might be, he didn't say.

Donnelly of the Center for Military Readiness argues that the demands of military life and combat weigh more heavily than social changes among civilians. "The claim that younger generations see this differently only applies to the civilian world," she says. "As long as we have need for a strong, cohesive military, as long as we have a need to engage an enemy in land combat, and as long as human beings remain the flawed beings that they are, I believe the law will indeed still be there."

The present campaign to lift the ban is "very intense," she acknowledges. But if it fails to succeed within the next two years, she predicts the ban is likely to remain in place for the foreseeable future.

Some critics of the ban agree. "Unless there's a major change of mood among our legislative leaders, or a president who is willing to make a big ruckus — a ruckus that likely would be extremely unpopular in parts of the country — how is it going to get changed?" asks Fidell, the military law expert at Yale.

Barring an intense campaign by a high-ranking former military figure, he says, only one other scenario would offer the possibility of change — but it wouldn't be a happy scenario. "If, God forbid, we had a substantially increased need for personnel, and everything was on the table other than conscription, that could be a galvanizing event. But I hope we don't face something like that, and I think our leaders are intelligent enough not to get us into that position."

Organizations leading the charge for allowing open gays and lesbians to serve argue that the combination of societal change, public support for opening the ranks and growing realization that homosexuals are already serving make change inevitable.

But immediate change is unlikely, say some critics of prohibition. "It's not the end of the game," says retired Lt. Gen. Kennedy. "Don't anyone come out of the closet right now. I don't think the individual sacrifice of careers is necessary to make it happen."

A loosening of restrictions — by executive order as the Palm Center advocates — would make plain that no catastrophe would ensue, says the center's Frank. "A few months down the road, [the president] could go to Congress and say, 'We have an official reality of officially gay service, and the sky hasn't fallen' — which is my prediction — 'and now, Congress, let's act to get this off the books.'"

So far Obama has rejected that approach. But even if he takes what some see as a slower approach, one expert says the ban's days are numbered.

"I cannot see it lasting 10 years," says Segal, the University of Maryland military sociologist, "because of the rate of social change. Society is becoming more tolerant at a rapid rate. The military reflects society, and the generational shift takes place more rapidly in the military than outside, because careers are shorter."

Change would have to come from Congress, whose members often enjoy long careers. But, Segal argues, citing what he calls growing public support for gays in the military, "If Congress sees its constituents moving in that direction, they're not likely to lead by example, but they are likely to follow public opinion."

NOTES

1. Dan Popkey, "Gay Boise Air Force Pilot 'outed' by false accusation," *Idaho Statesman*, Aug. 23, 2009, www.idahostatesman.com/273/story/874410.html.
2. 10 U.S. Code Sect. 654, http://law.justia.com/us/codes/title10/10usc654.html.
3. David Burrelli, " 'Don't Ask, Don't Tell:' The Law and Military Policy on Same-Sex Behavior," Congressional Research Service, Aug. 14, 2009, p. 10, www.fas.org/sgp/crs/misc/R40782.pdf.
4. "Report: More gay linguists discharged than first thought," The Associated Press, Jan. 13, 2005, www.msnbc.msn.com/id/6824206. Carol J. Williams, "No rush to end 'don't ask, don't tell,' " *Los Angeles Times*, May 20, 2009, p. A18.
5. Lymari Morales, "Conservatives Shift in Favor of Openly Gay Service Members," Gallup, June 4, 2009, www.gallup.com/poll/120764/conservatives-shift-favor-openly-gay-service-members.aspx. "More favor keeping gay ban in place," *USA Today*, Feb. 3, 1993, p. A8.
6. James J. Linday, *et al.*, "Gays and The Military: A Bad Fit," *The Washington Post*, April 14, 2009, www.washingtonpost.com/wp-dyn/content/article/2009/04/14/AR2009041402704.html.
7. " 'Don't Ask, Don't Tell': The Struggle Continues," McCormick Freedom Museum, Chicago, June 20, 2009. Recordings of the debate are not available from open sources, but a summary by an unnamed museum staffer is accessible at www.facebook.com/note.php?note_id=128287001752.
8. "Remarks by the President at LGBT Pride Month Reception," White House, June 29, 2009, www.whitehouse.gov/the_press_office/Remarks-by-the-President-at-LGBT-Pride-Month-Reception/.
9. William Branigin, "Supreme Court Turns Down 'Don't Ask' Challenge," *The Washington Post*, June 8, 2009, www.washingtonpost.com/wp-dyn/content/article/2009/06/08/AR2009060801368.html.
10. Brendan McGarry, "Troops oppose repeal of 'don't ask,' " *Army Times*, Dec. 29, 2008, www.armytimes.com/news/2008/12/military_poll_main_122908; Brendan McGarry, "2008 Military Times Poll: Wary about Obama," *Army Times*, Jan. 7, 2009, www.armytimes.com/news/2008/12/military_poll_main_122908.
11. Quoted McGarry, in "Troops oppose…," *ibid.*
12. *Ibid.*
13. *Ibid.*

14. "104 Generals and Admirals: Gay Ban Must End," Palm Center, Nov. 17, 2008, www.palmcenter.org/files/active/0/104Generals11-17-08.pdf; John M. Shalikashvili, "Gays in the Military: Let the Evidence Speak," *The Washington Post*, June 19, 2009, p. A25.

15. Allan Bérubé, *Coming out Under Fire: The History of Gay Men and Women in World War Two* (1990), p. 15.

16. Charles Moskos Jr., "From Citizens' Army to Social Laboratory," in Wilbur J. Scott and Sandra Carson, Stanley, eds., *Gays and Lesbians in the Military: Issues, Concerns, and Contrasts* (1994), p. 53.

17. Douglas Martin, "Charles Moskos, Policy Adviser, Dies at 74," *The New York Times*, June 5, 2008, p. B7.

18. " 'Don't Ask, Don't Tell': The Struggle Continues," *op. cit.*

19. James Dao, "Ex-Soldier Gets Life Sentence for Iraq Murders," *The New York Times*, May 21, 2009, www.nytimes.com/2009/05/22/us/22soldier.html.

20. "House Armed Services Subcommittee on Military Personnel Holds Hearing on a Review of Don't Ask Don't Tell Policy," CQ Congressional Transcripts, July 23, 2008.

21. "Qualification Standards for Enlistment, Appointment, and Induction," Department of Defense, July 11, 2007, www.dtic.mil/whs/directives/corres/pdf/130426p.pdf; "Enlisted Administrative Separations," Department of Defense, Aug. 28, 2008, www.dtic.mil/whs/directives/corres/pdf/133214p.pdf; "Separation of Regular and Reserve Commissioned Officers," Dec. 11, 2008, www.dtic.mil/whs/directives/corres/pdf/133601p.pdf.

22. Jody Feder, " 'Don't Ask, Don't Tell': A Legal Analysis," Congressional Research Service, Sept. 2, 2009, p. 2, www.fas.org/sgp/crs/misc/R40795.pdf.

23. "Enlisted Administrative Separations," and "Separation of Regular and Reserve...," *op. cit.*

24. Feder, *op. cit.*, p. 2.

25. "Press Conference with Secretary Gates En Route From Germany," U.S. Department of Defense, News Transcript, June 30, 2009, www.defenselink.mil/transcripts/transcript.aspx?transcriptid=4441.

26. "False 'National Security' Argument for Gays in the Military," Center for Military Readiness, September 2009, http://cmrlink.org/CMRDocuments/DoDDischarges-090809.pdf.

27. Nathaniel Frank, *Unfriendly Fire: How the Gay Ban Undermines the Military and Weakens America* (2009).

28. " 'Don't Ask, Don't Tell': The Struggle Continues...," *op. cit.*

29. "Homosexuals in the Military: Policies and Practices of Foreign Countries," General Accounting Office [later renamed Government Accountability Office], June, 1993, p. 3, http://archive.gao.gov/t2pbat5/149440.pdf.

30. *Ibid.*, pp. 3-4.

31. "Sexual Orientation and U.S. Military Personnel Policy: Options and Assessment," RAND (prepared for the office of the Secretary of Defense), 1993, p. xix, www.rand.org/pubs/monograph_reports/MR323/index.html.

32. "Countries That Allow Military Service by Openly Gay People," Palm Center, June, 2009, www.palm-center.org/files/active/0/CountriesWithoutBan.pdf.

33. Quoted in David Crary, "U.S. Allies Embrace Gay Military Personnel," The Associated Press, www.huffingtonpost.com/2009/07/13/us-allies-embrace-gay-mil_n_231075.html.

34. *Ibid.*

35. Reuven Gal, "Gays in the Military: Policies and Practices in the Israeli Defense Forces," in Scott and Carson, *op. cit.*, p. 181.

36. Moskos, *op. cit.*

37. Except where otherwise indicated, material on World War II in this subsection is drawn from Bérubé, *op. cit.*, and "Sexual Orientation and U.S. Military Personnel Policy...," *op. cit.*

38. "World War II: Women and the War," Women in Military Service for America Memorial Foundation Inc., undated, www.womensmemorial.org/H&C/History/wwii.html.

39. Randy Shilts, *Conduct Unbecoming: Gays & Lesbians in the U.S. Military* (2005), p. 425.

40. *Ibid.*

41. Quoted in Edward D. Sargent, "Homosexuals Protest At Bolling Over Probe," *The Washington Post*, Dec. 4, 1983, p. B3.

42. *Bowers v. Hardwick*, 478 U.S. 186 (1986). The Supreme Court overturned *Bowers* in its 2003 decision in *Lawrence v. Texas*. See www.law.cornell.edu/supct/html/historics/USSC_CR_0478_0186_ZS.html. Majority opinion quoted in Stuart Taylor Jr., "High Court, 5-4, Says States Have the Right to Outlaw Private Homosexual Acts," *The New York Times*, July 1, 1986, p. A1. Burger opinion quoted in Shilts, *op. cit.*, p. 540.

43. Burrelli, *op. cit.*

44. Curtis Wilkie, "Harvard tosses warmup queries to Clinton on eve of N.H. debate," *Boston Globe*, Oct. 31, 1991, p. A22; Gwen Ifill, "Clinton's Platform Gets Tryouts Before Friends," *The New York Times*, May 20, 1992, p. A21. Except where otherwise indicated, this subsection draws on Burrelli, *op. cit.*

45. Quoted in Michael Weisskopf, "Clinton Backs Early Military Retirement," *The Washington Post*, Nov. 12, 1992, p. A9.

46. John H. Cushman Jr., "Top Military Leaders Object to Lifting Homosexual Ban," *The New York Times*, Nov. 14, 1992, p. A9.

47. "Sexual Orientation and U.S. Military Personnel Policy," *op. cit.*, p. xvii.

48. Burrelli, *op. cit.*, p. 1.

49. *Ibid.*

50. "Enlisted Administrative Separations," and "Separation of Regular and Reserve Commissioned Officers," *op. cit.*

51. Quoted in "Review of the Effectiveness of the Application and Enforcement of the Department's Policy on Homosexual Conduct in the Military," Office of the Under Secretary of Defense (Personnel and Readiness), April, 1998, p. 2, www.dtic.mil/cgi-bin/GetTRDoc?AD=ADA353107&Location=U2&doc=GetTRDoc.pdf.

52. *Ibid.*

53. *Ibid.*

54. Elaine Sciolino, "Army Exonerates Officers in Slaying of Gay Private," *The New York Times*, July 19, 2000, p. A16.

55. Paul Richter, "Dismissal of Gays Rises in the Military," *The New York Times*, June 2, 2001, p. A12.

56. John Johnson, "9 Gay Linguists Discharged From the Army," *Los Angeles Times*, Nov. 16, 2002, p. B10.

57. "Report: More gay linguists discharged than first thought," *op. cit.*

58. *Ibid.*

59. Aaron Belkin, *et al.*, "How to End 'Don't Ask, Don't Tell': A Roadmap of Political, Legal, Regulatory, and Organizational Steps to Equal Treatment," Palm Center, May, 2009, www.palmcenter.org/files/active/0/Executive-Order-on-Gay-Troops-final.pdf. For background on stop-loss, see Pamela M. Prah, "Draft Debates," *CQ Researcher*, Aug. 19, 2005, pp. 661-684. Lawrence J. Korb, *et al.*, "Ending 'Don't Ask, Don't Tell': Practical Steps to Repeal the Ban on Openly Gay Men and Women in the U.S. Military," Center for American Progress, June 2009, www.americanprogress.org/issues/2009/06/dont_ask_dont_tell.html.

60. Morales, *op. cit.*

61. Aaron Belkin, "Self-Inflicted Wound: How and Why Gays Give the White House a Free Pass on 'Don't Ask, Don't Tell,'" Palm Center, July 27, 2009, www.palmcenter.org/files/active/0/SelfInflictedWound.pdf.

62. "Lt. Col. Victor Fehrenbach Discusses His Discharge Notice With Rachel Maddow," msnbc.com, May 19, 2009.

63. "Memorandum for Lt. Col. Victor J. Fehrenbach," Department of the Air Force, Headquarters of the 12th Air Force, Sept. 12, 2008, made available by Servicemembers Legal Defense Network.

64. Chairman's podcast, http://dodvclips.mil/index.jsp?auto_band=x&rf=sv&fr_story=FRdamp359676Ch.

65. " 'Don't Ask, Don't Tell:' The Struggle Continues," *op. cit.*

66. *Ibid.*

67. Gerry J. Gilmore, "Truman's Military Desegregation Order Reflects American Values, Gates Says," American Forces Press Service, July 23, 2008, www.defenselink.mil/news/newsarticle.aspx?id=50583.

"Sexual Orientation and U.S. Military Personnel Policy....," *op. cit.*, p. 20.

68. "Changing the Policy Toward Homosexuals in the U.S. Military," RAND Research Brief, 2000, www.rand.org/pubs/research_briefs/RB7537/index1.html.

69. "Statement by Secretary of Defense Les Aspin [and Powell] Before the House Armed Services Committee," July 21, 1993, http://dont.stanford.edu/regulations/aspin.pdf.

70. Jim Galloway, "Nunn: Open service for gays to come 'eventually,' " *Atlanta Journal-Constitution*, July 9, 2008.

71. "Colin Powell Interview," Global Public Square [TV], Dec. 14, 2008.

72. Galloway, *op. cit.*

BIBLIOGRAPHY

Books

Bérubé, Allan, *Coming Out Under Fire: The History of Gay Men and Women in World War Two*, Free Press, 1990.
This meticulously documented, groundbreaking classic was written by a founder of the San Francisco Lesbian and Gay History Project, who died in 2007.

Scott, Wilbur J., and Sandra Carson Stanley, *Gays and Lesbians in the Military: Issues, Concerns, and Contrasts*, Aldine de Gruyter, 1994.
The issues explored in this compilation — which emphasizes work by academics, including Charles Moskos, originator of "don't ask, don't tell" — remain current.

Shilts, Randy, *Conduct Unbecoming: Gays & Lesbians in the U.S. Military*, St. Martin's Press, 2005 edition.
Based on hundreds of interviews and documents, this lengthy but highly readable narrative focuses on the period during and after the Vietnam War; written by a journalist and author (now deceased) acclaimed for coverage of the onset of the AIDS crisis.

Articles

Brachear, Manya A., "Evangelicals fear new president," *Chicago Tribune*, Dec. 19, 2008, p. A6.
Fear that Obama might lift the military ban on open homosexuals adds to concerns about the incoming administration among socially conservative Christians.

Bumiller, Elisabeth, "In Military, New Debate Over Policy Toward Gays," *The New York Times*, May 1, 2009, p. A14.
A *Times* correspondent reports from the U.S. Military Academy at West Point on nuanced opinions about the possible end of the ban on open gays and lesbians.

Scarborough, Rowan, "Obama to delay repeal of 'don't ask, don't tell,' " *The Washington Times*, Nov. 21, 2008, p. A1.
An early and prescient report predicts that the Obama administration would not be pushing early to repeal the ban on gays in the military.

Stolberg, Sheryl Gay, "Gay Issues in View, Obama Is Pressed to Engage," *The New York Times*, May 7, 2009, p. A1.
Five months into the new administration, gay and lesbian political activists were sensing a lack of urgency by the new administration concerning homosexuals in the military and other matters of concern to them.

Vuoto, Grace, "Is Obama administration listening to the troops?," *The Washington Times*, July 30, 2009, p. B2.
An online survey by the Military Officers Association showed majority support for maintaining the ban, but the association removed the results from its Web site without explanation.

Reports and Studies

"Changing the Policy Toward Homosexuals in the U.S. Military," RAND, 2000, www.rand.org/pubs/research_briefs/RB7537/index1.html.
A Defense research think tank summarized a massive 1993 report that concluded that lifting the ban on gays serving openly in the military would not degrade military effectiveness.

"Homosexuals in the Military: Policies and Practices of Foreign Countries," General Accounting Office (now the Government Accountability Office), June 1993, http://archive.gao.gov/t2pbat5/149440.pdf.
Congress' investigative arm studied an issue that remains hotly debated, concluding that countries that allowed

homosexuals in their militaries reported no problems — a conclusion that prohibition supporters argue is irrelevant to the U.S. armed forces.

Burrelli, David F., " 'Don't Ask, Don't Tell': The Law and Military Policy on Same-Sex Behavior," Congressional Research Service, Aug. 14, 2009, www .fas.org/sgp/crs/misc/R40782.pdf.
The nonpartisan agency examines the legislative history and practical effects of the 1993 law and regulations on open homosexuals serving in the military.

Donnelly, Elaine, "Constructing the Co-Ed Military," Duke Journal of Gender Law & Policy, June 18, 2007, www.law.duke.edu/journals/cite.php?14+Duke+J.+Gender+L.+&+Pol%2527y+815.
A leading advocate of maintaining the ban on gays in the military provides a detailed explanation of her position.

Feder, Jody, " 'Don't Ask, Don't Tell': A Legal Analysis," Congressional Research Service, Sept. 2, 2009, www.fas.org/sgp/crs/misc/R40795.pdf.
The report focuses on the meaning, interpretation and legal support for the 1993 law and regulations.

Moradi, Bonnie, and Laura Miller, "Attitudes of Iraq and Afghanistan War Veterans Toward Gay and Lesbian Service Members," Palm Center, July 2009, www.palmcenter.org/files/active/0MoradiMillerAttitudesofIraqandAfghanistanWarVeterans.pdf.
Researchers find declining support in military ranks for the ban on homosexuals serving in the military. Data is based on an online survey — which ban supporters call an inadequate source.

For More Information

Center for Military Readiness, P.O. Box 51600, Livonia, MI 48151; (202) 347-5333; http://cmrlink.org. An advocacy organization providing material supporting maintenance of the ban on gays in the military.

Federation of American Scientists, 1725 DeSales St., N.W., Washington, DC 20036; (202) 546-3300; www.fas.org/sgp/crs/index.html. Posts Congressional Research Service (CRS) studies, which are not provided to the public.

Flag & General Officers For the Military, http://flagandgeneralofficersforthemilitary.com. Represents senior military retirees, who maintain close ties to the Center for Military Readiness.

Palm Center, University of California, Santa Barbara, CA 93106; (805) 893-5664; www.palmcenter.org. Leading think tank for studies seeking to show the ban is militarily ineffective and unjust.

Servicemembers Legal Defense Network, P.O. Box 65301, Washington, DC 20035; (202) 328-3244; www.sldn.org. Represents gay and lesbian military personnel facing discharge and other actions based on their sexuality.

VoteVets.org, 303 Park Ave. So., New York, NY 10010; (646) 415-8429; www.votevets.org. Iraq and Afghanistan veterans who advocate repealing the prohibition on gays and lesbians in the military.

6

Government and Religion

Thomas J. Billitteri

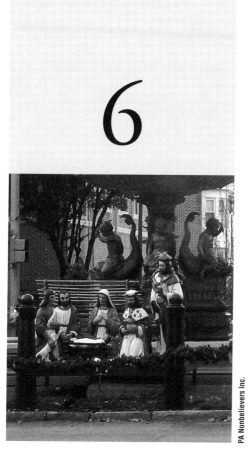

A Nativity scene in the town square in Chambersburg, Pa., during the 2009 holiday season was ordered removed by city officials. Conflicts over government and religion are as old as the nation itself, and new religion cases are coming before the U.S. Supreme Court.

PA Nonbelievers Inc.

From *CQ Researcher*, January 15, 2010.

In Chambersburg, Pa., this past holiday season the borough council removed a Nativity scene from the town square rather than bow to a non-believer's request to display an atheist symbol nearby. Protesters urged the council to reconsider. "This country was founded on Christian ethics," a pastor declared, adding, "I don't want our rights taken away as Americans."[1]

The crèche conflict was a small skirmish in a big, decades-long culture war over government and religion and the role of faith in civil society. The fighting shows no sign of abating as new cases come before the U.S. Supreme Court and fresh disputes arise over the use of government money for faith-based social-service programs. At the heart of the battle lies the question of whether the United States was formed as a Christian nation, as many conservatives contend, or whether the Founders meant to build a high wall of separation between church and state. (*See box on First Amendment, p. 129.*)

As unrelenting as the controversies remain, the search for common ground continues. On Jan. 12 a diverse group of secular and religious leaders — including Jews, Muslims and Christian evangelicals — released what was billed as "the most comprehensive joint statement of current law to date on legal issues dividing church and state." Produced by Wake Forest University's Center for Religion and Public Affairs, the 32-page document addresses issues ranging from whether elected officials may discuss their personal religious beliefs while operating in their official capacities to whether government property can be used for religious events.[2]

Among recent church-state battles:

- The Freedom From Religion Foundation, which represents atheists and agnostics, has sued to block a congressionally approved "In God We Trust" inscription above the entrance to the new visitor center at the U.S. Capitol.

The foundation's co-president, Annie Laurie Gaylor, called the engraving "an affront to the 15 percent of Americans who do not believe in God," adding, "Imagine if it said, 'In Allah We Trust,' how many Americans would be offended, and rightly so."[3]

But Sen. Jim DeMint, R-S.C., who pushed for the inscription, said, "The Founders based the Constitution and our laws on religious faith and principles that clear the way for individual freedom."[4]

- Efforts by Catholic bishops to block expansion of federal subsidies for abortion under new health-care legislation have sparked recriminations from liberal Democrats. "To limit our teaching or governing to what the state is not interested in would be to betray both the Constitution … and, much more importantly, the Lord Himself," said Cardinal Francis George, president of the U.S. Conference of Catholic Bishops.[5] But Rep. Lynn Woolsey, D-Calif., co-chair of the Congressional Progressive Caucus, suggested the bishops' "political hardball" was cause to question the church's tax-exempt status.[6]
- Intelligence reports written for former Defense Secretary Donald Rumsfeld and other officials contained cover sheets with biblical quotations, according to *GQ* magazine, which suggested that some in the Pentagon worried that if the covers were leaked, they could reinforce perceptions that the United States was fighting a war against Islam.[7] More broadly, publication of the cover sheets "may raise more questions about the proper role of religion in the military, and whether a Christian-influenced culture, rather than a neutral one, permeated some corners of the military," *The New York Times* noted. It cited earlier incidents including posting of a "Team Jesus" locker-room banner by an Air Force Academy coach and appearances by an Army general before evangelicals in which he compared the war against Islamic militants to a fight against Satan.[8]

The divide over religion and government is set against a shifting landscape of beliefs and religious affiliations among Americans. A 2007 survey by the First Amendment Center found that 65 percent of Americans believe the Founders intended the United States to be a Christian nation and that 55 percent think the Constitution establishes a Christian nation.[9]

Yet the share of Americans who profess to be Christians has been shrinking. The latest American Religious Identification Survey, conducted at Trinity College, found that 76 percent identified themselves as Christian in 2008, compared with 86 percent in 1990, and that 15 percent claimed no religious preference, up from 8 percent in 1990.[10]

The debate over the nation's ideological and religious roots often turns on hotly contested historical words and writings that include statements from the Founders, the Supreme Court and the French thinker Alexis de Tocqueville. For instance, those who say the Founders intentionally built a high wall between church and state often cite a 1797 U.S. anti-piracy treaty with Tripoli stating that "the government of the United States of America is not in any sense founded on the Christian Religion."[11] Those on the other side of the church-state divide often point to Supreme Court Justice David J. Brewer's comment in an 1892 decision that "this is a Christian nation."[12] (*See "At Issue," p. 141.*)

While history provides ammunition in the culture wars, however, it is policy issues such as gay marriage and stem-cell research, constitutional decisions by the courts and the actions of elected officials that keep new battles brewing.

When President Obama declared in Turkey last year that "we do not consider ourselves a Christian nation or a Jewish nation or Muslim nation" but a "nation of citizens who are bound by ideals and a set of values," outrage erupted in conservative circles.[13] Obama "was fundamentally misleading about the nature of America," former Republican House Speaker Newt Gingrich, R-Ga., said on Fox News. Sean Hannity, a co-host on the conservative network, said Obama is "out of touch with the principles that have made this country great."[14]

And when Republican Sen. John McCain, R-Ariz., declared during his recent White House bid that "since this nation was founded primarily on Christian principles, personally, I prefer someone who has a grounding in my faith" to be president, conservatives praised him while the left exploded in fury. "How can we trust someone to uphold the Constitution who doesn't even know what is in it?" declared Ira N. Forman, executive director of the National Jewish Democratic Council.[15]

The Supreme Court remains the final arbiter of the Constitution's meaning, but over the years the court has decided church-state cases in ways that sometimes have sown confusion. For example, in a pair of 2005 cases the court ruled that Ten Commandment displays in two Kentucky courthouses violated the First Amendment's prohibition against government establishment of religion but that a 40-year-old display of the Commandments at the Texas Capitol did not.

The two decisions are "difficult to reconcile," says Robert W. Tuttle, a professor of law and religion at the George Washington University Law School. Indeed, he says, "the opinions in those cases show the wide diversity of views on the court about the appropriate relationship between religion and civil government. It's often very hard to predict how a particular case will be decided."

That dynamic could well play out this year in two church-state cases before the court. In *Christian Legal Society v. Martinez,* the court must decide whether a public law school can deny student-funded meeting space and other benefits to a Christian student organization that requires members to affirm its core religious beliefs on homosexuality and other issues.[16] And in *Salazar v. Buono,* the court must decide whether an individual has legal standing to challenge the display of a cross on federal land as a violation of the Establishment Clause against government endorsement of religion and whether a congressional act directing that the property be transferred to a private party was a satisfactory remedy.[17]

Many Americans Don't Identify With Any Religion

The number of Americans who are non-theists or do not identify themselves with a religious group (collectively known as "Nones") more than doubled since 1990, to 34 million in 2008. When Americans who either don't know their religious identification or refuse to answer the question (and who resemble "Nones" in their beliefs) were included, the number rises to 46 million, or one in five adults, compared with one in 10 in 1990. The percentage of Christians dropped 10 points, to 76 percent, though the total number of Christians rose due to population increases and immigration.

Religious Self-Identification of the U.S. Adult Population, 1990-2008
(in millions)

	1990		2001		2008	
	Estimated No. of People	%	Estimated No. of People	%	Estimated No. of People	%
Total Christians	151.2	86.2	159.5	76.7	173.4	76.0
Other Religions	5.8	3.3	7.7	3.7	8.8	3.9
Nones	14.3	8.2	29.5	14.1	34.2	15.0
Don't know/ Refused	4.0	2.3	11.2	5.4	11.8	5.2
TOTAL	**175.4**	**100.0**	**207.9**	**100.0**	**228.2**	**100.0**

*Percentages may not add to 100 due to rounding.

Source: American Religious Identification Survey, Trinity College, March 2009

As controversy continues over the relationship between government and religion, here are some of the issues being debated:

Is the United States a "Christian nation"?

E. Ray Moore Jr., president of Frontline Ministries in Columbia, S.C., and a retired U.S. Army Reserve chaplain, has no doubts about the nation's religious roots. To buttress his case, he points to, among other things, Justice Brewer's 19th-century "Christian nation" words, the Constitution's reference to "in the Year of our Lord" and its exemption of Sundays for presidential action on bills.

"We were definitely founded as a Christian nation," says Moore, a Citadel graduate whose main focus these

Satisfaction With Religious Freedom Dropped

A majority of Americans feel the amount of religious freedom they have is "about right," but the percentage has dropped by 11 percentage points since 1997.

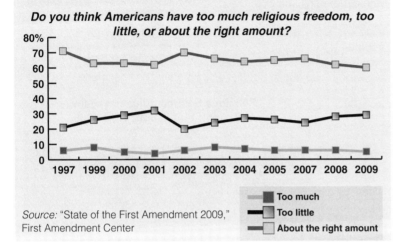

Do you think Americans have too much religious freedom, too little, or about the right amount?

Source: "State of the First Amendment 2009," First Amendment Center

- Too much
- Too little
- About the right amount

formed as a Christian nation, and there's vast evidence to the contrary," says the Rev. Barry Lynn, executive director of Americans United for Separation of Church and State, a Washington-based advocacy group.

Lynn cites the Tripoli treaty as one bit of evidence, along with opposition to a failed bid by patriot Patrick Henry to provide tax support for Christian churches. Lynn points out, too, that the Constitution has no references to God other than the "Year of our Lord" phrase, which he says was "grammatical" for the times and not "theological."

While the philosophical chords of the current church-state debate stretch back centuries, "it never gets settled because we don't have the kind of quality history education we ought to have in this country," Lynn

days is the Exodus Mandate Project, which urges Christians to withdraw their children from the public-school system and place them in Christian schools or home school them with a Christian emphasis. The public-school system, Moore argues, is "theologically and morally wrong, and it's failing academically."

Moore says the nation's Christian founding is "indisputable, incontrovertible and clear," though he notes that "elements of the Enlightenment" — an 18th-century philosophical movement that promoted rationalism — "were mixed in around the time of the Constitution."

Moore quotes the Old Testament book of Isaiah in arguing that church and state "need to be administratively separate," but he sees "no reason Christian values and beliefs cannot permeate public policy and law.

"We don't want the church as a body dictating to the government as an official body," he says. "But Christian principles and Christian morality should permeate government. The Ten Commandments should be foundational to all of our law."

Such views are anathema to those who advocate a high wall between religion and government. "There is absolutely no historical evidence for the view that we were

argues. "New generations grow up willing to believe any nonsense that is promoted that fits in with their vague sense that somehow religion is the cornerstone of the founding of the country."

But some scholars argue that both the Religious Right and secular left are sometimes at fault for oversimplifying history.

"I write as a Christian, and I teach at a church-related Christian school," says John Fea, an associate professor of American history at Messiah College, in Grantham, Pa., "but I don't think the evidence is there to suggest [the United States was founded] as a uniquely Christian nation. Most of the Constitution does not mention God at all, and when it does it talks about religious freedom or the Establishment Clause. So to suggest that in some ways [the Founders] were trying to create a republic that somehow uniquely privileged Christianity is simply ahistorical. There is simply no solid evidence to support that. There are many on the Christian right who claim to be historians who are playing fast and loose with the historical record."

Still, Fea says, "If you say the United States was founded at a time when a Christian culture dominated the British colonies or the new republic, you would be hard to argue with. There are many on the [secular left] who simply will not look at the historical record to see that all of these Founding Fathers believed religion needed to play a dominant role in the republic in order for it to survive. If you're going to create a republic of virtuous citizens — people who are willing to sacrifice their own self-interest for some greater good — the best system that teaches those principles is religion, in some cases particularly Christianity."

Ibrahim Hooper, national communications director for the Council on American-Islamic Relations, a Washington-based civil rights and advocacy group, argues that while "we are not a Christian nation, the history, the founding, the ethos of the nation is infused with Christianity, and that's not a bad thing. The Founders and those who have been important in American history have often been practicing Christians, and it's only natural that Christianity have an impact on our national experience in the same way a Muslim-majority nation is impacted by Islam — maybe not to that extent, but in the same general direction."

Still, Hooper says, "It's a stretch to go from saying that we have a historical base in Christianity to saying that theology has to impact our nation's policies. I wouldn't say that for Christianity or Islam or Judaism or any faith. We're a secular nation, and while people who make laws might draw inspiration from their spiritual beliefs, I don't think it's appropriate that the laws themselves would have a religious base."

Galen Carey, director of government affairs at the National Association of Evangelicals, a conservative group representing over 45,000 local churches in more than 40 denominations, says that although "a substantial majority" of U.S. citizens "are Christians and have been throughout our history, that doesn't make the country Christian."

Adds Carey, "The country has been shaped to a significant extent by people who are Christian, and many of

Understanding the First Amendment

The first 10 amendments to the U.S. Constitution are known as the Bill of Rights. The First Amendment includes two "religion clauses" — the so-called "Establishment Clause" limiting government promotion of religion and the "Free Exercise Clause" limiting the government's power to interfere with expressions of religious belief.

Experts say the two clauses are in tension with each other and that the U.S. Supreme Court has charted an uncertain course in applying each clause to specific situations.

The Bill of Rights was submitted to the states for ratification on Sept. 25, 1789, and adopted on Dec. 15, 1791, after ratification by three-fourths of the states.

The First Amendment
"Congress shall make no law respecting an establishment of religion, or prohibiting the free exercise thereof; or abridging the freedom of speech, or of the press; or the right of the people peaceably to assemble, and to petition the Government for a redress of grievances."

Getty Images/Chip Somodevilla

the ideals and values of our nation can be derived from Christian sources, though many others can be derived from other [sources]. We would say the people are Christians, nations are not Christian. People can participate in the political process and should try to contribute to the public discourse. But it's quite important that all people have religious freedom."

Tuttle, the George Washington University law professor, says that while the United States is predominantly a Christian nation from a demographic point of reference, it is "implausible" to claim the nation is Christian "in the sense of a system of government.

"The federal government was specifically not designed as a community of the saints or anything like that," he says. "It was designed to fulfill a very specific and secular purpose, which is governance of a diverse political community." It wasn't designed to be a government "that would have responsibility for all aspects of citizens' lives, including their religious lives."

Even so, Tuttle says, it is important to distinguish between the early philosophical foundation of the federal government and that of the states. When it comes to discussing religion and state government, he says, "it's a more complicated story." Well into the 19th century, Tuttle says, many states lacked constitutional provisions barring government establishment of religion, and some states imposed religious tests to determine who could hold office well into the 20th century.

It was only in the 1940s that the Supreme Court declared that the First Amendment's Free Exercise and Establishment clauses apply to the states. Even so, religious tests for public office persisted. A Maryland law requiring officeholders to declare a belief in God survived until 1961, when, in *Torcaso v. Watkins*, the U.S. Supreme Court struck it down.[18]

Should religious displays be allowed on public land?

Despite the Constitution's prohibition against government "establishment of religion," most Americans don't seem bothered when crèches, menorahs and other such religious symbols appear on public property. A 2008 Rasmussen poll found that 74 percent of adults thought such displays should be allowed.[19] The Pew Research Center has found similar popular support.[20]

Yet, the presence of religious symbols on government property has a long and sometimes conflicted history in the courts.

In 1980 the Supreme Court ruled that a Kentucky law requiring public schools to post a copy of the Ten Commandments in all classrooms was a violation of the Establishment Clause.[21] But in 1984, the court said it was constitutional for a Nativity scene to be displayed in a Rhode Island town square.[22]

"Since these two decisions in the 1980s, the Supreme Court and lower federal courts have issued somewhat unpredictable rulings, approving some religious displays while ordering others to be removed," the Pew Forum on Religion & Public Life noted in a 2007 review of religious display cases. (*See "Background" for a discussion of other key cases, p. 133.*)

Added Pew, "[t]he lack of clear guidelines reflects deep divisions within the Supreme Court itself. Some justices are committed to strict church-state separation and tend to rule that any government-sponsored religious display violates the Establishment Clause. These same justices also believe that, in some circumstances, the Establishment Clause may forbid private citizens

from placing religious displays on public property." But "[o]ther members of the court read the Establishment Clause far more narrowly, arguing that it leaves ample room for religion in the public square." Meanwhile, other justices have taken a middle path, arguing that "a religious display placed in a public space violates the Establishment Clause only when it conveys the message that the government is endorsing a religious truth."[23]

Some activists firmly oppose religious displays. Lynn of Americans United for Separation of Church and State, for example, argues that "a bright-line rule would make sense: If it's a government-sponsored event, icon or symbol, it should not be religious. When you put up a manger scene at Christmas and it's the government that owns it, it looks like the government is endorsing that religion," he argues.

Hooper, the Council on American-Islamic Relations spokesman, takes a broader view, arguing that "as long as everyone has equal access" to a site, "we're not opposed to it."

"It's really up to each religious community to make sure it has equal access," he adds. "We've dealt with this in the past as an organization. If a local library has a Christmas display, we don't ask people to go and tell them to take down the Christmas display. We say, 'Look, reserve it for the next time Ramadan comes along.' It's in our court, really."

Carey of the National Association of Evangelicals says that while the group is "not overly concerned about most of these issues," many cases concerning religious displays "do raise constitutional issues and need to be carefully studied on their merits.

"So much depends on context," says Carey, "There's a difference between 'In God We Trust' on our money or having a Nativity scene at city hall. You look at the context in the community."

What's needed is a "common sense" approach to the issue of religious displays, Carey argues. "We don't want the government to be in the position of establishing or favoring a particular religion." Many displays don't do much to do that, Carey says, "but if something were endorsing and furthering a particular religion, we would not be in favor of that."

In the crèche conflict in Chambersburg, Pa., the Nativity scene had been displayed for years in the town's Memorial Square, and some residents believe that's where it should have remained. "Jesus is the reason for the season," resident Kelly Spinner told a local media outlet. "They're taking that reminder away from us. I don't think it's fair. What's next? Santa Claus? A Christmas tree?"[24]

The council president, Bill McLaughlin, argued that Chambersburg was "a victim of the tyranny of the minority," adding that "the Constitution guarantees 'freedom of religion' " but says nothing about "freedom from religion."[25]

But a local Jewish resident noted that council members let him put a "Seasons Greetings" sign incorporating religious symbols from a variety of backgrounds on the town square in 1996. "You really can't pick and choose what goes up there," he said. "Once you let one group in, whether it's Christians, Jews, Muslims, then you have to let other groups in also."[26]

Lynn, commenting broadly on the issue of religious displays and not the Chambersburg flap, says that "if you truly say 'this courthouse lawn is open to everybody' — if you're really willing to do that — that I think the Constitution does permit, but I think that's a dopey idea." In places that have opened public spaces to displays of all persuasion, he says, "you get a cluttered lawn. People trip over stuff on their way to pay their parking tickets."

Among the most contentious religious-display issues in recent years has been the placement of religious mottoes on automobile license plates.[27] The Indiana legislature approved state-issued plates bearing the motto "In God We Trust" in 2006, and Florida followed suit in 2008.

In November, a federal judge ruled that South Carolina couldn't issue plates showing the image of a cross in front of a stained-glass window and bearing the words "I believe." U.S. District Judge Cameron Currie said a law approving the plates amounted to a "state endorsement not only of religion in general, but of a specific sect in particular."

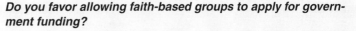

GOP Support for Faith-Based Funding Drops

In a philosophical role reversal, the percentage of Republicans who now favor government funding for faith-based groups has dropped over the past eight years while support has increased among Democrats, who were once less enthusiastic about government support.

Do you favor allowing faith-based groups to apply for government funding?

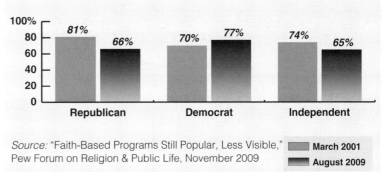

Source: "Faith-Based Programs Still Popular, Less Visible," Pew Forum on Religion & Public Life, November 2009

March 2001
August 2009

Lt. Gov. André Bauer, who had advocated the bill approving the plates, called the ruling "another attack on Christianity" and said Currie was a "liberal judge appointed by [President] Bill Clinton."[28]

But Currie ruled correctly in an "absolutely clear-cut" case," said Thomas Crocker, an assistant professor at the University of South Carolina Law School. Her decision was "not out to denigrate religion, but it's out of a historical understanding that problems for both politics and religion can flow from the state's entanglement with religious practices."[29]

Does government funding of faith-based programs violate the Constitution?

In 2001 President George W. Bush formed his "Faith-Based Initiative," designed to funnel federal taxpayer dollars to religious groups that provide social services ranging from homeless shelters to teen sex education.[30] Critics argued that the program threatened church-state separation, but defenders maintained that nothing in the Constitution prohibits church-sponsored social services from competing on a level playing field for government money.

Obama has vowed to build on the Bush program, saying during his 2008 campaign that "a partnership between

A long-running legal fight over the so-called Mojave Cross honoring World War I veterans will be decided by the U.S. Supreme Court. The cross was originally erected in the Mojave National Preserve in a remote part of California in 1934 by the Veterans of Foreign Wars and replaced several times by private parties.

the White House and grassroots groups — both faith-based and secular" — remained "a good idea." But Obama vowed to end one of the most controversial aspects of the Bush faith-based program: allowing religious organizations receiving government grants and contracts to hire workers on the basis of religion.

"If you get a federal grant, you can't use that grant money to proselytize to the people you help, and you can't discriminate against them — or against the people you hire — on the basis of their religion," Obama told an Ohio audience in 2008.[31]

But a year after taking office, Obama's own Office of Faith-Based and Neighborhood Partnerships has had a low profile. The president has not formally disavowed a 2002 Bush-era White House directive and a 2007 Justice Department memo arguing that hiring can be based on belief, though an Obama executive order says the head of the faith-based office may seek the Justice Department's opinion on individual cases.

The issue has led to a heated debate within religious and legal circles.

"[T]his issue has been controversial because it raises a direct conflict between two opposing viewpoints on church-state relations," Ira Lupu, a professor at the George Washington University Law School, told the Pew Research Center. "One viewpoint is that hiring on the basis of religion is discriminatory and that the government should never subsidize such discrimination. The opposing viewpoint, held by many faith-based groups, is that to maintain the distinctive character and nature of their respective religious missions, these groups must take religion into account when hiring employees."[32]

A group of 58 religious, educational, civil rights, labor and health groups has urged U.S. Attorney General Eric Holder to direct the Office of Legal Counsel to review and withdraw the 2007 memo, arguing that the document is based on an "erroneous" interpretation of the 1993 Religious Freedom Restoration Act "and threatens core civil rights and religious-freedom protections."[33] The 1993 act says the government may not "substantially burden" a person's free exercise of religion "without compelling justification."

Some religious groups argue that without the ability to hire according to beliefs, their social-service work will be undermined.

If organizations can't hire staff that share their mission, they will quickly lose their identity, says Carey of the National Association of Evangelicals, who worked in faith-based social-service programs for more than 25 years. He adds, "Nobody is telling Planned Parenthood they should have to hire staff that don't believe in contraception, so nobody should tell a religious group that they shouldn't also hire people who share" its religious beliefs.

Writing this fall on a *National Catholic Reporter* blog site, Michael Sean Winters, author of *Left at the Altar: How the Democrats Lost the Catholics and How the Catholics Can Save the Democrats*, argued that "if the government chooses to give funds to a Catholic organization because of the services it provides, that does not mean the government should be entitled to tell us whom we can hire.... A Catholic social-service provider may be efficient, it may be effective, it may alleviate suffering and do a lot of good, but unless its work springs from a shared faith commitment, it is not meaningfully Catholic."

But fellow blogger Maureen Fiedler, host of the public radio show "Interfaith Voices" and a member of the Sisters of Loretto religious community, argued that "if one is hiring a drug counselor, or someone to run a soup kitchen or a job-training office, it's a neutral job — religiously speaking — and there is no reason to discriminate on the basis of religion. In fact, since such salaries are paid with tax dollars, there is every reason not to discriminate."

George Washington University's Tuttle said he would be surprised if the Obama administration tackles the hiring question. "Why step in that one?" he asks rhetorically. The issue's complex and controversial nature "more than anything else explains the incredibly low profile" of Obama's faith-based program, Tuttle says. "What they've said is that the Justice Department is going to look at this and make decisions on a case-by-case basis."

Lupu, in an interview, said a strong political aspect of the debate over faith-based hiring has to do with some religious groups' beliefs about homosexuality.

"One of the deep undercurrents [of the issue] is a gay-rights question," Lupu says. "That's what's been driving the more heated politics of it, because part of what faith-based groups — some of them — don't want to do is have to hire without regard to sexual orientation. That is sort of the political undercurrent to this and has been all along."

Alongside the hiring question is the issue of how far religious groups receiving government funds can go in mixing religious activity or symbols into government-funded social-service programs. Critics argue that regulations on proselytizing that were issued by the Bush administration are unclear and ambiguous. An advisory task force composed of people with diverse views on church-state matters is reviewing the regulations and is expected to offer clarifications to Obama's Faith-Based and Neighborhood Partnerships program in mid-February, though it remains unclear whether the president will adopt the task force's recommendations.

Still, says Melissa Rogers, director of the Center for Religion and Public Affairs at the Wake Forest University School of Divinity and a task force member, "So far as I know, this is the first time a president or any governmental body has brought people together who have serious differences on certain church-state issues and asked them to try to find some common ground in this area."

BACKGROUND

Early Conflict

Conflict over the relationship between religion and government is as old as the nation itself.

"When the Constitution was submitted to the American public, 'many pious people' complained that the document had slighted God, for it contained 'no recognition of his mercies to us … or even of his existence,' " the Library of Congress noted in an online presentation of documents related to religion and the founding of the republic.[34]

While Article VI bars religious tests for federal office-holders, the Constitution (not including the Bill of Rights) is otherwise silent on religion. One reason, the Library of Congress notes, is that "many delegates [to the Constitutional Convention] were committed federalists, who believed that the power to legislate on religion, if it existed at all, lay within the domain of the state, not the national, government." Moreover, the delegates thought introducing religion into the Constitution would be a "tactical mistake" because of religion's "politically controversial" nature, the library says.

Even so, many of the Founders embraced religious expression. For instance, George Washington, an Episcopal vestryman, said in his 1796 Farewell Address that "of all the dispositions and habits which lead to political prosperity, religion and morality are indispensable supports.… It is substantially true that virtue or morality is a necessary spring of popular government."[35] Benjamin Franklin, in a 1787 speech asking the constitutional convention to begin each daily session with prayers, argued "that God governs in the Affairs of Men."[36]

Ratification in 1791 of the Bill of Rights — and its First Amendment stating that "Congress shall make no law respecting an establishment of religion, or prohibiting the free exercise thereof" — placed religion front and center in the national psyche. With the Bill of Rights, "the opportunity for conflict between federal and state religion policies expanded considerably," law professors Lupu and Tuttle noted in a 2006 scholarly article.[37]

That conflict came to full fruition after the 1868 ratification of the Fourteenth Amendment, which applied the Bill of Rights to the states.

"With the Fourteenth Amendment in place, and a new national understanding of the role and the authority of the federal government in preserving national unity

CHRONOLOGY

1600s-1800s *Religious-freedom policies take shape as the colonies break away from Britain.*

1644 Roger Williams, theologian and Rhode Island founder, declares a "wall of separation" exists "between the garden of the church and the wilderness of the world."

1787 Benjamin Franklin asks Constitutional Convention to begin daily sessions with prayer.

1791 Bill of Rights ratified, including First Amendment.

1797 U.S. anti-piracy treaty with Tripoli states "the government of the United States of America is not in any sense founded on the Christian Religion."

1892 Supreme Court Justice David J. Brewer writes "this is a Christian nation."

1940s-1950s *First Amendment's religious guarantees applied to the states even as religion becomes more prevalent in public domain.*

1940 Supreme Court rules in *Cantwell v. Connecticut* that First Amendment's "Free Exercise Clause" applies to the states.

1947 Supreme Court applies "Establishment Clause" to state and local governments (*Everson v. Board of Education*).

1954 Congress inserts "under God" into Pledge of Allegiance.

1956 "E Pluribus Unum" is replaced as national motto with "In God We Trust."

1960s-1980s *Key Supreme Court decisions shape intersection of government and religion; Religious Right gains prominence in politics.*

1961 Supreme Court strikes down Maryland law requiring office-holders to declare a belief in God.

1962 Landmark Supreme Court ruling (*Engel v. Vitale*) holds it is unconstitutional for state officials to require an official prayer to be recited daily in public school classes.

1971 Supreme Court establishes three-part test to decide Establishment Clause conflicts.

1979 Televangelist Jerry Falwell forms Moral Majority, rallying evangelicals to political activism.

1980 Supreme Court strikes down Kentucky law requiring posting of Ten Commandments in public classrooms.

1984 Supreme Court rules that a Christmas display in a Rhode Island shopping district has a legitimate "secular purpose."

1988 Christian Coalition founder Pat Robertson unsuccessfully seeks Republican presidential nomination.

1990s-2008 *Influence of Religious Right grows in national politics.*

1992 Christian Coalition produces voter guides for conservative Christians.

1997 Supreme Court allows federal program under which public school teachers offer secular remedial instruction inside parochial schools.

2001 George W. Bush elected president with help from evangelical voters.... Bush forms "Faith-Based Initiative."

2005 Supreme Court rules in *McCreary County v. ACLU of Kentucky* that display of Ten Commandments in Kentucky courthouses is unconstitutional but says in *Van Orden v. Perry* that a Texas monument inscribed with the Commandments is not.

2008 Presidential candidate Barack Obama endorses government funding for faith-based social services but promises changes to Bush-era initiative.

2009-Present *New government/religion cases come before Supreme Court.*

2009 President Obama says "we do not consider ourselves a Christian nation or a Jewish nation or a Muslim nation." ... Catholic bishops oppose abortion funding in health-care overhaul.... Supreme Court rules the placement of a permanent religious monument in a public park is protected government speech (*Pleasant Grove City v. Summum*).

2010 Texas education board votes on textbook proposals shaped with help of religious conservatives.... Supreme Court hears cases on cross on public land, Christian student group at public law school.

and individual freedom, the stage was set for the ensuing struggle over federal limitations on state power to formulate religion policy," Lupu and Tuttle wrote.[38]

Even before the Fourteenth Amendment's passage, though, church-state conflicts roiled the nation.

Some of the conflicts arose as part of "a complicated story in relation to the Civil War about religion and totalitarianism," Tuttle explained in an interview. "The South was identifying itself more strongly as Christian, over and against the particular 'godless North,' and some in the North were characterizing the South as being absolutists," accusing the South of a "lack of religious liberty."

A swelling tide of Catholic migration from Europe in the 19th century also spurred religious tensions. "In some states, the separation of church and state as a concept came to the forefront in response to Roman Catholic immigration," Tuttle says. "Nativists embraced this because they saw themselves losing out demographically, and the idea of the separation of church and state was a way to make sure that they didn't live in Catholic-run communities."

In 1875, James G. Blaine, speaker of the U.S. House of Representatives, proposed a constitutional amendment that would have barred states from providing funds for religious education — notably Catholic schools. The proposal, denounced by Catholics, failed, but some three dozen states passed their own constitutional amendments prohibiting state funding of religious groups, including religious schools.[39]

Meanwhile, passage of the Fourteenth Amendment had set the stage for bitter battles over the First Amendment's religion provisions, though it took many years for those conflicts to be fully realized in the Supreme Court. At first, the Fourteenth Amendment's application of the Bill of Rights to the states focused mainly on economic rights and corporate issues, not religious and other civil liberties. In fact, only two cases involving the religious Establishment Clause — one in 1899 involving federal funding of a religiously owned and run hospital, the other in 1908 involving federal funding of a Catholic school serving Sioux Indians — came before the high court before the mid-20th century.[40]

Religion's New Role

But beginning in 1940 the conflict over government and religion began to escalate in the courts. In a landmark decision that year in *Cantwell v. Connecticut*, a case involving free-speech rights of Jehovah's Witnesses, the Supreme Court ruled 9-0 that the First Amendment's Free Exercise Clause applies to the states.[41]

Then, in 1947, in *Everson v. Board of Education*, the court applied the Establishment Clause to state and local governments, upholding a New Jersey law allowing local school boards to reimburse parents for the cost of sending their children to public or private schools — including religious ones — on buses operated by a public transportation system.[42] Significantly, all the justices agreed that the Establishment Clause erected a high barrier between church and state, though a 5-4 majority concluded that reimbursement for busing to religious schools was allowed.

Notably, the court in *Everson* resurrected a central image from the early days of the republic that lies at the center of today's debate over religion and government: "In the words of [Thomas] Jefferson," Justice Hugo Black wrote, "the clause against establishment of religion by law was intended to erect 'a wall of separation between church and state.' " Black added: "The First Amendment has erected a wall between church and state. That wall must be kept high and impregnable. We could not approve the slightest breach."[43]

Jefferson's phrase "is as familiar in today's political and judicial circles as the lyrics of a hit tune," noted James Hutson, chief of the Library of Congress Manuscript Division. "This phrase has become well-known because it is considered to explain (many would say, distort) the 'religion clause' of the First Amendment."[44]

Meanwhile, just as the *Cantwell* and *Everson* decisions helped thrust religion into the forefront of the debate over the meaning of the Constitution and Bill of Rights, post-World War II cultural and political trends elevated the role of religion in civil society.

In 1953, President Dwight D. Eisenhower helped inaugurate the Presidential Prayer Breakfast, a controversial annual political event that continues today under the name of the National Prayer Breakfast.[45] In 1954, during the darkest days of McCarthy-era anti-communist fervor, Congress inserted "under God" into the Pledge of Allegiance.[46] In 1955 Congress added "In God We Trust" to paper currency, and the following year it made those words the official national motto, replacing "E Pluribus Unum" (Out of Many, One).[47]

In 1960, Democratic presidential candidate John F. Kennedy sought to reassure conservative ministers and

As Texas Textbooks Go, So May Go the Nation

Conservatives seek more treatment of religion in government and history classes.

While the Supreme Court is the most high-profile venue for deliberations on religion and government, conflicts in the states also can be significant.

In Texas, for example, the Board of Education is revising the statewide K-12 social studies curriculum amid debates among board members and outside reviewers, including several prominent religious conservatives, over how big a role religion should play in the teaching of history.

The action follows the board's adoption last March of new science-curriculum standards that validated the teaching of evolution but opened the way for teachers to critically assess aspects of evolutionary theory.

Curriculum decisions in Texas are significant because of the influence the state — the nation's biggest textbook market — has on teaching materials elsewhere. Publishers often use Texas standards, revised every decade, to shape textbooks they sell nationwide.

For the social studies curriculum, moderate or liberal members of the 15-member Texas education board appointed three so-called "expert reviewers" to make individual recommendations on the proposed curriculum, and three such reviewers were named by social conservatives on the board.

Reviewers named by moderate or liberal board members are professors of history or education at universities in

Texas, including former state historian Jesus F. de la Teja, chairman of the Texas State University history department.

Conservative reviewers include David Barton, former vice chairman of the Texas Republican Party and founder of WallBuilders, a Texas group whose stated goals include "educating the nation concerning the Godly foundation of our country."[1] Another is Massachusetts-based Presbyterian minister Peter Marshall, who describes his ministry as "dedicated to helping to restore America to its Bible-based foundations."[2]

Groups of teachers and academics finished drafts of the social studies standards in November, and a public hearing on the drafts was held on Jan. 13, 2010. Some, but not all, of the reviewers' suggestions were adopted in the drafts, though the board has final say over the curriculum content, a board spokeswoman said. The board is to take a first vote on the standards after the public hearing. New textbooks are scheduled to be adopted in Texas in 2012.

At least three conservatives on the education board have pushed for more treatment of religion in government and history classes. For example, former Chairman Don McLeroy has sought a new standard "that describes the Judeo-Christian Bible influence on the founding documents." And Chairwoman Gail Lowe, along with board member Barbara Cargill, want U.S. history classes to cover the Great Awakening, a time of religious fervor in colonial

other Protestants that his Roman Catholic faith would not hamper his ability to run the country, saying that presidential decisions should not be "limited or conditioned by any religious oath, ritual or obligation."

"I believe in an America where the separation of church and state is absolute — where no Catholic prelate would tell the president (should he be Catholic) how to act, and no Protestant minister would tell his parishioners for whom to vote ... and where no man is denied public office merely because his religion differs from the president who might appoint him or the people who might elect him," Kennedy said.[48]

Issues surrounding politicians' and presidents' views of religion continue today.

Supreme Court Decisions

Another Kennedy — Rep. Patrick J. Kennedy, D-R.I., son of the late Sen. Edward M. Kennedy — said in November he had been instructed by the Catholic bishop of Providence to refrain from receiving Communion because of his position on abortion.[49]

And Obama, the first president to refer to "non-believers" in an inaugural speech, this year chose not to have a National Day of Prayer service in the White House, drawing criticism from religious conservatives.

"President [Harry S.] Truman signed the first National Prayer Day proclamation, and President [Ronald] Reagan made it a permanent occasion," a *Los Angeles Times* blog

America that some conservatives contend helped spur the colonies to seek independence. [3]

In an early recommendation advocating coverage of the Great Awakening, Marshall, the Presbyterian minister and curriculum reviewer, wrote that "the leveling effect of the Gospel preaching . . . created a revulsion against the superior attitudes of British aristocracy and a revolt against British tyranny."

"You can't properly tell American history unless you teach the biblical motivations of the people who discovered the country, like Christopher Columbus; the people that settled it, like the Pilgrims and Puritans; the people who formed government, like the Founding Fathers," Marshall said. "My point in all of this is that children of this nation need to be taught the truth about the biblical worldview. The influence of the Bible and the Christian faith is absolutely gigantic in American history." [4]

But critics lambasted the curriculum-review process. The Texas Freedom Network, which describes itself as "a mainstream voice to counter the Religious Right," accused the board of education of including on the curriculum-review panel "absurdly unqualified ideologues who are hostile to public education and argue that laws and public policies should be based on their narrow interpretations of the Bible." [5]

John Fea, an associate professor of American history at Messiah College, also expressed concern. "Some of these

Conservative curriculum reviewer David Barton is founder of WallBuilders.

Christian-right people have political power. As long as they use the past to promote their political agendas — and to me to not be very good historians in the process — this kind of stuff is going to find its way into textbooks, and it's going to be an ongoing debate. I worry about historians just maybe getting too tired and just giving in."

—Thomas J. Billitteri

---

[1] Barton is well-known in evangelical circles for speeches and books arguing that America was founded as a Christian nation, and his online biography, at www.wallbuilders.com/ABTbioDB.asp, describes him as an "expert in historical and constitutional issues." However, his work has been sharply criticized by some mainstream scholars. See, for example, Mark Lilla, "Essay: Church Meets State," *The New York Times*, May 15, 2005, http://query.nytimes.com/gst/fullpage.html?res=9403E1D9 1730F936A25756C0A9639C8B63.

[2] Peter Marshall Ministries, http://petermarshallministries.com.

[3] Terrence Stutz, "3 take issue with social studies proposal; conservatives want greater mention of religion in classes," *Dallas Morning News*, Oct. 16, 2009.

[4] Quoted in Gary Scharrer, "What did Founding Fathers believe?," *Houston Chronicle*, Sept. 28, 2009, www.chron.com/disp/story.mpl/ metropolitan/6640410.html.

[5] "SBOE-Appointed Social Studies 'Experts' Lack Credentials, Denounce Public Education, Support," press release, Texas Freedom Network, April 30, 2009, www.tfn.org/siteNews2?page=NewsArticle& id=5778.

---

noted. Under President George W. Bush, it added, the day — the first Thursday of May —"was a political event, confirming a conviction that religion was a core tenet of Republican politics."[50]

"At this time in our country's history, we would hope our president would recognize more fully the importance of prayer," said Shirley Dobson, chairman of the National Day of Prayer Task Force and wife of James Dobson, founder of the conservative group Focus on the Family.[51]

But White House press secretary Robert Gibbs said that while Obama would sign a proclamation to recognize the day, "Prayer is something that the president does every day. I think the president understands, in his own life and in his family's life, the role that prayer plays."[52]

While public actions — a president's words or actions, say, or the content of the Pledge of Allegiance — often draw controversy, many of the most momentous moves on the relationship between government and religion have continued to occur in the Supreme Court.

Over the past 50 years a long string of decisions has shaped the boundaries of government involvement in religion and the rights of citizens to express their beliefs in public settings and on public property. Among the most controversial have been school-prayer cases. In 1962, in *Engel v. Vitale*, the Supreme Court ruled that a state could not compose an official prayer — even a voluntary, nondenominational one — for recitation at the start of the school day. The next year, in *Abington School District*

The Family: "What they want is government by God."

Author Jeff Sharlet talks about the secretive Christian group.

Jeff Sharlet is the author of the book The Family: The Secret Fundamentalism at the Heart of American Power, *which examines a secretive Christian group known as The Family, founded in 1935 to oppose union activity and whose members and associates include lawmakers and prominent businessmen. The group runs a house in Washington, D.C., known as C Street, which has served as a meeting place and residence for politicians such as South Carolina Gov. Mark Sanford, Nevada Sen. John Ensign and former Rep. Chip Pickering of Mississippi, all of whom have been in the news over accusations of extramarital affairs. Sharlet is a contributing editor for* Harper's *and* Rolling Stone *and since 2003 has been an associate research scholar at New York University's Center for Religion and Media. He spoke by phone with* CQ Researcher *contributing writer Barbara Mantel.*

CQ: What is "The Family?"

JS: It's the oldest and most influential religious organization in Washington, D.C. It is not partisan, in that it includes both Republicans and Democrats, although it is 90 percent Republicans, but it is political.

CQ: What is its mission?

JS: What they want is government by God. It doesn't mean theocracy, and it doesn't mean conspiracy. Rather, it refers to a government by God-chosen elites. These people may still be elected, but they are to seek authority for all their decisions, not just on social issues but on every issue, through the filter of a theology *The Family* describes as "Jesus plus nothing." What this amounts to in the real world is religion behind closed doors, the closed doors of C Street, the closed doors of the Cedars, its headquarters in Arlington, Va., the closed doors of its "prayer cells" — that is The Family's term — around the world.

CQ: How is The Family organized?

JS: The Family is different from other religious organizations in that they are only interested in elites. At the heart of it is a core group, like a board of directors, and at the center of that is a man called Doug Coe, said to be closer to Jesus and thus to the heart of power than anyone else in the world.

CQ: The Family openly organizes the annual National Prayer Breakfast and weekly fellowship groups for members of Congress.

JS: Those are fairly innocuous, but they are seen within the group as recruiting tools to bring men into closer relationships with The Family, the spiritual tutelage of Doug Coe or another senior leader and eventually into active political

v. Schempp, it held that a public school district cannot require students to start the school day with Bible reading and prayer. Many other cases have followed.

In terms of the Establishment Clause and government support for faith-based organizations, one of the most important rulings came in 1971 in *Lemon v. Kurtzman*, in which the court struck down programs in two states that subsidized teacher salaries and provided other aid for instruction in secular subjects in parochial and other private schools.[53]

In *Lemon*, the court established a three-part test, known as the "*Lemon* test," to decide conflicts over the Establishment Clause. The court said that to be in compliance, a statute "must have a secular legislative purpose; second, its principal or primary effect must be one that neither advances nor inhibits religion … [and] finally, the statute must not foster 'an excessive government entanglement with religion.' "

"The *Lemon* test would become an extremely influential legal doctrine, governing not only cases involving government funding of religious institutions but also cases in which the government promoted religious messages," a 2009 report by the Pew Forum on Religion & Public Life noted. "Over the years, however, many justices have

work towards The Family's goals. The next level would be a prayer cell, which is a small, gender- and oftentimes class-segregated group that meets on a much more frequent basis to review every aspect of members' lives. The prayer cells are not to take political action as prayer cells, but action is expected to grow out of the relationships forged in these private meetings.

CQ: Who are members of The Family?

JS: Sen. Jim Inhofe, Sen. John Ensign, Sen. Sam Brownback, Sen. Bill Nelson, a Democrat, Congressmen Joe Pitts and Zach Wamp. And in business, I don't want to say they are members but people who are very involved are Dennis Bakke [CEO of Imagine Schools, a company that operates charter schools in 10 states] and Thomas Phillips, former head of Raytheon. Overseas, probably the most prominent member in the news today is Yoweri Museveni [the president of Uganda].

CQ: Does The Family have a political agenda?

JS: They say they have no political agenda other than putting all nations on a Jesus footing. But when we look at what they've done and what they do, we see a 75-year project that has tended toward economic privatization, deregulation, free markets at any cost and all with Washington as, what the founder [Abraham Vereide] called, the world's Christian capital.

Author Jeff Sharlet.

Jeff Sharlet

CQ: Can you give some examples?

JS: The Family's first project was to break the spine of organized labor in the Northwest, where they began. In 1959, they designated a young Haitian leader and began organizing U.S. support for him. That was Papa Doc [Duvalier]. When Suharto came to power in Indonesia, killing hundreds of thousands of his own citizens in a coup, The Family called it a spiritual revolution and sent delegations of congressmen who became his champions in Washington. They have functioned like a lobby without registering as a lobby, and whether you think they are of concern depends on whether you value transparency and accountability in government.

CQ: The Family's house on C Street, known as the C Street Center, had been registered as a church but lost its tax-exempt status last fall. What happened?

JS: For years, The Family was using the tax-exempt status of the C Street Center to subsidize congressmen with below-market rents and to bring them into an intense community for spiritual counseling, policy talk and biblical-worldview discipline. The problem with the C Street house is that they were financially helping these congressmen and not acknowledging it.

— Barbara Mantel

criticized the test because the court has often applied it to require a strict separation between church and state."[54]

Through the years, various Supreme Court justices have proposed alternative standards for Establishment Clause cases, including an "endorsement test" put forth by Justice Sandra Day O'Connor under which courts would determine "whether the government intends to convey a message of endorsement or disapproval of religion."[55]

And some have scorned the *Lemon* test, none more colorfully than Justice Antonin Scalia. "Like some ghoul in a late-night horror movie that repeatedly sits up in its grave and shuffles abroad, after being repeatedly killed and buried, *Lemon* stalks our Establishment Clause jurisprudence once again," he wrote in a 1993 concurring opinion. "I agree with the long list of constitutional scholars who have criticized *Lemon* and bemoaned the strange Establishment Clause geometry of crooked lines and wavering shapes its intermittent use has produced."[56]

In recent years, the Supreme Court has softened the strict church-state separation standards set down in the *Lemon* case. In 1997, in *Agostini v. Felton*, the court, with O'Connor writing the 5-4 majority opinion, overturned an earlier ruling and determined that a federal program under which public school teachers offered secular remedial instruction inside parochial schools did not violate the Establishment Clause.[57] "More generally," the decision "held that the government may directly provide aid to religious institutions when the aid is secular and the government provides safeguards to ensure that recipients use the aid for secular purposes," the Pew Forum on Religion & Public Life said.[58]

In 2000, the court upheld a federal program that allocated money for instructional material and equipment to public and private schools, including Catholic and other religiously affiliated ones.[59] And in 2002, with the late conservative Chief Justice William H. Rehnquist writing for a 5-4 majority, the court upheld an Ohio school-voucher program allowing low-income parents to send their children to participating public or private schools, most of them religious institutions.[60]

Meanwhile, in cases involving religious displays on public property, the court has rendered what many scholars say have been inconsistent rulings over the years.

In 1980 it ruled that a Kentucky law requiring the posting of the Ten Commandments in each public classroom violated the Establishment Clause.[61] But in 1984 it ruled that a Christmas display in a Rhode Island city's shopping district had a legitimate "secular purpose" despite inclusion of a Nativity scene alongside a Santa house and Christmas tree because the display portrayed the historical origins of the Christmas holiday.[62] Five years later the court said a stand-alone Nativity scene inside a Pittsburgh courthouse, bearing a banner declaring "Gloria in Excelsis Deo" (Glory to God in the Highest), violated the Establishment Clause.[63]

The picture of what is and isn't constitutional became cloudier still in 2005 when the court issued a pair of contrasting decisions on displays of the Commandments. In one 5-4 decision, the justices said a decades-old six-foot-tall Ten Commandments monument on the Texas Capitol grounds did not violate the Establishment Clause.[64] In a companion 5-4 ruling, they said displays of the Commandments at two courthouses in Kentucky did violate the clause.[65]

"To the extent that the decisions provided guidelines for the further cases that are all but certain to follow," Linda Greenhouse of *The New York Times* wrote, "it appeared to be that religious symbols that have been on display for many years, with little controversy, are likely to be upheld, while newer displays intended to advance a modern religious agenda will be met with suspicion and disfavor from the court."[66]

Significantly, Scalia — among the court's most conservative justices and one likely to figure prominently in the *Salazar v. Buono* and *Christian Legal Society* cases now before the court — used the 2005 cases to expand on his views of religion and government.

"[T]here is nothing unconstitutional in a State's favoring religion generally, honoring God through public prayer and acknowledgement, or, in a non-proselytizing manner,

> The picture of what is and isn't constitutional became cloudier still in 2005 when the court issued a pair of contrasting decisions on displays of the Ten Commandments.

venerating the Ten Commandments," Scalia wrote in a concurring opinion in the Texas case.

Scalia voiced similar views in a long interview last fall with *Hamodia*, which bills itself as "the newspaper of Torah Jewry."

"It has not been our American constitutional tradition, nor our social or legal tradition, to exclude religion from the public sphere," Scalia said. "Whatever the Establishment Clause means, it certainly does not mean that government cannot accommodate religion, and indeed favor religion. My court has a series of opinions that say that the Constitution requires neutrality on the part of the government, not just between denominations, not just between Protestants, Jews and Catholics, but neutrality between religion and non-religion. I do not believe that. That is not the American tradition."[67]

CURRENT SITUATION

Clarification or Confusion?

Two cases before the Supreme Court this year could help clarify the court's overall direction in issues involving religion — or perhaps leave the legal waters as murky as ever.

Is the United States a Christian nation?

YES
Lt. Col. E. Ray Moore
Chaplain, U.S. Army Reserve (Ret.),
President, Exodusmandate.org

Written for *CQ Researcher*, January 2010

Was America founded as a Christian nation? The answer was once self-evident and a resounding "Yes!" If you had posed this question to Americans 40 years ago, they would have said, "Of course," and looked askance at anyone who suggested otherwise. The fact that the question meets with doubt today proves that the secular revolution to "de-Christianize" America is succeeding.

The indisputable historic fact is that America's culture, laws and civil institutions were founded on Christian principles. The vast majority of the Founders professed the Christian faith. *The Church of the Holy Trinity v. United States,* decided by the Supreme Court in 1892, confirms this. It has faded from public memory and has been expunged from federal jurisprudence. Those who would know whether America was a Christian nation should revisit this case.

The Supreme Court's unanimous decision in *Holy Trinity* stated that the government could not prosecute the church for hiring a foreign pastor, even though federal law expressly forbade hiring immigrants. The court said blocking the hiring would restrict the freedom of the Christian Church and religion in general and would violate the First Amendment. Moreover, Justice David Brewer wrote that to do so would pit the federal government "against religion."

Brewer stated, "Churches and church organizations ... abound .... A multitude of charitable organizations exist ... under Christian auspices .... These add a volume of unofficial declarations to the mass of organic utterances that this is a Christian nation." Brewer concluded the American people had established civil orders in accord with the laws of God, including the right to promote the Christian religion without interference from civil government.

Christianity teaches, and most Christians support, a jurisdictional separation between church and state, but not separation of God and government. A secular state is not American, not Christian, nor wise. Civil government must obey God's laws.

The meaning of the First Amendment has been upended. Often the term "separation of church and state" is used to bludgeon people of religious faith. The First Amendment was adopted, however, to block the federal government from over-reaching into the religious realm, not to control the church. The "wall of separation" concept meant keeping the federal government out of the church, not keeping Christian values out of government.

Christian America gave us religious liberty and freedom of conscience. When the secular revolution is complete, that liberty will no longer exist.

NO
Herb Silverman
President, Secular Coalition for America

Written for *CQ Researcher*, January 2010

America is a Christian nation in the same way it is a white nation. The majority of Americans are white and Christian, but we are not now nor have we ever officially been a white or Christian nation. Those who believe otherwise might be harkening back to the first Europeans who settled here.

Unlike our 18th-century Founders like Washington, Jefferson and Madison, the Pilgrims and Puritans were religious dissenters from Europe who sought freedom of worship for their own versions of Christianity, but not for religious freedom of others. Most of our early colonies also made blasphemy a crime, an offense that could be punishable by death.

In the American Revolution of 1776, political leaders in the soon-to-be United States not only declared independence from England but also declared something even more radical — that "Governments are instituted among men deriving their just powers from the consent of the governed." Americans rejected kings with a God-given authority to rule through "divine right."

In coming up with this new federal government, a minority faction in the Constitutional Convention of 1787 sought some recognition of Christianity, but more enlightened Founders disagreed. That's why there are only three references to religion in the Constitution. Article 6 says no religious test shall ever be required as a qualification to any office; the First Amendment says Congress shall make no law respecting an establishment of religion and limits the government's power to interfere with expressions of religious belief.

Our Founders did not want the new federal government to meddle in religion. They wisely established a secular nation whose authority rests with "We the People" (the first three words of the U.S. Constitution) and not with "Thou the Deity." We the people are free to worship one, many or no gods.

Unambiguous language from our Founders really should settle this debate over whether America is a Christian nation. In 1797 the Treaty of Tripoli was negotiated by George Washington, signed by John Adams and ratified unanimously by the Senate. It stated in part: "The government of the United States is not in any sense founded on the Christian religion." I wonder what part of "not" that Christian-nation advocates don't understand.

There have always been people who erroneously believe the Founders intended to establish a Christian nation. But the Framers were careful and thoughtful writers. Had they wanted a Christian republic, it seems highly unlikely that they would somehow have forgotten to include their Christian intentions in the supreme law of the land. And I defy anyone to find the words "God" or "Jesus" in the Constitution.

In December the court agreed to decide whether a public law school can deny formal recognition to a Christian student group that denies voting membership to homosexuals and requires its members to subscribe to its core religious beliefs.[68]

The case, *Christian Legal Society v. Martinez*, sets questions of religious freedom and freedom of association against the ability of a state-funded university to impose policies barring discrimination on the basis of religion and sexual orientation, among other grounds. As noted in the *Los Angeles Times*, "the case could set new rules for campus groups that receive funding through fees paid by the students."[69]

A student chapter of the Christian Legal Society (CLS), which bills itself as "a nationwide association of Christian attorneys, law students, law professors and judges," was denied recognition by the University of California's Hastings College of the Law in San Francisco.

CLS "says it welcomes all students to participate in its activities," *The New York Times* reported, but it bars students from voting membership or leadership roles "unless they affirm what the group calls orthodox Christian beliefs and disavow 'unrepentant participation in or advocacy of a sexually immoral lifestyle,' " including " 'sexual conduct outside of marriage between a man and a woman.' "[70]

Hastings officially recognizes roughly 60 student groups, which must agree to the school's antidiscrimination policy.[71] In losing formal recognition, CLS lost, among other things, the right to use reserved meeting rooms and school-funded travel costs for CLS leaders to attend national meetings, according to the *Los Angeles Times*.[72]

In March 2009, the 9th U.S. Circuit Court of Appeals supported Hastings, declaring that the law school "imposes an open-membership rule on all student groups — all groups must accept all comers as voting members even if those individuals disagree with the mission of the group. The conditions on recognition are therefore viewpoint neutral and reasonable."[73]

But in 2006, the 7th U.S. Circuit Court of Appeals came to an opposite conclusion in a case dealing with a CLS chapter at the University of Southern Illinois law school. "One of [CLS's] beliefs is that sexual conduct outside of a traditional marriage is immoral," Judge Diane S. Sykes wrote for the court. "It would be difficult for

CLS to sincerely and effectively convey a message of disapproval of certain types of conduct if, at the same time, it must accept members who engage in that conduct. CLS's beliefs about sexual morality are among its defining values; forcing it to accept as members those who engage in or approve of homosexual conduct would cause the group as it currently identifies itself to cease to exist."[74]

In the *Hastings* case, Kim Colby, senior counsel with the Center for Law & Religious Freedom, CLS's advocacy division, said "public universities shouldn't single out Christian student groups for discrimination. All student groups have the right to associate with people of like mind and interest. We trust the Supreme Court will not allow Hastings to continue to deprive CLS of this right by forcing the group to abandon its identity as a Christian student organization."[75]

But Ethan P. Schulman, a San Francisco lawyer for Hastings, said the Christian students are free to meet informally on campus, "The real question," Schulman said, "is whether a law school is obliged to subsidize a group with student fees that is committed to discriminating against some students. If their position is accepted by the court, it could force universities across the country to subsidize discriminatory organizations, including possibly hate groups or extremist groups."[76]

Oral arguments in the case will likely occur in March, with a decision due by the end of June.

Site of the Cross

Separately, in *Salazar v. Buono*, the justices are considering a cross originally erected in the Mojave National Preserve in 1934 by the Veterans of Foreign Wars (VFW) and replaced several times by private parties. Frank Buono, a former Park Service employee and a Roman Catholic, claimed the cross violated the Establishment Clause. While not objecting to the cross' presence on government property, Buono expressed offense at its display on federal land not made available for groups and individuals to put up other religious displays. In 1999 the Park Service turned down a request to build a Buddhist shrine near the cross.

A federal court agreed with Buono's constitutional claim, and the cross was covered, but that wasn't the end of the controversy. While the case was pending in federal district court, Congress designated the site a national memorial and prohibited the cross from being taken apart using federal funds. A year later, Congress transferred the parcel on which the cross sits to the VFW in exchange for a nearby piece of privately owned land. Buono sought to enforce the federal court order and block the property swap. More legal action followed, culminating in the case moving to the Supreme Court.

The court's decision is unlikely to rest on whether the cross is a violation of the Establishment Clause, many legal experts say. Instead, they say it may rest on whether Buono had standing to sue — in other words, whether he was legally entitled to bring his case in the first place — or whether the land swap was a proper remedy to the constitutional issue posed by the presence of the cross on federal land.

Either approach could pose challenges to the court. Some legal analysts say they hope the justices don't use the case to wade into the standing-to-sue doctrine because that area of the law already is muddled and difficult to parse. On the other hand, if the court rules that the land transfer solved the constitutional problems posed by the cross, the justices will need to reconcile its reasoning with past Supreme Court action, observers say.

The court "will at the very least have to explain how its decision is not overly formalistic and how it takes account of how people who visit the area are likely to interpret things," Vikram David Amar, associate dean for academic affairs at the University of California, Davis, law school, wrote in a column for FindLaw.

Amar noted that in 1985, in *Wallace v. Jaffree*, the court struck down an Alabama statute allowing a moment of silent prayer in public schools.[77] The court invalidated the law, Amar wrote, "in part because many observers plausibly understood the statute to be a substitute for the state-sponsored prayer statutes" struck down by federal courts in prior years. If the court viewed the Alabama law as "an impermissible circumvention of constitutional principle," Amar continued, "then at least the court will have to explain why the transfer of land in the *Buono* case should not be understood similarly."[78]

OUTLOOK

Continuing Battles

Conflicts over government and religion, many experts say, are unlikely to end anytime soon, if ever.

"As long as this debate remains politicized, we're going to continue to do battle in the culture wars," says Messiah College's Fea.

Those battles are raging on a variety of fronts, from gay-marriage laws to the moral implications of climate-change policy. One of the most visible and recent battles has occurred over Washington's efforts to overhaul the health-care system. The nation's Roman Catholic bishops have fought to prevent federal funds from being used for abortions, and critics have accused the bishops of undermining health-care reform.

"Why is it that the bishops are more concerned with restricting millions of American women from making health-care decisions that are best for them and their families than they are with ensuring that millions of Americans — women, men, children, immigrants, the poor, the middle class — get much-needed health insurance?" former Maryland Lt. Gov. Kathleen Kennedy Townsend wrote in *Politico* in December. "As a Catholic, I dare say it's because the Conference of Catholic Bishops has lost its way."[79]

But Carey, at the National Association of Evangelicals, declared in a *Washington Post* column, "Bravo to the Catholic bishops for their heroic efforts to protect immigrants, the poor, the sick, the elderly and the unborn as the current health-care debate unfolds. Their unflagging support for a consistent ethic of life is a powerful witness to a nation which too often seems to have lost its moral compass."[80]

Along with battles over abortion and health care, the culture wars may well feature more conflict over government funding for programs provided by religious organizations. The Supreme Court could wind up deciding whether federal policies on faith-based funding allow government to pay directly for services that have religious content, such as rescue-mission soup kitchens or church-run homeless shelters that include group prayer or religious tracts as part of their services.

How the court would rule in such a case is "very hard to predict," given its ideological diversity, Tuttle of George Washington law school says. A big question, he says, is how Justice Anthony Kennedy, who is often viewed as a swing vote on highly controversial cases, would vote.

Perhaps the most worrisome dimension of the culture wars comes at the intersection of religion, foreign policy and national security.

Some worry, for example, that efforts to cast the United States as a "Christian nation" will fuel perceptions among the world's Muslims that anti-terrorism campaigns in Iraq, Afghanistan and elsewhere are aimed at suppressing Islam. And after Army psychiatrist Nidal Malik Hasan, a Muslim, allegedly killed 13 and wounded dozens at Fort Hood, Texas, in November, commanders expressed concern about a backlash against U.S. soldiers who are Muslim.

"[W]hat happened at Fort Hood was a tragedy, but I believe it would be an even greater tragedy if our diversity becomes a casualty here," said Gen. George Casey, chief of staff of the Army. "And it's not just about Muslims. We have a very diverse army. We have a very diverse society. And that gives us all strength."[81]

NOTES

1. Roscoe Barnes III, "Protesters want nativity scene back on square," Hanover, Pa., *Evening Sun*, Dec. 1, 2009, www.eveningsun.com/localnews/ci_13895803.

2. "Religious Expression in American Public Life: A Joint Statement of Current Law," Center for Religion and Public Affairs, Wake Forest University Divinity School, Jan. 12, 2010, http://divinity.wfu.edu/rpa/. For background, see the following *CQ Researcher* reports: David Masci, "Religion and Politics," July 30, 2004, pp. 637-660; Brian Hansen, "Religion in the Workplace," Aug. 23, 2002, pp. 649-672, and Patrick Marshall, "Religion in Schools," Jan. 12, 2001, pp. 1-24.

3. Peter Urban, "GOP defends 'God' at Capitol Visitor Center," Gannett Washington Bureau, Nov. 17, 2009, www.azcentral.com/news/articles/2009/11/17/20091117gan-visitorcenter-ON.html.

4. Quoted in Lindsay Perna, "Atheists sue to stop 'In God We Trust' in Capitol visitor's center," *USA Today*, July 17, 2009, www.usatoday.com/news/religion/2009-07-17-atheist-capitol_N.htm.

5. Julia Duin, "Cardinal: lobbying health reform is duty," *Washington Times*, Nov. 17, 2009, www.washingtontimes.com/news/2009/nov/17/cardinal-sees-health-care-stance-as-a-duty/.

6. Rep. Lynn Woolsey, "Woolsey: IRS should scrutinize bishops," *Politico*, Nov. 9, 2009, www.politico.com/news/stories/1109/29336.html.

7. Robert Draper, "And He Shall Be Judged," *GQ*, June 2009, www.gq.com/news-politics/newsmakers/200905/donald-rumsfeld-administration-peers-detractors.

8. David E. Sanger, "Biblical Quotes Said to Adorn Pentagon Reports," *The New York Times*, May 18, 2009, www.nytimes.com/2009/05/18/us/18rumsfeld.html?scp=1&sq=biblical%20quotes%20said%20to%20adorn%20pentagon&st=cse.

9. " '07 survey shows Americans' views mixed on basic freedoms," First Amendment Center, Sept. 24, 2007, www.firstamendmentcenter.org/news.aspx?id=19031.

10. "American Religious Identification Survey 2008," March 2009, www.americanreligionsurvey-aris.org/2009/03/catholics_on_the_move_non-religious_on_the_rise.html.

11. "Treaty of Peace and Friendship," 1796, accessed at http://avalon.law.yale.edu/18th_century/bar1796.asp.

12. *Church of the Holy Trinity v. United States*, 143 U.S. 457.

13. "Joint Press Availability with President Obama and President Gul of Turkey," White House, April 6, 2009, www.whitehouse.gov/the_press_office/Joint-Press-Availability-With-President-Obama-And-President-Gul-Of-Turkey/.

14. "Age of Obama Threatening America's Safety?" Fox News, April 9, 2009, www.foxnews.com/story/0,2933,513599,00.html.

15. "Groups criticize McCain for calling U.S. 'Christian nation,' " CNN, Oct. 1, 2007, www.cnn.com/2007/POLITICS/10/01/mccain.christian.nation/.

16. *Christian Legal Society v. Martinez*, Docket No. 08-1371.

17. *Salazar v. Buono*, Docket No. 08-472.

18. *Torcaso v. Watkins*, 367 U.S. 488 (1961).

19. "74% Support Religious Displays on Public Property," *Rasmussen Reports*, Dec. 24, 2008, www.rasmussenreports.com/public_content/lifestyle/holidays/december_2008/74_support_religious_displays_on_public_property.

20. Ira C. Lupu, David Masci and Robert W. Tuttle, "Religious Displays and the Courts," Pew Forum on Religion & Public Life, June 2007, http://pewforum.org/assets/files/religious-displays.pdf. According to the report, a 2005 survey by the Pew Research Center found that 83 percent of Americans said displays of Christmas symbols should be allowed on government property, and another 2005 Pew poll found that 74 percent said they believed it was proper to display the Ten Commandments in government buildings.

21. *Stone v. Graham*, 449 U.S. 39.

22. *Lynch v. Donnelly*, 465 U.S. 668.

23. Lupu, *et al.*, *op. cit.*, pp. 2-3.

24. "Chambersburg Council Votes to Remove Nativity Scene," WHAG-TV, MSNBC.com, Nov. 24, 2009, http://your4state.com/content/fulltext/?cid=89441.

25. Quoted in *ibid.*

26. *Ibid.*

27. In South Carolina, state law allows private groups to have license tags bearing their own message, and the CEO of a group called the Palmetto Family Council filed a request with the state motor vehicles department to have an "I Believe" plate issued. See John Monk, " 'I Believe' tag might be resurrected," *The State*, Nov. 27, 2009, www.thestate.com/154/v-mobile/story/1045682.html.

28. John Monk, "Judge strikes down plate," *The State*, Nov. 11, 2009, www.thestate.com/513/story/1022683.html.

29. Quoted in *ibid.*

30. For background see Sarah Glazer, "Faith-Based Initiatives," *CQ Researcher*, May 4, 2001, pp. 377-400.

31. "Obama Delivers Speech on Faith in America," *The New York Times*, July 1, 2008, www.nytimes.com/2008/07/01/us/politics/01obama-text.html?scp=1&sq=obama%20delivers%20speech%20on%20faith%20in%20america&st=cse.

32. "Higher Law: Faith-Based Hiring and the Obama Administration," Pew Research Center, Feb. 2, 2009, http://pewresearch.org/pubs/1101/faith-based-hiring-obama-administration.

33. "Interfaith Alliance and Others Call on Attorney General to Review and Withdraw Memo That Threatens Crucial Religious Freedom Protections," news release, Interfaith Alliance, Sept. 17, 2009, www.interfaithalliance.org/news/320-interfaith-alliance-calls-on-attorney-general-to-review-and-withdraw-memo-that-threatens-crucial-religious-freedom-protections.

34. "Religion and the Founding of the American Republic," VI, "Religion and the Federal Government," Part 1, Library of Congress, www.loc.gov/exhibits/religion/rel06.html.

35. Washington's Farewell Address, 1796, accessed at http://avalon.law.yale.edu/18th_century/washing.asp. Source of Washington being an Episcopal vestryman is Library of Congress, *ibid.*

36. Library of Congress, *op. cit.*

37. Ira C. Lupu and Robert W. Tuttle, "Federalism and Faith," *Emory Law Journal*, Vol. 56, Issue 1, 2006, p. 20, www.law.emory.edu/fileadmin/journals/elj/56/1/Lupu___Tuttle.pdf.

38. *Ibid.*

39. "The Blaine Game: Controversy Over the Blaine Amendments and Public Funding of Religion," Pew Forum on Religion & Public Life, July 24, 2008, http://pewforum.org/events/?EventID=194. For further discussion and analysis of the Blaine Amendments, see Akhil Reed Amar, *The Bill of Rights* (1998), pp. 254-255.

40. In *Bradfield v. Roberts* (1899), the court said federal funding of a Catholic hospital was constitutional because the facility's main purpose was to provide secular care. In *Quick Bear v. Leupp* (1908) the court upheld federal support of a Catholic school serving a Sioux reservation because the money came from a Sioux trust fund. For background, see Ira C. Lupu, David Masci, Jesse Merriam and Robert W. Tuttle, "Shifting Boundaries: The Establishment Clause and Government Funding of Religious Schools and Other Faith-Based Organizations," Pew Forum on Religion & Public Life, May 2009, http://pewforum.org/newassets/images/reports/funding/funding.pdf.

41. *Cantwell v. Connecticut*, 310 U.S. 296 (1940).

42. *Everson v. Board of Education*, 330 U.S. 1 (1947).

43. The phrase "wall of separation" was coined by Roger Williams, a 17th-century Baptist theologian and founder of Rhode Island, who declared that a "wall of separation" existed "between the garden of the church and the wilderness of the world." Jefferson, in an 1802 letter to the Danbury [Conn.] Baptist Association suggesting that religious minorities need not worry about persecution, said the First Amendment builds "a wall of separation between church and state." See Lupu, *et al.*, footnote 40. In *Reynolds v. United States* (1878), in upholding a federal anti-bigamy statute in a case involving a Mormon leader, the Supreme Court alluded to Jefferson's "wall of separation" phrase, adding that "it may be accepted almost as an authoritative declaration of the scope and effect of the [First] amendment."

44. James Hutson, "'A Wall of Separation,'" *Library of Congress Information Bulletin*, June 1998, www.loc.gov/loc/lcib/9806/danbury.html.

45. See, for example, Jeff Sharlet, *The Family* (2009), p. 195.

46. David Greenberg, "The Pledge of Allegiance," *Slate*, June 28, 2002, www.slate.com/?id=2067499.

47. *Ibid.*

48. "Address of Sen. John F. Kennedy to the Greater Houston Ministerial Association," John F. Kennedy Presidential Library and Museum, Sept. 12, 1960, www.jfklibrary.org/Historical+Resources/Archives/Reference+Desk/Speeches/JFK/JFK+Pre-Pres/1960/Address+of+Senator+John+F.+Kennedy+to+the+Greater+Houston+Ministerial+Association.htm.

49. Ian Urbina, "Kennedy Discouraged from Communion by Bishop," *The New York Times*, Nov. 23, 2009, www.nytimes.com/2009/11/23/us/23kennedy.html?scp=1&sq=patrick%20kennedy&st=cse.

50. Johanna Neuman, "Obama ends Bush-era National Prayer Day service at White House," Top of the Ticket blog, *Los Angeles Times*, May 7, 2009, http://latimesblogs.latimes.com/washington/2009/05/obama-cancels-national-prayer-day-service.html.

51. Statement by Shirley Dobson quoted in *ibid.*

52. Quoted in *ibid.*

53. *Lemon v. Kurtzman*, 403 U.S. 602 (1971). See Lupu, Masci, Merriam and Tuttle, *op. cit.*, p. 5; and Kermit L. Hall, ed., *The Oxford Companion to the Supreme Court of the United States* (1992), p. 500.

54. Lupu, Masci, Merriam and Tuttle, *op. cit.*, p. 9.

55. *Lynch v. Donnelly*, 465 U.S. 668 (1984).

56. *Lamb's Chapel v. Center Moriches Union Free School District*, 508 U.S. 384 (1993).

57. *Agostini v. Felton*, 521 U.S. 203 (1997).

58. Lupu, Masci, Merriam and Tuttle, *op. cit.*, p. 5.

59. *Mitchell v. Helms*, 530 U.S. 793 (2000).

60. *Zelman v. Simmons-Harris*, 536 U.S. 639 (2002).

61. *Stone v. Graham*, 449 U.S. 39 (1980).

62. *Lynch v. Donnelly*, 465 U.S. 668 (1984).

63. *County of Allegheny v. ACLU*, 492 U.S. 573 (1989).

64. *Van Orden v. Perry*, 545 U.S. 677 (2005).

65. *McCreary County v. ACLU*, 545 U.S. 844 (2005).

66. Linda Greenhouse, "Justices Allow a Commandments Display, Bar Others," *The New York Times*, June 28, 2005, http://query.nytimes.com/gst/fullpage.html?res=9906E7DF153AF93BA15755C0A9639C8B63&sec=&spon=&&scp=2&sq=mccreary%20van%20orden&st=cse.

67. Y. M. Lichtenstein and T. Moskovits, "Justice Scalia: 'The American People Respect Religion,'" *Hamodia*, Sept. 16, 2009.

68. *Christian Legal Society v. Martinez*, 08-1371.

69. David G. Savage, "Supreme Court will decide appeal of Christian student group," *Los Angeles Times*, Dec. 8, 2009, www.latimes.com/news/nation-and-world/la-na-court-christians8-2009dec08,0,6381342.story.

70. Adam Liptak, "Rights and Religion Clash in Court," *The New York Times*, Dec. 8, 2009, www.nytimes.com/2009/12/08/us/08scotus.html?scp=1&sq=rights%20and%20religion%20clash&st=cse.

71. *Ibid.*

72. Savage, *op. cit.*

73. Accessed at www.scotusblog.com/wp/wp-content/uploads/2009/10/08-1371_ca9.pdf.

74. Accessed at http://caselaw.lp.findlaw.com/data2/circs/7th/053239p.pdf via Liptak, *op. cit.*

75. "U.S. Supreme Court agrees to hear lawsuit against UC-Hastings," press release, Christian Legal Society, Dec. 7, 2009, www.clsnet.org/center/updates/press-release-us-supreme-court-agrees-hear-lawsuit-against-uc-hastings.

76. Savage, *op. cit.*

77. *Wallace v. Jaffree*, 472 U.S. 38 (1985).

78. Vikram David Amar, "The Supreme Court Faces the Question of Who Can Sue to Challenge a Religious Display," FindLaw, Oct. 9, 2009, http://writ.news.findlaw.com/amar/20091009.html.

79. Kathleen Kennedy Townsend, "On health care, the bishops have lost their way," *Politico*, Dec. 8, 2009, www.politico.com/news/stories/1209/30311.html.

80. Galen Carey, "Bravo to the bishops," *The Washington Post*, Nov. 19, 2009, http://newsweek.washington-post.com/onfaith/panelists/galen_carey/2009/11/bravo_to_the_bishops.html?hpid=talkbox1.

81. "This Week with George Stephanopoulos," "Transcript: Gen. Casey, Steele vs. Kaine," ABC News, Nov. 8, 2009, http://abcnews.go.com/ThisWeek/Politics/transcript-steele-kaine/story?id=9023724.

BIBLIOGRAPHY

Books

Boyd, Gregory A., *The Myth of a Christian Nation*, Zondervan, 2005.
A conservative evangelical pastor argues that "a significant segment of American evangelicalism is guilty of nationalistic and political idolatry."

Kramnick, Isaac, and R. Laurence Moore, *The Godless Constitution*, Norton, 2005.
Two Cornell University professors offer, as the book's subtitle states, "a moral defense of the secular state."

Lilla, Mark, *The Stillborn God*, Knopf, 2007.
An intellectual historian explores the nexus of political theology and political philosophy over 400 years.

Meacham, Jon, *American Gospel*, Random House, 2006.
The *Newsweek* editor and historian writes that "religion shapes the life of the nation without strangling it."

Noll, Mark A., Nathan O. Hatch and George M. Marsden, *The Search for Christian America*, Helmers & Howard, 1989.
Evangelical Christian scholars offer a useful analysis of the nation's historical and religious origins.

Articles

Fea, John, "Is America a Christian Nation? What Both Left and Right Get Wrong," *History News Network*, Oct. 1, 2007, http://hnn.us/articles/42835.html.
A Messiah College history teacher argues that neither the Christian Right nor the secular left is immune to errors of historical thinking.

Johnson, Carrie, "Obama Cautious on Faith-Based Initiatives," *The Washington Post*, Sept. 15, 2009, p. 6A.
The Justice Department's Office of Legal Counsel has been considering a religious-freedom memo written during the George W. Bush administration.

Lichtenstein, Y. M., and T. Moskovits, "Justice Scalia: 'The American People Respect Religion,' " *Hamodia*, Sept. 16, 2009.
The Supreme Court justice tells the newspaper of Torah Jewry that "it has not been our American constitutional tradition, nor our social or legal tradition, to exclude religion from the public sphere."

Lind, Michael, "America is not a Christian nation," *Salon.com*, www.salon.com/opinion/feature/2009/04/14/christian_nation/.
President Obama's remark that "we do not consider ourselves a Christian nation or a Jewish nation or a Muslim nation" has "ample precedent in American diplomacy and constitutional thought."

Meacham, Jon, "The End of Christian America," *Newsweek*, April 4, 2009, www.newsweek.com/id/192583.
The percentage of Christians in the U.S. population is shrinking, and fewer people think the U.S. is a "Christian nation."

Sanders, Joshunda, "Christianity's role in history of U.S. at issue," *Austin American-Statesman*, Jan. 10,

2010, www.statesman.com/news/texas-politics/chris
tianity-s-role-in-history-of-u-s-172516.html.
Ideas submitted by Christian conservatives David Barton
and the Rev. Peter Marshall for revisions to the social
studies curriculum in Texas public schools could shape
how social studies are taught in the state for the next
decade.

Reports and Studies

**"Religious Expression in American Public Life: A
Joint Statement of Current Law," Center for Religion
and Public Affairs, Wake Forest University Divinity
School, Jan. 12, 2010, http://divinity.wfu.edu/rpa/.**
A diverse group of leaders from religious and secular
organizations, including Jewish, Muslim, Christian evangelical, mainline Protestant and Catholic, drafted a
32-page document billed as "the most comprehensive
joint statement of current law to date on legal issues
dividing church and state."

Kosmin, Barry A., Ariela Keysar, *et al.*, **"American
Nones: The Profile of the No Religion Population: A
Report Based on the American Religious Identification
Survey 2008," Trinity College, March 2009, www.amer
icanreligionsurvey-aris.org/reports/NONES_08.pdf.**
About 15 percent of American adults don't identify with
any particular religious group, while the proportion
among those ages 18-29 is higher.

**Lupu, Ira C., David Masci and Robert W. Tuttle,
"Religious Displays and the Courts," Pew Forum on
Religion & Public Life, June 2007, http://pewforum
.org/assets/files/religious-displays.pdf.**
Legal experts trace key court cases dealing with religious
displays in public areas.

**Lupu, Ira C., David Masci and Robert W. Tuttle,
"Shifting Boundaries: The Establishment Clause and
Government Funding of Religious Schools and Other
Faith-Based Organizations," Pew Forum on Religion
& Public Life, May 2009, http://pewforum.org/
newassets/images/reports/funding/funding.pdf.**
In the 18th century, public funding of religious activity
was attacked, legal scholars note in this broad historical
analysis.

For More Information

Americans United for Separation of Church and State,
518 C St., N.E., Washington, DC 20002; (202) 466-3234;
www.au.org. Advocacy group that supports separation of
church and state.

Christian Legal Society, 8001 Braddock Road, Suite 300,
Springfield, VA 22151; (703) 642-1070; www.clsnet.org.
Nationwide association of Christian attorneys, law students,
law professors and judges.

Council on American-Islamic Relations, 453 New Jersey
Ave., S.E., Washington, DC 20003; (202) 488-8787; www
.cair.com. Works to enhance understanding of Islam.

Exodus Mandate, P.O. Box 12072, Columbia, S.C. 29211;
(803) 714-1744; www.exodusmandate.org. Urges Christians
to withdraw their children from the public-school system
and place them in Christian schools or home school them
with a Christian emphasis.

First Amendment Center at Vanderbilt University, 1207
18th Ave. S., Nashville, TN 37212; (615) 727-1600; and
First Amendment Center/Washington, 555 Pennsylvania

Ave., N.W., Washington, DC 20001; (202) 292-6288; www
.firstamendmentcenter.org. Supports the First Amendment
through education, research and other activities.

Freedom From Religion Foundation, P.O. Box 750,
Madison, WI 53701; (608) 256-8900; www.ffrf.org. Advocacy group that supports separation of church and state.

National Association of Evangelicals, P.O. Box 23269,
Washington, DC 20026; (202) 789-1011; www.nae.net.
Represents more than 45,000 evangelical churches from more
than 40 denominations.

Pew Forum on Religion & Public Life, 1615 L St., N.W.,
Suite 700, Washington, DC 20036-5610; (202) 419-4550;
http://pewforum.org. Research group focusing on intersection
of religion and politics, law, domestic policy and world
affairs.

Secular Coalition for America, P.O. Box 66096, Washington, DC 20035-6096; (202) 299-1091; www.secular.org.
Advocates church-state separation and greater inclusion of
atheists, agnostics and other "non-theistic Americans."

7

Gun Rights Debates

Kenneth Jost

Private security guard Dick Heller, who challenged Washington, D.C.'s strict handgun ban, leaves police headquarters with a new gun permit on Aug. 18, 2008, after the U.S. Supreme Court struck down the ban. Although the decision transformed a decades-long debate over the Second Amendment, gun control and gun rights experts disagree on the likely impact of the ruling.

From *CQ Researcher*,
October 31, 2008.

Getty Images/Mark Wilson

J oseph Tartaro, the longtime executive editor of *Gun Week* magazine, looked out at a meeting room filled with hundreds of gun owners and gun rights advocates and announced that, at last, good times had arrived.

Thirty years earlier, Tartaro told the Second Amendment Foundation's annual conference in Phoenix on Sept. 28, only four states allowed the carrying of concealed weapons in public. And the District of Columbia had just enacted one of the strictest gun control laws in the country.

Today, explained Tartaro, the foundation's president, more than 40 states have so-called "shall issue" laws that allow carrying concealed firearms in public. And three months earlier — on June 26 — the Supreme Court had struck down Washington's handgun ban. The precedent-setting decision established an individual right to own and possess firearms for self-defense, at least in one's home.

"We've reached the good days," Tartaro continued. More handguns are being sold than at any other time in history. Long gun sales would be up too but for the bad economy. "People have discovered," he said, "that guns are not as scary as they thought they were."

"Law-abiding people should be able to defend themselves, their families and their communities," Tartaro concluded.[1]

Gun rights advocates indeed have much to celebrate thanks to the Supreme Court's *District of Columbia v. Heller* decision, which transforms a decades-long dispute over the meaning of the Second Amendment. The awkwardly phrased 27-word provision proclaims:

D.C. Gun Ban Case Split Supreme Court

The Supreme Court divided along ideological lines in its 5-4 decision striking down the District of Columbia's 32-year-old handgun ban. Justice Antonin Scalia wrote for a majority that included four other conservatives: Chief Justice John G. Roberts Jr. and Associate Justices Anthony M. Kennedy, Clarence Thomas and Samuel A. Alito Jr. Justice John Paul Stevens wrote the major dissenting opinion, joined by three other liberal justices: David H. Souter, Ruth Bader Ginsburg and Stephen G. Breyer.

Getty Images/Paul J. Richards (5)

| Roberts | Scalia | Kennedy | Thomas | Alito |

"The Constitution leaves the District of Columbia a variety of tools for combating [the problem of handgun violence], including some measures regulating handguns. But the enshrinement of constitutional rights necessarily takes certain policy choices off the table. These include the absolute prohibition of handguns held and used for self-defense in the home. . . . [I]t is not the role of this Court to pronounce the Second Amendment extinct."

District of Columbia v. Heller (From majority opinion by Justice Scalia)

Getty Images/Mark Wilson — AFP/Getty Images/Paul J. Richards — Getty Images/Mark Wilson — AFP/Getty Images/Brendan Smialowski

| Stevens | Souter | Ginsburg | Breyer |

"The Court would have us believe that over 200 years ago, the Framers made a choice to limit the tools available to elected officials wishing to regulate civilian uses of weapons, and to authorize this Court . . . to define the contours of acceptable gun control policy. Absent compelling evidence that is nowhere to be found in the Court's opinion, I could not possibly conclude that the Framers made such a choice."

District of Columbia v. Heller (From dissenting opinion by Justice Stevens)

Source: Supreme Court of the United States, www.supremecourtus.gov/opinions/07pdf/07-290.pdf.

"A well regulated Militia, being necessary to the security of a free State, the right of the people to keep and bear Arms, shall not be infringed."

Following a 1939 Supreme Court decision, federal courts had ruled all but uniformly for more than 60 years that the amendment's opening clause limited its scope to protecting the states' rights to organize militias. But the amendment did not establish an individual right to own or possess firearms, courts held. Under the so-called collective-right view, Congress and state and local governments remained largely free to regulate guns as they saw fit.

Gun rights advocates stepped up their efforts to challenge that doctrine in the 1960s and '70s. Over time, they gained support for their claim that the amendment established an individual right — first from many politicians, then from some academics and eventually from the general public.

The Supreme Court finally took up the issue after the federal appeals court for the District of Columbia struck down the D.C. gun ban in March 2007. The high court's 5-4 ruling gave gun rights advocates the victory they had awaited for so long.

Writing for the majority, Justice Antonin Scalia said the amendment established an individual right for "law-abiding, responsible citizens to use arms in defense of hearth and home." D.C.'s ban on handguns — the "quintessential self-defense weapon" — was invalid, he said, along with the law's provision requiring that any weapons in the home be either disassembled or trigger-locked.

Writing for the four dissenters, Justice John Paul Stevens said the ruling upset a "settled understanding" that the Second Amendment allowed virtually unlimited regulation of civilian use of firearms. He said the D.C. gun ban could be "just the first of an unknown number of dominoes to be knocked off the table."[2] (*See box, p. 150.*)

Leading advocates and experts disagree on the likely impact of the ruling. "Many laws [regulating guns] will be upheld — the laws that make more sense," says Alan Gura, the Alexandria, Va., lawyer who successfully represented D.C. private security guard Dick Heller and other plaintiffs in challenging the gun ban. "But laws that serve no legitimate governmental purpose but merely serve to harass gun owners, laws that make gun owning difficult or expensive — those laws are going to be struck down."

Gun control advocates are playing down the possibility that lots of gun regulations are now in constitutional jeopardy. They emphasize passages in Scalia's opinion that limit the Second Amendment right to weapons "in common use" and that leave standing laws setting "conditions and qualifications" on the commercial sale of arms.

"We're actually quite encouraged by comments that the majority made in the course of that decision offering some reassurance that some very broad categories of gun laws . . . are what the court called presumptively lawful," says Dennis Henigan, vice president for law and policy at the Brady Center to Prevent Gun Violence in Washington, the nonpartisan policy arm of the Brady Campaign to Prevent Gun Violence, a political action committee.

Americans Support Gun Rights, More Controls

More than three-quarters of Americans oppose amending the Constitution to ban individual gun ownership, but more than half support stricter gun control laws. Even more support specific measures such as keeping guns out of the hands of felons and requiring purchasers to wait several days before receiving a gun.

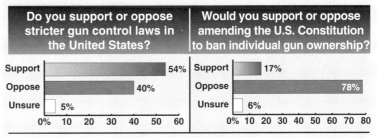

The exact words of the Second Amendment to the Constitution are: "A well regulated Militia, being necessary to the security of a free State, the right of the people to keep and bear Arms, shall not be infringed."

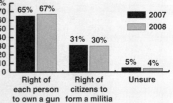

Do you think these words guarantee each person the right to own a gun, or do they protect the right of citizens to form a militia without implying that each individual has the right to own a gun?

Thinking about specific ways that the government has dealt with guns in the past, do you favor or oppose each of the following? . . .

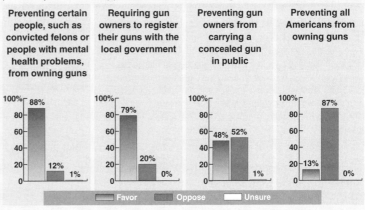

* Figures may not total 100 due to rounding.
Sources: CNN, Opinion Research Corporation, Quinnipiac University

Getty Images/Scott Olson

Chicago Mayor Richard Daley, right, examines assault weapons with Assistant Deputy Superintendent of Police Matt Tobias. The mayor opposes a lawsuit filed by the Second Amendment Foundation challenging a Chicago handgun ban similar to the recently overturned D.C. law. The city says the Supreme Court decision on Washington's ban applies only to federal jurisdictions, not to states and municipalities. Separately, the foundation is also challenging a San Francisco provision banning handguns in public housing.

A leading gun rights lawyer for the National Rifle Association (NRA) somewhat similarly plays down the likely impact of the ruling. "It's not as though all the gun regulations in the country are going to go by the wayside," says Stephen Halbrook, author of a number of pro-gun rights books and articles. But Halbrook says the court's decision represents a "tremendous moral defeat" for gun control advocates.

Other academic experts disagree. "In practice, the legislatures are not that limited in the kind of gun controls they can pass," says Gary Kleck, a professor at Florida State University's College of Criminology and Criminal Justice in Tallahassee, who describes himself as a supporter of "a moderate amount" of gun control. "They can do virtually everything they could before the decision."

But Philip Cook, a professor of economics and sociology at Duke University in Durham, N.C., and a supporter of stronger regulation, says gun control supporters are engaging in "happy talk" when they minimize the ruling's potential effects. "The decision has been a litigation magnet," says Cook. "At this point it remains hard to say how far the Supreme Court and the [federal] circuit courts are going to push this."

The Second Amendment Foundation, in fact, filed the first post-*Heller* lawsuit on the same day of the decision, challenging a Chicago handgun ban similar to the D.C. law. The NRA followed with a package of suits challenging handgun bans in Chicago and several nearby suburbs. Separately, the foundation and other gun rights groups challenged a San Francisco provision banning handguns in public housing.

Criminal defendants in federal courts are also citing the *Heller* decision to try to set aside sentence enhancements under federal provisions increasing prison terms for use or possession of guns by offenders. So far, judges appear to be rejecting those arguments. But the Supreme Court is set to hear arguments on Nov. 10 testing a federal law making it a crime for someone convicted of domestic violence to own a gun.

The ruling is also renewing the debate touched off by the Virginia Tech shootings in April 2007 over college and university rules prohibiting possession of firearms on campuses.* A student group advocating the right of licensed students to carry concealed weapons on campus claims to have attracted more than 30,000 members — but is also drawing criticism from gun control groups that

---

* On Oct. 25, two students were shot and killed outside a residence hall at Central Arkansas University. Four suspects were being held in what police say was not a random shooting. On Feb. 15, 2008, a former graduate student had shot and killed five students in a lecture hall at Northern Illinois University before shooting himself.

say increasing the number of firearms will make campuses less instead of more safe.[3] (*See sidebar, p. 160.*)

In Washington itself, the city council quickly responded to the Supreme Court decision by establishing a registration system for handguns while retaining other restrictions, including the requirement to store weapons disassembled or trigger-locked. The council adopted a significantly revised interim measure in September under the threat of a bipartisan measure in Congress to strip the district of all authority to regulate firearms. The new "emergency" legislation permits registration of semiautomatic pistols as well as single-shot pistols and eliminates the trigger-lock requirement. Those provisions are expected to be included in a permanent law to be adopted later. (*See sidebar, p. 156.*)

The *Heller* decision came at a time of relative quiet in the gun control debates — debates that often seem to be as much clashes of cultures and values as disagreements on law and policy. Gun control has receded as an issue over the past two years in Congress and state and local legislative bodies. Both major party presidential candidates endorsed the Supreme Court ruling to recognize individual rights under the Second Amendment: Republican John McCain strongly, Democrat Barack Obama more ambiguously. (*See sidebar, p. 163.*)

Even so, gun regulations remain a volatile issue in courts and legislative bodies around the country. Here are some of the principal questions on the agenda:

Should laws restricting ownership of firearms be relaxed?

Otis McDonald is a retiree in his 70s who lives on Chicago's far south side, a mixed-race area with middle-class homes and a relatively low crime rate. Still, McDonald recalls being threatened by members of a neighborhood gang outside his home a couple of years ago after reporting some information about a crime to police.

McDonald keeps a shotgun in his home for self-defense but under Chicago's ban on handguns has to store a pistol outside the city limits. Now, he is one of six Chicago residents who challenged the Chicago ordinance in federal court hours after the Supreme Court invalidated Washington's handgun ban.

Despite the high court ruling, Chicago is vigorously defending the measure. Mayor Richard Daley and Police Superintendent Jody Weiss have both criticized the

decision as a threat to public safety. The city's lawyers are slowing down the lawsuit and preparing legal arguments to save the city ban by arguing that the Supreme Court decision applies only to federal jurisdictions, not to states and municipalities.

Chicago will present "a full-blown analysis that the Second Amendment has not been incorporated against the states," says Michael Forti, a deputy corporation counsel in Chicago, referring to the legal doctrine of applying provisions of the Bill of Rights to the states. "We think this is an issue that is worth litigating."[4]

Most experts and advocates assume the Second Amendment will eventually be held applicable to state and local governments. "Very likely," says Duke University's Cook. "The court defined it as a personal right."

Douglas Berman, a professor at Ohio State University's Morris College of Law, agrees. He is helping represent defendants in efforts to use the newly recognized right to challenge gun-related sentence enhancements in state and federal courts. "I'll be surprised if this is another of the rights that is not incorporated," Berman says. "I don't think the *Heller* five did this just to strike down one District of Columbia law."

Even without a ruling on that preliminary issue, gun rights advocates are also scoring some victories. Three Chicago-area suburbs with gun-control bans — Evanston, Morton Grove and Wilmette — responded to suits filed by the NRA by either repealing or modifying their laws to permit handguns in the home for self-defense. The village of Oak Park, however, is joining with Chicago in defending its ordinance. The NRA's suits against Chicago and Oak Park have been consolidated with the McDonald case in a proceeding in U.S. District Court.[5]

Gun control advocates hope the Supreme Court decision will leave most gun regulations intact. "There are very few bans out there," says Joshua Horwitz, executive director of the Coalition to Stop Gun Violence. "If that is all it applies to, it's just not going to be that big a deal." The Brady Center's Henigan predicts lower courts will uphold "a wide variety" of gun regulations.

The NRA's Halbrook also doubts existing gun regulations will be shot down wholesale. "A lot of us are in agreement on a lot of gun laws," he says. But both the NRA and the somewhat harder-line Gun Owners of America are eyeing future challenges to local licensing systems — most prominently, New York City's — that make registering firearms very hard.

Most States Support Gun Rights

At least 40 states have laws preempting any local gun regulations or constitutional provisions guaranteeing firearm rights. Only seven states require handgun registration.

Provision	No. of States
Firearm rights constitutional provision	44
State firearm preemption laws	47
State right-to-carry-concealed provision	40
License required to permit or purchase	
Handgun	17
Long gun	6
Registration required	
Handgun	7
Long gun	6
State waiting period required	
Handgun	10
Long gun	5
Record of sale reported to state/local government	17

Source: "Compendium of State Laws Governing Firearms: 2007," National Rifle Association/Institute for Legislative Action

Licensing can be "a distinction without a difference," says Larry Pratt, Gun Owners' executive director. Florida State's Kleck says New York City makes it virtually impossible to register a gun except for former police officers or politically connected applicants.

Pratt says licensing schemes will be challenged eventually, but not right away. "You want to go one step at a time," he says. But Horwitz worries that passages in Scalia's opinion depicting the Second Amendment right as a check on governmental power leave licensing laws in jeopardy. "If the right is a core protection against the government, then licensing and registration may not be OK," he says.

The court's ruling also sets the stage for skirmishes over bans on specific types of weapons. "Bans on certain classes of weapons will be OK," Horwitz says. "It has to be fleshed out." Henigan notes that state courts interpreting gun rights provisions in their own state constitutions have generally upheld bans on sawed-off shotguns.

Some of these disputes are likely to be fought in legislative bodies. Speakers at the gun policy conference in Phoenix, for example, warned that a Democratic-controlled Congress might try to revive the federal ban on assault weapons that expired in 2004. But gun rights

advocates stress that the Supreme Court decision changes the rules for legal challenges.

The Supreme Court "held very clearly that the Second Amendment protects an individual right," says Pratt. "That will now be the template that all other gun cases will have to use."

Should laws regarding concealed weapons be relaxed?

Long before the Sept. 11, 2001, terrorist attacks on the United States, Atlanta had been enforcing a statewide law banning firearms at what is now Hartsfield-Jackson International Airport. Now, a gun rights organization in Georgia is trying to use a new state law legalizing possession of firearms in "public transportation" to permit airport visitors with a state firearms license to carry guns everywhere but in security zones.

"The city of Atlanta isn't obeying the state law," says John Monroe, the Atlanta attorney representing GeorgiaCarry.org and state Rep. Timothy Bearden, the freshman Republican legislator who sponsored the new law. The suit was filed July 1, the day the new law took effect.

City officials say the law does not apply to the airport and would be preempted by post-9/11 federal security measures if it did. U.S. District Judge Marvin Shoob agrees. The Atlanta airport — the busiest in the world — would be "less safe" if visitors could carry weapons, Shoob said on Aug. 11 in rejecting GeorgiaCarry's suit.[6]

Bearden, an NRA member and former police officer, touts the new law as the "biggest gun reform" in Georgia's history. The measure allows state firearm license holders to carry concealed weapons not only on transit system buses but also in state parks, state-owned buildings and most restaurants. Gov. Frank Perdue, a Republican, signed it into law on May 14 despite widespread calls from Democratic Atlanta Mayor Shirley Jackson and others to veto it.

Gun rights advocates are now citing the Supreme Court's *Heller* decision to help build on the gains they had already been making before the ruling to ease laws restricting concealed weapons in public places. "The Second Amendment recognizes a right not only to keep arms in the home but also to bear arms," says NRA attorney Halbrook.

Gun control advocates disagree. "There's nothing in that opinion that suggests that there's a right to carry guns on the street," says the Brady Center's Henigan. "It ought to be obvious that the implications of carrying a gun on the streets are different. There are a lot of risks to handguns. Carrying them outside the home transports those risks."

The Supreme Court decision, in fact, notes that most 19th-century courts interpreting gun rights provisions in state constitutions upheld laws prohibiting the carrying of concealed weapons. In the next sentence, however, Scalia left the question somewhat open by giving tentative approval only to laws forbidding the carrying of weapons in "sensitive places such as schools and government buildings."

GeorgiaCarry cited the Second Amendment in its lawsuit challenging the Atlanta airport ban, but Halbrook discounts the likelihood of raising constitutional claims in such cases. "I don't think you're going to see challenges under *Heller* to bans on very specific places," he says.

Halbrook does argue, however, that *Heller* raises a potential constitutional claim for carrying concealed weapons in most public places. "Responsible, trained persons — if they wish to do so — should have an entitlement to go through at least a registration process and carry guns for self-protection," he says.

"I don't think the populace would stand much for open carry," counters Horwitz of the anti-gun violence coalition. "It's awfully uncomfortable when people start carrying guns around." Still, Horwitz says the Supreme Court decision invites constitutional claims to carry firearms. "I don't think that's likely, but I really do think it's wide open," he says.

As the Georgia law illustrates, gun rights groups have been making gains on the issue in legislative bodies without having to go to court. Among its other provisions, the Georgia law also allows firearm license holders to bring guns to their jobs if stored in their cars. Florida also enacted a similar law this spring despite opposition from some employers who feared the measure would make workplaces less safe.

Speaking at the Second Amendment Foundation conference, Vice President Alan Gottlieb said gun rights advocates should press Congress to pass "a national concealed carry law so we will have the same rights that were given to law enforcement."

"The ultimate objective legislatively would be laws modeled after Vermont and Alaska, where there is specific recognition that people have a right to carry without any government involvement: no licenses, no permits," says Pratt of Gun Owners of America. "We keep trying to improve the situation so that people eventually have the same liberty that criminals do: carry without permits."

Meanwhile, the Atlanta airport suit prompted an Associated Press survey that found carrying firearms in the public areas of terminals is permitted at seven of the nation's busiest facilities. A spokesman for the federal Transportation Security Administration told the AP that the TSA has no position on guns at airports and no authority under federal law to ban them.[7]

Should criminal penalties for gun-related offenses be relaxed?

Randy Hayes was placed on probation after pleading guilty to battery in 1994 to settle a domestic violence complaint by his wife Mary Ann during a contentious divorce. Ten years later, Hayes found himself facing another domestic violence charge when Mary Ann called the Marion County, W. Va., sheriff's department after a dispute over his rights of visitation with their son.

Hayes might have resolved the new charge with another, similar plea and gotten the same kind of judicial tap on the wrist, except that a deputy sheriff found a rifle under Hayes' bed. That put Hayes in violation of a 1996 federal law — punishable by up to 10 years in prison — prohibiting possession of a firearm by anyone convicted of a crime of domestic violence.

The provision — known as the Lautenberg Amendment, after its principal Senate sponsor, Sen. Frank Lautenberg, D-N.J. — is one of many gun-related penalties embedded in federal criminal law. Gun rights advocates helped persuade Congress to enact those provisions. "It was a way of conservatives simultaneously saying we respect gun rights, but we also want to do something about gun violence," says Florida State's Kleck.

Now, criminal defense lawyers across the county are citing the Supreme Court's gun-rights decision in efforts to nullify convictions or enhanced sentences under some of these provisions. In particular, defense lawyers are arguing that so-called felon-in-possession convictions

D.C. Still Trying to Finesse Handgun Ban Revision

Gun ownership "is an individual right they have to respect," gun rights lawyer says.

Washington Police Chief Kathy L. Lanier.

Metropolitan Police Department

The District of Columbia faces the threat of renewed legal challenges as it works on a third rewrite of the district's 32-year-old handgun ban.

The D.C. council enacted a minimal rewrite of the ban on June 15, less than three weeks after the Supreme Court found the measure in violation of the Second Amendment's individual right to keep and bear arms. The council approved a broader revision on Sept. 16 to try to fend off a bipartisan effort in Congress to repeal the district's gun registration law altogether.

Now the council is working on permanent legislation to replace the "emergency" measure enacted in September and due to expire after 90 days. It was aimed at satisfying gun rights advocates by permitting registration of semiautomatic pistols and easing "safe-storage" requirements for pistols in the home.[1]

Despite the changes, Alan Gura, the victorious lawyer in the gun-ban case, says the interim Sept. 16 measure still does not comply with the Second Amendment. "There are still some problems," says Gura. "I think the council will either fix the problems, or they will have the problems fixed for them."

D.C. Mayor Adrian Fenty and Police Chief Cathy L. Lanier both promised immediately after the Supreme Court ruling to try to maintain the strictest possible handgun regulations while complying with the decision. The legislation approved by the 13-member council on June 15 closely tracked the Supreme Court's holding by creating a limited exception to the ban for the use of a handgun for self-defense in the home. It preserved the existing ban on possession of semiautomatic firearms by continuing to define them as prohibited machine guns.

The law — like the later 90-day emergency measure — also relaxed by as little as possible the previous requirement that firearms stored in the home be disassembled or equipped with a trigger-lock. As approved, the June 15 law lifted the

may infringe an ex-offender's Second Amendment right to self-defense in his or her home.[8]

So far, federal judges are rejecting those arguments. But a leading expert on federal sentencing law says the courts are not giving the arguments sufficient consideration. "*Heller* at the very least can and should be read as the vindication of those subject to harsh sanctions for gun possession to raise new constitutional questions to get around them," says Ohio State University's Berman, publisher of a blog on sentencing issues.[9]

Gun control advocates note that Scalia's majority opinion cited laws prohibiting possession of firearms by felons as presumptively valid even after the ruling. "The decision is very clear that criminal felons don't have Second Amendment rights," says Horwitz of the anti-gun violence coalition. "I don't think that's going to be a big change."

"It's ironic to see *Heller* being used in this way," adds the Brady Center's Henigan, "because it's a consistent theme of the gun lobby that the solution to gun violence is more aggressive penalties for gun violators."

The NRA's Halbrook emphasizes the group's support for stiff sentences for crimes committed with guns. "The NRA's focus always has been in favor of stern laws on criminals who use guns," he says. But he also says some federal provisions are overbroad.

Felon-in-possession laws are "safe and secure," Halbrook says, "with one condition: There are too many felonies and an increasing number of felonies being created by law." He notes that the federal felon-in-possession

requirement only when a firearm was being used against a "reasonably perceived threat of immediate harm."

At the same time, Chief Lanier issued somewhat restrictive regulations for registering handguns, which required applicants to take a written examination and submit to a criminal background check. For new purchases, an applicant had to complete the registration process before obtaining the weapon from a licensed dealer within Washington. Applicants could register only one handgun.

Gun rights advocates sneered at the council's minimal changes. "It took them some time to understand," Gura says. When Congress returned to Washington in September after a break for the Democratic and Republican national conventions, lawmakers from both parties pushed for a vote on a bill in the House of Representatives to repeal the district's ban on semiautomatic firearms and to repeal the registration process. Under the district's limited home rule, Congress can exercise its constitutional authority over the nation's capital by enacting legislation for the district or disapproving legislation approved by the council.

The council approved a second rewrite of the law on Sept. 16, the same day the House was to take up the override measure. Under the new version, the definition of machine gun was revised to eliminate semiautomatic weapons, applicants were permitted to register one pistol per month and the safe-storage rules were made advisory instead of mandatory. A new "child access provision," however, required that firearms be securely stored to prevent access by minors under age 16. Violators can be subject to a 180-day jail term and $1,000 fine or — if injury or death results to the child or anyone else — a five-year prison term and up to a $5,000 fine.[2]

Despite the council vote, the House approved the override measure in a post-midnight vote by a 266-152 margin, with 180 Republicans and 86 Democrats voting for it. D.C. Delegate Eleanor Holmes Norton — who has no vote on the House floor — strenuously opposed the measure as an infringement of home rule. Even as the House voted, however, it was widely assumed that senators friendly to the district would block a vote in the Senate.

Acting D.C. Attorney General Pete Nickles said the September measure should satisfy both the court and Congress. "Any legitimate concerns by Congress on district gun laws should be satisfied by the new laws," he said.

The council's Judiciary Committee held hearings on permanent legislation on Oct. 10 with an eye to a council vote on the matter in November. Gura is still wary. "The city council needs to accept that they lost, that this is an individual right that they have to respect and that failure to do so will lead to more adverse litigation consequences," he says.

---

[1] For recent coverage, see Mary Beth Sheridan, "Limit on Gun Law Passes; Senate Vote Unlikely," *The Washington Post*, Sept. 18, 2008, p. B2; Paul Duggan and Mary Beth Sheridan, "U.S. House, D.C. Council Wrestle Over Gun Control," *ibid.*, Sept. 17, 2008, p. A1.

[2] The legislation can be found on the district's Web site, http://dc.gov/mayor/pdf/showpdf.asp?pdfName=Second_Firearms_Control_Emergency_Amendment_Act_of_2008_Final.pdf.

---

law exempts persons convicted of antitrust violations, unfair trade practices or other business-related offenses.

For his part, Gun Owners' Executive Director Pratt says the group generally opposes the felon-in-possession charge and specifically favors repealing the Lautenberg domestic-violence provision. "Under the Lautenberg ban, people who have committed very minor offenses that include pushing, shoving or, in some cases, merely yelling at a family member can no longer own a firearm for self-defense," the group says on its Web site. "The Lautenberg gun ban should be repealed, not expanded."

The Supreme Court is set to consider a limited challenge to expansive enforcement of the Lautenberg Amendment on Nov. 10 when it considers Hayes' appeal of his felon-in-possession conviction. Charleston attorney Troy Giatris is arguing that Hayes' 1994 battery conviction was not domestic violence because the charge did not specifically include that element.

The 4th U.S. Circuit Court of Appeals agreed and threw out Hayes' felon-in-possession conviction in April 2007. The government asked the justices to review the decision, which it says conflicts with other federal appeals court rulings.

The government contends that limiting the Lautenberg Amendment to convictions for "domestic-violence specific laws" would "unnaturally" limit the scope of the provision. Giatris says he approves of the law but that it must be applied strictly. "Keeping guns out of the hands of lawbreakers is a good thing," he says, "but let's very clearly define who the lawbreakers are."

In a supporting brief filed on behalf of the Second Amendment Foundation, Gura, the winning lawyer in the *Heller* case, argues that defendants subject to gun-possession restrictions should at least be advised about the potential loss of Second Amendment rights before entering guilty pleas. On his blog, Professor Berman suggests that defendants arrested on the basis of guns found in home searches should consider raising Second Amendment claims.

Federal courts have proved unreceptive to such claims so far, according to Berman, citing Scalia's apparent endorsement of gun-rights restrictions on felons. "Unless and until lower courts are willing to rethink some pre-*Heller* precedents, it's not surprising that these defendants are not having much success so far," he says.

BACKGROUND

Rewriting History

The Supreme Court's decision to strike down the Washington, D.C., gun ban adopts what had been a non-mainstream view of the role of gun rights in England, colonial America and the United States. In this once minority viewpoint, the right to own and possess firearms was established in England and then embedded in the U.S. Constitution as an important bulwark of individual liberty, not only as protection for state militias. Gun bans, in this view, can amount to instruments of government oppression instead of domestic security.[10]

In Justice Scalia's telling of the history in the court's majority opinion, the Second Amendment derives from the conflict after the restoration of the English monarchy in 1661 between the Catholic kings Charles II and James II and their enemies in their predominantly Protestant adopted country. Charles and James sought to secure their power by using armed militias loyal to them while disarming Protestant militias.

James was overthrown in the Glorious Revolution of 1688, and his successors — his son-in-law William and daughter Mary — acceded to Parliament's passage of the omnibus English Bill of Rights. As a guarantee against further disarmament, Parliament included this provision: "That the subjects which are Protestants may have arms for their defense suitable to their conditions and as allowed by law."

Scalia depicts the provision as securing in England an individual right to firearms. In the 18th century, King George III sought to deny that right to the American colonists by disarming many of the inhabitants in rebellious areas in the tumultuous decades leading up to the American Revolution. Scalia cites various revolutionary-era writings from the colonists to support the conclusion that the Second Amendment preserved a pre-existing right to keep and bear arms that was understood at the time as an individual right, unconnected to service in a militia.

Scalia relies heavily on the work of a pro-Second Amendment historian, Joyce Lee Malcolm, now a professor at George Mason University Law School in Fairfax, Va. In his dissenting opinion, Justice Stevens cites the work of other legal historians — including Ohio State University's Saul Cornell and George Washington University Professor Emeritus Lois Schwoerer — to argue that Scalia has the history wrong. The English Bill of Rights provision was — by its terms — neither universal nor unlimited, Stevens notes. And — after criticizing Scalia for giving "short shrift" to Congress' deliberations on the Second Amendment — Stevens says that the prefatory Militia Clause reflects a "telling" decision by the draftsman, James Madison, to limit the amendment's scope and reject more broadly phrased proposals submitted by dissenters from some of the state constitutional conventions.

Scalia views comparable right-to-bear-arms provisions included in early state constitutions and 19th-century judicial interpretations of them as "universally" supporting the individual- rather than collective-right theory. He similarly treats the Supreme Court's two post-Civil War decisions touching on the Second Amendment as implicitly supporting an individual rights view; Stevens disagrees, saying the rulings merely declined to enforce the amendments against the states.

Whatever the legal import of the two decisions, Professor Gregg Lee Carter of Bryant University in Smithfield, R.I., notes that gun rights advocates point to both rulings as evidence of the unsavory motives behind limiting gun rights. In one, the court in 1876 found no basis for federal charges against members of an armed, white mob for massacring blacks who were defending an elected black official in Reconstruction-era Louisiana. In the other, the court in 1886 upheld the conviction of a German immigrant in Illinois for organizing an unauthorized militia aimed at protecting workers' right to unionize.[11]

CHRONOLOGY

Before 1960 *Second Amendment, ratified in 1791, establishes "right to keep and bear arms"; some view guarantee as individual right, others as collective right tied to "well-regulated militia."*

1939 Supreme Court upholds National Firearms Act, rules Second Amendment applies to weapons with "reasonable relationship" to militias.

1960s *Assassinations, crime surge prompt federal gun control law.*

1968 Gun Control Act of 1968 enacted after Martin Luther King Jr., Robert F. Kennedy killings; law bars interstate gun sales and sales to criminals, "mental defectives," others.

1970s *Lines harden in debates over gun regulations.*

1974 National Council to Control Handguns founded; later changes name to Handgun Control.

1976 Washington, D.C., bans registration of new handguns; ban survives two court challenges.

1977 National Rifle Association (NRA) leadership replaced by hard-line opponents of gun regulations.

1980s *Federal gun law eased; liberal law professor calls for re-examining Second Amendment.*

1981 White House press secretary Jim Brady seriously wounded, left partially disabled in attempted assassination of President Ronald Reagan; wife Sarah Brady becomes head of Handgun Control in 1985.

1986 Firearm Owners Protection Act eases ban on interstate gun sales; allows sales by licensed dealers away from principal place of business ("gun show loophole"); bans national firearms registry. . . . Armed Career Criminals Act provides for enhanced sentences for firearms possession by "prohibited persons," such as felons.

1989 University of Texas law Professor Sanford Levinson calls for re-examining scope, meaning of right to keep and bear arms.

1990s *Gun controls at federal level advance amid concern over mass shootings; many states pass right-to-carry laws.*

1990 Congress bans import of "assault weapons."

1993 Brady Handgun Violence Prevention Act requires five-day waiting period for background check on handgun purchasers; waiting period lapses in 1998 with creation of instant background checks.

1996 Lautenberg Amendment extends federal "felon-in-possession" offense to include persons convicted of misdemeanor crime of "domestic violence."

2000-Present *Bush administration backs individual right under Second Amendment; Supreme Court follows suit in striking down D.C. handgun ban.*

2000 Republican George W. Bush elected president with endorsement from NRA; Democrat Al Gore is seen by some to have been hurt in critical states by support for gun control.

2001 Federal appeals court in Texas endorses individual right to arms under Second Amendment but finds no bar to prosecution under Lautenberg Amendment.

2002 Bush administration endorses individual right under Second Amendment but successfully urges Supreme Court not to review Texas case.

2003 Six Washingtonians challenge handgun ban; district court judge upholds law in 2004; federal appeals court strikes it down in 2007.

2008 Supreme Court strikes down D.C. gun ban, 5-4; city council rewrites law. . . . Gun rights advocates challenge bans in Chicago, suburbs; defendants cite ruling in efforts to reduce gun-related penalties.

Student Group Supports 'Concealed Carry' on Campus

Opponents call arming students "a terrible and dangerous idea."

Texas State University student Michael Guzman remembers when he first heard there had been a shooting at Virginia Tech on April 16, 2007.

"I sort of dismissed it; I just thought, 'Ah, another school shooting,' " recalls Guzman, a former Marine. "But the next day when I started reading about it, I realized the full extent of what had happened. It just hit me how desensitized my generation has become about such a horrific thing and how defenseless I would be if something like that happened at my school."

So when Guzman heard about Students for Concealed Carry on Campus (SCCC), which was created the day after 32 students were killed at Virginia Tech, he joined immediately. Today the group claims more than 30,000 members on 200 college campuses; Guzman is the organization's president.

SCCC advocates that students with concealed-carry permits be allowed to carry firearms on their college campuses and seeks to advance its position through academic discussion.

"We want people to realize that there is a basis in empirical evidence to support our cause," Guzman said at the group's first national conference last August in Washington, D.C. "We're not just spouting inflamed rhetoric; there's logic and thought to how we feel."

But Brian Siebel, a senior attorney at the Brady Center to Prevent Gun Violence, calls arming students "a terrible and dangerous idea. College campuses are far safer than the rest of society. Why import the dangers of the outside society, where concealed carry is legal and gun violence is prevalent, onto safe, gun-free zones?"

Siebel is co-author of "No Gun Left Behind," a 2007 report arguing that college students' often-risky behavior is reason enough to block their access to firearms. A vocal critic of SCCC, the Brady Center contends that more firearms on campus would bring risks that far outweigh the benefits of protection in the event of another school shooting.[1]

SCCC argues that students should be able to defend themselves not only in a school shooting but also against the robberies and assaults that occur in and around college campuses. During protests held by the group in October 2007 and this past April, campus members across the country wore empty holsters to class for a week. Members are also asking their state and congressional lawmakers to support concealed carry on campus legislation.

Although no school has changed its rule since the organization has been formed, Liberty University in Lynchburg, Va., plans to consider the matter at its next Board of Trustees meeting in early March.

The SCCC is also working to change the law in Texas, where state lawmakers are considering proposed legislation that

Gun rights advocates view as similarly tainted the first 20th-century gun law: New York's Sullivan Law, the 1911 statute still on the books that requires a license to buy or carry a handgun. Gun rights advocates view the law not as an anti-crime measure but a xenophobic effort to keep weapons out of the hands of Italian immigrants.

Congress passed the first federal gun laws in the 1930s. The National Firearms Act of 1934 required registration by sellers or owners of "gangster-type" weapons such as sawed-off shotguns. The Federal Firearms Act of 1938 required a federal license for dealers in all weapons and ammunition; sales to convicted felons were prohibited.

One year later, the Supreme Court in *United States v. Miller* (1939) upheld convictions under the 1934 law for possession of unregistered sawed-off shotguns. Scalia and Stevens disagree on the meaning of the ruling. Stevens says the court held that the Second Amendment applies only to weapons with "some reasonable relationship" to a militia. But Scalia says the court's limited discussion of the amendment does not refute an individual right. Instead, he says, the ruling "stands only for the proposition that

would change the current no-guns-on-campus law. The group is organizing witnesses and experts to testify at future hearings and has support from Republican Gov. Rick Perry.

Utah currently is the only state that requires public universities to allow concealed carry. Utah authorized the policy after the state Supreme Court struck down the University of Utah's on-campus gun ban in 2006.

SCCC hopes that a change in legislation in Texas will have a domino effect, just as in the 1980s when Florida's new concealed-carry law for residents spurred other states to adopt similar legislation.

Another student group, Students for Gun Free Schools (SGFS), was formed last summer in response to SCCC by the friends and family of a Virginia Tech victim. The group's report, "Why Our Campuses are Safer Without Concealed Handguns," is available online. [2]

Congress, meanwhile, passed a law in December 2007 in response to the Virginia Tech shootings by seeking to improve background checks to prevent adjudicated mentally ill persons from purchasing handguns.

"This bill will make America safer without affecting the rights of a single law-abiding citizen," said the Senate's chief sponsor, New York Democrat Charles E. Schumer.

Rep. Carolyn McCarthy, D-N.Y., whose husband was killed by a gunman on the Long Island Railroad in New

Students grieve following the April 2007 shootings at Virginia Tech. Student Seung-Hui Cho killed 32 people and wounded many others before committing suicide.

York, said, "To me, this is the best Christmas present I could ever receive."

Although the bill won rare support from both the Brady Campaign to Prevent Gun Violence and the National Rifle Association, other groups said that in forging compromise with the gun lobby, the bill's authors unintentionally imposed an unnecessary burden on government agencies by enabling thousands of people to buy guns.

"Rather than focusing on improving the current laws prohibiting people with certain mental health disabilities from buying guns, the bill is now nothing more than a gun lobby wish list," said Kristen Rand, legislative director of the Violence Policy Center. "It will waste millions of taxpayer dollars restoring the gun privileges of persons previously determined to present a danger to themselves or others."[3]

— *Vyomika Jairam*

[1] Allen Roston and Brian Siebel, "No Gun Left Behind — The Gun Lobby's Campaign to Push Guns into Colleges and Schools," Brady Center to Prevent Gun Violence, May 2007.

[2] "Why Our Campuses are Safer Without Concealed Handguns," Students for Gun Free Schools, www.studentsforgunfreeschools.org/SGFSWhyOurCampuses-Electronic.pdf.

[3] Laurie Kellman, "Congress OKs Va Tech-Inspired Gun Bill," The Associated Press, Dec. 20, 2007.

the Second Amendment right, whatever its nature, extends only to certain types of weapons."[12]

Drawing Lines

Battle lines formed between gun rights and gun control groups beginning in the 1960s and hardened through the rest of the 20th century. The sharp divisions first emerged as Congress considered and eventually enacted a tough, federal gun control law in response to the assassinations and the urban crime and unrest of the 1960s. They hardened in the 1970s with the birth of the

handgun control movement and the takeover of the National Rifle Association by hard-line opponents of gun regulations. Gun owners gained ground in Washington in the 1980s and continued to make progress in the states in the 1990s, even as gun control advocates were winning some significant victories in Congress.

Lee Harvey Oswald's use of a mail-order rifle to assassinate President John F. Kennedy in Dallas on Nov. 22, 1963, prompted calls for a federal gun law that bore fruit five years later in the wake of public outrage over the

Mom checks out a Glock at the National Rifle Association's annual meeting in Louisville, Ky., on May 16, 2008. The NRA has filed a package of suits challenging handgun bans in Chicago and several nearby suburbs.

shooting deaths of two other national leaders: the Rev. Martin Luther King Jr. and Sen. Robert F. Kennedy, D-N.Y. The Gun Control Act of 1968 banned mail-order sale of guns. It also prohibited the interstate sale of pistols or ammunition and of long guns unless contiguous states authorized such sales. In addition, the law imposed an outright ban on possession of guns by "prohibited persons," including felons, fugitives, alcoholics, drug users, "mental defectives" or juveniles. Congress, however, rejected President Lyndon B. Johnson's call for federal licensing and firearms registration.

The organized gun control movement that began to emerge in the 1970s owed its creation to two victims of gun violence. Mark Borinsky founded the National Council to Control Handguns in 1974 after being robbed at gunpoint as a graduate student in Chicago. Pete Shields, a Republican businessman, joined the organization after his son's murder during San Francisco's so-called Zebra killings of 1973-1974 and eventually became its executive director and later chairman. It later changed its name to Handgun Control, Inc., and in 2001 to the Brady Campaign to Prevent Handgun Violence. It originally worked with but later separated from the harder-line National Coalition to Ban Handguns, now known as the Coalition to Stop Gun Violence.

On the opposite side, the National Rifle Association — originally formed in 1871 as a shooting association — had been actively opposing federal gun laws at least since the 1930s. The NRA leadership had angered many of its members, however, by endorsing some federal controls during deliberations on the 1968 law. NRA Executive Committee member Harlon Carter began urging a firmer stand against any gun controls in 1972. He gained support for his views thanks to editorials criticizing the NRA leadership in the association's own publication, *The American Rifleman*, and in editor Tartaro's magazine, *Gun Week*. The dispute came to a head in the so-called "Revolt at Cincinnati" at the NRA's annual meeting in 1977, which ousted the existing leadership and turned what Carter called "the new NRA" into a single-issue group denounced by critics as "the gun lobby."

Gun rights advocates gained some ground after the attempted assassination of President Ronald Reagan in 1981 but suffered significant setbacks during the rest of the decade. Most important, Congress eased federal gun restrictions with the Firearms Owners Protection Act of 1986 — also known as the McClure-Volkmer Act after its principal Senate and House sponsors. The law allowed interstate gun sales if the purchase is legal in the buyer's home state. It also created what critics call the "gun show loophole" by allowing licensed firearms dealers to sell guns away from their principal place of business. And it included a specific prohibition on creating a national gun registry. In line with the NRA's lobbying stance, Congress in the same year included provisions in the Armed Career Criminal Act to increase sentences for possession of firearms by "prohibited persons" under the 1968 act.

Gun control advocates rebounded with significant successes in Washington in the 1990s. The Jan. 17, 1989, killing of five schoolchildren in Stockton, Calif., by a man armed with a semiautomatic assault rifle spurred Congress the next year to ban the import of specified semiautomatic weapons designated as "assault weapons." Three years later — with a Democratic president and Democratic-controlled Congress for the first time since 1981 — the Brady Handgun Violence Prevention Act established a federal background check and five-day waiting period to purchase a handgun. The five-day wait lapsed with establishment of the National Instant Criminal Background Check System in 1998.

In the states, meanwhile, gun rights advocates had been pressing arguments that shooting sprees such as the Stockton killings could be prevented or minimized by liberalizing laws to allow carrying of weapons. Through

McCain and Obama Both Support Gun Rights

But NRA calls Obama "anti-gun."

Democrat Barack Obama and Republican John McCain both endorse an individual right to possess guns under the Second Amendment — and so do their two national party platforms. Both presidential candidates also endorsed the Supreme Court's June decision in the *Heller* case that struck down Washington, D.C.'s handgun ban.

Despite those parallels between the two candidates' positions, the National Rifle Association is endorsing McCain while warning in more than $2 million worth of advertising that Obama would be "the most anti-gun president in American history."

From the opposite perspective, the Brady Campaign to Prevent Gun Violence is backing Obama, saying that he would make it "harder for dangerous people to get dangerous weapons" and complaining that McCain has "pandered to the gun lobby."

The opposing groups' interest in gun issues is not shared by the public at large. Guns barely register when voters are asked to identify major issues in the presidential campaign. Among 15 issues specifically listed in a CNN poll of voters in June 2008, guns ranked 12th among those who listed it as "extremely important." In nearly two years of campaigning, Obama and McCain have given the issue only passing attention and are giving it even less attention in the final weeks of a race now concentrated almost solely on economic issues. [1]

Gun rights advocates complain of the lack of attention. "Do you realize we've gone through all three presidential debates, and not one moderator asked a question about the Second Amendment or the *Heller* case?" NRA Executive Vice President/CEO Wayne LaPierre asks on the group's Web site.

LaPierre notes that McCain but not Obama signed a brief submitted by 54 senators in the *Heller* case urging the Supreme Court to strike down the Washington, D.C., gun ban. After the decision, McCain called the ruling "a landmark victory." Obama said he had "always" believed in an individual right under the Second Amendment but also voiced support for "commonsense, effective safety measures."

The Democrats' platform, adopted in August, promises to "preserve Americans' continued Second Amendment

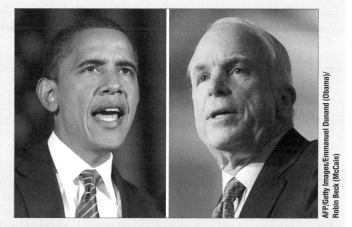

Sens. Barack Obama, D-Ill., and John McCain, R-Ariz., both endorsed the Supreme Court's *Heller* decision striking down the D.C. gun ban.

right to own and use firearms." But it also calls for reinstating the federal ban on so-called assault weapons, improving federal background checks for gun purchasers and closing the "gun show loophole" permitting sales between individuals without a background check.

The Republican platform, approved in September, promises to "uphold the right of individual Americans to own firearms." It goes on to oppose federal licensing or national gun registration and to condemn "frivolous lawsuits" against gun manufacturers. It says gun control "only . . . penalizes law-abiding citizens" and is "ineffective at reducing violent crime."

As senators, McCain supported and Obama opposed a measure to shield gun makers from liability suits. McCain opposed the assault weapon ban adopted in 1994 but did vote for background checks. As a state senator in Illinois, Obama supported a ban on semiautomatic weapons.

McCain pleased gun rights advocates by speaking to the NRA convention in May and by picking Alaska Gov. Sarah Palin — an NRA member — as his vice presidential running mate. Obama antagonized gun owners with a remark at a private fund-raiser talking about "bitter" people who "cling" to guns and religion because of economic frustration.

---

[1] Some background drawn from Glen Johnson, "Gun control a gray issue between McCain, Obama," The Associated Press, Oct. 15, 2008.

the 1990s, a growing number of states passed right-to-carry laws.

Going to Court

Gun rights advocates had been emphasizing a supposed individual right under the Second Amendment throughout the political debates over gun regulations since the 1960s, but they failed to win any court rulings backing the argument. Gradually, however, they picked up support from unexpected quarters: first from a liberal law professor, then from two Supreme Court justices and finally in 2001 and 2002 from the federal government itself. By the time the Supreme Court considered the D.C. handgun ban in March 2008, the individual rights view seemed likely to carry the day — and the only question remained how far the justices would go in setting constitutional limits on gun regulation.

The expansion of the individualist view of the Second Amendment beyond the circle of gun owners and their political supporters can be dated to the publication of a law journal article by a well-known liberal professor in 1989. In "The Embarrassing Second Amendment," Sanford Levinson, a professor at the University of Texas Law School, argued that gun control supporters like himself needed to acknowledge that the amendment did set some constraints on government regulation of guns. More than a decade later, the prominent liberal Harvard law Professor Laurence Tribe came to a similar conclusion and renounced his previous view of the amendment.[13]

Two conservative Supreme Court justices, Scalia and Clarence Thomas, signaled their support for the individual rights view in the 1990s. Thomas called for considering the issue in a concurring opinion in the court's 1997 decision striking down the Brady Act's requirement that local law enforcement agencies conduct background checks on gun purchasers. Scalia explicitly adopted the individual rights view in a passage in his book published the same year, *A Matter of Interpretation.*[14]

The 2000 presidential election brought to the White House a Republican, George W. Bush, who had been endorsed by the NRA and who was seen by some political observers to have owed his victory to pro-gun rights voters in such states as Tennessee and West Virginia. The Bush administration proved to be supportive of gun rights positions, most significantly when Attorney General John Ashcroft issued a memorandum in 2001 specifically endorsing the individual rights view of the Second Amendment. In 2002, the government formally notified the Supreme Court of its change of position in a filing in a criminal case from Texas testing the constitutionality of the ban on gun possession by domestic-violence defendants.

The case, *United States v. Emerson*, resulted in the first federal appeals court decision to adopt the individual rights view. Timothy Emerson, a Texas physician, had challenged his prosecution for possessing a gun while under a domestic violence restraining order. In a lengthy opinion, the 5th U.S. Circuit Court of Appeals in 2001 said that the Second Amendment guaranteed an individual right to possess firearms but that the domestic-violence restriction passed constitutional muster. Emerson appealed to the Supreme Court, where the government echoed support for the individual rights view while urging the justices to allow Emerson's case to go to trial. The court declined to hear the case.[15]

A clearer Second Amendment challenge emerged in 2003, when six Washington, D.C., residents took on the 1976 handgun ban. U.S. District Judge Emmet Sullivan upheld the law in 2004, citing the Supreme Court's 1939 decision in *Miller.* In 2007, however, the D.C. Circuit Court of Appeals ruled the law unconstitutional in a 2-1 decision written by a prominent conservative judge. The Second Amendment "protects an individual right to keep and bear arms," Laurence Silberman wrote, and the complete ban on handguns violated that right.

Washington officials appealed to the Supreme Court even while gun control advocates acknowledged the risk of an adverse ruling. The case attracted more than 60 friend-of-the-court briefs — with two-thirds of them calling for the law to be struck down. The Bush administration urged the justices to recognize an individual right but give D.C. a second chance to justify the law. The justices' questions during the March 18, 2008, arguments, however, strongly indicated that the court's five conservatives agreed with the individual rights view and saw the city's ban as a clear violation of the right.

Scalia and Stevens dramatically summarized their respective opinions in the case as the court ended its term on June 26. Based on textual and historical analysis, Scalia said the Second Amendment established an individual right to possess firearms in the home for self-defense.

"It is not the role of this Court to pronounce the Second Amendment extinct," Scalia said as he concluded.

Will wider availability of handguns increase public safety?

YES   **Gary Kleck**
*Professor, College of Criminology and
Criminal Justice, Florida State University*

NO   **Philip J. Cook**
Professor of Public Policy, Duke University
Jens Ludwig
*Professor of Social Service Administration, Law
and Public Policy, University of Chicago*

Written for *CQ Researcher*, October 2008

Written for *CQ Researcher*, October 2008

It is unlikely that the Supreme Court's recent Second Amendment decision will noticeably affect national gun ownership rates, but it could increase levels in the handful of local areas that had previously banned handguns, such as Washington, D.C., and Chicago. It is therefore worth reviewing what the best evidence indicates about the likely effects of changes in gun availability.

No one is proposing to legalize the possession or acquisition of guns by convicted criminals, which is currently forbidden in every state. Thus, any weakening of legal restrictions on guns in the foreseeable future is likely to pertain only to those individuals not previously convicted of crimes.

This distinction is important because research has consistently indicated that gun possession and use has both violence-increasing and violence-decreasing effects, and that which of these effects dominates depends on whether the guns are possessed or used by criminals or non-criminals. Gun possession among non-criminals has overwhelmingly violence-reducing effects, while gun possession among criminals has mixed effects.

Research has unanimously indicated that defensive gun use is effective. Victims who use guns during crimes are less likely to be injured or lose property than those who use other resistance strategies or do not resist at all — and almost always without wounding or killing the criminal. Victim gun use does not provoke offenders into greater violence, nor does it result in offenders taking guns from victims and using them against the victims.

Gun ownership may also deter some criminals from even attempting some crimes in the first place, for fear of confronting an armed victim. Criminals interviewed in prison indicate they have at times refrained from committing crimes because they believed a potential victim might have a gun. Likewise, crime rates have dropped substantially after highly publicized instances of prospective victims arming themselves, being trained in gun use or using guns against criminals. Further, burglars in the United States are more careful to avoid residences where the victims are home than burglars in nations with lower gun ownership; burglaries against unoccupied homes cannot result in injury to the residents.

Gun availability among non-criminals tends to increase public safety. More guns among non-criminals does provide more guns for criminals to steal, and thus might increase criminal gun levels, but the statistically strongest research indicates that higher overall gun levels have either no net effect on violent-crime rates or mild crime-reducing effects.

One of the most hotly contested issues in the larger debate on gun control is whether guns in a community have a positive or negative effect on crime. Now, as a result of the *Heller* decision, the issue may be tested, as gun regulations are challenged on Second Amendment grounds in one jurisdiction after another.

If gun regulations are relaxed and more residents of large, crime-prone cities acquire handguns for self-defense, the rates of assault, robbery, and rape will not be noticeably affected. What will be affected is the assailants' choice of weapon. An increase in gun ownership fuels the secondary market by which guns flow to youths and criminals through loans among family and friends, off-the-books sales and theft. Of course, gun prevalence may have other effects as well — if criminals are concerned about encountering an armed victim, they may desist (the "deterrence" argument). But theoretical arguments are not enough to resolve this issue.

Fortunately, the empirical evidence is very strong, thanks to the discovery of a new proxy for gun prevalence. It turns out that the percentage of suicides with guns is very highly correlated with household gun ownership rates, both across jurisdictions and over time. That discovery has opened the door for empirical research that was previously hamstrung by the lack of a good measure of local gun prevalence. Now we know with certainty that in areas where more households own guns, young men are more likely to carry guns, and more robberies and assaults are likely to involve guns. And that is not good news.

Increased gun use will result in a higher murder rate. When an assailant uses a gun instead of a knife or club, it greatly increases the chance that the victim will die. Guns do not cause violence, but they intensify violence. We have found, using long-term studies in large U.S. counties, that an increase in gun prevalence increases the gun murder rate but has no effect on the non-gun murder rate, so the net result is an increase in the overall murder rate. A 10 percent increase in gun prevalence results in a 1-3 percent increase in murders, all other things equal. We were able to rule out the possibility that this result reflects reverse causation, although we cannot be absolutely sure in the absence of randomized field experiments.

Sadly, the *Heller* decision may provide something akin to a grand experiment with increased gun prevalence.

He stressed that other regulations could survive, including registration and licensing, limits on carrying weapons in "sensitive" places and categorical bans on possession by felons and the mentally ill.

Stevens countered that the ruling would force courts to second-guess decisions by elected officials about gun regulations. "This Court should stay out of this political thicket," he warned.

CURRENT SITUATION

Testing *Heller's* Reach

A decade-long legal battle over gun shows at the Alameda County Fairgrounds in California is emerging as the case likely to yield the first ruling on whether the newly recognized Second Amendment gun-possession right limits state and local gun regulations.

Gun show promoters Russell and Sallie Nordyke are citing the Supreme Court's decision in the District of Columbia gun ban case in their effort to invalidate a county ordinance that effectively bans gun shows at the fairgrounds by prohibiting guns on any county-owned property.

The Supreme Court's *Heller* decision applies only to Washington, D.C. — a federal jurisdiction — and leaves open the question whether the Second Amendment also applies to state and local governments. The Nordykes are asking the 9th U.S. Circuit Court of Appeals to rule that the Second Amendment should be "incorporated" against the states and then to strike down the county's ordinance as an unconstitutional local government restriction on gun possession rights.[16]

"The Founding Fathers believed that the right of self-defense was the premier human right and that it included the right to possess arms for self-defense," says Don Kates, a longtime gun rights advocate who joined as co-counsel in the Nordykes' case on behalf of the Second Amendment Foundation. "Once you accept those premises, why would you not incorporate it?"

The county's lawyers, however, contend that the Second Amendment should not be enforced against the states under the Supreme Court's current approach to the incorporation doctrine because the right was not well established in English common law and is not regarded as fundamental in the states today.

Two men wearing guns stop for lunch in Vermillion, Ohio, in December 2003 during a demonstration in support of legislation permitting concealed weapons in the state. That law was passed in 2004. A new Ohio law that took effect on Sept. 8, 2008, follows passage of the 2004 law and a 2006 measure preempting local gun regulations.

"States are all over the map in the degree to which they regulate firearm use," says Peter Pierce, a Los Angeles attorney handling the Second Amendment aspect of the case for the county. "So it's very difficult to say that there's any degree of uniformity in the states."

The long history of the Nordykes' suit makes it more likely to yield an early ruling on applying the Second Amendment to the states than the challenges to local gun bans filed immediately after the Supreme Court's decision on June 26. A federal judge in Chicago is in the early stages of presiding over three consolidated suits — two challenging Chicago's handgun ban and a separate suit against a similar ban in suburban Oak Park.

The NRA originally included San Francisco in a suit challenging a handgun ban imposed by the San Francisco Housing Authority. Because the city has been dismissed from the suit, the Second Amendment incorporation issue dropped out.[17]

Alameda County banned guns on county-owned property a year after a gang-related shootout at the fairgrounds in Pleasanton on July 4, 1998. Nine people were wounded and seven others injured from a resulting stampede.

The ordinance was sponsored by County Supervisor Mary King, who had earlier introduced a measure specifically banning gun shows at the fairgrounds. After the ordinance was enacted, Sallie Nordyke, owner with her husband Russell of T.S. Trade Shows, said the measure would likely put them out of business if followed by other counties.

Today, Alameda County Counsel Richard Winnie defends the ordinance as a public safety measure not only for the fairgrounds but also for many other county-owned facilities. "The county government deals with social welfare issues, a lot of places where there are conflicts," Winnie says. "It's very important to make sure the public feels safe, and guns are a situation where people feel endangered."

The Nordykes' case has wound its way through both federal and state courts. The 9th Circuit rejected the Nordykes' claim that the ordinance violated their free speech rights to promote the use and sale of guns. The federal court also rejected a Second Amendment claim on the strength of a prior 9th Circuit ruling, but two judges criticized the earlier decision. On a referral from the 9th Circuit, the California Supreme Court also rejected the Nordykes' argument that state law preempted the county's ordinance.

Both sides have now filed new briefs discussing the *Heller* case. The three-judge 9th Circuit panel has yet to schedule arguments.

Even if the Second Amendment is held applicable to the states, one expert predicts most state and local government regulations will still be upheld. "You're not going to see a major revolution," says Ohio State history Professor Cornell. "You can't have wholesale bans on handguns. Almost anything else that can survive the political process is going to pass constitutional muster."

Gaining in the States

Ohio gun rights advocates are resting on their accomplishments after winning enactment of a new law — signed by Democratic Gov. Ted Strickland — that further eases state gun regulations.

The new law, which took effect Sept. 8, follows two other major victories in the past four years: a 2004 law permitting carrying of concealed weapons and a 2006 measure preempting any local gun regulations. The preemption measure took effect in March 2007 after the Ohio General Assembly had overridden a veto by Republican Gov. Robert Taft.

"The past 18 months have been the best there have ever been," says Ken Hanson, an attorney who is legislative chair for the Buckeye Firearms Association. Hanson says the group has no current legislative agenda at the state level, pleading "fatigue" after "years and years" of fighting.

The state's lone, prominent gun control lobbyist concedes that gun rights forces gained the upper hand with passage of the concealed carry law in 2004 and have been picking up additional victories since then.

"They nitpick at it, and it goes downhill from there," says Toby Hoover, executive director of the Ohio Coalition Against Gun Violence. "The reality is that they don't want any regulation."

Ohio was relatively late in passage of concealed-carry and preemption legislation, but the two laws are emblematic of the successes that gun rights advocates have won at the state level. The NRA counts 47 states with laws preempting local gun regulations: all but Hawaii, Illinois and Nevada. It counts 40 states as having "right to carry" laws — 11 of those enacted since 2000. (*See chart, p. 154.*)

Laws differ from state to state. Ohio's law preempts localities from banning guns in public parks, according to a 4-3 ruling by the state's Supreme Court in September. By contrast, the California Supreme Court's 2002 ruling in the Alameda County fairgrounds case allows localities to ban guns on publicly owned property.

Ohio passed its concealed carry law in 2004 after what Hoover describes as a 10-year legislative struggle. "We didn't really have much good news before then," Hanson concedes.

The measure is typical of so-called shall-issue laws, which generally require authorities to issue permits to carry concealed handguns to any applicant meeting specified requirements. The Ohio law requires applicants to be at least 21 years of age, to have taken at least 12 hours of firearms training and to have demonstrated competency through written and shooting examinations. A criminal background check is required. No permits are to be issued to anyone convicted of a felony, a drug offense or certain violent misdemeanors.

Taft signed the concealed-carry law. Two years later, he vetoed the preemption measure, citing home-rule concerns. The veto override was the first in Ohio in 28 years, according to Hanson.

Strickland, a Democrat from rural southeastern Ohio with what Hanson calls an "A-plus" rating on gun issues, signed the 2008 measure into law. It relaxes various restrictions on where concealed weapons can be carried and also denies landlords the right to prohibit guns on rented premises. In addition, the measure enacts a so-called "castle defense" provision, expanding the scope for using deadly force in self-defense in one's home or car.

Hanson, who lives just outside Columbus, attributes gun rights advocates' successes to a new political attitude toward gun issues among legislators in both parties. "The legislators started to realize the gun issue was nothing to lose and everything to gain," he says. "When [legislators] do vote pro-gun, they gain contributions and volunteers."

For her part, Hoover sees the issue as one that divides rural and urban lawmakers. "We have a lot of big cities," says Hoover, who lives in Toledo. "The rural areas don't really understand the crime problems in big cities. The legislature felt they had the right to tell the local governments that they had no right to govern on this issue, so they passed a preemption."

Gun rights advocates push for concealed-carry laws by pointing to a personal desire for self-defense, while gun control supporters warn they are likely to increase gun violence and accidents. Many experts concede the evidence is inconclusive. "Most of the research shows it doesn't make much of a difference one way or the other," says Harry Wilson, a professor of political science at Roanoke College in Virginia.

Gun rights advocates were already advancing in the states before the Supreme Court's decision in the *Heller* case. One gun control advocate believes the court's decision may help gun rights supporters' cause despite the passage in the court's opinion signaling approval of many gun regulations.

"Most state legislators will hear a message that when it comes to gun controls, gun bans — the Supreme Court has said you can't go there," says Horwitz of the Coalition to Stop Gun Violence.

OUTLOOK

Missing the Bull's-Eye?

The Supreme Court's decision in the Washington, D.C., gun ban case may change the political and legal background on gun issues less than it might seem to portend after an initial reading. It recognizes an individual right under the Second Amendment already largely accepted by the American public and then quickly signals likely acceptance of a range of restrictions on the possession or carrying of firearms.

Despite the court's cautionary passage, gun rights advocates are hopeful that lower courts will rely on the decision to begin striking down other gun restrictions once — as they assume — the Second Amendment is held applicable to the states. "Judges have been told to get re-educated," says Gun Owners' Executive Director Pratt. "Read the doggone amendment and learn what the words mean."

From the opposite perspective, gun control supporters are saying that the decision could help aid their cause by eliminating the fear that restrictions could merely be a first step toward gun bans. "Over the long haul, it may make it more difficult for the gun lobby to frame the debate as a cultural debate," says the Brady Center's Henigan.

Outside experts, however, are discounting the likelihood of significant shifts, either legally or politically. "Everybody will continue to believe what they've always believed," says Florida State Professor Kleck. Roanoke College's Wilson agrees. "Five years from now, we'll be pretty much where we are today," he says.

"Things may loosen up a bit," Wilson adds. "We will have seen a couple more cases go up to the [Supreme] Court." But gun rights advocates, he says, "will be taking cases they're pretty certain they can win."

Gura, the winning lawyer in the D.C. gun ban case, expects messier litigation that over time will result in advances for gun rights. "We're going to see a number of frivolous and silly cases making bizarre Second Amendment claims that are not going to work," he says, citing, in particular, cases challenging felon-in-possession law. "But there are also going to be some cases that will advance and define the right to arms as practical and meaningful."

Skirmishes will continue in state legislatures, Wilson says, but they will be fights "at the fringes." Nationally, the opposing interest groups have opposing agendas. Gun rights advocates imagine a national concealed carry law; gun control supporters put highest priority on closing the "gun show loophole."

A new Congress with what is widely predicted to be a bigger Democratic majority may be somewhat more receptive to gun control proposals. The new president — Obama or possibly even McCain — is unlikely to be as supportive of gun rights groups as the Bush administration has been.

Nevertheless, gun issues seem unlikely to rank high on the agenda for either the president or Congress after Inauguration Day, Jan. 20, 2009. The economy is still expected to be in distress, wars will be continuing in Iraq and Afghanistan and a plateful of other unattended issues — domestic and international — will be crying for attention.

Gun control advocates appear to be resting their hopes on Democrats controlling both ends of Pennsylvania Avenue. "With a change in administration and a change in Congress, you may very well have a change of momentum for stronger gun laws, just as we had during the Clinton administration," says Henigan.

"It remains the case that the vast majority of the American people support stronger gun laws," he says. "The vast majority of gun owners support stronger gun laws."

But Wilson doubts that Democrats will see a political advantage in taking on the issue. "The Democrats don't want to touch this with a 10-foot pole," he says.

Meanwhile, the NRA's Halbrook scoffs at gun control supporters' hope for a coming-together on gun issues. "There's going to be continued controversy," he says. "Those who wish to restrict or ban handguns — now they're going to say everything is reasonable. It's the same stuff, basically."

"Each side sees it as a slippery slope," says E. Stewart Moritz, an associate professor at Akron University School of Law in Ohio, who teaches a course on firearms regulation. "Because of that, every inch of ground is so hard-fought. They don't know how to stop."

NOTES

1. Reporting in Phoenix by freelance journalist Noble Sprayberry.

2. The decision is *District of Columbia v. Heller* 554 U.S. — (2008), www.supremecourtus.gov/opinions/07pdf/07-290.pdf. For a detailed account, see Kenneth Jost, "Second Amendment Confers Individual Right to Firearms," *The Supreme Court Yearbook 2007-2008* (November 2008). For previous coverage, see these *CQ Researcher* reports: Bob Adams, "Gun Control Debate," Nov. 12, 2004, pp. 949-972; Kenneth Jost, "Gun Control Standoff," Dec. 19, 1997, pp. 1105-1128; Richard L. Worsnop, "Gun Control," June 10, 1994, pp. 505-528.

3. For background, see Kenneth Jost, "Gun Violence," *CQ Researcher*, May 25, 2007, pp. 457-480.

4. The case, *McDonald v. City of Chicago*, 1:2008cv03645, is pending before U.S. District Court Judge Milton Shadur.

5. See Deborah Horan, "Under fire, suburbs vote down gun bans," *Chicago Tribune*, Aug. 12, 2008, p. 1.

6. The case is *GeorgiaCarry.Org, Inc. v. City of Atlanta*, 1:08:CV-2171-MHS (U.S. Dist. Ct. N.D. Ga.). For documents, see www.georgiacarry.org or www.asherafuse.com, the Web site of the private law firm defending the city in the case. For coverage, see Bill Rankin, "Ban on guns at airport to stay," *Atlanta Journal-Constitution*, Aug. 12, 2008, p. 1A. Shoob's formal order dismissing the complaint on Sept. 26 is now being appealed to the 11th U.S. Circuit Court of Appeals.

7. Shannon McCaffrey, "In many US airports, guns are OK outside security," The Associated Press, Oct. 15, 2008. The list includes Dallas/Fort Worth, Detroit, Los Angeles, Minneapolis/St. Paul, Philadelphia, Phoenix and San Francisco.

8. For early coverage, see Mark Sherman, "Guns ruling spawns legal challenges by felons," The Associated Press, July 19, 2008.

9. "Sentencing Law and Policy," http://sentencing.typepad.com/sentencing_law_and_policy/. The blog includes a number of *Heller*-related entries, some of them compiled from a separate blog, "The Volokh Conspiracy," published by UCLA law Professor Eugene Volokh (www.volokh.com).

10. Background drawn in part from narrative chronology in Gregg Lee Carter, *Gun Control in the United States: A Reference Handbook* (2006). On the English history, from an individual rights perspective, see Joyce Lee Malcolm, *To Keep and Bear Arms: The Origins of an*

Anglo-American Right (1994); on American history, from a "civic participation" perspective, see Saul Cornell, *A Well-Regulated Militia: The Founding Fathers and the Origins of Gun Control* (2006).

11. See Carter, *op. cit.*, pp. 128-129. The decisions are *United States v. Cruikshank*, 92 U.S. 542 (1876) and *Presser v. Illinois*, 116 U.S. 252 (1886).

12. The decision is *Miller v. United States*, 307 U.S. 174 (1939).

13. For an overview, see Adam Liptak, "A Liberal Case for the Individual Right to Own Guns Helps Sway the Federal Judiciary," *The New York Times*, May 7, 2007, p. A1. Levinson's article, originally published in *Yale Law Journal*, Vol. 99, pp. 637-659 (1989), can be found online on a number of pro-gun rights Web sites.

14. See *Printz v. United States*, 521 U.S. 898, 936 (1997); Antonin Scalia, *A Matter of Interpretation: Federal Courts and the Law* (1997), pp. 136-137.

15. The case is *United States v. Emerson*, 270 F.3d 303 (5th Cir. 2001). For coverage, see Linda Greenhouse, "Justices Reject Case on Right to Bear Arms," *The New York Times*, June 11, 2002, p. A24.

16. The case is *Nordyke v. King*, Civ. 07-15673 (9th Cir.); documents can be found on Hoffmanmag.com, a blog published by a pro-gun rights businessman, Gene Hoffman Jr. (www.hoffmang.com/firearms/Nordyke-v-King). For coverage, see Bob Egelko, "Gun show promoters may appeal weapons ban at fairgrounds," *San Francisco Chronicle*, April 20, 2007, p. B2.

17. For a wrap-up, see Judy Keen, "NRA suits push cities to drop gun bans," *USA Today*, Sept. 11, 2008, p. 3A.

BIBLIOGRAPHY

Books

Burbick, Joan, *Gun Show Nation: Gun Culture and American Democracy*, New Press, 2006.
A professor of English and American studies at Washington State University in Pullman critically examines the role of guns in American culture after extensive travels to gun shows, gun stores and gun rights conventions. Includes detailed notes.

Carter, Gregg Lee, *Gun Control in the United States: A Reference Handbook*, ABC-Clio, 2006.
The comprehensive reference work opens with expository chapters on the social and political landscape of gun control and the practical operation of gun regulations. Carter chairs the Department of History and Social Sciences at Bryant University in Rhode Island. Includes detailed chronology, federal and state laws, organization list and other reference materials.

Cornell, Saul, *A Well-Regulated Militia: The Founding Fathers and the Origins of Gun Control in America*, Oxford University Press, 2006.
A professor of history at Ohio State University examines the debates in the United States over the right to be armed from the Revolutionary era and the writing of the Second Amendment through the 19th century. Cornell believes neither side in contemporary gun rights debates is "faithful to the original understanding" of the amendment. Includes detailed notes.

Jacobs, James B., *Can Gun Control Work?* Oxford University Press, 2002.
The director of the Center for Research in Crime and Justice at New York University critically examines the on-the-ground practicalities of gun control. Jacobs, a professor of law, cautions against believing that some ideal gun control solution would substantially reduce violent crime. Includes notes, 16-page bibliography.

Malcolm, Joyce Lee, *To Keep and Bear Arms: The Origins of an Anglo-American Right*, Harvard University Press, 1994.
Malcolm, now a professor at George Mason University School of Law, traces the right to be armed from its origins in 17th-century England through the writing of the Second Amendment. Malcolm says the right "has not worn well" in either England or the United States. Includes detailed notes. Malcolm's more recent work, *Guns and Violence: The English Experience* (Harvard University Press, 2002), closes with two chapters analyzing and proposing a resolution of the gun control debate in the United States.

Spitzer, Robert J., *The Politics of Gun Control* (4th ed.), CQ Press, 2008.
A professor of political science at the State University of New York-Cortland provides a comprehensive overview of gun control issues with new material on, among other

things, state right-to-carry and "shoot-first" self-defense laws. Includes chapter notes.

Wilson, Harry L., Guns, *Gun Control, and Elections: The Politics and Policy of Firearms***, Rowan & Littlefield, 2007.**

A professor of public affairs at Roanoke College tries to provide a balanced account of the political and policy debate over gun control. Wilson ends up taking the gun rights perspective but criticizes "scare tactics" by gun rights advocates and gun control groups alike. Includes chapter notes, 16-page list of works cited.

Reports and Studies

"The Second Amendment and the Right to Bear Arms After *DC v. Heller*," *UCLA Law Review***, Vol. 56, No. 5 (forthcoming, June 2009).**

A symposium scheduled for Jan. 23, 2009, at the University of California-Los Angeles Law School will include invited papers from a range of leading experts and advocates representing all sides of the gun rights debate.

"Unintended Consequences: What the Supreme Court's Second Amendment Decision in *D.C. v. Heller* **Means for the Future of Gun Laws," Brady Center to Prevent Gun Violence, Oct. 20, 2008, www.bradycenter.org/ xshare/pdf/ heller/post-heller-white-paper.pdf.**

The 17-page "white paper" argues that the Supreme Court's decision in the D.C. gun ban case may aid efforts to enact and enforce "reasonable" gun laws by alleviating fears of broader gun bans. Gun rights organizations such as the National Rifle Association, Gun Owners of America and Second Amendment Foundation have not produced comparable overviews of the impact of the *Heller* decision but do provide various analyses and commentaries on their Web sites.

Wilkinson, J. Harvie III, "Of Guns, Abortions, and the Unraveling Rule of Law," *Virginia Law Review* **(spring 2009); available on Social Science Research Network (http://papers.ssrn.com/sol3/papers.cfm?abstract_ id=1265118).**

The conservative former chief judge of the 4th U.S. Circuit Court of Appeals accuses the Supreme Court of "a failure to adhere to a conservative methodology" in the *Heller* decision. Wilkinson's article drew many comments on legal blogs, including criticism on such conservative blogs as *National Review Online* (http://bench .nationalreview.com/) and the Volokh Conspiracy (www .volokh.com).

For More Information

Brady Campaign to Prevent Gun Violence, 1225 Eye St., N.W., Suite 1100, Washington, DC 20005; (202) 898-0792; www.bradycenter.org. Political action committee dedicated to ending gun violence without banning all guns; the Brady Center to Prevent Gun Violence (same address) is the organization's affiliated non-partisan policy arm.

Centers for Disease Control and Prevention, 1600 Clifton Rd., Atlanta, GA 30333; 1-800-232-4636; www .cdc.gov. Agency of the U.S. Department of Health and Human Services that works to protect public health and safety by providing information to help enhance health decisions; maintains statistics on deaths and injuries resulting from firearm use.

Coalition to Stop Gun Violence, 1424 L St., N.W., Suite 2-1, Washington, DC 20005; (202) 408-0061; www.csgv .org. Coalition of 45 national organizations — including religious organizations, child welfare advocates and public health professionals — pushing a progressive agenda to reduce firearms death and injury.

Gun Owners of America, 8001 Forbes Place, Suite 102, Springfield, VA 22151; (703) 321-8585; www.gunowners .org. Nonprofit lobbying organization defending Second Amendment rights of gun owners.

National Rifle Association, 11250 Waples Mill Rd., Fairfax, VA 22030; 1-800-672-3888; www.nra.org. Promotes the safety, education and responsibility of gun ownership and the rights of Americans under the Second Amendment to own and carry guns.

Second Amendment Foundation, 12500 N.E. 10th Place, Bellevue, WA 98005; (425) 454-7012; www.saf.org. Educational and legal policy center dedicated to promoting a better understanding of Americans' constitutional rights under the Second Amendment to possess firearms.

8

Housing the Homeless

Peter Katel

Nursing assistant Leida Ortiz is working three part-time jobs and getting back on her feet after becoming homeless in July and living with her two children in a motel room for two weeks. At a recent briefing on Capitol Hill, she urged housing advocates to work to expand the emergency housing program that helped her family.

From *CQ Researcher*,
December 18, 2009.

L eida Ortiz was getting by. She lived with her sister and both of their children in an apartment in Worcester, Mass. Then, in the spring of 2007, her factory-worker father was diagnosed with stomach cancer, so Ortiz moved back into the home her parents owned to help her mother care for her father.

After he died, in December of that year, Ortiz and her mother couldn't afford the mortgage payments on the house. A move back to her sister's didn't work out, so Ortiz and her two children began sharing an apartment with a roommate. But she wasn't making enough from her part-time job as a nursing assistant to kick in her $400 share of the rent.

The roommate asked her and her 11-year-old son, Joseph, and 5-year-old daughter, Angelina, to leave.

"I became homeless in July," Ortiz said. "I cried every night, wondering if my kids were going to end up in different schools somewhere else. We were living out of our bags. We didn't know where we were going to end up next. The kids, they see that you're stressed, they get stressed. They see you putting yourself to sleep every night crying."

Speaking at a Capitol Hill briefing held by an advocacy group in early December, Ortiz recounted a happy ending to her family's two-week stay at a motel. She urged the assembled housing advocates and congressional staffers to work to expand the "prevention and rapid rehousing" program that she credited for her family's rescue.

Now working three part-time jobs, the 30-year-old Ortiz hardly fits the picture of "homeless" that hit the national consciousness in the early 1980s — seemingly unemployable people suffering

173

California Has Largest Homeless Population

Nearly 160,000 people in California are homeless, more than twice as many as New York, the state with the next-largest homeless population. Seventeen states have more than 10,000 homeless people, while 11 states have fewer than 2,000.

Homeless Population by State
(on a single night in January 2008)

Legend:
- 0-1,999
- 2,000-9,999
- 10,000-19,999
- 20,000-59,999
- 60,000+

Source: "The 2008 Annual Homeless Assessment Report to Congress," U.S. Department of Housing and Urban Development, July 2009

mental illness or addiction or both. But in an economic climate shadowed by massive unemployment, some experts see working families facing threats to their housing stability that easily can escalate into homelessness, as in Ortiz's case. "When you're going into a recession starting with a limited supply of affordable housing, with families who are precariously housed and at risk, it's the perfect storm for families," says Mary K. Cunningham, a housing specialist at the nonpartisan Urban Institute think tank.

In 2008, homelessness among people in families rose by 9 percent over the number from the previous year, the U.S. Department of Housing and Urban Development (HUD) reported in an annual survey on homelessness.[1]

Overall, about 1.6 million people slept in homeless shelters or other temporary housing in the United States in 2008, the report said.[2] Whether that rough estimate shows an increase or decrease from the 1980s can't be determined, Cunningham says, given the vast differences in methodology from then until now.

Whatever the case, housing advocates are united in the belief that government action can eliminate homelessness once and for all. Conservatives tend to be more skeptical, though ideology isn't a reliable guide to views on homelessness.

"It is immoral," Cheh Kim, a staff member for Sen. Christopher Bond, R-Mo., told the Capitol Hill briefing. "People need to understand that anybody can slip into homelessness. Just go into shelters and talk to people and realize that a lot of them were middle-income, or owned small businesses, and because of one little thing in their life, they just fell down."

To be sure, Kim's overall view was that Congress has been responding effectively to the persistence of homelessness. A major piece of evidence: a $1.5 billion appropriation in mid-2009 for a new Homelessness Prevention and Rapid Re-Housing Program (HPRP).

But Joel Segal, a staffer for Rep. John Conyers, D-Mich., argued at the briefing that congressional attitudes remain an obstacle to a definitive solution to homelessness. "A majority of people in Congress do think that homeless people want to be homeless," Segal told Kim and the rest of those present. "That's who they see in the streets pushing the baskets. Trust me on this — they do not know who's in those shelters, because most members of Congress are raising money from very wealthy donors.'"

Notwithstanding the staffers' emphasis on shelters, the growing consensus among advocates for the homeless is that a danger exists of policy makers focusing too heavily on shelters. That approach, they say, would effectively mean continuing to channel mentally unstable and chronically homeless people into shelters instead of expanding a newer strategy of building permanent facilities designed to meet their needs. And families in unstable housing situations — perhaps "doubled up" in relatives' homes — should be kept out of shelters in the first place.

"What we've learned over the past 10 years is that building up a bigger shelter system is a sort of self-fulfilling prophecy," says Nan Roman, president of the National Alliance to End Homelessness.

A number of sources report rising housing instability among families. HUD experts studying present-day trends see a link between the economic crisis and the growing number of families in shelters.[3] The National School Boards Association said in January 2009 that 724 of the country's nearly 14,000 school districts had already served 75 percent or more of the number of homeless students they'd served during the 2007-2008 school year.[4]

Districts track the trend because the Education for Homeless Children and Youth Act requires schools to provide the same level of education to students without fixed addresses as to all other children and youth. Schools can also use grants made under the law to provide homeless students with medical and dental care and other services.

A constellation of other laws authorizes programs designed for the "chronically" homeless, for households who can't afford decent housing and for veterans without homes.

This year, Congress added new forms of assistance, including the Homeless Emergency Assistance and Rapid Transition to Housing (HEARTH) Act for families facing imminent loss of housing or recently made homeless. The law also promotes the construction of so-called "supportive housing" for the long-term homeless, who need mental health services and similar services along with roofs over their heads.

Meanwhile, about 2 million families nationwide receive substantial help in paying their rents under the Section 8 Housing Choice Voucher Program, in place since 1974 and revamped in 1998. For many housing advocates, Section 8 vouchers represent a speedy way to expand the supply of affordable housing, the lack of

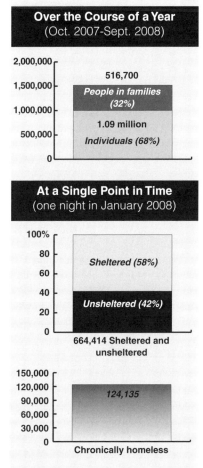

Total No. of Homeless

About 1.6 million persons used a shelter or transition housing, including half a million individuals in families.

Over the Course of a Year
(Oct. 2007-Sept. 2008)

516,700
People in families (32%)
1.09 million
Individuals (68%)

At a Single Point in Time
(one night in January 2008)

Sheltered (58%)
Unsheltered (42%)

664,414 Sheltered and unsheltered

124,135
Chronically homeless

Source: Department of Housing and Urban Development, July 2009

which they view as a major contributor to homelessness.

Some conservative policy experts say the problem isn't a shortage of affordable housing but deeply rooted poverty — a condition they call ill-suited for resolution by housing subsidies. "The idea that housing is unaffordable and that we've done nothing about it — give me a break," says Howard Husock, vice president of the Manhattan Institute for Policy Research, a New York think tank. "What we've done to make housing more affordable over the past 30 years is so extensive that I would inquire of advocates what more they would have government do."

Even so, HUD, which administers three of those programs, calculates that a family with one full-time, minimum-wage worker can't afford a two-bedroom apartment anywhere in the country.[5]

As a practical matter, a one-earner family means a household headed by a single mother — the population segment that by all accounts is the most economically and socially vulnerable to deep poverty. The HUD annual report says that families in shelters are typically headed by a single mother.[6]

Ortiz, the once-homeless single mother in Worcester, Mass., says that she was able to start turning her life around only after her city's housing program helped her find an $850-a-month apartment, which she pays for with the help of a $700 monthly subsidy from the "rapid rehousing" program.

Before that, she says. "I couldn't get more work hours because of my kids getting out of school at 4:10. I didn't have anybody reliable enough to drop them off for me or pick them up if I did get a full-time job, and after-school programs cost so much."

Homeless in Nation's Capital Face Cold Winter

Funding cuts may reduce number of beds in shelters.

Mark Raymond is worried. He says funding cuts will prevent his organization's huge 1,350-bed shelter in Washington — among America's largest — from adequately serving homeless men and women in the nation's capital.

"Lots of programs that were started last year and this year are not to be funded next year," says Raymond, director of administrative offices at the Community for Creative Non-Violence.

In late September, Clarence Carter, director of the city's Department of Human Services, announced a $12 million cut in homeless-services funding for fiscal 2010. D.C. Council member Tommy Wells, D-Ward 6, contended the cut could be as large as $20 million. [1] Either way, homeless shelters say they will have to scramble to find enough beds for the lethally cold hypothermia season.

The current economy has forced more people onto the streets, including more families in which jobs have been lost and no savings exist. The slow housing market means an increasing number of electricians and construction workers are unemployed. [2] Half the homeless adults in Washington don't receive regular income, including Social Security and disability checks. The 20 percent who are employed have a median monthly income of $524.

According to a January 2009 survey, 6,228 homeless people live in shelters or transitional housing in the District, a 3 percent increase over 2008. [3] In July the total included 703 homeless families and more than 1,400 homeless children. Last year, homelessness among families

across the nation rose 9 percent but 25 percent in the District. [4]

The number of teenagers without a place to live is also rising. But so is awareness of their plight. Recently, rappers Flava Flav, once homeless himself, and Chuck D., of the band Public Enemy, shared a Thanksgiving meal with the young residents at the Sasha Bruce House in Washington, which features programs for children ages 11-17. Typically, youths are reunited with their families or transitioned into more permanent care. Counseling services are provided, particularly as children without families transition into adulthood.

The two entertainers encouraged the youngsters to stay in school. "It takes three times as much to get your education later as now, so do it now," Chuck D told the teens crowded around him. Later, Public Enemy performed, and Flava Flav stressed the importance of volunteerism. "If you're successful and can't talk to younger people in need, you got a problem," he said.

During his term, former Mayor Anthony A. Williams called for an end to homelessness by 2014. [5] A major component of his "Homeless No More" plan, now being implemented by current Mayor Adrian M. Fenty, is providing housing and financial support to those most at risk of becoming homeless. In early December, the District distributed $7.5 million in federal stimulus money to house homeless families and help struggling families remain in their homes. The money, from federal Homeless Prevention and Rapid Re-Housing funds awarded to the District in July, will help

Once she and her family got a place of their own, she found a friend who could pick up the children twice a week, allowing Ortiz to work two part-time jobs as a nursing assistant, and one in a party-supply store. In addition, she's studying for the GED, planning to then enroll in medical-technology training.

"Things are slowly falling into place for me," she says. "A shelter would have been no way for my kids to live. It's not the same as having your house."

As homeless advocates and public officials struggle with rising numbers of homeless families, here are questions being debated:

Can government end homelessness?

Homelessness has remained a social and political issue since it surfaced in the late 1970s and exploded in the early '80s.

The fact that more than a million and a half people every year experience homelessness makes plain that all

680-800 households. [6] Those who have been homeless the longest and those with the most severe disabilities will be housed first. Proponents of the plan say programs in Denver, San Francisco, and Portland, Ore., have proven that providing housing and counseling is more humane and cost-effective than putting people in shelters.

Martha Burt and Sam Hall — researchers at the Urban Institute, a Washington think tank — endorse Fenty's focus on permanent supportive housing, but they caution he needs to keep the momentum going if homelessness is to be ended in the next four years. [7] However, Michael Ferrell, executive director of the District of Columbia Coalition for the Homeless, says ending homelessness by 2014 is "very highly unlikely" and calls for a multipronged approach.

"The first prong has to be prevention strategies, and quite frankly, that's preferable to addressing the problem on the back end," he says. Homeless individuals and families should be rehoused as soon as possible, he explains, but the long-term goal should be to provide enough rental assistance or subsidies for up to 12 months to prevent homelessness from occurring in the first place.

But Raymond cautions against shifting the focus away from shelters. "So many people need subsidized housing," he says, "that there is a year-and-a-half, two-year waiting list. Shelters are absolutely still necessary."

The shift towards permanent supportive housing instead of shelters, however, is a national trend. Philip F. Mangano, until recently executive director of the U.S. Interagency

A homeless man settles in at a Metro station in Washington, D.C., in May 2009. More than 6,000 homeless people live in shelters or transitional housing in the District.

Council on Homelessness, had focused on getting people out of shelters and into homes. "When you ask the consumer what they want, they don't simply say a bed, blanket and a bowl of soup," he said. "They say they want a place to live. We have resources being provided to us at record levels. If you look at the numbers for chronic homelessness, we're winning." [8]

— Emily DeRuy

[1] Darryl Fears, "Officials Squabble, Service Providers Scramble; No Matter How You Do the Math, Advocates Say, Less Money Means More People on Streets," *The Washington Post*, Oct. 6, 2009, p. B2.

[2] Mary Otto, "A Growing Desperation; Housing, Economic Slumps May Portend Rise in Ranks of Region's Homeless, Survey Shows," *The Washington Post*, Jan. 25, 2008, p. B1.

[3] "A Summary of the 2009 Point in Time Enumeration for the District of Columbia," The Community Partnership for the Prevention of Homelessness, www.community-partnership.org/docs/TCP%20 Fact%20Sheet%20Point%20in%20Time%202009.pdf.

[4] "In the News," Washington Legal Clinic for the Homeless, www.legal-clinic.org/about/inthenews.asp.

[5] Anthony A. Williams, "Homeless No More: A Strategy for Ending Homelessness in Washington, D.C. by 2014," U.S. Department of Health and Human Services, www.hrsa.gov/homeless/statefiles/dcap.pdf.

[6] Darryl Fears, "District to Disburse $7.5M in Stimulus Money to Help Homeless," *The Washington Post*, Nov. 30, 2009.

[7] Martha Burt and Sam Hall, "What It Will Take to End Homelessness in D.C.," The Urban Institute, July 13, 2008, www.urban.org/publications/901185.html.

[8] Derek Kravitz, "Homelessness Official Wins Praise with Focus on Permanent Housing; Detractors Cite Mangano's Frequent Travel, Including Trips Abroad," *The Washington Post*, Dec. 30, 2008, p. A13.

the attention focused on the problem over the past three decades hasn't eliminated it. To some conservatives, the persistence of homelessness despite myriad government programs suggests they may be doing more to perpetuate the problem than to solve it — if a solution is possible at all, which some conservatives doubt.

Nevertheless, conservatives don't automatically reject government programs, especially those aimed directly at people shuttling between the street and

shelters. In fact, the government committed itself to ending "chronic" homelessness in 10 years when Republican George W. Bush was in office (*see p. 188*).

Housing advocates on the liberal side argue for expanding that goal to ensure that no families suffer loss of their homes, or, in the worst-case scenario, get help in acquiring new housing. That strategy is embodied in the expansion of the McKinney-Vento Homeless Assistance Act that President Obama signed into law in May. It provides "homelessness prevention" aid to families living in unstable housing conditions — moving in with relatives, for example.

Now, the housing advocates are pushing for more funding, arguing that as more families benefit, builders will respond. "The government can stimulate the housing market in a way to allow homeless people to become housed," says Linda Couch, deputy director of the National Low Income Housing Coalition. She advocates expanding government subsidies designed to make housing affordable for low-wage workers.

Responses that go beyond helping individuals cope with financial emergencies are also well within government's capability, Couch argues. "We know how to build housing," she says. "It's not rocket science, it's just too expensive for people earning the minimum wage, or even two times the minimum wage. Work doesn't pay enough."

Conservative analysts don't necessarily reject strategies designed to boost the purchasing power of low-wage workers. But they argue that such measures shouldn't be lumped in with responses to homelessness.

"Government should strive to end homelessness of single individuals — people who live on the street, who have mental illness and substance abuse problems," says Husock, at the Manhattan Institute. People who aren't on the street but who face housing crises, he argues, can be helped more effectively by programs that don't limit assistance to housing subsidies. "Let's say a blue-collar, two-parent family has been hurt by this recession," Husock says. "Why would we want to say, 'Here's a chit for housing?' All you can use that for is to rent an apartment from a landlord who is willing to take you. Why wouldn't we say we are increasing unemployment insurance, or the value of the earned-income tax credit, and you can use that money as you see fit? If you want to live with his parents for a year while you save, why wouldn't you have that choice?"

But the line isn't hard and fast between policy experts who are skeptical of government's capacity to end all homelessness, and those who argue that government programs can prevent homelessness as well as rescue the homeless from the street.

Roman has no preference for housing-only assistance over other kinds of aid. "Housing affordability has an income dimension and a supply dimension," she says. "You could make housing cheaper or figure out some way to supplement people's income through vouchers or tax credits — however you want to do it."

The bottom line, Roman says, is that the government can rescue long-term homeless people from the streets, even while ensuring that people who have homes don't lose them. "Do I think homelessness can be ended? Yes," she says. "People will always have housing crises, but I don't think there's any particular reason we can't end homelessness. I remember a time when we didn't really have homelessness."

Policy experts who advocate reducing government's efforts at social engineering doubt that politicians and bureaucrats can achieve anything close to a definitive result. "I don't think government can end homelessness," says Michael D. Tanner, a senior fellow at the Cato Institute, a libertarian think tank.

But government could protect more people from homelessness by making affordable housing more available, argues Tanner, who specializes in domestic policy. County and city governments could modify zoning restrictions that, for instance, prohibit apartment building construction in some localities.

Should the definition of homeless include people in unstable housing situations?

The ways in which laws and policies define a condition also specify who will — and who won't — benefit from programs designed as remedies.

"Homeless" might seem to be an easily defined term. But some argue for expanding its definition to those with housing, albeit in unstable situations. Skeptics question whether that would blunt the effectiveness of programs designed to get unsheltered people off the streets.

The activists who first drew attention in the late 1970s to the homeless were advocating on behalf of the lost souls on skid rows in virtually every city, the looked-down-upon people often described as hoboes, vagrants and bums. They slept in parks, bus stations or cardboard boxes in alleys or — at best — ultra-cheap hotels known as "flop houses" or "cage hotels" (featuring cubicles with wire-mesh roofs to prevent stealing).

At about the same time, concerns were also raised about veterans of the recently ended Vietnam War. Then came the recession of 1981-1982, and worries about homelessness began to focus on people who'd never been homeless before but were losing their houses after losing

Most Sheltered Homeless People Are Men

Nearly two-thirds of the people living in shelters in 2008 were men. One-fifth were under age 18, and 43 percent were disabled.

Percentage of All Sheltered Homeless Persons, 2008

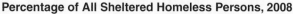
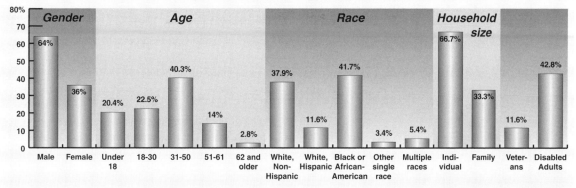

Source: "The 2008 Annual Homeless Assessment Report," U.S. Department of Housing and Urban Development, July *2009*

their jobs. (The unemployment rate rose to 10.8 percent in December 1982, compared to 10.0 percent this November.)[7]

Citing an apparent connection between economic trends and threats to the housing stability of working Americans, some housing program advocates began arguing for a more expansive definition of homelessness.

But HUD, the federal agency most directly involved in the issue today, defines the term literally: A homeless person is someone who "lacks a fixed, regular and adequate nighttime residence," and who spends nights in a shelter of some kind, including places not designed for that use.[8]

That definition, however, doesn't control all federal law on homelessness. When it comes to public school students, the 2000 McKinney-Vento Homeless Assistance Act, which created most homelessness-related programs, effectively defines homelessness more expansively. Children who can enroll in programs for helping homeless children and youth include those who are sharing housing with others because of economic hardship; who are living in hotels, trailer parks or campgrounds out of necessity; who are awaiting foster care placement or those whose parents are migrant workers.[9]

The Runaway and Homeless Youth Act uses a still-broader definition. It makes young people eligible for

transitional housing if they're 16-21 years of age, or for short-term shelter if under 18 and not living with relatives.[10]

As these interpretations of the word show, defining the term is the critical step in deciding who can benefit from government programs. "It's a waste of breath to argue with people who want an expansive definition that makes it look like we should do more, and with the others who want a restricted agenda so it makes it look like we should do less," says Christopher Jencks, a professor of social policy at Harvard University's Kennedy School of Government. "Both sides have agendas."

At the same time, Jencks favors the approach of housing advocates who want government to issue more housing subsidies. "I'm not sure that making the number bigger is the way to go," he says. "Do we want to say that 4 million people are homeless?"

Some housing advocates argue that a broader definition of homelessness applied to all government programs would, in fact, reflect reality. "We believe that everyone has a right to a home," says Couch of the National Low-Income Housing Coalition. "In my mind that doesn't include a van, or a garage or couch-surfing. It would be a real shame, after all we've learned about the importance of stable housing if, in response to the spike in family homelessness, we started building shelters."

Couch adds that HUD officials, along with lawmakers who specialize in housing issues, understand that building more facilities designed for the street-dwelling homeless population wouldn't respond adequately to the housing instability that threatens families who may have roofs over their heads but may also have to change lodgings frequently. "I think reason will prevail," Couch says. "People in housing know that homelessness is solved by housing."

Some of those who favor narrowing the scope of anti-homelessness programs argue that defining homelessness beyond the plain meaning of the word opens the door to unfocused strategies.

"In Hong Kong they talk about 'street sleepers,'" says Husock of the Manhattan Institute. "It's a very accurate description, and a useful one to distinguish them from people who are sharing accommodations with other family members."

People who are doubled-up clearly experience stress, Husock acknowledges. But it doesn't resemble the perils faced by people in the streets. "We should not confuse that issue with the problems faced by very-low-income people," he says. "Two or three generations under one household roof — it's not a common-sense definition of homelessness."

But even some who agree that the definition of homeless should be kept narrow also advocate that people at risk of becoming homeless — and currently bedding down at a relative's or friend's house where they're "doubled up" — should get assistance under homelessness prevention programs. That approach wouldn't require expanding the definition of "homeless."

"There are lots of people who are literally homeless," says Roman of the National Alliance to End Homelessness. "A substantial percentage of them are not sheltered at all. That's who is homeless. People who are doubled up and at risk of homelessness, we would not be in favor of calling homeless."

Are housing subsidies the best way to help families facing homelessness?

Since 1974, the Section 8 Housing Choice Voucher program has been the major federal provider of housing for low-wage workers. Its rental subsidy means recipients don't have to pay more than 30 percent of their income for housing. Through the voucher, the government pays the difference between that 30 percent and the monthly rent.

About 2 million U.S. households currently receive subsidies, which go to poor families who can document their inability to rent decent housing. But most cities also maintain waiting lists, some of them years long, because demand for vouchers outstrips supply. Overwhelmingly, housing experts say, the biggest share of vouchers go to households headed by single mothers, who make up the greatest share of low-income families threatened by housing instability. Vouchers may be simple in concept, but Section 8 isn't simple in operation. "The system is governed by hundreds of pages of regulations and guidance that make the program, some argue ... difficult to administer," the Congressional Research Service (CRS) reported last year.[11]

The program owes its complexity to its dual mission. Section 8 was designed to provide decent housing to poor people, with the longer-range aim of helping them climb out of poverty. But affordable housing alone may not be enough for some people to make that climb. Recognizing the key role of education in giving young people a chance at a better future, the so-called "portability" feature of Section 8 allows voucher recipients to live wherever a landlord will accept them (the feature also allows families to move to another state for a job).

"Portability offers the possibility for families with vouchers to move from areas of high concentrations of poverty, poor schools, and little opportunity to areas with low concentrations of poverty, good schools and more opportunity," the CRS report said. It added, "Researchers and advocates for low-income families have argued that the mobility potential of portability has not been fully reached. They argue for more funding for mobility counseling and performance standards that encourage mobility efforts."[12]

Some housing advocates argue that expanding the long-established program offers the fastest way to open affordable housing to more families. Rep. Maxine Waters, D-Calif., is sponsoring a bill to add 150,000 more vouchers next year. The National Low-Income Housing Coalition, which is backing the legislation, sees the legislation as the first step toward a larger goal of doubling the number of vouchers to 4 million by 2020.

"We know that vouchers solve homelessness," says Couch, at the National Low-Income Housing Coalition.

"Often, homeless families need nothing other than a voucher. They don't need transportation or job training. Vouchers are a surefire way not only to prevent homelessness but also to get people out of that situation as quickly as possible."

An expansion is especially needed now, Couch argues, because the recession is hitting low-wage households so hard. "Typically, about 10 percent of people cycle off the program every year," she says. "But in the recession, what we've seen is that, because people's incomes aren't going up, they're staying in the program longer than normal. The waiting lists in a lot of places are frozen."

Not all those who object to the proposed expansion oppose vouchers on principle. Rep. Barbara Capito, R-W. Va., the ranking Republican on the House Financial Services' Housing and Community Opportunity Subcommittee, voted against the Waters bill in the House Financial Services Committee. "It's a critical program, particularly at a time of economic challenge," Capito says. "I'd like to see the vouchers work better for people, but I'm concerned the Section 8 could swallow up the HUD budget."

Capito says adding 150,000 vouchers would lessen the housing agency's ability to deal with other issues, including substandard housing, which she calls a serious problem in her district. But the cost of the proposed voucher expansion is "way out of control," she says.

Deeper objections to Section 8 focus on what critics call the program's tendency to make beneficiaries dependent on the vouchers. "It makes much more sense to supplement the earnings of those at the low end of the income scale," says the Manhattan Institute's Husock. "It's much

Housing Issues Central to Homelessness

Lack of affordable housing is seen as the biggest cause of homelessness — and the main solution — by officials from a majority of 27 U.S. cities surveyed. Most of the officials also called for permanent housing for the disabled and better-paying jobs.

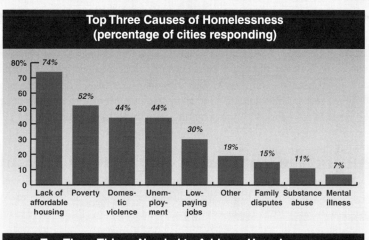

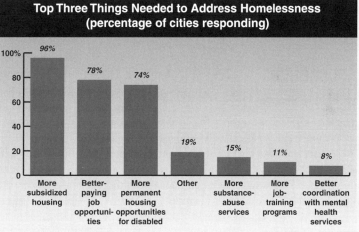

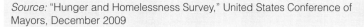

Source: "Hunger and Homelessness Survey," United States Conference of Mayors, December 2009

more efficient. If people have cash in their pocket, they can find something to rent."

Built into Husock's preferred approach is that recipients of income supplements would, by definition, have incomes — that is, they would have jobs. People suffering unstable housing who don't have jobs have other problems that aren't best solved by simply subsidizing apartments for them, he argues. Job training or help in job-seeking would be of more help. "Housing as a solution to the problem of poverty — it's not self-evident to me why that would be the best solution."

People who deal with individuals' housing problems agree to some extent with Husock's categorizations. "There are families who have substance-abuse problems, domestic violence, extreme disability issues such as a child with cerebral palsy," says Marta Beresin, a staff attorney with the Washington Legal Clinic for the Homeless. But she adds that a number of families in these circumstances couldn't be helped by income supplements tied to employment. "There are families where the head of household may not qualify for disability benefits but may have a lot of issues that make it difficult to hold down a steady job — domestic violence, mental health, kids with lot of health issues."

Those conditions, Beresin agrees, spring from deeply rooted poverty. But she differs with Husock on how to give families afflicted with these woes a toehold on a better existence. For these households, "The only way they're ever going to get out of a shelter is with a housing subsidy."

BACKGROUND

The Right to Shelter

The sight of homeless people in big cities began to arouse public concern in the late 1960s and post-Vietnam War era when social activism was at its peak. At the end of the decade, a New York lawsuit played a key role in the emergence of homelessness as a national issue with legal and political dimensions.

Robert M. Hayes, a lawyer with the white-shoe Wall Street law firm Sullivan & Cromwell, filed a class action lawsuit against the city and state in 1979 on behalf of homeless men — represented by six homeless plaintiffs — demanding a right to shelter. Some shelter space was available, but government policy at the time was to deny shelter in order to pressure homeless people to find temporary housing on their own.[13]

In 1979, Judge Andrew R. Tyler of the New York Supreme Court (equivalent to district courts in other states) ruled that the U.S. and New York constitutions required that shelter space be available for every homeless man.

Technically, the ruling applied only to homeless men in the skid row area of New York known as the Bowery. But after the judge made his initial ruling to the case, Hayes and government lawyers settled the suit by agreeing that government was obliged to provide shelter for all men with no homes (women were included later). Underscoring the urgency of the homelessness issue, Robert Callahan, who led the list of named plaintiffs, died on the street before the settlement was reached.

The August 1981, court-approved agreement led to a vast expansion of shelter space in New York. When Hayes had gone to court, shelter space was scattered around the cheap, dormitory-style hotels known as "flophouses." By 1988, when demand for shelter reached a peak, city refuges could house as many as 10,000 people in 24 shelters. The accommodations went far beyond a place to sleep, meals and bathing facilities. The shelters also offered health care, mental health counseling, drug rehabilitation and job-training programs.

By 1981, homeless men and women were fixtures in cities across the country, often camping out in downtown areas and parks. Many were former residents of mental institutions who were turned out and left on their own after a wave of "deinstitutionalizations" prompted by horror stories about conditions in institutions. Some scholars say that President Ronald W. Reagan's administration further added to the ranks of the homeless by drastically cutting back on the number of recipients of federal disability payments, among them people too mentally ill to work. The administration also cut federal funds for public housing.[14]

New York's growing homeless population inspired activists and lawyers elsewhere. Pinning down the numbers proved difficult. Jencks, at Harvard University's Kennedy School, estimated that the nation's homeless population grew from 100,000 in 1980 to 200,000 in 1984 to 400,000 in 1987-1988.[15]

Mitch Snyder, a Washington-based advocate for the homeless, had put the number of homeless at 2 million to 3 million, but he later acknowledged the estimate had "no meaning, no value."[16]

Snyder dedicated himself to awakening the national conscience and challenging the political system. Starting in the late 1970s, he had begun organizing demonstrations designed to call attention to the unmet needs of homeless men and women in the streets of the nation's

C H R O N O L O G Y

1978-1980s *As homelessness grows into a major social and political-legal problem, advocates win important legal rights for those lacking permanent housing.*

1978 Washington, D.C., activist Mitch Snyder leads a takeover of the National Visitors' Center by the homeless, forcing the city to open more shelter space.

1979 Wall Street lawyer Robert M. Hayes sues New York City and state, demanding a right to shelter for homeless men; initial ruling in case named for homeless plaintiff Robert Callahan is favorable to the homeless.

1981 Callahan dies while sleeping on the street.... In a landmark agreement, New York settles the case by agreeing to provide shelter for everyone who is homeless.

1982 Philadelphia law guarantees the homeless a right to shelter.... As deep recession brings unemployment, homelessness surges.

1983 Callahan agreement is amended to apply to women.

1984 After more attention-getting protests organized by Snyder and fellow activists, Washington voters pass the nation's first referendum guaranteeing overnight shelter to homeless people.

1987 President Ronald W. Reagan signs into law the McKinney (later renamed McKinney-Vento) Homeless Assistance Act, which becomes the major source of federal funds to help the homeless.

1990s *Persistent homelessness leads academics and think-tank analysts to crunch data in an effort to understand causes and possible cures and leads the Bill Clinton administration to step up its rhetoric on the issue.*

1993 Martha R. Burt of the Urban Institute concludes that a shortage of affordable housing for working Americans clearly is one cause of the long-running homelessness crisis.... Homeless 43-year-old Yetta M. Adams freezes to death outside Washington, D.C., headquarters of the U.S. Department of Housing and Urban Development (HUD).

1994 Partly in response to Adams' death, the Clinton administration unveils a plan to reduce homelessness by one-third.

1998 Congress revamps Section 8 housing voucher program to require that vouchers for rental assistance go to very poor families.

2000s *Idea that government can eliminate homelessness gains strength, but the economic crisis at the end of the decade threatens to deepen the problem.*

2002 George W. Bush administration vows to end chronic homelessness in 10 years.

2003 Administration hands out $48 million in grants to programs designed to get chronically homeless people off the streets.

2007 HUD count shows number of chronically homeless dropped since 2006 by about 30,000 to approximately 124,000.... Service providers begin warning of the potential for massive homelessness among Iraq-Afghanistan veterans.

2008 As recession grips the nation, progress on reducing the ranks of the chronically homeless halts; number remains essentially flat from previous year.... Bush creates National Housing Trust Fund, designed to finance affordable housing.

2009 Family homelessness is up 9 percent, apparently due to recession, with veterans slightly overrepresented among the homeless.... National School Boards Association reports growth in student homelessness in more than 700 school districts.... President Barack Obama signs law creating new Homelessness Prevention and Rapid Re-Housing program, funded with $1.5 billion.... U.S. Conference of Mayors says about three-quarters of a group of cities show rise in family homelessness and decline or leveling off of homelessness among individuals.... Advocacy groups launch drive to push Congress to appropriate another $1 billion to the program for fiscal 2010-2011.

Scotland's Homeless and the Right to Housing

Long-term housing soon will be available to almost everyone.

Scotland probably comes closer than any other country to implementing a right to housing for the homeless, according to American homeless advocates. [1] Since 1977, legally enforceable rights to housing have been on the books in Scotland, as well as England and Wales. But until recently the right was limited to "priority" categories of the most vulnerable people — families with children, the elderly, disabled and those displaced in natural disasters, among others. [2]

In 2003, Scotland forged ahead of the rest of Britain and greatly expanded the kinds of homeless individuals for whom the government has a duty to provide accommodation, including single adults. Scotland's uniquely expansive definition of homelessness "has no equivalent anywhere in Europe," according to Tom Mullen, a professor of law at the University of Glasgow. [3]

By 2012 the right to long-term permanent housing will extend to virtually all homeless people in Scotland under the revised law. In the interim, local authorities have a legal duty to provide immediate temporary shelter for all homeless persons and long-term permanent housing for a greatly expanded class of priority groups.

In 2004, the priority-need category was expanded to include homeless youth ages 16-17; 18-20-year-olds in danger of sexual or financial exploitation or drug abuse; adults discharged from prison, the armed forces or a hospital; adults with personality disorder, and those at risk from domestic abuse, violence or harassment.

"On paper we have the most progressive homelessness legislation in Europe, if not, possibly, the world," concedes Chris Campbell, deputy chief executive of the Scottish Council for Single Homeless, an umbrella group for homeless-service organizations.

But the challenge of making it work on the ground, he says, includes "changing public attitudes about the deserving vs. the undeserving: Someone's been on the waiting list paying their rent on time: Should they come before or second to someone who in their eyes is going to squander that tenancy with a drug issue?"

Homeless advocates say the tension comes essentially over allocating a scarce, desirable resource — public housing,

which doesn't carry the same stigma as in the United States — and finding enough government money to increase the supply of affordable housing.

In 2005, a government-appointed monitoring group found that a shortage of affordable housing was a major obstacle to implementing the new law. [4] Towns short of housing have resorted to sending families to bed and breakfasts or towns up to 200 miles away, according to homeless advocates.

The shortage has produced one of the most commonly heard criticisms of the law. "Imagine a small town in Scotland with a family which has been there quite a long time and has made an application to move into social [public] housing. They see someone who is not from that area getting housing in front of them — quite legitimately because they're homeless. That can cause a problem," says Graeme Brown, director of Shelter Scotland, a homeless advocacy and advice organization.

Reluctance among some local government officials to shift toward the statute's more inclusive definition of those eligible for help has also been cited by government monitors as impeding the law's goals. [5]

Before passage of the 2003 act, those who did not fit into priority categories were entitled only to advice and assistance — not housing — which some observers viewed as a way of rationing scarce housing. [6]

Another rationing device was the lower-priority status the law gave to "intentional homelessness." The category was developed in response to local authorities' fears that large numbers of people would give up their existing accommodation to secure a better house under the legislation. After 2012, those deemed "intentionally homeless" are the only remaining group entitled only to temporary, not permanent, housing. [7]

Immediately after passage of the act, the number of homeless applications surged — a 34 percent increase in 2005-06 over the beginning of the decade. Some experts attribute the rise to more people becoming aware they were now eligible for help.

Homelessness figures in 2008-09 show a slight increase, but the steep rise seen earlier in the decade has now leveled off, coinciding with policy changes making housing rights available to more single adults, according to the Scottish government.[8]

"To be fair, local government has gotten better at preventing homelessness," Brown says. "The highly visible homeless sleeping on the streets that we saw 10 years ago in Edinburgh and Glasgow has declined."

Two innovative Scottish programs hold out hope of keeping people in their homes in these times of rising foreclosures — which hit 6,500 households last year. Under the 2003 law, a lender who is about to foreclose on a homeowner or a landlord about to evict a tenant must inform the local government authority immediately. The idea is to give officials time to prevent eviction or find alternative housing.

Scotland has also pioneered an innovative mortgage-to-rent scheme, since imitated by England and Wales. Local nonprofit groups funded by government purchase a house that is about to be foreclosed upon and rent the house back to the residents. With funding limited, however, it will help only 250-300 of the 4,500 households that may be repossessed this year, according to the Scottish government.

In a recent law journal article on the 2003 legislation, attorney Eric S. Tars of the National Law Center on Homelessness and Poverty, in Washington, D.C., applauded a Scottish applicant's ability to sue if local government has not met its statutory duty to provide him housing — a right denied to Americans.[9]

But in Scotland's far less litigious society, suits are rare. If someone comes to Shelter Scotland for help after their local authority has wrongly denied them housing, "we find that almost always the [local] council will back down" after they are contacted, Gavin Corbett, Shelter Scotland's head of policy, said in an e-mail. Shelter could threaten the council with a judicial review of its decision in a higher court, but it rarely comes to that.

The lack of litigiousness may reflect greater social consensus around the issue of homelessness in Scotland than even in the rest of Great Britain, says Brown. "Culturally and politically, even in these post-industrial days, Scotland

Homeless people live under a bridge along the River Clyde in Glasgow, Scotland. Scotland has greatly expanded the government's obligation to house the homeless.

is still more of a nation concerned about their fellow citizens," he says in his lilting Scottish brogue. Speaking by phone from Edinburgh, where it was raining, he added, "This is a northern European country; you need a roof over your head."

The law's ultimate success hinges on whether local governments manage to house the expanded universe of citizens who will qualify for help by the law's target date of 2012 — still an open question, homeless advocates say.[10]

— Sarah Glazer

[1] Eric S. Tars and Caitlin Egleson, "Great Scot!" *Georgetown Journal on Poverty Law & Policy*, winter 2009, pp. 187-216, www.nlchp.org/view_report.cfm?id=314.

[2] The 1977 act, enacted under a Labor government, applied to all of Great Britain. Homeless rights under the act were reduced later under Conservative governments in 1979-1997 in England and Wales, but not Scotland, and largely restored under Labor in 2002.

[3] Tom Mullen, "The Right to Housing in Scotland," Homeless in Europe, European Federation of National Organizations Working with the Homeless, autumn, 2008. The law is the Homelessness, Etc. (Scotland) Act of 2003, www.feantsa.org/files/Month%20Publications/EN/Magazine_Homeless_in_Europe_EN/Homeless%20in%20Europe_Autumn08_EN.pdf.

[4] *Ibid.*

[5] *Ibid.*, and Tars and Egleson, *op. cit.*, p. 203.

[6] Mullen, *op. cit.*

[7] *Ibid.*, p. 197. However, temporary housing can last up to one year, with further help after that.

[8] E-mail from Scottish Housing and Support Division.

[9] Tars and Egleson, *op. cit.*, p. 215. The law provides a legally enforceable duty on the local government to meet the housing needs of its residents. Applicants unhappy with a decision may seek judicial review. However, in a judicial review a court cannot substitute its own opinion for that of the decision makers. It can strike down a decision on the grounds that the decision maker has exceeded or abused powers or failed to perform the duty delegated or entrusted or exhibited bias. (E-mail from Scottish Housing and Support Division.)

[10] Local authorities have targets to increase their numbers of priority-need assessments until all of those assessed as homeless have the same rights. Statistics published by the Scottish government in September indicate local authorities have increased their priority assessments to 83 percent of homeless households across Scotland.

capital, often sleeping on steam-heat exhaust grates located near federal buildings.

Headline-grabbing protests that Snyder sparked — as a leader of a onetime anti-Vietnam War organization, the Community for Creative Nonviolence — included a December 1978 takeover of the National Visitors Center, near Union Station, by homeless people. The action forced the city to provide more shelter space.[17]

In November 1981 — three months after the New York settlement — Snyder led a group of about 150 activists and homeless people in building and occupying a tent camp they called "Reaganville" in Lafayette Park, across from the White House. In naming the camp after President Reagan, the activists were trying to evoke the Great Depression, when the jobless and homeless built camps they called "Hoovervilles," after President Herbert Hoover.

The next year, Philadelphia enacted an ordinance that also guaranteed the right to shelter, and in 1984 Washington finally acted. Partly in response to Snyder's and other protests, Washington voters in 1984 passed the nation's first referendum measure guaranteeing "adequate overnight shelter" to homeless people — a statutory equivalent of the New York legal agreement.[18]

Beyond Shelter

The major federal response to rising homelessness came in the form of the Stewart B. McKinney Homeless Assistance Act, which Reagan signed in 1987. (It was retitled in 2000 as the McKinney-Vento Homeless Assistance Act.)[19]

The law authorized programs designed to expand or upgrade shelters and created a series of initiatives aimed at meeting other needs of the homeless population, including: HUD homeless assistance grants for emergency shelters; supportive housing for disabled people and SRO (single-room occupancy) rehabilitation; Veterans Administration and Department of Labor programs for homeless veterans who needed medical care and job-seeking help; Health and Human Services grants and medical care; and Education Department programs for homeless children and youth.[20]

The 1987 law made up the biggest part of the federal attempt to cope with homelessness, but some separate programs had already existed, and others were created later. These included services to homeless youth, provided under a 1974 law; grants to homelessness-prevention projects in local communities, authorized by a 1983 law; a series of programs aimed at homeless veterans, created over several years; and a Social Security Administration program begun in fiscal 2003 designed to help chronically homeless people apply for disability payments.

As Congress legislated, policy experts at universities and think tanks were trying to determine the size of the homeless population and its sub-groups and whether socioeconomic changes played a part in the growth of homelessness. They zeroed in on changes in the housing market, the job market and care of the mentally ill.

By the early 1990s, a consensus had formed among liberals and centrists that the decreasing availability of affordable housing was the root cause of non-chronic homelessness among families and others.

"There is an absolute shortage of appropriate rental units to accommodate poorly housed families," wrote Martha R. Burt, a scholar at the Urban Institute think tank, in a 1993 book that analyzed voluminous data on housing availability, cost and other factors. She found, however, that families made up perhaps as little as 12 percent, of the homeless population.[21]

The bulk of the homeless were single men, almost all weighed down by mental illness, addiction or both — disabilities that had led to long periods of reliance on shelters or the streets. It was these chronically homeless who had been largely responsible for drawing attention to the issue.

They continued to do so, even in death. On Nov. 29, 1993, a homeless woman named Yetta M. Adams, 43, died of exposure on a bench outside the Washington headquarters of HUD Secretary Henry G. Cisneros, prompting new government attention.

In response, the Clinton administration launched a wave of spending — grants totaling $11 million to 187 homeless-assistance programs in 44 states. And in May 1994, the administration unveiled a plan aimed at reducing chronic homelessness by one-third.

Ending Homelessness

The Clinton plan didn't fulfill the expectations created by its announcement. Some programs took effect, said Donald Whitehead, executive director of the National Coalition for the Homeless, but "many other initiatives were never implemented, [and] HUD ended up with no real, substantial increase in new funding."[22]

Nonetheless, the idea took hold that the government could do more than simply respond to homelessness. In 2000, the National Alliance to End Homelessness released a 10-year plan to eliminate homelessness. "Housing has become scarcer for those with little money," the organization said. "Earnings from employment and from benefits have not kept pace with the cost of housing for low income and poor people. Services that every family needs for support and stability have become harder for very poor people to afford or find."[23]

The plan centered on mobilizing government and private organizations to provide housing and related services designed to reverse the conditions that the alliance saw as the core of the problem.

But the new Bush administration took a narrower approach. In 2002 it set a goal of ending chronic homelessness in 10 years. To carry it out, the administration revived the Interagency Council on Homelessness, which had been formed in 1987 but fell into inactivity in the 1990s.[24]

In a series of other actions designed to meet the 10-year goal, the administration in 2003 made grants totaling $48 million to programs designed to help chronically homeless people get jobs, permanent housing, substance-abuse treatment and mental health services.[25]

Over the following years, the Bush administration maintained its focus on the chronically homeless. For example, in evaluating grant applications for building housing for the chronically homeless, HUD gave preference to state and local agency applicants that had developed 10-year plans of their own.

Six years after the Bush administration launched its 10-year campaign, chronic homelessness seemed to be diminishing. From 2006 to 2008, for instance, the national one-night count of homeless people that HUD conducts every January showed a decrease from 155,623 to 124,135 chronically homeless people both in shelters and in other locations, such as streets and bus stations. (Despite the seeming precision of those numbers, HUD'S "point-in-time" count is an estimate, given the difficulty of locating every single homeless person on a single night.)[26]

From 2007 to 2008, however, HUD's count of the chronically homeless was virtually unchanged.[27]

"Ending chronic homelessness has been a national policy objective that has been supported by significant

Tracy Munch (above) and her fiancé were evicted last February from the house they were renting in Adams County, Colo., after the owner stopped paying his mortgage. They managed to borrow enough money to rent another house for themselves and their four children, but not in time to avoid eviction.

investments in developing permanent supportive housing," HUD said in its report, which was released this year. "For several years communities have reported declines in the number of persons experiencing chronic homelessness."[28]

Meanwhile, some organizations advocating a push to eliminate homelessness in all its forms were working to expand the definition of "homelessness." The goal was to enlarge the community of people who would benefit from programs aimed at the people who weren't included in the "chronic" segment of the homeless population.

In 2008, Rep. Gwen Moore, D-Wis., introduced a bill to expand the McKinney-Vento law's definition of "homeless" to include individuals or families who would "imminently lose" their housing and couldn't afford a new house or apartment, plus anyone fleeing domestic violence or another threat to life.

Moore's bill would also have authorized community programs to serve families with children, or children on their own, who were defined as homeless in other laws. The effect would have been to include people who had experienced prolonged periods without stable housing, and could be expected to remain in that condition because of chronic disabilities, chronic physical or mental health problems, addiction, histories of domestic violence, or multiple barriers to employment.

The legislation passed the House, but the Senate took no action on the measure.[29]

War and Recession

In the last two years of the Bush administration the economic and political climate in which politicians and advocates debated and crafted anti-homelessness measures was changing fast.

The foreclosure crisis that started in 2007, with millions of homeowners beginning to default on mortgages, led to the Wall Street meltdown and what economists began calling the Great Recession.[30]

The same HUD report that showed a decline in the number of chronically homeless people also seemed to contain an early warning about families. The report showed that the number of homeless people in families increased from 2007 to 2008 by 43,000, to 516,724, a 9 percent jump. And the number of families in shelters with children rose from 130,968 in 2007 to 159,142. "The most common demographic features of sheltered family members are that adults are women, children are young, the family identifies itself as belonging to a minority group, and the family has two or three members," the report said.[31]

The statistics confirmed anecdotal reports that had been circulating among advocates for low-income families. As a result, the advocacy organizations were able to bolster the argument they'd been making for increasing homelessness assistance and prevention funds to individuals and families who fell outside the "chronically homeless" category. Until then, says Roman of the National Alliance to End Homelessness, "We didn't have the data."

Economic conditions alone would have been enough to suggest that the ranks of the homeless would include growing numbers of low-income households hit by job loss or cutbacks in working hours. But another factor was present as well — the appearance of a new cohort of combat veterans. As men and women began returning from Iraq and Afghanistan, many in the veterans' and housing policy communities began warning against a repetition of what many believed to be a plague of homelessness among Vietnam vets.

Researchers in the 1990s had concluded that homeless veterans of the Southeast Asia war were not as numerous as many had thought.[32] Still, the reality of

any veterans from the new century's wars wandering streets or sleeping in shelters was widely considered a reflection of failure by government's veteran-care and social services agencies. "We're beginning to see, across the country, the first trickle of this generation of warriors in homeless shelters," Phil Landis, chairman of Veterans Village of San Diego, a residence and counseling center, told *The New York Times* in 2007. "But we anticipate that it's going to be a tsunami."[33]

So far, no tidal wave has hit. But the HUD annual report does show that veterans account for 11.6 percent of the adult population that uses shelters, but a lesser share — 10.5 percent — of the national adult population. "The estimated number of homeless veterans should be watched closely," the report adds, "as the number of veterans returning from recent combat increases during the next few years."[34]

CURRENT SITUATION

Fund Drive

Housing advocacy groups are campaigning for increased federally funding for homelessness programs. But many are pessimistic due to the state of the economy, the growing government deficit and the Obama administration's growing list of priorities, including the newly announced Afghanistan troop surge.

At the same time, the gravity of the economic crisis may persuade politicians that homelessness has become more than a niche issue. "I can count on one hand the number of staffers who are actually invested, passionate, care about housing," Kim, the aide to Missouri Republican Sen. Bond, told a Capitol Hill briefing in early December organized by the National Alliance to End Homelessness. He added, "Now with the foreclosure crisis, there are probably people who are a little more sensitive to it."

Alliance president Roman went even further. Enactment earlier in the year of the Homelessness Prevention and Rapid Rehousing Program (HPRP) — designed to help families avoid losing their housing — marked a major shift in government strategy, she said. "We may actually come out of this difficult period with a better homelessness system than we went into it with, if we're able to take advantage of the opportunity presented by HPRP."

Should homelessness be redefined by HUD to include more youths and families?

YES

Phillip Lovell
Vice President for Education, Housing, and Youth Policy First Focus

Written for *CQ Researcher*, Dec. 15, 2009

"Not homeless enough." That's the message sent to over 550,000 children who are considered homeless by the Department of Education and other agencies but are not homeless enough for the Department of Housing and Urban Development (HUD). Yes, you read that correctly. A child can be homeless enough for one federal agency, but not for another.

Increasingly, the homeless are families who lose their homes and temporarily "double up" with others or stay in motels, often because shelters are full. They do not live in "unstable housing situations." They have lost their homes, cannot afford another apartment and do not know where or when their next move will take place. No one staying in this type of temporary, often unsafe, situation can be said to have a home. Denying this fact is disastrous.

In 2007, a youth whom I will call John became homeless. Desperate, he accepted an offer to stay with an adult for two months. John was raped repeatedly and, as a result, contracted HIV.

When I met John, he looked like a normal kid. He was receiving a scholarship to help him go to college and was bright, articulate and smiling. He did not look homeless. But he was no less homeless, vulnerable or deserving of federal support.

The president recently signed legislation making modest improvements to the HUD definition. Now, a family in a doubled up or motel situation is considered homeless if they can only stay in their housing for 14 days. Additionally, families can be considered homeless if they are fleeing situations where the health and safety of children are jeopardized.

Neither provision would have helped John. He stayed in his doubled up situation until another temporary situation became available — well above the 14-day maximum. And the only way he would qualify for assistance under the health and safety clause is by being raped. This is unacceptable.

In the end, this is about our children. This is about keeping them safe and making sure they have the basic necessities of life. Congress must change HUD's definition of homelessness to reflect reality. A narrow definition masks the real problems facing our communities. Homelessness cannot be defined away.

It will be some time before Congress considers this issue again. In the meantime, HUD is required to issue regulations on the newly passed definition of homelessness. For all those who may follow in John's footsteps, let us hope HUD does so in a way that protects as many children, youth and families as possible.

NO

Howard Husock
Vice president for policy research Manhattan Institute for Policy Research and author, America's Trillion-Dollar Housing Mistake: The Failure of American Housing Policy

Written for *CQ Researcher*, Dec. 15, 2009

Without doubt, the collapse of the U.S. housing market has caused hardship. Owners are stuck with homes worth less than the price they paid. Others have moved in with parents and extended families. We cannot, however, address our housing situation clearly by using emotional descriptions as arguments for a vast expansion of subsidized housing — which would be both difficult to afford and, just as significantly, ill-advised social policy.

The term "homelessness" dates to the early Reagan administration, when two trends overlapped. The deinstitutionalization of those suffering from mental illness or alcohol and substance abuse problems — begun as a liberal policy in the 1960s — utterly failed. Many people wound up living on the streets, becoming the public image of "homelessness." At the same time, reductions in public assistance forced some very low-income (primarily single-parent) households to double-up with relatives or live in more crowded conditions. Such households never fit the common-sense definition of homeless — known in Britain as "street-sleeping." But advocates of subsidized housing began to include them in estimates of homelessness — and, in some cities, they began to be admitted in large numbers to public group-living quarters (the very term "shelters" perpetuated the image that such households were living on the street). Those households also received priority for a rapidly expanding housing-voucher program, which allowed them to pay public housing rents for private apartments. This, in turn, ballooned the Section 8 voucher program — to the point that its budget now surpasses that for cash welfare assistance.

Now those who want to further expand such housing assistance are using the foreclosure and delinquency spike as a rationale for expanding that same housing-voucher program — by using the image of the recession-strapped working family as the new face of homelessness. Such problems are being addressed through federal efforts to modify loans and other methods. Doubling the size of the housing-voucher program is not likely even to reach such families.

Far better to continue to take steps to help the truly homeless — the mentally ill who should be assisted through housing combined with social services — and to adjust the voucher program by converting it to a cash payment expansion of the Earned Income Tax Credit. Let's help those of low income but not by costly, ineffective and inaccurately labeled remedies.

AFP/Getty Images/Jewel Samad

Homeless people pitch camp beside a Las Vegas street last April. Across the nation, another group of people is joining the growing number of low-income households hit by job loss and homelessness: men and women returning from the wars in Iraq and Afghanistan.

Accordingly, Roman and her allies are urging Congress to add another $1 billion to the HPRP, on top of the $1.5 billion appropriated earlier this year.

They also want lawmakers to allocate $1 billion to the National Housing Trust Fund (NHTF), created by a 2008 law to provide funds to build or rehabilitate rental housing for households with very low incomes. The request is in line with a plan endorsed by the Obama administration for fiscal 2010-2011. "We will work with Congress to identify a financing source for the Housing Trust Fund, which will help provide decent housing for families hardest hit by the current economic downturn," HUD Secretary Shaun Donovan said in October.[35]

Rep. Barney Frank, D-Mass., chairman of the House Banking Committee, and Sen. Jack Reed, D-R.I., a member of the Housing, Transportation, and Community Development Subcommittee, have introduced bills to make the $1 billion allocation.

In the last month of 2009, the National Low-Income Housing Coalition was drumming up a grassroots campaign to pressure lawmakers into committing themselves to the trust fund legislation. "Our goal is to create an early-December blizzard of phone calls from all over in a compressed period of time to demonstrate strong and urgent support for an initial infusion of money for the NHTF," the coalition told its members.[36]

Advocacy groups are also pressing for the appropriation of $2.4 billion under the Homeless Emergency Assistance

and Rapid Transition to Housing (HEARTH) Act. Enacted in 2009, but without funding for 2009-2010, HEARTH authorizes homeless-assistance grants and supportive housing for homeless people with disabilities.

In addition, with the Temporary Assistance to Needy Families (TANF) system up for reauthorization in 2010, housing advocates are asking Congress to add funding for states with effective strategies against family homelessness. TANF was created under the Clinton administration as a new version of welfare aid to families with children.

Metropolitan Trends

Several big and medium-size cities are showing the same trend in homelessness that HUD reported in mid-2009. Homelessness among single individuals is declining or remaining flat, but more families are losing their homes, the U.S. Conference of Mayors reported in early December.[37]

"The recession and a lack of affordable housing were cited as the top causes of family homelessness in the surveyed cities," the organization said.[38]

The survey covered 27 cities from October 2008 to Sept. 30, 2009, including Boston, Chicago, Dallas and Los Angeles, as well as Gastonia, N.C., Louisville and St. Paul, Minn., among the smaller cities. About three-fourths of the cities reported an uptick in family homelessness — ranging from 1 percent in Salt Lake City to 41 percent in Charleston, S.C. Seventy-four percent of the municipal governments reported a lack of affordable housing as the top cause of homelessness.

Developments among families stood in sharp contrast to the trend for individuals. In 64 percent of the responding cities (16 cities), individual homelessness was reported decreased or at the same level as the previous year. Norfolk, Va., reported the highest increase, of 18 percent.

However, the survey isn't a precision instrument, as the Conference acknowledged. For instance, Los Angeles reported a 68 percent decline in family homelessness, basing that result on censuses it conducted in 2007 and 2009. "The steep decline … conflicts with anecdotal evidence from Los Angeles homeless service providers, who say the number of families seeking shelter has swelled recently because of the recession."

And the reported national drop in individual homelessness has at least one major exception. In New York, which didn't participate in the survey, lawyers representing homeless men and women took city government to court in early December, charging failure to live up to the landmark Callahan agreement of 1981. The city isn't keeping up with demand for shelter space, lawyers for the Legal Aid Society and the Coalition for the Homeless charged.

"The extreme situation now is reminiscent of problems that we haven't seen in years," Steven Banks, attorney in chief for Legal Aid, told *The New York Times.* "It's a failure to plan, and it's having dire consequences for vulnerable women and vulnerable men."[39]

A motion by the lawyers cited reports by monitors for the coalition. For example, they said two shelters in late September hadn't provided beds for 15 men. At another shelter in late October, 52 men slept in chairs or on the floor; 14 men were bused to shelters with beds, but 38 were left bedless for the night. At yet another shelter, two women slept on a dining room table.

Robert V. Hess, the city's commissioner of homeless services, called the motion "alarmist." He told *The Times:* "We've seen an uptick in demand, so our system, as you might expect, is a little tight. We're confident that we'll continue to be able to meet demand and meet our obligations throughout the winter."[40]

Capacity in the adult shelter system was at 99.6 percent on Dec. 8, Hess told *The Times.* The shelters held 4,934 men and 2,041 women that day. Not included were military veterans in short-term housing; chronically homeless people who've entered a program designed for them; and 30,698 people in families who were in short-term housing set aside for them.

Concerning the monitors' reports, Hess said that some of those without beds had refused them, or had arrived at shelters after 2 a.m. Of a report that some women were taken by bus to a shelter where they had less than five hours to sleep, Hess called the account "potentially correct."

Small-Town Woes

Homelessness is often considered a big-city phenomenon, but it's hitting rural communities and small towns as well.

"More companies are downsizing or closing," says Kay Moshier McDivitt, adviser to the Lancaster County Coalition to End Homelessness, in the heart of Pennsylvania's Amish country. "Now our demand has increased beyond our ability to respond."

Employment prospects in the area, a major tourist destination, are dominated by low-wage service jobs, which leave little cushion against job loss. Some service workers spend up to 75 percent of their incomes for housing, McDivitt says.

Speaking at the December Capitol Hill briefing organized by the National Alliance to End Homelessness, McDivitt said that in October and November of 2009 the coalition had received 1,500 requests for help paying rent or mortgages — a 400 percent increase over 2008. "Most of our families when they first become homeless spend a year or more moving among family and friends. By the time we see our families, they have often been homeless for a year or more, with lots of instability. They are ready for permanence and stability."

Demand for help has risen so sharply the coalition is setting up its first family shelters. Until now, McDivitt said, HPRP funds have enabled the county to help families pay rent so they never become homeless. But, she adds, "We expect family homelessness is going to increase."

A slightly less pessimistic assessment came from Kathy Wahto, executive director of Serenity House of Clallam County, Wash., which helps the homeless in Port Angeles, northeast of Seattle.

There, despite persistent poverty, a state-funded homelessness-prevention program had helped lower homelessness by about 40 percent over the past three years. But the recession has cut a major source of revenue for that program — document recording fees on real estate transactions. "That's $200,000 in revenue we're not going to have," Wahto said.

HPRP partly made up for the loss with an $89,000 infusion. "The ending of homelessness in our county was in sight," Wahto said. "We don't want to go backwards."

OUTLOOK
'Modestly Positive' Trends

Housing advocates who've been pushing for years to expand homelessness services tend toward optimism about the medium-term future.

"If you had asked me last year if we would have $1.5 billion for HPRP, I would have said no," says the Urban Institute's Cunningham. "A lot of positive things are coming out of the present administration."

She concedes that homelessness programs are competing for money and attention in a time of crisis on several fronts. But it's within the administration's reach to go a long way toward eliminating homelessness, she says. "If you look at the research, the bottom line is, we know how to end homelessness. We just need the political will to do it."

Husock of the Manhattan Institute takes a somewhat more skeptical view, though not an entirely bleak one. "I would guess we would be closer to the status quo than any kind of big change," he says. But he says he's encouraged by the openness of HUD Secretary Donovan to programs in Atlanta and elsewhere that combine housing assistance with work requirements of the kind that transformed the welfare system.

"To me, Atlanta is pointing the way to the future," Husock says. Overall, he says, "The trend has been modestly positive."

The Cato Institute's Tanner takes a dimmer view, based on what he calls continuing attachment to regulatory controls that he argues slows construction of affordable housing. "I don't see any policy to expand the availability of low-income housing through eliminating rent control or zoning regulations."

That aside, he argues that the extent of homelessness over the next decade will largely be determined by the state of the economy. "If you get long-term economic growth, you'll get a lower number of people homeless because they lost their jobs."

On that point at least, virtually everyone agrees.

"How about you give me a prediction about where we'll be on the unemployment rate in 10 years," says Jencks of Harvard's Kennedy School of Government. "I would love to believe we won't be in this fix."

One nuance to the question, though, is that providing more services to homeless people may not result in an immediate reduction in their numbers. "Conservatives tend to argue, and they're not completely off-base, that when you do more, you're going to get more homeless people," Jencks says. "I don't take that as defeat. A lot of people are living in terrible circumstances, and if you give them the opportunity not to live with a belligerent brother-in-law, they will. Is that a waste? I don't think so."

Among those who deal daily with the heartaches and complexities of individual and family housing crises, the depth of the economic crisis leads to caution in forecasting when a homelessness turnaround might occur.

"A number of people are falling into poverty, and a number of governments are being hit by the recession and having to cut programs," says Beresin of the Washington Legal Clinic for the Homeless. "It takes a long time to bounce back from all that — not to mention that we've decided to send 30,000 more troops into Afghanistan."

In Washington, Beresin notes, some construction projects for affordable housing have been stopped in their tracks because a city government program that provides funding is itself short of revenue, which comes from a real-estate transaction tax. "D.C. definitely can't do it alone," she says. "It needs federal dollars, and if those aren't going to be there because the government is prioritizing other things, we don't have much control over that."

Still and all, among advocates who deal with Congress, the prevailing mood tends toward optimism. "In 10 years, I think there will be fewer homeless people," says Roman of the National Alliance to End Homelessness. "We've learned a lot about how to run a much better homeless system. We could probably get about half the way to ending homelessness with that."

The other half may be harder to solve. "The affordable housing crisis is the driver," she says. "When we didn't have that gap, we didn't have homeless people. People have lots of problems, but they used to be able to afford a place to live, and now they can't."

NOTES

1. "The 2008 Annual Homeless Assessment Report to Congress," U.S. Department of Housing and Urban Development, July 2009, p. v, www.hudhre.info/documents/4thHomelessAssessmentReport.pdf. HUD reported on 2008 in mid-2009; the 2009 report is scheduled for release in 2010.

2. *Ibid.*

3. "Affordable Housing," U.S. Department of Housing and Urban Development, Dec. 3, 2009, www.hud.gov/offices/cpd/affordablehousing/.

4. Ellie Ashford, "Districts Cope With Rising Numbers of Homeless Students," School Board News, National School Boards Association, January 2009, www.nsba.org/HPC/Features/AboutSBN/SbnArchive/2009/

January-2009/Districts-cope-with-rising-numbers-of-homeless-students.aspx.

5. "Affordable Housing," *op. cit.*

6. "The 2008 Annual Homeless Assessment," *op. cit.*, p. 31.

7. "Labor Force Statistics from the Current Population Survey," U.S. Bureau of Labor Statistics, updated monthly, http://data.bls.gov/PDQ/servlet/Survey OutputServlet.

8. "Federal Definition of Homeless," U.S. Department of Housing and Urban Development, March 3, 2009, www.hud.gov/homeless/definition.cfm.

9. Libby Perl, *et al.*, "Homelessness: Targeted Federal Programs and Recent Legislation," Congressional Research Service, Jan. 15, 2009, p. 2, http://web.mit .edu/lugao/MacData/afs.lugao/MacData/afs/sipb/con trib/wikileaks-crs/wikileaks-crs-reports/RL30442.pdf.

10. *Ibid.*

11. Maggie McCarty, "Section 8 Housing Choice Voucher Program: Issues and Reform Proposals in the 110th Congress," Congressional Research Service, p. 3, http://wikileaks.org/leak/crs/RL34002 .pdf.

12. *Ibid.*, p. 10.

13. Details of the lawsuit and its effects are drawn from Kim Hopper, *Reckoning With Homelessness* (2003), pp. 186-191; Lyn Stolarwski, "Right To Shelter: History of the Mobilization of the Homeless as a Model of Voluntary Action," *Nonprofit and Voluntary Sector Quarterly*, 1988, http://nvs.sagepub.com/cgi/ reprint/17/1/36.pdf; Robin Herman, "Pact Requires City to Shelter Homeless Men," *The New York Times*, Aug. 27, 1981, p. A1; Charles Kaiser, "A State Justice Orders Creation of 750 Beds for Bowery Homeless," *The New York Times*, Dec. 9, 1979.

14. For background, see Charles S. Clark, "Mental Illness," *CQ Researcher*, Aug. 6, 1993, pp. 673-696. Chris Koyanagi, "Learning From History: Dein-stitutionalization of People With Mental Illness as Precursor to Longterm Care Reform," Kaiser Commission on Medicaid and the Uninsured, August 2007, p. 8, www.kff.org/medicaid/upload/7684.pdf.

15. Christopher Jencks, *The Homeless* (1994), pp. 16-17. For background, see William Triplett, "Ending Homelessness," *CQ Researcher*, June 18, 2004, pp. 541-564.

16. *Ibid.*, pp. 1-2.

17. Paul W. Valentine, "Street People in Visitor Center Vex U.S.," *The Washington Post*, Dec. 7, 1978, p. B1; Paul W. Valentine, "City Agrees to Provide More Homeless Shelters," *The Washington Post*, Dec. 16, 1978, p. D1.

18. Sandra G. Boodman, "City Softens Opposition to Shelter Initiative," *The Washington Post*, Nov. 8, 1984, p. A58.

19. Except where otherwise indicated, this subsection is drawn from Perl, *et al.*, *op. cit.*

20. *Ibid.*

21. Burt, *op. cit.*, pp. 16-17.

22. Quoted in Triplett, *op. cit.*

23. "A Plan, Not a Dream: How to End Homelessness in Ten Years," National Alliance to End Homelessness, June 1, 2000, www.endhomelessness.org/content/ article/detail/585.

24. Maggie McCarty, *et al.*, "Homelessness: Recent Statistics, Targeted Federal Programs, and Recent Legislation," Congressional Research Service, May 31, 2005, pp. 17-18, www.fas.org/sgp/crs/misc/ RL30442.pdf.

25. *Ibid.*, pp. 17-18.

26. "The 2008 Annual Homeless Assessment Report to Congress," *op. cit.*

27. *Ibid.*

28. *Ibid.*, p. 5.

29. HR 7221, *CQ Billtrack*, Nov. 17, 2008.

30. For background, see Marcia Clemmitt, "Mortgage Crisis," *CQ Researcher*, Nov. 2, 2007, pp. 913-936; Peter Katel, "Straining the Safety Net," *CQ Researcher*, July 31, 2009, pp. 645-668.

31. "The 2008 Annual Homeless Assessment Report to Congress," *op. cit.*, pp. 31, 42.

32. For background, see Peter Katel, "Wounded Veterans," *CQ Researcher*, Aug. 31, 2007, pp. 697-720.

33. Quoted in Erik Eckholm, "Surge Seen in Number of Homeless Veterans," *The New York Times*, Nov. 8, 2007, www.nytimes.com/2007/11/08/us/08vets.html.

34. "The 2008 Annual Homeless Assessment Report to Congress," *op. cit.*, p. 28.

35. "Administration Calls on Congress to Approve Key Housing Measures," U.S. Department of Housing and Urban Development, press release, Oct. 29, 2009, http://treas.gov/press/releases/tg336.htm.

36. "Please Call Congress December 1 or 2 for NHTF Money," National Low Income Housing Coalition, undated, http://capwiz.com/nlihc/issues/alert/?alertid=14407651.

37. "Hunger and Homelessness Survey: A Status Report on Hunger and Homelessness in America's Cities, a 27-City Survey," United States Conference of Mayors, December 2009, www.usmayors.org/pressreleases/uploadsUSCMHungercompleteWEB2009.pdf.

38. "U.S. Cities See Sharp Increases in the Need for Food Assistance; Decreases in Individual Homelessness," United States Conference of Mayors, Dec. 8, 2009, www.usmayors.org/pressreleases/uploadsRELEASE-HUNGERHOMELESSNESS2009FINALRevised.pdf.

39. Quoted in Julie Bosman, "Advocates Say City is Running Out of Beds for the Homeless," *The New York Times*, Dec. 10, 2009, www.nytimes.com/2009/12/10/nyregion/10homeless.html?_r=1&ref=nyregion.

40. Quoted in *ibid*.

BIBLIOGRAPHY

Books

Burt, Martha R., *Over the Edge: The Growth of Homelessness in the 1980s*, Russell Sage Foundation, 1993.
One of the leading scholars of homelessness wrote an early and influential analysis of its causes and extent.

Hopper, Kim, *Reckoning With Homelessness*, Cornell University Press, 2003.
Homelessness can be approached historically, through first-hand observation or anthropologically; one anthropologist blended all three approaches.

Husock, Howard, *America's Trillion-Dollar Housing Mistake: The Failure of American Housing Policy*, Ivan R. Dee, 2003.
A policy expert for the conservative-leaning Manhattan Institute critically analyzes federal subsidized-housing programs as a strategy that has promoted dependency instead of independence and social advancement.

Jencks, Christopher, *The Homeless*, Harvard University Press, 1994.
Writing from a perspective that remains relevant today, an influential policy scholar examines the causes and possible remedies for homelessness.

Articles

Bazar, Emily, "Tent cities filling up with casualties of the economy," *USA Today*, May 5, 2009, p. A1.
Money troubles are driving thousands of homeless people into tent encampments around the country, a national newspaper reports.

Chong, Jia-Rui, "Some vets of recent wars find homelessness at home," *Los Angeles Times*, June 29, 2009, p. A4.
A growing number of Iraq-Afghanistan combat veterans are winding up homeless, often because of the psychological effects of their battlefield experiences.

Eckholm, Erik, "More Homeless Pupils, More Strained Schools," *The New York Times*, Sept. 6, 2009, p. A1.
School systems are scrambling to meet the needs of children and youth living in various types of temporary housing, ranging from trailers in campgrounds to friends' and relatives' homes.

Fears, Darryl, "15 Homeless People Get Apartments Next Month," *The Washington Post*, Sept. 29, 2009, p. B4.
As part of a nationwide policy to provide "supportive housing" to chronically homeless people, Washington is moving forward with a plan to provide permanent housing for mentally ill people who had been living on the street.

Patterson, Thom, "U.S. seeing more female homeless veterans," *CNN*, Sept. 25, 2009, www.cnn.com/2009/LIVING/09/25/homeless.veterans.
As growing numbers of women return from the front lines, some are joining the ranks of homeless male veterans.

Rubin, Bonnie Miller, "Homeless, unless you count storage space," *Los Angeles Times*, Nov. 15, 2009, p. A12.

A reporter finds a Chicago-area family fallen on hard times whose illegal home is a storage locker, except on rare occasions when they can rent a motel room for a night.

Urbina, Ian, "Recession Drives Surge in Youth Runaways," *The New York Times*, Oct. 26, 2009, p. A1.

The number of teenagers living on their own — usually in perilous circumstances — is growing because of family stresses aggravated by the economic crisis.

Reports

"The 2008 Annual Homeless Assessment Report to Congress," U.S. Department of Housing and Urban Development, July 2009, www.hudhre.info/documents/4thHomelessAssessmentReport.pdf.

The federal government's annual study provides a wealth of statistics and analysis.

Cunningham, Mary K., "Preventing and Ending Homelessness — Next Steps," Urban Institute, February 2009, www.urban.org/publications/411837.html.

A longtime specialist provides a detailed summary of programs and recommends further measures.

DeHaven, Tad, "Three Decades of Politics and Failed Policies at HUD," Cato Institute, Nov. 23, 2009, www.cato.org/pub_display.php?pub_id=10981.

A budget analyst for the libertarian think tank recounts the history of scandals at the main federal agency in charge of program to alleviate homelessness.

Duffield, Barbara and Phillip Lovell, "The Economic Crisis Hits Home: The Unfolding Increase in Child and Youth Homelessness," National Association for the Education of Homeless Children and Youth, First Focus, December 2008, www.naehcy.org/dl/TheEconomicCrisisHitsHome.pdf.

Children's rights organizations examine the growth in homelessness and unstable housing among young people.

Perl, Libby, *et al.*, "Homelessness: Targeted Federal Programs and Recent Legislation," Congressional Research Service, Jan. 15, 2009, http://wikileaks.org/leak/crs/RL30442.pdf.

Specialists for Congress' research arm provide a wealth of detail about legislation designed to reduce homelessness.

For More Information

Manhattan Institute for Policy Research, 52 Vanderbilt Ave., New York, NY 10017; (212) 599-7000; www.manhattan-institute.org. A conservative leaning think tank on urban issues that tends to be skeptical about federal housing and homelessness policies.

National Alliance to End Homelessness, 1518 K St., N.W., Washington, DC 20005; (202) 638-1526; naeh@naeh.org. Works on legislation and program design and publishes research on causes and effects of homelessness.

National Center on Homelessness Among Veterans, U.S. Department of Veterans Affairs, 810 Vermont Ave., N.W., Washington, DC 20420; (800) 827-1000; www1.va.gov/Homeless/. Publishes information on federal homeless programs as well as research on veterans and homelessness.

National Coalition for the Homeless, 2201 P St., N.W., Washington, DC 20037; (202) 462-4822; www.national

homeless.org/index.html. Helps organize voter-registration drives for the homeless and other national campaigns.

National Law Center on Homelessness & Poverty; 1411 K St., N.W., Washington, DC 20005; (202) 638-2535; www.nlchp.org. Pursues judicial and legislative remedies to problems tied to homelessness.

U.S. Department of Housing and Urban Development, 451 7th St., S.W., Washington, DC 20410; (202) 708-1112; http://portal.hud.gov/portal/page/portal/HUD/topics/homelessness. Publishes detailed data on homelessness and government programs.

Urban Institute, 2100 M St., N.W., Washington, DC 20037; (202) 833-7200; www.urban.org/housing/index.cfm. A nonpartisan think tank that studies homelessness and policies designed to reduce or end it.

9

Prisoner Reentry

Peter Katel

Inmate William Gray learns work skills at the Department of Corrections reentry facility in Plainfield, Ind. Many experts say reentry programs designed to help ex-prisoners land on their feet are an answer to the nation's rising prison population and high recidivism rate. But with states battered by the recession, relatively few reentry programs have been started.

From *CQ Researcher*, December 4, 2009.

W hen the big question comes — and it will — don't slouch in your chair, look down and mumble that you were in the wrong place at the wrong time. "That doesn't work," Hillel Raskas tells a quiet group of new residents at a pre-release center in the Washington suburb of Rockville, Md.

Instead, when the job interviewer asks if you've been convicted of a crime, Work-Release Coordinator Raskas advises the nine men and two women to sit up straight, look him in the eye and say: "Here's something I need to tell you. I have a conviction; I sold a few drugs, I made a mistake. I'm in a work-release program. I've been approved to work. I'm ready to work. I know what I need to do. I'm the right man, I'm the right woman. I'll be here every day."

With that approach, Raskas says, you'll have a real shot at the job.

If the newcomers at the Montgomery County corrections department's Pre-Release Center manage to get employed, put their pasts behind them and never enter another prison or jail, they will be among the fortunate 48 percent of America's growing army of ex-prisoners — 725,000-strong in 2007 — who are not re-incarcerated.[1]

The revolving-door nature of crime and punishment is plaguing lawmakers and policy experts nationwide. Caught up in the Great Recession, they're trying to dig their way out of budget disasters, and only Medicaid soaks up more state general fund money than prison systems — an estimated $47 billion in fiscal 2008.[2]

In this atmosphere, calls to improve ex-prisoners' "reentry" chances are ringing more loudly than ever. With or without help,

Prisoner Releases Almost Equal Admissions

More than 750,000 prisoners were admitted to federal and state prisons in 2007, quadruple the number in 1980. In 1980, the number of released prisoners was 87 percent of the total number admitted that year. By 2007, releases had reached 96 percent of admissions.

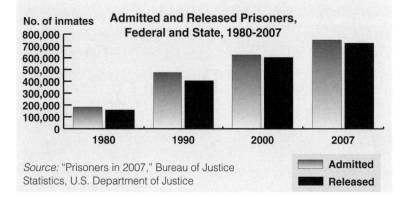

Admitted and Released Prisoners, Federal and State, 1980-2007

No. of inmates

Source: "Prisoners in 2007," Bureau of Justice Statistics, U.S. Department of Justice

Admitted
Released

95 percent of all prisoners in the United States are released. Reentry programs are designed to help them navigate the range of demands and needs they face — from finding a job and a place to live to dealing with drug or alcohol habits or psychological problems connected with past crimes. The emphasis on practical solutions largely distinguishes "reentry" from "rehabilitation" — a term mostly used in connection with attempts to help prisoners learn new skills and attitudes while they're incarcerated.

"We've got an unprecedented volume of people coming out of prison and jail," says Michael Thompson, director of the Council of State Governments' Justice Center, which has been working with state governments on the issue since 2001. At the same time, "Policy makers are looking at very high failure rates of people coming out of prison. That's obviously a public-safety problem. And states don't have the money to keep growing the prison and jail population. Suddenly you've got more momentum for improving reentry success rates than ever before."

It's no secret why so many prisoners are being released. As crime rates began rising in the 1970s, politicians began passing tough-on-crime laws that sent prison and jail populations soaring. At the same time, rehabilitation programs came to be seen as ineffective in curbing crime and fell out of favor. Prisons' main mission became

punishment and removal from society. Even as prison populations soared, remedial education programs served fewer and fewer prisoners, the nonprofit Urban Institute reported in 2004.[3]

Although crime rates had begun falling by the early '90s, the effects of toughened sentencing laws still resonate: U.S. prisons and jails held more than 2 million prisoners by 2003 — the world's largest prison population, both per capita and in absolute terms. By 2007, America's prison population had grown to nearly 2.3 million.

In this climate, reentry programs are gaining ground. "As few as 10 years ago, very few state departments of corrections had divisions devoted to reentry," Thompson says. "But today every department of corrections in the country will identify for you a person in charge of administering reentry programs."

"In order to reduce recidivism you can't hand them 100 bucks, a new suit and a bus ticket," says Florida state Sen. Victor D. Crist, a Tampa Republican (no relation to Gov. Charlie Crist) who helped toughen sentencing laws in the 1990s, but who argues that Florida doesn't do enough to get soon-to-be-released prisoners ready for their new lives. "You've got to help them establish a work ethic, cultivate meaningful skills and transition from life in the big house."

All reentry programs share those broad objectives, but the scale and scope vary widely. Michigan, for example, launched in 2005 what has grown into the statewide Michigan Prison ReEntry Initiative (MPRI), designed to provide each released prisoner with a "transition plan" as well as services designed to help with employment, housing and other matters. Coupled with early releases of some prisoners, MPRI is allowing the state to close up to three state prisons and five prison camps.[4]

Some observers are holding the applause, however. "We're suspicious," says Mel Grieshaber, executive director of the Michigan Corrections Organization, the prison employees' union. "We support the objective of keeping bad people from committing other crimes, and it seems to us that more objective data should be available to prove that it's working."

Some liberals are also raising questions. "I'm very supportive of reentry, but it leaves out the question of sentencing policy, which is driving prison numbers in the first place," says Marc Mauer, executive director of the Sentencing Project, which advocates alternatives to incarceration. "As long as we continue to send so many people to prison and increasingly keep them there for long periods of time, reentry is just trying to bail out the problem."

Still, reentry has risen to the top of the agenda in nearly all states. Kansas, New York and other states are also reducing their prison populations and recidivism rates by, among other things, expanding reentry services. Even Texas — long known for a hard-line approach to crime and punishment — rejected a prison expansion plan in 2007, creating instead the $241 million Justice Reinvestment Initiative designed in part to lower recidivism.[5]

At the other extreme is California, which took no steps to lower an ever-expanding prison population — now the nation's highest at about 150,000 inmates, many of them parole violators — until federal judges in August ordered the state to do so. (*See "Current Situation," p. 212.*) The state's latest plan to reduce its prison population by 40,000 over two years does include some reentry assistance.[6]

But even where reentry programs are being expanded, most newly released prisoners — and the neighborhoods to which nearly all of them return — still face enormous obstacles. "These communities — already struggling with poor schools, poor health care and weak labor markets — are now shouldering the burden of reintegrating record numbers of returning prisoners," says Jeremy Travis, president of John Jay College of Criminal Justice in New York.[7]

Though states make their own laws and build their own prisons, the federal government plays an influential role, in part via the grant-making process. The Justice

Many Inmates Didn't Finish High School

More than 40 percent of inmates in the nation's prisons and jails in 1997 had not completed high school or its equivalent, according to the most recent data available from the U.S. Justice Department. By comparison, only 18 percent of the general population over age 18 had not finished 12th grade.

Educational Attainment of Inmates

Education level	Total incarce- rated	State	Federal	Local jail inmates	Proba- tioners	General popu- lation
High school or less	41.3%	39.7%	26.5%	46.5%	30.6%	18.4%
GED	23.4	28.5	22.7	14.1	11.0	n/a
High-school diploma	22.6	20.5	27.0	25.9	34.8	33.2
Postsecondary	12.7	11.4	23.9	13.5	23.6	48.4

Source: Caroline Wolf Harlow, "Educational and Correctional Populations," Bureau of Justice Statistics, U.S. Department of Justice, January 2003

Department has disbursed $28 million in grants this year to reentry programs.

"Even a modest reduction in recidivism rates would prevent thousands of crimes and save hundreds of millions of taxpayer dollars," U.S. Attorney General Eric Holder told the Vera Institute of Justice, last July.[8]

In promoting reentry, the Obama administration is following in the footsteps of its two predecessors. In 1999, President Bill Clinton's Attorney General Janet Reno formally launched what her then-adviser Travis calls the "reentry movement." And to the surprise of many, President George W. Bush — a classic tough-on-crime politician — took up the cause in his 2004 State of the Union address. "America is the land of second chances, and when the gates of the prison open, the path ahead should lead to a better life."[9]

Inescapable socioeconomic realities pose a major obstacle. Only 46 percent of all prison and jail inmates have high-school diplomas or GEDs.[10]

"Eighty percent of the people who come to CEO [Center for Employment Opportunities] have reading and math scores below eighth grade," says Mindy S. Tarlow, executive director of the New York-based nongovernmental job placement program for ex-prisoners.

But while reentry programs and prison downsizing may appeal to cash-strapped state lawmakers, economic

Jobs Program Reduced Recidivism Slightly

About 6 percent fewer ex-prisoners who participated in a jobs program were arrested, convicted or incarcerated within three years, compared with ex-prisoners who did not participate (left). The program provided coaching in life and jobs skills and assistance in finding a job. Among nearly 300,000 prisoners released in 15 states in 1994, more than two-thirds were rearrested within three years (right).* The recidivism rate was slightly lower in 1983.

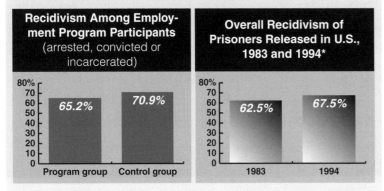

Recidivism Among Employment Program Participants (arrested, convicted or incarcerated)

Program group: 65.2%
Control group: 70.9%

Overall Recidivism of Prisoners Released in U.S., 1983 and 1994*

1983: 62.5%
1994: 67.5%

*The recidivism results are based on a 2002 study of 1994 data, which are the most recent available. The 272,111 former inmates released in 1994 represented two-thirds of all prisoners released in the United States that year.

Sources: Patrick A. Langan and David J. Levin, "Recidivism of Prisoners Released in 1994," Bureau of Justice Statistics, June 2002; Cindy Redcross, "Transitional Jobs for Ex-Prisoners," Association for Public Policy Analysis and Management, November 2009.

conditions are hindering reentering prisoners' job hunts. That's especially true for people like a man in his early 40s who was among Raskas' trainees at the Montgomery County Pre-Release Center. *(See sidebar, p. 208.)* The former career drug dealer is finishing a three-year sentence for possession of cocaine with intent to distribute. His record shows four other drug charges and a few relatively minor offenses.

"I wasted a lot of time in life," he tells staff members. But he says he has turned a page and wants to support himself legally. "I actually don't have a problem working."

Center staff will help him refine that sales pitch. Recession or not, they say, someone somewhere is always hiring. Raskas, a former businessman and congressional staffer, tells his class that he's helped 1,400 people with backgrounds similar to theirs find work. "Eighty-five percent of people leave here with a job."

As criminal justice officials and reentry advocates struggle with how to help prisoners reestablish themselves in their communities, here are some of the questions being debated:

Are state governments doing enough to help prisoners reenter society?

The basic argument for expanding reentry programs is simple: Virtually all prisoners will be released except those serving life sentences without the possibility of parole or facing execution. But if at least half of them will be returning to prison or jail, reducing that number by helping ex-prisoners gain a foothold in the outside world would be good for them — and for society.

Supporters of expanded reentry programs point out that even as state governments face budgetary strains ranging from serious to catastrophic, they can cut long-term prison costs by spending on reentry instead of on prison space, which is more expensive. States spend an average of $22,650 yearly to maintain one prisoner.[11]

However, to make that case to state legislatures, advocates must show hard data on which kinds of reentry programs lower recidivism most effectively. But solid numbers only now are being assembled and reported. Recidivism among New York's CEO program participants, for instance, was 5.7 percent lower over a three-year period than in a control group of ex-prisoners not in the program. *(See sidebar, p. 210.)*

But even without precise statistics on which kinds of programs are most effective, plenty of evidence shows approaches that don't work, say reentry program advocates.

For example, California imposes parole supervision on virtually all released prisoners — but doesn't have money for intensive supervision. The result: 66 percent of ex-prisoners returned to prison in

2003-2004 — compared with a national rate of 40 percent at that time. Two-thirds of those sent back to prison had violated parole conditions, according to a recent Justice Department study, which showed a dearth of reentry services.

"It is estimated that two-thirds or more of all California parolees have substance-abuse problems, and nearly all of them are required to be drug tested," the study's authors reported. "Yet few of them will participate in appropriate treatment while in prison or on parole."[12]

Former prison inmate and California Republican state legislator Pat Nolan, now vice president of Prison Fellowship, a Christian rehabilitation group, calls the combination of newly released prisoners with drug problems and a near-absence of treatment programs "one of the great scandals of our current California prison system."[13]

Nolan argues that the rigid enforcement of parole conditions such as no drug use means that ex-prisoners get sent back for relatively minor offenses. "Drug possession — bam, you take them [back] to prison," he says. "This guy can have a job, be supporting his family; he shouldn't use drugs, but do you want to disrupt his life, send him back to prison, for a first [parole] offense?"

But some prison system veterans say more reentry programs won't necessarily produce ex-prisoners better prepared to reenter society. "You can't make someone rehabilitate himself," says Gary B. King, a 19-year veteran of the Florida Corrections Department, one of the country's biggest prison agencies. "Over the years, what I have seen as the most rehabilitative thing we do is when we hold people accountable for their actions; when an inmate commits an infraction we apply administrative sanctions. The more we make them follow the rules while they're in prison, and do that across the board, the more we prepare them for going back into society."

King is now a classification officer who supervises individual prisoners' disciplinary records, progress reports and participation in educational or other programs at Columbia Correctional Institute, a medium-security institution near Lake City, Fla. He doubts a stronger emphasis on rehabilitation and reentry would make a big dent in Florida's recidivism rate. Nevertheless, he acknowledges that work-release programs do make sense for some prisoners nearing the end of their sentences, so they can experience the very different world outside prison. "Some inmates inside an institutional setting can do very well because their daily schedule is regimented, and they are quarantined from bad behavior and substance abuse," he says. "Once at liberty to do as they please and associate with whomever they please, they do not do well. Some inmates do not seem to handle well the responsibility that comes with freedom."

Yet even Crist, the conservative Republican Florida state senator, argues that the slim chances some prisoners have of staying out of trouble after release shouldn't block the state from expanding reentry programs for inmates who could benefit. "About one-third of the inmate population are hardened; you're going to have very little impact on them," he says. "Another two-thirds [deserve] a running chance."

Moreover, some prisoners with violent pasts may do well on the outside. "Somebody can go to prison with a first-degree felony and serve time and have an excellent track record and go through psychological testing and work release and have an excellent chance in the community," he says.

But some conservative experts who support reentry expansion on principle question how well helping hardcore prisoners reenter can be carried out in practice. "We don't know a lot about what works," says David B. Mulhausen, a senior policy analyst at the conservative Heritage Foundation's Center for Data Analysis. "Usually, the impact is rather small, and other communities haven't always been successful in replicating it."

Moreover, Mulhausen is skeptical about what he views as the political leanings of reentry advocates. "A lot of people [favoring] reentry programs really don't like prison," he says. "They don't give credit to the fact that the drop in crime we've had in the past several years is partly due to incarceration."

But the Sentencing Project, the leading alternatives-to-incarceration organization, says that while imprisonment plays a role in the drop in crime, that role may be smaller than Mulhausen and others assert. Crime dropped by about 12 percent in 1998-2003 in states with high imprisonment — and declined by the same rate in states in which incarceration diminished or stayed the same.

"There was no discernible pattern of states with higher rates of incarceration experiencing more significant declines in crime," project staffers wrote.[14]

Parole Violations in Calif. Boost Recidivism

Two-thirds of California's offenders return to prison within three years, with nearly a third sent back for parole violations — a much higher rate than in other large states. A big reason for the higher violation rate is that virtually all offenders released in California go on parole supervision, while most large states do not have that policy. In addition, California has a large population of young offenders with criminal records, who tend to have higher recidivism rates.

Three-Year Recidivism Rates in California vs. Selected Big States

State	Returned to Jail or Prison		
	New Crime	Technical Violation	Total
	(by percentage)		
California	37%	32%	69%
Florida	32	8	40
Illinois	40	4	44
New York	49	14	63
North Carolina	45	8	53
Texas	31	7	38

Source: Ryan G. Fischer, "Are California's Recidivism Rates Really the Highest in the Nation? It Depends on What Measure of Recidivism You Use," Center for Evidence-Based Corrections, University of California-Irvine, September 2005

Should government or private organizations provide subsidized jobs for ex-prisoners?

Jobs are a major focus of virtually all reentry programs, and the No. 1 objective of most newly released prisoners. Their prospects are bleak, however, since their résumés indicate that they are former jail or prison inmates, and many have been outside the conventional workforce for most, if not all, of their lives and often have little education.

"Compared with the general population, those in prison were approximately twice as likely not to have completed high school or attained a GED," the Urban Institute reported in 2004. "And four times the number of young males in the general population had attended some college or postsecondary courses, compared with incarcerated males."[15]

Moreover, the vast expansion of the prison population far outpaced programs designed to help prisoners improve their prospects upon release, the institute concluded. "Only about half of the total inmate population receives educational or vocational training, a proportion that has been decreasing over time."[16]

But even where programs do exist, training and coaching can't improve the grim employment environment that ex-prisoners enter upon leaving jails and prisons.

However, researchers find that former prisoners who land jobs do a better job of staying out of trouble. "Respondents who were employed and earning higher wages after release were less likely to return to prison the first year out," another group of Urban Institute researchers reported last year.[17]

For some reentry advocates, the best way to keep recidivism down — even in a dismal job climate — is to subsidize temporary jobs for ex-inmates in order to get them on the employment track. The nonprofit Joyce Foundation of Chicago created experimental "transitional jobs" programs in 2006 in Chicago, Detroit, Milwaukee and St. Paul in order to acquire data on whether the strategy — based on providing jobs for about four months to a total of about 1,800 ex-prisoners — helped participants avoid returning to prison. Results are expected in 2010.[18]

Director Tarlow of New York's CEO program argues that subsidizing jobs can attract public and political support, even when workers without prison records are having a hard time landing a job. "The cost of putting somebody in prison is five to six times greater than the cost of serving someone at CEO," Tarlow says. "You can't talk about the cost of CEO outside the context of not having CEO."

Moreover, she adds, "The more dire the fiscal situation is, the more likely it is that [a state] government will take risks. In extremely difficult economic times, when prisons are overcrowded and incredibly expensive to run, so many people get incarcerated when they come out. Why? Because they don't have a job."

But Grieshaber, at the Michigan union for prison system employees, cites the state's 15.3 percent unemployment rate as a definitive obstacle to providing subsidized jobs.[19] "With this kind of unemployment, it's just impossible," he says.

Michigan's wide-ranging reentry program includes job-search assistance, Grieshaber notes. "But if anybody brought up subsidizing jobs — my goodness," he says. "You've already got people complaining about prisoners getting paid for working in the prisons."

Others also warn that the present bleak employment climate isn't the right political environment for a subsidized-jobs strategy. "There are people out of work who have never broken any law and aren't being offered that kind of job," Nolan of Prison Fellowship says.

But when the jobs picture improves, "I can see the advantage of a subsidized job," he says, especially for ex-prisoners with no formal employment experience who must learn to function in a workplace before they enter the labor market. "A lot of people have never had a job. A job teaches them discipline, showing up on time, to call if they're going to be late."

Others argue against subsidizing jobs. Montgomery County, Md., Corrections and Rehabilitation Director Art Wallenstein, an ardent reentry advocate, says a subsidized-jobs program would entangle his agency in political complications. "I don't want reentry to get bogged down on the issue of whether our unemployed are more valuable than your unemployed," he says. "I can live without subsidized jobs."

Wallenstein isn't philosophically opposed to the subsidized-jobs strategy but argues that they're not essential. "I believe there are jobs out there," he says. "We can get offenders workforce-ready if we don't rely on magic but

Prison Population Tops 2.2 Million Inmates

Nearly 2.3 million inmates were in custody in state and federal prisons and local jails in 2007. Slightly more than half were in state prisons, and about a third were in local jails.

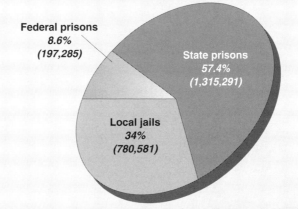

Number of U.S. Inmates, December 2007

Federal prisons
8.6%
(197,285)

State prisons
57.4%
(1,315,291)

Local jails
34%
(780,581)

Source: Heather C. West and William J. Sabol, "Prisoners in 2007," Bureau of Justice Statistics, Dec. 31, 2008

on tested, workforce-development programs that prepare people to engage in the job market. We don't need a leg up for offenders."

Do reentry programs significantly reduce recidivism?

Reentry programs have a major selling point: reducing recidivism. "The high recidivism rates that translate into thousands of new crimes each year could easily be averted through improved reentry efforts," New York City Mayor Michael Bloomberg told a Summit on Reentry and Employment held by the U.S. Conference of Mayors last year in New York.

"To keep inmates on the right path once they leave, we will link them to the benefits they need immediately upon release. They've paid their debt — but with no prospects, sadly, too many of them will return to jail. Let's help them build their future — which will help keep all of us safe."[20]

Experts readily acknowledge, however, that data is not yet available on which reentry strategies produce the best results. In Michigan, for instance, reentry program

AP Photo/The Herald-Palladium/John Madill

AP Photo/Steven Senne

Second Chances

Former inmate Tony Monk (top, foreground) landed a job at Regal Finishing in Coloma, Mich., after completing the state's Prisoner Reentry Initiative Program. He holds tractor headlight reflectors coated at the Regal plant. His boss, Jim Kodis, left, says Regal co-workers' support of Monk was critical to his success. Joshua Gomes (bottom) is a free man thanks to a new Rhode Island law that allows certain prisoners to get out early if they commit to rehabilitation programs. Gomes, 24, of Central Falls, R.I., went to prison after stealing a man's wallet and robbing a convenience store to feed his cocaine habit. He served about half of his two-year sentence.

participants haven't been free long enough "to draw anything other than preliminary conclusions about recidivism findings," Dennis Schrantz, deputy director of the Michigan corrections department, told the House

Appropriations Subcommittee on Commerce, Justice, Science and Related Agencies last March.[21]

But, in a sign of how the pendulum has swung from the days in which longer sentences were seen as the best approach to fighting crime, Schrantz also told lawmakers that the model of widespread and lengthy incarceration clearly was ineffective. "Prisoners who serve longer terms do not recidivate less frequently," he said. "Rearrest rates for former prisoners who serve one, two, three, four or five years in prison are nearly the same."[22]

However, so many politicians and policy experts are singing the praises of reentry that even some of those advocates worry that the concept could be dismissed as a fad, especially by prison system personnel.

"One of the problems we face with the corrections folks is that reentry has become the flavor of the month," says Nolan of Prison Fellowship. "They're basically tired of being guinea pigs. Frankly, reentry can mean all things to all people, so I can understand the jaundiced response."

"We want programs that work," says Grieshaber of the Michigan correction employees' union. "We're just suspicious that you don't get an honest evaluation when there are these massive budget pressures. We're kind of — 'Proceed with caution' on the whole thing."

More pointedly, Grieshaber questions whether politicians' recent call for greater emphasis on reentry is purely budget-driven. "If we didn't have these dramatic budget pressures, would we be letting all these prisoners out?" he asks. "A lot of us think the answer would be 'no.'"

But in Colorado, Attorney General John Suthers, a conservative Republican, argues that saving money by cutting recidivism is a worthwhile objective. "The vast majority of inmates going into prison every year are recidivists," he says. "If you can significantly reduce that, you can make tremendous savings."

Suthers acknowledges that recidivism declines are measured in small quantities. "Don't kid yourself — you're not going to reduce recidivism by 10 percent to 50 percent," he says. "But I do think 5 percent to 10 percent is possible, and well worth the effort."

Ordinary citizens might not consider that much of a drop. James M. Byrne, a professor of criminology at the University of Massachusetts, noted that although drug treatment, educational and other programs could cut "criminal behavior" by about 10 percent, bigger reductions would require social programs in "high-crime/poverty pocket" areas.[23]

"I suspect that the general public — already wary of the prospects for individual offender change — will be expecting a bit more for their investment in rehabilitation than marginal reductions in offender recidivism," Byrne told the House Appropriations subcommittee's March hearing on reentry programs.

Some optimists say the widespread emphasis on reentry programs could evolve into an approach with enormous potential. "The next frontier," says John Jay College president Travis, "is community-level intervention.

"People return to settings that are governed by institutions like family and peer groups and social interactions," he says. "Are they welcomed back home or shunned? Do we pay attention to the availability of positive peer group networks as opposed to the old gang on the corner?"

BACKGROUND

Crime Boom

Starting in the early 1970s, and fueled in the '80s by growing drug-related violence, the nation's crime rate skyrocketed, and fear of crime grew into a leading issue in cities and states — and eventually in Congress.[24]

After growing steadily throughout the 1960s, crime shot up in the '70s and '80s. By 1990, the violent crime rate had more than quadrupled — from 160.9 per 100,000 population in 1960 to 731.8.[25]

During this period, harsh new anti-drug laws played a key role in boosting prison populations. In 1980, just 19,000 drug offenders were in state prisons and 4,900 in federal institutions. By 2003, state prisons held 250,900 drug offenders — 20 percent of the prisoner population, up from 6 percent in 1980. And drug offenders made up 55 percent of federal prisoners — up from 25 percent in 1980.[26]

Starting in the mid-1980s, a crack epidemic and the resulting massive government response played a role in filling the prisons. But the groundwork had been laid years before crack appeared on the scene. A new attitude about incarceration had replaced the old doctrine of rehabilitation, which held that psychological counseling and other prison programs could transform convicts into law-abiding citizens.

Academic research seemed to support the new view that rehabilitation didn't work and that prisons should punish rather than rehabilitate. Robert Martinson, an influential sociologist at City University of New York, wrote in 1974 that "with few and isolated exceptions, the rehabilitative efforts that have been reported so far have had no appreciable effect on recidivism."[27]

However, Martinson revised his sweeping conclusion four years later. In many cases psychological counseling in prison did keep recipients from returning to crime, he wrote in 1978. But by then Martinson's initial assessment had been embraced. And the idea that trying to rehabilitate lawbreakers was a waste of time fit in well with an increasingly popular view that criminals didn't need counseling — they needed to be locked up, and locked up longer.

In the 1970s, politicians of all ideological stripes were blaming the steady rise in crime on what they called a breakdown in the criminal justice system. One of Congress' leading liberals, Sen. Edward M. Kennedy, D-Mass., lent his voice to the chorus — which also included Republican President Gerald R. Ford — demanding lengthier sentences.

"'Revolving door' justice convinces the criminal that his chances of actually being caught, tried, convicted and jailed are too slim to be taken seriously," Kennedy wrote in an op-ed piece in *The New York Times* in 1975. "Our existing criminal justice system is no deterrent at all to violent crime in our society."[28]

Mandatory Minimums

Kennedy and many others pointed to laws throughout the country that mandated "indeterminate" sentences for specific crimes, such as prison terms of five to 15 years. Prison and parole authorities would decide when and if an inmate was rehabilitated enough to be released.[29]

But the approach was conditioned on the results of rehabilitative programs that were often shoddy and poorly financed. Conservatives viewed parole boards as irresponsible or naïve — falling for convicts' tales of reformation and letting hardened criminals back on the street.

1970s-1980s *Escalating crime prompts many states and Congress to set harsh minimum sentences.*

1970 Nation's violent crime rate more than doubles, jumping from 160.9 incidents per 100,000 population in 1960 to 363.5 per 100,000.

1973 New York state's "Rockefeller Drug Laws" establish long, fixed sentences for drug offenses.

1974 Influential study by sociologist Robert Martinson concludes that prison rehabilitation programs have "no appreciable effect on recidivism;" four years later, he reverses his conclusion.

1977 Liberal Sen. Edward M. Kennedy, D-Mass., introduces legislation mandating minimum sentences.

1983 All but two states have enacted mandatory minimum sentences.

1984 Congress passes Sentencing Reform Act, setting minimum sentences for a range of federal crimes.

1986 Crack cocaine epidemic coupled with intense media coverage prompts Congress to establish longer sentences for sales of crack than of powder cocaine.

1990s *Prison population booms, even as crime rates start falling.*

1990 Federal and state prison population soars to more than 739,000 inmates, more than double the 1980 population of about 315,000.

1991 Sister of a man imprisoned for five years for growing marijuana starts Families Against Mandatory Minimums, which helps lead campaign to change sentencing laws.... Federal Judge J. Lawrence Irving of San Diego resigns to protest mandatory minimums.

1993 Violent-crime rate begins falling after years of steady increase.

1999 U.S. Attorney General Janet Reno calls for the criminal justice system to help ex-inmates reenter society.

2000s *Prison system costs and high recidivism rates prompt some states to expand reentry programs; President George W. Bush prods Congress to pass Second Chance Act with funding for reentry projects.*

2002 Major Justice Department recidivism study finds that 67 percent of ex-prisoners in 15 biggest states are rearrested within three years, and 47 percent are convicted of new crimes and sent back to prison.... National Institute of Drug Abuse official says there is no physiological difference between the effects of crack cocaine and cocaine powder.

2003 Justice Department keeps focus on recidivism and soaring prison populations with announcement that federal and state prisons and local jails hold more than 2 million people.

2004 Violent crime rate drops to 463 incidents per 100,000 population, from 747 per 100,000 in 1993.... President Bush calls America "the land of the second chance" and advocates federal support for reentry programs.

2005 New York legislature authorizes (but doesn't require) judges to lower some Rockefeller Drug Law sentences — to 12 to 24 years for selling 3 oz. of crack cocaine, for instance, from the former mandatory 25 years to life.

2007 Number of prisoners released from federal and state prisons reaches more than 725,000.... Texas legislature rejects prison-construction plan in favor of spending on parole supervision and alternatives to incarceration.

2008 Bush signs Second Chance Act.... Total state spending to operate prisons rises to $47 billion, even as some states cut prison costs.

2009 Justice Department awards $28 million in Second Chance Act grants to programs across the country.... Senate and House committees hold hearings on strengthening reentry programs.... Two-thirds of ex-prisoners in California are reincarcerated for parole violations, according to new recidivism study.... Plan to cut California's prison population proposes new parole standards to avoid reincarceration.... Michigan expands statewide reentry program, pursues plans to close eight prisons.

Liberals, for their part, decried a system in which authorities had virtually total power to decide when a prisoner could be freed. The system lent itself to abuse, these critics said, especially since evaluating whether a prisoner had been rehabilitated was a highly subjective exercise.

By the time Kennedy called for a new system of "mandatory minimum" sentences, some states already had begun using that method, including New York. The state's so-called Rockefeller Drug Laws of 1973 had been championed by liberal-leaning Republican Gov. Nelson A. Rockefeller, who touted the harsh measures as a weapon against growing use of heroin.

The laws applied to all illegal drugs — cocaine as well as heroin (marijuana was removed from the list in 1977). Judges were required to impose sentences of 15 years to life for anyone convicted of selling two ounces of a drug, or possessing four ounces (amounts were later changed). The laws triggered a sixfold increase in the state prison population, from about 10,000 inmates in 1973 to more than 61,000 in 1992. By 1997, about a third of New York prisoners had been sentenced on drug charges — up from 9 percent in 1980.[30]

As criticism of "indeterminate" laws mounted, Congress spent years devising ways to assure standardized sentences in federal court, so that two people convicted for the same crime before different judges would receive equal punishment. A 1977 measure sponsored by Kennedy also would have restricted parole. Congress took no action on the bill.[31]

The 1980 election of conservative Republican President Ronald W. Reagan reenergized the movement to toughen federal sentencing. In 1984, Congress passed the Sentencing Reform Act (SRA), which ordered judges to follow a series of "mandatory minimum" sentences for some crimes involving drugs and firearms. Additional minimum sentences were added later for other crimes. And the law abolished parole for all offenders serving time in federal prisons who had been convicted of federal crimes committed after Nov. 1, 1987.

"The SRA and the guidelines make rehabilitation a lower priority than other sentencing goals," said a history published by the U.S. Sentencing Commission, which the law established.[32]

The law-and-order trend was reinforced in the mid- and late-1980s after crack cocaine arrived on the scene. The cheap, smokable form of cocaine spawned a crime wave in the nation's inner cities as dealers fought for turf and addicts committed crimes. But mass-media reports supported the then widely accepted notion that crack's chemical properties triggered greater violence than other drugs.

Acting on that belief, Congress passed a 1986 law imposing a mandatory sentence of five years for selling five grams of crack (the weight of two pennies) — the same penalty imposed for selling 500 grams (about a pound) of powder cocaine. And someone convicted of selling 11 lbs. of powder cocaine got the same sentence as a person convicted of selling less than 2 oz. of crack — 10 years.[33]

Nearly two decades later, the view of crack as especially associated with violence still held sway in some law-enforcement circles. In 2002, Deputy Attorney General Larry D. Thompson told the U.S. Sentencing Commission that crack was more addictive than powder cocaine.[34] But Glenn Hanson, the acting director of the National Institute on Drug Abuse, testified that crack and powered cocaine's had precisely the same physiological effects.[35]

Incarceration Boom

The Sentencing Reform Act ensured that more federal offenders were serving time and for longer sentences. By 2002, 86 percent of federal offenders were sent to prison — up from 69 percent in 1987 — and time served doubled from about 25 to 50 months.[36]

State lawmakers were moving to the same beat: By 1983, 48 states had enacted mandatory-minimum sentencing laws, and at least five had eliminated parole. By 1994, 11 states had enacted "three strikes" laws imposing life sentences with no parole for people convicted of a third felony (in some cases, a third violent felony).[37]

As the wave of get-tough laws washed over the country, the handful of critics decrying the social and economic effects of driving up imprisonment got little support. "Many states realize corrections costs are out of control, and they're looking for ways to save money," Alvin J. Bronstein, director of the American Civil Liberties Union's National Prison Project, said in 1994. "But at the same time they're talking about 'three strikes and you're out,' treating juveniles as adults and jamming through other laws that will jack up [prison] costs."[38]

In fact, an unprecedented expansion of prison systems was occurring across the country. In the 1980s, the federal

Halfway House Puts Focus on Jobs

"If you want to change your life, this is where you can do it at."

Making pizzas for slightly more than minimum wage — it's not a job that puts a spring in the step of a middle-aged man who has lived the life of a drug dealer.

"It's a humbling experience, to say the least," says the man, a resident at the Montgomery County Pre-Release Center (PRC), a halfway house in the Washington suburb of Rockville, Md. "The money I make in a week, I used to make that in a couple of hours."

The man, who asks to be called Mr. Nolton, tends to think carefully before he speaks. A couple of decades cycling in and out of jail and prison make you cautious, he explains. "Most of my adult life has been drug sales and incarceration," he says. "Pretty much, I'm at the end of my rope, in the sense that I would like to have something wholesome in my life as well as make my family proud, and try to make the best of whatever 'normal' life is."

Mr. Nolton is fairly typical of the older residents at PRC, who are accepted in the final four to six months of their sentences. Although Maryland state prison inmates and some federal prisoners are allowed to apply, Montgomery County jail inmates make up the majority of the approximately 170

A sculpture captures the mission of the Montgomery County Pre-Release Center: Lunchbox in hand, a former prisoner kisses his wife good-bye as he goes to work.

residents at the center, most of whom have been incarcerated previously. The center sits just a block from the shopping centers and restaurants of bustling Rockville Pike. The nicely landscaped building looks like a small office and bears no identification as an outpost of the Montgomery County Correction and Rehabilitation Department.

"The population here is exactly representative of the population of the jail," says Director Stefan LoBuglio. PRC staff evaluate applicants for potential danger to the community, but the center is willing to accept people with long criminal records if there is evidence they can be trusted to stay out of trouble.

Founded in 1969 and well-known to advocates of prisoner reentry programs, the center emphasizes the practical in getting its residents — don't call them inmates — ready for the outside world. They start off living in two-person rooms, not cells or dormitories, and residents can earn their way up a waiting list for a single room with private bathroom by following rules, which include looking for a job every day until finding one.

To be sure, staff members wear badges on their belts, unauthorized departure is classified as escape and residents

and state prison population more than doubled, from 315,974 to 739,980; by 2000 it was more than 1 million. For the entire 20-year period, the nation saw a 318 percent increase in the number of people incarcerated.[39] To keep up, the number of state prisons rose from 592 in 1974 to 1,023 — a 73 percent increase.[40]

As the size of the incarcerated population kept expanding, critics tried repeatedly to mobilize opposition to the trend. "While there is surprising agreement within the

criminal justice community that we lock up too many people and that we keep them in prison far too long, the United States seems to be on the verge of embarking on the most extensive prison construction program in the history of the world," journalist Michael Specter wrote in 1982 in *The Nation*, a left-liberal magazine.[41]

In 1986, a group of lawyers founded The Sentencing Project, a Washington-based advocacy and research organization, which lobbied to eliminate mandatory-minimum

are tested for alcohol three times a day and for drugs three times a week. But such restrictions come off as fairly mild to people whose days were filled until recently with the sounds of cell doors clanking, and with outdoor views of fences and barbed wire.

Above all, while prisons and jails are designed mainly to keep their populations locked up, the PRC's main mission is to help residents get out of jail and stay out — by helping them find jobs. Because today's job-application process has become virtually totally Web-centric, all residents have access to computers — restricted to job searches — and are required to obtain free Hotmail e-mail addresses — to make monitoring easier.

Residents who need computer training get instructions in Web navigation and associated skills. Those who need help in regaining their driver's licenses can call on PRC staff for that as well.

And the center offers guidance in résumé-writing. "We have a lady who comes in on Wednesday," Work Release Coordinator Hillel Raskas tells a class of new arrivals. "She can make a résumé for anybody."

Raskas hands out a sample résumé that lists a "Career Exploration Certificate" from the Maryland Education Department at Jessup, Md. That's the location of a state prison, but leaving out that bit of information is all right, he says. He adds, though, that when an application asks about a criminal record, fill in the correct information. "Write, 'Will explain in interview.' Do not lie, do not leave it blank."

Residents at the Montgomery County center can use computers only for job searches. Computer training and help with résumé writing are also available.

CQ Press/Peter Katel

Some lucky residents have former jobs to go back to. One young man is expecting to return to a catering business. Another, also barely out of his teens, said a cousin had arranged a supermarket job.

On a recent afternoon, a resident in his 20s walks into Unit Manager Chris Johnson's office and tells her with a big smile that he's landed a job after six weeks of looking — a $10-an-hour gig in a call center. "I probably could have gotten a job quicker if I didn't set my sights so high," he says. His ambition was understandable. Before he was sentenced to about five years on a drug conviction, he had been a computer engineering student.

Was his criminal record a problem in landing the job? "No, they're understaffed and overloaded," he tells Johnson. Still, she calls to verify the job offer and to make sure the employer knows of the young man's conviction. Everything checks out, and within days the man starts working.

While Mr. Nolton admits he does get a bit weary of the rules, he acknowledges that he owes a lot to the PRC. For one thing, the center banks his earnings, so he expects to have about $500 saved up by the time his sentence is up in five months. So he'll be able to rent a studio apartment.

"This place is really based on the individual," he says. "If you want to change your life and you want a good way back into the community, this is where you can do it at."

— *Peter Katel*

sentences as well as the disparity between crack and powder cocaine sentences.

Eventually, a few members of the law-enforcement community began speaking out against the toughened sentencing laws, especially those applying to drug offenses. "You've got murderers who get out sooner than some kid who did some stupid thing with drugs," said U.S. District Judge J. Lawrence Irving of San Diego, who was appointed to the bench by President Ronald Reagan in 1982 and

resigned in 1991 rather than continue to hand down mandatory sentences. "These sentences are Draconian. It's a tragedy."[42]

But the prevailing law-enforcement view in the 1990s was summed up by Paul McNulty, then a spokesman for the First Freedom Coalition, which advocated tough drug laws, and later a deputy attorney general in the George W. Bush administration. "You can't get convicted [under] a drug law unless you knew what you were doing,"

Reentry Experts Try to Answer '$64,000 Question'

"We still have much to learn about what works."

Advocates of reentry programs don't promise miracles — they know that reentry is a game of inches. In New York, an unspectacular-sounding 5.7 percent fewer ex-prisoners who participated in a reentry program sponsored by the Center for Employment Opportunities (CEO) were rearrested than ex-prisoners who didn't participate.[1]

That might strike a layman as a small-bore result. But Dan Bloom, who directed the CEO evaluation for MDRC, a social-policy research organization, and is running a bigger analysis of job-focused reentry programs in four Midwestern cities, calls the statistic "promising," noting that, "A 5 percent difference is what you tend to see in social programs."

In addition, he says, because the cost of keeping a prisoner incarcerated is quite high, "You don't need a big difference in recidivism to potentially save a lot of money." A cost-benefit analysis of the CEO results is under way.

The data Bloom is collecting ultimately may help answer questions about the most effective ways to help ex-prisoners.

"There is so little [data] out there," Amy L. Solomon, a senior research associate at the Urban Institute's Justice Policy Center, recently told the Senate Subcommittee on Crime and Drugs. "We still have much to learn about what works."[2]

Criminal-justice specialists have been acknowledging as much for some time. "The $64,000 question still remains: Which programs should government agencies, nonprofit organizations and faith-based communities invest in?" wrote Joan Petersilia, a professor at Stanford University

Law School and a noted expert on probation and parole systems.[3]

Criminal-justice system veterans, however, have learned to temper expectations. "Programs can't replace good parenting," says Colorado Attorney General John Suthers, former director of the state's prison system. He argues that recidivism reductions of 5 to 10 percent — though a worthwhile achievement — represent the limit of what reentry programs can achieve.

"If you want to look at a profile of America's prison population," Suthers says, "you can talk about minorities, drug problems, but the single defining characteristic is that two-thirds of them grew up in a home where they lived with their natural father." But for those who came from broken homes and didn't get solid early education, "It's too late for those guys," he says.

Suthers is a conservative Republican, but his conclusion is widely shared across the ideological spectrum.

But some still argue that more than modest results can be expected from reentry programs. "If we could implement effective programs for all returning prisoners, with all the resources needed, we could expect recidivism reductions of about 15-20 percent," said Jeremy Travis, president of John Jay College of Criminal Justice in New York City and a leading advocate of expanding reentry services.[4]

Whether the expectations are high or low, lawmakers — who control most program funding — demand statistics. In Michigan, which has one of the country's most comprehensive programs — the Michigan Prisoner ReEntry Initiative (MPRI) — administrators know better data is

McNulty said in 1993. "After everything this country has been through with drug trafficking, it's very hard for people to look at these supposedly sympathetic cases and say, 'Gee, we feel sorry for you.'"[43]

Reentry Reality

As the debate over sentencing and incarceration policies sharpened during the 1990s, little attention was paid to

the fact that eventually nearly all prisoners are released. Only when U.S. Attorney General Reno raised the issue in 1999 did the question of how to reduce recidivism begin getting sustained attention.

"Too often, offenders leave prison and return to the community without supervision, without jobs, without housing," Reno said. "They quickly fall back into their old patterns of drug usage, gang activities and other crimes."[44]

needed. "We cannot yet establish an empirical link between observed outcomes and MPRI processes, activities and spending," Dennis Schrantz, the state's deputy director of corrections, told a House subcommittee in March.[5]

On a more positive note, Schrantz said results thus far suggest MPRI is "contributing significantly to observed differences in outcomes, even though we cannot yet establish the causal links."[6]

For example, Schrantz noted, the number of parolees sent back to prison for new crimes dropped to 98 per 1,000, the lowest rate in four years; the number of prisoners returned to prison for "technical" parole violations dropped to 89 per 1,000, the lowest level since 1992; and increases in the overall prison population fell to an average of 150 new prisoners a year from 2003-2007, in contrast to annual average growth of 1,925 prisoners from 1984-2002.[7]

Statistics also are important for ferreting out the approaches that actually may do more harm than good. Counterintuitively, programs that deal exclusively with nonviolent, first-time offenders are especially risky, says Michael Thompson, director of the Council of State Governments' Justice Center.

"Take a 40-year-old guy busted for writing bad checks, who has a fairly stable home life and a job — and a drinking problem," Thompson says. "The reentry program says, 'I'm going to put you in intensive alcohol treatment and make sure your parole officer visits you often. So the guy's got to leave his job to go to the parole office, and the parole officer visits his job site, and the guy gets fired. So he's back in the

Stanford University Law School Professor Joan Petersilia calls for more evaluations of reentry programs.

www.law.stanford.edu/

bar drinking. If we'd left him alone, he probably would have been fine."

Even as politicians and policy makers hunger for data, some experts have been urging researchers to expand their research goals beyond recidivism. Statistics should try to measure the extent of social reintegration, argued Petersilia. "For example, evaluations should measure whether clients are working, whether that work is full- or part time and whether the income derived is supporting families," she wrote. "We should measure whether programs increase client sobriety and attendance at treatment programs. We should track whether programs help convicts become involved in community activities, in a church, or in ex-convict support groups or victim sensitivity sessions."[8]

— *Peter Katel*

[1] Data furnished by MDRC.

[2] Testimony before hearing on "The First Line of Defense: Reducing Recidivism at the Local Level," Senate Judiciary Subcommittee on Crime and Drugs, Nov. 5, 2009, Webcast available at http://judiciary.senate.gov/about/subcommittees/crime.cfm.

[3] Joan Petersilia, "What Works in Prisoner Reentry? Reviewing and Questioning the Evidence," *Federal Probation*, September 2004, www.uscourts.gov/fedprob/September_2004/whatworks.html.

[4] Testimony before hearing on "Successful Prisoner Reentry," House Appropriations Subcommittee on Commerce, Justice, Science, and Related Agencies," March 12, 2009.

[5] Testimony before hearing on "Innovative Prisoner Reentry Programs," House Appropriations Subcommittee on Commerce, Justice, Science, and Related Agencies, March 11, 2009.

[6] *Ibid.*

[7] *Ibid.*

[8] Petersilia, *op. cit.*

Borrowing from the "drug court" model that began in Miami when she was chief prosecutor there, Reno proposed that state and local governments set up "reentry courts." She envisioned judges approving reentry plans for individual ex-prisoners and monitoring progress along the lines of a parole system."[45]

The court idea didn't spread widely. But Reno's proposal helped intensify the growing concern over the massive

incarceration expansion that had been under way for more than two decades.

The fact that crime was going down perhaps helped to shift attitudes. The violent crime rate plummeted from 747 crimes per 100,000 in 1993 to 454 in 2008.[46]

Amid the crime downturn came the startling news in 2003 that the nation's prison and jail population had passed the 2 million mark — the world's highest. "When violent crime rates were higher, many politicians were afraid to be seen as soft on crime," *The New York Times* said in an editorial. "But now that crime has receded and the public is more worried about taxes and budget deficits, it would not require extraordinary courage for elected officials to do the right thing and scale back our overuse of jails and prison cells."[47]

In the following years, nearly half the states softened sentencing laws or probation-parole policies, mostly by diverting nonviolent drug offenders to non-prison treatment programs, expanding alternatives to incarceration for nonviolent offenders and reducing time served behind bars while expanding probation and parole supervision.[48]

Meanwhile, matters took an unexpected turn at the federal level. Activists who had been advocating federal support for state reentry programs had concluded that the George W. Bush administration, out of an ideological distrust for alternatives to incarceration and preoccupation with war and terrorism, would not support reentry programs. But in his 2004 State of the Union address, Bush said, referring to the 600,000 prisoners expected to be released that year: "If they can't find work or a home or help, they are much more likely to commit crime and return to prison."[49]

Bush proposed a $300 million "reentry initiative" to expand job training and placement, provide temporary housing and connect newly released prisoners to mentors to help guide them after incarceration. Support from the president and other conservative Republicans was critical to the passage of the Second Chance Act of 2007. The bipartisan alliance that pushed the bill through Congress included prison-reform advocates such as former National Institute of Justice director Travis and the Prison Fellowship's Nolan. Many religious conservatives, who counted Bush as an ally, saw a spiritual reason to give offenders a second chance.

House and Senate versions were sponsored by bipartisan groups that included Sens. Sam Brownback, R-Kan., and Patrick Leahy, D-Vt., and Reps. Danny Davis, D-Ill., and Chris Cannon, R-Utah. Nevertheless, the bill didn't make its way to Bush's desk until 2008, among other reasons because Sen. Tom Coburn, R-Okla., put a "hold" on it in 2006, stopping its progress in the Senate for a time. He said he supported the legislation but argued that other federal programs served the same purpose. In fiscal 2008-2009, Congress appropriated $25 million for Second Chance Act grants and pilot projects across the country.[50]

CURRENT SITUATION

Upgrading Skills

Even as reentry advocates fight to spread basic programs around the country, some in the movement are starting to expand their goals.

In New York, a program is trying to take ex-prisoners beyond the world of low-paid, entry-level jobs. "I don't think anybody knows more than we do at the CEO how hard it is to get folks that first full-time job when they get out of prison, but it's not enough," says Center for Employment Opportunities executive director Tarlow. "People need to develop real careers and career pathways."

The CEO is in the second year of a fledgling program designed to open doors to high-paid, skilled trades, such as electrical work, plumbing and refrigeration. Criminal records aren't a bar to employment in those industries, as a rule. But trade school graduation is a prerequisite. Getting into trade school means passing tests, which can be an obstacle for people whose reading and math skills typically top out at middle-school levels.

That's where the CEO Academy comes in. Open to CEO participants working at entry-level jobs, the academy holds weeknight and Saturday classes in reading and math — geared toward helping participants pass trade-school entrance exams.

But it's a tough slog. The first 12-week class began with 35 participants. By the end of the session only 13 students remained. Eventually, 11 students entered trade school, and nine finished.

"Nothing is a slam dunk," says Marta Nelson, CEO's director of policy and planning, who directs the program. Setbacks that have forced students out of the program, she says, include the shock of doing classroom work after many years out of school, health problems and rearrests — sometimes for something as simple as "leaving the state to visit a son and violating parole."

However, the second academy class of 62 had 42 graduates, and 31 were expected to graduate from trade school in late November. The program is now recruiting for a third class of 100.

So far, two trade-school graduates have landed skilled jobs with contractors. But CEO expects that number to go up now that a full-time employment counselor has been hired for the program.

AT ISSUE

Can reentry and rehabilitation programs reduce recidivism?

YES
Jeremy Travis
*President, John Jay College of
Criminal Justice*

From testimony before House Appropriations Subcommittee on Commerce,
Justice, Science and Related Agencies, March 12, 2009

The challenge we face is daunting: to make significant reductions in [the] very high rate of rearrest. The rate of failure — as defined by rearrest — is significantly higher in the initial months following release. If the risk of failure is highest in the first six months, then we should devote our efforts and resources to reducing the rate of failure in those months. It's a very simple but revolutionary concept: We align our resources to match the risk.

We know far more than we did a few decades ago about program effectiveness. Research allows us to see the potential for measurable reductions in recidivism. In fact, according to the best estimates of researchers in this field, if we could implement effective programs for all returning prisoners, with all the resources needed, we could expect recidivism reductions of about 15-20 percent. And, we can also state with great confidence that these investments would be cost-effective: They would pay for themselves by reducing future criminal justice and corrections costs.

We should not be satisfied with these results. In my opinion, we can only achieve results that match the magnitude of the reentry phenomenon if we recognize that our approach has been too timid. We have been constrained by a medical model that focuses on individual-level interventions, rather than also embracing an ecological model that focuses simultaneously on the community context within which individuals are struggling to thrive after prison. The next chapter of innovation in this area should test ideas that attempt to change the environment to which individuals return home.

Around the country, there are a number of demonstration projects that are testing a very new reentry model — a community-based approach to reentry. Recognizing that some communities are experiencing very high rates of incarceration and reentry, these projects approach reentry as a community phenomenon. These programs create coalitions of community organizations to interact with every person returning home from prison. They attempt to create a different climate in the neighborhood, one promoting successful reintegration.

These demonstration efforts represent a new frontier in reentry innovation. They do not focus exclusively on individual-level interventions. Rather, they create a coalition of support for individuals returning from prisons and jails, bring together law enforcement and community leaders, communicate clearly about the consequences of illegal behavior and provide a clear pathway out of a life of antisocial conduct.

NO
James M. Byrne
*Professor, Department of Criminal Justice and
Criminology, University of Massachusetts*

From testimony before House Appropriations Subcommittee on Commerce,
Justice, Science and Related Agencies, March 12, 2009

Rehabilitation is back in vogue in the United States. Individual-offender rehabilitation is being presented to the public at large — and to federal and state policy makers — as the single-most-effective crime-control strategy. The argument is simple, seductive and not all that offender-friendly: Don't provide convicted offenders with treatment because it will help them as individuals. We need to provide rehabilitation because the provision of rehabilitation has been demonstrated to significantly reduce the likelihood of re-offending, which makes us — and our communities — safer. We are doing it for ourselves and our communities.

Some would argue that this represents one of the big lies of individual-offender rehabilitation, because even significant reductions in the recidivism [rate] in this country will not likely change the crime rates of most communities, because [ex-] offenders do not live — in large numbers — in most communities. They live in a small number of high crime/ poverty pocket neighborhoods in a handful of states. Since residents of these communities do not have the social capital to adequately address the long-standing problems found in high-risk, poverty pocket areas, the prospects for community change are bleak.

We do know that traditional probation and parole programs are not as effective today as they were 30 years ago; we just don't know why. Any serious discussion of new strategies for addressing the prison reentry problem must begin with an examination of the reasons why these programs are ineffective.

Although the reported [results] for prison treatment and programs are modest (a 10 percent reduction in recidivism upon release using standard follow-up measures), there is reason to anticipate improvements in these effects in prison systems designed to focus on offender change rather than short-term offender control.

I suspect that the general public — already wary of the prospects for individual-offender change — will be expecting a bit more for their investment in rehabilitation than marginal reductions in offender recidivism. If we cannot demonstrate the link between participation in the next generation of individual-offender rehabilitation programs and community protection, then support for rehabilitation, tenuous at best, will quickly dissipate. While the general public appears to believe in the possibility of individual-offender change, I think you will find that most of us are skeptical about the probability of individual-offender change, particularly among individuals with serious substance-abuse and/or mental health problems.

Getty Images/Justin Sullivan

Inmates are stacked three-high in a gymnasium at Mule Creek State Prison in Ione, Calif. A panel of federal judges recently ordered California to reduce its prison population over two years from 150,000 to about 115,000. All California prisoners must be released on parole, so parole officers have little time to supervise or assist prisoners. Thousands of parolees a year are sent back to prison for parole violations.

CEO may be in a better position than most reentry programs to move ex-prisoners beyond the low-wage job scene. Established in the late 1970s as a project of the Washington-based Vera Institute of Justice, the organization has been on its own since 1996, funded by foundation grants and government contracts.

As participants work in their subsidized jobs, CEO helps them find work in the open economy. "We focus on small- to medium-size businesses that don't have human-resources departments, and act as their HR department," Tarlow says. "Say they want to hire a person off the street who doesn't have a felony conviction. They'd have to do a background check; it costs them to advertise. With us, I'm saying right up front that my client has a felony conviction, but I'm telling you this person is working right

now; I've got his attendance record right in front of me. And in the worst-case scenario, if it doesn't work out, I'll send you another person the next day."

California Meltdown

The country's biggest prison system has become the national example for what not to do when a state runs out of money to keep expanding incarceration.

The situation in California shows states "what will happen if they ignore the problem or say, 'There's not much we can do,' " says Michael Thompson, director of the Council of State Governments' National Justice Center, which advises states on reentry.

In mid-November, in the latest installment of a long-running crisis and legal battle, Gov. Arnold Schwarzenegger's administration finally came up with a plan to reduce the state's prison population over two years from 150,000 to about 115,000 — or 137 percent of the prisons' 84,000 capacity.[51] The reduction was ordered by a panel of federal judges.[52]

The bulging population partly reflects the state's overwhelmed parole system. California is one of a handful of states that require all prisoners to be released on parole, effectively swamping parole officers who have little time to supervise or assist prisoners. Consequently, thousands of parolees a year are sent back to prison for violating the terms of their release. But with reentry services facing severe budgetary pressures, even more released prisoners may end up back behind bars. (*See chart, p. 202.*)

California's Division of Adult Probation Operations, which runs reentry services, expects to lose $41 million in funding, which director Robert Ambroselli said will be accomplished by delaying the activation of new reentry program sites, but no closures of current programs. "However … the implementation of other new programs is not being considered at this time," he pointed out.[53]

Existing programs — which help with housing, drug counseling and job searches — served about 18,449 parolees in California during the first nine months of 2009.

Though those services won't be expanded, a new state plan will exempt "low-level, lower-risk offenders" from being placed on active parole, which will reduce the number of offenders returning to prison for parole violations, according to the state Corrections and Rehabilitation Department.[54]

But the new plan apparently didn't resolve the political conflict over criminal-justice policy that accompanied the steady expansion of the prison population. Schwarzenegger will propose legislation next year that lawmakers rejected in 2009, which would — among other things — raise the threshold for grand theft from $400 to $950, allowing people convicted of stealing less to be sent to jail instead of prison. Those proposals prompted Republican Assemblyman Jim Nielsen to call the plan an "egregious compromise of justice." He wants the state to build more prisons.[55]

Meanwhile, a Democratic lawmaker has proposed changing the sentencing guidelines. And state Sen. Mark Leno, a Democrat from the San Francisco Bay Area, complained that the plan calls for 2,400 new prison beds and transferring 5,000 inmates to privately owned prisons.

"Building new beds doesn't address the problem that caused the symptom," he said.[56]

OUTLOOK

Change in Tone

The growing emphasis on reentry is changing the tone and substance of the long-polarized criminal-justice policy debate. Conservatives typically have insisted on locking up criminals for longer sentences, while liberals generally oppose mass incarceration and focus on social inequities that influence most offenders' backgrounds.

Traces of that debate certainly remain, but the focus has shifted to questions on how to boost reentry programs by, among other things, improving prisoners' and ex-prisoners' skills and expanding parole supervision to include reentry assistance.

"I won't say that reentry will be a well-oiled machine, but it will be a significant part of the rehabilitation process," says Florida state Sen. Crist, a Republican. For one thing, he predicts, the economy will need more of the kinds of labor ex-prisoners can provide.

"[With] the United States getting tougher on immigration, there's going to be a significant reduction of entry-level workers for jobs that most Americans don't want to do," Crist says. "And with technology advancing and more people in the educational system and moving toward higher-paying opportunities, there's going to be a need

for construction, lawn care and restaurant workers — all these things have to be done by somebody."

At the policy end, however, officials must decide which reentry methods work best. "Right now is the crossroads," says Thompson, of the Council of State Governments' Justice Center. "The federal government is making a significant investment in testing and promoting certain reentry strategies, and states are deciding whether to scale back or build in some of these areas."

Meanwhile, he adds, "Corrections professionals recognize that if they don't generate the gains that leaders in the field said were possible, they'll have missed the key window of opportunity. And if they close the window, they'll exacerbate the prison-population problem."

Nolan of Prison Fellowship acknowledges that when ex-prisoners commit crimes it poses setbacks for reentry programs. "Things like that hurt the movement," he says.

Overall, however, Nolan is confident the reentry movement will lower recidivism. "Jesus wouldn't call us to something ineffective," he says.

However, an advocate of lowering the reliance on prison warns that reentry programs probably won't make a major dent in the national prison population. "It's slowly starting to shift," says Marc Mauer, executive director of the Sentencing Project, "but the scale is so enormous that it will take a much more substantial policy shift to turn things around. There's no reason to expect a change in the next five years."

And prison staffers are still skeptical about reentry programs. "Our guys are saying lots of bad characters are getting released," says Grieshaber of the Michigan corrections workers' union. "That's our bias. But we're holding our breath hoping we don't have a lot of bad things happening out there. I'm not talking about one dramatic thing — that can happen. I'm talking about an aggregation of events, where after a year or two you say, 'Oh, my God.' "

Skeptics are still to be found in the policy world as well. "I would suspect that the number of people released from prison will continue to be high," says Mulhausen of the Heritage Foundation. "Reentry is now the buzzword. In 10 years we'll probably be talking about a whole new thing."

But, in a sign of how the reentry movement has created a change in tone, Mulhausen adds, "I'm willing to admit that some things work, but they often don't work spectacularly well. We should do these programs, but they're not the magic bullet."

Still, some veterans of the prisoner reentry world are confident that prospects for improvement are excellent.

Tarlow of the Center for Employment Opportunities draws a connection between the reentry movement and the welfare reform law of 1996. The act forced mothers on public assistance into the workforce, in theory setting a better role model for their children.[57] The next step, she says, is to examine the effects on children of having their fathers incarcerated.

"People have come to realize that children have two parents, and that the father often has a connection to the criminal justice system," Tarlow says. "I believe that 10 years from now, this burgeoning movement about the importance of young men, who are fathers, coming home from jail and prison and needing work will really take hold," she says. "I think you're going to see an easier path from prison to work."[58]

NOTES

1. Heather C. West and William J. Sabol, "Prisoners in 2007," Bureau of Justice Statistics, Department of Justice, updated May 12, 2009, www.ojp.usdoj.gov/bjs/pub/pdf/p07.pdf. Pre-2000 statistics furnished by Bureau of Justice Statistics (not available online).

2. Christine S. Scott-Hayward, "The Fiscal Crisis in Corrections: Rethinking Policies and Practices," Vera Institute of Justice, July 2009, p. 3, www.vera.org/files/The-fiscal-crisis-in-corrections_July-2009.pdf.

3. Amy L. Solomon, et al., "From Prison to Work: The Employment Dimensions of Prisoner Reentry," Urban Institute, Justice Policy Center, 2004, p. 8, www.urban.org/UploadedPDF/411097_From_Prison_to_Work.pdf.

4. Jim Suhr, "States target prisons for cuts, raising worries," The Associated Press, July 28, 2009; "The Michigan Prisoner ReEntry Initiative Progress Snapshot," March 2009, www.fce.msu.edu/Family_Impact_Seminars/pdf/FIS-Spring2009/Family_Impact_Seminar_MPRI_Snapshot_030809.pdf.

5. Jamal Thalji, "Legislators Look West for Prison Solution," St. Petersburg Times, Nov. 18, 2009, p. B1;

"Justice Reinvestment in Texas," Council of State Governments Justice Center, April 2009, http://justicereinvestment.org/states/texas/pubmaps-tx.

6. Bob Egelko, "State submits plan to reduce prison population," San Francisco Chronicle, Nov. 13, 2009, www.sfgate.com/cgi-bin/article.cgi?f=/c/a/2009/11/12/MNMV1AJNHV.DTL; "Defendants' Response to Three-Judge Court's Oct. 21, 2009 Order," Case3:01-cv-01351-TEH Document2274, Nov. 12, 2009, www.cdcr.ca.gov/News/2009_Press_Releases/docs/11-12_Filed-Stamped_Filing.pdf.

7. "Successful Prisoner Reentry," House Appropriations Committee, Subcommittee on Commerce, Justice, Science and Related Agencies, March 12, 2009.

8. "Remarks as Prepared for Delivery by Attorney General Eric Holder," July 9, 2009, www.justice.gov/ag/speeches/2009/ag-speech-090709.html.

9. "State of the Union Address," Miller Center of Public Affairs, University of Virginia, Jan. 20, 2004, http://millercenter.org/scripps/archive/speeches/detail/4542.

10. Caroline Wolf Harlow, "Education and Correctional Populations," Bureau of Justice Statistics, U.S. Justice Department, January 2003, www.ojp.usdoj.gov/bjs/pub/pdf/ecp.pdf.

11. James J. Stephan, "State Prison Expenditures, 2001," Bureau of Justice Statistics, U.S. Justice Department, June 2004, www.ojp.gov/bjs/pub/pdf/spe01.pdf.

12. Ryken Grattet, et al., "Parole Violations and Revocations in California: Analysis and Suggestions for Action," Federal Probation, June 2009, pp. 2-4, http://ucicorrections.seweb.uci.edu/sites/ucicorrections.seweb.uci.edu/files/Parole%20Violations%20and%20Revocations%20in%20CA.pdf.

13. Jennifer Warren, "He found a calling in prison," Los Angeles Times, July 5, 2007, p. A1.

14. Ryan S. King, et al., "Incarceration and Crime: A Complex Relationship," Sentencing Project, 2005, pp. 3-4, www.sentencingproject.org/doc/publications/inc_iandc_complex.pdf.

15. Solomon, et al., op. cit.

16. Ibid.

17. Christy Visher, *et al.*, "Employment After Prison: A Longitudinal Study of Releasees in Three States," Urban Institute, Justice Policy Center, October 2008, www.urban.org/UploadedPDF/411778_employment_after_prison.pdf.

18. "Transitional Jobs Reentry Demonstration," The Joyce Foundation, July 2009, www.mdrc.org/publications/522/policybrief.pdf.

19. "Michigan Unemployment Rate (Seasonally Adjusted)," September 2009, Michigan.gov, www.milmi.org.

20. Kathy Amoroso, "Mayors Highlight Innovative Strategies for Aiding Prisoner Reentry at National Summit," United States Conference of Mayors, March 10, 2008, http://usmayors.org/usmayornewspaper/documents/03_10_08/pg14_prisoner_reentry.asp.

21. "Successful Prisoner Reentry," *op. cit.*

22. *Ibid.*

23. *Ibid.*

24. Except where otherwise indicated, this subsection draws on Doris Layton MacKenzie, *What Works in Corrections: Reducing the Criminal Activities of Offenders and Delinquents* (2006).

25. "Reported Crime in the United States," Bureau of Justice Statistics, updated Jan. 12, 2009, http://bjs-data.ojp.usdoj.gov/dataonline/Search/Crime/State/statebystaterun.cfm?stateid=52. For background, see Peter Katel, "Prison Reform," *CQ Researcher*, April 6, 2007, pp. 289-312.

26. Marc Mauer and Ryan S. King, "A 25-year Quagmire: The War on Drugs and its Impact on American Society," The Sentencing Project, September 2007, pp. 9-10, www.sentencingproject.org/doc/publications/dp_25yearquagmire.pdf. For background see Peter Katel, "War on Drugs," *CQ Researcher*, June 2, 2006, pp. 481-504.

27. Quoted in MacKenzie, *op. cit.*

28. Edward M. Kennedy, "Punishing the Offenders," *The New York Times*, Dec. 6, 1975.

29. Except where otherwise indicated, this subsection draws on MacKenzie, *op. cit.*

30. Aaron D. Wilson, "Rockefeller Drug Laws Information Sheet," Partnership for Responsible Drug Information, Aug. 7, 2000, www.prdi.org/rocklawfact.html.

31. Paul J. Hofer, *et al.*, "Fifteen Years of Guidelines Sentencing: An Assessment of How Well the Federal Criminal Justice System is Achieving the Goals of Sentencing Reform," U.S. Sentencing Commission, November 2004, pp. 1-35, www.ussc.gov/15_year/15_year_study_full.pdf.

32. *Ibid.*, p. 13.

33. Mauer and King, *op. cit.*, pp. 9, 22. Laura Murphy, "Testimony to U.S. Sentencing Commission," March 19, 2002, www.aclu.org/racial-justice_drug-law-reform_immigrants-rights_womens-rights/testimony-washington-national-office-.

34. "Summary of Public Hearings on Cocaine Sentencing Policy," U.S. Sentencing Commission, 2002, pp. E-1-E-2, www.ussc.gov/r_congress/02crack/AppE.pdf.

35. *Ibid.*, p. E-3.

36. *Ibid.*, pp. 138-139.

37. Larry Rohter, "In Wave of Anticrime Fervor, States Rush to Adopt Laws," *The New York Times*, May 10, 1994, p. A1; Stuart Taylor Jr., "Strict Penalties for Criminals: Pendulum of Feeling Swings," *The New York Times*, Dec. 13, 1983, p. A1.

38. Quoted in William Claiborne, "Making Sentences Fit the Prisons," *The Washington Post*, July 16, 1994, p. A1.

39. Sarah Lawrence and Jeremy Travis, "The New Landscape of Imprisonment: Mapping America's Prison Expansion," Urban Institute, April 2004, p. 7, www.urban.org/UploadedPDF/410994_mapping_prisons.pdf.

40. *Ibid.*, p. 8.

41. Michael Specter, "The Untried Alternative to Prisons," *The Nation*, March 13, 1982, p. 300.

42. Alexandra Marks, "Rolling back stiff drug sentences," *The Christian Science Monitor*, Dec. 8, 1998, p. 1.

43. Dirk Johnson, "As Mandatory Terms Pack Prisons, Experts Ask, Is Tougher Too Tough?" *The New York Times*, Nov. 8, 1993, p. A16.

44. Quoted in Michael J. Sniffen, "Reno Wants Prisoner Release Help," The Associated Press, Oct. 14, 1999.

45. Quoted in *ibid.* For background, see Mary H. Cooper, "Drug-Policy Debate," *CQ Researcher*, July 28, 2000, pp. 593-624.

46. "Crime in the United States by Volume and Rate per 100,000 Inhabitants, 1989-2008," FBI Uniform Crime Report, September 2009, www.fbi.gov/ucr/cius2008/data/table_01.html.

47. "Two Million Inmates, And Counting," *The New York Times*, April 9, 2003, p. A18.

48. Ryan S. King, "Changing Direction? State Sentencing Reforms 2004-2006," The Sentencing Project, March 2007, www.sentencingproject.org/doc/publications/sentencingreformforweb.pdf.

49. "State of the Union Address," *op. cit.*

50. "President Bush to Sign Unprecedented Prisoner Reentry Legislation," Reentry Policy Council, Council of State Governments, April 8, 2008, http://reentrypolicy.org/announcements/bush_sign_SCA; "Appropriations Update," Reentry Policy Council, undated, www.reentrypolicy.org/government_affairs/second_chance_act#OVERVIEW; Chris Suelleontrop, "The Right Has a Jailhouse Conversion," *The New York Times Magazine*, Dec. 24, 2006, p. 47.

51. Egelko, *op. cit.*

52. Carol J. Williams, "State gets two years to cut 43,000 from prisons," *Los Angeles Times*, Aug. 5, 2009, p. A1.

53. "Defendants' Response to Three-Judge Court's October 21, 2009 Order," *op. cit.*

54. "CDCR Files Response to Federal Three Judge Panel on Prison Management Plan," California Department of Corrections and Rehabilitation, Nov. 12, 2009, www.cdcr.ca.gov/News/2009_Press_Releases/Nov_12.html.

55. Quoted in Egelko, *op. cit.*

56. Quoted in *ibid.*

57. For background, see Sarah Glazer, "Welfare Reform," *CQ Researcher*, Aug. 3, 2001, pp. 601-632.

58. For background, see Kathy Koch, "Fatherhood Movement," *CQ Researcher*, June 2, 2000, pp. 473-496.

BIBLIOGRAPHY

Books

Kleiman, Mark A.R., *When Brute Force Fails: How to Have Less Crime and Less Punishment*, Princeton University Press, 2009.
A leading criminal justice policy expert, now at the University of California, Los Angeles, examines measures designed to lessen reliance on incarceration, including recidivism reduction.

MacKenzie, Doris Layton, *What Works in Corrections: Reducing the Criminal Activities of Offenders and Delinquents*, Cambridge University Press, 2006.
A University of Maryland criminologist examines the literature on reentry programs to find and analyze effective approaches.

Petersilia, Joan, *When Prisoners Come Home: Parole and Prisoner Reentry*, Oxford University Press, 2009.
A national expert on prisons examines reentry systems as they now exist and how to improve them.

Travis, Jeremy, *But They All Come Back: Facing the Challenges of Prisoner Reentry*, Urban Institute Press, 2005.
The leading advocate of reentry, now president of John Jay College of Criminal Justice in New York City, makes a case for expanding reentry programs.

Articles

Barnett, Ron, "Incarcerated getting educated," *USA Today*, Sept. 25, 2009, p. A3.
State prisons across the country are stepping up education programs to better inmates' reentry chances.

Bell, Dawson, "Prisons — 2nd Chance: 2 Succeed, 2 Struggle," *Detroit Free Press*, May 25, 2009, p. A7.
In part of a package of stories about Michigan's reentry system, a reporter chronicles the experiences of four newly released prisoners.

Buntin, John, "Job Freedom: Can the lessons of welfare reform be applied to the prison system?" *Governing*, August 2009, www.governing.com/article/job-freedom.
A reporter for a magazine for government administrators examines the single-minded dedication to finding jobs

that characterizes a county-run pre-release center in Maryland.

Freedman, Samuel G., "Unlikely Allies on a Former Wedge Issue," *The New York Times*, June 28, 2008, p. B5.
A religion columnist reports on Christian conservatives joining forces with liberal advocates of alternatives to incarceration.

Gramlich, John, "At least 26 states spend less on prisons," *Stateline.org*, Aug. 11, 2009, www.stateline.org/live/details/story?contentId=418338.
A news service covering state governments reports on a trend of cutting back spending on prisons.

Miller, Carol Marbin, "Prison system change sought," *The Miami Herald*, June 24, 2009, p. B1.
Support builds in Florida for reducing incarceration by methods that include expanding reentry programs.

Rothfeld, Michael, "Gov. says prisons 'collapsing,'" *Los Angeles Times*, Aug. 20, 2009, p. A4.
California's governor paints a grim picture in the wake of a riot at a severely overcrowded state prison.

Reports and Studies

Brazzell, Diana, and Nancy G. La Vigne, "Prisoner Reentry in Houston: Community Perspectives," The Urban Institute, May 2009, www.urban.org/UploadedPDF/411901_prisoner_reentry_houston.pdf.
The high-crime communities to which most ex-prisoners return reflect the tensions of reentry.

"Criminal Justice Primer: Policy Priorities for the 111th Congress," The Sentencing Project, 2009, www.sentencingproject.org/doc/publications/cjprimer2009.pdf.
A leading think tank advocating alternatives to prison presents a case for increased reentry funding, among other issues.

Harlow, Caroline Wolf, "Education and Correctional Populations," Bureau of Justice Statistics, U.S. Justice Department, April 15, 2003, www.ojp.usdoj.gov/bjs/pub/pdf/ecp.pdf.
A federal statistician details an issue widely discussed in policy circles — the educational shortcomings of most prison inmates.

"The Power of Work: The Center for Employment Opportunities Comprehensive Prisoner Reentry Program," Center for Employment Opportunities and MDRC, March 2006, www.mdrc.org/publications/426/full.pdf.
A New York-based nonprofit describes its strategy for helping ex-prisoners find work.

Visher, Christy, *et al.*, "Employment After Prison: A Longitudinal Study of Releasees in Three States," Urban Institute, Justice Policy Center, October 2008, www.urban.org/UploadedPDF/411778_employment_after_prison.pdf.
Reentry researchers present results on the importance of prison jobs and job-training to post-prison employment success

For More Information

Center for Employment Opportunities, 32 Broadway, 15th Floor, New York, NY 10004; (212) 422-4430; www.ceoworks.org/index.php. Helps connect ex-prisoners with the job market.

Heritage Foundation, 214 Massachusetts Ave., N.E., Washington, DC 20002-4999; (202) 546-4400. A research and educational institute that formulates and promotes conservative public policies.

Michigan Prisoner ReEntry Initiative, Michigan Department of Corrections (MDOC), 206 E. Michigan Ave., Grandview Plaza, Lansing, MI 48933; (517) 373-3653; www.michigan.gov/reentry. Offers detailed information on reentry operations and goals.

National Institute of Justice, 810 7th St., N.W., Washington, DC 20531; (202) 307-2942; www.ojp.usdoj.gov/nij/ topics/corrections/reentry/welcome.htm. Provides a variety of studies and other information on reentry.

National Reentry Resource Center, 100 Wall St., 20th Floor, New York, NY 10005; (646) 383-5721; info@national reentryresourcecenter.org. Offers all kinds of technical assistance to local governments.

Prisoner Reentry Institute, John Jay College of Criminal Justice, 555 W. 57th St., 6th Floor, New York, NY 10019; (212) 484-1399; www.jjay.cuny.edu/centers/prisoner_reen try_institute/2705.htm. Publishes research and holds conferences, all aimed at a specialist audience.

Urban Institute, 2100 M St., N.W., Washington, DC 20037; (202) 833-7200; www.urban.org/Pressroom/prisonerreentry .cfm. A nonpartisan social-policy organization that sponsors extensive research on reentry.

10

Tea Party Movement

Peter Katel

Republican Scott Brown celebrates in Boston on Jan. 19, 2010, after winning a special election to fill the seat of the late U.S. Sen. Edward M. Kennedy. Tea Party activity typically occurs in Republican territory — "red states" — in the South, West and Midwest. But Tea Party activists also cite Brown's upset election in Massachusetts, considered among the bluest of blue states, as indicative of their broad appeal.

From *CQ Researcher*, March 19, 2010.

I t's lock and load time, a pumped up Dana Loesch told several thousand attendees at the Conservative Political Action Conference (CPAC) in Washington last month. "We're in the middle of a war. We're fighting for the hearts, minds and souls of the American people."

Forget politeness, the St. Louis-based radio host and Tea Party activist told the equally energized crowd. "It's all about amplifying your voice." Conservatives, she said, should declare often and loudly, "'I don't like Barack Obama.'"

And as for the president's supporters, said the 31-year-old home-schooling mother, "Make them uncomfortable.... Attack, attack, attack. Never defend."

Many tea partiers may favor a softer approach, but Loesch's take-no-prisoners intensity reflects the dynamic and triumphant spirit emanating from the country's newest political trend, which arose in early 2009 in reaction to economic stimulus legislation, corporate bailouts and the Democrats' health insurance reform effort.

Indeed, as CPAC's enthusiastic embrace of Loesch and other tea partiers makes clear, the Tea Party movement is on the cutting edge of a conservative surge that aims to undercut, or even defeat, the Obama administration and what foes call its big-government, socialist agenda. Tea partiers are also trying to push the national Republican Party to the right, with Tea Party-affiliated candidates this year running in GOP primaries for at least 58 congressional and state offices, including three governorships. (*See map, p. 222.*)

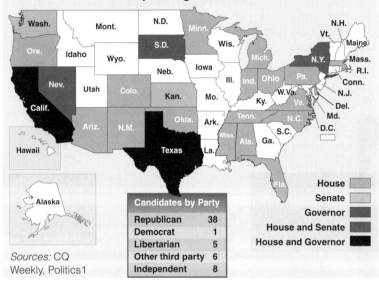

Tea Partiers Running in 25 States

At least 58 candidates — mostly Republican — in 25 states in the upcoming election say their beliefs align with those of the Tea Party movement. Most are running for House seats, but three candidates are in contention for governorships.

States with Tea Party-aligned Candidates in Upcoming Elections

Candidates by Party

Republican	38
Democrat	1
Libertarian	5
Other third party	6
Independent	8

House
Senate
Governor
House and Senate
House and Governor

Sources: CQ Weekly, Politics1

left acknowledge that the Tea Party campaign for Brown could have stirred support among Republican and GOP-leaning independents.

"At a time of heavy recession and joblessness, giving banks a bailout rankles people across the spectrum," says Joseph Lowndes, a University of Oregon political scientist. "A lot of Brown supporters might have been in that camp."

But a vote for Brown doesn't equate to Tea Party membership, he adds, because the movement's sharply defined conservative political perspective doesn't travel well across the left-right divide. "A lot of people who are independents and disenchanted with Obama aren't going to be tea partiers," he says.

The decentralized and loosely defined Tea Party movement takes its name from the Boston Tea Party — the 1773 protest against British taxation. Tea Party Patriots is a national grassroots organization that claims to support more than 1,000 community-based Tea Party groups around the country. The Patriots-organized Tax Day protests last year drew 1.2 million people, says Tea Party activist Jenny Beth Martin of Woodstock, Ga., a founder of the group. She and her husband lost their home and filed for bankruptcy in August 2008 after their business failed. They owed $510,000 to the Internal Revenue Service (IRS). "We've been hit by the financial crisis and the recession," Martin told Fox News, just like other "everyday Americans."[3]

Martin was especially angered by the federal bailouts of ailing banks and financial institutions by the outgoing Bush administration just before the 2008 presidential election and then of the auto companies in 2009 by the incoming Obama administration. After her husband's temp firm failed, "We started cleaning houses and repairing computers to make ends meet," she told Fox News, while big corporations that were struggling got billions in aid from the federal government. "We were saying, these businesses they were bailing out, there's already a

A major wing of the movement, Tea Party Patriots, has helped set up a fundraising arm, Liberty Central, in the Washington suburb of Burke, Va. Its president and CEO is Virginia Thomas, wife of Supreme Court Justice Clarence Thomas. She appeared on the same CPAC platform with Loesch and two other movement members. Obama's "hope and change agenda certainly became a leftist agenda pretty fast," she said. "We saw what they were doing, and it was just a big ol' power grab."[1]

The movement proved itself a political force to be reckoned with in the special Senate election in January of Republican Scott Brown for the Massachusetts Senate seat held by the late liberal Democratic lion, Edward M. Kennedy.[2]

"The Tea Party movement had a lot to do with that election," says John Hawkins, publisher of the online *Right Wing News.* "[Brown] had millions and millions of dollars flooding in from the Internet, which showed people getting energized and excited." And some on the

[bankruptcy] process in place," she said. "We've gone through it. It sucks and it's not fun, but its part of how the system works."

Grassroots anger at political and business elites has fueled political movements on both the right and left throughout history. A prolific right-leaning blogger, University of Tennessee law professor Glenn Harlan Reynolds, even views the Tea Party as continuing another tradition — the Great Awakening evangelical religious movements that have emerged periodically throughout American history. "It's a symptom of dissatisfaction with politics as usual," he says.

But Republican Indiana Gov. Mitch Daniels is more cautious. "I wouldn't overestimate the number of people involved," he told *The New York Times*, also offering faint praise to tea partiers' "net positive" effects on the party.[4]

Indeed, doctrines supported by some Tea Party followers would give pause to many politicians. Featured speakers at a Nashville Tea Party convention in February included, aside from former Alaska Gov. Sarah Palin, Web news entrepreneur Joseph Farah, who said Obama may not qualify for the presidency because of his possible foreign birth. Another speaker, ex-Republican Rep. Tom Tancredo of Colorado — known for his anti-immigrant stance — urged voter literacy tests, a discriminatory practice rooted in the Jim Crow South. "Because we don't have a civics literacy test to vote," Tancredo said, "people who couldn't even spell 'vote' — or say it in English — put a committed socialist ideologue in the White House named Barack Hussein Obama."[5]

Tea Partiers Have 'Unfavorable' View of Obama

More than three-quarters of Tea Party supporters have unfavorable views of President Obama, compared with a third of all Americans. Forty-four percent of tea partiers think erroneously that the administration has raised taxes, compared with 24 percent of all Americans.

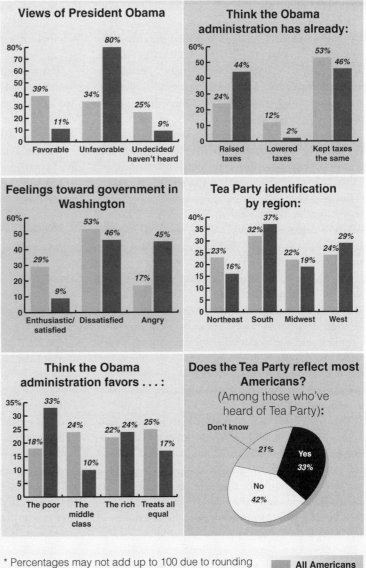

* Percentages may not add up to 100 due to rounding or respondents who didn't answer

Source: CBS News/NY Times Poll, Feb. 11, 2010

For some on the left, the Tancredo and Farah appearances — along with xenophobic and racist signs and slogans that have popped up at other Tea Party events — represent the core identity of the movement. "Tea Partiers have unjustly and unfairly targeted the Latino community to further their political agenda," say the organizers of a new Facebook community called *Cuéntame* ("tell me about it").[6]

Others insist that anti-immigrant xenophobia represents only a fringe. "I was concerned that the anti-immigrant people would try to hijack the Tea Party movement, and they have tried," said Grover Norquist, president of Americans for Tax Reform and a longtime Washington-based conservative who favors liberalized immigration policies. "Not succeeded to date."[7]

In any event, most Tea Party activists stayed away from the $549-per-person Nashville event, organized by the group Tea Party Nation, a social-networking site focusing on social issues that some other Tea Party activists discourage; among Tea Party Nation's "strategic partners" is Farah's *WorldNetDaily*. "It wasn't the kind of grassroots organization that we are, so we declined to participate," said Mark Meckler, a cofounder of Tea Party Patriots (TPP).[8]

The TPP network, which represents the movement's mainstream, steers away from social issues and instead has forged a consensus largely on economic matters: Government spending should be cut, government should be limited and the free-market system should prevail. (*See box, p. 226.*) Specifically, members argue, the federal government shouldn't expand its role in a health-care system that they say already provides adequate care to the poor and the elderly.

"Even if this bill were to have me insured tomorrow, it's still not the right thing to do for America," says Georgia TPP activist Martin. Although she and her husband lost their health coverage when his business failed, they oppose pending health-care legislation on the grounds it would add to the federal budget. "There are a lot of people in this movement who are unemployed. They don't want to burden future generations."

Martin shares a background in Republican politics with many other Tea Party activists — and a critical attitude toward the party. "There's no question the GOP has lost the mantle of fiscal responsibility and small government," writes John M. O'Hara, a former Labor Department staffer in the George W. Bush administration. But, he adds, "The GOP is the most likely breeding ground for the fiscally responsible constitutionalists the Tea Party movement — and America — craves."[9]

A rally O'Hara helped to organize last year in Washington was part of a series of protests that launched the movement. A cable TV moment provided the mobilizing spark: On Feb. 19, 2009, CNBC business reporter Rick Santelli launched a tirade against a plan by the new Obama administration to help homeowners facing foreclosure.

"How about this, President and new administration?" Santelli yelled from the floor of the Chicago Board of Trade. "Why don't you put up a Web site to have people vote on the Internet as a referendum to see if we really want to subsidize the losers' mortgages."[10]

Santelli went on: "We're thinking of having a Chicago Tea Party in July. All you capitalists that want to show up to Lake Michigan, I'm gonna start organizing." Within four days, Santelli's rant had been viewed 1.7 million times on the CNBC Web site.[11]

O'Hara and others used Twitter and other social-network links to find compatriots and launched their rallies on Feb. 27. Protesters showed up in more than a dozen cities — including Atlanta, Fort Worth, Nashville, New York, St. Louis, San Diego Omaha and Tampa.[12] Later events included a Sept. 12 march on Washington promoted by conservative Fox News commentator Glenn Beck.

But fledgling activist Keli Carender — who blogs as "Liberty Belle" — beat them all to the punch. The 30-year-old Republican convert organized a Feb. 16 rally in her hometown, liberal Seattle, against the Obama administration's economic stimulus bill, which she dubbed "porkulus."[13]

Carender's playful approach — she distributed pulled pork at the event — seems distant from Loesch's militancy at the CPAC convention. So distant, in fact, that the conservative *Washington Examiner* issued a warning that echoed the remarks of some in the Republican establishment. "The approach [Loesch] suggests . . . could easily be mistaken for a rallying cry for angry yelling," the paper said. "She must realize that when it comes to making change, it's not about who yells loudest but who actually makes people want to listen. Claiming that the tea parties and conservative activists have declared war on the left only serves to marginalize the right."

As the tea partiers gear up to challenge politics as usual in the 2010 congressional elections later this year, here are some of the questions being raised about the movement:

Does the Tea Party represent only a narrow segment of the population?

Some Tea Party activists are quite candid about what they see as the movement's base. "They've been listening to Rush Limbaugh for years, they've been railing against the mainstream media for years, they've been voting Republican for years," J. P. Freire, a *Washington Examiner* editor and Tea Party activist, said at a Washington panel discussion in February organized by the America's Future Foundation, which trains young conservatives in economics. "I'm talking about mom-and-pop suburban dwellers."

Indeed, some key Tea Party issues do coincide with key Republican positions: The federal budget deficit is out of control; the administration's health-care proposal is unnecessary and fiscally risky; the $787 billion stimulus represented a grave threat to the nation's economic health.

Only three Republican senators voted for the stimulus. And party leaders have been arguing ever since that the stimulus didn't fulfill Obama's promise to jumpstart the economy and create and save jobs. Celebrating Republican gubernatorial victories in New Jersey and Virginia last November, GOP Chairman Michael Steele condemned "an incredibly arrogant government in Washington that has put our country, our freedoms and our economy at risk with unprecedented spending."[14]

Tea partiers insist they don't just blame Obama and the Democrats for excessive spending. "There was a loss of enthusiasm for Republicans" triggered by deficit spending, says blogger and law professor Reynolds, who co-founded Porkbusters, a political initiative that attacked Republicans as well as Democrats for allegedly wasteful spending. "It was one of the things that cost them Congress, and cost them the whole 2008 election."

Tea Party activity typically occurs in Republican territory —"red states" — in the South and Midwest. Like the GOP itself, Tea Party event attendees are overwhelmingly white. But Tea Party activists also cite

Brown's upset election in Massachusetts, considered among the bluest of blue states, as indicative of their broad appeal.

"A lot of Democrats voted for Scott Brown," says Reynolds. "And he had massive Tea Party support. That is at least an indicator we're moving beyond the red state-blue state thing."

While labeling the Tea Party a red-state trend "isn't entirely false," he says, the number of "disaffected Democrats" is growing. "I actually think you'll see this spread to an insurgency in the Democratic Party." The theory is that the Tea Party appeals to a bipartisan sense that Congress and the White House are listening only to powerful lobbyists and not looking out for the interests of the average American.

But non-tea partiers view the movement as fitting comfortably within the Republican fold. "Given the pretty fervent conservatism that exists in this group, it is unlikely that there are a significant number of Democrats in it," says John Sides, a political scientist at George Washington University who studies political polarization. "You may be able to find people who say they voted for Obama, but I don't think that is the central tendency of the movement."

In fact, he argues, the concentration of conservatism in suburbs and smaller cities will make it difficult for the Tea Party to build strength in big urban centers. But the movement could play a big role in areas that are up for grabs. "You can imagine that activism by the Tea Party could have a measurable impact on 'blue dog' [conservative, usually Southern] Democrats in close races," he says.

Indeed, a cofounder of the TPP points to the movement's popularity outside of red-state America. "Three of the five coordinators in New York City are Democrats," says Georgia activist Martin. And she says she's ready for the emergence of a New York politician of either party who supports Tea Party principles but who is too socially liberal to win an election in her state.

Martin spent years as a Republican Party volunteer, heading Sen. Saxbe Chambliss' reelection campaign in her county. But she deplored his vote for the TARP (Troubled Asset Relief Program) bill — the emergency "bank bailout" legislation enacted in October 2008, signed into law by George W. Bush a month before Obama was elected. She has renounced completely

Tenets of the Tea Party

The Tea Party Patriots organization says its impetus comes from "excessive government spending and taxation," according to the TPP's Web site. Here are the group's three core values:

"Fiscal Responsibility — Fiscal Responsibility by government honors and respects the freedom of the individual to spend the money that is the fruit of their own labor. . . . Such runaway deficit spending as we now see in Washington, D.C., compels us to take action as the increasing national debt is a grave threat to our national sovereignty and the personal and economic liberty of future generations.

Constitutionally Limited Government: We, the members of the Tea Party Patriots, are inspired by our founding documents and regard the Constitution of the United States to be the supreme law of the land. . . . Like the founders, we support states' rights for those powers not expressly stated in the Constitution. As the government is of the people, by the people and for the people, in all other matters we support the personal liberty of the individual, within the rule of law.

Free Markets: A free market is the economic consequence of personal liberty. The founders believed that personal and economic freedom were indivisible, as do we. Our current government's interference distorts the free market and inhibits the pursuit of individual and economic liberty. Therefore, we support a return to the free-market principles on which this nation was founded and oppose government intervention into the operations of private business."

Source: Tea Party Patriots, www.teapartypatriots.org

you would like to use, you don't push them out."

Will the Tea Party movement reshape the Republican Party?

It remains to be seen whether the Tea Party can foment national political change. But some political observers think the movement is well-placed to drive the GOP rightward, especially on economic policy issues. Others say it's a fringe faction that ultimately will lose steam.

One outcome is fairly certain: The Tea Party movement would be seriously undercut if it evolved into a third political party — historically the route taken by new movements that want to broaden the national debate. Most Tea Party activists argue against such a move. "If you create a third party you guarantee that it's going to split Republican votes and guarantee socialist Democrat victories," says *Right Wing News* publisher Hawkins. He predicts that the Tea Party instead will effectively take over the GOP.

To be sure, the prevailing view in liberal circles is that the Republican Party has already moved far to the right. Even some senior Republicans are delivering much the same message.

"To those people who are pursuing purity, you'll become a club not a party," Republican Sen. Lindsey Graham of South Carolina told *Politico*, a Washington-based online newspaper, last November. He spoke following the failed attempt by Conservative Party candidate Doug Hoffman to win a congressional seat in upstate New York, replacing the Republican incumbent, who was judged by the party establishment as too liberal. (Democrat Bill Owens won the seat.)

"Those people who are trying to embrace conservatism in a thoughtful way that fits the region and the state and the district are going to do well," Graham said. "Conservatism is an asset. Blind ideology is not."[15]

partisan activity and doesn't exempt the GOP from criticism on big spending. But she acknowledges, "I think the Republican Party is probably the one most Tea Party people more closely align with."

Georgetown University historian Michael Kazin says the movement's espousal of strict market principles determines the Tea Party's political makeup. "It's hard to think of too many people who voted for Barack Obama who really care about the budget deficit."

Kazin, who specializes in populism and other social movements, draws a distinction between the Tea Party and other grassroots upsurges. "Social movements aren't as connected to one of the main parties as this one seems to be. I know that leaders of the Republican Party are trying to appear more moderate, but clearly if you have tens or hundreds of thousands of people whose views

Some Washington-based conservatives question the possibility that any movement based on political principles can exert deep and lasting influence on the political process, where fulltime participants tend to act as much — or more — from self-interest as from ideology.

A movement that channels itself into a party inevitably suffers the dilution of its ideas, a conservative writer argued during the February panel discussion in Washington organized by the America's Future Foundation. "Politics is a profession, and the temptation, once we're in charge, is to say, 'We're going to fix everything, we're going to solve everything,' not realizing that people involved in these parties are human beings and susceptible to compromise," said Kelly Jane Torrance, literary editor of the Washington-based *American Conservative* magazine.

The absence of a Tea Party institutional presence makes its absorption by professional politicians inevitable, she added. "People seem to need a charismatic leader or organizer or an institution, which is why I think the movement is basically being eaten up by the Republican Party," she said.

But some Tea Party activists argue that promoting their ideas within the GOP is essential if the movement is to avoid being marginalized. "There's got to be communication with the political party establishment," says Karin Hoffman, a veteran Republican activist from Lighthouse Point, Fla. "The Democratic Party has done everything to ridicule the movement," she says, while the GOP platform "matches what the grassroots movement feels."

Hoffman orchestrated a Washington meeting this February between 50 Tea Party-affiliated activists and Republican Chairman Steele. Hoffman says she's on guard against the danger of Tea Party activists becoming nothing more than Republican auxiliaries.

"I've not been happy with how Republicans have behaved," she says, citing the reduced-price system for prescription drugs under Medicare that President Bush pushed through in 2003. "We don't need an increase in government."

Disillusionment with Bush is commonplace among tea partiers, who tend to have been Bush voters in 2000 and 2004. The shift in their support — or, alternatively, their view that he abandoned principles they thought he shared with them — underscores the potential obstacles

to reshaping national parties. "Even with a relatively diffuse organization, they can have influence just because of visibility, and can pull conventions and rallies," says Sides of George Washington University. "But that's not a recipe for transformational change."

Sides cites the history of the Club for Growth, an organization of economic conservatives that rates lawmakers on their votes on taxes, spending and related issues. "No one would say that the Club for Growth has been able to remake the Republican Party," Sides says, "but it has exerted influence in certain races."

Republican consultant and blogger Soren Dayton disputes that view. "If you look at the electoral and policy successes of the conservative movement — look at the Republican Party," Dayton said at the America's Future Foundation event. "Abortion, guns and taxes are settled issues. If you're an activist on these issues, the point is actually changing the minds of Democrats."

The reason for that ideological victory is easy to identify, Soren said. "We're winning these [electoral] fights on the ground because the Republican Party is solid — because it's been taken over in certain significant ways by conservatives."

Does the Tea Party attract conspiracy theorists?

Advocates of ideas and policies from far outside the mainstream are the bane of grassroots movements of any stripe. A classic case is the takeover in the 1960s of the New Left by self-styled revolutionaries, who cited Communist Vietnam and China as economic and political models.

Conservative movements, for their part, have always faced the danger of identification with far-right defenders of segregation and, more recently, with those who question President Obama's legitimacy on the grounds of his supposed foreign birth — a notion that has been laid to rest.

Tensions over ideas tinged with discredited notions about race and conspiracies surfaced publicly at the controversial Tea Party convention in Nashville. Speechmakers included Tancredo, the former Republican House member from Colorado. He advocated voter-literacy tests — a now-illegal procedure that was part of segregation law in the Deep South designed to deny black citizens the right to vote. And *WorldNetDaily*'s Farah insisted that Obama's birthplace remains an unsettled issue. "The president refuses to produce documents proving he meets the Constitution's natural-born citizen requirement," *WorldNetDaily* said in paraphrasing his argument.[16]

The publication reported that "the crowd cheered wildly, whistled and applauded" when Farah made his claim. But observers from both right and left reported a different impression.

Jonathan Raban, writing in the left-leaning *New York Review of Books*, said the favorable response was not universal: "I saw as many glum and unresponsive faces in the crowd as people standing up to cheer."[17] And conservative blogger, columnist and professor Reynolds says, "I did not hear a single person say a good thing about Farah or the 'birther' issue."

In fact, the dispute went public. After his speech, Farah engaged in a heated argument outside the convention hall with Andrew Breitbart, publisher of the conservative *Breitbart.com* news and commentary sites.[18] Breitbart called Farah's focus on Obama's citizenship "a fundamentally controversial issue that forces a unified group of people to have to break into different parts."[19]

The surfacing of the tensions among the tea partiers did lend substance to press reports of fringe constituencies attaching themselves to the movement, whose primary concerns publicly center on economic policy.

Les Phillip, a Tea Party candidate for the Republican nomination for a House seat in Alabama, blames the mainstream media for characterizing the Tea Party constituency as "white, racist old men." To be sure, he says, "You do have some folks on the far right." But, he adds, "Most are in the center."

Himself a black immigrant from Barbados, Phillip calls Farah's insistence on the Obama birth issue a diversion. But he voices sympathy for Tancredo's call for voter-literacy tests, despite their unsavory history. "I know more about the country than many people who were born here," he says. "If you're going to be a voter, you need to understand the history and governing documents and how the government should work."

Nevertheless, Lowndes of the University of Oregon argues that racial fears and xenophobia do play a role in some Tea Party movements, whose agendas may vary widely from place to place. "Certainly one does get the sense that the movement is made up mostly of older folks, 50 and older," he says. "I think these are people who are most likely to be uncomfortable with cultural differences and certainly with racial differences."

Racial and cultural concerns may outweigh suspicion of the business establishment, which used to predominate among many of today's Tea Party supporters. They also denounce excessive government intrusion in citizens' lives, though typically with little reference to the Patriot Act, the Bush-era law that expanded government's surveillance and monitoring authority over e-mail and other communications. "If these folks are concerned about overweening executive power, then why did the movement not arise during the Bush years?" Lowndes asks.

Hawkins of *Right Wing News* counters that the same kind of inconsistency shadows the liberal activist world. Antiwar marches and protests of all kinds marked the Bush presidency, he observes. Yet, with tens of thousands of U.S. troops fighting hard in Afghanistan and still present in Iraq, "Where's the antiwar movement?" he asks.

Similarly, he argues, the presence of fringe activists who attach themselves to a broader cause is no less a problem on the left than on the right. "There's a very tiny percentage of people who generally are not welcome at tea parties," Hawkins says, adding that he distinguishes members or sympathizers of the militia movement from those who question Obama's presidential eligibility. "I guarantee you that, percentage-wise, there are as many Democrats who think Bush stole the election in 2004 as people who think Barack Obama is not a citizen. I would put those as complete equivalents."

Sides, of George Washington University argues, however, that the Tea Partys' big tent may limit the movement's effectiveness for reasons that go beyond issues of political respectability. The presence of the "birthers" and some militia members, along with people concerned about taxes and spending, likely will add to what he sees as a fundamental weakness. "There is an extraordinarily diffuse organizational structure with a lot of internecine conflict," he says. "That makes coalescing extremely difficult."

BACKGROUND

People's Party

Historians trace the origins of populism to the early years of the new republic. President Andrew Jackson, who served two terms (1829-1837), helped formulate the fear

C H R O N O L O G Y

1830s-1900s *Movements expressing citizen outrage at government and business elites begin.*

1832 President Andrew Jackson vetoes a bill to expand the national bank, calling it a tool of the "rich and powerful."

1892 People's Party of America (populists) formed in St. Louis by small farmers, evangelical Christians, labor unions and alcohol prohibition advocates.

1896 Populists unite with Democratic Party behind presidential candidate William Jennings Bryan, who is defeated.

1908 People's Party dissolves, unable to develop an urban base to match its rural constituency.

1930s-1950s *Populist politicians begin directing anger toward government, and sometimes ethnic minorities, and away from big business.*

1938 The Rev. Charles E. Coughlin, a Catholic priest with a large radio following, switches from support of President Franklin D. Roosevelt's New Deal to virulent opposition.

1954 After leaping to prominence by accusing the State Department and other agencies of harboring Soviet loyalists, Sen. Joseph R. McCarthy wrecks his career by charging the U.S. Army is also protecting communists.

1955 Liberal academics alarmed by McCarthyism argue that far-right tendencies lurk within all populist-oriented movements.

1960s-1970s *Civil rights and antiwar movements prompt middle-class whites to become Republicans.*

1966 Activists in Oakland, Calif., form Black Panther Party, embodying the worst fears of many middle-class whites about surging left-wing radicalism and "black power."

1968 Violence at Democratic National Convention in Chicago deepens divide between pro- and anti-Vietnam War Democrats and further alienates middle-class whites from protest movements .... Alabama Gov. George C. Wallace

wins 13 percent of ballots for his third-party candidacy, built on anti-Washington message.

1969 Referring to Americans turned off by protesters, President Richard M. Nixon calls on "great silent majority" to support his plan to end the war.

1972 Sen. George S. McGovern, D-S.D., the Democratic presidential candidate, wins only one state as incumbent Nixon successfully ties Democrats to privileged, unpatriotic elites who look down on "good, decent people."

1979 Former Gov. Ronald Reagan, R-Calif., wins the presidency, largely by appealing to the "silent majority" constituency identified by Nixon.

1990s-2000s *Populism returns as a third-party movement, and then as a group with strong political party ties.*

1992 Texas billionaire H. Ross Perot launches himself as a third-party presidential candidate, attacking deficit spending and outsourcing of jobs abroad .... Perot wins 19 percent of the vote, drawing votes from both winning candidate Bill Clinton and the defeated George H. W. Bush.

2008 Congressionally approved financial bailout creates discontent among grassroots Republicans and Democrats.

2009 Seattle woman outraged by Obama administration-proposed economic stimulus holds protest against "porkulus." ... CNBC reporter Rick Santelli calls for a "tea party" while denouncing administration's rescue plan for homeowners facing foreclosure .... Dozens of activists network to plan "tea party" demonstrations on Feb. 27 .... Tea Party activists take part in town hall meetings with lawmakers, denouncing administration's health-care proposal .... Fox News commentator Glenn Beck promotes a "9/12" rally in Washington, which draws heavy crowd of Tea Party supporters.

2010 Tea Party activists contribute to surprise election victory of Republican Sen. Scott Brown in Massachusetts .... "Tea Party Nation" convention in Nashville sparks dissension in movement due to high ticket price and presence of anti-immigration and "birther" speakers .... Tea Party opponents begin organizing Coffee Party alternative.

Tea Partiers Take Aim at Health Reform

Movement plans a replay of last summer's town hall meetings.

Joblessness hovers near 10 percent. Yet in a country where most Americans get health insurance through their employers, opposing health insurance reforms proposed by congressional Democrats at the urging of President Barack Obama has been a driving force in the Tea Party movement.

"The Tea Party … did help destroy health reform," Kelly Jane Torrance, literary editor of the *American Conservative*, claimed at a Washington panel discussion in February. "I think that's an amazing accomplishment."

Torrance's remarks at the America's Future Foundation event may have been premature. Since the event, prospects for passage of the legislation seem to have improved.

With a congressional recess starting on March 29, tea partiers are aiming for a replay of last summer's fractious "town hall" meetings with legislators, when the movement's opposition to health reform — especially its added cost to the deficit — first erupted. "We're gonna hit 'em when we know they're back in [the] district, and we're gonna hit 'em hard," Tom Gaitens, a Tampa Tea Party organizer, told Fox News.

Final passage of the legislation before the recess would short-circuit that plan. But the prospects are uncertain.

In any event, plans to destroy the health-care plan, a longtime centerpiece of the Democratic agenda, might seem counter-intuitive, given that the Tea Party hopes to grow — in a country with up to 45 million uninsured residents.[1]

Among them is Tea Party organizer Jenny Beth Martin of Woodstock, Ga. Martin's family lost health coverage when her husband's business failed more than two years ago. When one of the Martins' children gets sick, "We tell the doctor we don't have insurance, and make arrangements to pay cash," Martin says.

The hardships brought on by the Great Recession hit even deeper for Martin's family. She and her husband lost their home, and for a while the couple was cleaning houses to make ends meet.

Nevertheless, she opposes the Obama plan. "I think that we do need health insurance reform," she says. "I just don't think this bill is a good idea."

Her political response, even in the face of personal hardship, illustrates a major facet of the movement, and of American conservatism in general. "People don't connect the economic crisis to the need for any kind of government intervention," says Joseph Lowndes, a political scientist at George Washington University. "People come to this movement with a pretty strong level of conservatism in place already. So there is that irony: to some extent these movements are facilitated by a poor economy, but their reaction … does not embrace the government's effort to fix things."

---

that a financial elite threatened popular control of national institutions.[20]

Jackson's distrust of "money power" led him to veto a bill to extend the charter of a privately owned national bank that served the federal government as well as private interests. "It is to be regretted that the rich and powerful too often bend the acts of government to their selfish purposes," his veto message said.[21]

Jackson's admonition resounded for generations. But it wasn't until the late 19th century that a national political movement was organized to wrest control of the country from intertwined political and business classes. The People's Party of America, formed in 1892 in St. Louis, united an array of activists that included small farmers from the South and Great Plains who were overwhelmed by debt; the Woman's Christian Temperance Union, which advocated alcohol prohibition; two early union organizations, the Knights of Labor and the American Federation of Labor; and evangelical Christians with socialist politics.

All saw themselves as oppressed by big business and its political allies. The prohibitionists viewed big business as profiting from the vice of alcoholism. But the Populists — as they were dubbed — dodged the issue of race because they counted on Southern supporters of segregation.

Still, the Populist alliance generated enough enthusiasm to drive a presidential campaign in the 1892 election. The Populist candidate, former Union Army officer James

John Hawkins, publisher of the *Right Wing News* Web site, suggests another reason for conservative distrust of the health-reform plan. "I think people fear there is going to be a massive decrease in the quality of care," he said. "The idea that you'll cover more people, but the quality won't drop and it won't cost more — people don't believe that."

And, Hawkins says, conservatives understand another deep-seated element of American political culture. "People don't, with good reason, trust the competence of government."

Martin opposes health reformers' plans to penalize businesses that don't provide health insurance for employees and to raise taxes to help subsidize mandatory coverage for those who couldn't afford it. Although the legislation hasn't been finalized, proposals so far would pay for the expanded insurance coverage by raising taxes on high-end health insurance plans or on wealthy Americans (those earning more than $250,000 a year). Martin also does not like the proposal to delay implementation of benefits until 2014, after some higher taxes take effect (though a prohibition would be immediate on insurance companies refusing clients with pre-existing conditions).[2]

A tea partier protests President Obama's health-care reform plans before his arrival at Arcadia University in Glenside, Pa., on March 8, 2010.

AP Photo/Mark Stehle

Martin does favor making coverage "portable," not dependent on employment — which would be compatible with the Obama plan, in principle. And she agrees that individuals who can't qualify for insurance could benefit from high-risk insurance pools, which some states have set up. Tea Party organizer John M. O'Hara laid out these and other proposals in a book on the movement.[3]

The book doesn't propose dismantling Medicare, the massive health-care subsidy program for the elderly, and neither does Martin. "It's there now, and we need to deal with it as it is."

And, she adds, "I don't think there is anything wrong with government providing safety nets. I understand that sometimes things happen to people."

— *Peter Katel*

[1] Carl Bialik, "The Unhealthy Accounting of Uninsured Americans," *The Wall Street Journal*, June 24, 2009, http://online.wsj.com/article/SB124579852347944191.html#articleTabs%3Darticle. Some question that U.S. Census Bureau estimate, in part because it includes illegal aliens who wouldn't be covered under a new law.

[2] Alec MacGillis and Amy Goldstein, "Obama offers a new proposal on health care," *The Washington Post*, Feb. 23, 2010, p. A1.

[3] John M. O'Hara, *A New American Tea Party: The Counterrevolution Against Bailouts, Handouts, Reckless Spending, and More Taxes* (2010), pp. 175-201.

B. Weaver, garnered 8.5 percent of the national vote, an impressive showing for a third-party candidate.

Realizing that their party stood no chance of winning the presidency on its own, the Populists forged an electoral alliance in 1896 with the Democratic Party (founded by Jackson). The Democrats' nominee was William Jennings Bryan, who had worked closely with the Populists as a House member from Nebraska.

Known for his spellbinding oratory, Bryan wanted the U.S. currency based on both gold and silver, not just gold. That would lower the value of debt-ridden farmers' obligations by lowering the value of the dollar.

"Having behind us the commercial interests and the laboring interests and all the toiling masses," Bryan said in his electrifying speech to the Democratic Convention that nominated him, "we shall answer their demands for a gold standard by saying to them, you shall not press down upon the brow of labor this crown of thorns. You shall not crucify mankind upon a cross of gold."[22]

However, the Democrat-Populist alliance proved no match for the Republicans. Populists' weaknesses included their strong ties to the Farm Belt and support of strict Protestant moral codes — turn-offs to big-city voters, many of them Catholic immigrants.

Republican William McKinley won the election, which marked the high point of the People's Party's fortunes. By 1908 it had dissolved.

Sarah Palin Shines at Tea Party Convention

Some see her as a potential party leader.

Tea partiers pride themselves on their lack of formal leadership, but that hasn't stopped speculation about who will emerge to lead the movement. So far, the speculation largely has zeroed in on Sarah Palin. And the former vice-presidential candidate's insistence that she isn't seeking a leadership role hasn't squelched the topic.

In fact, Palin has actually fueled the speculation, possibly inadvertently. After her surprise resignation last year as Alaska's governor and the publication of *Going Rogue*, her best-selling book, she addressed the Tea Party's February convention in Nashville — the only speech she's given this year at an overtly political event. Her political ideas, to the extent she has spelled them out, seem consistent with the tea partiers' call for lower taxes and smaller government.

In the eyes of Tea Party activists who skipped Nashville — in part because they objected to its $500-plus ticket price — Palin made a mistake in going. That view was even more prevalent after the influential online political newspaper *Politico* reported she had received $100,000 for the speech. "This has nothing to do with the grassroots movement — nothing," said Robin Stublen, who helped organize a Tea Party group in Punta Gorda, Fla.[1]

Palin didn't deny that account, but she wrote in *USA Today* that "any compensation for my appearance will go right back to the cause."[2] She didn't specify the precise destination for the money.

Some tea partiers saluted her presence in Nashville and its effects on the movement. "I think the Tea Party is gaining respect when we're able to attract some of the quality representation … a caliber of person such as this," said Bob Porto, an attendee from Little Rock.[3]

Palin's star power certainly generated media attention for the convention, even though a relatively modest 600 people attended, and the convention was controversial within the movement. Her speech, in fact, was carried live on C-SPAN, CNN and Fox News.

Palin made a point of waving off the idea that she wants to take the helm. "I caution against allowing this movement to be defined by any one leader or politician," she said. "The Tea Party movement is not a top-down operation. It's a ground-up call to action that is forcing both parties to change the way they're doing business, and that's beautiful."[4]

For all of her attention-getting capabilities, Palin comes with baggage. A new book by Steve Schmidt, top strategist for the McCain-Palin campaign, described her as dishonest. And another book, by journalists Mark Halperin and John Heilemann reported that she was ignorant of even basic national and international matters. "[S]he still didn't really understand why there was a North Korea and a South Korea," Heilemann said on CNN.[5]

Even a friendlier figure, Stephen F. Hayward of the conservative American Enterprise Institute, warned Palin that she's nowhere near as ready for a national position as Ronald Reagan was. "Palin has as much as admitted that she needs to acquire more depth, especially on foreign policy," he wrote in *The Washington Post*. "One thing above all is required: Do your homework. Reagan did his."[6]

Right Turn

Populist leaders spoke eloquently of corporate oppression, a classic issue of the left. But their handling of race would seem to place them on the political right. While Tom Watson, a Georgia Populist leader, made joint speaking appearances with black populists (who had their own organization), he defended Jim Crow laws, as did party rank and file. (After the party ceased to exist, Watson incited and then defended the lynching of Jewish factory manager Leo Frank of Atlanta, wrongly accused of the rape and murder of a 13-year-old girl.)[23]

In other respects, the Populists' attacks on big business, as well as ties to the early labor movement, marked them as left-liberal. President Franklin D. Roosevelt's New Deal policies of 1933-1940 drew on the Populists' doctrines. They influenced his campaigns to impose regulatory controls — such as creation of the Securities and Exchange Commission — on the "economic royalists" of Wall Street. And his administration's agricultural policies, which sought

But in Nashville, the crowd loved her, wrote Jonathan Raban in the liberal *New York Review of Books.* Many had been cool not only to the anti-immigrant talk of Tom Tancredo, the former Colorado congressman and 2008 GOP presidential candidate, but also the Obama-birthplace suspicions of Web news entrepreneur Joseph Farah, Raban reported.

But the crowd embraced Palin. "A great wave of adoration met the small black-suited woman .... The entire ballroom was willing Sarah to transport us to a state of delirium with whatever she chose to say."[7]

The speech was something of a letdown, Raban added, because Palin's delivery was better suited to the TV cameras than to the live audience. Still, she got a big sendoff. "The huge standing ovation ('Run, Sarah, Run!') was more for the concept of Palin ... than it was for the lackluster speech," Raban wrote.[8]

Palin hasn't revealed whether she'll run for president in 2012, but she pointedly avoids denying it. "I won't close the door that perhaps could be open for me in the future," she told Fox News.[9]

However, University of Tennessee law professor Glenn Harlan Reynolds, who covered the Nashville convention for the Web-based *Pajamas TV,* warned that Palin's popularity could exact the same price that he argues President Obama has made his political allies pay for hero-worshipping him.

"The biggest risk that the Tea Party movement faces is that it will create its own Obama in the person of Sarah

Sarah Palin answered questions from attendees at the National Tea Party Convention in Nashville on Feb. 6, 2010.

Getty Images for NASCAR/Jerry Markland

Palin and get a similar result," he says. "She made a point of saying she didn't want to be their leader, and most people agreed. But the tendency of people to run after a charismatic leader is probably genetically hardwired."

— Peter Katel

[1] Quoted in Chris Good, "Is Palin's Tea Party Speech a Mistake?" *The Atlantic,* Feb. 4, 2010, www.theatlantic.com/politics/archive/2010/02/is-palins-tea-party-speech-a-mistake-tea-partiers-have-mixed-opinions/35360/.

[2] Ben Smith and Andy Barr, "Tea partiers shell out big bucks for Sarah Palin," *Politico,* Jan. 12, 2010, www.politico.com/news/stories/0110/31409.html; Sarah Palin, "Why I'm Speaking at Tea Party Convention," *USA Today,* Feb. 3, 2010, http://blogs.usatoday.com/oped/2010/02/column-why-im-speaking-at-tea-party-convention-.html.

[3] *Ibid.*

[4] "Sarah Palin Speaks at Tea Party Convention," CNN, Feb. 6, 2010, http://transcripts.cnn.com/TRANSCRIPTS/1002/06/cnr.09.html.

[5] Jonathan Martin, "Steve Schmidt: Sarah Palin has trouble with truth," *Politico,* Jan. 11, 2010, www.politico.com/news/stories/0110/31335.html.

[6] Steven F. Hayward, "Would Reagan Vote for Sarah Palin?" *The Washington Post,* March 7, 2010, p. B1.

[7] Jonathan Raban, "At the Tea Party," *New York Review of Books,* March 25, 2010, www.nybooks.com/articles/23723.

[8] *Ibid.*

[9] Quoted in "Palin says 2012 presidential bid a possibility," CNN, Feb. 8, 2010, www.cnn.com/2010/POLITICS/02/07/palin.presidential.run.tea.party/index.html.

to stabilize prices by subsidizing farmers for not overproducing, also grew out of the Populists' search for solutions to farmers' financial woes.[24]

Nevertheless, Watson's career had shown that populism can whip up hatred as well as inspire ordinary citizens to demand that government serve their interests, as was exemplified during the Roosevelt era by the career of the Rev. Charles E. Coughlin, a figure of far greater influence than Watson. The Catholic priest from Royal Oak, Mich., went from being a New Deal supporter to a furious critic, whose weekly radio speeches became wildly popular. He

then took a sharp right turn into anti-Semitism in 1938, attempting to link Jews to communism — a longtime target of his wrath — and financial manipulation.[25]

Dislike of Jews was commonplace in pre-World War II America, but Coughlin's calls for action against Jews found little support outside the ranks of his hardcore supporters. He raised enough concern in the Catholic hierarchy, however, to lead the archbishop of Detroit to order Coughlin to end his radio broadcasts in 1941. And in 1942, at the U.S. Justice Department's request, the church ordered him to stop publishing his weekly newspaper.

Although the infamous "radio priest" never returned to the public arena, he left his mark. In depicting communism as a menace to ordinary Americans, Coughlin anticipated the early-1950s career of Sen. Joseph R. McCarthy, R-Wis., and his supporters. To be sure, some of McCarthy's followers abhorred anti-Semitism; *National Review* founder William F. Buckley Jr., a leading defender of McCarthy, was credited with purging that prejudice from mainstream conservatism.[26] Ethnic hatred aside, McCarthy owed an intellectual debt to Coughlin with his portrayal of working people preyed upon by communist-inspired elites or outright communist agents.

McCarthy himself saw his career go down in flames in 1954 after a conflict with the U.S. Army in which the senator accused the military of harboring communists. But McCarthyism left a foundation upon which later conservative politicians built, writes Georgetown historian Kazin.

By stirring up distrust of the highly educated graduates of elite schools who predominated in the top reaches of public life — especially the foreign policy establishment — McCarthy and his allies caused serious alarm among liberal academics. McCarthyism "succeeded in frightening many liberals into mistrusting the very kinds of white Americans — Catholic workers, military veterans, discontented families in the middle of the social structure — who had once been foot soldiers of causes such as industrial unionism, Social Security and the GI Bill."[27]

The 'Silent Majority'

The tensions fanned by McCarthy burst into flame in the mid-1960s. Some of the most active and visible leaders of the civil rights movement — such as Stokely Carmichael of the Student Non-Violent Coordinating Committee — adopted the "black power" slogan. The term was elastic — covering everything from affirmative action to armed self-defense — but many whites heard a threat.

Adding to the tension, the Black Panther Party, formed in 1966 in Oakland, Calif., paraded with firearms to illustrate its goal of "self-defense" against police officers and soon embraced the Cuban and North Korean versions of communist doctrines.[28]

The anti-Vietnam War movement also was gathering strength on college campuses, where potential male foot soldiers benefited from draft deferments, unlike working-class high school graduates who weren't going on to college. Antiwar activists also began openly advocating draft-dodging and draft resistance, some even burning their draft cards in protest — stirring outrage among many among the World War II-Korean War generations.

Political and social tensions exploded in 1968. First, the April 4 assassination of civil rights leader the Rev. Dr. Martin Luther King Jr. led to rioting in black communities across the country, notably in Washington, D.C., where the National Guard was called out to quell the violence. Also that spring, tensions over the Vietnam War within the Democratic Party — and within the country as a whole — came to a head during the Democratic Convention in Chicago, marked by large antiwar demonstrations and violent police repression. Although Vice President Hubert H. Humphrey won the nomination, his campaign against Republican Richard M. Nixon was hobbled by the escalation of the war under outgoing President Lyndon B. Johnson.

Nixon's victory enabled him to indulge a deep grudge against the East Coast-based Democratic political elite. In 1969, soon after taking office, he used a term that echoed old-school populist rhetoric, urging the "great silent majority" to support his peace plan.[29] In effect, Nixon was effectively telling ordinary Americans repelled by the civil disorder and protests that they were the backbone of the nation, despite all the noise generated by the demonstrators.

But another high-profile politician tapped even deeper into the vein of outrage that ran through blue-collar America. Gov. George C. Wallace of Alabama had propelled himself into the national spotlight by dint of his fervent resistance to the civil rights movement. As the presidential candidate of the American Independent Party, he tried to expand his segregationist appeal (he later repudiated Jim Crow) to cast himself as the voice of the common American. He demonstrated his familiarity with his constituency by ticking off its members' occupations: "The bus driver, the truck driver, the beautician, the fireman, the policeman and the steelworker, the plumber and the communications worker and the oil worker and the little businessman." They knew more about the nation's problems, he said, than snobbish politicians, academics and journalists.[30]

As a third-party candidate, Wallace had no chance of winning, but he garnered nearly 10 million votes — 13 percent of ballots — showing that his appeal ran strong.[31] Many of those Wallace votes would have gone to Nixon if the Alabama governor hadn't launched his third-party bid, and Nixon concluded that he didn't want to face that challenge again.[32]

Enduring Appeal

In 1972 Wallace had plans for another presidential run. But the outsider candidate apparently wasn't above making insider deals. In a book on Nixon's presidential campaigns, author Rick Perlstein reports that Nixon made moves to benefit Wallace in exchange for the Alabaman dropping his third-party strategy and running instead in the Democratic presidential primary. As a Democratic candidate, Wallace wouldn't siphon off Republican votes in the general election, as he had in 1968.[33]

In the summer of 1971, Wallace met with Nixon during a flight to Alabama from the president's vacation home in Key Biscayne, Fla. Three months later, a federal grand jury investigating alleged tax fraud by Wallace's brother dissolved without issuing indictments. Shortly thereafter, the Justice Department announced — "suddenly and improbably," in Perlstein's words — that Alabama's civil rights enforcement plan was superior to other states' plans.

In January 1972 Wallace announced he would run for the Democratic presidential nomination. In Florida, the first primary, he won first place in a five-man race, with 42 percent of the vote.

In the end, Wallace (who was shot and paralyzed midway through the campaign) won only two primaries outside the Old Confederacy, in Michigan and Maryland. The Democratic nomination went to Sen. George S. McGovern of South Dakota, an anti-Vietnam War candidate.

Unfortunately for McGovern, he came to symbolize a social gap between hard-working, ordinary Americans, and pampered liberals and radicals. In fact, he had earned a Distinguished Flying Cross as a bomber pilot in World War II and hardly fit the stereotype.[34]

But McGovern's supporters did include the liberal wing of the Democratic Party, Hollywood stars among

them. So the "McGovern Democrats" neatly symbolized one side of the social gap that right-wing populists had identified, and that Nixon had done his best to widen. "It is time that good, decent people stop letting themselves be bulldozed by anybody who presumes to be the self-righteous moral judge of our society," Nixon said in a radio address shortly before Election Day.[35]

His strategy proved spectacularly successful. McGovern won only one state, Massachusetts, and Washington, D.C. But Nixon's even more spectacular political downfall during the Watergate scandal prevented him from taking advantage of his victory. He was forced to resign in 1974.

Though President Ronald Reagan, another Republican, adopted Nixon's "silent majority" paradigm, Reagan's overall optimism effectively sanded off the doctrine's sharp edges. And Reagan didn't have to contend with directing an unpopular war.

During the 1992 reelection campaign of Reagan's successor (and former vice president), President George H. W. Bush, another populist figure emerged, Texas billionaire H. Ross Perot. In his brief but influential third-party campaign for president, Perot declared, "America today is a nation in crisis with a government in gridlock. We are deeply in debt and spending beyond our means."[36]

A pro-choice, law-and-order conservative, Perot paid little attention to social issues. Instead, he emphasized the need to cut government spending and strongly opposed the proposed North American Free Trade Agreement (NAFTA) with Mexico and Canada. Business' "job is to create and protect jobs in America — not Mexico," he said shortly before formally announcing.[37]

And he decried what he saw as the lavish perks of government service. "We have government turned upside down, where the people running it act and live at your expense like royalty, and many of you are working two jobs just to stay even."[38]

Perot's intolerance for criticism and a strong authoritarian streak (he praised Singapore, notorious for its rigid enforcement of laws on personal behavior) limited his appeal. Still, he wound up with 19 percent of the vote, including 29 percent of all votes by independents. "He showed the nation's ruling elites," wrote *The Washington Post*'s John Mintz, "that millions of Americans are deeply disturbed by what they believe is a breakdown in American society."[39]

New Coffee Party Drawing Supporters

"People are tired of the anger."

An alternative to the Tea Party is taking shape, as citizens who oppose its message and tactics are forming their own grassroots network — the Coffee Party.

The Tea Party's nascent rival takes a deliberately toned-down approach to political conflict. "We've got to send a message to people in Washington that you have to learn how to work together, you have to learn how to talk about these issues without acting like you're in an ultimate fighting session," founder Annabel Park, who launched the movement from a Coffee Party Facebook page, told *The New York Times* recently.[1]

Tea partiers put themselves on the map with rallies, pointed questions to politicians at town hall meetings and election campaign organizing. How the coffee partiers plan to project themselves into the national debate isn't clear yet. But there's no question that the effort grows out of the liberal, Democratic Party-oriented part of the political spectrum — a counterpart to the veteran Republicans who launched the Tea Party. Park, a documentary filmmaker in the Washington suburb of Silver Spring, Md., had worked on the Obama campaign.

By mid-March, when enthusiasts nationwide held a coordinated series of get-togethers in — of course — coffee shops across the country, the Coffee Party page had collected more than 100,000 fans. "Coffee partiers seem to be more in favor of government involvement — as in envisioning a greater role for government in the future of health care — but denounce the "corporatocracy" that holds sway in Washington," *The Christian Science Monitor* reported from a Coffee Party meeting in Decatur, Ga.[2]

Whether the Coffee Party grows into a full-fledged movement, there's no denying the initial appeal. The organizer of a Dallas-area gathering in March had expected 15 people at most. She got 40. "This is snowballing," Raini Lane said. "People are tired of the anger, tired of the hate."[3]

— Peter Katel

---

[1] Quoted in Kate Zernike, "Coffee Party, With a Taste for Civic Participation, Is Added to the Menu," *The New York Times*, March 2, 2010, p. A12.

[2] Patrik Jonsson, "'Coffee party' movement: Not far from the 'tea party' message?" *The Christian Science Monitor*, March 13, 2010, www.csmonitor.com/USA/Politics/2010/0313/Coffee-party-movement-Not-far-from-the-tea-party-message.

[3] Quoted in Cassie Clark, "Coffee Party energizes fans," *Dallas Morning News*, March 14, 2010, p. B2.

Political professionals had assumed Perot would draw far more Republican votes away from Bush than Democratic ones from Bill Clinton. But post-election surveys showed that Perot voters — often casting what amounted to protest votes — came from both Republican- and Democratic-oriented voters.

"Those who said they voted for Perot," *The Washington Post* reported, "split almost evenly between Bush and Clinton when asked their second choice."[40]

CURRENT SITUATION

The Election Test

Across the country, Tea Party-affiliated candidates — or those who claim the movement's mantle — are running for a range of Republican nominations, in races that will test both the movement's strength and its potential to influence GOP politics. The races will also set the stage for the 2012 Republican presidential nomination.

So far, at least one potential Republican candidate seems to think the Tea Party will have run its course by then. Former Massachusetts Gov. Mitt Romney is criticizing populism among both Republicans and Democrats. "Populism sometimes takes the form of being anti-immigrant … and that likewise is destructive to a nation which has built its economy through the innovation and hard work and creativity of people who have come here from foreign shores," Romney told *The Boston Globe*.[41]

Some candidates seeking Tea Party votes do take an anti-immigrant line. In Arizona, former Rep. J.D. Hayworth is challenging veteran Sen. John McCain, the GOP

AT ISSUE

Does the Tea Party movement represent another Great Awakening?

YES
Glenn Harlan Reynolds
Professor of Law, University of Tennessee

NO
Joseph Lowndes
*Professor of Political Science,
University of Oregon*

Written for *CQ Researcher*, March 2010

In the 18th and 19th centuries, America experienced two Great Awakenings, in which mainstream religious institutions — grown too stodgy, inbred and self-serving for many — faced a sudden flowering of new, broad-based religious fervor. Now we're experiencing a third Great Awakening, but this time it's political, not religious, in nature.

Nonetheless, the problem is the same: The existing institutions no longer serve the needs of broad swaths of the public. The choice between the two parties is increasingly seen as a choice between two gangs of thieves and charlatans. While Americans always joked about corruption and venality in politics, now those jokes don't seem as funny.

The Tea Party movement is one symptom of this phenomenon: Millions of Americans are aligning themselves with a bottom-up insurgency angered by bailouts, growing deficits and the treatment of taxpayers as cash cows. Though often treated as a red-state phenomenon, the Tea Party movement is strong even in deep-blue states like Massachusetts, where Scott Brown was elected to the Senate, or California, where one out of three voters told a recent poll that they identified with the Tea Party.

But the Tea Party movement is a symptom of a much broader phenomenon, exemplified by earlier explosions of support for Howard Dean via Meetup and Barack Obama and Sarah Palin via Facebook. They were triggered by the growing sense that politics has become a cozy game for insiders, and that the interests of most Americans are ignored.

Thus, Americans are becoming harder to ignore. Over the past year they've expressed their dissatisfaction at Tea Party rallies and town hall meetings, and at marches on Washington and state capitals. And they're planning what to do next, using the Internet and talk radio.

Traditional politics is still wedded to 20th-century top-down models, where mailing lists, organizations and message control are key. But in the 21st century, the real energy is at the grassroots, where organization can take place on the fly. When Tea Party activists decided to support Brown, they sent him money through his Web site, and put together an online "Moneybomb" campaign to bypass the Republican Party, which got behind Brown's seemingly quixotic campaign only after the momentum was established by the grassroots.

Coupled with widespread dissatisfaction at things as they are, expect a lot more of this grassroots activism, in both parties, over the coming years.

Written for *CQ Researcher*, March 2010

The Tea Party movement is indeed revivalist, but it revives not the egalitarian impulses of the 1740s or 1830s that fed the zeal of the Revolution and abolition. Rather it rehashes a tradition of racial, antigovernment populism that stretches from George Wallace's American Independent Party through Reagan Democrats to Sarah Palin Republicans.

In this tradition's origins mythology, a virtuous white citizenry became squeezed between liberal elites above and black dependents below as a result of civil rights and Johnson's Great Society. Since then, these Americans have resented taxation and social welfare, linking it to those whom they believe are recipients of special rights and government coddling. Thus, for the tea partiers and their immediate forebears the state is what monopoly capital was for 19th-century populists: a parasitic entity controlling their lives through opaque and malevolent machinations. It is worth noting that a significant percentage of tea partiers appear to be in their 60s or older — placing them in the generation that expressed the most negative reaction to the advances of the civil rights movement.

Why are we seeing this wave of protest now? The Tea Party movement has emerged out of the confluence of two momentous events: an enormous economic crisis and the election of a black president. The dislocations produced by the former have stoked the latent racial nationalism ignited by the latter. Obama represents both aspects of modern populist resentment — blackness and the state, and his perceived coziness with Wall Street taps into outrage felt toward banks right now. Add to this Glenn Beck's continual attacks on Obama and progressivism more generally, and you get a demonology that allows tea partiers to see tyranny wherever they look. (If "demonology" seems too strong a word here, look no further than the grotesque Joker-ized image of Obama over the word "Socialism" that has been omnipresent at Tea Party rallies.)

Will this movement transform the landscape? Third-party movements have impact when they can drive a wedge into the two-party system, creating a crisis that reframes the major political questions of the day. But the stated principles of the various Tea Party groups show them to be entirely consistent with the social conservative wing of the GOP. And there is a great overlap in leadership ties and funding sources as well, making it likely that the movement will find itself reabsorbed by the party with little independent impact.

Chris Van Hollen, D-Md., chairman of the influential House Democratic Congressional Campaign Committee, helps guide House Democrats' fundraising and strategizing. He thinks the Tea Party activists may be driving the Republicans to the right and that primary victories by Tea Party-style Republicans could spell victory for centrist Democrats in November.

candidate for president in 2008. "In Arizona, you can't ignore the Republican animus against Sen. McCain on immigration," Jason Rose, a spokesman for Hayworth, told *Roll Call*, a Washington political newspaper.[42]

Meanwhile, another Tea Party-backed candidate, Mike Lee, is challenging Republican Sen. Bob Bennett of Utah, whose backers include the state's senior senator, Republican Orrin Hatch. And in Kentucky, Tea Party enthusiast Rand Paul (son of libertarian Rep. Ron Paul, R-Texas) is competing against a Republican officeholder, Secretary of State Trey Grayson, for the GOP nomination to a Senate seat left open by a Republican retirement. Florida's GOP Gov. Charlie Crist, whom tea partiers consider insufficiently conservative, is fighting hard for the Senate nomination against Marco Rubio, a lobbyist and former state legislator who has become a national star among conservative Republicans. "America already has a Democrat Party, it doesn't need two Democrat parties," Rubio told CPAC in February.[43]

And Sen. Jim DeMint, the South Carolina Republican who has become a Senate liaison for the Tea Party, made clear to the CPAC crowd where his sympathies lie, tacitly

drawing a parallel between Crist and Sen. Arlen Specter of Pennsylvania. who defected from the GOP last year to save his seat. "I would rather have 30 Marco Rubios in the Senate than 60 Arlen Specters."[44]

In the Deep South, where the Tea Party runs along the same conservative Republican tracks, two Tea Party-friendly candidates for Congress are opposing each other in north Alabama. "A lot of Tea Party activists are split between Les Phillip and Mo Brooks," says Christie Carden, who organized a Tea Party group in Huntsville. So far, at least, she and her fellow members have not endorsed either candidate.

Complicating matters, a third Republican is running as well. Incumbent Parker Griffith was welcomed into the GOP fold after he switched from Democrat to Republican last December. Party-establishment backing for Griffith makes sense, given the GOP's interest in providing a defector with a favorable reception, says blogger and Tennessee law professor Reynolds. But, he adds, "One of the Tea Party complaints is that there is too much *realpolitik*" — or compromising — in the GOP establishment.

Elsewhere, even where Tea Party candidates might have traction, Republican organizations won't necessarily welcome them with open arms. "The Republican Party in Pennsylvania is pretty good at controlling its side of the ballot," says Dan Hirschorn, editor and publisher of the Philadelphia-based political news site *pa2010*. "When ... Tea Party candidates are in a race where there already are establishment Republicans, the political landscape the Tea Party candidates face is really formidable."

Democrats view the tension between party professionals and conservative insurgents as a potential advantage. "You've got these very divisive primaries," Rep. Chris Van Hollen, D-Md., chairman of the House Democratic campaign organization, told *CQ Weekly*. "In many instances it's driving the primary way to the right."[45]

In some districts, Van Hollen suggested, primary victories by Tea Party-style Republicans could spell victory for centrist Democrats.

Political Realities

Fresh from his victory in Massachusetts, Sen. Brown is now a certified hero to Republicans, especially the Tea Party movement, which worked its heart out for him. Brown's victory was made all the sweeter by its location in the heart of blue-state America. But his first vote on Capitol Hill has conservatives talking about political realities.

Less than three weeks after he formally took office on Feb. 4, Brown joined four other Republicans in voting for a $15-billion jobs bill pushed by the Obama administration and Democratic Senate leader Harry Reid of Nevada. "I came to Washington to be an independent voice, to put politics aside and to do everything in my power to help create jobs for Massachusetts families," Brown said after the vote. "This Senate jobs bill is not perfect. I wish the tax cuts were deeper and broader, but I voted for it because it contains measures that will help put people back to work."[46]

His words did nothing to stem the tide of rage that poured onto his Facebook page — 4,200 comments in less than 24 hours after his Feb. 22 vote, the vast majority of them furious. As gleefully documented by the liberal *Huffington Post* news site, the comments included "LYING LOW LIFE SCUM HYPOCRITE!" and "YOU FAILED AT THE FIRST CHANCE" and "You sir, are a sellout."

But Michael Graham, a radio talk-show host and *Boston Herald* columnist in the Tea Party fold, mocked the outrage. "This is still Massachusetts," Graham wrote. "Brown will have to win a general election to keep this seat.... This one, relatively insignificant vote sent a powerful message to casual, Democrat-leaning voters that Brown isn't in the GOP bag.... It's brilliant politics."[47]

Graham is a political veteran, unlike many tea partiers. The movement, in fact, prides itself on its many political neophytes. "These are not people," Tea Party activist Freire, the *Washington Examiner* editor, said at the Washington panel discussion in February, "who are used to getting engaged in the process."

Although the panel discussion preceded Brown's vote by about a week, it delved into the tension between principles and pragmatism that surfaced after Brown's move. Other conservative lawmakers also have disappointed conservative backers, Freire noted. Rep. Paul Ryan, R-Wis., Freire said, "is a pretty reliable guy when it comes to his fiscal conservatism; he still voted for the bailout."

Third-Party Option

Democrats are nourishing the fond if unlikely hope that the Tea Party will turn into a full-fledged political party.

"[That] would have a negative effect on Republicans, as would threatening to do that and influencing Republican candidates to move further to the right," says Neil Oxman of Philadelphia, cofounder of The Campaign Group political consulting firm.

For that reason, the third-party idea has not caught fire among tea partiers. "We don't need another party," says Carden, the Huntsville organizer. "We just need to use the vehicles for political change that are already there."

History points to that course as the most promising. Socialists, conservatives, libertarians and other political movements have long used third-party campaigns to build national support or at least publicize their ideas. Winning the White House isn't the goal.

In state races, candidates outside the two major parties have won, though such cases at the moment can be counted on one hand. Sen. Bernard Sanders of Vermont, a socialist who ran as an independent, is serving his first Senate term after 16 years in the House. Another senator, lifelong Connecticut Democrat Joseph I. Lieberman, is technically an independent, but he dropped that affiliation after losing a primary race to an Iraq War opponent.

The outcome of a bitter political fight in upstate New York last November would seem to confirm the two-party strategy as best for Republicans. In a special election to fill a newly vacated "safe" GOP House seat, the choice of a Republican legislator raised the hackles of conservatives nationwide, who viewed her as too liberal on abortion and gay rights. Instead, they backed a Conservative Party candidate — who eventually lost to Democrat Owens. His backers included the onetime Republican candidate Dede Scozzafava, who denounced what she viewed as betrayal by the GOP.[48]

"This election represents a double blow for national Republicans and their hopes of translating this summer's Tea Party energy into victories at the ballot box," Van Hollen, the Democratic Congressional Campaign Committee chairman, said.[49]

In New York state, Conservative Party candidate Hoffman's backers included Sarah Palin and former Rep. Dick Armey of Texas, a Tea Party booster and former House Republican leader who is president of FreedomWorks, a Washington-based activist-training organization whose politics run along Tea Party lines.

The New York debacle was followed by Brown's triumph in Massachusetts. That Brown ran as a Republican seemed to confirm the wisdom of channeling Tea Party activism into GOP campaigns.

Republican strategy guru Karl Rove, the top campaign and White House adviser to former President George W. Bush, is warning Tea Party groups to stay in the Republican fold. "There's a danger from them," he told *USA Today* recently, "particularly if they're used by political operators ... to try and hijack" elections.[50]

Rove could have had Nevada in mind. There, a candidate from the "Tea Party of Nevada" has filed to oppose Senate Majority Leader Reid in the GOP primary.

Leaders of Nevada's Tea Party movement told the conservative *Washington Times* that they don't recognize the names on the Tea Party of Nevada filing documents. They claimed the third party was created on Reid's behalf to siphon Republican votes. But the candidate said by mail, "I am not for Harry Reid....

My candidacy is real." The Reid campaign didn't return a call to the *Times*' reporter.[51] Whatever the sincerity of the Nevada Tea Party, grassroots conservatives elsewhere who are disenchanted with the GOP argue that the best course is to fight within the party. "Use the Republican Party to your advantage," Chicago tea partier Eric Odom wrote on his blog. "Move in and take it over."[52]

OUTLOOK

Short Life?

In the hyperspeed political environment, evaluating the 10-year prospects for a newly emerged movement is an iffy proposition. Still, a consensus is emerging that the Tea Party's ideas will last longer than the movement itself.

"These ideas are endemic in American political culture," says Sides of George Washington University. "Whether we will be able to attach them to a movement or an organization we call the Tea Party is an open question."

Georgia Tea Party activist Martin acknowledges the movement may dissolve over the next decade. "If there isn't a movement 10 years from now, I hope it's faded away because people understand what the country's core values are and don't need to be reminded."

Whatever the state of national consciousness in the near future, the life cycle of social movements in their most influential phase arguably has never been very long,

even before the pace of modern life quickened to its present pace. "In their dynamic, growing, inspirational, 'we-can-change-the-world' stage, they last five to seven years," says Kazin of Georgetown University.

The labor union movement's high point ran from 1933 to 1938, Kazin says. And the civil rights movement in its nationwide, unified phase ran from just 1960 to 1965. "And those were movements that were more independent of a political party structure," he adds.

As a movement closely linked to the Republican Party, the Tea Party's future will depend greatly on the course of the 2010 elections, Kazin argues. And which GOP candidates are nominated for president in 2012 will offer an even clearer gauge of the movement's influence.

Hawkins of *Right Wing News* thinks he knows where the Tea Party will be in 10 years. "I tend to doubt it will exist," he says. "It will have been absorbed into the Republican Party."

But the University of Oregon's Lowndes argues that beyond the country's Republican strongholds, the Tea Party won't acquire enough influence to reconfigure the entire party. "It will shape politics in certain places, and shape the Republican Party, but it won't take it over."

For now, however, Lowndes credits the Tea Party with effectively pulling together strands of discontent. "With enormous power concentrated in the executive branch and in corporations, there is a sense of powerlessness at work that can be picked up and interpreted different ways by different folks," he says. "These people have found a language for it that the left has not."

Jonah Goldberg, high-profile editor of *National Review Online*, urged conservatives during the America's Future Foundation panel discussion in February to come to terms with the nature of the political system. "The American people aren't as conservative as we would like them to be, and they never will be," he said, despite what seem to be favorable conditions for the right that largely grow out of the Tea Party's success.

"Things are so much better than they seemed to be a little while ago," he continued. "Will Republicans blow it? They have a great history of that. One of the things that movements do is try to keep politicians honest. That's going to be hard work because politicians are politicians."

Reynolds of the University of Tennessee Law School acknowledges that the Tea Party's promise may go unfulfilled. Conservative hopes ran high after the 1994

Republican takeover of Congress midway through the first Clinton administration, he notes. "But that didn't have long-lasting legs."

On the other hand, Reynolds says, the Reagan legacy has been long-lasting. "And this is probably bigger," he says of the Tea Party.

But there are no guarantees, he cautions. "A lot of people are involved in politics who never were before. In 10 years, some will have gone back to their lives. Of the people who stay in, the odds are that many will become politicians as usual. The question is how much this will happen."

NOTES

1. Kathleen Hennessey, "Justice's wife launches 'tea party' group," *Los Angeles Times*, March 14, 2010, www.latimes.com/news/nation-and-world/la-na-thomas142010mar14,0,3190750,full.story.

2. Mark Leibovich, "Discipline Helped Carve Path to Senate," *The New York Times*, Jan. 21, 2010, www.nytimes.com/2010/01/21/us/politics/21brown.html.

3. Zachary Ross, "Top Tea Partier, Husband, Owed IRS Half a Million Dollars," *Talking Points Memo*, Oct. 8, 2009, http://tpmmuckraker.talkingpoints-memo.com/2009/10/top_tea_partier_husband_owed_irs_half_a_million_do.php.

4. Jeff Zeleny, "Daniels Offers Advice to Republicans," *The New York Times*, The Caucus (blog), March 9, 2010, http://thecaucus.blogs.nytimes.com/2010/03/09/daniels-offers-advice-to-republicans/.

5. "Tom Tancredo's Feb. 4 Tea party speech in Nashville," *Free Republic*, Feb. 5, 2010, http://freerepublic.com/focus/f-news/2445943/posts.

6. Cuéntame, www.facebook.com/cuentame?v=app_11007063052.

7. John Maggs, "Norquist on Tea and Taxes," *National Journal*, Feb. 4, 2010, http://insiderinterviews.nationaljournal.com/2010/02/-nj-were-you-surprised.php.

8. *Ibid.* Also see Tea Party Nation, teapartynation.com; and Kate Zernike, "Seeking a Big Tent, Tea Party Avoids Divisive Social Issues," *The New York Times*, March 13, 2010, p. A1.

9. John M. O'Hara, *A New American Tea Party: The Counterrevolution Against Bailouts, Handouts, Reckless Spending, and More Taxes* (2010), pp. 256-257.

10. "Rick Santelli Rant Transcript," www.reteaparty.com/2009/02/19/rick-santelli-rant-transcript/.

11. *Ibid.*; Brian Stelter, "CNBC Replays Its Reporter's Tirade," *The New York Times*, Feb.23, 2009, p. B7.

12. Mary Lou Pickel, "Tea Party at the Capitol," *Atlanta Journal-Constitution,* Feb. 28, 2009; Aman Batheja, "Several hundred protest Obama stimulus program in Fort Worth," *Fort Worth Star-Telegram*, Feb. 28, 2009; "Tea Party Time," *New York Post*, Feb. 28, 2009, p. 16; Tim O'Neil, "Riverfront tea party protest blasts Obama's stimulus plan," *St. Louis Post-Dispatch*, Feb. 28, 2009, p. A7; Christian M. Wade, "Tax Protesters Converge on Federal Courthouse," *Tampa Tribune*, Feb. 28, 2009, p. A4; "Protesters bemoan stimulus funds at Tenn. Capitol," The Associated Press, Feb. 28, 2009.

13. Kate Zernike, "Unlikely Activist Who Got to the Tea Party Early," *The New York Times*, Feb. 27, 2010, www.nytimes.com/2010/02/28/us/politics/28keli.html.

14. Quoted in David M. Halbfinger and Ian Urbina, "Republicans Bask in Glow of Victories in N.J. and Va.," *The New York Times*, Nov. 5, 2009; Janet Hook, "Stimulus bill battle is only the beginning," *Los Angeles Times*, Feb. 15, 2009, p. A1.

15. Quoted in Manu Raju, "Lindsey Graham warns GOP against going too far right," *Politico*, Nov. 4, 2009, www.politico.com/news/stories/1109/29131.html.

16. Chelsea Schilling, " 'Government wants to be your one and only god,' " *WorldNetDaily*, Feb. 6, 2010, www.wnd.com/index.php?pageId=124326.

17. Jonathan Raban, "At the Tea Party," *New York Review of Books*, March 25, 2010, www.nybooks.com/articles/23723.

18. For background, see Peter Katel, "Press Freedom," *CQ Researcher*, Feb. 5, 2010, pp. 97-120.

19. Quoted in David Weigel, "Birther Speaker Takes Heat at Tea Party Convention," *Washington Independent*, Feb. 6, 2010 (includes audio clip of argument), http://washingtonindependent.com/75949/birther-speaker-takes-heat-at-tea-party-convention.

20. Except where otherwise indicated, this subsection is drawn from Michael Kazin, *The Populist Persuasion: An American History* (1998).

21. Quoted in Daniel Feller, "King Andrew and the Bank," *Humanities*, National Endowment for the Humanities, January-February, 2008, www.neh.gov/news/humanities/2008-01/KingAndrewandtheBank.html.

22. "Bryan's 'Cross of Gold' Speech: Mesmerizing the Masses," *History Matters*, undated, http://history-matters.gmu.edu/d/5354/.

23. Steve Oney, "The Leo Frank case isn't dead," *Los Angeles Times*, Oct. 30, 2009, http://articles.latimes.com/2009/oct/30/opinion/oe-oney30. Except where otherwise indicated, this subsection is drawn from Kazin, *op. cit.*

24. William E. Leuchtenburg, *Franklin D. Roosevelt and the New Deal* (1963), pp. 33, 255, 335-336.

25. For background, see Peter Katel, "Hate Groups," *CQ Researcher*, May 8, 2009, pp. 421-448.

26. Douglas Martin, "William F. Buckley Jr., 82, Dies," *The New York Times*, Feb. 28, 2008, p. A1.

27. Kazin, *op. cit.*, p. 193. For background on the G.I. Bill, see "Record of 78th Congress (Second Session)," *Editorial Research Reports*, Dec. 20, 1944, available at *CQ Researcher Plus Archive*; K. Lee, "War Veterans in Civil Life," *Editorial Research Reports*, Vol. II, 1946; and William Triplett, "Treatment of Veterans," *CQ Researcher*, Nov. 19, 2004, pp. 973-996.

28. Todd Gitlin, *The Sixties: Years of Hope, Days of Rage* (1993), pp. 348-351.

29. Quoted in Kazin, *op. cit.*, p. 252.

30. *Ibid.*, pp. 234-235.

31. Richard Pearson, "Former Ala. Gov. George C. Wallace Dies," *The Washington Post*, Sept. 14, 1998, p. A1, www.washingtonpost.com/wp-srv/politics/daily/sept98/wallace.htm.

32. Rick Perlstein, *Nixonland: The Rise of a President and the Fracturing of America* (2008), pp. 631-632.

33. Except where otherwise indicated, this subsection draws from *ibid.*

34. "George McGovern Interview," The National World War II Museum, undated, www.nationalww2museum.org/wwii-community/mcgovern.html.

35. Quoted in Perlstein, *op. cit.*, pp. 732-733.

36. H. Ross Perot, "What Americans Must Demand," *The Washington Post*, March 29, 1992, p. C2.

37. Quoted in John Dillin, "Possible Presidential Bid by Perot Is Seen Posing a Threat to Bush," *The Christian Science Monitor*, March 24, 1992, p. 1.

38. Quoted in *ibid.*

39. John Mintz, "Perot Embodied Dismay of Millions," *The Washington Post*, Nov. 4, 1992, p. A26; Jeffrey Schmalz, "Clinton Carves a Wide Path Deep Into Clinton Country," *The New York Times*, Nov. 4, 1992, p. B1.

40. Thomas B. Edsall and E. J. Dionne, "White, Younger, Lower-Income Voters Turn Against G.O.P.," *The Washington Post*, Nov. 4, 1992, p. A21.

41. Quoted in Sasha Issenberg, "In book, Romney styles himself wonk, not warrior," *Boston Globe*, March, 2, 2010, www.boston.com/news/nation/washington/articles/2010/03/02/mitt_romneys_no_apology_is_not_light_reading?mode=PF.

42. Emily Cadei, "Sands of GOP Discord in Arizona," *Roll Call*, Jan. 28, 2010.

43. Quoted in Liz Sidoti, "Excited GOP: Energy on the right, divisions within," The Associated Press, Feb. 19, 2010. Adam Nagourney and Carl Hulse, "Re-energized, G.O.P. Widens Midterm Effort," *The New York Times*, Jan. 25, 2010, p. A1; Thomas Burr, "GOP's Armey backs Lee, scolds Bennett," *Salt Lake Tribune*, Feb. 18, 2010.

44. Quoted in *ibid.*

45. Quoted in Joseph J. Schatz, "Reading the Leaves," *CQ Weekly*, March 1, 2010, pp. 480-489.

46. Quoted in James Oliphant, "Scott Brown's 'tea party' fans feel burned by jobs vote," *Los Angeles Times*, Feb. 23, 2010, http://articles.latimes.com/2010/feb/23/nation/la-na-scott-brown24-2010feb24.

47. Michael Graham, "Still right cup of tea," *Boston Herald*, Feb. 25, 2010, www.bostonherald.com/news/opinion/op_ed/view.bg?articleid=1235356.

48. Jeremy W. Peters, "Conservative Loses Upstate House Race in Blow to Right," *The New York Times*, Nov. 3, 2009, www.nytimes.com/2009/11/04/nyregion/04district.html?_r=1&scp=9&sq=HoffmanScozzafava&st=cse.

49. Quoted in *ibid.*

50. Judy Keen, "Rove: 'Tea Party' may be risk to GOP," *USA Today*, March 10, 2010, p. A1.

51. Quoted in Valerie Richardson, "New party brings its own 'tea' to election," *The Washington Times*, Feb. 22, 2010, p. A1.

52. Quoted in Kate Zernike, "In Power Push, Movement Sees Base in G.O.P.," *The New York Times*, Jan. 15, 2010, p. A1.

BIBLIOGRAPHY

Books

Continetti, Matthew, *The Persecution of Sarah Palin: How the Elite Media Tried to Bring Down a Rising Star*, Sentinel, 2009.
An editor of the conservative *Weekly Standard* chronicles the rise of Tea Party-friendly Palin from a sympathetic perspective.

Kazin, Michael, *The Populist Persuasion: An American History*, Cornell University Press, 1998.
A Georgetown University historian traces the forms that an enduring American distrust of elites has taken.

O'Hara, John M., *A New American Tea Party: The Counterrevolution Against Bailouts, Handouts, Reckless Spending, and More Taxes*, John Wiley & Sons, 2010.
A manifesto in book form by one of the first Tea Party activists tells of the movement's formation and ideas.

Perlstein, Rick, *Nixonland: The Rise of a President and the Fracturing of America*, Scribner, 2008.
A non-academic historian adds to the Tea Party story with this account of Nixon and his appeal to the "silent majority."

Articles

Barstow, David, "Tea Party Lights Fuse for Rebellion on Right," *The New York Times*, Feb. 15, 2010, www.nytimes.com/2010/02/16/us/politics/16teaparty.html.
A lengthy, detailed report traces the formation of a Tea Party undercurrent of conspiracists and militia members.

Continetti, Matthew, "Sarah Palin and the Tea Party, Cont.," *Weekly Standard*, Feb. 8, 2010, www.weeklystandard.com/print/blogs/sarah-palin-and-tea-party-cont.
The author of a sympathetic book on Palin argues she made a powerful case for herself as a 2012 presidential candidate.

Good, Chris, "Some Tea Partiers Question Meeting With Steele," *The Atlantic*, Politics site, Feb. 16, 2010, www.theatlantic.com/politics/archive/2010/02/some-tea-partiers-question-meeting-with-steele/36027/.
Some Florida tea partiers questioned the movement credentials of a political activist who organized a meeting with Michael Steele, the controversial Republican national chairman.

Hennessey, Kathleen, "Justice's wife launches 'tea party' group," *Los Angeles Times*, March 14, 2010, www.latimes.com/news/nation-and-world/la-na-thomas14-2010mar14,0,3190750,full.story.
This is the first report of the Tea Party activism of Virginia Thomas, wife of Supreme Court Justice Clarence Thomas.

Markon, Jerry, " 'Wired' conservatives get the message out," *The Washington Post*, Feb. 1, 2010, p. A1.
Tea Party organizers made extensive use of social networking tools and Republican connections in getting the movement up and running, a political correspondent reports.

Naymik, Mark, "GOP stumbles with Tea Party as movement gains foothold," *Cleveland Plain Dealer*, Feb. 21, 2010, p. A1.
A leading newspaper in a key political state reports on ambivalent relations between tea partiers and the Republican Party.

Parker, Kathleen, "The GOP's misguided hunt for heretics," *The Washington Post*, Feb. 24, 2010, www.washingtonpost.com/wp-dyn/content/article/2010/02/23/AR2010022303783.html.
A conservative columnist warns of a tendency to zealotry and intolerance among tea partiers.

Rucker, Philip, "GOP woos wary 'tea party' activists," *The Washington Post*, Jan. 20, 2010, p. A4.
Republican officials are courting Tea Party members, Washington's leading newspaper reports.

Sidoti, Liz, "Primary time: Let the political family feuds begin," *The Associated Press*, Jan. 30, 2010.
The Tea Party movement's political strength will be tested in some key primary elections, a political correspondent reports.

Tanenhaus, Sam, "The Crescendo of the Rally Cry," *The New York Times*, Jan. 24, 2010, Week in Review, p. 1.
A *Times* editor who writes on the history of conservatism examines the Tea Party movement in light of past populist surges.

Wilkinson, Howard, "Tea Partiers aim to remake local GOP," *Cincinnati Enquirer*, Jan. 30, 2010.
Tea partiers in southwest Ohio are making a concerted effort to take over Republican precinct organizations.

Zernike, Kate, "Seeking a Big Tent, Tea Party Avoids Divisive Social Issues," *The New York Times*, March 13, 2010, p. A1.
Some Tea Party activists deliberately bypass controversial social issues, a correspondent specializing in the Tea Party reports.

Reports

"AEI Political Report," *American Enterprise Institute for Public Policy Research*, February 2010, www.aei .org/docLib/Political-Report-Feb-2010.pdf.
A compilation of survey results from a variety of sources includes data on public knowledge of the Tea Party.

For More Information

Coffee Party, www.coffeepartyusa.com. A new network of Tea Party opponents.

FreedomWorks, 601 Pennsylvania Ave., N.W., North Building, Washington, DC 20004; (202) 783-3870; www .freedomworks.org. Created by former House Republican Leader Dick Armey, the conservative organization trains local activists.

Politics1, 409 N.E. 17th Ave., Fort Lauderdale, FL 33301; www.politics1.com/index.htm. Comprehensive political site offering a guide to races involving Tea Party candidates.

Right Wing News, rightwingnews.com. Independent Web site covers Tea Party movement, often critically.

Talkingpointsmemo, www.talkingpointsmemo.com. Democratic-oriented news site provides critical but fact-based coverage of Tea Party.

Tea Party Patriots, www.teapartypatriots.org. An extensive network of Tea Party groups around the country offering movement news and views from its Web site.

11

Financial Bailout

Thomas J. Billitteri and Phil Mattingly

A trader at the New York Stock Exchange on Sept. 16 follows one of the market's worst single-day declines. The continued volatility of the U.S. stock market signals that investors are not yet convinced the government's $700 billion financial bailout will work. In the past 15 months, several major U.S. banks have failed, and Americans have lost some $2 trillion in retirement savings that were invested in the market.

From *CQ Researcher*,
May 18, 2010.

A nger was palpable this fall as Congress scrambled to quell a financial wildfire that began in the overheated home-mortgage market, raged through Wall Street, spread ominously to Main Street and then flared into a global financial catastrophe.

"We were told that markets knew best, and that we were entering a new world of global growth and prosperity," declared Sen. Charles E. Schumer, D-N.Y., chairman of the Joint Economic Committee. "We now have to pay for the greed and recklessness of those who should have known better."[1]

Such emotions have been widespread in the wake of the nation's — and perhaps the world's — worst financial crisis since the Great Depression. But agreement on the root causes and likely outcome of the crisis has been harder to find.[2]

Early this month Congress overcame bitter ideological differences and passed a $700 billion bailout bill that permitted an immediate infusion of $250 billion into the banking system. Along with other loans, the government's potential tab for rescuing the American economy totaled at least $1 trillion in mid-October.[3] The federal government also announced on Oct. 23 it would guarantee up to $2.8 billion in debt and money market deposits.

Initially, the bailout's chief aim was to buy up "toxic" loans on lenders' books in the hopes of thawing the nation's frozen credit markets. As the crisis spread overseas, however, European central bankers — led by British Prime Minister Gordon Brown — began infusing their shaky banks with cash. Treasury Secretary Henry M. Paulson Jr. followed suit, committing the government to pumping $250 billion directly into U.S. banks to induce them to begin

Credit-Default Swaps Dominate Markets

The unregulated market for complex financial instruments known as credit-default swaps is estimated to be worth some $55 trillion, more than twice the value of the U.S. stock market and more than the combined values of the stock market, mortgage securities and U.S. Treasury instruments.

Value of Various Markets

(in $ trillions)

* As of June 2008

** As of 2007

Sources: The New York Times, February 2008, International Swaps and Derivatives Association

lending to each other again — vital to easing the nation's credit woes and bolstering confidence in the financial system.

As policy makers grasped for new options, experts remained divided over how much the plan will ultimately cost taxpayers, who should be held accountable for creating the economic debacle in the first place and whether the rescue plan would prevent a deep recession — an increasingly unlikely prospect.

The financial storm had been brewing for months, but it broke wide open in September with a shocking cascade of events over several tumultuous weeks. In the United States alone:

- Fannie Mae and Freddie Mac were seized by the federal government, which promised to inject up to $100 billion into each firm as concerns grew over the two mortgage titans' cash reserves;
- The investment bank Lehman Brothers collapsed in the biggest bankruptcy in U.S. history;
- Brokerage house Merrill Lynch narrowly averted Lehman's fate by selling to Bank of America;

- Global insurer American International Group (AIG) was propped up with an initial $85 billion federal bridge loan (since raised to as much as $123 billion);
- Washington Mutual failed, in the biggest bank collapse in U.S. history;
- Struggling Wachovia Bank planned to sell out to Wells Fargo, and
- Goldman Sachs and Morgan Stanley converted to commercial banks subject to stringent federal regulation, leaving Wall Street without major investment banks.

As the crisis intensified, Federal Reserve Chairman Ben S. Bernanke, Secretary Paulson and President George W. Bush urged quick congressional action. In a prime-time televised speech on Sept 24, Bush warned that without a rescue plan, "America could slip into a financial panic" and "a distressing scenario" of business failures, job losses and home foreclosures would follow.

But support for a bailout was far from universal, even within the president's own party. Sen. Jim Bunning, a Kentucky Republican, said spending $700 billion in taxpayer money to "prop up and clean up the balance sheets of Wall Street" is "financial socialism" and "un-American."[4]

Still, many experts viewed the bailout as painful but necessary. "We have to do something," said Tony Plath, an associate professor of finance at the University of North Carolina at Charlotte. "We can't let the American system melt down."

The crisis has clearly spooked Main Street. A CNN/Opinion Research Corp. poll released on Oct. 6 found that nearly six in 10 Americans thought an economic depression was likely.[5]

How the financial system reached the brink of collapse is a complex story that economists and congressional leaders will be untangling for years. But as the crisis deepened, experts pointed to a variety of likely and alleged culprits, including:

A collapsing real estate market — Spurred by record-low interest rates earlier this decade, lenders fueled a massive housing bubble, betting that borrowers — even ones with bad credit or lacking the documented means to repay — could refinance based on ever-rising home values. That gamble proved catastrophically wrong. When home prices fell, millions of homeowners found themselves owing more than their homes were worth, sparking a flood of mortgage defaults and fore-closures.[6] That squeezed lenders who had made subprime, "Alt-A" and other shaky loans as well as invest-ment banks that borrowed heavily to buy mortgage-backed securities based on such loans. (*See glossary, p. 253.*)

Fannie Mae and Freddie Mac — Some blame the Federal National Mortgage Association and Federal Home Loan Mortgage Corporation for fueling the market for reckless lending. The government-backed companies own or guarantee $5.4 trillion in mortgage loans — about 45 percent of the nation's total. Fannie alone bought or guar-anteed at least $270 billion in risky loans between 2005 and 2008, *The New York Times* reported.[7]

Credit-default swaps — Ultimately, many experts say, the crisis was caused by little understood, unregu-lated, insurance-like contracts that are intended to guar-antee against loan defaults. Subprime and other loans were backed by trillions of dollars in credit swaps. When home buyers began defaulting, financial institutions that sold the swaps lacked enough capital to make good on the guarantees, and investors who had purchased risky mortgage-backed securities were left hanging.

Plunging confidence in the financial system — Many major financial institutions, both in the United States and overseas, borrowed heavily to invest in mort-gages, and their highly leveraged positions put them at risk of insolvency when defaults rose. As the financial crisis intensified, banks found it harder and harder to raise new capital to avert trouble. Meanwhile, investors and creditors began worrying that all kinds of assets on the books of financial institutions — not just residential

Home Prices on the Decline

Home prices in 20 major U.S. cities doubled from 2000 to 2006. Prices, however, have steadily declined since 2006.

Source: S&P/Case-Shiller Home Price Indices

real estate — might be grossly overvalued, further erod-ing confidence. When banks even became leery of lend-ing to each other, consumer and business credit began freezing up.

The failure of government regulators — The 1999 repeal of the Glass-Steagall Act, a Depression-era law that split commercial banking from investment activi-ties, helped set the stage for the current crisis, some experts say. Others cite what they argue was Congress' failure to rein in Fannie Mae and Freddie Mac. Critics also point to the 2000 Commodity Futures Modernization Act, which prohibited regulation of most swaps. Also under scrutiny is a 2004 Securities and Exchange Commission (SEC) decision to loosen capital rules for brokerage units of investment banks, which freed bil-lions of dollars for investments in mortgage-backed secu-rities, credit derivatives and other instruments.[8]

Whatever the policy roots of the crisis, its resolution has been maddeningly elusive. In the days following the rescue plan's passage, the Dow Jones Industrial Average suffered its worst single-week decline in its 112-year his-tory. Stock markets around the world also plunged, a grim reminder that the crisis is global and threatens not only major European and Asian economies but emerging markets and poor nations as well.

In the United States, many economists remained skeptical that the infusions of capital and the purchase of toxic assets would lead banks to lend anew and get the economy moving again.

"Rather than jump into this morass again, a lot of commercial banks are going to opt for liquidity on their balance sheets," says a skeptical Robert Ekelund, professor emeritus of the economics of regulation at Auburn University.

Indeed, many see more pain ahead for the financial system and U.S. economy, including rising defaults on credit cards.[9] "We have to be prepared that it gets a lot worse," said Jamie Dimon, chief executive of JP Morgan Chase.[10]

As policy makers struggle to contain the damage from the economic crisis, these are some of the questions being asked:

Will the bailout plan work?

On the first full day of stock trading after the bailout's passage on Oct. 3, the Dow plunged some 800 points before rebounding to "only" a 370-point loss. The sell-off rattled global markets, and President Bush sought to reassure a nervous world.

"It's going to take a while to restore confidence in the financial system," he said. "But one thing people can be certain of is that the bill I signed is a big step toward solving this problem."[11]

In fact, many see the $700 billion rescue bill as a necessary, albeit expensive, evil.

"The rescue plan is a smart thing," says Gregory Hess, a professor of public economics at Claremont McKenna College, in California. "You have to give credit markets every chance to create confidence and unwind the systemic uncertainty in the market. What monetary policy does and what finance does is that literally we're just trading pieces of paper. And until the Fed and the Treasury can create confidence and those pieces of paper are meaningful and trustworthy, we're not going to get out of this credit collapse."

But others are skeptical about the bailout plan. "What we really need to do is save the homeowners," says L. Randall Wray, an economics professor at the University of Missouri-Kansas City and a visiting senior scholar at the Jerome Levy Economics Institute at Bard College, in Annandale-on-Hudson, N.Y. "Several hundred billion into the hands of consumers will do a lot more than $700 billion in the hands of Wall Street."

The government's new plan to inject $250 billion into banks, announced Oct. 14, is probably an improvement over the original plan to just buy toxic assets, Wray says, but "it is still based on the unwarranted hope that severely troubled banks will now want to lend, and that overindebted firms and households want to borrow. That is why I favor putting income into the hands of consumers over relief for Wall Street."

Writing in *The Wall Street Journal*, Martin Feldstein, chairman of the Council of Economic Advisers in the Reagan administration and now a Harvard economics professor, said the bailout plan "does nothing to stop" what he called "the fundamental cause of the crisis: the downward spiral of house prices that devastates household wealth and destroys the capital of financial institutions that hold mortgages and mortgage-backed securities."[12]

Feldstein said a successful economic plan "must do more than buy back impaired debt from financial institutions." He urged a system of limited federal mortgage-replacement loans for struggling borrowers that would "break the downward spiral of house prices."

The global nature of the financial crisis has made it all the more difficult to control. Economists point out that while the United States has a centralized way to deal with systemic financial problems, a unified plan is much more difficult to execute in Europe, with its many separate national governments.

Still, the fate of the global financial system depends on how effectively nations can engineer a coordinated response to the crisis. (*See sidebar, p. 256.*)

"We're all in this together," says James J. Angel, an associate professor of finance at Georgetown University. "Our economic markets are interconnected, our financial markets are interconnected and weakness in one area quickly translates to weakness in other areas."

In the United States, Angel says, the bailout plan alone "is not a panacea that will fix all our problems." But the plan, in combination with other government action, "means we now have the tools to clean up the mess," he says.

Among those tools, Angel says, is Hope for Homeowners, a measure Congress passed last summer to help certain borrowers refinance their mortgages. He also points to a Federal Reserve decision, made in early October amid a rapidly weakening economy, to buy unsecured short-term commercial debt from eligible companies in an effort to revive moribund credit markets.[13]

Still, Angel says, "Having and using the tools are two different things. There's a lot of implementation work that needs to be done, and done well, to get things moving again."

Some experts have argued that buying toxic loans from banks could backfire by revealing the true value of assets that financial companies have on their books.[14]

"Ironically, the intervention could even trigger the additional failures of larger institutions, because some institutions may be carrying troubled assets on their books at inflated values," Peter R. Orszag, director of the Congressional Budget Office, told the House Budget Committee about a week before the bailout was signed into law. "Establishing clearer prices might reveal those institutions to be insolvent."[15]

In the long run, Ekelund, the emeritus Auburn professor, says he thinks credit eventually will thaw and banks will regain enough confidence in borrowers that they will start lending freely again. But he fears that when that happens banks will resort to old habits, figuring that "if they make mistakes, they'll be bailed out."

Did Fannie Mae and Freddie Mac cause the financial crisis?

As policy makers look ahead to the effects of the bailout plan, they also are looking back at the causes of the economic crisis, including the bitterly debated role of Fannie Mae and Freddie Mac.

The two quasi-federal entities don't lend money directly but rather buy mortgages from lenders, enabling lenders to replenish capital in order to make more home loans. Fannie and Freddie package some loans into mortgage-backed securities for sale to investors. In other cases, they buy and hold loans in their own portfolios.

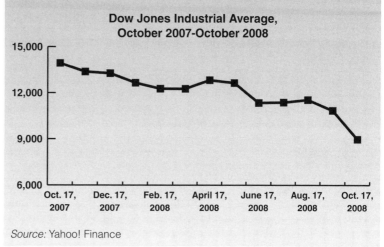

Dow Jones Average Has Plummeted

The Dow Jones Industrial Average — a performance index for 30 of the largest U.S. companies — is widely regarded as a bellwether for the health of the U.S. economy. The "Dow" has dropped precipitously — about 5,000 points, or 36 percent — from a year ago. The index recently dipped below 9,000 for the first time since 2003.

Dow Jones Industrial Average, October 2007-October 2008

Source: Yahoo! Finance

As "government-sponsored enterprises," Fannie and Freddie serve both the profit motives of shareholders and an affordable-housing mission that is subsidized by the federal government. Their special status in the secondary mortgage market, long protected by millions of dollars in lobbying expenditures and campaign contributions, has allowed Fannie and Freddie to borrow at lower rates than their commercial competitors and maintain lower cash reserves to cushion risk.

Their special status also has led investors to think the government stood behind Fannie and Freddie's debts, giving the two entities a competitive edge over purely private companies. That "implicit guarantee" was never in writing until this summer, though, when Congress authorized the Treasury to bail out Fannie and Freddie as they appeared to be heading toward insolvency.

Fannie and Freddie's financial trouble stemmed from their investments in risky subprime and Alt A mortgage loans. James B. Lockhart, director of the companies' regulator, the Federal Housing Finance Agency, told a congressional panel in September that despite regulators' "repeated warnings about credit risk," Fannie and Freddie in 2006 and 2007 "bought or guaranteed many more low-documentation, low-verification and non-standard [adjustable rate] mortgages than they had in the past." In the first half of 2007, about a third of Fannie and Freddie's new business was in Alt-A and other risky loans, compared with 14 percent in 2005, Lockhart said.[16]

Investors that bought mortgage-backed securities from Fannie and Freddie — including banks in China and elsewhere — stood to lose billions of dollars, and their pressure on the U.S. government reportedly helped persuade Treasury to take over the mortgage giants in early September.

In the 12 months ending June 30, Washington-based Fannie and McLean, Va.-based Freddie had combined losses of $14 billion, according to *The Wall Street Journal*, which said the losses came "largely because they lowered their credit standards and purchased or guaranteed dubious home loans."[17]

The companies' downward cycle ended in the government bailout, which the Congressional Budget Office initially estimated last summer at $25 billion but whose eventual tab could run far more, depending on the outcome of the housing crisis and the value of the assets underlying loans that Fannie and Freddie bought or guaranteed.

Critics of Fannie and Freddie have long argued that their government strings should be cut. (*See "At Issue," p. 263*.) Accounting scandals earlier this decade, multimillion-dollar compensation packages paid to Fannie and Freddie executives and the emerging details of the companies' risky loan business have fed calls for them to be privatized. But advocates of Fannie and Freddie, including Democrat Barney Frank, chairman of the House Financial Services Committee, contend that the companies' congressionally mandated affordable-housing mission is too important to leave to purely commercial companies.

Now, with the nation's credit markets essentially frozen, that mission has become a lightning rod for Fannie and Freddie's detractors. Conservatives have accused congressional Democrats of protecting Fannie and Freddie from tougher regulation, but Frank called the charge "nonsense," arguing that when Republicans held a majority in Congress they didn't pass stiffer regulations of the companies.[18]

But the critics are relentless. The companies and their Washington supporters "are largely to blame for our current mess," charged Charles W. Calomiris, a professor of finance and economics at Columbia Business School and a scholar at the conservative American Enterprise Institute, and Peter J. Wallison, an institute senior fellow and former Treasury Department general counsel in the Reagan administration.[19]

"[T]o curry congressional support" after accounting scandals earlier this decade, Fannie and Freddie "committed to increased financing of 'affordable housing' [and] became the largest buyers of subprime and Alt-A mortgages between 2004 and 2007," they wrote. "In so doing, they stimulated the growth of the subpar mortgage market and substantially magnified the costs of its collapse."[20]

Calomiris and Wallison are not alone in that view. "You ended up with a larger market for these subprime loans than you would have otherwise had," argues Hans Bader, counsel for special projects at the free-market-oriented Competitive Enterprise Institute.

Jeffrey A. Miron, a senior lecturer in economics at Harvard University, also puts Fannie and Freddie "at the center of the crisis." Miron, who joined 166 academic economists in opposing the bailout plan, wrote that "[t]he government implicitly promised these institutions that it would make good on their debts, so Fannie and Freddie took on huge amounts of excessive risk. Worse . . . Congress pushed mortgage lenders and Fannie/Freddie to expand subprime lending. The industry was happy to oblige, given the implicit promise of federal backing, and subprime lending soared.[21]

But others argue that Fannie and Freddie's purchases of risky mortgages, while imprudent, were more a reflection of their attempt to compete in what became a highly aggressive commercial mortgage market, not the main cause of it.

William K. Black, associate professor of economics and law at the University of Missouri-Kansas City School of Law, points out that Fannie and Freddie bought their risky loans almost exclusively from commercial companies. "Fannie and Freddie aren't making these mortgages," he says. "Somebody has to originate all this toxic waste."

Most of the bad loans in the market weren't bought by Fannie and Freddie but by investment and commercial banks and wealthy investors, Black says. Of the bad loans Fannie and Freddie did buy, if they hadn't done so, others would have, he says.

Most loans on Fannie and Freddie's books are high-quality, though they had enough "nonprime" mortgage-backed securities to render them insolvent, Black says. "Were those bad investments? You betcha. Does that prove Fannie and Freddie had some unique weakness? Well, no, they're about the fifth step in the food chain."

Mark Thoma, an associate professor of economics at the University of Oregon, argues that Fannie and Freddie "were followers, not leaders" of the subprime mortgage debacle.

Thoma contends that pressure from an unregulated "shadow industry" of hedge funds, investment banks and other institutions gave lenders a financial incentive to make risky loans. To remain competitive in a quickly evolving mortgage market, he says, Fannie and Freddie entered the subprime market in a big way, straying from their traditional practice of buying conventional loans made to people with good credit.

"I'm not going to defend them and say they didn't take on risk they shouldn't have," Thoma says. "It's just that they didn't start the problem."

Some conservative commentators have asserted that the 1977 Community Reinvestment Act (CRA), which encourages financial institutions to lend in low- and moderate-income neighborhoods, pushed Fannie and Freddie to support mortgages or people who couldn't repay. But others disagree.

"The notion that the Community Reinvestment Act is somehow responsible for poor lending decisions is absurd," wrote Daniel Gross, a columnist for *Newsweek* and *Slate*. While acknowledging that Fannie and Freddie were part of a culture of reckless lending, he said Wall Street investment banks created a demand for subprime loans and made those loans "for the same reason they made other loans: They could get paid for making the loans, for turning them into securities and for trading them — frequently using borrowed capital."[22]

Judith A. Kennedy, president of the National Association of Affordable Housing Lenders, also challenged the notion that the CRA led to the subprime

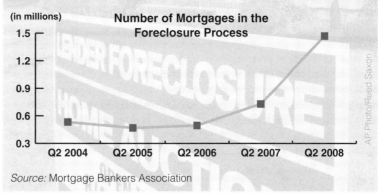

Foreclosures Rising Steadily

Nearly 1.5 million residential mortgages were in foreclosure in the second quarter of 2008, nearly twice as many as in the same period a year earlier and nearly triple the total from four years earlier.

Number of Mortgages in the Foreclosure Process

(in millions)

Source: Mortgage Bankers Association

mess. She blamed "the proliferation of unregulated mortgage originators during the housing boom, financed in part by . . . Fannie Mae and Freddie Mac."[23]

While CRA lending by banks "involves loans that help people with low or moderate incomes buy homes of high quality and lasting value," Fannie and Freddie "were determined to thwart the spirit, if not the letter, of a 1992 federal law that permitted them to take 'less than the return earned on other activities' to assist 'mortgages on housing for low- and moderate-income families,'" Kennedy asserted. "Instead of taking less of a return, Fannie Mae and Freddie Mac decided to take more of a return on affordable housing by issuing more than $400 billion in debt to finance higher-cost, higher-yield subprime mortgages, helping to fuel the subprime feeding frenzy."

Should Congress adopt tougher regulatory reforms?

Many argue that a failure of the regulatory system lies at the heart of the financial crisis.

"Wall Street is driven by two emotions, fear and greed," says John Bohn, a California Public Utilities Commission member and former head of both Moody's Investors Service, a major credit rating company, and the Export Import Bank of the United States. "When the fear of excessive risk goes away, greed does what it is expected to do. That is what happened. The whole mess is a monumental failure of regulation. One can blame all sorts of players, but it goes to the heart of the regulatory/ political process. The fox was in the henhouse and dining in splendid fashion for a long time. If one looks for one major player who is at the heart of the problem, it is the SEC, which was supposed to police how all the new capital was to be used. It failed utterly."

Indeed, in late September the inspector general of the SEC issued a blistering report concluding that the commission had failed in its mission to oversee Bear Stearns, the Wall Street investment bank that collapsed in March.[24]

In 2006 the SEC "identified precisely the types of risks that evolved into the subprime crisis in the United States less than one year later" but "did not exert influence over Bear Stearns to use this experience to add a meltdown of the subprime market to its risk scenarios," the report said.[25]

Sen. Charles Grassley, R-Iowa , called the report, plus another on the SEC's regulation of brokerage companies, "another indictment of failed leadership.

"We had it at Fannie Mae and Freddie Mac, it was throughout Wall Street and these reports document the failure of regulators at the SEC to either make its oversight program work or seek authority from Congress so that it could work."[26]

Regulation of the financial markets has been a central theme in this year's presidential race, too, with Democratic candidate Sen. Barack Obama of Illinois and Republican Sen. John McCain of Arizona trading bitter accusations.

The crisis "is a final verdict on the failed economic policies of the last eight years, strongly promoted by President Bush and supported by Sen. McCain, that essentially said that we should strip away regulation, consumer protections, let the market run wild and prosperity would rain down on all of us," Obama said at the second presidential debate on Oct. 7.[27]

McCain charged that "the match that lit the fire was Fannie Mae and Freddie Mac. . . . [T]hey're the ones that, with the encouragement of Sen. Obama and his cronies and his friends in Washington, went out and made all these risky loans, gave them to people that could never afford to pay back."[28]

One of the most contentious issues emerging from the financial collapse is whether a 1999 bill to dismantle the Depression-era Glass-Steagall Act touched off today's crisis. The 1933 law had erected a wall between commercial banking and the investment business. But the law was gradually weakened in the 1980s and '90s and finally repealed in 1999 with the Gramm-Leach-Bliley Act, passed by a Republican-controlled Congress and signed by Democratic President Bill Clinton.

Some lawmakers who fought repeal of Glass-Steagall insist they were right.

"They could have put bamboo shoots under my fingernails, and I never would have voted for it," said Rep. John L. Mica, R-Fla., one of the few Republicans to vote against repeal efforts. "The financial industry put a full-court press on and said, 'Oh, we can't compete in other financial markets, and other countries are doing it, and it's going to be the end of banking and finance as we know it.' But it has come home to roost."[29]

But many others say it is misguided to implicate Glass-Steagall's repeal in today's crisis.

"I don't see that [the repeal] had anything to do with the current crisis," Clinton told *Business Week.* What's more, he said the ability to mix banks and brokerages actually helped to blunt the effects of this year's Wall Street collapse. "Indeed, one of the things that has helped stabilize the current situation as much as it has is the purchase of Merrill Lynch by Bank of America, which was much smoother than it would have been if I hadn't signed that bill."[30]

Bader of the Competitive Enterprise Institute says, too, that while the wreckage on Wall Street has many causes, deregulation of the financial-services industry through repeal of Glass-Steagall wasn't one of them. "Diversification is a good thing," he says. "The more isolated you are economically, the more [prone] you are to go bankrupt. You have more bank collapses when you have more artificial restrictions."

Others point out that the big institutions that collapsed this year, such as Bear and Lehman, were not commercial banks that ran into problems because of risky stock transactions — the problem that Glass-Steagall was designed to address.

David Leonhardt, an economics columnist for *The New York Times*, argued that it wasn't so much that Gramm-Leach-Bliley spawned the current crisis but rather that congressional Republicans and the Clinton administration failed to create effective new financial regulations in its wake. "[O]ne act of deregulation, even a big one, and the absence of other, good regulations aren't the same thing," he wrote. "The nursemaid of the current crisis isn't so much what Washington did . . . as what it didn't do."[31]

Glossary of Key Financial Terms

Alternative-A mortgage: "Alt-A" mortgages are considered riskier than prime mortgages — which only lend to individuals with high credit scores — but less risky than subprime mortgages, which go to those with low credit. Borrowers tend to have higher credit — sometimes "A-rated" — than subprime borrowers, but the application process often involves little or no documentation of income.

Collateralized debt obligation (CDO): An unregulated, investment-grade security backed by a pool of bonds, loans and other assets. Each CDO has various levels of risk, known as tranches. The higher the risk, the higher the reward so long as the underlying investments are free from default.

Credit-default swap: An unregulated type of "insurance" in which a buyer makes a series of payments in exchange for the right to receive a payoff if a credit instrument goes into default. Many sellers of swaps for mortgage-backed securities could not pay their buyers after subprime borrowers defaulted on their mortgages.

Leverage: Borrowing large amounts of capital to complete a broad range of transactions.

Mortgage-backed security: An asset-backed security whose cash flow is determined by the principal and interest payments of a set of mortgage loans. Payments are made over the lifetime of the underlying loan.

Prime mortgage: A high-quality mortgage eligible for purchase or securitization in the secondary mortgage market. Such loans have a low default risk and are only made to borrowers with good credit.

Stated income loan: A mortgage — sometimes called a "liar loan" — where the lender does not verify the borrower's income. Mainly intended for people who have difficulty documenting their income, they are particularly easy targets for fraud.

Subprime mortgage: Carries a higher interest rate and generally goes to borrowers with a history of loan delinquency or default, bankruptcy or those with limited debt experience.

— Darrell Dela Rosa

Leonhardt said Gramm-Leach-Bliley did encourage mergers that fueled banks with capital, some of which wound up in the subprime market. But he saved his most stinging rebuke for the Bush administration and former Chairman Alan Greenspan's Federal Reserve, whose "near-religious belief in the powers of the market led them to conclude that the mere fact that a company was willing to make an investment made that investment OK."

Looking past the immediate carnage on Wall Street, the University of Missouri's Wray says the system for overseeing financial institutions needs far more funding to hire enough examiners to police increasingly complex and opaque institutions.

What's more, Wray says the highly fractured regulatory framework, made up of agencies as diverse as the Office of Thrift Supervision, the Federal Reserve and various state regulators, needs complete revamping.

"We have to make sure the regulated institutions can't play one regulator against another," he says.

Roger Leeds, director of Johns Hopkins University's Center for International Business and Public Policy, says the financial crisis magnifies a longstanding "failure of the regulatory structure and framework to keep up with the enormous changes that have been taking place in the global financial system." Although the system has been "pretty vigilant" when it comes to commercial banks, he says, "banks are not the only important financial intermediaries anymore, and everybody knows that."

Leeds says the regulatory system was designed for an era when commercial banks were the mainstays of the financial sector. However, in recent years, he says, a highly diffuse network of investment banks, insurance companies, hedge funds and other financial intermediaries have become as important as commercial banks, but they have not been subjected to the same level of regulatory oversight and supervision.

For example, rules on leverage, capital adequacy and full disclosure of so-called off-balance-sheet transactions are lacking, Leeds says. Also, he says, although the Securities and Exchange Commission has oversight responsibility for investment banks, it has been "largely absent for at least the last eight years." And, he says, the institutional framework for financial regulation is "egregiously fragmented. There are too many regulatory institutions, and coordination among them is inadequate — they don't talk to each other very effectively."

Adds Hess of Claremont McKenna College, "We did not keep up with the pace of financial innovation. We need to regulate as new products are being developed, not after we've found out which ones don't work."

BACKGROUND

First Sparks

Henry Paulson said that when he became Treasury secretary in 2006 he could see that "some kind of market turbulence" was about due but that he "didn't expect quite

this." Still, he told his colleagues, "[W]hen there's a lot of dry tinder out there, you never know what spark is gonna light the tinder."[32]

Some of the first sparks were struck early this decade. After the collapse of the technology-stock bubble in the late 1990s and the terrorist attacks of September 2001, the Federal Reserve started slashing interest rates to stimulate borrowing and spending. At the end of 2001 the discount rate — the rate the government charges commercial banks for short-term loans — was down to a paltry 1.25 percent.

Rates that low filter down to mortgages, says Ekelund, the Auburn professor emeritus. "You're going to have growth, but growth is going to be at the expense and stability of the financial system."

Meanwhile, banks, pension funds and other financial institutions in the United States and around the world

C H R O N O L O G Y

1920s-1930s *Stock market collapse and Depression reshape federal financial policy.*

1929 Stocks crash, heralding decade of economic decline.

1933 Glass-Steagall Act separates commercial and investment banking.

1938 Federal National Mortgage Association (Fannie Mae) established.

1960s-1970s *Inflation, war and other economic pressures spur policy changes.*

1968 Congress shifts Fannie Mae ownership entirely to private investors.

1970 Congress creates Freddie Mac to compete with Fannie Mae.

1980s *Recession and high interest rates batter financial companies.*

1982 "Collateralized mortgage obligations" are invented to bundle and sell mortgages to financial institutions. . . . Restrictions eased on savings and loan associations ("thrifts").

1984 Government rescues Continental Illinois National Bank and Trust.

1987 Alan Greenspan becomes Federal Reserve chairman. . . . Stock market crashes.

1989 Congress creates Resolution Trust Corp. to take over insolvent thrifts.

1990s *Financial institutions are deregulated.*

1992 Office of Federal Housing Enterprise Oversight created to supervise Fannie and Freddie.

1998 Losses on derivatives trading sink Long-Term Capital Management, but Greenspan opposes new regulations.

1999 Gramm-Leach-Bliley Act repeals Glass-Steagall Act, enabling banks to own securities firms and insurance companies.

2000s *Reckless lending policies fuel housing bubble that explodes into global crisis.*

2000 Commodity Futures Modernization Act deregulates derivatives.

2001 Federal Reserve slashes interest rates after tech-stock bubble and terrorist attacks hurt U.S. economy.

2003, 2004 Freddie Mac admits misstating earnings; accounting scandal hits Fannie Mae.

2001-2006 Housing prices in many cities double; home-equity loans boost consumer spending. . . . Subprime and other risky loans are growing share of residential mortgages.

CHRONOLOGY (CONTINUED)

2005 Congress rejects tighter regulation of Fannie, Freddie.

2007 Bear Stearns closes two big investment funds hit by subprime losses.

2008 March: Fed approves $29 billion loan to help JP Morgan Chase acquire Bear Stearns. . . . July 30: President Bush signs legislation authorizing Treasury to purchase Fannie, Freddie common stock and debt. . . . Sept. 7: U.S. seizes Fannie, Freddie. . . . Sept. 15: Lehman Brothers files for bankruptcy; Merrill Lynch agrees to sale to Bank of America. . . . Sept. 16: Fed bails out American International Group. . . . Sept. 18: Fed Chairman Henry Paulson Jr. announces $700 billion plan to buy banks' "toxic" debt. . . . Sept. 25: Washington Mutual collapse is biggest bank failure in history. . . . Sept. 29: House rejects bailout plan; negotiations resume. . . . Oct. 1: Senate passes revised bailout; House follows on Oct. 3, and Bush signs bill. . . . Oct. 10: Dow Jones Industrial Average ends worst week ever. . . . Oct. 13: Dow surges 936 points after European and U.S. leaders agree to support their financial systems. . . . Oct. 14: Treasury announces $250 billion plan to recapitalize U.S. banks. . . . Oct. 23: Government promises to provide $2.5 trillion to protect money market deposits and many loans. . . . Nov. 15: International meeting on economy called for in Washington by President Bush.

2008

Nov. 24 Bush administration decides to inject Citigroup Inc. with another $20 billion in Troubled Asset Relief Program (TARP) money and guarantees up to $306 billion of the company's toxic mortgage assets.

Dec. 1 National Bureau of Economic Research announces that the U.S. has been in a recession since December 2007.

Dec. 11 Bernard Madoff, 71, legendary Wall Street trader, is arrested after admitting to running a $50 billion Ponzi scheme. He is later sentenced to 150 years in prison.

Dec. 13 Bush administration deploys $13.4 billion to bail out General Motors and Chrysler.

2009

Jan. 16 U.S. Senate, at the request of then-President-elect Barack Obama, votes to release the second half of the $700 billion TARP money.

Feb. 11 Treasury Secretary Timothy Geithner unveils Obama administration's revised bank bailout and economic rescue package.

Feb.18 Administration announces $50 billion program designed to stem the foreclosure crisis.

March 3 Fed and Treasury announce the creation of the Term Asset-Backed Securities Loan Facility, a program aimed at thawing the frozen lending market.

May 7 Federal Reserve releases the results of the "stress tests" conducted on the 19 largest U.S. banks. The results of the tests, which were roundly criticized, help calm the markets as investors determine the banks are not as bad off as originally thought.

June 17 Administration releases its proposal to overhaul the financial regulatory system. The "White Paper" would eventually be followed by proposed legislative text that would serve as the basis for congressional efforts.

Aug. 25 President Obama announces his nomination of Ben Bernanke for a second term as Federal Reserve chairman.

Dec. 2 Bank of America announces that it will return all of its $45 billion in federal bailout money. Citigroup follows less than two weeks later.

Dec. 11 House passes its bill to overhaul the financial regulatory system.

2010

Jan. 21 Administration announces the "Volcker Rule" — named for former Federal Reserve Chairman Paul Volcker — a legislative proposal designed to bar commercial banks from trading on their own accounts.

February 1 Fed allows five of its primary crisis programs to expire.

Feb. 23 Federal Deposit Insurance Corp. announces that 702 banks are on its "problem" list. FDIC Chairman Sheila Bair tells reporters that she expects an uptick in bank failures from the 2009 level of 140.

March 23 Senate Banking Committee approves, along party lines, legislation proposed by Chairman Christopher Dodd, D-Conn., to overhaul U.S. financial regulations.

April 27 Goldman Sachs executives and traders are brought before the Senate Permanent Subcommittee on Investigations for a highly publicized hearing on their role during the financial crisis. Subcommittee also explores the failures of credit rating agencies and failed mortgage lenders.

April 28 Senate Republicans allow debate on a financial overhaul bill to begin on the Senate floor.

May 6 U.S. stock market suffers worst drop in the Dow Jones Industrial Average since 1987; electronic malfunctions and fears of European default are blamed.

Global Financial Markets Face Meltdown

British Prime Minister Brown plays key rescue role.

The global banking and credit crisis bears a distinct "Made in America" tag, in the eyes of many foreign leaders and economists.

Denunciations by Russian Prime Minister Vladimir Putin were no surprise. As plunging prices in October forced Russia's two principal stock markets to shut down, he declared, "Trust in the United States as the leader of the free world and the free economy and confidence in Wall Street as the center of that trust has been damaged, I believe, forever. There will be no return to the previous situation."[1]

Friends of the United States were almost as critical. "The American banking system is going to have to reinvent itself," said Peter Mandelson of Britain, the European Union's trade commissioner. "It's going to be consolidated, it's going to operate in a different way, it's going to have to operate with more responsibility, less risk," as October's perilous month began.[2]

But as U.S. and European banks approached cardiac arrest on Oct. 10 after a devastating week of stock market losses, America-bashing took a back seat to collaboration.

Global financial markets were "on the brink of systemic meltdown," warned Dominique Strauss-Kahn, managing director of the International Monetary Fund (IMF).[3] "The days of finger-pointing and schadenfreude are over, former Federal Reserve Chairman Paul Volcker commented in *The Wall Street Journal*.[4]

French Finance Minister Christine Lagarde told the Council on Foreign Relations, "I'm not in the blame game, and it is pointless to do so. The first lesson to be learned is humility."[5]

Over the weekend, the Federal Reserve and European central banks engineered a joint reduction in interest rates and an agreement to pour more funds into endangered banks. Finance ministers from the six largest economies met in Washington with President George W. Bush and pledged cooperation.

The decisive move, however, was taken singly by British Prime Minister Gordon Brown's government. On Oct. 13 it bought majority control of the Royal Bank of Scotland and 40 percent stakes in HBOS, the holding company that owns the Scottish Bank and Lloyds/TSB for £50 billion ($81 billion).[6]

Britain's sudden move toward bank nationalization trumped the Bush administration's strategy, developed by Treasury Secretary Henry M. Paulson Jr., which focused on acquiring bad bank debt rather than infusing banks with much-needed cash, or liquidity — in effect, a partial federal takeover.

Britain was followed by France, Germany and Spain, all making similar investments in their nation's banks in return for shares of the financial institutions, and the United States was obliged to follow, analysts said. Otherwise, it risked a flight of investment capital from the United States toward European banks with seemingly greater government protection. Luxembourg, the Netherlands and Iceland have also intervened with governmental rescues of endangered banks.[7]

But Europe's share of the $4 trillion in new debt issued by major nations in the crisis will be harder to bear because their levels of taxation are relatively higher than in the United States, says David Smick, publisher of *The International Economy* quarterly. "The bottom line is that the Europeans have reason to be angry with the United States. The credit crisis has placed them in a fiscal stranglehold," Smick said in a statement.

On Oct. 13, Paulson moved the United States in line, announcing a $250 billion federal injection into the banking system by acquiring shares of Citigroup, Bank of America, Wells Fargo, Goldman Sachs, JP Morgan Chase and smaller banks and promising to make new loan guarantees, in order to unfreeze bank lending.

"The Europeans not only provided a blueprint but forced our hand," Harvard University Professor Kenneth S. Rogoff told *The New York Times*.[8]

"Today's actions are not what we ever wanted to do," Paulson acknowledged, "but today's actions are what we must do to restore confidence to our financial system."[9]

Stock markets around the world responded initially to the weekend's actions with a global exhale of relief. The Dow Jones Industrial Average in the United States soared a record 936 points on Oct. 13, and other stock markets in

Europe and Asia registered double-digit gains. But the euphoria has not lasted.

Whatever the outcome of the October intervention, many world leaders and financial experts are declaring that the crisis has ended the 30-year domination of international economic policy by the laissez-faire, pro-market philosophies championed by the United States.

"The financial crisis continues to make victims," wrote Paul De Grauwe, an economics professor at Belgium's University of Leuven.[10] They include the U.S.-led belief in the supremacy of markets and its corollary hostility toward regulation, he said. "Helped by the missionary zeal of successive American administrations and pushed by international financial institutions, country after country freed their financial markets from pernicious government controls, hoping to share in these economic wonders. The credit crisis has destroyed the idea."

"People around the world once admired us for our economy, and we told them if you wanted to be like us, here's what you have to do — hand over power to the market," said Nobel Prize-winning U.S. economist Joseph Stiglitz. "The point now is that no one has respect for that kind of model anymore, given this crisis. And, of course, it raises questions about our credibility. Everyone feels they are suffering now because of us."[11]

French President Nicolas Sarkozy said on Sept. 25 that the crisis marked "the end of a world that was built on the fall of the Berlin Wall and the end of the Cold War — a big dream of liberty and prosperity." He called for "new balance" between the market and government regulation, adding, "The idea that markets are always right was a mad idea."[12]

Hindsight may not yield all the answers in a new global economy that faces several years or more of recession or stagnant growth, according to the IMF. "Many advanced economies are close to or are moving into recession; growth in emerging economies also is weakening," said IMF First Deputy Managing Director John Lipsky.[13]

Economist Dennis Snower, president of Germany's Kiel Institute, argues that the crisis signals a move away from the U.S. dollar as the world's dominant currency, a role it has held since the end of World War II.[14] The staggering initial costs of the U.S. rescue plan may drive America's 2009 federal deficit above $775 billion, estimates University of Wisconsin economist Menzie Chinn, or more than quadruple the amount in fiscal 2007.[15] That will make the U.S. even more dependent upon foreigners — and foreign central

banks in particular — to purchase enough U.S. Treasury bonds and notes to balance the budget.

The critical issue is whether wealthy and developing nations have learned the necessity of working together, said the IMF's Strauss-Kahn. "All kinds of cooperation have to be commended. All lonely acts have to be avoided, if not condemned."[16]

— Peter Behr

[1] Quoted in "US image damaged forever over economy woes," The Associated Press, Oct. 9, 2008.

[2] Peter Wilson, "Europe wants US Power shift," *The Australian,* Oct. 1, 2008, p. 36.

[3] Edmund Conway, "IMF warns of world financial system 'meltdown,' " *The Telegraph,* Oct. 12, 2008.

[4] Paul Volcker, "We Have the Tools to Manage the Crisis; Now we need the leadership to use them," *The Wall Street Journal,* Oct. 10, 2008, http://online.wsj.com/article/SB122360251805321773.html.

[5] Harry Dunphy, "French minister says no one to blame for crisis," The Associated Press, Oct. 10, 2008.

[6] "European stocks rally on G7 plan," "ABC Premium News" (Australia), Oct. 13, 2008.

[7] Nelson D. Schwartz, "Nations Move on Plans to Shore Up Banks," *The New York Times,* Oct. 14, 2008.

[8] Mark Landler, "U.S. Investing $250 billion to Bolster Banks," *The New York Times,* Oct. 14, 2008.

[9] Statement by Treasury Secretary Henry M. Paulson Jr., Oct. 14, 2008, www.ustreas.gov/press/releases/hp1205.htm.

[10] Paul De Grauwe, "Cherished myths have fallen victim to economic reality," *CEPS Commentary,* Centre for European Policy Studies, July 24, 2008.

[11] Anthony Faiola, "The End of American Capitalism?" *The Washington Post,* Oct. 10, 2008, p. A1.

[12] Peter Gumbel, "The Meltdown Goes Global," *Time,* Oct. 20, 2008, p. 32.

[13] John Lipsky, "Navigating the Storm," *The Washington Post,* Oct. 10, 2008, p. A19.

[14] Gumbel, *op. cit.*, and "The Dollar Issue," *The International Economy,* spring 2008, pp. 22-37, www.international-economy.com/Spring2008 archive.htm. For background, see Peter Behr, "The Troubled Dollar," *CQ Global Researcher,* October 2008, pp. 271-294.

[15] Menzie Chinn, "The Budget Deficit . . . and Macro Policies Going Forward," *Econbrowser,* Oct. 12, 2008, www.econbrowser.com/archives/2008/10/the_budget_defi.html.

[16] Jim Puzzanghera and Maura Reynolds, "Financial Crisis: In Fear's Grip; Calls grow for global strategy; No country can solve the credit crisis alone, an IMF official says," *Los Angeles Times,* Oct. 10, 2008.

were flush with trillions of dollars in assets. Indeed, according to International Monetary Fund economist Ceyla Pazarbasioglu, the global pool of capital amounts to an astonishing $70 trillion — nearly twice the amount available worldwide in 2000.[33]

Trillions of dollars were flooding into the United States from burgeoning markets in the Middle East, China (which joined the World Trade Organization in 2001) and elsewhere. With money sloshing through the U.S. and global economy and mortgage rates at lows not seen since the 1960s, home buyers stampeded into the market. As they did, institutional investors here and abroad — looking for profitable ways to invest — piled into mortgage-backed securities.

Home buyers included many well-qualified borrowers looking for owner-occupied homes, but also speculators and people with little means to sustain a monthly mortgage payment. Lenders were happy to accommodate them all — even borrowers with weak credit or other financial obstacles. In one example cited by *The Washington Post*, a mortgage broker told of securing a $500,000 loan for a $35,000-a-year McDonald's employee.[34]

Soaring Home Prices

Soaring home prices kept this fire burning. In many major cities, prices more than doubled between 2000 and 2006, according to the S&P/Case-Shiller Home Price Indices. In hot markets like Los Angeles and Miami they shot up even more.

As long as prices were climbing, borrowers, lenders and mortgage investors felt safe. They figured homeowners could always refinance, based on homes' growing market value, or sell at a profit. The risks of default seemed low. Some lenders were making loans that exceeded a house's value, figuring home prices would rise at least enough to cover balloon payments that would come due in a few years.

But such assumptions were wrong. Builders had rapidly expanded the supply of available homes and condos, outstripping demand. Meanwhile, the economy was slowing, interest rates were edging higher and the hot real estate market had cooled. Soon, home prices were flattening, falling or in some places plummeting. In Boston and San Diego, the bubble began deflating in late 2005. By 2007 it was losing air everywhere, and fast.

The subprime crisis began gathering strength in early 2007 and then accelerated. The share of loans that entered the foreclosure process rose from 0.38 percent in the second quarter of 2005 to more than double that rate in the third quarter of 2007, according to the Mortgage Bankers Association (MBA). It reached 1.08 percent in the second quarter of this year, according to the MBA's latest data. That means foreclosures began on more than one of every 100 loans in that quarter — a figure that represents billions of dollars in losses for lenders and investors.

With losses mounting, financial institutions such as UBS, Citigroup, Merrill Lynch and JP Morgan Chase took massive mortgage-related write-downs.

Then this past March came an event that would shake Wall Street to its foundation. The investment bank Bear Stearns, founded before the Great Depression, collapsed under the weight of subprime mortgage investments largely made with borrowed money. Bear sold for a mere $10 per share to JP Morgan Chase in a deal that included as much as $29 billion in federal support. A year earlier, Bear Stearns' shares had traded for $170 apiece.[35]

"This is like waking up in summer with snow on the ground," Ron Geffner, a former Securities and Exchange Commission enforcement lawyer, told *The New York Times.*[36]

Takeover of Fannie, Freddie

As stunning as Bear's collapse was, it was not as shocking as the wholesale reordering of the Wall Street terrain that would follow.

In September came the government's seizure of Fannie Mae and Freddie Mac after weeks of speculation that the mortgage behemoths could fail — with explosive consequences for the already teetering housing market.

Then, in rapid succession, came more bad news: On Sept. 15, real estate-related losses brought down Lehman Brothers, a Wall Street icon founded before the Civil War. The same day, the nation's biggest brokerage, Merrill Lynch, also crippled by mortgage investments, rushed into the embrace of Bank of America.

On Sept. 16 the Federal Reserve announced it was taking control of the global insurer American International Group. AIG's main insurance business was profitable; its troubles stemmed from credit-default swaps, which AIG sold to other institutions to guarantee their risky mortgage investments against default.

New Rescue Plan Dwarfs Earlier Bailouts

Aid recipients ranged from railroads to cities.

The Bush administration's recent $1 trillion package to rescue the nation's banks, financial markets and largest insurer is worth more than the total of eight major bailouts undertaken by the federal government since 1970. The second-largest bailout occurred in 1989, when President George W. Bush's father, President George H. W. Bush, asked for about $160 billion to finance the breakup of the nation's troubled savings and loans.

During the Great Depression, the government also played a key role in trying to resuscitate the economy, launching programs ranging from the Works Progress Administration and Social Security to Fannie Mae.

Franklin D. Roosevelt's New Deal created the Emergency Banking Act, which helped reopen banks under the Treasury's supervision, making loans available when necessary. The sweeping New Deal also created the Farm Security Administration, Resettlement Administration, Rural Electrification Administration and Tennessee Valley Authority to help those living in severe poverty.

In addition to program assistance, the government also implemented numerous reforms designed to prevent future crises, such as the Federal Deposit Insurance Corporation (FDIC), the Economy Act, which cut the salaries of federal employees in order to balance the budget, and the National Industrial Recovery Act, which allowed blue-collar workers the right to collective bargaining.

The biggest government bailouts since 1970 were:

- **Penn Central Railroad ($676.3 million)** — Arguing that it provided crucial national defense and transportation services, the big railroad appealed to the Federal Reserve for aid in 1970 as it teetered on the verge of bankruptcy. President Richard M. Nixon and the Fed asked Congress for financial assistance, but lawmakers refused. The railroad declared bankruptcy in June, freeing it from its debts. To counteract the impact on the economy of the unpaid debts, the Fed agreed to provide commercial banks with $676.3 million to allow them to meet customers' credit needs.
- **Lockheed Corp. ($250 million)** — In August 1971 Congress passed the Emergency Loan Guarantee Act, which enabled the government to provide funds for any major business in crisis but was primarily used to bail out Lockheed, a struggling aircraft manufacturer. The company received $250 million based on concerns its failure would create significant job losses

in California, contribute to a decline in GNP and harm national defense.

- **Franklin National Bank ($1.75 billion)** — After the Long Island bank posted an operating loss of $63.6 million in 1974, the Fed loaned it $1.75 billion.
- **New York City ($2.3 billion)** — With the city in crisis throughout the 1970s, President Gerald R. Ford signed the New York City Seasonal Financing Act, which authorized $2.3 billion in loans.
- **Chrysler Corp. ($1.5 billion)** — The nation's third-largest automaker asked the government for aid after losing $1.1 billion in 1979. The Chrysler Loan Guarantee Act provided $1.5 billion in loans to help rescue Chrysler from insolvency; U.S. and foreign banks matched that amount.
- **Continental Illinois National Bank and Trust Company ($4.5 billion)** — The bank suffered significant losses in 1984 after purchasing $1 billion in energy loans from the failing Penn Square Bank of Oklahoma. The Fed and FDIC devised a $4.5 billion plan to rescue the bank, which included replacing its top executives.
- **Savings and Loan Associations ($160.1 billion)** — Following the widespread failure of 747 savings and loan institutions, or "thrifts," Congress passed the Financial Institutions Reform Recovery and Enforcement Act to finance their dissolution.
- **Airline Industry ($15 billion)** — The Air Transportation Safety and Stabilization Act was signed into law by President George W. Bush to compensate airlines for the mandatory grounding of aircraft after the Sept. 11 terrorist attacks. The act released $5 billion in compensation along with more than $10 billion in loan guarantees or other credit instruments.
- **Current Financial Crisis ($1 trillion)** — In the fallout from a subprime mortgage meltdown and subsequent liquidity crisis, the federal government lent JP Morgan Chase up to $29 billion to help it acquire rival investment bank Bear Stearns; seized Fannie Mae and Freddie Mac after pumping $200 billion into the two mortgage giants; took over the nation's largest insurer, American International Group, after providing it with $123 billion to avoid a liquidity crisis; authorized the Treasury Department to spend up to $700 billion to purchase "toxic" mortgage-backed securities from Wall Street and invest in the nation's banks to unlock a credit freeze.

— Darrell Dela Rosa

On Sept. 25 Washington Mutual collapsed and was sold by federal regulators to JP Morgan Chase. In a bankruptcy filing, a holding company for the 119-year-old firm listed more than $8 billion in debt, according to Bloomberg.com.[37]

Citing data from *Inside Mortgage Finance*, an industry newsletter, Bloomberg said WaMu was the second-biggest provider of so-called payment-option adjustable-rate mortgages, with $54 billion in WaMu's portfolio in the first quarter. Such instruments allow borrowers to miss part of their payment and add that amount to their loan's principal — meaning borrowers could owe more than their house is worth when home prices fall.

Soon after Washington Mutual's demise, Wachovia, one of the nation's largest commercial banks, went up for sale. Wachovia had recently purchased a major seller of subprime loans. In fact, Bloomberg said, Wachovia eclipsed WaMu in payment-option adjustable loans.[38]

Meanwhile, alarm was spreading through Washington that a massive credit crisis could topple the entire U.S. and global economies. On Sept. 16, the Reserve Primary Fund, a $65 billion money-market fund — a kind of savings vehicle long viewed as rock-solid — said it had "broken the buck" — its customers' accounts had fallen to 97 cents on the dollar because some investments had dropped in value.[39]

Startled government officials feared that customers would rush to cash in their money-market accounts, signaling a broad-scale financial panic. And if money funds — a key source of business credit — began shrinking, the chain reaction would shake the entire economy.

Rescue Plan

With chaos engulfing Wall Street and Washington, Fed Chairman Bernanke and Treasury Secretary Paulson hastily called a meeting on Capitol Hill on the evening of Sept. 18, where they put forth the outline of the $700 billion rescue plan. "If we don't do this," Bernanke reportedly said, "we may not have an economy on Monday."[40]

A week later, as congressional leaders sparred over details of a bailout, President Bush was even more blunt about the economy's prospects. "If money isn't loosened up," he warned, "this sucker could go down."[41]

Passage of the rescue plan on Oct. 3 did little — at least initially — to control what had become a global calamity. Over eight days in early October the Dow plunged 22 percent, posting the worst week in its 112-year history.[42] Overseas markets also sank. On the weekend of October 12, world leaders, meeting in Washington and elsewhere, scrambled to find a way to solve the crisis.

A plan to inject billions of dollars of capital into banks here and abroad seemed to restore some degree of confidence, and stocks began to recover some of their losses, but in mid-October the Dow Jones Industrial Average was roughly 40 percent below its high a year earlier.

Fears of a prolonged recession here and abroad rivaled concern over the subprime crisis.

As officials continued to seek solutions, they also were trying to untangle what led to the worst economic calamity since the Great Depression.

Lawrence White, an economics professor at New York University, says that investment banks and other financial firms ran into deep trouble when the real estate market declined because they had borrowed heavily to cash in on the mortgage boom. Some investment banks had borrowing levels — or leverage ratios — as much as 30 times their equity.

Institutions that had borrowed heavily and had a thin capital cushion for safety were vulnerable to even a small rise in defaults, White said.

When an institution is operating on a high leverage ratio, all it takes is a small decline in the value of an institution's assets to make creditors nervous about getting repaid, White says. And when those creditors panic, they pull back on lending, starting a chain reaction that ripples through the entire economy.

Leveraging — borrowing massive amounts of capital in order to complete a broad range of financial transactions — is commonplace on Wall Street. But it can turn deadly when the underlying assets that are used as collateral plummet in value, forcing borrowers to prematurely liquidate their investment or try to borrow more funds on far more onerous terms. Leverage "is how you make the most money in good times, and how you lose the most in bad times," says Johns Hopkins University's Leeds.

Leeds points, for example, to the spectacular failure in 1998 of the giant hedge fund Long-Term Capital Management. It borrowed heavily to invest in sophisticated, seemingly sound financial instruments. When Russia suddenly defaulted on its short-term debt obligations — just a year after an Asian financial crisis — global investors fled to higher-quality investments that rendered Long-Term Capital's complex risk-management models useless. Within weeks the hedge fund lost more than $4 billion and collapsed, causing the Federal Reserve to intervene to avert a larger systemic crisis.

That collapse was a miniature version of today's crisis, many say. Yet Congress and federal regulators failed to grasp its lesson, Leeds says. "There was lots of talk about more tightening of disclosure, placing limits on leverage and so forth, and nothing happened," he says.

Besides excessive leverage, experts say another catalyst for today's crisis is "securitization," or the packaging by banks of illiquid debt obligations they are owed and creating tradable securities that are then sold to investors.

Bankers have been securitizing mortgages, student loans and credit card debt for decades, to great benefit. Lenders are able to move the loans off their balance sheets, freeing up capital so they can make more loans. And because investors are buying into a diversified pool of risk, the chances of getting stung by defaults are reduced.

But securitization also creates perverse incentives for lenders to take unwise risks. "Because the assets — mortgages for example — are no longer long-term commitments of the bank, there is less incentive to conduct rigorous due diligence on the borrower's creditworthiness," says Leeds. "Bankers are more willing to take these risks, knowing they are not going to be holding that asset for 20 or 30 years." In the current crisis, however, institutions haven't been able to sell many of those securitized assets because the market has been frozen.

The sale of mortgages packaged as collateralized debt obligations (CDOs) to Wall Street investment banks, pension and hedge funds, insurance companies and other investors mushroomed as the housing industry boomed. Lenders "were making these loans hand over fist without worrying very much about the long-term consequences because the risk wasn't going to be on their balance sheet — or at least that's what they thought," says Leeds. And "regulators were complicit by not imposing stricter disclosure requirements."

But some experts warned that CDOs suffered from a lack of transparency. "The danger in these products is that in changing hands so many times, no one knows their true makeup, and thus who is holding the risk,"

said Joshua Rosner, a managing director at Graham Fisher & Company, a New York research firm."[43]

Institutional investors borrowed heavily to buy CDOs, holding them in their own portfolios or reselling them to other investors. To hedge against losses, investors bought arcane, unregulated insurance contracts called credit-default swaps, in which buyers of swaps pay a premium to a "counterparty" that agrees to pay off a loan if the original borrower defaults. But sellers of swaps weren't required to hold cash reserves against the swaps, and when payments to buyers of the insurance-like instruments became necessary, they couldn't always pay off.

The market for credit-default swaps and other "credit derivatives" had a value of $55 trillion at mid-year, according to the International Swaps and Derivatives Association.[44] But credit swaps are unregulated, and critics have pointed to them as a prime culprit in the financial crisis.

Last month SEC Chairman Christopher Cox urged Congress to regulate the swaps, saying the market was "ripe for fraud and manipulation."[45] *The New York Times* noted that the government bailed out American International Group primarily because AIG was a counterparty to large amounts of swaps with global financial institutions.[46]

Helping to fuel the frenzy for collateralized debt obligations backed by subprime loans were big credit agencies that rate long-term debt. Even though CDOs were packed with potentially bad loans, the agencies often gave those securities high marks.

This summer, after a 10-month investigation, the SEC said in a scathing report that the major rating firms, Moody's Investor Services, Standard & Poor's Ratings Services and Fitch Ratings, had stumbled in their duty to protect investors.

"We've uncovered serious shortcomings at these firms, including a lack of disclosure to investors and the public, a lack of policies and procedures to manage the rating process and insufficient attention to conflicts of interest," said Cox. "When the firms didn't have enough staff to do the job right, they often cut corners."[47]

In one case, an analyst at a credit-ratings firm e-mailed a colleague that the firm's model didn't capture "half" of a certain deal's risk, but that "it could be structured by cows and we would rate it." In another case, a manager said the rating agencies were creating an "even bigger monster — the CDO market. Let's hope we are all wealthy and retired by the time this house of cards falters."[48]

Cox said the "good news" was that the credit-rating agencies' problems were "being fixed in real time." But not everyone agreed. "There was an utter failure and breakdown of control in these companies, and the SEC failed to catch any of it," said Rosner of Graham Fisher. "I'm certain there's a hell of a lot more incriminating e-mails. The SEC is glossing it over."[49]

CURRENT SITUATION

Red Ink

As extreme volatility continues to rock global markets, financial institutions are swimming in red ink.

This October Citigroup, a global financial company with interests ranging from investment banking to credit cards, reported a $2.8 billion third-quarter loss, the fourth period in a row it has had write-downs on investments and bigger consumer-loan losses.[50]

The New York Times noted that "every major region of the world where Citigroup operates, with the exception of the one anchored by the Middle East, reported a decline in revenue."[51]

Many eyes are on the United States and the prospects that its bailout plan will help reverse the steep economic decline that has spread worldwide. That may not be clear for a while, though. Earlier this month, federal officials, as well as investors and businesses, were still waiting to see how well the infusion of capital into banks would work.

Many banks remain leery of lending, and some banks are hanging on to their cash to shield themselves against future losses from credit-card defaults. Citing the latest Federal Reserve figures, *The Washington Post* said the rate of credit-card loans going bad rose 54 percent in the second quarter of this year from the same period in 2007.[52]

Meanwhile, it remains to be seen how deep a recession the U.S. economy is facing, but some government officials, including Fed Chairman Bernanke, are pushing for a new stimulus package to head off a steep decline.

"With the economy likely to be weak for several quarters, and with some risk of a protracted slowdown, consideration of a fiscal package by Congress at this juncture seems appropriate," Bernanke told the House Budget Committee on Oct. 20.[53]

It also remains to be seen how much the government might pay under the bailout plan for toxic mortgage debt on the books of lenders.

Valuing the bad debt is perhaps the trickiest part of the bailout effort. If the government pays too much, taxpayers will lose. If it doesn't pay enough, the bailout might not help banks enough or unthaw frozen credit markets. And because confidence in the credit markets and the economy has been at rock-bottom, some loans may be perceived as worthless even though borrowers are making scheduled payments and may continue to do so.

Moreover, many bad loans have been sliced up and packaged into complex securities along with solid loans, which makes it difficult to arrive at accurate valuations.

Financial experts continue to propose various ideas for putting the rescue plan into action. Many economists applauded Paulson's move to use $250 billion of the bailout money to buy equity in the banks, and some even recommended he spend the entire $700 billion on buying equity stakes in banks instead of toxic mortgage assets.

"I hope they won't buy any bad loans, and that they will keep this $700 billion to recapitalize the banking industry," said William Isaac, who chaired the FDIC during President Ronald Reagan's first term. For every dollar of equity the government buys, he said, banks can lend $10. "If all they do is buy bad loans, you don't get leverage out of that. If you buy $250 billion of capital, you increase bank lending capacity by $2.5 trillion."[54]

Earlier this month, for example, *The Wall Street Journal* reported that Treasury officials were mulling selling bundles of bad debt to partnerships owned jointly by investors and the government as opposed to selling debt directly to the private sector. *The Journal* noted that similar transactions were executed by the Resolution Trust Corp. during the savings and loan crisis of the late 1980s and early '90s, the last big real-estate bust.[55]

The S&L debacle cost taxpayers and the thrift industry more than $150 billion.[56]

Fate of Fannie, Freddie

In the longer term, policy makers must decide what to do about Fannie Mae and Freddie Mac, the quasi-government companies placed in federal conservatorship last month.

Should Fannie Mae and Freddie Mac be privatized?

YES
Lawrence J. White
Professor of Economics, Stern School of Business, New York University; former member, Federal Home Loan Bank Board

Written for *CQ Researcher*, September 2008

During the current market anxiety, the two mortgage giants, Fannie Mae and Freddie Mac, should remain as is: nationalized. But their proper place in the longer run is clear: They should be truly privatized.

Recall their previous status: They were nominally "normal" corporations, with shares traded on the New York Stock Exchange. But they had so many special features — each was a creature of federal legislation, which spelled out special privileges and obligations for the two companies — that they were "government-sponsored enterprises."

The financial markets treated their debt as special, so that they were able to borrow at rates about 0.40 percent lower than their stand-alone finances would have justified. In turn, the interest rates on the "conforming" mortgages that they could buy — to securitize and resell, or to hold — were about 0.25 percent lower than otherwise.

The political popularity of any arrangement that made mortgages cheaper but did not represent a federal budgetary outlay was understandable. Whether this represented good public policy is questionable.

In any event, the hybrid private/public nature of the two companies was unsustainable. They experienced conflicting pressures to earn good returns for their shareholders and also to support affordable housing. Low capital levels certainly allowed high returns but also meant that they couldn't weather the mortgage debacle that has engulfed the U.S. economy.

For the future, they should be fully privatized, with no special ties to government. Their existing organizations should remain intact, since they were relatively good — despite some lapses — at their secondary mortgage market operations.

All future debt incurred by Fannie and Freddie should be explicitly non-guaranteed. Cautious lenders will insist that they maintain higher capital levels and/or pay higher interest rates, and they will shrink relative to their recent sizes. That is all to the good.

Simultaneously, the valuable social function of encouraging low- and moderate-income families to become homeowners should be under the aegis of government, with substantial and transparent on-budget appropriations. That is good public policy, and good government.

Let the private sector do what it does best. Let the government perform the appropriate social function. Mixing the two was toxic. Let's not make that mistake again.

NO
Dean Baker
Co-director, Center for Economic and Policy Research

Written for *CQ Researcher*, September 2008

Fannie Mae was set up by the Roosevelt administration 70 years ago to create a national mortgage market and thereby make home ownership more affordable. By all accounts, Fannie Mae and its twin, Freddie Mac, accomplished this goal. They have made mortgage loans cheaper and more widely available to tens of millions of homeowners.

These institutions failed to recognize the largest housing bubble in the history of the world. This failure left them exposed to the bubble's collapse and eventually threw them into the hands of the government. The question is whether it now makes sense to either privatize them outright or return them to their public/private status.

Privatization would end the role that these institutions played in promoting access to mortgage credit. Without Fannie and Freddie, we could expect to see a jump in mortgage interest rates nationwide. In the absence of the national market created by Fannie and Freddie there would be pockets with especially high interest rates. The private sector has no interest in assuring the general availability of mortgages.

Of course, we could allow private banks to issue mortgage-backed securities with a government guarantee, but unless we are anxious to see another financial collapse, this would not be a wise route to follow. It would be crazy to trust banks to act responsibly, and our current regulatory system is certainly not sufficient to rein in the wizards of Wall Street.

The serious question, then, is what the public could possibly gain by returning to the mixed public/private system. There seems little obvious gain from adding the private component to these institutions. Ordinarily, we look to the private sector because it is more innovative, and private entrepreneurs are more willing to take risk.

This is a case where innovation and risk-taking are not wanted. The basic task should be very mundane — buying up standard mortgages and packaging them into securities. Risk-taking is what got Fannie and Freddie into trouble. In fact, Fannie and Freddie's economists might have been more open to those of us warning about the housing bubble if their companies were not making so much money on loans to bubble-inflated markets.

In addition to risk, the private side adds costs: The dividends and high executive compensation in private financial companies are effectively a tax on homeowners.

In short, by accident, we ended up in a better place with Fannie and Freddie. Keep them public.

The decision will turn on the views of Congress and, ultimately, the next president.

Critics, including Sen. McCain and other key congressional conservatives, argue that the government has no business putting taxpayers at risk to maintain Fannie and Freddie. But advocates of Fannie and Freddie, including Massachusetts Rep. Frank of the House Financial Services Committee, contend their affordable-housing mission is too important to jeopardize.

In coming months, policy makers will face three broad choices of what to do with Fannie and Freddie:

- Keep them as government-sponsored entities;
- Nationalize them, with the federal government assuming the risks of mortgage finance but also potentially reaping the profits; or
- "Privatize" them by breaking them up into smaller chunks, cutting off their government support and turning them loose to compete in the open market.

Claremont McKenna College's Hess favors privatization. But at a minimum, he says, the government should require Fannie and Freddie to maintain a larger capital cushion to cover mortgage defaults and to shun all but high-quality mortgages. In addition, he says policy makers should reduce Fannie and Freddie's dominance of the loan-purchase and loan-guarantee business by encouraging more competition from commercial companies.

"There's always a public responsibility for housing," but if the federal government wants to subsidize home ownership, it "should put that explicitly on its books and not create institutions with the potential for unlimited liability for the federal government," Hess says.

Sheila Crowley, president of the National Low-Income Housing Coalition, says she has worried about the potential for the government's seizure of Fannie and Freddie to curtail their contributions to low-income housing programs and ultimately force Fannie and Freddie into the private sector, ending their public affordable-housing mission. Still, Crowley is "optimistic that when the dust settles after the reworking of the housing finance system promised by the next Congress, none of those things will have come about."

Crowley also argues that Fannie and Freddie have helped temper the effects of the credit crisis by buying mortgages that private investors haven't wanted to touch.

"In this time of financial turmoil, the percentage of all mortgages bought by Fannie and Freddie has skyrocketed because the private sector backed out," she argues. "If you want stability, you need to have some way to temper the erratic nature of the market."

Placing Blame

As policy makers continue to plot a course for economic recovery, they will have to decide who to hold accountable for the turmoil. Earlier this month *The Washington Post* reported that Justice Department officials promised to untangle the credit-default swaps and other arcane transactions that helped spark the crisis but would "generally seek criminal charges against individual brokers and bankers, rather than companies themselves."[57]

"Mindful of the fallout from the last wave of business fraud cases six years ago, authorities are leaning against seeking indictments of major banks and insurers that may have inflated the value of their mortgage-related investments," said *The Post*. "Instead, prosecutors will look for such garden-variety crimes as false statements and insider trading by executives who tried to disguise financial problems or pad their wallets."

That may be of little solace to retirees who have seen their savings sharply eroded because of the crisis.[58]

Over the past 15 months, declines in the stock market have erased some $2 trillion in Americans' retirement savings, the Congressional Budget Office's Orszag told lawmakers early this month.[59]

"Americans were counting on much of this wealth for their retirement," said committee Chairman Rep. George Miller, D-Calif. "Now it is gone — as is their ability to adequately fund their retirement.... Retirement and financial experts now predict that retirees and older workers who rely on financial investments for retirement income may suffer more than any portion of the American population in the coming years."[60]

And those looking toward retirement aren't the only ones facing trouble.

The decline in home prices has left roughly 12 million households — nearly one in six — owing more on their mortgages than their homes are worth, increasing the chances of more defaults, *The Wall Street Journal* reported.[61]

Among those who bought their homes within the past five years, 29 percent owe more than the homes are worth,

The Journal reported, citing an estimate by Zillow.com, a real-estate Web site.

Said Mark Zandi, Economy.com's chief economist: "It is very possible that there will ultimately be more homeowners under water in this period than any time in our history."[62]

OUTLOOK

Major Changes?

With financial markets deeply unsettled and debt-burdened lenders awaiting implementation of the bailout bill, the future course of the financial crisis is anything but clear. But experts say one thing is certain: The economic turmoil will alter the nation's financial, regulatory and political landscape in ways that would have been unimaginable only a few months ago.

Many observers expect a big push for greater disclosure of the risks inherent in exotic financial instruments, notably credit-default swaps.

Also under close inspection will be lavish executive compensation packages, which featured prominently in angry congressional hearings on Lehman Brothers and AIG this month.[63]

More broadly, the government's entire regulatory framework will be under review.

"It was a lack of regulation that allowed these firms to take on risk and got them into trouble," says University of Oregon economist Thoma. A way to achieve more efficient oversight is to consolidate the current hodge-podge of federal agencies that now oversee the financial sector — the Federal Deposit Insurance Corp., Federal Savings and Loan Insurance Corp., Comptroller of the Currency, and so on — into a new omnibus regulator whose purview would extend to "shadow industry" entities like hedge funds and investment banks, Thoma argues.

No matter how policy makers reform the financial system, said Norman Ornstein, a fellow at the American Enterprise Institute, the concept of "moral hazard" must be taken into account. Ornstein was referring to "situations where no adverse consequences flow from risky behavior or failure; and where wrongheaded, risky behavior that goes unpunished begets even more wrongheaded, risky behavior."

Moral hazard "must become a core concept of governance in the next regulatory regime," Ornstein argued in a recent blog. "The most important thing when restoring the long-term health of the financial system is to recreate the balance between risk and reward, and between benefits for exemplary performance and punishment for malfeasance or nonfeasance."[64]

As the financial crisis continues to unfold, it is likely that more and more observers — both in the United States and overseas — will be asking whether the failure of major financial institutions and the history-making involvement of government in private markets spell the "end of capitalism," a phrase that lately has turned up in blogs and news commentaries with increasing frequency.

What's more likely, many experts say, is the end of U.S. supremacy. "The history of capitalism is filled with credit crises, panics, financial meltdowns and recessions," *Newsweek* columnist Fareed Zakaria pointed out. The financial crisis "doesn't mean the end of capitalism. But it might well mean the end of a certain kind of global dominance for the United States."

Zakaria went on to say that "the real fallout" from the crisis "will be the delegitimization of American power. People around the world once saw the United States as the most modern, sophisticated and productive economy in the world. Now they wonder, was this all a house of cards? They listened to American policy makers with respect, even awe. Today, they wonder if these officials know what they are doing."[65]

UPDATE

The U.S. Congress closed in mid-May 2010 on a sweeping plan to overhaul the regulatory structure of the financial system, as–lawmakers, regulators and prosecutors escalated their efforts to identify and punish those at fault for the worst financial crisis since the Great Depression.

Many of the federal rescue programs deployed at the height of the crisis have begun to slowly wind down, as the nation's largest banks paid back the majority of the funds received through the $700 billion Troubled Asset Relief Program (TARP) and the Federal Reserve has slowly and methodically closed down its myriad of rescue program.[66]

Senate Banking Committee Chairman Christopher Dodd, a Connecticut Democrat, was shepherding a financial overhaul bill through the U.S. Senate aimed at addressing many of the regulatory failures that precipitated the economic collapse of 2008, including:

- New authority for federal regulators to wind down systemically risky financial firms;
- Creation of a new agency to regulate consumer financial products like mortgages and credit cards, and
- The first regulatory structure for the $615 trillion over-the-counter derivatives market.[67]

The process has been long, and has taken several turns, in the wake of the crisis that saw legendary Wall Street firms like Bear Stearns, Lehman Brothers and Merrill Lynch bailed out or in bankruptcy. Legislative action, which started with proposals from the Obama administration and wound its way through the House and Senate, was kick-started by two seminal events in the spring.

President Barack Obama, on March 23, 2010, signed into law an overhaul of the U.S. health care system. The debate preceding the signing ceremony polarized the country—and largely stalled the administration's other legislative priorities. The day after signing the health care bill into law, Obama hosted a meeting with Dodd and House Financial Services Committee Chairman Barney Frank, D-Mass., signaling the administration's desire to pivot and direct its focus to the financial overhaul debate.[68] What has followed has been regular engagement from the president and his deputies, bolstering the efforts of Senate Democrats to push through the largest financial regulation bill since the 1930s.

"I'm much more optimistic. In light of what happened on health care, I think, frankly, the outcome there . . . has strengthened our hand in reaching out to people who would like to be part of the solution," Dodd told reporters after the meeting.

Just a few weeks after the White House meeting, congressional Democrats received another boost.

Goldman Sachs Group, the storied Wall Street investment bank, was sued by federal regulators on April 16 for fraud. The Securities and Exchange Commission (SEC) made arguably the biggest waves in the fallout from the financial crisis, alleging the New York-based firm, and one employee in particular, had crafted financial instruments for clients that were designed to fail. Those products, linked to the subprime housing market, were created and sold to investors without Goldman disclosing that hedge fund manager John Paulson was betting against the vehicles, according to the SEC. Paulson's firm, Paulson & Co., worked with Goldman in creating the trade that earned the fund an estimated $1 billion.[69]

Two panels tasked with investigating the financial crisis contributed to the public outrage, The Senate Permanent Subcommittee on Investigations held a highly publicized full day hearing on Goldman Sachs' role in the crisis, bringing top executives and high profile traders to Capitol Hill to testify.[70] At the same time, the Financial Crisis Inquiry Commission, created to investigate and report to Congress on the causes of the financial crisis, continued to question Wall Street chief executives and companies involved in the collapse.[71]

As Congress moved to complete its regulatory overhaul, the economic crisis continued to mushroom in other parts of the world. With Greece teetering on the edge of default, European finance ministers agreed on a rescue package of nearly $1 trillion.[72] Europe's economic woes played at least some role in exacerbating one of the worst stock market plunges in U.S. history. The Dow Jones Industrial Average fell 998 points in 10 minutes on May 6. While the market recovered somewhat, it was a shock to market watchers, lawmakers and regulators alike, who, weeks after the event, still had not pinned down exactly what caused the drop.[73]

The legal proceedings and instability only served to bolster Senate Democrats as they pushed forward with an overhaul measure that would create a federal mechanism to wind down and systemically resolve risky financial firms like Bear Stearns and American International Group (AIG)—two financial firms that required federal bailouts in 2008. The bill took an unexpectedly tough turn, as the anger at Wall Street appeared to translate into more stringent regulations.[74]

Much of the political ire directed at the financial-services industry came as a result of record earnings from Wall Street's largest firms as the country struggled with an unemployment rate the hovered near 10 percent. Goldman Sachs, even as it faced the fraud charges, recorded $3.46 billion in profit in the first quarter of 2010.[75] The firm, along with Bank of America and JPMorgan Chase, did not experience a single day of trading losses during the quarter.[76] But as the largest firms returned to profit, the majority of the banking industry remained plagued by loan defaults that had extended into the commercial real estate market. The Federal Deposit Insurance Corp., in February, announced that a record 702 banks were on its "problem" bank list. U.S. regulators closed 140 lenders in 2009, and FDIC Chairman Sheila Bair has said the agency expects that number to rise this year.[77]

But the public outrage at the bailouts extended beyond Wall Street. Federal Reserve Chairman Ben S. Bernanke, one of the architects of the proposals credited with pulling the U.S. back from the brink of an economic collapse, faced a difficult confirmation process after Obama re-nominated the former Princeton professor for a second term as Fed chief. Thirty senators voted against the nomination—the most in history, as Bernanke found out firsthand the political trouble the Fed was facing.

The central bank deployed some of the widest-ranging rescue programs at the height of the financial crisis, most of which did not require congressional approval and involved little reporting or transparency. Those programs, including the purchase of $1.25 trillion in mortgage-backed securities, are credited with stabilizing the economy. The Fed also cut its benchmark interest rate virtually to zero. But while the actions were considered integral to propping up the economy, they also resulted in a populist backlash that threatened not only the chairman but the institution itself. Members of Congress moved to cut the Fed's authority and increase transparency through the regulatory overhaul.[78]

The administration received a boost on two fronts as 2009 came to a close, when the House took the first steps in the regulatory overhaul process, passing a bill that tracked closely with an administration proposal outlined six months earlier.

"We are sending a clear message to Wall Street: The party is over," House Speaker Nancy Pelosi, D-Calif., said after the 223 to 202 tally, which failed to attract a single Republican vote.[79]

Bank of America and Citigroup also began the process of paying back their combined $90 billion in federal bailout money. Banks have now paid back $135.8 billion, or around 65 percent of the funds disbursed as part of TARP's Capital Purchase Program.[80] Many of the institutions, most notably those on the receiving end of "exceptional assistance" from the federal government, paid back the money to escape the executive compensation curbs imposed by Kenneth Feinberg, the administration's Special Master for Executive Compensation. Feinberg, in October 2009, cut the annual salaries of the top executives of the seven companies receiving "exceptional" amounts of taxpayer aid by an average of 90 percent.[81]

But the administration's problems still remained numerous, and two of its biggest—mortgage giants Fannie Mae and Freddie Mac—continued to bring some of the worst political and economic news. The institutions, which are now wholly owned by the federal government, have taken the brunt of the mortgage crisis, as mounting losses on defaulting mortgages have led to $146 billion in federal bailout money.[82] On Dec. 24, 2009, the Treasury Department announced it would remove the caps on the amount of money the government could provide. That sparked more criticism from House and Senate Republicans who blame the two companies' quasi-government status and dual business mandate—to finance affordable housing and earn a profit for investors—for creating much of the financial crisis.[83]

The housing crisis, which sat at the core of the economic collapse, continued to plague the country, as the Obama administration attempted to find an answer to the mounting foreclosures. Fannie and Freddie served a primary role in the administration's $50 billion federal foreclosure relief program, but over more than a year, little headway had been made in solving a problem that was expected to lead to 4.5 million foreclosure filings in 2010.[84]

The Bush administration and Treasury Secretary Henry M. Paulson gave way to the Obama administration in January 2009. The new administration began action on its financial stability plans before it even took office, embarking on a successful lobbying campaign for Congress to release the second $350 billion of the TARP funds. Shortly after Obama took office on January 20, Timothy F. Geithner, the president of the Federal Reserve Bank of New York, took over for Paulson at Treasury.

The Obama administration faced a daunting battle. The banking system remained far from stable and just a month before the inauguration, the National Bureau of Economic Research, officially announced that the country was in the midst of a recession. The recession had begun a year earlier, as the onset of the mortgage crisis began to take shape throughout the world.[85]

The recession that would eventually push the nation's unemployment rate over 10 percent also would help root out one of the most prolific frauds in U.S. history. Bernard Madoff, a legendary Wall Street trader, was arrested in December after admitting to running a Ponzi scheme estimated to cost investors at least $50 billion. Madoff, the former chairman of the Nasdaq stock market, evaded the SEC for nearly two decades.

Andrew Calamari, a senior enforcement official at New York's SEC, described the scheme as "a stunning fraud that appears to be of epic proportions."[86]

The Madoff arrest came as the Bush administration continued to deploy new programs on a seemingly daily basis to wall off the crisis. The administration, in December 2008, chose to deploy more than $13 billion in TARP money as a temporary bailout of the automotive industry.[87] The Treasury, Fed and FDIC came together to produce several programs designed to both keep the largest Wall Street firms from failing, but also to spur lending in an economy that was facing an overall credit freeze.[88]

Citi, AIG and Bank of America all took extra bailout money and guarantees to survive the crisis. Citi and Bank of America each took a total of $45 billion in TARP money.[89] Citi received $306 billion in federal loan loss guarantees, while B of A, attempting to complete its purchase of another failing Wall Street giant—Merrill Lynch—received $118 billion in guarantees. The federal government remains on the hook for $182.3 billion to AIG.[90]

NOTES

1. Quoted in David Stout, "Fed Chief Calls Delay a Threat to the Economy," *The New York Times*, Sept. 25, 2008.

2. For background, see Kenneth Jost, "Financial Crisis," *CQ Researcher*, May 9, 2008, pp. 409-432.

3. Mark Landler and Eric Dash, "Drama Behind a $250 Billion Banking Deal," *The New York Times*, Oct. 15, 2008.

4. "Opening Statement of Sen. Jim Bunning, Banking, Housing and Urban Affairs Committee Hearing on Turmoil in the U.S. Credit Markets," Sept. 23, 2008, http://bunning.senate.gov/public/index.cfm?Fuse Action=NewsCenter.NewsReleases&ContentRecord_ id=8fe55864-a113-e3fa-47d4-d7778f175c00.

5. Chris Isidore, "Poll: 60% say depression 'likely,'" CNNMoney.com, Oct. 6, 2008, http://money.cnn .com/2008/10/06/news/economy/depression_poll/ index.htm.

6. For background see Marcia Clemmitt, "Mortgage Crisis," *CQ Researcher*, Nov. 2, 2007, pp. 913-936.

7. Charles Duhigg, "Pressured to Take More Risk, Fannie Reached Tipping Point," *The New York Times*, Oct. 5, 2008.

8. Stephen Labaton, "Agency's '04 Rule Let Banks Pile Up New Debt," *The New York Times*, Oct. 3, 2008.

9. See, for example, "Zachary A. Goldfarb, "Banks Hoard Cash as Credit Card Defaults Rise," *The Washington Post*, Oct. 16, 2008, p. 1D. For background see Marcia Clemmitt, "Regulating Credit Cards," *CQ Researcher*, Oct. 10, 2008, pp. 817-840.

10. Quoted in *ibid.*

11. Press Release, "President Bush Meets with Small Business Owners in Texas, Discusses Economy," White House, Oct. 6, 2008, www.whitehouse.gov.

12. Martin Feldstein, "The Problem Is Still Falling House Prices," *The Wall Street Journal*, Oct. 4, 2008.

13. See Edmund L. Andrews and Michael M. Grynbaum, "Fed Announces Plan to Buy Short-Term Debt," *The New York Times*, Oct. 7, 2008.

14. Frank Ahrens, "Bailout Could Deepen Crisis, CBO Chief Says," *The Washington Post*, Sept. 25, 2008, p. 4D.

15. Statement of Peter R. Orszag, "Federal Responses to Market Turmoil," House Budget Committee, Sept. 24, 2008, http://budget. house.gov/hearings/2008/ 09.24.08_Orszag_Testimony.pdf, quoted in *ibid*.

16. Testimony of James B. Lockhart III, director, Federal Housing Finance Agency, before Senate Committee

on Banking, Housing and Urban Affairs, Sept. 23, 2008, http://banking.senate.gov/public/_files/LOCKHARTStmt92308.pdf.

17. James R. Hagerty, "Fannie, Freddie Share Spotlight in Mortgage Mess," *The Wall Street Journal*, Oct. 16, 2008.

18. *Ibid.*

19. Charles W. Calomiris and Peter J. Wallison, "Blame Fannie Mae and Congress for the Credit Mess," *The Wall Street Journal*, Sept. 23, 2008.

20. For background, see Jane Tanner, "Affordable Housing," *CQ Researcher*, Feb. 9, 2001, pp. 89-112.

21. Jeffrey A. Miron, "Commentary: Bankruptcy, not bailout, is the right answer," CNN, www.cnn.com/2008/POLITICS/09/29/miron.bailout/index.html.

22. Daniel Gross, "Subprime suspects," *Slate*, Oct. 7, 2008, www.slate.com/id/2201641/.

23. Judith A. Kennedy, "At the Root of the Subprime Mess," letter to the editor of *The Washington Post*, Oct. 4, 2008, p. 16A. Her letter was in response to a column by the *Post's* Charles Krauthammer. The column is "Catharsis, Then Common Sense," *The Washington Post*, Sept. 26, 2008, p. 23A.

24. Kara Scannell, "SEC Faulted for Missing Red Flags at Bear," *The Wall Street Journal*, Sept. 27-28, 2008, p. 1A.

25. *Ibid.*

26. Quoted in *ibid.*

27. Transcript, "The Second Presidential Debate," *The New York Times*, Oct. 7, 2008.

28. *Ibid.*

29. Ryan Grim, "Lawmakers regret deregulating," *Politico*, Sept. 25, 2008.

30. Maria Bartiromo interview with Bill Clinton, *Business Week*, Oct. 6, 2008, p. 19.

31. David Leonhardt, "Washington's Invisible Hand," *The New York Times*, Sept. 28, 2008.

32. "Paulson Warns of 'Fragile' Economy," CBS News, Sept. 28, 2008, www.cbsnews.com/stories/2008/09/28/60minutes/printable4483612.shtml.

33. Quoted in Ira Glass, "The Giant Pool of Money," in "This American Life," episode no. 355, National Public Radio, October 2008.

34. Alec Klein and Zachary A. Goldfarb, "The Bubble," *The Washington Post*, June 15, 2008, p. 1A.

35. Andrew Ross Sorkin, "JP Morgan Pays $2 a Share for Bear Stearns," *The New York Times*, March 2008. www.nytimes.com/2008/03/17/business/17bear.html.

36. Quoted in *ibid.*

37. Jef Feeley and Steven Church, "Washington Mutual Lists $8 Billion Debt in Bankruptcy," Bloomberg, Sept. 27, 2008, www.bloomberg.com/apps/news?pid=20601087&sid=a_WW5ZH_P_A0&refer=home#.

38. *Ibid.*

39. Diana B. Henriques, "Money Market Fund Says Customers Could Lose Money," *The New York Times*, Sept. 17, 2008.

40. Joe Nocera, "36 Hours of Alarm and Action as Crisis Spiraled," *The New York Times*, Oct. 2, 2008, www.nytimes.com/2008/10/02/ business/02crisis.html?hp.

41. Paul Kane and Lori Montgomery, "Talks Falter on Bailout Deal," *The Washington Post*, Sept. 26, 2008, p. 1A.

42. E. S. Browning, Diya Gullapalli and Craig Karmin, "Wild Day Caps Worst Week Ever for Stocks," *The Wall Street Journal*, Oct. 11, 2008.

43. Gretchen Morgenson, "Will Other Mortgage Dominoes Fall?" *The New York Times*, Feb. 18, 2007. See also, Joseph R. Mason and Joshua Rosner, "How Resilient Are Mortgage-Backed Securities to Collateralized Debt Obligation Market Disruptions," www.hudson.org/files/publications/Mason_RosnerFeb15Event.pdf.

44. Press release, "ISDA Mid-Year Market Survey Shows Credit Derivatives at $54.6 Trillion," International Swaps and Derivatives Association, www.isda.org/press/press092508.html.

45. Andrew Ross Sorkin, ed., *DealBook*, "S.E.C. Chair: Regulated Credit-Default Swaps Now," *The New York Times*, Sept. 23, 2008.

46. *Ibid.*

47. Press release, "SEC Examinations Find Shortcomings in Credit Rating Agencies' Practices and Disclosure to Investors," Securities and Exchange Commission,

July 8, 2008, www.sec.gov/news/press/2008/2008-135.htm.

48. "Summary Report of Issues Identified in the Commission Staff's Examinations of Select Credit Rating Agencies," Securities and Exchange Commission, July 2008, p. 12, www.sec.gov/news/studies/2008/craexamination070808.pdf.

49. Quoted in Greg Farrell, "SEC slams credit-rating agencies over standards," *USA Today*, July 8, 2008.

50. Eric Dash, "$2.8 Billion Loss Reported at Citigroup on Write-Downs," *The New York Times*, Oct. 17, 2008.

51. *Ibid.*

52. Goldfarb, "Banks Hoard Cash as Credit Card Defaults Rise," *op. cit.*

53. Edmund L. Andrews, "Bernanke Says He Supports New Stimulus for Economy," *The New York Times*, Oct. 21, 2008, p. 1A.

54. Quoted in Clea Benson, "Rescue Takes On A New Purpose," *CQ Weekly*, Oct. 20, 2008, pp 2804-2805.

55. Lingling Wei and Anton Troianovski, "U.S. May Help Private Funds To Purchase Troubled Assets," *The Wall Street Journal*, Oct. 8, 2008.

56. Timothy Curry and Lynn Shibut, "The Cost of the Savings and Loan Crisis: Truth and Consequences," *FDIC Banking Review*, Vol. 13, No. 2, 2000, www.fdic.gov/bank/analytical/banking/2000dec/brv13n2_2.pdf.

57. Carrie Johnson, "Prosecutors Expected To Spare Wall St. Firms," *The Washington Post*, Oct. 3, 2008, p. 1D.

58. For background see Alan Greenblatt, "Pension Crisis," *CQ Researcher*, Feb. 17, 2006, pp. 145-168, and Barbara Mantel, "Consumer Debt," *CQ Researcher*, March 2, 2007, pp. 193-216.

59. Nancy Trejos, "Retirement Savings Lose $2 Trillion in 15 Months," *The Washington Post*, Oct. 8, 2008.

60. House Education and Labor Committee, "Chairman Miller Statement at Committee Hearing on the Impact of the Financial Crisis on Workers' Retirement Security," Oct. 7, 2008, http://edlabor.house.gov/statements/2008-10-07-GMHearingStatement.pdf.

61. James R. Hagerty and Ruth Simon, "Housing Pain Gauge: Nearly 1 in 6 Owners 'Under Water,' " *The Wall Street Journal*, Oct. 8, 2008.

62. Quoted in *ibid.*

63. For background, see Thomas J. Billitteri, "Curbing CEO Pay," *CQ Researcher*, March 9, 2007, pp. 217-240.

64. Norman Ornstein, "Ornstein on the Economy's Moral Hazard Meltdown," The Plank blog, *The New Republic*, Oct. 8, 2008.

65. Fareed Zakaria, "The Age of Bloomberg," *Newsweek*, Oct. 13, 2008.

66. Neil Irwin, "Federal Reserve edges away from crisis measures," The Washington Post, Dec. 17, 2009, www.washingtonpost.com/wp-dyn/content/article/2009/12/16/AR2009121600255.html.

67. "Senate Banking Committee Summary of Wall Street Bill," http://banking.senate.gov/public/_files/FinancialReformSummaryAsFiled.pdf.

68. Sewell Chan, "Financial overhaul is next priority of Democrats," The New York Times, March 24, 2010, www.nytimes.com/2010/03/25/business/25regulate.html.

69. Louise Story and Gretchen Morgenson, "S.E.C. accuses Goldman of Fraud in housing deal," The New York Times, April 17, 2010, www.nytimes.com/2010/04/17/business/17goldman.html

70. Louise Story, "Panel's blunt questions put Goldman on defensive," The New York Times, April 28, 2010, www.nytimes.com/2010/04/28/business/28goldman.html.

71. Sewell Chan, "For crisis panel, the creativity is verbal instead of financial," The New York Times, April 8, 2010, www.nytimes.com/2010/04/09/business/09notebook.html.

72. James Kanter and Landon Thomas, "E.U. details $957 billion rescue package," The New York Times, May 9, 2010, www.nytimes.com/2010/05/10/business/global/10drachma.html?scp=18&sq=europe%20%241%20trillion&st=Search.

73. Alexander Twin, "Glitches send Dow on wild ride," CNNMoney.com, May 6, 2010, http://money.cnn.com/2010/05/06/markets/markets_newyork/index.htm.

74. Eamon Javers and Meredith Shiner, "Nightmare on Wall Street," Politico, May 6, 2010, www.politico.com/news/stories/0510/37318.html.

75. Ken Sweet, "Goldman Sachs first-quarter earnings surge," Fox Business, April 20, 2010, www.foxbusiness.com/story/markets/industries/finance/goldman-sachs-quarter-earnings-surge/.

76. Eric Dash, "4 big banks score perfect 61-day run," The New York Times, May 11, 2010, www.nytimes.com/2010/05/12/business/12bank.html.

77. Michael R. Crittenden, "Lending falls at epic pace," The Wall Street Journal, Feb. 24, 2010, http://online.wsj.com/article/SB200014240527487041881045750833320054615 58.html.

78. Mark Felsenthal, "Senate backs Bernanke for second term at Fed," Reuters, Jan. 28, 2010, www.reuters.com/article/idUSTRE60P5KC20100128

79. Brady Dennis, "House votes 223 to 202 to approve sweeping bill to overhaul financial regulatory system," The Washington Post, Dec. 12, 2009, www.washingtonpost.com/wp-dyn/content/article/2009/12/11/AR2009121102754.html.

80. "Treasury Department Report to Congress," March 31, 2010, www.financialstability.gov/docs/FSOB/FINSOB%20Quarterly%20Report%2003311 0.pdf.

81. Betsy Stark, Jake Tapper and Matthew Jaffe, "Obama's pay czar Ken Feinberg to slash executive compensation at 7 bailout firms," ABC News, Oct. 22, 2009, http://abcnews.go.com/Politics/Business/obamas-pay-czar-ken-feinberg-slash-executive-compensation/story?id=8887792.

82. Nick Timiraos, "Fannie Mae needs $8.4 billion more," The Wall Street Journal, May 11, 2010, http://online.wsj.com/article/SB10001424052748703880304575236030191182938.html.

83. Rebecca Christie and Jody Shenn, "U.S. Treasury ends cap on Fannie and Freddie lifeline," Bloomberg News, Dec. 25, 2009, www.bloomberg.com/apps/news?pid=20601208&sid=abTVUSp9zbAY

84. John Gittelsohn, "Half of U.S. home loan modifications to default again," Bloomberg News, March 25, 2010, www.bloomberg.com/apps/news?sid=aVYxPZ56vjys&pid=20601087.

85. Neil Irwin, "NBER: U.S. in recession that began last December," The Washington Post, Dec. 1, 2008, www.washingtonpost.com/wp-dyn/content/article/2008/12/01/AR2008120101365.html.

86. David Lieberman, "Investors remain amazed over Madoff's sudden downfall," USA Today, Dec. 15, 2008, www.usatoday.com/money/markets/2008–12–14-ponzi-madoff-downfall_N.htm.

87. David Sanger, David M. Herszenhorn and Bill Vlasic, "Bush aids Detroit, but hard choices wait for Obama," The New York Times, Dec. 19, 2008, www.nytimes.com/2008/12/20/business/20auto.html?_r=1&_r.

88. Joint Agency press statement, U.S. Treasury Department, Oct. 14, 2008, www.ustreas.gov/press/releases/hp1206.htm.

89. Bradley Keoun, "Citigroup gets guarantees on $306 billion of assets," Bloomberg News, Nov. 24, 2008, www.bloomberg.com/apps/news?sid=a_rp_i7EWcH8&pid=20601068.

90. Paritosh Bansal and Clara Ferreira Marques, "AIG, Pru in talks to restructure AIA deal," Reuters, May 11, 2010, http://news.yahoo.com/s/nm/20100511/bs_nm/us_prudential_aig.

BIBLIOGRAPHY

Books

Morris, Charles R., *The Trillion Dollar Meltdown,* *Public Affairs,* **2008.**
A noted financial writer explains how arcane financial instruments and policy misjudgments brought the global financial system to the brink of ruin.

Phillips, Kevin, *Bad Money: Reckless Finance, Failed Politics, and the Global Crisis of American Capitalism,* **Viking, 2008.**
A prolific policy analyst and scholar finds the "most worrisome thing about the vulnerability of the U.S. economy . . . is the extent of official understatement and misstatement."

Stanton, Thomas H., *Government-Sponsored Enterprises,* **AEI Press, 2002.**
A fellow at Johns Hopkins University's Center for the Study of American Government argues that hybrid

organizations like Fannie Mae and Freddie Mac "used their market power" to resist government regulatory efforts.

Wallison, Peter J., ed., *Serving Two Masters, Yet Out of Control*, AEI Press, 2001.
A fellow at the conservative American Enterprise Institute presents articles by various experts analyzing the favored positions occupied by Fannie Mae and Freddie Mac.

Articles

"End of illusions," *The Economist*, July 17, 2008, www.economist.com/finance/displaystory.cfm?story_id=11751139.
Fannie Mae and Freddie Mac "did not stick to their knitting," says this insightful analysis of the problems facing the government-sponsored enterprises.

Cresswell, Julie, "Protected by Washington, Companies Ballooned," *The New York Times*, July 13, 2008, p. A1.
A reporter traces the influence of "Fannie and Freddie's sprawling lobbying machine" on Capitol Hill and elsewhere.

Dilanian, Ken, "How Congress set the stage for a fiscal meltdown," *USA Today*, Oct. 13, 2008, p. A1.
Congress' actions on Fannie Mae and Freddie Mac and credit-default swaps and other derivatives became major factors in the financial crisis.

Duhigg, Charles, "At Freddie Mac, Chief Discarded Warning Signs," *The New York Times*, Aug. 5, 2008, p. A1.
CEO Richard F. Syron didn't heed warning signals that might have shielded the company from turmoil.

Goodman, Peter S., "Taking Hard New Look at a Greenspan Legacy," *The New York Times*, Oct. 9 2008, p. A1.
Many economists say that if Alan Greenspan had made different decisions as Federal Reserve chairman, the financial crisis might have been tempered or avoided.

Grim, Ryan, "Lawmakers regret deregulating," *Politico*, Sept. 25, 2008, www.politico.com/news/stories/0908/13887.html.
Lawmakers discuss Congress' 1999 decision to repeal the Depression-era Glass-Steagall Act.

Laing, Jonathan R., "Swept Away: How Fannie Mae keeps its losses from sullying the bottom line," *Barron's*, May 17, 2004.
The venerable financial weekly says Fannie Mae's accounting methods, "while legal . . . obfuscate rather than illuminate" the company's financial condition.

Landler, Mark, and Eric Dash, "Drama Behind a $250 Billion Banking Deal," *The New York Times*, Oct. 15, 2008, p. A1.
The reporters detail how Treasury Secretary Henry M. Paulson Jr. forced major banks to accept government intervention.

Morgenson, Gretchen, "Behind Insurer's Crisis, Blind Eye to a Web of Risk," *The New York Times*, Sept. 28, 2008, p. A1.
While the housing collapse touched off the financial emergency, credit derivatives made the system vulnerable, the veteran financial writer concludes in an examination of giant insurer American International Group.

Reports and Studies

Laurenti, Adolfo, "Fannie Mae and Freddie Mac: A Fall from Grace," *Mesirow Financial*, July 24, 2008, www.mesirowfinancial.com/economics/laurenti/themes/globalmkts_0708.pdf.
An economist sees a risk "that the government, and politics, will play too large instead of too small a role in financial markets as we struggle to deal with [the Fannie and Freddie] crisis in an election year."

Office of Federal Housing Enterprise Oversight, "2008 Report to Congress," www.ofheo.gov/media/annualreports/ReporttoCongress2008.pdf.
The regulator of Fannie Mae and Freddie Mac reviews the government-sponsored enterprises' operations and financial performance.

For More Information

American Enterprise Institute, 1150 17th St., N.W., Washington, DC 20036; (202) 862-5800; www.aei.org. Conservative think tank focusing on economic policy and other public-policy issues.

Center for Economic and Policy Research, 1611 Connecticut Ave., N.W., Suite 400, Washington, DC 20009; (202) 293-5380. Liberal think tank focusing on economic policy and other public-policy issues.

Federal Home Loan Mortgage Corp. (Freddie Mac), 8200 Jones Branch Dr., McLean, VA 22102; (703) 903-2000; freddiemac.com. Government-sponsored enterprise that owns or guarantees mortgage loans.

Federal National Mortgage Association (Fannie Mae), 3900 Wisconsin Ave., N.W., Washington, DC 20016; (202) 752-7000; www.fanniemae.com. The larger of the two government-sponsored enterprises that own or guarantee mortgage loans.

International Swaps and Derivatives Association, 360 Madison Ave., 16th Floor, New York, NY 10017; (212) 901-6000; www.isda.org. Trade group for the derivatives industry, which includes credit-default swaps.

Mortgage Bankers Association, 1331 L St., N.W., Washington, DC 20005; (202) 557-2700; www.mbaa.org. Trade association for the real estate finance industry.

National Association of Affordable Housing Lenders, 1667 K St., N.W., Suite 210, Washington, DC 20006; (202) 293-9850; www.naahl.org. Supports greater private lending and investing in low- and moderate-income communities.

National Low Income Housing Coalition, 727 15th St., N.W., 6th Floor, Washington, DC 20005; (202) 662-1530; www.nlihc.org. Advocates access to affordable housing for the lowest-income households.

12

Interrogating the CIA

Kenneth Jost

The CIA's questioning of accused al Qaeda terrorist Abd al-Rahim al-Nashiri may be among the cases ordered reexamined by Attorney General Eric H. Holder Jr. to see whether CIA operatives exceeded official interrogation guidelines. With al-Nashiri shackled, a CIA debriefer racked an unloaded pistol next to al-Nashiri's head. Later, he revved a power drill near a naked and hooded al-Nashiri.

From *CQ Researcher*,
October 31, 2008.

Abd al-Rahim al-Nashiri, the accused mastermind of the bombing of the *USS Cole* in October 2000, was captured by Central Intelligence Agency (CIA) operatives in the United Arab Emirates in November 2002 and taken to a secret CIA prison in Thailand. Immediately upon arrival, around Nov. 15, al-Nashiri — identified as the chief of operations in the Persian Gulf for the terrorist group al Qaeda — was subjected to one or more of the harsh measures that the CIA calls "enhanced interrogation techniques" and that human-rights advocates say can amount to torture.

Al-Nashiri continued to be harshly interrogated until Dec. 4 — including two instances of waterboarding, or simulated drowning, on his 12th day in custody — and then for another two weeks later in the month. By then, the agents deemed al-Nashiri to be "compliant" and turned him over to a "debriefer" from CIA headquarters.

By the end of the month, however, the debriefer — untrained in interrogation and not authorized to use any of the 10 enhanced techniques sanctioned by the CIA and the Justice Department under President George W. Bush — determined that al-Nashiri was "withholding" information. He decided, after consultation with an unnamed individual, to go beyond the approved interrogation methods. With al-Nashiri shackled, the debriefer entered the cell with an unloaded pistol and racked the weapon "once or twice" next to al-Nashiri's head. "Probably" on the same day, the debriefer entered the cell again and, with al-Nashiri naked and hooded, revved a power drill.

Interrogation Techniques Included Waterboarding

Ten "enhanced interrogation techniques" were approved by the Department of Justice for use by Central Intelligence Agency (CIA) interrogators. The legal memorandum approving the techniques, dated Aug. 1, 2002, was signed by Jay Bybee, assistant attorney general for the Office of Legal Counsel, and prepared by his deputy, John Yoo.

Attention grasp — Detainee is grasped with both hands, one hand on each side of collar opening, in "a controlled and quick motion," and in the same motion drawn toward interrogator.

Walling — Detainee is pulled forward and then "quickly and firmly" pushed into flexible false wall so that shoulder blades hit wall. Head and neck are supported with rolled towel to prevent whiplash.

Facial hold — Detainee's head is immobilized by interrogator placing open palm on either side of detainee's face; interrogator's fingertips "are kept well away from" detainee's eyes.

Facial or insult slap — With fingers "slightly spread apart," the interrogator's hand "makes contact with" area between tip of detainee's chin and bottom of corresponding earlobe.

Cramped confinement — Detainee is placed in confined space, typically a small or large box, usually dark; confinement can last up to two hours in small space, up to 18 hours in larger space.

Insects — "Harmless" insect is placed in confinement box with detainee.

Wall standing — Detainee stands about 4 to 5 feet from wall with feet spread to shoulder width, arms stretched out in front of him, and fingers resting on wall to support body weight. Not allowed to reposition hands or feet.

Stress positions — Detainee sits on floor with legs extended straight out in front of him with arms raised above head or kneels on floor while leaning back at 45-degree angle.

Sleep deprivation — "Will not exceed 11 days at a time."

Waterboarding — Detainee is bound to bench with feet elevated above head; head is immobilized and interrogator places cloth over detainee's mouth and nose while pouring water onto cloth in controlled manner. "Airflow is restricted for 20 to 40 seconds, and the technique produces the sensation of drowning and suffocation."

Source: CIA, Inspector General, "Special Review: Counterterrorism Detention and Interrogation Activities (September 2001-October 2003)," May 7, 2004.

The debriefer made no report of the episode to CIA headquarters in Langley, Va., outside Washington. But CIA officers who arrived in January heard of the incident and reported it to Langley, prompting an investigation by the CIA's inspector general (IG), John Helgerson, and a referral to the Justice Department for possible prosecution.

After review by prosecutors in the U.S. attorney's office in Alexandria, Va., however, the government in September 2003 formally decided not to bring criminal charges and left any discipline up to the CIA.

Now, six years later, the case may be one of those that Attorney General Eric H. Holder Jr. has asked a respected career prosecutor to reexamine. On Aug. 24 Holder announced his decision to reopen cases in which CIA agents may have gone beyond official guidelines, just as the agency was itself releasing under court order a 158-page report documenting more than a dozen instances of possible abuse over the first two years of the CIA's controversial interrogation program. The other "unauthorized" techniques described in the report included a staged mock execution, a threat to sexually abuse a detainee's mother, a threat to kill another's children and the choking of another prisoner to the point of losing consciousness.[1]

The IG's report — first released in May 2008 but with much heavier redactions than in the new version — was part of the latest batch of documents on the Bush administration's treatment of suspected terrorists unearthed by two Freedom of Information Act (FOIA) lawsuits filed by the American Civil Liberties Union (ACLU) beginning in 2004. ACLU officials are praising Holder's decision to reopen the cases against CIA agents but say more needs to be done. The latest information "further underscores the need for a comprehensive investigation into the torture of detainees and those who authorized it," says Jameel Jaffer, director of the ACLU's National Security Project.[2]

President Obama decided on Jan. 22 — his second full day in office — to bar the use of waterboarding or

CIA Report Evaluates Interrogation Techniques

Here are major conclusions from a May 2004 report by the Central Intelligence Agency's inspector general on counterterrorism and interrogation activities from September 2001 through October 2003:

- Program provided intelligence that helped identify and apprehend terrorists and warned of planned terrorist attacks on U.S., other countries.
- Office of General Counsel "worked closely" with Justice Department to determine legality of "enhanced interrogation techniques" (EITs) and also "consulted" with White House and National Security Council regarding techniques.
- Justice Department legal opinion "consists of finely detailed analysis" to support conclusion that EITs, "properly" carried out, would not constitute torture; opinion did not address whether practices were consistent with U.S. voluntary undertaking to prevent "cruel, inhuman or degrading" treatment.
- A number of agency officers are concerned that they "may be vulnerable" to legal action in the United States or abroad and that the U.S. government "will not stand behind them."
- Officers are concerned that future public revelation of the program is "inevitable" and "will seriously damage" reputations of personnel, agency.
- Agency "generally" provided "good guidance and support" to officers using EITs, in particular at "these [redacted] foreign locations."
- Agency in early months of program "failed to provide adequate guidance, staffing, guidance and support"

to agents involved in interrogation at [redacted location(s)].

- "Unauthorized, improvised, inhumane, and undocumented detention and interrogation techniques were used [redacted] referred to the Department of Justice (DoJ) for potential prosecution."
- Agency "failed to issue in a timely manner comprehensive written guidelines for detention and interrogation activities."
- "Such written guidance as does exist … is inadequate."
- Waterboarding was used during interrogation of two detainees "in a manner inconsistent with" the Justice Department's legal opinion; one key al Qaeda terrorist [Khalid Shaikh Mohammed] was subjected to waterboarding 183 times and denied sleep for 180 hours. In this and another instance, "the technique of application and volume of water used differed from the DoJ opinion."
- CIA's Office of Medical Services provided "comprehensive medical attention," but did not issue formal medical guidelines until April 2003.
- EITs may have been applied "without justification" in some instances based not on analytical assessments but on agents' "presumptions" about individual's knowledge.
- Agency faces "potentially serious long-term political and legal challenges" because of use of EITs and government's inability to decide what it will ultimately do with detainees.

Source: "Counterterrorism Detention and Interrogation Activities," Office of Inspector General, Central Intelligence Agency, May 7, 2004

---

any of the other enhanced techniques by CIA or military interrogators. "We believe we can abide by a rule that says, we don't torture, but we can effectively obtain the intelligence we need," Obama said in a White House ceremony on Jan. 22 attended by a group of former military officers assembled by human-rights groups. He also promised to close the prison camp at the Guantánamo Bay Naval Base in Cuba within one year.[3]

Republicans and national security-minded conservatives immediately began attacking the Obama policies, with former Vice President Dick Cheney assuming the highest-profile role among the critics. Cheney is continuing his attacks on the president since Holder's decision to reopen the CIA cases. He calls Holder's action "political" and credits use of the harsh methods with preventing any attacks on the United States following the Sept. 11, 2001, attacks.

"My sort of overwhelming view is that the enhanced interrogation techniques were absolutely essential in saving thousands of American lives and preventing further attacks against the United States," Cheney said on "Fox News Sunday" on Aug. 30. "I think they were directly responsible for the fact that for eight years we had no further mass casualty attacks against the United States."[4]

Seven former CIA directors raised the stakes in the controversy with a letter on Sept. 18 asking Obama to reverse Holder's decision to reopen the investigations. The group, including CIA directors in Republican and Democratic administrations, said the investigation of previously closed cases was unfair to the officers involved, would "seriously damage" other officers' willingness to "take risks to protect the country" and would damage the ability to obtain cooperation from foreign intelligence agencies.

Obama rebuffed the suggestion in an appearance on one of several Sunday talk shows on Sept. 20. "I appreciate the former CIA directors wanting to look after an institution that they helped to build," he told host Bob Schieffer on the CBS program "Face the Nation." "But I continue to believe that nobody's above the law. And I want to make sure that, as president of the United States, I'm not asserting in some way that my decisions overrule the decisions of prosecutors who are there to uphold the law."

At the same time, *The Washington Post* reported that the investigation may be narrower than once thought, with perhaps only two or three cases being seriously considered for possible indictments. *The Post* based the story on two unnamed sources who were described as having been briefed on the investigation.[5]

In the Jan. 22 session, Obama appointed an interagency task force to be headed by Holder to recommend new policies on interrogation and detainee transfers. The task force's recommendations announced by Holder on Aug. 24 reaffirmed Obama's decision to bar any interrogation techniques other than those outlined in the latest version of the *U.S. Army Field Manual*. The manual — revised in 2006 by the Bush administration after the disclosure of abuses of Iraqi prisoners by U.S. military personnel at the Abu Ghraib prison outside Baghdad — details 17 different techniques of interrogation and bars any use of physical force or degrading treatment against prisoners. (*See story, p. 281.*)

Holder said the task force, including members of the intelligence community, was unanimous in concluding that the manual provides "adequate and effective means of conducting interrogations." Obama accepted the task force's further recommendation to take interrogation of so-called high-value detainees away from the CIA and assign the responsibility to a new group comprising specially trained experts from several agencies that will be housed at the FBI and overseen by the National Security Council.[6]

Obama also drew sharp criticism earlier for revoking and then directing the Justice Department to release controversial legal opinions from its Office of Legal Counsel (OLC) that concluded the CIA's enhanced interrogation techniques were legal and did not constitute torture under U.S. or international law. The release of the memos in the ACLU's FOIA suit — with the most graphic description until then of the CIA's harsh techniques — came after a strong plea by CIA Director Leon Panetta to withhold or heavily edit the documents. Instead, the memos were released on April 16 with few redactions.

In releasing the memos, however, Obama appeared to rule out prosecutions of CIA operatives who conducted interrogations according to the techniques he was ordering discarded. "It is our intention," Obama said in the April 16 statement, "to assure those who carried out their duties relying in good faith upon legal advice from the Department of Justice that they will not be subject to prosecution."[7]

At the same time, Obama reiterated his opposition to a broad reexamination of the Bush administration's counterterrorism policies. Obama described the events as "a dark and painful chapter in our history," but added, "Nothing will be gained by spending our time and energy laying blame for the past."

Nevertheless, some lawmakers and many civil liberties and human-rights groups continue to press for a full investigation of the Bush policies either by a special congressional committee or a bipartisan, independent commission comparable to the commission that reexamined events leading up to the 9/11 terrorist attacks. "An independent commission would take a broader look at the policies that have troubled so many people and look at how we can avoid going in that direction again," says Virginia Sloan, president and founder of the bipartisan Constitution Project.

Meanwhile, Obama is making only slow progress toward meeting his goal of closing the Guantánamo prison camp by Jan. 20, 2010. The review of individual cases is moving slowly, other countries are reluctant to accept transferred detainees and Republican politicians are opposing relocating any of the detainees to U.S. soil.

The national security issues complicate Obama's political standing as he tries to move the country out of the economic doldrums and push an ambitious domestic agenda through Congress.

Here are some of the questions being debated:

Should CIA agents be prosecuted for exceeding interrogation guidelines?

Abdul Wali, an Afghan farmer, turned himself in to U.S. authorities in June 2003 after learning he had been implicated in rocket attacks on the U.S. military base at Asadabad, near the Pakistani border. But David Passaro, a former Special Forces medic working on contract as a CIA interrogator, got angry when Wali was unable to answer his questions.

Witnesses said the enraged Passaro repeatedly struck Wali with a foot-long flashlight and his fists and kicked him in the groin while wearing combat boots. Wali died two days later. Today, Passaro is serving time in a federal prison after a federal jury in North Carolina convicted him in August 2006 of assault.[8]

The CIA itself referred Passaro's case to the Justice Department for possible prosecution, and then CIA Director Michael Hayden stressed after the verdict that Passaro's conduct was "neither authorized nor condoned" by the agency. The agency also referred other cases to Justice, but career prosecutors in the U.S. attorney's office in Alexandria decided not to bring criminal charges in any of the others.

Attorney General Holder's Aug. 24 decision to designate John Durham, a career federal prosecutor from Connecticut, to take a second look at those cases is drawing heavy criticism from the intelligence community, including high-ranking CIA officials from Democratic and Republican administrations.

AFP/Getty Images/Brendan Hoffman

Former Vice President Dick Cheney harshly criticizes President Obama's decision to bar waterboarding and other enhanced techniques used by CIA and military interrogators. Cheney labels Attorney General Eric Holder's decision to reopen the CIA interrogation cases "political" and credits the harsh methods with preventing any attacks on the United States following the Sept. 11, 2001, attacks.

Jeffrey Smith, the CIA's general counsel for two years under President Bill Clinton, warns that prosecutions could set a "dangerous precedent" of using criminal law to settle policy differences at the expense of career officials. And former CIA Inspector General Helgerson says a successful prosecution would be "very difficult" because of the Justice Department's approval of the interrogation program. "I do not believe there was any criminal intent among those involved," Helgerson told *The Washington Post* after the release of his 2004 report on interrogation practices.[9]

In his television interview, Cheney cited the previous investigations, including the prosecution of Passaro, as evidence of a political motivation in Holder's action. Robert Alt, a senior legal fellow with the conservative Heritage Foundation, also notes that any prosecution would face substantial legal hurdles, including the five-year statute of limitations for most federal offenses. "When you put all that together and you hear the howl from the political left about the need for more action, it begins to look political," says Alt, deputy director of Heritage's Center for Legal and Judicial Studies.

Civil liberties and human-rights advocates defend Holder's action in part by criticizing what they describe as the Bush administration's politicization of the Justice

Department. "I'm not convinced that those prosecutors had access to all the facts," says Elisa Massimino, chief executive officer and executive director of Human Rights First. "I'm not convinced that they were operating in the appropriate legal framework to make those decisions."

ACLU lawyer Alex Abdo notes that Holder has only asked for a review of the cases and would have to decide later whether to bring any prosecutions. A legal fellow with the ACLU's National Security Project, Adabo dismisses accusations of political motivations. "The question of whether the law was broken is strictly a legal question, not a political one," he says.

Cheney also warned of the effect the decision is having on the morale of CIA officers. "We ask those people to do some very difficult things. Sometimes, they put their own lives at risk," Cheney said in the Fox News interview. "And if they are now going to be subject to being investigated and prosecuted by the next administration, nobody's going to sign up for those kinds of missions."

Massimino counters that CIA morale suffered because the agency was given the assignment to interrogate the high-value detainees using legally questionable tactics that Cheney famously characterized shortly after the 9/11 attacks as "the dark side."

"There were a lot of people at the CIA who were devastated by the idea that they were the agency that would go to what Vice President Cheney called the dark side, that they were the agency that would violate the law," Massimino says. "People who are concerned about the morale, where were those people when there was pressure on people at the agency to go beyond the law? Why didn't they stand up then for the morale of the intelligence officers who are trying to serve their country honorably?"

Cheney and other critics also warn that the review of the CIA cases is merely a first step toward possible criminal investigations against others in the Bush administration involved in the interrogation policies, including Justice Department lawyers who sanctioned the enhanced interrogation techniques. Many critics "will not be satisfied until they see former Bush administration officials paraded in orange jump suits," says Alt.

In fact, the ACLU and Human Rights First are among the groups pressing for broader inquiries. "Given what's on the public record, we should be investigating attorneys in the Department of Justice and other senior officials who were the architects of the CIA's enhanced interrogation program," says Abdo.

Should the CIA be allowed to use "enhanced interrogation techniques" when questioning "high-value" detainees?

With Democratic majorities in both chambers, Congress in 2008 moved to prohibit any of the "enhanced interrogation techniques" that CIA operatives had been using against selected "high-value" detainees. But President Bush vetoed the measure, saying the harsh measures were needed to overcome resistance techniques learned by al Qaeda members during training.

"It is vitally important," Bush said in the March 8, 2008, veto message, "that the Central Intelligence Agency be allowed to maintain a separate and classified interrogation program."[10]

In his Jan. 22 executive order, President Obama accomplished what Congress had sought by limiting all interrogations to those practices authorized in the *U.S. Army Field Manual.*[11] Seven months later, Holder announced that the task force Obama had appointed to review the policy reaffirmed the president's decision. "The task force concluded that the *Army Field Manual* provides appropriate guidance on interrogation for military interrogators and that no additional or different guidance was necessary for other agencies," Holder said.

Despite Obama's decision, the debate over the legality and effectiveness of the CIA interrogation program is continuing. Cheney and other defenders of the practices say the CIA interrogations produced valuable intelligence after proper review and approval by the Justice Department. As evidence, they point to the CIA inspector general's bottom-line conclusion that the agency's interrogations provided "actionable intelligence" that helped identify and apprehend terrorists and warned of planned terrorist attacks against the United States or other countries.

In his interview, Cheney said that two of the most valuable al Qaeda detainees — Khalid Shaikh Mohammed and Abu Zubaydah — provided information only after being subjected to some of the enhanced interrogation techniques (EITs). "The evidence is overwhelming that the EITs were crucial in getting them to cooperate," he said.

Army Prohibits Force in Questioning Prisoners

The U.S. Army's 384-page field manual on "human intelligence (HUMINT) collection" details more than a dozen "approaches" to questioning an enemy prisoner of war (EPW) or detainee, none entailing physical force, coercion or threat of violence. The manual, as revised in September 2006, included specific prohibitions against abusive practices documented at the Abu Ghraib prison in Iraq, including forced nudity and use of military dogs to harass or intimidate prisoners. Here are the approaches listed in the manual:

Direct approach: HUMINT collector "asks direct questions." Effective 90 percent of time during World War II, 95 percent of time in Operation Desert Storm in Iraq (1991); preliminary studies indicate "dramatically less successful" in Afghanistan (2001-2002) and Iraq (2003).

Incentive approach: HUMINT collector "may use incentives to enhance rapport and to reward the source for cooperation and truthfulness." May not state or imply that basic rights under international, national law are contingent on cooperation.

Emotional approaches: HUMINT collector "can often identify dominant emotions that motivate the EPW/detainee." These approaches are:

Emotional love approach: HUMINT collector "focuses on the anxiety felt by the source . . . , his isolation from those he loves, and his feelings of helplessness." Has "a chance of success" if source can be shown what he can do to improve the situation of the object of his emotion: family, homeland, comrades.

Emotional hate approach: HUMINT collector must "build on [source's hate] so the emotion overrides the source's rational side." Hate may be directed to his country's regime, immediate superiors, officers in general or fellow soldiers.

Emotional fear-up approach: HUMINT collector "identifies a preexisting fear or creates a fear" within source and "links" elimination or reduction of fear to source's cooperation. Must be "extremely careful" not to threaten or coerce source.

Emotional fear-down approach: HUMINT collector "mitigates existing fear in exchange for" source's cooperation.

Emotional-pride and ego-up approach: HUMINT collector "exploits a source's low self-esteem" by flattery. "This should produce positive feelings on the part of the source," who "will eventually reveal pertinent information to solicit more favorable comments. . . ."

Emotional-pride and ego-down approach: HUMINT collector attacks ego or self-image of source, who in defense "reveals information to justify or rationalize his actions."

Emotional-futility: HUMINT collector convinces source that resistance is futile.

Other approaches: Most "require considerable time and resources." They are:

We Know All: HUMINT collector "subtly" convinces source that questioning is perfunctory because information is already known.

File and Dossier: HUMINT collector prepares dossier with all known information about source and uses the file to convey impression that source is only confirming information already known.

Establish Your Identity: HUMINT collector accuses source of being "infamous individual" wanted on more serious charges; source then attempts to establish his true identity in an effort to clear himself.

Repetition: HUMINT collector repeats question and answer several times; source then answers "fully and truthfully . . . to gain relief from the monotony. . . ."

Rapid Fire: HUMINT collector asks rapid-fire questions to confuse source, who "will tend to contradict himself" and then be caught in inconsistencies.

Silent: HUMINT collector says nothing, looks squarely at source and waits for source to break eye contact.

Change of Scenery: Source is removed from "intimidating" atmosphere to "setting where he feels more comfortable speaking."

Mutt and Jeff: Requires two HUMINT collectors, both "convincing actors." One adopts formal, unsympathetic stance ("bad cop"); the second gains source's confidence by scolding colleague's stance ("good cop"). No violence or threats may be used.

False Flag: Goal is to trick detainee into cooperating by convincing him he is being interrogated by non-U.S. forces; use must be approved by superiors; no "implied or explicit threats" that non-cooperation will result in harsh treatment by non-U.S. entities.

Source: U.S. Department of the Army, *Human Intelligence Collection Operations*, September 2006, www.army.mil/institution/armypublicaffairs/pdf/fm2-22-3.pdf.

Critics of the practices reject the now-repudiated Justice Department advisories that said the techniques did not constitute torture as defined by U.S. law. They also question whether the enhanced techniques were necessary to obtain information from detainees. As evidence, they point to the caveat in the CIA inspector general's report that the effectiveness of the techniques in eliciting information that would not have been obtained otherwise "cannot be so easily measured."[12]

"What the report doesn't say and doesn't conclude is that torture was responsible for the information that was obtained or that the intelligence could not have been obtained without torture," says ACLU lawyer Abdo.

After years of secrecy, the operational details of the CIA interrogation program are now coming to light with the release of the inspector general's report and a second document: a Dec. 30, 2004, description of the program for the Justice Department written by an unidentified lawyer. The 19-page background paper — written after the Bush administration's decision in 2003 to discontinue use of waterboarding — groups the techniques then in use into three categories: "conditioning techniques," including nudity, sleep deprivation and "dietary manipulation"; "corrective techniques," including facial slap, abdominal slap, facial hold and attention grasp; and "coercive techniques," including "walling," water dousing, stress positions, wall standing and cramped confinement.

The paper describes the use of the techniques sequentially from less to more severe. The objective, the paper says, is to place the detainee in "a state of learned helplessness and dependence conducive to the collection of intelligence in a predictable, reliable, and sustainable manner."

The Justice Department memos in August 2002 concluded the techniques did not constitute torture under applicable federal law, which prohibits actions "under the color of law intended to inflict severe physical or mental pain or suffering." In his Fox News interview, Cheney stressed the Justice Department's approval of the enhanced techniques, but also agreed to a question from host Chris Wallace that he was "comfortable" with the program even when interrogators went beyond the authorized practices. Cheney has also been reported to be planning to write in his forthcoming memoir that he

disagreed with Bush's decision to discontinue use of waterboarding.[13]

Today, waterboarding has few vocal defenders, but the legal status of the other harsh interrogation techniques remains a subject of dispute. "Most of the techniques fall pretty clearly on the legal side of the torture line," says Alt at the Heritage Foundation. "Most fall into the category of mind games, which is what interrogation is."

But the ACLU's Abdo says the techniques "in combination" amounted "either to torture or cruel, inhuman and degrading treatment, both of which are prohibited by international law as well as our own laws." The prohibition against inhuman treatment was added by the Detainee Treatment Act of 2005, enacted after the Justice Department memo and the period covered by the CIA inspector general's report.

For now, the legal debate is moot, since the Obama administration decided to limit interrogation to the non-coercive techniques permitted under the *Army Field Manual*. The White House asked that the interrogation issue be kept out of a pending bill to reauthorize intelligence activities.

As for the debate on the need for the techniques or their effectiveness, Benjamin Wittes, a Brookings Institution senior fellow who has studied the interrogation of post-9/11 detainees, says the answer may be unknowable.

"It's very hard to do a controlled experiment," Wittes says. "The CIA wasn't trying to do a controlled experiment. They were trying to get actionable intelligence and save lives."

Should Congress authorize an in-depth investigation of past detention and interrogation practices?

A little more than a year after the Sept. 11 terrorist attacks, Congress in November 2002 passed legislation to create an independent, bipartisan commission to examine why the government had failed to prevent the attacks and what could be done to guard against future attacks. President Bush reluctantly agreed to the measure, which Democrats in Congress had pushed with strong backing from many of the families of the nearly 3,000 people killed in the attacks.

The commission's report, issued in July 2004, identified a host of intelligence failures under Bush as well as

President Clinton that underestimated the threat posed by al Qaeda and missed clues to the group's plan to hijack airplanes and crash them into landmark buildings in the United States. The commission recommended a number of steps to guard against future attacks, including the creation of a new national intelligence director with authority over both the CIA and FBI. That step was one of several that were eventually adopted.[14]

A coalition of 18 civil liberties and human-rights advocates is pressing for a similar investigation of the Bush administration's detention and interrogation policies. "We can't entirely move forward unless we look back and find out what happened," says Sloan of the Constitution Project. "The American people don't know what was done in their name, and we're entitled to know."[15]

Sloan approves of Obama's decision to change detention and interrogation policies but says a broad inquiry is needed for Congress to consider legislative changes. "That's an executive branch decision that the president has made, but another president could change that," she says.

Proposals for an independent commission have support among some Democratic lawmakers, including House Speaker Nancy Pelosi, D-Calif. But Pelosi's counterpart, Senate Majority Leader Harry Reid, D-Nev., prefers investigations by individual congressional committees. Republican lawmakers generally oppose any look back as unnecessary and politically motivated. "I don't see what we're going to learn that congressional leaders didn't already know," House Minority Leader John Boehner of Ohio remarked in April.[16]

For his part, President Obama has generally opposed any broad inquiry into the Bush administration policies. "We should be looking forward, not backwards," Obama said in an April 21 news conference, five days after release of the Justice Department memo. But he went on to indicate a preference for an independent commission over congressional committees as a forum for any investigation. "I think it's very important for the American people to feel as if this is not being dealt with to provide one side or another political advantage but rather is being done in order to learn some lessons so that we move forward in an effective way," he said.

Conservatives echo the concerns about political recriminations from any broad investigation. "Part of the question is whether it's needed to get at the truth or whether it

CIA Director Leon Panetta warns that "exceptionally grave damage" to national security could result — including exposing individual CIA officers to "grave risk" — if additional documents about the CIA detention and interrogation program are released under a Freedom of Information Act request by the American Civil Liberties Union and other groups. President Obama opposes a broad reexamination of the Bush administration's counterterrorism policies.

becomes a political rehashing," says the Heritage Foundation's Alt. "Given the time that has elapsed, one wonders whether it's not simply an attempt to criminalize or vilify differences with the past administration."

ACLU lawyer Abdo counters that a broad investigation is needed to compile "an accurate historical record of what took place during the last eight years." The ACLU favors a select congressional committee for that purpose. "It's unlikely that anybody could compile as accurate and comprehensive a record as Congress," he says.

Sloan says the coalition has a "slight preference" for an independent commission over congressional inquiries. "So much in Congress gets politicized and bogged down," she says. "We thought a commission that would be independent of that kind of politics would be better."

Whatever forum might be used for an investigation, Sloan says Congress should use the results to draft legislation. "If you don't have laws, then you're leaving things to the discretion of the executive branch," she says, "and that seems to be what got us into trouble in the first place."

BACKGROUND

Eliciting the Truth

The use of coercive interrogation techniques dates to ancient times, and so too the debate over their value in eliciting the truth. In the Western world, pain has been wielded as an instrument of judicial interrogation by the ancient Greeks and Romans, European monarchs and 20th-century dictators. For several centuries, the Roman Catholic Church inflicted pain on presumed heretics to educe confessions. Throughout, some have argued that — apart from moral considerations — coercion is an inefficient technique that often produces unreliable information from subjects willing to say anything to stop the pain.[17]

As University of Wisconsin history professor Alfred W. McCoy notes, torture was practiced by the ancient Greeks on slaves and by the Romans on slaves and freemen alike. The third-century Roman jurist Ulpian defined *quaestio* (torture) as "the torment and suffering of the body in order to elicit the truth," but recognized its limitations. Some people have "such strength of body and soul" that there is "no means of obtaining the truth from them," he wrote, while others "are so susceptible to pain that they will tell any lie rather than suffer it."[18]

Torture fell out of use in Christian Europe during the first millennium, but resurfaced among civil and ecclesiastical authorities by the 12th and 13th centuries. The Catholic Church's "inquisitions" aimed at suppressing heretical movements took on torture as an instrument of interrogation under a papal bull issued by Pope Innocent IV in 1252. One of the techniques used by the Italian Inquisition was to suspend the subject by rope in five degrees of escalating severity — hence, the modern term "third degree." Church manuals prescribed techniques of interrogation. In one, Nicholas Eymerich, 14th-century inquisitor general of Aragon, cataloged 10 techniques of "evasion and deception" by heretics; he went on to specify methods for interrogators to counter them that entailed physical intimidation as well as psychological manipulation.

Civil authorities in Europe also used torture from medieval times into the 18th and 19th centuries both as coercive interrogation and public punishment. England's King Henry VIII and Queen Elizabeth I both used torture against their opponents; the Tower of London housed a rack and other instruments of torture. In Paris, the Bourbon kings confined prisoners in the Bastille under torture-like conditions.

Legal acceptance of torture began to recede with its abolition by Prussia in 1754. Ten years later, the Italian penal reformer Cesare Beccaria denounced torture as "a sure route for the acquittal of robust ruffians and the conviction of weak innocents." By the late 19th century, the French author Victor Hugo felt justified in declaring that torture "has ceased to exist." The widespread use of torture by such 20th-century dictatorial regimes as the Soviet Union and Nazi Germany, however, proved the reports of its demise to be exaggerated.

The United States has no acknowledged experience with legally sanctioned torture, but coercive interrogation was a widespread if unacknowledged law enforcement practice as late as the mid-20th century. "Our police, with no legal sanction, employ duress, threat, bullying, a vast amount of moderate physical abuse and a certain degree of outright torture," the author and social critic Ernest Jerome Hopkins wrote in 1931.[19] In a succession of cases beginning in 1936 and continuing through the 1950s, the Supreme Court began throwing out convictions based on confessions that police secured either by physical or psychological coercion. Frustrated with the case-by-case adjudications, the court in 1966 laid down the famous Miranda rule requiring police to notify suspects of their rights. Chief Justice Earl Warren, a former district attorney, stressed that the rule was aimed at preventing the use of physical beatings or incommunicado interrogation to coerce confessions from suspects in custody.[20]

World War II gave the United States its first sustained experience with interrogating wartime captives. Far removed from the battlefield, the government built two special detention centers in the United States to interrogate German and Japanese prisoners. The two facilities — Fort Hunt, in Northern Virginia near Washington, D.C., and Camp Tracy, near Stockton, Calif. — were kept secret during and for decades after the war. During the war, the military even delayed or avoided telling the International

C H R O N O L O G Y

Cold War *Central Intelligence Agency established, given covert roles in propaganda, subversion; disclosures of CIA operations often bring controversy.*

1947 National Security Act of 1947 establishes CIA to collect and analyze intelligence; mandate expanded next year to include covert propaganda, support for anti-communist movements.

1950s *CIA's MKUltra program experiments with interrogation techniques using hypnosis, drugs and physical coercion; terminated in late 1960s, records destroyed in 1973.*

1963 Secret CIA manual — *Kubark counterintelligence interrogation-July 1963* — details "coercive" interrogation techniques.

Mid-to-late 1960s *Widespread torture carried out by South Vietnamese forces in Operation Phoenix, CIA-designed counterinsurgency program.*

1960s-1970s *CIA-trained and funded police forces in Latin America are accused of abuse, torture.*

1983 Secret CIA "Human Resource Exploitation Training Manual" details non-physical methods for coercive interrogation: "debility, disorientation and dread."

1997 CIA declassifies interrogation manuals in response to threatened Freedom of Information Act suit by *Baltimore Sun.*

2001-Present *CIA given lead role in interrogating "high-value" terrorism suspects after Sept. 11 attacks; gains permission for "enhanced" techniques that critics say amount to torture.*

September 2001 Vice President Dick Cheney says U.S. will have to "work the dark side" to combat al Qaeda (Sept. 16); President George W. Bush signs order directing CIA to interrogate "high-value" detainees (Sept. 17).

Fall-winter 2001-2002 CIA arranges to hold future detainees in secret prisons overseas.

March 2002 Abu Zubaydah, purported adviser to Osama bin Laden, captured in Pakistan; CIA proposes using "enhanced interrogation techniques."

2002 Justice Department approves use of 10 "enhanced" CIA interrogation techniques." . . . Abd al-Rahim al-Nashiri, accused mastermind of *USS Cole* bombing, captured, taken to secret prison in Thailand, subjected to waterboarding; later threatened with pistol, power drill.

2003 CIA inspector general opens investigation of interrogation practices (January), later refers some cases to Justice Department for prosecution. . . . Khalid Shaikh Mohammed (KSM), alleged architect of 9/11 attacks, captured in Pakistan (March), waterboarded 183 times; dispute continues about value of information elicited by enhanced techniques.

April-May 2004 Photos of abuse of Iraqi prisoners in U.S. military prison outside Baghdad provoke outcry in U.S., around world. . . . CIA report questions implementation of interrogation program; notes agents' concern about potential backlash if disclosed.

November-December 2005 *Washington Post* publishes first detailed story on CIA secret prisons. . . . CIA destroys 92 videotapes of interrogation of KSM, others. . . . Detainee Treatment Act prohibits "cruel, inhuman or degrading" treatment by military, but not CIA, interrogators.

August 2006 CIA contractor David Passaro convicted of assault in death of Afghan farmer Abdul Wali after interrogation in June 2003; later given prison term. . . . Bush orders 14 remaining "high-value" detainees in CIA prisons transferred to Guantánamo Bay Naval Base, Cuba.

March 2008 Bush vetoes bill passed by Congress barring enhanced interrogation techniques by CIA; says techniques vital to war on terror.

2009 President Obama bars enhanced-interrogation techniques, orders CIA prisons closed; promises closure of Guantánamo within one year. . . . Obama declassifies Justice Department memos approving use of enhanced interrogation techniques; rules out prosecution of agents who followed guidelines. . . . CIA inspector general's report declassified in August, yields detailed picture of CIA interrogation program. . . . Attorney General Eric H. Holder Jr. asks career prosecutor to review CIA interrogation cases where agents exceeded guidelines; move brings strong criticism from Republicans, conservatives and former CIA officials.

'Extraordinary Rendition' of Terrorists Challenged

Detainees say they were abducted and tortured.

The Obama administration continues to invoke a "state secrets" privilege to block a federal lawsuit seeking damages from a CIA-contractor airline for transporting prisoners to foreign countries where they were allegedly tortured.

The two-year-old lawsuit in a federal appeals court in California is one of several American Civil Liberties Union (ACLU) efforts to challenge the practice known as "extraordinary rendition." Under President George W. Bush, the Central Intelligence Agency (CIA) was accused of transferring suspected terrorists, often apprehended in foreign countries under questionable circumstances, to countries known to abuse or torture prisoners.

The Obama administration has continued to hand over suspected terrorists to other countries but is vowing to prevent abuses against U.S.-captured detainees by more frequent inspection of foreign prison facilities. ACLU lawyers say those efforts are inadequate because prisoners held in other countries are unlikely to report abuse to visiting U.S. monitors.[1]

Meanwhile, Justice Department lawyers are asking the federal appeals court in San Francisco to reconsider its April 28 decision to allow five former or current detainees to pursue a lawsuit charging Jeppesen Dataplans, a Bay-area airline, with knowingly assisting the CIA in forcibly transporting them to other countries to be tortured. A federal judge in San Jose had granted the government's motion to dismiss the suit on "state secrets" grounds, a privilege the government can use to limit evidence or even throw out a suit altogether if state secrets might be disclosed. However, the 9th U.S. Circuit Court of Appeals overturned that decision.

In rejecting the privilege for now, the three-judge panel said the subject of the suit — the agreement between the government and the airline, a Boeing subsidiary — was not secret. The ruling, which the government now wants the full appeals court to hear, left the question open as to whether the government can invoke the privilege in regard to specific evidence as the case proceeds.[2]

Committee of the Red Cross about the camps — a violation of the Geneva Conventions. Interrogators emphasized rapport-building instead of coercion. "I never laid hands on anyone," one of the Fort Hunt veterans told a *Washington Post* reporter in 2007. But the interrogators also gathered intelligence by secretly monitoring and recording the prisoners' cellblock conversations.[21]

Mind Control

The Cold War between the United States and two communist states — the Soviet Union and China — featured the use of interrogation on both sides for multiple purposes. The principals used interrogation to gather intelligence and to create propaganda. They also fostered the use of interrogation by proxy states to suppress or intimidate domestic opposition. The CIA was a prime player in secretly developing techniques of interrogation in the 1950s and '60s that became intensely controversial when publicly disclosed in later decades.[22]

The CIA was created in 1947, and the next year given a broad congressional charter to collect and analyze intelligence and carry out covert operations overseas without disclosing its budget, staffing or other information. As the new agency was taking shape, the nations of the world were also laying the foundations of a new framework of international law, including the Universal Declaration of Human Rights in 1948 and the rewritten and expanded Geneva Conventions in 1949. Included in the fourth Geneva Convention regarding treatment of civilians was a new provision that barred the use of "physical or mental

The lead plaintiff in the case, Ethiopian-born British citizen Binyam Mohamed, was arrested by Pakistani authorities in 2002, turned over to U.S. authorities and transferred to Morocco. He claims he was tortured during 18 months of captivity there before being transferred to U.S. facilities in Afghanistan and then in Guantánamo Bay, Cuba. He was finally released in February 2009. Of the other four plaintiffs, two remain in prison, one in Egypt, one in Italy; two others have been released.

The ACLU filed a similar suit in 2005 on behalf of Khaled el-Masri, a German citizen who said he was abducted in Macedonia and taken to a secret CIA prison in Afghanistan where he was tortured. El-Masri

Khaled el-Masri, a German citizen, says he was abducted and tortured by the CIA.

was eventually released without charges; he was apparently confused with a suspected terrorist with a similar name.

The federal appeals court in Richmond, Va., cited the state secrets privilege in dismissing el-Masri's earlier suit against former CIA Director George Tenet and three CIA-contractor airlines; the Supreme Court declined to hear el-Masri's appeal in October 2007. The ACLU is now asking the Inter-American Commission on Human Rights to hear

the case; the government has two months from the Aug. 27 filing to respond.

Attorney General Eric Holder announced on Sept. 23 new limits on the use of the state secrets privilege. It will be invoked only to prevent "genuine and significant harm" to national security or foreign policy, Holder said, and not to conceal violations of law or prevent embarrassment to the government. The policy was described as applying to cases after Oct. 1 — apparently ruling out any direct effect on the *Jeppesen* case.[3]

---

[1] See David Johnston, "Renditions to Continue, but With Better Oversight, U.S. Says," *The New York Times*, Aug. 25, 2009, p. A8.

[2] The decision is *Mohamed v. Jeppesen Dataplan, Inc.*, 08-15693 (9th Cir. 2009), as amended Aug. 31, 2009, www.ca9.uscourts.gov/datastore/opinions/2009/08/31/08-15693.pdf. See Bob Egelko, "U.S. fights rendition suit against Bay Area firm;" *San Francisco Chronicle*, Aug. 10, 2009, p. C1.

[3] See Department of Justice, "Attorney General Establishes New State Secrets Policies and Procedures," Sept. 23, 2009, www.usdoj.gov/opa/pr/2009/September/09-ag-1013.html. For advance coverage, see Carrie Johnson, "Obama to Set Higher Bar for Keeping State Secrets," *The Washington Post*, Sept. 23, 2009, p. A1.

---

coercion" for any purpose, including "to obtain information from them or third parties." The official commentators described the provision, Article 31, as "an important step forward in international law."

Despite this international law prohibition, the CIA worked over the course of two decades to develop new interrogation techniques using hypnosis, drugs and various forms of physical discomfort. The initiatives stemmed in part from information about the use of hypnosis, drugs and electroshock by Nazi interrogators during World War II. They gained urgency from the belief that the Soviet and Chinese regimes had developed mind-control techniques that — whether applied to Soviet citizens in the Stalinist-era "show trials" or to U.S. prisoners in the Korean War — could induce the subjects to say almost

anything the interrogators wanted them to say. Edward Hunter, a journalist secretly on the CIA's payroll, gave a frightening name to the techniques with his 1951 book *Brainwashing in Red China.*[23]

In his critical account, University of Wisconsin history professor McCoy chronicles a secret program code named MKUltra, whose findings and techniques were later codified in a 1963 manual called *Kubark*. The program used human subjects in experiments with the newly discovered hallucinogen LSD and with such sensory-deprivation techniques as isolation in a cramped box or water tank. Drug-induced interrogation proved to be a blind alley, but sensory deprivation proved more efficacious in inducing a state of helplessness in the subjects. McCoy describes the CIA's discovery of "no-touch torture" as "the first real

Terrorism Suspects Transferred from Secret Sites

Fourteen "high-value" terrorism suspects were transferred from secret CIA sites to the prison camp at the Guantánamo Bay Naval Base in Cuba in September 2006. Five have been charged with helping plan the Sept. 11 terrorist attacks on the United States; the government is deciding whether to continue prosecuting them in special military tribunals or move the trials to a regular federal court. Formal charges have not been brought against the other nine detainees. The now disbanded combatant status review tribunals at Guantánamo confirmed their status as "enemy combatants."

Here are the 14 "high-value" detainees and the role the government alleges they played in terrorism:

The five 9/11 detainees — Each defendant is charged with conspiracy and a number of separate offenses including murder in violation of the law of war, attacking civilians, destruction of property in violation of the law of war and terrorism.

Khalid Shaykh Muhammad: principal al Qaeda operative directing 9/11 attacks.

Walid Bin Attash: linked indirectly to the 1998 U.S. Embassy bombings in Tanzania and Kenya and the *USS Cole* bombing in 2000.

Ramzi Bin al-Shibh: coordinator of 9/11 attacks.

Mustafa al-Hawsawi: linked to detailed computer records of al Qaeda members, finances.

Ammar al-Baluchi: linked to arrangements for 9/11 attacks.

The other nine high-value detainees yet to be charged are:

Ahmed Khalfan Ghailani: linked to bombing of U.S. Embassy in Tanzania.

Mohd Farik bin Amin ("Zubair"): arranged financing for bombing of J. W. Marriott Hotel in Jakarta, Indonesia, in 2003.

Al Nashiri, Abd Al Rahim Hussein Mohammed: linked to *Cole* bombing.

Bashir bin Lap ("Lillie"): linked to planning of bombing of J. W. Marriott Hotel.

Rjduan bin Isomuddiiu ("Hambali"): linked to bombings in Indonesia, efforts to topple Malaysian government.

Zayn al Abidin Muhammad Husayn ("Abu Zubaydah"): Head of al Qaeda training camps in Afghanistan; diary entries include unacted-on plans for attacks within United States.

Guleed Hassan Ahmed: al Qaeda cell leader in Djibouti.

Majid Khan: linked to alleged al Qaeda money-laundering plot.

Abu Faraj al-Libi: deputy to al Qaeda's 3rd in command.

Source: Combatant Status Review Tribunals/Administrative Review Boards, U.S. Department of Defense, Oct. 17, 2007; accessed online on Sept. 21, 2009. Note: The DOD's name spellings are used; variations are often used in the news media.

---

revolution in the cruel science of pain in centuries."

The official directing the program was Richard Helms, assistant deputy director of operations in the 1950s and later the director of the CIA from 1966 to 1973. In one of his final acts in office, Helms directed the destruction of all documents pertaining to the program — in advance of imminent journalistic and congressional investigations of the agency.

By then, however, the CIA had come under intense criticism for its role in a counterinsurgency program in the Vietnam War known as Operation Phoenix. The CIA-designed program as carried out by the South Vietnamese entailed the use of outright torture, including beatings and electric shocks; the South Vietnamese attributed nearly 41,000 deaths to the program. In hearings on his nomination to succeed Helms as CIA director in 1973, William Colby, who had served as the CIA's chief of pacification in Vietnam, told the Senate Foreign Relations Committee he was aware of reports of abuse but had instructed CIA personnel not to participate.[24]

McCoy depicts the CIA as guilty of "propagating torture" also through a program in the 1960s and '70s that funneled aid to police forces in pro-American governments. The program was housed in the Office of Public Safety in the Agency for International Development (U.S. AID), but was headed by a former CIA official and operated in what McCoy describes as "close coordination with the agency's intelligence mission." Latin American countries sent police recruits to a clandestine academy in Washington for training. A report by what was then the General Accounting Office (GAO) in 1976 acknowledged allegations that the academy "taught or encouraged the use of torture," but made no formal finding on the claims. Amnesty International, however, claimed to have documented widespread torture by police in at least two dozen countries that had received aid under the program.

Allegations of CIA complicity in torture were renewed in the 1980s — notably, in Latin America. A *New York Times* report on the CIA's role in counterinsurgency in Honduras in 1988 prompted a closed-door hearing by the Senate Intelligence Committee that disclosed to lawmakers — but not the public — a CIA instructional manual on interrogation used in at least seven Latin American countries in the 1980s. *The Human Resource Exploitation Training Manual*, adapting methods outlined in *Kubark* two decades earlier, cautioned against physical torture in favor of non-physical coercive techniques: "debility, disorientation, and dread." The 1983 manual suggests, among other techniques, "persistent manipulation of time," "disrupting sleep schedules" and "serving meals at odd times." The CIA declassified and released both manuals in 1997 in response to the threat of a Freedom of Information Act suit by *The Baltimore Sun*.[25]

'Using Any Means'

Within weeks of the 9/11 attacks, the CIA was tasked with helping capture and then interrogate high-ranking officials in the al Qaeda terrorist network despite the agency's lack of recent experience in questioning adversaries. Some "high-value" detainees were kept in secret prisons and questioned using the "enhanced" techniques approved by the Justice Department despite concerns among some operatives about the reaction to their eventual disclosure. With information leaking out, the Bush administration eventually discarded the harsh measures and in September 2006 transferred the remaining 14 detainees from CIA prisons to Guantánamo. Even with the Obama administration's change in policy, however, some Bush officials and supporters of the former administration continue to defend both the legality and effectiveness of the interrogations.[26]

Vice President Cheney set the mood for the administration's war on terror with his statement on NBC's "Meet the Press" on Sept. 16, 2001, that the government would "have to work through sort of the dark side if you will. . . . It's going to be vital for us to use any means at our disposal,

basically, to achieve our objective," Cheney said.[27] Against that backdrop, the CIA seemed the logical choice for any off-the-books counterterrorism work. And the agency had an interest in restoring its reputation after a major pre-9/11 failure: The CIA had failed to notify domestic law enforcement of the entry into the United States of two known al Qaeda operatives who later became two of the 9/11 hijackers.

As journalist Jane Mayer relates in her sharply critical book, *The Dark Side*, the agency had focused on where to house high-value detainees in late 2001 and early 2002, before it even had anyone in custody. Guantánamo, chosen to hold those captured by the military in Afghanistan, was rejected as too visible; a suggestion to use perpetually circumnavigating aircraft was rejected as impractical. Eventually, friendly governments were asked and agreed to provide secret sites for the detainees transported under the so-called "extraordinary rendition" program. Thailand, Lithuania, Poland and Romania were later identified, but none acknowledged their role.

Meanwhile, the agency had turned to a retired military psychologist, John Mitchell, to prepare a paper on al Qaeda's resistance techniques. Mitchell and his partner and fellow psychologist John Bruce Jessen had served in the Air Force in a program called Survival, Evasion, Resistance, Escape (SERE) that trained U.S. service members in countering coercive techniques that an adversary might employ. As the CIA inspector general's report notes, the pair "developed a list of new and more aggressive EITs that they recommended for use in interrogations."[28]

The capture of the senior al Qaeda operative Abu Zubaydah in Pakistan in late March 2002 provided the template for the CIA's enhanced interrogations. Zubaydah, an al Qaeda veteran believed to be personally close to Osama bin Laden, was captured in a joint raid by FBI, CIA and Pakistani law-enforcement and intelligence officers outside Faisalabad. With the badly wounded Zubaydah in custody, the FBI team was pushed aside by a CIA team headed by Mitchell. The measures used on Zubaydah, including being confined in a coffin-like box and waterboarded, formed the basis of the Aug. 2, 2002, Office of Legal Counsel opinion sanctioning a total of 10 enhanced techniques. The memo carried the signature of Jay Bybee, who had the rank of assistant attorney general as head of the office, but was actually written by his deputy, John Yoo, a soft-spoken but hard-edged proponent of expansive presidential power on leave from the University of California's Berkeley Law School.

According to later information, Nashiri became the second detainee to be waterboarded following his capture in November 2002. The inspector general's investigation of the program began in January 2003; the report is ambiguous as to whether the account of Nashiri's treatment was the catalyst. Even with the internal probe going on, however, CIA interrogators conducted the most extensive use of coercive measures two months later after the capture of the highest-value detainee: Khalid Shaikh Mohammed.

The self-described mastermind of the 9/11 hijackings, KSM, as he came to be known, was captured on March 1, 2003, in Rawalpindi, Pakistan, thanks to a $25 million reward paid to an informant. The inspector general's report states that he was waterboarded 183 times, but the remainder of the account of his treatment is redacted in the version released in August. Mohammed himself later described being kept naked for more than a month, chained to a wall in a painful crouch, subjected alternately to extreme heat or cold and doused with water. Mohammed's interrogation is the focal point of the dispute over the need or effectiveness of these coercive measures. Supporters say KSM provided invaluable information but only after use of the enhanced techniques. Opponents say he was glad to boast of his role in al Qaeda but also deliberately fed false information to his interrogators.

As some in the agency had feared, the details of the CIA interrogations slowly leaked out, but only after pictures of abuses of Iraqi prisoners by U.S. military personnel at Abu Ghraib prison gained worldwide attention in April and May 2004. It also was revealed that leaders of the congressional intelligence oversight committees, who had been secretly briefed on the CIA's activities, had raised no public objections.

By 2005, CIA and military interrogators were being publicly implicated in deaths of detainees in Afghanistan and Iraq. In the most notorious case, Manadel al-Jamadi, an Iraqi suspected in the bombing of a Red Cross office in Baghdad, died in November 2003 during interrogation by Navy SEALS and a CIA interrogator. An image of Jamadi's ice-packed corpse with a smiling U.S. service member standing over it was among the Abu Ghraib photos published in 2004. In February 2005, The Associated Press reported that Jamadi died while hung from

his wrists — a technique dubbed "Palestinian hanging." In October, the ACLU reported that documents obtained in Freedom of Information Act litigation showed at least 44 detainees' deaths during interrogation, with 21 of those classified in official autopsies as homicides. A report by the group Human Rights First published in February 2006 raised the number of deaths to 100, with 34 classified as homicides.[29]

The controversies spawned by the Abu Ghraib photographs and detainees' deaths helped drive Congress to pass the Detainee Treatment Act of 2005, with a ban on "cruel, inhuman or degrading treatment" of detainees. The provision was written by Sen. John McCain, the Arizona Republican who was held by North Vietnam as a prisoner of war for five years, and reluctantly accepted by President Bush. But the ban applied only to military interrogators, not to the CIA.

Meanwhile, *The Washington Post* had published in November 2005 a well-informed story on the CIA's secret prisons and its program of "extraordinary renditions."[30] Unbeknownst to the public at the time, the International Committee for the Red Cross (ICRC), officially designated under the Geneva Conventions to monitor wartime captives, was denied any access to the detainees despite repeatedly expressing concerns about their whereabouts. ICRC monitors were first allowed to visit the detainees in October 2006, after their transfers to Guantánamo. In a confidential report written in February 2007 and disclosed by author-journalist Mark Danner in March 2009, the ICRC described the prisoners' allegations of their treatment as amounting to "torture and/or cruel, inhuman or degrading treatment."[31]

Bush's decision in September 2006 to transfer the high-value detainees to Guantánamo symbolized the retreat on the issue. But the prisoners were still kept separate from other detainees. And through the end of the administration, both Bush and Cheney continued to defend the interrogation program as the key to having prevented al Qaeda from any subsequent attacks on U.S. soil.

CURRENT SITUATION

Fighting Over Disclosure

The Obama administration is continuing to resist disclosure of some details of the CIA's interrogation program, even after disavowing the harsh measures used on some "high-value" detainees and shutting down the secret prisons once used to hold them.

The administration is invoking national security and other grounds in federal court filings to block release of hundreds of documents that the ACLU and other civil liberties and veterans' groups are seeking from the CIA through Freedom of Information Act (FOIA) litigation.*

The documents withheld include President George W. Bush's original Sept. 17, 2001, order authorizing the CIA's detention and interrogation program and scores of messages between CIA headquarters and field operatives on implementation of the program. Also being withheld are some documents pertaining to the CIA's destruction of 92 videotapes of the interrogations in November 2005 and the contents of the tapes.[32]

John Durham, a career federal prosecutor in Connecticut, was designated in 2008 by Attorney General Michael Mukasey to conduct an independent investigation of the destruction of the tapes; Durham was then chosen by Attorney General Holder to review the cases involving CIA interrogation of detainees.

President Obama has declassified and ordered the release of some of the documents sought in the litigation, including the CIA inspector general's critical May 2004 report on the program. In court filings, however, CIA Director Panetta and an agency FOIA officer are warning that further releases could do "exceptionally grave damage" to national security, endanger cooperation with foreign intelligence services and expose individual CIA officers to "grave risk."

The legal scrapping on the CIA issues is playing out in front of a federal judge in New York City, Alvin Hellerstein, who previously chastised the Bush administration for its "glacial pace" in responding to the ACLU litigation. Hellerstein is scheduled to hear arguments on Sept. 30 on the ACLU's objections to some redactions in three Justice Department memos released on April 16 and to the withholding of the documents pertaining to the destruction of the videotapes.[33]

Meanwhile, in a separate part of the FOIA litigation, the government is asking the Supreme Court to block the release of photographs of abuse of prisoners held by the military in seven facilities in Afghanistan and Iraq. The New York-based 2nd U.S. Circuit Court of Appeals ruled in September 2008 in favor of the ACLU's FOIA request for the photographs, which are in addition to photographs already released of prisoners at Abu Ghraib being abused.

The Justice Department originally decided not to appeal, but in May Obama said that release of the photos could harm U.S. service members abroad by inflaming anti-American sentiment. The government is arguing the photographs fall within the Freedom of Information Act's exemption for "information compiled for law enforcement purposes" that "could reasonably be expected to endanger the life or physical safety of any individual." In its ruling, the appeals court said the government's use of the exemption was too broad.[34]

In the CIA case, the government's legal arguments are based on four other exemptions from the information act, which protect classified information, information specifically exempted by other statutes, attorney-client communications and personnel and medical files. In broader terms, the CIA's most recent court filing, on Aug. 31, warns that further disclosures regarding the interrogation program are "reasonably likely to degrade the [U.S. government's] ability to effectively question terrorist detainees." In addition, the agency says that disclosure of cooperation from other countries "would damage the CIA's relations with these foreign governments and could cause them to cease cooperating with the CIA on such matters."

ACLU lawyers call the administration's stance in the litigation inconsistent with President Obama's past criticisms of the Bush administration's policies. "It's disappointing that the government continues to withhold these vital documents that would fill in the remaining gaps in the public record," says ACLU legal fellow Abdo.

From the opposite side, the administration has faced pressure from within the CIA and from past CIA directors to limit disclosures. Former CIA Director Hayden was one of four past heads of the agency who contacted the White House in April to urge the president not to release the Justice Department memos approving use of the enhanced interrogation techniques. Appearing on "Fox News Sunday" at the time, Hayden said the disclosures were making it "more difficult for CIA officers to defend the nation."[35]

---

* Other plaintiffs in the litigation are the Center for Constitutional Rights, Physicians for Human Rights, Veterans for Common Sense and Veterans for Peace.

Did harsh CIA interrogations amount to torture?

YES
David Kaye
*Executive Director, UCLA School of Law
International Human Rights Program*

Written for *CQ Researcher*, September 2009

Senior officials in the Bush administration initiated and authorized a policy of harsh treatment of terrorism suspects held by the United States. Recent documents released by the Obama administration — some only released under court orders — demonstrate that CIA interrogation techniques included waterboarding, extensive sleep deprivation, forced confinement in extremely small spaces, threats with handguns and power drills, threats against the lives and well-being of detainees' family members, severe stress positions, "walling" detainees by slamming them against fixed spaces during interrogations, forced standing and shackling, exposure to cold and other forms of torture or cruel, inhuman or degrading treatment.

In my opinion, these techniques constituted torture or, at a minimum, cruel or inhuman treatment prohibited by U.S. law.

Since the United States had long been at the forefront of objecting to torture under any circumstance, it should not be a surprise that the U.S. government, prior to 2001, had joined many treaties that prohibit torture — including the 1949 Geneva Conventions, the 1966 International Covenant on Civil and Political Rights and the 1984 Convention Against Torture — and enacted domestic laws criminalizing it. The anti-torture statute in the U.S. Code prohibits acts "specifically intended to inflict severe physical or mental pain or suffering," defining such mental pain or suffering as, among other things, "the threat of imminent death." The War Crimes Act similarly prohibits torture and cruel or inhuman treatment (such as "serious physical abuse"). Neither permits any sort of exceptional circumstance to justify torture.

As a bipartisan report of the Senate Armed Services Committee underscored last year, the Justice Department under President Bush distorted the meaning of these criminal laws beyond recognition, approving harsh techniques that the United States has condemned in other contexts. Many of the abuses noted above are prohibited under any good-faith reading of U.S. law, some plainly constituting torture. Take waterboarding, which creates a profound sensation of drowning and imminent death: Even one application amounts to the kind of physical and mental abuse prohibited by U.S. law, but interrogators applied it 83 times to one detainee and 183 times to another, according to the CIA inspector general.

While the argument against prosecuting CIA agents for these acts may be understandable, the argument that these techniques are permitted by U.S. law is simply wrong. As we consider the kind of detention policy our country deserves, defining our past conduct in the proper terms — that is to say, recognizing it as torture, cruel and inhumane — is an important step forward.

NO
Jeffrey F. Addicott
*Director, Center for Terrorism Law, St. Mary's
University School of Law*

From testimony submitted to Senate Judiciary Subcommittee on Administrative Oversight and the Courts, May 13, 2009.

In the context of the Department of Justice legal memorandums that approved certain CIA enhanced interrogation techniques, the issue is whether they amounted to "torture" — especially the use of "waterboarding" on high-value al-Qaeda detainees.

Since the detainees are not entitled to prisoner of war status, international law does not forbid interrogation. By its very nature, even the most reasonable interrogation process places the detainee in emotional duress and causes stress to his being — both physical and mental. Allegations of "torture" roll off the tongue with ease. Recognizing that not every alleged incident of interrogation or mistreatment necessarily satisfies the legal definition of torture, it is imperative that one view such allegations with a clear understanding of the applicable legal standards set out in law and judicial precedent.

In this manner, allegations or claims of illegal interrogation practices can be properly measured as falling above or below a particular legal threshold. In my legal opinion, the so-called CIA enhanced interrogation practices approved by the Department of Justice in several detailed legal memorandums did not constitute torture under international law or U.S. domestic law.

The 1984 U.N. Convention Against Torture and Other Cruel, Inhuman or Degrading Treatment or Punishment is the primary international agreement governing torture. It defines torture as:

"[A]ny act by which severe pain or suffering, whether physical or mental, is intentionally inflicted on a person for such purposes as obtaining . . . information or a confession."

Even the worst of the CIA techniques — waterboarding — would not constitute torture under the Torture Convention. (CIA waterboarding lasted no more than 40 seconds and appears similar to what we have done hundreds of times to our own military special-operations soldiers in training courses.)

As foreboding as the term enhanced interrogation techniques may sound, responsible debate must revolve around legal case law associated with interpreting the Torture Convention and not simply cases that use the word torture.

For example, in *Ireland v. United Kingdom,* the European Court of Human Rights ruled by a sweeping vote of 13-3 that certain British interrogation techniques used against suspected Irish terrorists — which included wall-standing for up to 30 hours and subjection to loud noises — were not torture. If the British techniques were deemed not to constitute torture by this leading court, then even the worst of the American interrogation techniques fell far below what the British interrogators practiced.

Human-rights advocates, however, say the public needs still more information about the detention and interrogation programs. "We've learned a lot," says John Sifton, a human-rights investigator and attorney in New York City. But, he adds, "there's still a lot of things that are unclear."[36]

Meanwhile, the ACLU filed a new FOIA suit in federal court in New York City on Sept. 22 seeking records from the Pentagon and the CIA on prisoners held at Bagram Air Force Base in Afghanistan. In announcing the suit, ACLU staff attorney Melissa Goodman described Bagram as "the new Guantánamo," but complained that the public "is still in the dark" about basic facts about the facility, including the number of prisoners and rules and conditions of confinement. The ACLU said that the Defense Department had identified a list of prisoners, but declined to release it on national security and privacy grounds.[37]

Getting to Trial?

The government is weighing its next move in the trial of the five CIA "high-value" detainees charged with helping plan the Sept. 11 attacks. In question is whether to continue prosecuting them in special military tribunals or move the trial to a regular federal court.

Justice Department attorneys disclosed the pending decision in court filings on Sept. 16 that opposed a motion by one of the detainees, Ramzi bin al-Shibh, seeking to bar all proceedings before the military commission already convened at Guantánamo to try the five. While opposing the motion, the lawyers also filed a new motion asking the military judges to temporarily stay the proceedings in order for the government to decide by mid-November whether to shift the trial to a civilian federal court.

The lawyers noted that Congress is currently considering changes to the Military Commissions Act, the 2006 law that added new procedural safeguards to the military commissions set up by the Bush administration in order to comply with a Supreme Court decision.[38] In addition, the lawyers pointed to "upcoming decisions" on the forum for the trial that would be made within 60 days by Attorney General Holder in consultation with Defense Secretary Robert Gates.[39]

The requested continuance — which the military judge granted on Sept. 21 — is the third delay since January in the government's highest-profile proceeding against detainees rounded up in other countries by the Bush administration. The lead defendant is Khalid Shaikh Mohammed, the accused chief planner of the 9/11 attacks and one of three CIA detainees known to have been waterboarded.

The trial was thrown into disarray on Dec. 8 when all five defendants said they wanted to plead guilty to the broad conspiracy charges filed against them in February 2008. The proceedings were put on hold, however, to allow the tribunal time to determine whether bin al-Sibh and a second defendant, Mustafa Ahmed al-Hawsawi, were mentally competent to decide to proceed without an attorney. Mohammed and two others had already been granted permission to represent themselves.

President Obama moved to put all the military commissions on hold after taking office in January as part of his promise to close Guantánamo within a year. He tasked Holder with deciding how to proceed against what were then the camp's remaining 241 prisoners. Since then, 14 inmates have been transferred to other countries and about 80 others approved for resettlement.

Bin al-Shibh has been described as the coordinator of the 9/11 attacks. Al-Hawsawi is alleged to have assisted, another of the defendants, Ali Abd al-Aziz Ali, in handling financial arrangements for the hijackers. Aziz Ali, also known as Ammar al-Baluchi, is a nephew of Mohammed and allegedly acted as his lieutenant for the operation. The fifth defendant, Waleed bin Attash, also known as Khallad, is alleged to have helped select and train some of the hijackers.

A sixth defendant, Mohammed al-Qahtani, was originally charged, but his case was dismissed in May 2008 without explanation. Al-Qahtani has been identified as the "twentieth hijacker" in the attacks because he tried to enter the United States before Sept. 11 but was denied entry. In January 2009, the presiding military judge, Susan Crawford, said she dismissed charges against al-Qahtani because she concluded he had been tortured at Guantánamo.[40]

The five remaining defendants are among 14 detainees from CIA sites who were transferred to Guantánamo in September 2006. The government has not brought formal charges against the other nine, who are challenging their detentions in federal habeas corpus proceedings. All nine were given hearings before the now disbanded combatant status review tribunals at Guantánamo, which confirmed their status as "enemy combatants."

As part of its Freedom of Information Act litigation, the ACLU obtained redacted transcripts in June of some of those proceedings, including testimony by Mohammed and three others that they had been tortured or abused while in U.S. custody. Transcripts released during the Bush administration had deleted all references to abuse, the ACLU said. The transcripts quote Mohammed as saying he used to "make up stories" for CIA interrogators after being tortured. Al Nashiri, one of the waterboarded detainees, said that interrogators would "drown me in water."[41]

ACLU lawyers favor shutting down the military commissions altogether. "We have said from the beginning that these are illegitimate proceedings," says Denny LeBoeuf, head of the John Adams Project, a joint venture with the National Association of Criminal Defense Lawyers that is providing attorneys for detainees in the 9/11 and other capital cases.

LeBoeuf says that any evidence obtained by torture will not be allowed in either the military commissions or in federal courts, but that other evidence will be admissible. "There'll be civilian lawyers, there'll be military lawyers and they'll argue about what evidence should be admitted." In the end, she adds, "some people will get convicted."

OUTLOOK
Change and Continuity

Four days after releasing details of the harsh interrogation measures used by the CIA against suspected terrorists, President Obama visited the agency's headquarters on a politically sensitive morale-boosting mission.

"Don't be discouraged by what's happened in the last few weeks," Obama told the assembled employees on April 20. The government's willingness to acknowledge "serious mistakes" and "move forward," Obama said, "is precisely why I am proud to be president of the United States, and that's why you should be proud to be members of the CIA."[42]

Four months later, Obama's attorney general undercut the president's efforts to reassure CIA employees by asking a federal prosecutor to investigate agency operatives who may have gone beyond the "enhanced interrogation techniques" that the Justice Department authorized.

"Morale at the agency is down to minus 50," said A. B. "Buzzy" Krongard, the third-ranking CIA official at the time of the use of harsh interrogation practices.[43]

"The agency feared this day would come," says Amy Zegart, a professor of public policy at UCLA who has studied intelligence agencies' role in counterterrorism. "They did everything that was legally authorized by the Department of Justice and politically sanctioned by the White House. And now they feel they're being hung out to dry."

Some human-rights advocates are applauding Holder's decision to refer the CIA interrogation cases for further investigation. "It's important for the United States to be able to return to a system of operating under law," says Human Rights First executive director Massimino.

Many want Holder to go further. Human-rights investigator Sifton calls for an investigation of "any and all violations of law that took place in connection with the detention and interrogation program," including possible obstruction of justice by officials at the Justice Department and White House up to and including Vice President Cheney and President Bush. "No one wants to go after low-level CIA officers," Sifton says. "That's not accountability. That's scapegoating."

Others, however, disagree with Holder's decision. "I'm opposed to prosecutions," says Joseph Marguiles, a veteran human-rights advocate who is representing Abu Zabaydah. Like other human-rights advocates, however, Marguiles strongly favors a full investigation by a congressional committee or independent commission.

Among the new proposals to emerge in that regard is a suggestion by Fred Hiatt, editorial page editor of the *Post*, for a "truth commission" to be chaired by two retired Supreme Court justices: Sandra Day O'Connor and David H. Souter. "A fair-minded commission," Hiatt wrote on Aug. 30, "could help the nation come to grips with its past and show the world that America is serious about doing so."[44]

The prospects for a full-blown investigation of that sort, however, appear to be dim. "I don't get any sense that the Obama administration is willing to see this full discussion take place," says Marguiles. "In fact, there's every indication they don't want it to take place." For her part, Zegart doubts that an investigation could produce a "sober" assessment in what she calls "this partisan, poisonous atmosphere."

National-security law expert Robert Chesney at the University of Texas Law School in Austin says Obama has tried to navigate the political shoals with measured steps in revising the Bush administration's counterterrorism policies. Obama has scrapped the "enhanced interrogation techniques" but continues to defend the power to detain enemy combatants with limited judicial review. He has changed review procedures at the prison camp at Bagram Air Force base in Afghanistan, but continues to oppose habeas corpus rights for the detainees there. The government is also continuing to invoke the state-secrets privilege in such cases as one in federal court in California seeking to hold CIA-contractor airlines liable for their role in transporting detainees to other countries.

"People are going to find what they want to find," says Chesney, who served this summer with the task force that Obama created on detention policy. "If they want to see continuity [with the Bush policies], they are going to see continuity. If they want to see change, they're going to see change."

The CIA's role in future interrogations remains to be worked out with the new high-value detainee information group that Obama created and placed under the FBI instead of the CIA. The plans call for interagency cooperation, but Zegart calls the plan a "terrible idea." "Since when did interagency processes work well in intelligence?" she asks.

In his visit to Langley, however, Obama tried his best to reassure the agency that it is still needed in dealing with terrorist threats. "We're going to have to operate smarter and more effectively than ever," Obama said in closing. "So I'm going to be relying on you, and the American people are going to rely on you."

NOTES

1. "Special Review: Counterterrorism Detention and Interrogation Activities (September 2001-October 2003)," Inspector General, Central Intelligence Agency, May 7, 2004, http://luxmedia.vo.llnwd.net/o10/clients/aclu/IG_Report.pdf. For coverage, see these stories by Peter Finn, Jory Warrick and Julie Tate in *The Washington Post*: "CIA Report Calls Oversight of Early Interrogations Poor," Aug. 25, 2009, p. A1; "CIA Releases Its Instructions on Breaking a Detainee's Will," Aug. 26, 2009, p. A1.

2. For background on the ACLU litigation, see Scott Shane, "A.C.L.U. Lawyers Mine Documents for Truth," *The New York Times*, Aug. 30, 2009, sec. 1, p. 4. The ACLU maintains a comprehensive archive of documents in the litigation: www.aclu.org/safe-free/torture/index.html. For a compilation of some of the documents and a narrative overview, see Jameel Jeffer and Amrit Singh, *Administration of Torture: A Documentary Record from Washington to Abu Ghraib and Beyond* (2007).

3. For background, see these *CQ Researcher* reports: Kenneth Jost, "Closing Guantánamo," Feb. 27, 2009, pp. 177-200; Kenneth Jost and the *CQ Researcher* Staff, "The Obama Presidency," Jan. 30, 2009, pp. 73-104; Peter Katel and Kenneth Jost, "Treatment of Detainees," Aug. 25, 2006, pp. 673-696. See also Seth Stern, "Torture Debate," *CQ Global Researcher*, September 2007, pp. 211-236.

4. For transcript, see www.foxnews.com/story/0,2933,544522,00.html. For coverage of comments from others, see Rachel L. Swarns, "Cheney Offers Sharp Defense of C.I.A. Tactics," *The New York Times*, Aug. 31, 2009, p. A1.

5. See Carrie Johnson, Jerry Markon and Julie Tate, "Inquiry Into CIA Practices Narrow," *The Washington Post*, Sept. 19, 2009, p. A1. The full text of the letter can be found on RealPolitics.com: www.realclearpolitics.com/politics_nation/cialetter0918.pdf. For Obama's reply, see CBS "Face the Nation," Sept. 20, 2009, www.cbsnews.com/stories/2009/09/20/ftn/main5324077.shtml?tag=cbsnewsTwoColUpperPromoArea.

6. "Special Task Force on Interrogations and Transfer Policies Issues Its Recommendations to the President," Department of Justice, Aug. 24, 2009, www.usdoj.gov/opa/pr/2009/August/09-ag-835.html. For coverage, see Anne E. Kornblut, "New Unit to Question Key Terror Suspects," *The Washington Post*, Aug. 24, 2009, p. A1.

7. See "Statement of President Barack Obama on Release of OLC Memos," April 16, 2009, www.whitehouse.gov/the_press_office/Statement-of-President-Barack-Obama-on-Release-of-OLC-Memos/. For coverage, see Mark Mazzetti and Scott Shane, "Memos Spell Out Brutal Mode of C.I.A.

Interrogation," *The New York Times*, April 17, 2009, p. A1.

8. Estes Thompson, "Ex-CIA Contractor Guilty in Afghan Death," The Associated Press, Aug. 18, 2006. Passaro was convicted of assault with a dangerous weapon and assault with intent to inflict serious injury. He was sentenced in 2007 to eight-and-a-half-years in prison, but the 4th U.S. Circuit Court of Appeals on Aug. 10, 2009, ordered resentencing on the ground that Judge Terence Boyle had not justified a sentence longer than recommended under the federal sentencing guidelines.

9. See Jeffrey H. Smith, "CIA Accountability," *The Washington Post*, Aug. 24, 2009, p. A15; Walter Pincus and Jory Warrick, "Ex-Intelligence Officials Cite Low Spirits at CIA," *ibid.*, Aug. 30, 2009, p. A2.

10. The veto message appears in the *Congressional Record* on March 10, 2008: http://fas.org/irp/congress/2008_cr/veto.html. For coverage, see Steven Lee Myers, "Bush Vetoes Bill on C.I.A. Tactics, Affirming Legacy," *The New York Times*, March 9, 2008, p. A1.

11. "Executive Order — Ensuring Lawful Interrogations," Jan. 22, 2009, www.whitehouse.gov/the_press_office/EnsuringLawfulInterrogations/.

12. "Special Review," *op. cit.*, p. 100.

13. Barton Gellman, "Cheney Uncloaks His Frustration With Bush," *The Washington Post*, Aug. 13, 2009, p. A1.

14. *The 9/11 Commission Report: Final Report of the National Commission on Terrorist Attacks Upon the United States*, 2004. For background, see Kenneth Jost, "Re-examining 9/11," *CQ Researcher*, June 4, 2004, pp. 493-516.

15. Other groups include Amnesty International USA, Human Rights First, Human Rights Watch, Open Society Institute, Physicians for Human Rights and Rutherford Institute. For a complete list, see www.commissiononaccountability.org/.

16. Quoted in Bennett Roth, "Democrats Split on Interrogation Inquiry," *CQ Weekly*, April 27, 2009, p. 978.

17. Background drawn from Alfred W. McCoy, *A Question of Torture: CIA Interrogation, from the Cold War to the War on Terror* (2006), pp. 16-20; Pauletta Otis, "Educing Information: The Right Initiative at the Right Time by the Right People," in Intelligence Science Board, "Educing Information: Interrogation: Science and Art; Foundations for the Future: Phase 1 Report," December 2006, pp. xv-xx. See also Stern, *op. cit.*; David Masci, "Torture," *CQ Researcher*, April 18, 2003, pp. 345-368.

18. McCoy, *op. cit.*, p. 16.

19. Ernest Jerome Hopkins, *Our Lawless Police* (1931), quoted in Richard A. Leo, "From Coercion To Deception: The Changing Nature of Police Interrogation in America," *Crime, Law and Social Change*, Vol. 18 (1992), p. 35.

20. The decision is *Miranda v. Arizona*, 384 U.S. 436 (1966).

21. Petula Dvorak, "Fort Hunt's Quiet Men Break Silence on WWII," *The Washington Post*, Oct. 6, 2007, p. A1; Roni Gehlke, "New book out about Byron's Camp Tracy," *Contra Costa* (Calif.) *Times*, July 8, 2009. The referenced book is Alexander Corbin, *The History of Camp Tracy: Japanese WWII POWs and the Future of Strategic Interrogation* (2009).

22. For background, see McCoy, *op. cit.*, chs. 2 & 3; Laura L. Finley, "The Central Intelligence Agency and Torture," in *The Torture and Prisoner Abuse Debate* (2008).

23. McCoy, *op. cit.*, pp. 24-25.

24. *Ibid.*, pp. 68-69.

25. See Gary Cohn, Ginger Thompson and Mark Matthews, "Torture was taught by CIA," *The Baltimore Sun*, Jan. 27, 1997.

26. Background drawn from Jane Mayer, *The Dark Side: How the War on Terror Turned Into a War on American Ideals* (2008). See also "Special Review," *op. cit.* Approximately 100 prisoners were held at the secret CIA sites at one time or another.

27. Quoted in Mayer, *op. cit.*, pp. 9-10.

28. "Special Review," p. 13; the report does not identify Mitchell and Jessen by name. See also Mayer, *op. cit.*, pp. 157-158.

29. See Seth Hettena, "Iraqi Died While Hung From Wrists," The Associated Press, Feb. 17, 2005; "U.S. Operatives Killed Detainees During Interrogations in Afghanistan and Iraq, CIA, Navy Seals and Military Intelligence Personnel Implicated," American Civil Liberties Union, Oct. 24, 2005, www.aclu.org/intl-humanrights/gen/21236prs 20051024.html; Human Rights First, "Command's Responsibility: Detainee Deaths in U.S. Custody in Iraq and Afghanistan," February 2006, www.humanrightsfirst.org/us_law/etn/dic/exec-sum.aspx. For an account of Jamadi's interrogation and death, see Mayer, *op. cit.*, pp. 238-258. Mark Swanner, the CIA interrogator, has denied any wrongdoing; Mayer said the agency's inspector general referred the case to the Justice Department "for possible criminality," but no charges were brought.

30. Dana Priest, "CIA Holds Terror Suspects in Secret Prisons," *The Washington Post*, Nov. 2, 2005, p. A1. Priest won a Pulitzer Prize for her reporting on the sites.

31. Mark Danner, "U.S. Torture: Voices from the Black Sites," *New York Review of Books*, April 9, 2009. The ICRC keeps its reports confidential to preserve its impartiality with individual governments. After Danner obtained the report, the *New York Review* posted the complete document on its Web site: www.nybooks.com/icrc-report.pdf.

32. See Mark Mazzetti, "U.S. Says CIA Destroyed 92 Tapes of Interrogations," *The New York Times*, March 3, 2009, p. A16.

33. The consolidated cases are *American Civil Liberties Union v. Dep't of Defense*, 04 Civ. 4151, and *American Civil Liberties Union v. Dep't of Justice*, 05-9620. For coverage of Panetta's declaration, see R. Jeffrey Smith, "CIA Urges Judge to Keep Bush-Era Documents Sealed," *The Washington Post*, June 9, 2009, p. A1.

34. The Supreme Court case is *U.S. Defense Dep't v. American Civil Liberties Union*, 09-160. For coverage, including links to the government's petition and the lower court ruling, see Lyle Denniston, "Transparency in wartime at issue," SCOTUSBlog, Aug. 24, 2009, www.scotusblog.com/wp/transparency-in-wartime-at-issue/. See also Adam Liptak, "Obama's About-Face on Detainee Photos Leads to Supreme Court," *The New York Times*, Sept. 15, 2009, p. A13.

35. "Fox News Sunday," April 19, 2009, www.foxnews.com/story/0,2933,517158,00.html.

36. See John Sifton, "What's Missing from the CIA Docs," *The Daily Beast*, Aug. 25, 2009, www.thedailybeast.com/blogs-and-stories/2009-08-25/whats-missing-from-the-cia-docs/.

37. The case is *ACLU v. Dep't of Defense*, 09 CV 8071 (S.D.N.Y.) For background, see Bagram FOIA (8/13/2009), www.aclu.org/safefree/detention/40715res20090813.html.

38. The decision is *Hamdan v. Rumsfeld*, 548 U.S. 557 (2006). For an account, see Kenneth Jost, *The Supreme Court Yearbook 2005-2006.*

39. For coverage, including a link to the government's filing, see Lyle Denniston, "Decision soon on 9/11 trials," SCOTUSBlog, Sept. 16, 2009, www.scotusblog.com/wp/decision-soon-on-911-trials/. See also David Johnston, "U.S. Seeking 3rd Delay on Guantánamo Cases," *The New York Times*, Sept. 17, 2009, p. A17, from which some background has been drawn.

40. Bob Woodward, "Detainee Tortured, U.S. Official," *The Washington Post*, Jan. 14, 2009, p. A1.

41. See "Newly Released Detainee Statements Provide More Evidence of CIA Torture Program," June 15, 2009, www.aclu.org/safefree/torture/39868prs 20090615.html. For coverage, see Julian E. Barnes and Greg Miller, "Detainee says he lied to the CIA," *Los Angeles Times*, June 16, 2009, p. A1.

42. The text of the speech is on the CIA's Web site: www.cia.gov/news-information/speeches-testimony/president-obama-at-cia.html. For coverage, see Peter Baker and Scott Shane, "Pressure Grows to Investigate Interrogations," *The New York Times*, April 21, 2009, p. A1.

43. See Pincus and Warrick, *op. cit.*, p. A2.

44. Fred Hiatt, "Time for a Souter-O'Connor Commission," *The Washington Post*, Aug. 30, 2009, p. A21.

BIBLIOGRAPHY

Books

Finley, Laura L., *The Torture and Prisoner Abuse Debate*, Greenwood Press, 2008.
The book, part of Greenwood's "Historical Guides to Controversial Issues in America," includes chapters on the origins of torture, the CIA and torture and abusive interrogations and detentions in Afghanistan and Iraq and at Guantánamo. Finley teaches in the women's studies department at Florida Atlantic University. Includes chapter notes, seven-page bibliography.

Mayer, Jane, *The Dark Side: How the War on Terror Turned Into a War on American Ideals*, Doubleday, 2008.
The book details the origins and implementation of harsh interrogation practices by military and CIA interrogators after Sept. 11 and strongly criticizes the practices on legal, moral and pragmatic grounds. Mayer is an author and staff writer for *The New Yorker*. Includes notes, bibliography.

McCoy, Alfred W., *A Question of Torture: CIA Interrogation, from the Cold War to the War on Terror*, Metropolitan Books, 2006.
A professor of history at the University of Wisconsin traces the history of the CIA's controversial interrogation practices. Includes notes, 23-page bibliography.

Wittes, Benjamin, *Law and the Long War: The Future of Justice in the Age of Terror*, Penguin, 2008.
A leading researcher on national security argues for legislation to authorize administrative detention of suspected enemy combatants and some methods of interrogation at least for the CIA beyond those authorized in the *U.S. Army Field Manual*. Wittes is a research fellow at the Brookings Institution and a member of the Hoover Institution's National Security Task Force. His paper co-authored with Stuart Taylor Jr., "Looking Forward, Not Backward: Refining American Interrogation Law," is being published in *Legislating the War on Terror: An Agenda for Reform* (Brookings, 2009).

Articles

Herman, Arthur, "The Gitmo Myth and the Torture Canard," *Commentary*, June 2009, www.commentarymagazine.com/viewarticle.cfm/the-gitmo-myth-and-the-torture-canard-15154?search=1.
The historian and longtime *Commentary* contributor argues that reports of abusive interrogation by the military and CIA have been exaggerated, part of a "Gitmo myth" created to "ruin the Bush administration" and "blacken" the United States' reputation.

Sullivan, Andrew, "Dear President Bush," *The Atlantic*, October 2009, p. 78, www.theatlantic.com/doc/200910/bush-torture.
The well-known author-journalist lays out a searing critique of detention and interrogation practices by the military and the CIA and asks former President George W. Bush to support "a full accounting and report from an independent body."

Reports and Studies

"Educing Information: Interrogation: Science and Art; Foundations for the Future: Phase 1 Report," Intelligence Science Board NDIC Press, December 2006, www1.umn.edu/humanrts/OathBetrayed/Intelligence%20Science%20Board%202006.pdf.
The official advisory body at the National Defense Intelligence College laments the limited knowledge about the efficacy of specific interrogation techniques and recommends scientific studies on the questions. Includes introductory essays, 10 scientific papers and annotated bibliography.

"Inquiry Into the Treatment of Detainees in U.S. Custody," Senate Armed Services Committee, Nov. 20, 2008, as declassified April 20, 2009, http://graphics8.nytimes.com/packages/images/nytint/docs/report-by-the-senate-armed-services-committee-on-detainee-treatment/original.pdf.
The report provides the most thorough accounting to date of the harsh interrogation practices approved at the highest levels of the Bush administration.

For More Information

American Civil Liberties Union, 125 Broad St., 18th Floor, New York, NY 10004; (212) 607-3300; www.aclu.org. Works to defend and preserve individual rights and liberties guaranteed by the Constitution.

Constitution Project, 1200 18th St., N.W., Suite 1000, Washington, DC 20036; (202) 580-6920; www.constitutionproject.org. Promotes bipartisan dialogue to reach consensus on difficult legal and constitutional issues.

Heritage Foundation, 214 Massachusetts Ave., N.E., Washington, DC 20002; (202) 546-4400; www.heritage .org. Public policy research institute promoting conservative positions on free enterprise, limited government and a strong national defense.

Human Rights First, 333 Seventh Ave., 13th Floor, New York, NY 10001; (212) 845-5200; www.humanrightsfirst .org. Nonprofit international human-rights organization promoting laws and policies that advance universal rights and freedoms.

National Security Archive, The George Washington University, 2130 H St., N.W., Washington, DC 20037; (202) 994-7000; www.gwu.edu/~nsarchiv. Non-governmental research institute serving as a repository for government documents relating to national security and intelligence.

13

Prosecuting Terrorists

Kenneth Jost

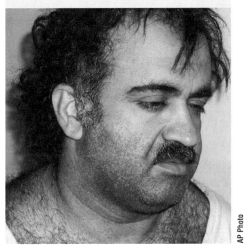

Republican lawmakers say al Qaeda terrorist Khalid Sheikh Mohammed, seen shortly after his capture in Pakistan in 2003, should be treated as an enemy combatant and tried in the military commissions established during the Bush administration. But administration officials and Democratic lawmakers say criminal prosecutions have produced hundreds of convictions since 9/11 compared to only three in the military system.

From *CQ Researcher*,
October 31, 2008.

He has been described as Osama bin Laden's chief executive officer, the man who conceived the plan to crash hijacked airliners into buildings symbolic of America's political, military and financial power.

Some 18 months after the 9/11 attacks, Pakistani intelligence agents, working with the U.S. Central Intelligence Agency, captured Kuwait-born Khalid Sheikh Mohammed at an al Qaeda safe house in Rawalpindi. Rousted out of bed in the middle of the night, he looked like a street person — not the scion of a well-to-do Pakistani family once known for its expensive tastes and elegant dress.[1]

For the next three years, KSM — as U.S. officials and news media dubbed him — was held at a secret CIA site, reportedly in Poland, where interrogators waterboarded him 183 times in the first month of his captivity. In September 2006 he was transferred to the U.S. prison camp at the Guantánamo Bay naval base in Cuba, to be held awaiting trial.

The trial — on 2,973 counts of murder and other charges — began before a military judge on June 5, 2008, but was thrown into disarray six months later, when Mohammed announced that he and his four co-defendants wanted to plead guilty. A month later, the judge, Army Col. Stephen Henley, agreed to put the trial on hold in response to President Obama's decision, on his first full day in office, to suspend the military trials of all suspected "enemy combatants" being held at Guantánamo.

Now, a year after Obama's interim move, the proceedings against KSM remain in limbo thanks to the full-throttle controversy that

Military Commissions Convicted Three

Three of the terrorism suspects who were detained at Guantánamo Bay — Ali Hamza Ahmad Suliman al Bahlul, Salim Ahmed Hamdan and David Hicks — have been convicted after trials before military commissions. Hicks, known as the "Australian Taliban," and Hamdan, identified as the driver for al Qaeda leader Osama bin Laden, have served their sentences already and been released to their home countries. Al Bahlul awaits a decision on his appeal to his life sentence before a U.S. military judge panel. Hamdan's appeal of his conviction is pending before the same panel; Hicks waived his right of appeal after pleading guilty.

Terrorists Convicted in Military Commissions at Guantánamo Bay

al Bahlul

Nationality:	Yemeni
Conviction date:	Nov. 3, 2008
Charges:	35 counts of solicitation to commit murder, conspiracy and providing material support for terrorism.
Current status:	Sentenced to life in prison; appeal pending before panel of military judges; argued Jan. 26.

AFP/Getty Images

Hamdan

Nationality:	Yemeni
Conviction date:	Aug. 6, 2008
Charges:	Providing material support for terrorism.
Current status:	Returned to Yemen and released; appeal pending before panel of military judges; argued Jan. 26.

AFP/Getty Images

Hicks

Nationality:	Australian
Conviction date:	March 30, 2007
Charges:	Providing material support for terrorism.
Current status:	Returned to Australia and released.

Getty Images

Source: News reports

erupted after Attorney General Eric Holder announced plans to try the five alleged 9/11 conspirators in a federal court in New York City. In announcing his decision on Nov. 13, Holder said the defendants would "answer for their alleged crimes in a courthouse just blocks away from where the twin towers [of the World Trade Center] once stood."[2]

New York City Mayor Michael Bloomberg and Police Commissioner Raymond Kelly welcomed Holder's decision, but many New Yorkers expressed concerns about the costs and risks of a sensational trial in Lower Manhattan. Some families of 9/11 victims also voiced criticism, saying enemies of the United States deserved military tribunals, not civilian courts.

Holder faced a buzz saw of criticism when he appeared before the Senate Judiciary Committee a week later to defend his decision — which he said he made without consulting the White House. Sen. Jeff Sessions of Alabama, the committee's ranking Republican, called the decision "dangerous," "misguided" and "unnecessary."[3]

Criticism of the decision intensified — and became even more overtly politicized — after the Christmas Day arrest of Umar Farouk Abdulmutallab for the attempted bombing of a Northwest Airlines flight bound from Amsterdam to Detroit. Republican lawmakers and former GOP officials, including former Vice President Dick Cheney and former Attorney General Michael Mukasey, strongly criticized the decision to treat Abdulmutallab as a criminal suspect instead of as an enemy combatant. A major focus of the criticism was the decision to advise Abdulmutallab of his Miranda rights not long after his arrest. (*See sidebar, p. 310.*)

GOP lawmakers raised the stakes on the issue by introducing legislation in Congress to prohibit the use of any funds to try KSM in civilian courts. With administration officials and Democratic lawmakers making little headway in quieting the criticism, the White House let it be known in early February that Obama was personally reviewing the planned location for the trial as part of the broader issue of where and how to try the remaining prisoners at Guantánamo.[4]

The trials have been delayed by controversies that began immediately after President George W. Bush decided to use the base to house alleged enemy combatants captured in the Afghanistan war or rounded up from other locations. Instead of using civilian courts or regular military courts — courts-martial — Bush used his power as commander in chief to create military commissions to try the detainees, with fewer procedural rights than courts-martial.[5]

Critics, including a wide array of civil liberties and human rights organizations, denounced the military commissions as a second-class system of justice. They also lent their support to legal challenges filed by some of the prisoners that eventually resulted in Supreme Court decisions guaranteeing judicial review of their cases and forcing some changes in the rules for the commissions.

Because of the legal uncertainties, the military commissions did not produce their first conviction until March 2007 when David Hicks, the so-called Australian Taliban, pleaded guilty to providing material support for terrorism. Two other Guantánamo prisoners were convicted on material-support counts the next year: Salim Ahmed Hamdan, former driver to bin Laden, and Ali Hamza Ahmad Suliman al Bahlul, an al Qaeda filmmaker and propagandist. (*See box at left.*)

Even as the Guantánamo cases moved at a glacial pace, the Bush administration was using federal courts to prosecute hundreds of individuals arrested in the United States on terrorism-related charges. Among the first was Richard Reid, the so-called shoe bomber, who was charged with attempting to blow up a commercial aircraft en route to the United States on Dec. 22, 2001. Reid, an admitted al Qaeda supporter, is now serving a life sentence.

At various points, Bush himself touted the administration's record of convicting hundreds of individuals in

Guidelines Adopted for Detainee Prosecutions

The Justice and Defense departments adopted broadly written guidelines in July 2009 to be used in deciding whether a Guantánamo detainee was to be tried in a civilian court or before a military tribunal. The protocol begins with "a presumption that, where feasible, referred cases will be prosecuted in" federal criminal courts. The two-page agreement lists three categories of factors to be considered in deciding whether "other compelling factors make it more appropriate to prosecute a case in a reformed military commission":

Strength of interest, including where the offense occurred, where the defendant was apprehended and which agency or agencies investigated the case.

Efficiency, including protection of intelligence sources, foreign policy concerns and "legal or evidentiary problems that might attend prosecution in the other jurisdiction."

Other prosecution considerations, including the charges that can be brought and the sentences that can be imposed in one or the other forum.

Source: "Determination of Guantánamo Cases Referred for Prosecution," July 20, 2009, www.justice.gov/opa/documents/taba-prel-rpt-dptf-072009.pdf

terrorism-related cases in criminal courts. In a budget document in 2008, the Justice Department put the number of convictions or guilty pleas at 319 out of 512 individuals prosecuted.[6]

More recently, a report written for Human Rights First counted 195 convictions or guilty pleas in al Qaeda- or Taliban-related terrorism cases through July 2, 2009, along with 19 acquittals or dismissals. The report, written by two lawyers who had previously served as federal prosecutors in New York, concluded that the criminal justice system "is well-equipped to handle a broad variety of cases arising from terrorism" associated with al Qaeda or similar groups.[7] (*See sidebar, p. 318.*)

Despite that record, GOP lawmakers, ex-Bush administration officials and conservative experts and advocates are arguing strongly for the use of military commissions to try Abdulmutallab and, apparently, most of the prisoners held at Guantánamo. "Wartime alien enemy combatants should be tried by military commissions in the safety of Guantánamo Bay," says Andrew McCarthy, a contributing editor with *National Review Online* and former federal prosecutor.[8]

While in the U.S. attorney's office in Manhattan, McCarthy was lead prosecutor in the 1995 trial of Omar Abdel Rahman, the so-called Blind Sheik, along with nine others for plotting to blow up various civilian targets in the New York City area. Rahman was convicted of seditious conspiracy and is now serving a life sentence.[9]

Human rights advocates, however, say military commissions have failed to produce results while tarnishing the United States' image both at home and abroad. "The only choice should be trial in civilian courts," says Laura Olson, senior counsel for the rule of law program at the Washington-based Constitution Project. "They're both tougher and more reliable than military commissions."

The Obama administration says civilian trials are the presumptive forum for terrorism cases but is continuing the use of what it calls "reformed" military commissions for some cases. A protocol adopted jointly by the Justice and Defense departments in July 2009 says forum selection will depend on a number of factors, including the agency or agencies involved in the investigation and the charges and sentences available in one or the other forum. Holder designated several Guantánamo prisoners for trial by military commissions on the same day he announced the decision to try KSM in New York City. (*See box, p. 307.*)

Meanwhile, administration officials also are saying that 50 or more Guantánamo prisoners may be held indefinitely without trial because they cannot be prosecuted successfully but are too dangerous to release.[10] Conservatives say the prolonged detentions are justifiable as long as the United States is effectively at war with al Qaeda. Civil liberties advocates strongly disagree.

President Obama cheered human rights groups with his initial moves on counterterrorism policies, especially his pledge to close the Guantánamo prison camp within a year. Now that the deadline has been missed and other policies recalibrated, Obama is drawing some complaints from liberal advocacy groups along with sharp criticism from Republicans and conservative groups for the planned use of federal courts to try enemy combatants.

Here are some of the major issues the administration faces:

Should suspected terrorists be tried in civilian courts?

When the FBI got wind of a group of Yemeni Americans who had trained at an al Qaeda camp in 2001 and returned to their homes in the Buffalo, N.Y., suburb of Lackawanna, Bush administration's officials were divided on what to do.

Vice President Dick Cheney and Defense Secretary Donald Rumsfeld wanted to use troops to arrest the men and treat them as enemy combatants to be tried before a military commission. President Bush, however, sided with Attorney General John Ashcroft and FBI Director Robert Mueller, who favored using federal agents to arrest the men and trying them in a federal court.

In the end, the men were arrested without incident on Sept. 14, 2002, and over the next year pleaded guilty and received prison sentences ranging from seven to 10 years for supporting a foreign terrorist organization. They also cooperated with authorities in providing information about al Qaeda, and three of them testified in the 2008 military commission trial of the al Qaeda filmmaker Bahlul.[11]

Supporters of criminal prosecutions — including but not limited to human rights and civil liberties groups — say prosecutions such as the Lackawanna Six case prove civilian courts can mete out effective, tough justice in terrorism-related cases without shortchanging constitutional rights.

"The criminal justice system is reasonably well-equipped to handle most international terrorism cases," New York attorneys Richard B. Zabel and James J. Benjamin Jr. wrote in the Human Rights First report in May 2008. A year later, the two former federal prosecutors reiterated that civilian court prosecutions had generally led to "just, reliable results" without causing security breaches or other harms to national security.[12]

National security-minded critics and some non-ideological experts counter that the rights accorded defendants in the criminal justice system do pose potential obstacles to successful prosecutions in some terrorism cases. "Civilian trials should be a secondary option," says David Rivkin, a former Justice Department official in the Bush administration now affiliated with the hawkish Foundation for the Defense of Democracies. Among other problems, Rivkin says classified information is harder to protect in a civilian court than in a military commission despite a federal law, the Classified Information Procedure Act (CIPA), which limits disclosure in federal trials.

"The federal courts have some real limitations," agrees Benjamin Wittes, a research fellow at the Brookings Institution and author of several influential reports about war-on-terror policies. He cites as examples the beyond-a-reasonable-doubt standard used in criminal prosecutions and the stricter standard on use of evidence obtained under coercive interrogation. Still, Wittes adds, the problems are "not as big as conservatives claim."

Critics assailed the decision to try the 9/11 conspiracy case in New York City in particular as a security risk. Rivkin complains of "the logistical nightmare" that would be created by a trial in a major metropolitan area such as New York.

When Holder visited New York to discuss plans for the trial in December, however, a Justice Department spokesman declared, "We have a robust plan developed by both federal and local officials to ensure that these trials can be safely held in New York, and everyone is committed to doing that."[13]

Above any practical considerations, however, critics such as Rivkin say simply that criminal prosecutions signal a wrong approach in the nation's fight against al Qaeda. "This is a long and difficult war," he says. "It is essential for any administration to inculcate the notion that this is a real war. And it is utterly jarring in that context to take enemy combatants, particularly high-value ones, and treat them as common criminals."

Benjamin counters that the criminal justice system in fact amounts to one of the United States' most effective weapons in the war on terror. "We are at war," he says. "One of the unique features of this particular war is that many of the people on the other side are violating our criminal law. If we can develop the evidence and successfully put them away, why in the world would we foreclose ourselves from doing that?"

Should suspected terrorists be tried in military tribunals?

Attorney General Holder's decision to try seven Guantánamo detainees in military commissions represents only a modest step toward resolving the cases of the remaining prisoners there. (*See box, p. 317.*) But the trials, if completed, would more than double the number of cases resolved by military tribunals since President Bush authorized them less than two months after the 9/11 attacks.

Supporters say history, law and national security justify the use of military tribunals to try enemy combatants. They blame opponents for the legal controversies that have limited their use so far.

"The record has been underwhelming," concedes ex-Justice Department attorney Rivkin. "Why should we be surprised? There has been a concentrated effort from day one to litigate against them."

Human rights and civil liberties groups counter that the military tribunals were flawed from the outset and, despite some recent reforms, still have significant problems and will face additional legal challenges.

"They remain vulnerable to constitutional challenge," says Olson of the Constitution Project. "We're going to have to go through this litigation for years and years."

In contrast to the three men convicted so far by military commissions, the prisoners that Holder designated in his Nov. 13 announcement for trial by military commissions include figures alleged to have played significant roles in al Qaeda operations. They include Abd al Rahim al Nashiri, a Yemeni accused of plotting the October 2000 attack on the *USS Cole*, and Noor Uthman Mohammed, a Sudanese alleged to have assisted in running an al Qaeda training center in Afghanistan.

The accusations against some of the others, however, depict them as hardly more than al Qaeda foot soldiers. The group includes Omar Khadr, the youngest Guantánamo detainee, who was captured at age 15 after a firefight in Afghanistan. Now 23, the Canadian citizen faces a charge of providing support for terrorism by throwing a grenade that killed a U.S. soldier. The charge goes against the United Nations' position that children should not be prosecuted for war crimes.[14]

In announcing his decisions on the legal forum to be used, Holder gave no explanation of the reasons for designating some of the prisoners for trial by military commissions. But he did say that recent changes approved by Congress for the commissions "will ensure that commission trials are fair, effective and lawful." Those changes

AFP/Getty Images/Don Emmert

Omar Abdel Rahman, the so-called Blind Sheik, was convicted in a civilian criminal trial in 1995 along with nine others for plotting to blow up various civilian targets in the New York City area. Rahman is now serving a life sentence. Andrew McCarthy, the then-lead prosecutor for the U.S. attorney's office, is now a contributing editor with National Review Online, a conservative publication. He now says, "Wartime alien enemy combatants should be tried by military commissions in the safety of Guantánamo Bay."

include limits on use of hearsay and coerced testimony and greater access for defendants to witnesses and evidence.

Despite the changes, human rights advocates continue to oppose use of the military commissions. "We don't quarrel with military justice," says Ben Winzer, a staff attorney with the American Civil Liberties Union's (ACLU) national security project. "The problem is that even the modified military commissions are being used to paper over weaknesses in the government's evidence."

"Most of the growing pains have been alleviated;" counters Rivkin. "The solution now is to stand them up,

make them work, give them the right resources and get out of the way."

For his part, Brookings Institution expert Wittes says the military commissions "have significantly underperformed to date" and continue to face a host of practical and legal difficulties. "We worry that the military commissions will present issues of their own, particularly with respect to challenges to the lawfulness and integrity of the system itself," he says. "And the rules have been used so little that there are a lot of issues about how the system works."

Among the most important pending issues is the question whether material support of terrorism — a mainstay of criminal prosecutions — is an offense that can be tried in a military tribunal. The review panel established to hear appeals from the military commissions currently has that issue under advisement after arguments in two cases in January.

"No one questions that these are crimes, but there are special rules that come into play when we start talking about what crimes military commissions can prosecute," says Stephen Vladeck, a law professor at American University in Washington. "I think there are far fewer cases in which the government realistically has a choice between civilian and military courts than we might think, if for no other reason than the jurisdiction of military commissions is actually tightly circumscribed by the Constitution."

Should some Guantánamo detainees be held indefinitely without trial?

In his first major speech on how to deal with the Guantánamo prisoners, President Obama called in May 2009 for "prolonged detention" for any detainees "who cannot be prosecuted yet who pose a clear danger to the American people." Obama said he would work with Congress to "construct a legitimate legal framework" for such cases, but added: "I am not going to release individuals who endanger the American people."[15]

In the nine months since, neither Congress nor the president has put any appreciable work into possible legislation on the issue. Now, administration officials are estimating 50 or more detainees will have to be held without trial, but they have not listed names or described procedures being used to designate individuals for that category.

Khalid Sheikh Mohammed and the 9/11 Attacks

Khalid Sheikh Mohammed, self-described mastermind of the Sept. 11 terrorist attacks, faces trial in federal court on 2,973 counts of murder and other charges along with his four co-defendants. Kuwait-born KSM first claimed to have organized the 9/11 attacks during interrogations in which he was waterboarded 183 times. In March 2007, at a hearing at the Guantánamo Bay prison, he said he was responsible for the attacks "from A to Z" — as well as for 30 other terrorist plots. The five co-defendants now face nine charges including conspiracy, terrorism, providing material support for terrorism and murder. Controversy erupted over Attorney General Eric Holder's plan to hold the trial in New York City, and the location of the trial is now being reconsidered. KSM's four co-defendants are:

- **Ramzi Bin al-Shibh (Yemen)** — Alleged "coordinator" of the attacks after he was denied a visa to enter the United States.
- **Walid bin Attash (Saudi Arabia)** — Charged with selecting and training several of the hijackers of the attacks.
- **Ali Abdul Aziz Ali (Pakistan)** — Allegedly helped hijackers obtain plane tickets, traveler's checks and hotel reservations. Also taught them the culture and customs of the West.
- **Mustafa Ahmed al-Hawsawi (Saudi Arabia)** — Allegedly an organizer and financier of the attacks.

The ACLU and other human rights groups immediately denounced Obama's remarks on the issue and continue to oppose detention without trial. The administration's conservative critics approve of holding some prisoners without trial but fault the administration for its efforts to transfer others to their home countries or other host nations because they might return to hostilities against the United States.

"The term is detention for the duration of hostilities," says Rivkin. "Those rules have been in place since time immemorial. They are not meant to punish anybody; they are designed to prevent someone from going back to the battlefield."

Rivkin says the policy of transferring prisoners to other countries — begun by the Bush administration and continued by Obama — amounts to "a revolving door" for terrorists. "We know for sure that they go back to combat," Rivkin says. "This is the first war in human history where we cannot hold in custody a captured enemy. That's a hell of a way to run a war."

ACLU lawyer Winzer calls Obama's detention-without-trial proposal "an extraordinarily controversial statement in a country governed by the rule of law." Anyone "truly dangerous" should be and likely can be prosecuted, Winzer says. "Our material-support laws are so broad

that if we don't have legitimate evidence to convict [detainees] under those laws, it's hard to accept that they are too dangerous to release."

Allegations that some of the released Guantánamo prisoners have returned to hostilities against the United States stem from studies released by the Pentagon during the Bush administration and sharply challenged by some human rights advocates. The final of three studies, released in January 2009 only one week before Bush was to leave office, claimed that 61 out of 517 detainees released had "returned to the battlefield."

But an examination of the evidence by Mark Denbeaux, a law professor at Seton Hall University in South Orange, N.J., and counsel to two Guantánamo detainees, depicts the Pentagon's count as largely unsubstantiated. In any event, Denbeaux says the Pentagon's count is exaggerated because it includes former prisoners who have done nothing more after their release than engage in propaganda against the United States.[16]

Supporters of detention without trial cite as authority the first of the Supreme Court's post-9/11 decisions, *Hamdi v. Rumsfeld*.[17] In that 2004 ruling, a majority of the justices agreed that the legislation Congress passed in 2001 to authorize the Afghanistan war included authority for the detention of enemy combatants. In the main opinion, Justice Sandra Day O'Connor said a detainee was entitled to some opportunity to contest allegations against him, but did not specify what kind of procedure.

The court rulings appear to support the government's power "to hold people indefinitely without charge if they are associated with al Qaeda or the Taliban in the same way that a solider is associated with an army," says Benjamin, coauthor of the Human Rights First report. Law professor Vladeck agrees, but says the number of people in that category is likely to be "small."

Brookings Institution expert Wittes defends the practice "philosophically" but acknowledges practical problems, including public reaction both in the United States and abroad. "The first risk is that it's perceived as the least legitimate option, domestically or internationally," he says. "It's not the way you like to do business."

The evidence needed to justify detention has been the major issue in the dozens of habeas corpus petitions filed by Guantánamo prisoners. Federal district judges in Washington who have been hearing the cases have mostly decided against the government, according to a compilation coauthored by Wittes.[18]

Wittes has long urged Congress to enact legislation to define the scope of indefinite detention. In an unusual interview, three of the judges handling the cases agreed. "It should be Congress that decides a policy such as this," Judge Reggie Walton told the online news site *ProPublica*.[19]

But David Cole, a law professor at Georgetown University in Washington and prominent critic of the detention policies, disagrees. The issues, Cole says, "require careful case-by-case application of standards. It's a job for judges, not Congress."[20]

BACKGROUND

Power and Precedent

The United States faced the issue of how to deal with captured members or supporters of al Qaeda or the Taliban with no exact historical parallel as guidance. The use of military tribunals for saboteurs, spies or enemy sympathizers dated from the American Revolution but had been controversial in several instances, including during the Civil War and World War II. After World

War II, military commissions became — in the words of Brookings expert Wittes — "a dead institution." The rise of international terrorism in the 1980s and '90s was met with military reprisals in some instances and a pair of notable U.S. prosecutions of Islamist extremists in the 1990s.[21]

As commander of the revolutionary army, Gen. George Washington convened military tribunals to try suspected spies — most notably, Major John André, Benedict Arnold's coconspirator, who was convicted, sentenced to death and hanged. During the War of 1812 and the First Seminole War (1817-1818). Gen. Andrew Jackson was criticized for expansive use of his powers as military commander — most notably, for having two British subjects put to death for inciting the Creek Indians against the United States. During the occupation of Mexico in the Mexican-American War, Gen. Winfield Scott established — without clear statutory authority — "military councils" to try Mexicans for a variety of offenses, including guerrilla warfare against U.S. troops.

The use of military tribunals by President Abraham Lincoln's administration during the Civil War provoked sharp criticism at the time and remains controversial today. Lincoln acted unilaterally to suspend the writ of habeas corpus in May 1861, defied Chief Justice Roger Taney's rebuke of the action and only belatedly got Congress to ratify his decision. More than 2,000 cases were tried by military commissions during the war and Reconstruction. Tribunals ignored some judicial orders to release prisoners. Lincoln, however, overturned some decisions that he found too harsh. As the war continued, the Supreme Court turned aside one challenge to the military commissions, but in 1866 — with the war ended — held that military tribunals should not be used if civilian courts are operating.[22]

During World War II, President Franklin D. Roosevelt prevailed in three Supreme Court challenges to expansive use of his powers as commander in chief in domestic settings. Best known are the court's decisions in 1943 and 1944 upholding the wartime curfew on the West Coast and the internment of Japanese-Americans. Earlier, the court in 1942 had given summary approval to the convictions and death sentences of German saboteurs captured in June and tried the next month before hastily convened military commissions. Roosevelt's order convening the seven-member tribunals specified that the death

CHRONOLOGY

1970s-2000 *International terrorism era begins, with attacks on civilian aircraft, facilities; prosecutions in foreign, U.S. courts get mixed results.*

1988 Bombing of Pan Am Flight 103 over Scotland kills 270, including 189 Americans; Scottish court later convicts and sentences to life former head of Libyan secret service; ill with cancer, released from Scottish jail in 2009.

1995 Civilian court convicts Omar Abdel Rahman and nine others for conspiring to blow up World Trade Center, other sites, in 1993.

1997 Ramzi Ahmed Yousef draws life sentence after 1997 conviction in civilian court for masterminding 1993 trade center bombing.

2000-Present *Al Qaeda launches 9/11 attacks; Bush, Obama administrations prosecute terrorism cases mainly in civilian courts.*

September-October 2001 Nearly 3,000 killed in al Qaeda's Sept. 11 attacks. . . . Congress on Sept. 14 gives president authority to use force against those responsible for attacks.

November-December 2001 President George W. Bush on Nov. 13 authorizes military commissions to try enemy combatants captured in Afghanistan, elsewhere. . . . U.S. Naval Base at Guantánamo Bay is chosen as site to hold detainees. . . . Zacarias Moussaoui indicted in federal court in Virginia on Dec. 11 for conspiracy in 9/11 attacks. . . . "Shoe bomber" Richard Reid arrested Dec. 21 for failed attack on American Airlines Flight 63.

2002 First of about 800 prisoners arrive in Guantánamo; first of scores of habeas corpus cases filed by detainees by mid-spring. . . . José Padilla arrested at Chicago airport May 8 in alleged radioactive bomb plot; case transferred to military courts. . . . John Walker Lindh, "American Taliban," sentenced Oct. 4 by a civilian court to 20 years in prison.

2003 Federal judge in Boston sentences Reid to life in prison on Jan. 31.

2004 Supreme Court rules June 28 that U.S. citizens can be held as enemy combatants but must be afforded

hearing before "neutral decisionmaker" (*Hamdi v. Rumsfeld*); on same day, court rules Guantánamo detainees may use habeas corpus to challenge captivity (*Rasul v. Bush*).

2006 Moussaoui is given life sentence May 3. . . . Supreme Court rules June 29 that military commissions improperly depart from requirements of U.S. military law and Geneva Conventions (*Hamdan v. Rumsfeld*). . . . Congress passes Military Commissions Act of 2006 in September to remedy defects.

2007 First conviction in military commission: Australian David Hicks sentenced on March 30 to nine months after guilty plea to material support for terrorism. . . . Padilla convicted in federal court Aug. 16 on material support counts; later sentenced to 17 years.

2008 Supreme Court reaffirms June 12 habeas corpus rights for Guantánamo detainees (*Boumediene v. Bush*). . . . Two more convictions of terrorists in military commissions: Hamdan convicted on material support counts Aug. 6, sentenced to 7-1/2-year term; al Qaeda propagandist Ali Hamza al Bahlul convicted Nov. 3, given life sentence.

January-June 2009 President Obama pledges to close Guantánamo within a year, suspends military commissions pending review (Jan. 21). . . . Obama in major speech says some detainees to be held indefinitely without trial (May 21).

July-December 2009 Defense and Justice departments agree on protocol to choose civilian or military court (July 20). . . . Military Commission Act of 2009 improves defendants' protections (October). Attorney General Eric Holder announces plan to try Khalid Sheikh Mohammed (KSM), four others in federal court in Manhattan for 9/11 conspiracy (Nov. 13); other alleged terrorists designated for military commissions; plan for N.Y. trial widely criticized. . . . Umar Farouk Abdulmutallab arrested Dec. 25 in failed bombing of Northwest Flight 253; decision to prosecute in civilian court criticized, defended.

2010 Administration mulls change of plans for KSM trial. . . . U.S. appeals court backs broad definition of enemy combatant in first substantive appellate-level decision in Guantánamo habeas corpus cases (Jan. 5). . . . Military review panel weighs arguments on use of "material support of terrorism" charge in military commissions (Jan. 26).

The Case Against the 'Christmas Day' Bomber

Critics say prosecutors mishandled Abdulmutallab's arrest.

Caught in the act of trying to bomb a Northwest Airlines aircraft, Umar Farouk Abdulmutallab would appear to offer prosecutors a slam dunk under any of several terrorism-related charges. Indeed, there were dozens of witnesses to his capture.

But the case against the baby-faced Nigerian-born, Yemeni-trained al Qaeda supporter became enmeshed in post-9/11 American politics almost immediately after his Christmas Day flight landed in Detroit.[1]

President Obama invited the subsequent criticism by initially labeling Abdulmutallab as "an isolated extremist" on Dec. 26 before learning of his training in al Qaeda camps in Yemen and history of extreme Islamist views. Homeland Security Secretary Janet Napolitano compounded the administration's political problems by saying on Dec. 27 that Abdulmutallab's capture showed that "the system worked" — a statement she quickly worked hard to explain away, given that a U.S. airliner had nearly been bombed.

The administration also faced criticism for intelligence analysts' failure to block Abdulmutallab from ever boarding a U.S.-bound aircraft after having received a warning from the suspect's father, a prominent Nigerian banker, of his son's radicalization. Obama moved to stanch the criticism by commissioning and quickly releasing a review of the intelligence agencies' "failure to connect the dots" and by ordering other steps, including a tightening of airline security procedures.

The politicization of the case intensified, however, with a broadside from former Vice President Dick Cheney sharply attacking the administration's decision to treat Abdulmutallab as a criminal suspect instead of an enemy combatant to be tried in a military tribunal. Obama "is trying to pretend we are not at war," Cheney told *Politico*, the Washington-based, all-politics newspaper.

"He seems to think if he has a low-key response to an attempt to blow up an airliner and kill hundreds of people, we won't be at war. He seems to think if he gives terrorists the rights of Americans, lets them lawyer up and reads them their Miranda rights, we won't be at war."[2]

White House press secretary Robert Gibbs responded promptly by accusing Cheney of playing "the typical Washington game of pointing fingers and making political hay." But the response did nothing to stop Republican politicians and conservative commentators from keeping up a drumbeat of criticism for several weeks into the new year, focused in particular on the decision to advise Abdulmutallab of his right to remain silent and to confer with a lawyer.

The criticism appears to have been based in part on an erroneous understanding of when FBI agents advised the 21-year-old Abdulmutallab of his Miranda rights. For weeks, critics said he had been "Mirandized" within 55 minutes of his arrest. Only in mid-February did the administration release a detailed, materially different timeline.[3]

penalty could be imposed by a two-thirds majority instead of the normal unanimous vote. The Supreme Court heard habeas corpus petitions filed by seven of the eight men but rejected their claims in a summary order in the case, *Ex parte Quirin*, on July 31. Six of the men had been executed before the justices issued their formal opinion on Oct. 29.[23]

International law governing wartime captives and domestic law governing military justice were both significantly reformed after World War II in ways that cast doubt on the previous ad hoc nature of military

commissions. The Geneva Conventions — signed in 1949 and ratified by the Senate in 1954 — strengthened previous protections for wartime captives by, among other things, prohibiting summary punishment even for combatants in non-traditional conflicts such as civil wars. The Uniform Code of Military Justice, approved by Congress in 1950, brought civilian-like procedures into a system previously built on command and discipline. The United States went beyond the requirements of the Geneva Conventions in the Vietnam War by giving full prisoner-of-war status to enemy captives, whether they belonged

The administration's account showed that Abdulmutallab was questioned for 55 minutes and provided some information about his rights before being taken away for surgery. When he returned after the four-hour procedure — a total of nine hours after his arrest — Abdulmutallab declined to answer further questions.

Without regard to the precise timing, critics said Abdulmutallab should have been treated outside the criminal justice system to maximize his value as a source of intelligence. Former Attorney General Michael B. Mukasey said the administration had "no compulsion" to treat Abdulmutallab as a criminal defendant "and every reason to treat him as an intelligence asset to be exploited promptly." The administration claimed that Abdulmutallab did begin providing actionable intelligence after family members were brought to the United States from Nigeria, but Mukasey said the five-week time lag meant that "possibly useful information" was lost.[4]

Administration supporters noted, however, that the Bush administration handled all suspected terrorists arrested in the United States as criminal defendants with the concomitant necessity to advise them of their Miranda rights. The administration's defense was substantiated by John Ashcroft, Mukasey's predecessor as attorney general. "When you have a person in the criminal justice system, you Mirandize them," Ashcroft told a reporter for *Huffington*

U.S. Marshals Service via Getty Images

Umar Farouk Abdulmutallab, a 23-year-old Nigerian, is charged with attempting to blow up a Northwest Airlines flight as it was landing in Detroit last Christmas Day.

Post when questioned at the conservative Tea Party Conference in Washington in mid-February.[5]

Administration critics appeared to say little about the precise charges brought against Abdulmutallab. He was initially charged in a criminal complaint Dec. 26 with two counts: attempting to blow up and placing an explosive device aboard a U.S. aircraft. Two weeks later, a federal grand jury in Detroit returned a more detailed indictment charging him with attempted use of a weapon of mass destruction and attempted murder of 269 people. If convicted, he faces a life sentence plus 90 years in prison. No trial date is set.

— *Kenneth Jost*

[1] Some background drawn from a well-documented Wikipedia entry: http://en.wikipedia.org/wiki/Umar_Farouk_Abdulmutallab.

[2] Mike Allen, "Dick Cheney: Barack Obama 'trying to pretend,'" *Politico*, Dec. 30, 2009, www.politico.com/news/stories/1209/31054.html, cited in Philip Elliott, "White House Hits Back at Cheney Criticism," The Associated Press, Dec. 30, 2009.

[3] Walter Pincus, "Bomb suspect was read Miranda rights nine hours after arrest," *The Washington Post*, Feb. 15, 2010, p. A6.

[4] Michael B. Mukasey, "Where the U.S. went wrong on Abdulmutallab," *The Washington Post*, Feb. 12, 2010, p. A27.

[5] Ryan Grim, "Ashcroft: 'When You Have a Person in the Criminal Justice System, You Mirandize Them,'" *Huffington Post*, Feb. 19, 2010, www.huffingtonpost.com/2010/02/19/ashcroft-when-you-have-a_n_469384.html.

to the regular North Vietnamese army or the guerrilla Vietcong.

International terrorism grew from a sporadic problem for the United States in the 1970s to a major concern in the 1980s and '90s. The results of foreign prosecutions in two of the major incidents in the '80s left many Americans disappointed. An Italian jury imposed a 30-year sentence in 1987 on Magid al-Molqi after the Palestinian confessed to the murder of U.S. citizen Leon Klinghoffer during the 1985 hijacking of the cruise ship *Achille Lauro*; the prosecution had sought a life term. The bombing of

Pan Am Flight 103 over Scotland in 1988 — and the deaths of 189 Americans among the 270 victims — resulted in the long-delayed trial of Abdel Basset Ali al-Megrahi, former head of the Libyan secret service. Megrahi was indicted in 1991 in the United States and Scotland, extradited only after protracted diplomatic negotiations and convicted and sentenced to life imprisonment in 2001. He was released on humanitarian grounds in 2009, suffering from purportedly terminal pancreatic cancer.

Two prosecutions in the United States stemming from the 1993 bombing of the World Trade Center produced seemingly stronger verdicts. Omar Abdel Rahman, the so-called Blind Sheik, was convicted in federal court in New York City along with nine others in 1995 for conspiracy to carry out a campaign of bombings and assassinations within the United States. Abdel Rahman is now serving a 240-year prison sentence. Two years later, Ramzi Ahmed Yousef was convicted on charges of masterminding the 1993 bombing and given a life sentence. Even after the second verdict, however, questions remained about whether the plot had been sponsored by a foreign state or international organization.[24]

Challenge and Response

The Bush administration responded to the 9/11 attacks by declaring an all-out war on terrorism that combined separate strategies of detaining captured "enemy combatants" at Guantánamo outside normal legal processes and prosecuting hundreds of individuals in federal courts on terrorism-related charges. The improvised system of military tribunals at Guantánamo drew political and legal challenges that stalled their work, resulting in only three convictions late in Bush's time in office. Meanwhile, criminal cases proceeded in federal courts with relatively few setbacks and little hindrance from criticism by some civil libertarians of overly aggressive prosecutions.[25]

Even as the Guantánamo military tribunals were being formed, the administration was initiating criminal prosecutions in other al Qaeda or Taliban-related cases. In the most important, the government indicted Zacarias Moussaoui, sometimes called the 20th hijacker, on Dec. 11, 2001, on conspiracy counts related to the 9/11 attacks. The prosecution dragged on for more than four years, extended by Moussaoui's courtroom dramatics and a fight over access to classified information that ended with a ruling largely favorable to the government. The trial ended on May 3, 2006, after a jury that had deliberated for seven days imposed a life sentence instead of the death penalty — apparently rejecting the government's view of Moussaoui as a central figure in the 9/11 attacks.

Two other early prosecutions ended more quickly. British citizen Richard Reid, the so-called shoe bomber, was charged in a federal criminal complaint on Dec. 24, 2001, two days after his failed explosive attack on American Airlines Flight 63. In January, Attorney General John Ashcroft announced that U.S. citizen John Walker Lindh,

the so-called American Taliban captured in Afghanistan, would be tried in a civilian court in the United States. Both men entered guilty pleas in 2002; Lindh was given a 20-year sentence while Reid was sentenced in January 2003 to life in prison.

The government started two other early cases in the criminal justice system and moved them into the military system only to return later to civilian courts. Ali Saleh Kahlah al-Marri, a Qatari student attending college in Illinois, was detained as a material witness in December 2001 and indicted two months later on credit-card charges. Bush's decision in 2003 to designate him as an enemy combatant led to a protracted appeal that the Obama administration resolved in 2009 by indicting al-Marri on a single count of conspiracy to provide material support for terrorism. In a similar vein, U.S. citizen José Padilla was arrested at the Chicago airport on May 8, 2002, on suspicion of plotting a radioactive attack; designated an enemy combatant a month later and then indicted after drawn-out legal challenges that reached the Supreme Court. Padilla was convicted of terrorism conspiracy charges and given a 17-year prison sentence; al-Marri drew 15 years after pleading guilty.

Meanwhile, the military tribunals had been stymied by a succession of legal challenges before the Supreme Court and responses by the administration and Congress to the justices' rulings. In the pivotal decision in Hamdan's case, the court ruled in June 2006 that the military commissions as then constituted were illegal because the president had not shown a need to depart from established rules of military justice.[26] Reconstituted under the Military Commissions Act of 2006, the tribunals finally produced their first conviction in March 2007 when the Australian Hicks pleaded guilty to a single material-support count. Under a plea agreement and with credit for time served, he was allowed to return to Australia to serve the remaining nine months of a seven-year sentence.

Two more convictions followed in 2008, both after trials. Hamdan was convicted in August of conspiracy and material support but acquitted of more serious charges and given an unexpectedly light sentence of 61 months. With credit for time served, he was transferred to his native Yemen in late November to serve the last month of his term. Earlier, a military tribunal on Nov. 3 had convicted Bahlul of a total of 35 terrorism-related counts after the former al Qaeda propaganda chief essentially boycotted the proceedings. The panel returned the verdict in the morning and then deliberated for an hour before sentencing the Yemeni native to life imprisonment.

As the Bush administration neared an end, the Justice Department issued a fact-sheet on the seventh anniversary of the 9/11 attacks touting its "considerable success in America's federal courtrooms of identifying, prosecuting and incarcerating terrorists and would-be terrorists." The report listed the Padilla and Moussaoui cases among eight "notable" prosecutions in recent years. It also briefly noted the department's cooperation with the Defense Department in developing procedures for the military commissions, defending against challenges to the system and jointly bringing charges against KSM and other high-value detainees.[27]

In an important post-election setback, however, a federal judge in Washington ruled on Nov. 20, 2008, in favor of five of the six Algerians whose habeas corpus petitions had led to the Supreme Court decision guaranteeing judicial review for Guantánamo detainees. Judge Richard Leon said the government had failed to present sufficient evidence to show that the six men, arrested in Bosnia in January 2002, had planned to travel to Afghanistan to fight against the United States. He found sufficient evidence, however, that one of the prisoners had acted as a facilitator for al Qaeda. Three of the five were returned to Bosnia in December; two others were transferred to France in May and November 2009.[28]

Change and Continuity

In his first days in office, President Obama began fulfilling his campaign pledge to change the Bush administration's legal policies in the war on terror. Obama's high-profile decisions to set a deadline for closing Guantánamo, shut down the secret CIA prisons and prohibit enhanced interrogation techniques drew support from Democrats and liberals and sharp criticism from Republicans and conservatives. By year's end, the roles were reversed, with support from the right and criticism from the left of Obama's decision to continue use of military tribunals and claim the power to detain suspected terrorists indefinitely without trial. Meanwhile, the government was continuing to win significant terrorism-related convictions in federal courts but suffering setbacks in many habeas corpus cases brought by Guantánamo prisoners.

Even with the Guantánamo and interrogation policies under attack, the Justice Department was achieving some significant successes in prosecutions that carried over from the Bush administration. The new administration side-stepped a Supreme Court test of the power to detain U.S. residents by transferring al-Marri to civilian courts in late February and securing his guilty plea in April. Also in April, Wesam al-Delaema, an Iraqi-born Dutch citizen, was given a 25-year prison sentence for planting roadside bombs aimed at U.S. troops in his native country. Al-Delaema had fought extradition from the Netherlands and was to be returned there to serve what was expected to be a reduced sentence. The case marked the first successful prosecution for terrorist offenses against U.S. forces in Iraq.

In May, the government won convictions — after two prior mistrials — in its case against the so-called Liberty City Six (originally, Seven), who were charged with plotting to blow up the Sears Tower in Chicago and selected federal buildings. The jury in Miami convicted five of the men but acquitted a sixth. On the same day, a federal jury in New York City convicted Oussama Kassir, a Lebanese-born Swede, of attempting to establish a terrorist training camp in Oregon. Material-support charges were the major counts in both cases. Kassir was sentenced to life in September; of the six defendants in the Miami case, sentences handed down on Nov. 20 ranged from 84 to 162 months.

By summer, the Justice Department conceded that it would be late with an interim report on closing Guantánamo. In acknowledging the delay in a background briefing on July 20 — the eve of the due date for the report — administration officials claimed some progress in resettling some of the detainees but confirmed expectations to hold some of the prisoners indefinitely. The administration did release the two-page protocol from the Defense and Justice departments on prosecuting Guantánamo cases, with its stated "presumption" in favor of civilian prosecutions "where feasible." The memo outlined a variety of factors to consider in choosing between civilian courts or "reformed" military commissions. With Guantánamo dominating the coverage, the memo drew little attention.[29]

Meanwhile, federal judges in Washington, D.C., were giving mixed verdicts as more of the long-delayed habeas corpus cases by Guantánamo detainees reached decision stage.[30] In the first of the rulings after Obama took office,

Material-Support Law Called Anti-Terror "Weapon of Choice"

Critics say the broadly written law criminalizes lawful speech.

Oussama Kassir never took up arms against U.S. forces in Afghanistan and never carried out a terrorist attack against Americans in the United States or abroad. But he is serving a life prison sentence today after a federal court jury in New York City found him guilty of attempting to establish a jihadist training camp in Oregon and distributing terrorist training materials over the Internet.

To put Kassir behind bars, federal prosecutors used a broadly written law that makes it a crime to provide "material support" — broadly defined — to any group designated by the government as a "terrorist organization." The law, first passed in 1994 and amended several times since, accounts for roughly half of the al Qaeda-related terrorism convictions since 2001, according to a study by two ex-prosecutors written for the Washington-based group Human Rights First. [1]

The material-support law is "the anti-terror weapon of choice for prosecutors," says Stephen Vladeck, a law professor at American University in Washington, D.C. "It's a lot easier to prove that a defendant provided material support to a designated terrorist organization than to prove that they actually committed a terrorist act."

Kassir, a Lebanese-born Swedish citizen, was convicted on May 12, 2009, after a three-week trial. The evidence showed he came to the United States in 1999 and bought a parcel of land in Oregon with plans to take advantage of lax U.S. gun laws to train Muslim recruits in assembling and disassembling AK-47 rifles. He also established six different Web sites and posted materials about how to make bombs and poisons.

The defense denied that Kassir conspired to train recruits and claimed the Web sites contained only readily available information. The jury deliberated less than a day before returning guilty verdicts on a total of 11 counts. U.S. District Judge John Keenan sentenced him to life imprisonment on Sept. 15. [2]

On the same day as the Kassir verdict, a federal court jury in Miami returned guilty verdicts against five of the so-called "Liberty City Six," who had been charged with plotting to blow up the Sears Tower in Chicago and selected federal buildings. In the Human Rights First report, New York lawyers Richard Zabel and James J. Benjamin Jr. note that the trial shows the importance of the material-support charge because prosecutors won convictions against only two defendants on an explosives charge and against only one defendant for seditious conspiracy.

Zabel and Benjamin, who both served in the U.S. attorney's office in New York City, say the material-support law has similarly been used to convict defendants for such actions as providing broadcasting services to a terrorist organization's television station or traveling to Pakistan for training in a jihadist camp. The law was also invoked against Lynne Stewart, a well-known defense lawyer, for transmitting messages to her terrorism-case client, Omar Abdel Rahman, the "Blind Sheik."

The law defines material support to include not only financial contributions but also any "property" or "service," including "personnel" and "training, expert advice or assistance." Medicine and religious materials are exempted.

Some civil liberties and humanitarian groups contend the law sweeps too broadly. Material support is defined "so expansively and vaguely as to criminalize pure speech furthering lawful, nonviolent ends," the bipartisan Constitution

Judge Leon ruled on Jan. 28 that evidence of serving as a cook for al Qaeda was sufficient to hold a prisoner for "material support" of terrorism. In 14 cases over the next year, however, the government lost more — eight — than it won (six). In five of the cases granting habeas corpus, judges found the government's evidence either insufficient or unreliable. In one, the judge specifically found the government's evidence had been obtained by torture or under the taint of prior torture. In the two other cases, one of the detainees was found to have been expelled from al Qaeda, while the other was no longer a threat because he was cooperating with U.S. authorities.

Project says in a recent report. The report recommends amending the law to exempt "pure speech" unless intended to further illegal conduct. It also calls for giving groups the opportunity to contest designation as a terrorist organization. [3]

Appellate courts have generally upheld broad readings of the statute. In a decision in December 2007, however, the San Francisco-based U.S. Court of Appeals for the Ninth Circuit ruled that some of the law's terms —"training," "service," and "expert advice or assistance" — were impermissibly vague or overbroad.

The ruling came in a suit filed originally in 1998 by the Humanitarian Law Project on behalf of individuals or U.S.-based groups that sought to provide assistance to two designated terrorist organizations: the Kurdistan Workers' Party in Turkey or the Liberation Tigers of Tamil Eelam in Sri Lanka. The plaintiffs claimed they wanted to counsel both groups on use of international law and nonviolent conflict resolution.

The Supreme Court agreed to hear the government's appeal of the case as well as the plaintiffs' cross-appeal of the part of the ruling that upheld a broad construction of the term "personnel." The case was argued on Feb. 23; a decision is due by the end of June. [4]

Meanwhile, a military appeals panel is weighing challenges to the use of material-support counts in military commission proceedings. The United States Court of Military Commission Review heard arguments on Jan. 26 in appeals by two of the three men convicted so far in military commissions: Salim Ahmed Hamdan, former driver for al Qaeda leader Osama bin Laden, and al Qaeda filmmaker and propagandist Ali Hamza Ahmad Suliman al Bahlul.

AFP/Getty Images/Vadim Kramer

Oussama Kassir is serving a life sentence after a federal court jury in New York City found him guilty last year of attempting to establish a jihadist training camp in Oregon and distributing terrorist training materials over the Internet.

Hamdan, who was freed in late 2008 after about seven-and-a-half years in captivity, and al Bahlul, who was sentenced to life imprisonment, both contend that material support for terrorism is outside the military tribunals' jurisdiction because it is not a traditional war crime. The cases were argued before separate three-judge panels, which gave no indication when rulings would be expected. [5]

— Kenneth Jost

[1] Richard B. Zabel and James J. Benjamin Jr., "In Pursuit of Justice: Prosecuting Terrorism Cases in the Federal Courts," Human Rights First, May 2008, p. 32, www.humanrightsfirst.info/pdf/080521-USLS-pursuit-justice.pdf. See also by same authors "In Pursuit of Justice: Prosecuting Terrorism Cases in the Federal Courts: 2009 Update and Recent Developments," July 2009, www.humanrightsfirst.org/pdf/090723-LS-in-pursuit-justice-09-update.pdf. Background drawn from both reports.

[2] The press release by the U.S. Attorney for the Southern District of New York can be found at www.humanrightsfirst.org/pdf/090723-LS-in-pursuit-justice-09-update.pdf. See also "Man convicted in NY of trying to start terror camp," The Associated Press, May 12, 2009.

[3] "Reforming the Material Support Laws: Constitutional Concerns Presented by Prohibitions on Material Support to 'Terrorist Organizations,' " Constitution Project, Nov. 17, 2009, www.constitutionproject.org/manage/file/355.pdf.

[4] The case is *Holder v. Humanitarian Law Project*, 08-1498. For materials on the case, including links to news coverage, see SCOTUSWiki, www.scotuswiki.com/index.php?title=Holder_v._Humanitarian_Law_Project.

[5] Material in Bahlul's case can be found at www.defense.gov/news/CMCRHAMZA.html/; materials in Hamdan's case at www.defense.gov/news/commissionsHamdan.html.

In order to prevent leaks, Holder made his decision to try KSM in a federal court with little advance notice to New York City officials. He explained later to the Senate Judiciary Committee that a federal court trial would give the government "the greatest opportunity to present the strongest case in the best forum." The explanation left Republicans, conservatives and many New Yorkers unconvinced of the benefits, dismayed at the potential costs and appalled at the idea of according full legal rights to a self-proclaimed enemy of the United States. Civil liberties and human rights groups applauded the decision while giving little attention to Holder's simultaneous move to try the alleged *USS Cole* plotter and others in military commissions that the groups had called for abolishing.

The political attacks over the administration's handling of Abdulmutallab's case added to the pressure against trying KSM in New York City. Behind the scenes, Justice Department officials were looking for alternate, more remote sites for a possible civilian trial. And by February Holder was being deliberately ambiguous about whether the case would be tried in a civilian court at all.

"At the end of the day, wherever this case is tried, in whatever forum, what we have to ensure is that it's done as transparently as possible and with adherence to all the rules," Holder said on Feb. 11.[31] "If we do that, I'm not sure the location or even the forum is as important as what the world sees in that proceeding."

CURRENT SITUATION

Watching Appeals

Lawyers for the government and for Guantánamo detainees are watching the federal appeals court in Washington and a specially created military appeals panel for the next major developments on the rules for prosecuting terrorism cases.

The government scored a major victory in early January when the U.S. Circuit Court of Appeals for the District of Columbia decisively backed the government's power to detain a low-level member of a pro-Taliban brigade captured during the Afghanistan war and held at Guantánamo for more than eight years.

Later in the month, the U.S. Court of Military Commission Review heard arguments on Jan. 26 from two of the men convicted so far in the military tribunals challenging the government's power to prosecute material support for terrorism in military instead of civilian courts. Separate three-judge panels convened to hear the appeals by al Qaeda propagandist Bahlul and former bin Laden driver Hamdan gave no indication when they would rule on the cases.

With several other habeas corpus cases pending before the D.C. Circuit, the appeals court is likely to determine both the direction and the pace of the next stage of the litigation from Guantánamo prisoners, according to Brookings Institution scholar Wittes.

If other judges follow the lead of the conservative-dominated panel in the Jan. 5 decision, many of the outstanding issues regarding the government's power to hold enemy combatants could be resolved quickly, Wittes says. But different rulings by panels in other cases could add to what he calls the "cacophony" surrounding the habeas corpus cases and force the Supreme Court to intervene to resolve the conflicts.

The appeals court's decision rejected a habeas corpus petition by Ghaleb Nassar Al-Bihani, a Yemeni native who served as a cook for a Taliban brigade. He argued that he should be released because the war against the Taliban has ended and, in any event, that he was essentially a civilian contractor instead of a combatant.

In a 25-page opinion, Judge Janice Rogers Brown rejected both arguments. Brown, a strongly conservative judge appointed by President George W. Bush, said Bihani's admitted actions of accompanying the brigade to the battlefield, carrying a weapon and retreating and surrendering with the brigade showed that he was "both part of and substantially supported enemy forces."

As for the status of the war, Brown said, it was up to Congress or the president to decide whether the conflict had ended, not the courts. In a significant passage, Brown also said that U.S. instead of international law determined the president's authority to hold enemy combatants. "The international laws of war as a whole have not been implemented domestically by Congress and are therefore not a source of authority for U.S. courts," Brown wrote.

Judge Brett Kavanaugh, another Bush-appointed conservative, joined Brown's opinion. Judge Stephen Williams, who was appointed by President Ronald Reagan, agreed on the result but distanced himself from Brown's comments on the impact of international law. He noted that Brown's "dictum" — the legal term for a passage unnecessary to the decision in the case —"goes well beyond what the government has argued in the case."[32]

Wittes says the ruling is "a huge development if it stands." The appellate panel, he says, was "signaling" to the federal district court judges in Washington handling habeas corpus cases to "lighten up" on the government. District court judges have ruled against the government in somewhat over half of the cases decided so far.

The appeals court for the military commissions was created by the 2006 law overhauling the rules for the

Cole Bombing Case, Six Others Set for Tribunals

Abd al Rahim al Nashiri, the alleged mastermind of the October 2000 suicide attack on the *USS Cole*, is one of seven Guantánamo detainees designated by Attorney General Eric Holder for trial by military commissions. Seventeen U.S. sailors were killed in the attack on the warship as it lay docked in Aden, Yemen.

The Saudi-born al-Nashiri, now 45, allegedly served as al Qaeda's chief of operations in the Arabian peninsula before his capture in the United Arab Emirates in November 2002. He was held in a secret CIA prison (reportedly in Thailand) until being brought to Guantánamo in 2006.

The CIA has confirmed that al-Nashiri was waterboarded. He claims that he falsely confessed to the *Cole* attack and six other terrorist incidents as a result. It is also reported that he was the target of a mock execution by CIA interrogators.

The six other prisoners designated for trial by military commissions are:

- **Ahmed al Darbi (Saudi Arabia)** — Accused of plotting to bomb oil tankers in the Strait of Hormuz.
- **Mohammed Kamin (Afghanistan)** — Charged with planting mines in Afghanistan.
- **Omar Khadr (Canada)** — Accused of killing a U.S. soldier with a grenade in Afghanistan in 2002; Khadr was 15 at the time.
- **Noor Uthman Mohammed (Sudan)** — Charged with assisting in running al Qaeda training center.
- **Obaidullah (Afghanistan)** — Charged with possessing anti-tank mines.
- **Ibrahim al Qosi (Sudan)** — Accused of acting as Osama bin Laden's bodyguard, paymaster and supply chief.

tribunals, but it had no cases to review until after Hamdan's and Bahlul's convictions in 2008.

In their appeals, both men claim that their convictions for material support for terrorism were improper because the offense is not a traditional war crime prosecutable in a military court. Bahlul also argues that the First Amendment bars prosecuting him for producing a video documentary for al Qaeda that recounts the bombing of the *USS Cole* and calls for others to join a jihad against the United States.

The government counters by citing cases from the Civil War and World War II to argue that providing support to unlawful enemy combatants has been prosecutable in military courts even if the term "material support for terrorism" was not used. As to Bahlul's free-speech argument, the government contends that the First Amendment does not apply to enemy "propaganda."[33]

Bahlul is also challenging the life sentence imposed in November 2008; Hamdan was freed later that month after being credited with the seven years he had already been held at Guantánamo.

Wittes says the government has "a big uphill climb" on the material-support issue. He notes that in the Supreme

Court's 2006 decision in Hamdan's case, four of the justices questioned whether military tribunals could try a conspiracy charge, another of the generally phrased offenses the government has used in terrorism cases. Material support for terrorism would be harder to justify, he says.

Wittes adds that it is important to resolve the issue quickly if the military commissions are to be used in other cases. "What you don't want to happen is to have a whole lot of people sentenced in military commissions and then find out that the charges are invalid," he says.

Making a Deal?

The Obama administration may be on the verge of deciding to try Khalid Sheikh Mohammed and four other alleged 9/11 conspirators in a military tribunal in an effort to gain Republican support for closing the Guantánamo prison camp.

Administration officials are reportedly near to recommending that Obama reverse Attorney General Holder's Nov. 13 decision to hold the 9/11 conspiracy trial in federal court in hopes of securing support for closing Guantánamo from an influential Republican senator, South Carolina's Lindsey Graham.[34]

Should terrorism suspects ordinarily be tried in civilian courts?

YES
Laura Olson
Senior Counsel, Rule of Law Program Constitution Project

Written for *CQ Researcher*, March 2010

Civilian courts are the proper forum for trying terrorism cases. Trial in our traditional federal courts is a proven and reliable way to provide justice, while ensuring our national security. This is in stark contrast to the new military commissions that were re-created for the third time in the Military Commissions Act (MCA) of 2009. Like their predecessors, these new commissions remain vulnerable to constitutional challenge.

We should not place some of the most important terrorism trials, and arguably the most important criminal trials, in our nation's history in the untested and uncertain military commissions system.

Since 2001, trials in federal criminal courts have resulted in nearly 200 convictions of terrorism suspects, compared to only three low-level convictions in the military commissions. Two of those three are now free in their home countries. This record demonstrates that prosecutions in our traditional federal courts are tough on terrorists.

To date, the rules to accompany the MCA of 2009 remain to be approved. Therefore, military commission judges are without guidance on how to proceed with these cases. Meanwhile, our traditional federal courts move ahead, applying long-established rules on procedure and evidence. For example, the Classified Information Procedures Act (CIPA) elaborates the procedures by which federal courts admit evidence while protecting national security information from improper disclosure. The MCA of 2009 incorporates CIPA procedures on dealing with classified information into the military commissions system, but military judges have little or no experience with these procedures. Federal judges have worked with CIPA for the last 30 years.

Our Constitution provides a safe and effective way to prosecute terrorism suspects. In fact, Ahmed Kfalfan Ghailani, a former Guantánamo detainee, is now being held in New York City for his trial in federal court there. The judge has issued a protective order on all classified information, and there have been no reports of any increased safety risks or expenses associated with this trial.

I agree with the nearly 140 former diplomats, military officials, federal judges and prosecutors and members of Congress, as well as bar leaders, national-security and foreign-policy experts, and family members of the 9/11 attacks that signed Beyond Guantánamo: A Bipartisan Declaration. This unique and bipartisan group is in favor of trying terrorism suspects in our traditional federal courts. Federal trials are the only way to ensure swift and constitutional trials of terrorism suspects.

NO
Sen. John McCain, R-Ariz.
From statement in support of the Enemy Belligerent Interrogation, Detention and Prosecution Act, March 4, 2010

This legislation seeks to ensure that the mistakes made during the apprehension of the Christmas Day bomber, such as reading him a Miranda warning, will never happen again and put Americans' security at risk.

Specifically, this bill would require unprivileged enemy belligerents suspected of engaging in hostilities against the U.S. to be held in military custody and interrogated for their intelligence value by a "high-value detainee" interagency team established by the president. This interagency team of experts in national security, terrorism, intelligence, interrogation and law enforcement will have the protection of U.S. civilians and civilian facilities as their paramount responsibility. . . .

A key provision of this bill is that it would prohibit a suspected enemy belligerent from being provided with a Miranda warning and being told he has a right to a lawyer and a right to refuse to cooperate. I believe that an overwhelming majority of Americans agree that when we capture a terrorist who is suspected of carrying out or planning an attack intended to kill hundreds if not thousands of innocent civilians, our focus must be on gaining all the information possible to prevent that attack or any that may follow from occurring. . . . Additionally, the legislation would authorize detention of enemy belligerents without criminal charges for the duration of the hostilities consistent with standards under the law of war which have been recognized by the Supreme Court.

Importantly, if a decision is made to hold a criminal trial after the necessary intelligence information is obtained, the bill mandates trial by military commission, where we are best able to protect U.S. national security interests, including sensitive classified sources and methods, as well as the place and the people involved in the trial itself.

The vast majority of Americans understand that what happened with the Christmas Day bomber was a near catastrophe that was only prevented by sheer luck and the courage of a few of the passengers and crew. A wide majority of Americans also realize that allowing a terrorist to be interrogated for only 50 minutes before he is given a Miranda warning and told he can obtain a lawyer and stop cooperating is not sufficient. . . .

We must ensure that the broad range of expertise that is available within our government is brought to bear on such high-value detainees. This bill mandates such coordination and places the proper focus on getting intelligence to stop an attack, rather than allowing law enforcement and preparing a case for a civilian criminal trial to drive our response.

Graham, a former military lawyer, has strongly advocated use of military tribunals for detainees held at Guantánamo but has not joined other Republicans in attacking Obama's pledge to close the facility. GOP lawmakers have been pushing legislative proposals to block use of funds for closing Guantánamo or for holding the 9/11 conspiracy trial in federal court.

The administration's possible reversal on the KSM trial is drawing a heated response from civil liberties and human rights groups. The decision would "strike a blow to American values and the rule of law and undermine America's credibility," according to the ACLU.

Elisa Massimino, president and CEO of Human Rights First, says failure to support Holder's decision would set "a dangerous precedent for future national security policy."

In the wake of the strong criticism of holding the KSM trial in New York City, Justice Department lawyers and others had been reported to be holding onto the plan for a federal court trial, but in a different location. Among the sites reported to have been under consideration were somewhere else in southern New York, Northern Virginia and western Pennsylvania.[35]

Any of those sites would satisfy the constitutional requirement that trial of a federal criminal case be held in "the district wherein the crime shall have been committed." Besides the World Trade Center in New York City, the 9/11 hijackers also crashed a plane into the Pentagon in Northern Virginia and into a rural location in western Pennsylvania.

Graham, first elected to the Senate in 2002, argued during the Bush administration for a greater role for Congress in defining detention policies. Since Obama's election, he is widely reported to have formed a working relationship on several issues with White House chief of staff Rahm Emanuel, a former colleague in the House of Representatives. Emanuel was described in a flattering profile in *The Washington Post* and elsewhere as having disagreed with Obama's pledge to close Guantánamo and with Holder's decision to try KSM in federal court.[36]

Beyond the KSM trial and Guantánamo issue, Graham is continuing to call for congressional legislation to govern the handling of detention issues. "I want Congress and the administration to come up with a detainee policy that will be accepted by courts and so that the international community will understand that no one is in jail by an

FEMA News Photo/WireImage/Andrea Booher

Controversy erupted after Attorney General Eric Holder announced plans to try the five alleged 9/11 conspirators in a federal court "just blocks away from where the twin towers [of the World Trade Center] once stood." New York City Mayor Michael Bloomberg and Police Commissioner Raymond Kelly welcomed Holder's decision, but many New Yorkers expressed concern about the costs and risks of a sensational trial in Lower Manhattan.

arbitrary exercise of executive power," Graham told *The New York Times.*[37]

As outlined, the legislation would authorize holding terrorism suspects inside the United States without charging them with a crime or advising them of Miranda rights; establish standards for choosing between military or civilian court for prosecution; and authorize indefinite detention under standards subject to judicial review. Civil liberties and human rights groups remain opposed to indefinite-detention proposals.

Administration officials were quoted in news accounts as saying Obama hopes to have the KSM trial issue resolved before he begins a trip to Asia on March 18. But officials quoted in *The Washington Post* cautioned against expecting a "grand bargain" with Graham on the full range of detention issues in the near future.

OUTLOOK

Bringing Justice to Bear

When he defended the administration's decision to try Khalid Sheikh Mohammed in a civilian court, deputy national intelligence director John Brennan made clear that he expected the trial would be fair and just, but the result certain and severe.

"I'm confident that he's going to have the full weight of American justice," Brennan said on NBC's "Meet the Press" on Feb. 7. Asked by host David Gregory whether Mohammed would be executed, Brennan initially skirted the question but eventually concluded, "I'm convinced and confident that Mr. Khalid Sheikh Mohammed is going to meet his day in justice and before his maker."[38]

Despite the assurance from Brennan, Attorney General Holder and other administration officials, Americans apparently lack the same confidence in the federal court system. An ABC/*Washington Post* poll conducted in late February showed Americans favoring military over civilian trials for terrorism suspects by a margin of 55 percent to 39 percent. In a similar poll in the fall, Americans showed a statistically insignificant preference for military trials: 48 percent to 47 percent.[39]

A survey by Democratic pollsters similarly finds a majority of respondents opposed to Obama's policy on interrogation and prosecution of terrorism suspects (51 percent to 44 percent). But the survey, conducted in late February for the Democratic groups Democracy Corps and Third Way, also found majority approval of Obama's handling of "national security" (57 percent to 40 percent) and "fighting terrorism" (54 percent to 41 percent).

In a memo, leaders of the two organizations advise Obama to move the issue away from "civilian" versus "military" trials. Instead, they say the administration should "place the debate over terrorism suspects into the broader context of tough actions and significant results."[40]

Even before the memo's release, civil liberties and human rights groups were following the strategy in public lobbying of Obama as the administration was weighing where to hold the KSM trial. In a March 5 conference call for reporters arranged by Human Rights First, three

retired military officers all depicted the military commissions as an unproven forum for prosecuting terrorists. "This is not ready for prime time," said Human Rights First President Massamino.

The ACLU followed with a full-page ad in the Sunday edition of *The New York Times* that compared the 300 terrorism cases "successfully handled" in the criminal justice system to "only three" in military commissions. "Our criminal justice system will resolve these cases more quickly and more credibly than the military commissions," the March 7 ad stated.

Meanwhile, former prosecutor McCarthy conceded in a speech sponsored by a college-affiliated center in Washington, "I don't think the military commission system performed well. By and large, the civilian system has performed well."

Speaking March 5 at the Kirby Center for Constitutional Studies and Citizenship at Hillsdale College in Michigan, McCarthy nevertheless reiterated that discovery procedures available to defendants argued against use of criminal prosecutions. "When you're at war, you can't be telling the enemy your most sensitive national intelligence," the *National Review* columnist said. Massamino noted, however, that a new military commissions law passed in 2009 dictates that defendants are to have access to evidence "comparable" to that provided in civilian courts.

The White House now says a decision on the KSM trial is "weeks" away. On Capitol Hill, Sen. Graham is continuing to push for a deal that would swap Republican support for closing Guantánamo for the administration's agreement to try KSM and other high-level terrorism suspects in military commissions. But Graham has yet to gain any public support for the plan from GOP colleagues.

McCarthy mocks Graham's proposed deal. He says the White House has already "stood down" on the military commissions issues and is only deferring a decision in hopes of getting GOP support for closing Guantánamo. "It makes no sense to horse-trade when Obama was being pushed toward military commissions by reality," McCarthy writes.[41]

Fellow conservative Rivkin also expects military commissions to become the norm for terrorism suspects. "My hope is that we'll come to our senses," he says. The current policies "are not consonant with the traditional law-of-war architecture, and they're not consistent with prevailing in this war."

Liberal groups continue to strongly oppose use of military commissions, but acknowledge congressional politics may determine decision-making. "There's no question that Congress has been trying to hold hostage the president's national security agenda," Massamino says.

For his part, former Assistant U.S. Attorney Benjamin doubts that military commissions will prove as useful as conservatives expect. "It would be great if the military commissions develop into a forum that works," he says. "But I have my doubts about how quickly or how smoothly that will happen."

NOTES

1. Some background information drawn from Farhan Bokhari, *et al.*, "The CEO of al-Qaeda," *Financial Times*, Feb. 15, 2003. See also the Wikipedia entry on Khalid Sheikh Mohammed and sources cited there, http://en.wikipedia.org/wiki/Khalid_Sheikh_Mohammed.

2. Quoted in Devlin Barnett, "NYC trial of 9/11 suspects faces legal risks," The Associated Press, Nov. 14, 2009. For Holder's prepared remarks, see U.S. Department of Justice, "Attorney General Announces Forum Decisions for Guantánamo Detainees," Nov. 13, 2009, www.justice.gov/ag/speeches/2009/ag-speech-091113.html.

3. Quoted in Carrie Johnson, "Holder Answers to 9/11 Relatives About Trials in U.S.," *The Washington Post*, Nov. 19, 2009, p. A3. See also Charlie Savage, "Holder Defends Decision to Use U.S. Court for 9/11 Trial," *The New York Times*, Nov. 19, 2009, p. A18.

4. See Anne E. Kornblut and Carrie Johnson, "Obama to help pick location of terror trial," *The Washington Post*, Feb. 12, 2010, p. A1.

5. For background, see these *CQ Researcher* reports: Kenneth Jost, "Closing Guantánamo," Feb. 27, 2009, pp. 177-200; Peter Katel and Kenneth Jost, "Treatment of Detainees," Aug. 25, 2006, pp. 673-696; and Kenneth Jost, "Civil Liberties Debates," Oct. 24, 2003, pp. 893-916.

6. "FY 2009 Budget and Performance Summary: Part One: Summary of Request and Performance," U.S. Department of Justice, www.justice.gov/jmd/2009summary/html/004_budget_highlights.htm. See also Mark Hosenball, "Terror Prosecution Statistics Criticized by GOP Were Originally Touted by Bush Administration," *Declassified* blog, Feb. 9, 2010, http://blog.newsweek.com/blogs/declassified/archive/2010/02/09/terror-prosecution-statistics-criticized-by-gop-were-originally-touted-by-bush-administration.aspx.

7. Richard B. Zabel and James J. Benjamin Jr., "In Pursuit of Justice: Prosecuting Terrorism Cases in the Federal Courts: 2009 Update and Recent Developments," Human Rights First, July 2009, www.humanrightsfirst.org/pdf/090723-LS-in-pursuit-justice-09-update.pdf. See also by the same authors, "In Pursuit of Justice: Prosecuting Terrorism Cases in the Federal Courts," Human Rights First, May 2008, www.humanrightsfirst.info/pdf/080521-USLS-pursuit-justice.pdf.

8. Andy McCarthy, "No Civilian Trial — In NYC or Anywhere Else," *Conservative Blog Watch*, Jan. 30, 2010, www.conservativeblogwatch.com/2010/01/30/no-civilian-trial-in-nyc-or-anywhere-by-andy-mccarthy.

9. See Benjamin Weiser, "A Top Terrorism Prosecutor Turns Critic of Civilian Trials," *The New York Times*, Feb. 20, 2010, p. A1.

10. See Del Quentin Wilber, " '08 habeas ruling may snag Obama plans," *The Washington Post*, Feb. 13, 2010, p. A2.

11. The defendants and their respective sentences were Mukhtar Al-Bakri and Yahya Goba (10 years each), Sahim Alwan (9-1/2 years), Shafal Mosed and Yaseinn Taher (eight years each) and Faysal Galab (seven years). For a full account, see Matthew Purdy and Lowell Bergman, "Where the Trail Led: Between Evidence and Suspicion, Unclear Danger: The Lackawanna Terror Case," *The New York Times*, Oct. 12, 2003, sec. 1, p. 1. See also Lou Michel, "Lackawanna officials say troops in city was bad idea," *Buffalo News*, July 26, 2009, p. A1.

12. *In Pursuit of Justice, op. cit.*, p. 2; *In Pursuit of Justice: 2009 Update, op. cit.*, p. 2.

13. Quoted in Bruce Golding, "Holder tours federal courthouse ahead of 9/11 terror trial," *The New York Post*, Dec. 9, 2009.

14. See Peter Finn, "The boy from the battlefield," *The Washington Post*, Feb. 10, 2010, p. A1.

15. "Remarks by the President on National Security," National Archives, May 21, 2009, www.whitehouse .gov/the_press_office/Remarks-by-the-President- On-National-Security-5-21-09/. For coverage, see Sheryl Gay Stolberg, "Obama Would Move Some Terror Detainees to U.S.," *The New York Times*, May 22, 2009, p. A1.

16. Department of Defense comments on the study are at www.defense.gov/Transcripts/Transcript.aspx? TranscriptID=4340. See also Joseph Williams and Bryan Bender, "Obama Changes US Course on Treatment of Detainees," *The Boston Globe*, Jan. 23, 2009, p. A1. See Mark Denbeaux, Joshua Denbeaux and R. David Gratz, "Released Guantánamo Detainees and the Department of Defense: Propaganda by the Numbers?," Jan. 15, 2009, http://law.shu.edu/ publications/GuantánamoReports/propaganda_ numbers_11509.pdf.

17. The case is 542 U.S. 507 (2004). For an account, see Kenneth Jost, *Supreme Court Yearbook 2003-2004*, CQ Press.

18. Benjamin Wittes, Robert Chesney and Rabea Benhalim, "The Emerging Law of Detention: The Guantánamo Habeas Cases as Lawmaking," Brookings Institution, Jan. 22, 2010, www.brook ings.edu/papers/2010/0122_Guantánamo_wittes_ chesney.aspx. See Benjamin Wittes and Robert Chesney, "Piecemeal detainee policy," *The Washington Post*, Jan. 27, 2010, p. A17.

19. Chisun Lee, "Judges Urge Congress to Act on Indefinite Detention," *ProPublica*, Jan. 22, 2010, www.propublica.org/feature/judges-urge-congress- to-act-on-indefinite-terrorism-detentions-122. Walton, an appointee of President George W. Bush, was joined in the interview by Chief Judge Royce Lamberth, an appointee of President Ronald Reagan, and Judge Ricardo Urbina, an appointee of President Bill Clinton.

20. David Cole, "Detainees: still a matter for judges," *The Washington Post*, Feb. 9, 2010, p. A16.

21. Background drawn in part from Jennifer K. Elsea, "Terrorism and the Law of War: Trying Terrorists as War Criminals before Military Commissions," Congressional Research Service, Dec. 11, 2001, www .fas.org/irp/crs/RL31191.pdf. See also Louis Fisher, *Military Tribunals and Presidential Power: American Revolution to the War on Terrorism* (2005). Wittes' quote is from his book *Law and the Long War: The Future of Justice in the Age of Terror* (2008), p. 42.

22. The decision is *Ex parte Milligan*, 71 U.S. 2 (1866). *The New York Times'* contemporaneous account is reprinted in Kenneth Jost, *The New York Times on the Supreme Court 1857-2006* (2009), CQ Press, pp. 58-59.

23. The citation is 317 U.S. 1 (1942). The opinion was issued on Oct. 29, almost three months after the July 31 decision. The rulings on the curfew and internments are *Hirabayashi v. United States*, 320 U.S. 81 (1943), and *Korematsu v. United States*, 323 U.S. 214 (1944).

24. Joseph P. Fried, "Sheik Sentenced to Life in Prison in Bombing Plot," *The New York Times*, Jan. 18, 1996, p. A1, and Christopher S. Wren, "Jury Convicts 3 in a Conspiracy to Bomb Airliners," *The New York Times*, Sept. 6, 1996, p. A1. See also Benjamin Weiser, "Judge Upholds Conviction in '93 Bombing," *The New York Times*, April 5, 2003, p. A1.

25. Accounts drawn from *Pursuit of Justice* (2008), *op. cit.*, supplemented by Wikipedia entries or con- temporaneous news coverage.

26. The decision is *Hamdan v. Rumsfeld*, 548 U.S. 557 (2006). For an account, see Kenneth Jost, *Supreme Court Yearbook 2005-2006*, CQ Press.

27. U.S. Department of Justice, "Fact Sheet: Justice Department Counter-Terrorism Efforts Since 9/11," Sept. 11, 2008, www.justice.gov/opa/pr/2008/ September/08-nsd-807.html.

28. The Supreme Court decision is *Boumediene v. Bush*, 553 U.S. — (2008). For an account, see Kenneth Jost, *Supreme Court Yearbook 2007-2008*, CQ Press. For Leon's decision granting habeas corpus to five of the six prisoners, see "Emerging Law of Detention," *op. cit.*, p. 99; William Glaberson, "Judge Declares Five Detainees Held Illegally," *The New York Times*, Nov. 21, 2008, p. A1.

29. See Peter Finn, "Report on U.S. Detention Policy Will Be Delayed," *The Washington Post*, July 21, 2009, p. A2.

30. For summaries of individual cases, see "Emerging Law of Detention," *op. cit.*, appendix II, pp. 88-105.

31. Quoted in Kornblut and Johnson, *op. cit.*

32. The decision is *Al Bihani v. Obama*, D.C. Cir., Jan. 5, 2010, http://pacer.cadc.uscourts.gov/docs/common/opinions/201001/09-5051-1223587.pdf. For coverage, see Del Quentin Wilber, "Court upholds ruling to detain Yemeni suspect," *The Washington Post*, Jan. 6, 2010, p. A3.

33. Material in Bahlul's case can be found at www.defense.gov/news/CMCRHAMZA.html/; materials in Hamdan's case had not been posted by the deadline for this report.

34. See Anne E. Kornblut and Peter Finn, "Obama aides near reversal on 9/11 trial," *The Washington Post*, March 5, 2010, p. A1; Charlie Savage, "Senator Proposes Deal on Handling of Detainees," *The New York Times*, March 4, 2010, p. A12.

35. Richard A. Serrano, "Experts make case for N.Y. terror trial," *Los Angeles Times*, March 3, 2010, p. A12.

36. Jason Horwitz, "Obama's 'enforcer' may also be his voice of reason," *The Washington Post*, March 2, 2010, p. A1.

37. Savage, *op. cit.* (March 4).

38. Transcript: www.msnbc.msn.com/id/35270673/ns/meet_the_press//.

39. http://blogs.abcnews.com/thenumbers/2010/03/911-and-military-tribunals.html

40. "The Politics of National Security: A Wake-Up Call," Democracy Corps/Third Way, March 8, 2010, www.democracycorps.com/strategy/2010/03/the-politics-of-national-security-a-wake-up-call/?section=Analysis. The memo was signed by Stanley B. Greenberg, James Carville and Jeremy Rosner of Democracy Corps, and Jon Cowan, Matt Bennett and Andy Johnson of Third Way.

41. Andrew McCarthy, "Hold the Champagne on Military Commissions — It's a Head Fake," *The Corner*, March 5, 2010, http://corner.nationalreview.com.

BIBLIOGRAPHY

Books

Fisher, Louis, *Military Tribunals and Presidential Power: American Revolution to the War on Terrorism*, University of Kansas Press, 2005.
The veteran separation-of-powers specialist at the Library of Congress examines the development of the president's wartime authority in legal matters. Includes chapter notes, 10-page bibliography and list of cases.

Wittes, Benjamin, *Law and the Long War: The Future of Justice in the Age of Terror*, Penguin Press, 2008.
A leading researcher on national security at the Brookings Institution provides a critical examination of detention and interrogation policies along with his arguments for Congress to pass legislation to authorize administrative detention of suspected enemy combatants and to create a national security court to try terrorism cases. Includes detailed notes. Wittes is also editor of *Legislating the War on Terror: An Agenda for Reform* (Brookings, 2009).

Yoo, John, *War by Other Means: An Insider's Account of the War on Terror*, Kaplan, 2005.
Yoo, a law professor at the University of California-Berkeley who served as deputy assistant attorney general for the Office of Legal Counsel during the George W. Bush administration, provides a combative account of his role in detention and interrogation policies and a strong argument for presidential wartime powers vis-à-vis Congress and the courts. Includes detailed notes. Yoo's other books include *Crisis and Command: The History of Executive Power from Washington to George W. Bush* (Kaplan, 2009); and *The Powers of War and Peace: Foreign Affairs and the Constitution after 9/11 (University of Chicago* (2005).

Articles

Mayer, Jane, "The Trial," *The New Yorker*, Feb. 5, 2010, www.newyorker.comreporting/2010/02/15/100215fa_fact_mayer.
The magazine's prolific staff writer details the legal reasoning behind, and political implications of, Attorney General Eric Holder's decision to prosecute Khalid Sheikh Mohammed and four other alleged 9/11 conspirators in a civilian court instead of a military tribunal.

Reports and Studies

Elsea, Jennifer K., "Comparison of Rights in Military Commission Trials and Trials in Federal Criminal Courts," Congressional Research Service, Nov. 19, 2009, http://assets.opencrs.com/rpts/R40932_20091119.pdf.

The 23-page report provides a side-by-side comparison of the rights accorded to defendants respectively in federal criminal courts under general federal law or in military commissions under the Military Commissions Act of 2009. Elsea, a legislative attorney with CRS, also wrote two previous reports on military commissions: "The Military Commissions Act of 2006 (MCA): Background and Proposed Amendments" (Sept. 8, 2009), http://assets.opencrs.com/rpts/R40752_20090908.pdf; and "Terrorism and the Law of War: Trying Terrorists as War Criminals before Military Commissions" (Dec. 11, 2001), www.fas.org/irp/crs/RL31191.pdf.

Laguardia, Francesca, Terrorist Trial Report Card: September 11, 2001-September 11, 2009, Center on Law and Security, New York University School of Law, January 2010, www.lawandsecurity.org/publications/TTRCFinalJan14.pdf.

The series of reports studies data from federal terrorism prosecutions in the post-9/11 years and analyzes trends in the government's legal strategies.

Wittes, Benjamin, Robert Chesney and Rabea Benhalim, "The Emerging Law of Detention: The Guantánamo Habeas Cases as Lawmaking," Brookings Institution, Jan. 22, 2010, www.brookings.edu/papers/2010/0122_guantanamo_wittes_chesney.aspx.

The comprehensive report examines and identifies unsettled issues in decisions by federal courts in Washington, D.C., in several dozen habeas corpus cases filed by Guantánamo detainees. Wittes is a senior scholar and Benhalim a legal fellow at Brookings; Chesney is a law professor at the University of Texas-Austin.

Zabel, Richard B., and James J. Benjamin Jr., "In Pursuit of Justice: Prosecuting Terrorism Cases in the Federal Courts: 2009 Update and Recent Developments," Human Rights First, July 2009, www.humanrightsfirst.org/pdf/090723-LS-in-pursuit-justice-09-update.pdf.

The 70-page report by two New York City lawyers who formerly served as federal prosecutors finds federal courts to have a "track record of serving as an effective and fair tool for incapacitating terrorists." The report updates the authors' original, 171-page report, "In Pursuit of Justice: Prosecuting Terrorism Cases in the Federal Courts" (May 2008), www.humanrightsfirst.info/pdf/080521-USLS-pursuit-justice.pdf.

On the Web

Two newspapers — *The New York Times* and *The Miami Herald* — maintain Web sites with comprehensive information on Guantánamo detainees: http://projects.nytimes.com/guantanamo and www.miamiherald.com/guantanamo/. The Pentagon maintains a Web site on military commissions: www.defense.gov/news/courtofmilitarycommissionreview.html.

For More Information

American Civil Liberties Union, 125 Broad St., 18th Floor, New York, NY 10004; (212) 549-2500; www.aclu.org. Advocates for individual rights and federal civilian trials for suspected terrorists.

Brookings Institution, 1775 Massachusetts Ave., N.W., Washington, DC 20036; (202) 797-6000; www.brookings .edu. Public policy think tank focusing on foreign policy and governance.

Constitution Project, 1200 18th St., N.W., Suite 1000, Washington, DC 20036; (202) 580-6920; www.constitu tionproject.org. Promotes bipartisan consensus on significant constitutional and legal issues.

Foundation for Defense of Democracies, P.O. Box 33249, Washington, DC 20033; (202) 207-0190; www.defend democracy.org. Nonpartisan policy institute dedicated to promoting pluralism, defending democratic values and opposing ideologies that threaten democracy.

Human Rights First, 333 Seventh Ave., 13th Floor, New York, NY 10001; (212) 845 5200; www.humanrightsfirst .org. Advocates for the U.S. government's full participation in international human rights laws.

National Institute of Military Justice, Washington College of Law, American University, 4801 Massachusetts Ave., N.W., Washington, DC 20016; (202) 274-4322; www.wcl.american .edu/nimj. Promotes the fair administration of justice in the military system.

14

U.S.-China Relations

Roland Flamini

Bustling Shanghai — with twice the number of high rises as Manhattan — reflects China's phenomenal growth. Some economists worry that China holds nearly $900 billion in U.S. Treasury securities, refuses to fairly value its currency and maintains an annual trade advantage over the U.S. of more than $230 billion.

From *CQ Researcher*,
October 31, 2008.

President Bill Clinton's trip to China in July 1998 was a splashy, 10-day display of America's power and prestige. Clinton arrived in Beijing with an entourage that included his wife, Hillary, and daughter Chelsea, five Cabinet secretaries, more than 500 White House staffers, members of Congress and security personnel, plus a swarm of journalists. His meetings with China's leaders turned into vigorous and lively debates. At Beijing University, Clinton delivered a forthright speech on human rights and answered questions from Chinese students, all of which was televised live nationwide. The authorities released a number of dissidents, and as the American visitors toured China's landmarks large crowds turned out to greet them.[1]

But that was then. President Obama's China visit in November 2009 was a low-key, four-day affair, part of a swing through Southeast Asia. Wife Michelle and daughters Malia and Sasha remained at home in Washington. His one direct contact with the Chinese public, a town meeting with 500 Chinese students in Shanghai, was deemed a local event and not broadcast nationwide. Throughout his stay, Obama made no public statement on human rights — although he did criticize China's Internet censorship, without mentioning China by name. In Beijing, his joint press appearance with his Chinese host, President Hu Jintao, was limited to a statement from each leader, with no press questions taken. Like Clinton, Obama visited the Forbidden City, but only after it was emptied of tourists.

In the years between the two presidential visits, China has emerged as the world's third-largest economy after the United States and Japan, and a force to be reckoned with in global affairs. And

Trigger Points in the East and the West

China shares a western border with Pakistan, which buys 36 percent of all China's arms exports — the largest share. Security experts worry that some of those arms may end up in the hands of anti-American insurgents in Afghanistan. In the east, concern focuses on the buildup of China's naval fleets and its bellicose comments about U.S.-supported Taiwan.

Sources: The World Factbook, *Central Intelligence Agency*

while the United States and Europe continue their uphill struggle to recover from the world recession, China is back on track, posting a phenomenal 11.9 percent growth rate for the first quarter of 2010 — well above the annual 8 percent its leaders consider crucial to keeping unemployment and social unrest at bay.[2]

Last year, China overtook Germany as the world's top exporter. China is now America's second-biggest trading partner after Canada, with $62.3 billion in trade to date in 2010 (up from $52.5 billion during the same period in 2009).[3] But China is also the leading trading partner of the European Union, Japan, Brazil and India, reflecting the global reach of its burgeoning commercial activity. It is second only to the United States in energy consumption, has overtaken the U.S. as the biggest producer of greenhouse gasses on the planet and is also the No. 1 market for automobile sales.

The string of accomplishments has tilted the balance of the world's most important bilateral relationship in favor of the Chinese. With America's economy weakened, its military mired in two long and costly wars and its trade imbalance with China heavily in the red (-$238 billion) Obama's trip was fashioned to Beijing's specifications — brief and businesslike. Because China holds more than $877 billion of U.S. Treasury securities, commentators likened the visit to a debtor meeting with his bank manager.

Persuading the Chinese to increase the value of their currency was high on Obama's talks agenda. Concerned American manufacturers and unions say China deliberately keeps the renminbi (also referred to as the yuan) low against the dollar, giving China's goods an unfair advantage in U.S. and other foreign markets. China's refusal to adopt a floating currency system, according to experts, leads to so-called goods "dumping" by Chinese exporters — making their goods cheaper and undercutting foreign manufacturers.

The dispute over pricing has led to a tit-for-tat tariff battle. The United States currently imposes special tariffs and duties on 95 categories of goods imported from China — the highest for any country.[4]

When — shortly before Obama's visit — the United States announced stiff penalties on $3.2 billion in steel

China at a Glance

Area: 9.6 million sq. km. (slightly smaller than the U.S.)

Population: 1.34 billion (July 2009 est.); U.S.: 308 million

Birth rate: 14 births/1,000 population (2009 est.); United States: 13.82 births/1,000 population (2009 est.)

Ethnic groups: Han Chinese 91.5%; Zhuang, Manchu, Hui, Miao, Uyghur, Tujia, Yi, Mongol, Tibetan, Buyi, Dong, Yao, Korean, and other nationalities 8.5% (2000 census)

Religions: Mainly Daoist (Taoist) and Buddhist; Christian 3%-4%, Muslim 1%-2%

Languages: Standard Chinese or Mandarin (Putonghua, based on the Beijing dialect) about 70%; Yue (Cantonese), Wu (Shanghainese), Minbei (Fuzhou), Minnan (Hokkien-Taiwanese), Xiang, Gan, Hakka dialects, minority languages

Government: Communist state. President and vice president elected by National People's Congress for five-year terms. Unicameral National People's Congress with 2,987 seats; members elected by municipal, regional and provincial people's congresses and People's Liberation Army to five-year terms.

Economy: GDP: $8.8 trillion (2009 est.); United States: $14.43 trillion (2009 est.)

Exports: mining and ore processing, iron, steel, aluminum, other metals, coal; machine building; armaments; textiles and apparel; petroleum; cement; chemicals; fertilizers; consumer products, including footwear, toys, electronics; food processing; transportation equipment, including automobiles, rail cars and locomotives, ships and aircraft; telecommunications equipment, commercial space launch vehicles, satellites.

Unemployment rate: 4.3% (Sept. 2009 est.); United States: 9.3% (2009 est.)

Military expenditures: 4.3% of GDP (2006); United States: 4.06% of GDP (2005 est.)

Sources: The World Factbook, *Central Intelligence Agency*

pipe from China for use in oil and gas fields, the Ministry of Commerce denounced the move as "protectionist" and said it was looking into whether American sedans and big sport utility vehicles on sale in China were subsidized by the United States government. "By not recognizing China as a market economy, the U.S. is acting in a discriminatory manner," stated ministry spokesman Yao Jian.[5]

Not so, said U.S. Steelworkers Union president Leo Gerard. "We're fed up with [the Chinese] cheating on our trade laws. Penalties for these transgressions are long overdue."[6]

A February meeting between the Dalai Lama — Tibet's exiled leader — and President Obama miffed the Chinese government, which maintains that Tibet is an inherent part of China and refuses to recognize Tibetan independence.

On the foreign-policy front, the Obama administration needs China's help in containing Iran's nuclear ambitions. The next planned step in Washington's high-priority attempt to stymie the ruling ayatollahs' efforts to produce nuclear weapons is tight U.N. sanctions to block Iran from acquiring any more of the technology it still needs. As one of the five veto-wielding, permanent members of the U.N. Security Council, China possesses an indispensable vote needed to pass any U.N. sanctions resolution. (The other members are the United States, Russia, Britain and France.)

But Iran is China's third-largest crude oil supplier, shipping 460,000 barrels a day in 2009 and about the same this year. China's National Petroleum Corp. also has sizable investments in Iranian oil production.[7] In Beijing, the Chinese shared Obama's concern that Iran should become a nuclear power but resisted his pressure to cooperate. Since then they have agreed to help in drafting a U.N. resolution — but have said nothing about voting for it. The president also raised U.S. concern over China's lack of respect for copyright laws and patent rights — a perennial Western complaint. Despite some new legislation to protect intellectual property, the production of knock-offs of famous brand names and the piracy of music, films and electronic game software remains a full-blown industry.[8]

In China's latest copyright scandal, the embarrassed organizers of Shanghai's $40 billion Expo 2010, which opened on May 1, recently withdrew the trade fair's promotional theme song after being deluged with protests that it had been plagiarized from a Japanese pop song.[9]

Such controversies are hardly new, but as China's economy and military have become more robust, so has its belief that it is operating from a position of strength, and the United States from growing weakness. "I think it is a common perception in the region that U.S. influence has been on the decline in the last decade, while Chinese influence has been increasing," Jeffrey Bader, director of Asian affairs at the National Security Council, declared prior to Obama's Asian trip. "And one of the messages that the president will be sending in his visit is that we are an Asia-Pacific nation and we're there for the long haul." Coming from a senior White House adviser the admission was revealing.[10]

In the end there was very little give by the Chinese leadership on either trade or Iran. Obama also made a pitch to the Chinese for what he described as "a positive, constructive and comprehensive relationship that opens the door to partnership on the big global issues of our time: economic recovery, development of clean air energy, stopping the spread of nuclear weapons and the surge of climate change, the promotion of peace in Asia and around the globe."[11]

Zbigniew Brzezinski, a former U.S. national security adviser who advised the Obama election campaign, described Obama's proposal more succinctly as a Washington-Beijing G-2 partnership. But the Chinese seemed lukewarm to Obama's power-sharing offer. "China fundamentally has not promoted the idea that China and the U.S. will form the two major powers," says Feng Zhongping, the head of the European section of the Beijing-based Chinese Institute of Contemporary International Relations. "China believes that the idea that [China and the United States] could undertake the responsibility of administering the world is incorrect."[12]

As experts try to read the tea leaves on the future of U.S.-China relations, here are some of the questions being asked:

Is a U.S.-China partnership actually possible?

Until the early 1970s, when President Richard M. Nixon made his historic trip to China, the two countries were virtual enemies — militarily and ideologically. Today, as China becomes a global powerhouse and a challenge to U.S. commercial and political interests, the relationship is deeply complex.

"It may be a cliché, but there are issues on which the United States and China have a common interest, and other issues with divergent interests, and difficulties are going to persist for some time, and occasionally there will be some friction," says China specialist Bonnie Glaser at Washington's Center for Strategic and International Studies. "But China does not want to have an unstable, unhealthy relationship with the United States. It's extremely important to the Chinese to have good relations."

To underline this, Chinese officials pointed out to the author that in Beijing Obama signed 11 bilateral agreements, including those on nuclear proliferation, economic cooperation, climate change, participation in multinational anti-pirate patrols in the Horn of Africa, visits between U.S. and Chinese forces (the U.S. carrier *USS Nimitz* visited Hong Kong in February), plus a joint commitment to strengthen people-to-people exchanges. As part of an enlarged U.S. academic-exchange program, Obama has promised to send 100,000 American students to China — roughly the same number of Chinese currently studying in the United States.[13]

The Chinese leadership's determination to avoid even the impression of giving in to pressure is almost a conditioned reflex because this would mean a dreaded loss of face.

Thus when Obama in Beijing held out the prospect of a closer partnership to tackle the major global issues, the response was noncommittal. Four months later, President Hu came to Washington to attend the Nuclear Security Summit. In a one-on-one with Obama, according to the official Xinhua news agency, he put forward a five-point proposal "to establish a partnership to jointly deal with common challenges."

Hu's overture covered much the same ground as Obama's, but only up to a point: The second of his five

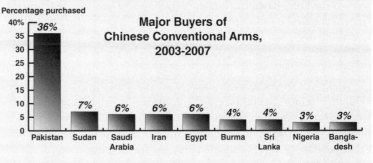

China Sells Most Arms to Pakistan

Pakistan purchased more than a third of all Chinese conventional arms from 2003-2007 — by far the largest share. The second-largest buyer was Sudan, followed by Iran, Saudi Arabia and Egypt.

Percentage purchased

Major Buyers of Chinese Conventional Arms, 2003-2007

Pakistan	36%
Sudan	7%
Saudi Arabia	6%
Iran	6%
Egypt	6%
Burma	4%
Sri Lanka	4%
Nigeria	3%
Bangladesh	3%

Source: "Military Power of the People's Republic of China, 2009," Office of the Secretary of Defense

points stressed that each country "would respect the other's core interests and major concerns," a point not specifically made by Obama, and one that left wide latitude for divergence. Two of these interests were Tibet and Taiwan, which "concern China's sovereignty and territorial integrity and its interests," Xinhua stated, and which the United States should "handle with caution."[14]

This balance-of-interests approach by the Chinese is typically — and almost cryptically — expressed by Kaiser Kuo, an associate researcher at Beijing's World Politics Institute. "Sino-American competition and cooperation are increasingly intertwined," Kaiser says. "There is cooperation within competition, and competition within cooperation. There is no absolute cooperation or competition. Therefore, we should not completely reject competition — and we should strengthen cooperation."[15]

In Washington, President Hu also hinted that China might be considering a revaluation of its currency, "based on its own economic and social-development needs." In other words, not because Washington is pressing for it.[16]

Hu also agreed that Beijing should cooperate on the wording of an Iran sanctions resolution. But in Beijing, Chinese Foreign Ministry spokeswoman Jiang Yu repeated China's position that "dialogue and negotiations are the best way."[17]

But some analysts think U.S.-Chinese relations may be less about cooperation and more about an ascendant China challenging the United States in areas once firmly in America's sphere of influence. "Obama and his policy makers are required to face up to a new reality," commented the Seoul-based English-language *Korean Times*, "in which China is jockeying for the world's No. 2 position while the U.S., the world's sole superpower, is waning, especially in the aftermath of the global financial and economic crisis."[18]

Unlike U.S.-Soviet relations during the Cold War, the challenge is not ideological. Still, according to the Congressional Research Service, "China's growing 'soft power' — primarily diplomatic and economic influence in the developing world — has become a concern among many U.S. policy leaders, including members of Congress."[19]

Because of its voracious demand for raw materials, Chinese trade with Latin America — the United States' back yard — grew tenfold between 2002 and 2007. In 2008, Chinese trade with Latin America ($142 billion) was a sixth of U.S. trade with the region — but growing at a faster rate. China's footprint in Africa is even larger in terms of both financial aid and investments.[20] But more significant from Washington's point of view is Beijing's increasing involvement in the Middle East.

In 2009, exports of Saudi Arabian crude to China were higher than to the United States, as Beijing courted the world's largest oil producer — and longtime U.S. ally.

"Saudi Arabia used to be very much an American story, but those days are over," said Brad Bourland, head researcher at Jadwa Investment in Riyadh, Saudi Arabia. The Saudis "now see their relationship with China as very strategic, and very long term."[21]

In a recent interview, Xu Xueguan, director of North American affairs at the Chinese Foreign Ministry's huge headquarters in Beijing, told the author he couldn't understand why China had not been included in the so-called Quartet, the coalition of the United Nations, European Union, United States and Russia that is seeking a peaceful solution to the Israel-Palestine confrontation. When the Quartet was set up eight years ago, China did not yet have the clout to insist on being included. More recently, Beijing has expressed interest in becoming the fifth member of the U.N.-sponsored peace effort, without success — at least so far.

Is a confrontation with China inevitable, as some predict?

The Chinese leadership is "gunning for a paradigm shift in geopolitics. In particular, Beijing has served notice that it won't be shy about playing hardball to safeguard what it claims to be 'core national interests,' " writes Willy Lam, a China specialist at the Washington-based Jamestown Foundation think tank.[22] At the top of those national interests is Taiwan which, *The Economist* magazine said recently, "has been where the simmering distrust between China and America most risks boiling over."[23]

The chance of a war between China and the United States is generally regarded as remote. The Chinese threat to the United States is indirect — for example, if China should decide to use force to annex Taiwan, and America intercedes — as it is committed to do even though the United States does not recognize the island as an independent state.

China hands like Elizabeth Economy, director of Asia Studies at the Council on Foreign Relations think tank in Washington, downplay the new "Red Scare." Economy argues that the West — particularly the United States — has "completely lost perspective on what constitutes reality in China today." Economy concedes that "there is a lot that is incredible about China's economic story, but there is a lot that is not working well on both the political and economic fronts," distorting the real picture.

In other words, China has enough problems without provoking the challenge of an international nemesis. The Chinese leadership appears to worry about a fragile society: A persistent nightmare is that a sudden significant spike in unemployment, officially kept at 4 percent (but possibly higher because of the huge, hard-to-track migrant-worker population) could lead to widespread unrest.[24]

Still, looking at the Chinese as the potential aggressors, does China have the capacity for a military confrontation with the United States?

In the past five years China has spent hundreds of billions of dollars modernizing its armed forces, with special emphasis on the navy. China's 1.7 million Chinese under arms is considerably more than the 1.4 million in the U.S. armed forces, but in 2009 the U.S. defense budget was $738 billion and China's estimated at between $69.5 billion and $150 billion.[25]

The government insists it seeks a peaceful solution to the issue of uniting Taiwan to the mainland, but the Chinese have built up a formidable fleet of submarines and developed anti-ship missiles to counter a possible U.S. defense of the Taiwan Strait. The Americans will be ready for them. In its annual report to Congress on China's military power, the Pentagon said it was "maintaining the capacity to defend against Beijing's use of force or coercion against Taiwan."

Beyond the strait, the Pentagon reported, "China's ability to sustain military power . . . remains limited."[26] The Pentagon's annual report is a source of irritation to the Chinese, who routinely denounce it. This year, the Xinhua news agency dismissed the assessment as "a largely subjective report with distorted facts and groundless speculation."[27]

Less hypothetical is the threat to the U.S. government's computer system. The Pentagon's 2009 report said U.S. government computers had been the target of "intrusions that appear to have originated" in China, although not necessarily from the military.[28] And in his annual "Threat Assessment" to the Senate Select Committee on Intelligence, Director of National Intelligence Dennis C. Blair warned in February that "malicious cyber activity is occurring on an unprecedented scale with extraordinary sophistication."

As a result, Blair added, the United States "cannot be certain that our cyberspace infrastructure will remain available and reliable during a time of crisis." Blair did not refer to China directly at that point. However, later in his assessment he called "China's aggressive cyber activities" a major concern.[29]

In January, after Google reported that hackers in China had targeted the computers of more than 30 U.S.

U.S. Trade Deficit With China Has Surged

The United States imports far more from China than it exports, causing a significant and growing trade gap. U.S-China trade rose rapidly after the two nations reestablished diplomatic relations and signed a bilateral trade agreement in 1979 and provided mutual most-favored-nation treatment beginning in 1980. In recent years, China has been one of the fast-growing U.S. export markets, and it is expected to grow even further as living standards continue to improve and a sizable Chinese middle class emerges.

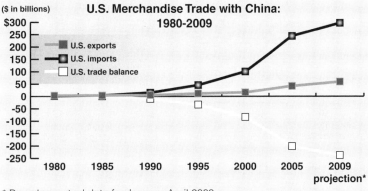

($ in billions)

U.S. Merchandise Trade with China: 1980-2009

- U.S. exports
- U.S. imports
- U.S. trade balance

* Based on actual data for January-April 2009

Source: Wayne M. Morrison, "China-U.S. Trade Issues," Congressional Research Service, June 23, 2009

corporations, including its own, and that the e-mail accounts of human rights activists had also been hacked, Secretary of State Hillary Rodham Clinton called on the Chinese government to investigate and to make its findings public.[30] (*See sidebar, p. 340.*)

U.S. officials and business executives warn that a trade war could also erupt if the Chinese don't yield to international pressure and raise the aggressive undervaluation of the renminbi, kept artificially low to favor Chinese exports. China's cheap currency is a serious problem for the global economy by undercutting exports throughout the industrial world, including the United States, and contributing to the trade imbalance. (President Obama has contended that if China lets the renminbi appreciate, U.S. exports would increase.)

The Obama administration has so far avoided picking a public fight with China over its currency — even to the extent of postponing indefinitely a Treasury Department report on worldwide currencies originally due out on April 15. Without any movement by Beijing on the currency front, the report could well label China a "currency manipulator." If that happens, Sen. Charles E. Schumer, D-N.Y., is ready with draft legislation that would place more tariffs on Chinese goods.

Chinese Commerce Minister Chen Deming recently told *The Washington Post* that the United States would lose a trade war with China. "If the United States uses the exchange rate to start a new trade war," he said, "China will be hurt. But the American people and U.S. companies will be hurt even more."[31]

One way for America to increase its exports, said Chen, would be to remove the restrictions on high-tech goods with possible military applications, which the United States imposed following Beijing's repressive crackdown on student demonstrations in 1989 in Tiananmen Square — something the Obama administration shows no signs of doing.

Has China's "market authoritarian" model of government emerged as an alternative to Western democracy?

Despite predictions, China's emergence from isolation and its spectacular economic growth have not led to democratization. Instead, China has developed what Stefan Halper, director of the Atlantic Studies Program at Cambridge University, calls "a market authoritarian form of government, in which the free market is allowed to operate, but the government holds a very firm hand on political activity in the country."

In so doing, says Halper, author of the recent book *The Beijing Consensus*, the Chinese have produced an alternative to the Western democratic system that is thought to go hand in hand with a free-market economy. Non-democratic countries around the world like Egypt,

China's U.S. Holdings Greatly Increased

Since the early 2000s, China's holdings of U.S. securities— including U.S. Treasury securities and corporate stocks and bonds — have risen above $1.2 trillion — an increase of more than 500 percent. While China's U.S. holdings have helped the United States meet its investment needs, some policymakers worry they could give China increased leverage over the U.S. on political and economic issues.

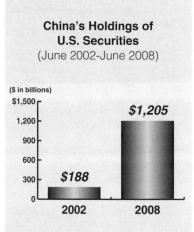

China's Holdings of U.S. Securities
(June 2002-June 2008)

Source: Wayne M. Morrison, "China-U.S. Trade Issues," Congressional Research Service, June 23, 2009

Indonesia, Myanmar and Malaysia must find much to envy in a country that has achieved a 9 percent growth rate yet "managed to control its media, the legislature and the dissident voices, and has achieved global prominence," Halper adds.

The Chinese system "offers a seductive model that is eagerly taken up by the leaders of countries that have not yet settled on democratic structures," writes Australian China hand Rowan Callick in *The American*, the magazine of the American Enterprise Institute, a conservative Washington think tank. The Chinese model attracts autocrats because "their broader populations become content and probably supportive because their living standards are leaping ahead."[32]

China, however, has no interest in exporting its form of government. Its dealings with the rest of the world are dominated by the single-minded pursuit of one objective: economic development. As a ubiquitous lender and financial aid donor, China finds the door open in developing countries because Beijing's money comes with no strings attached about human rights and democracy — which is hardly the case with financial assistance from either the United States or the European Union.

Chinese money "is made available relatively easily and quickly without the political, economic, social and environmental conditions . . . that U.S. and European donors typically impose," says the Congressional Research Service report on China's foreign trade.[33]

But envious autocratic leaders should take note: Authoritarian capitalism may only work up to a point, writes Thomas P.M. Barnett, author of the recent book *Great Powers: America and the World after Bush*. He argues that when an economy starts to mature and needs to become more efficient, productive and innovative-based —"then we're talking intensive growth . . . something that nobody ever has been able to plan, because it lives and breathes on fierce competition, which only a true free market, accompanied by democracy, can supply."[34]

Moreover, under closer scrutiny, China's economic success has fragile underpinnings, with some doubting its long-term sustainability. For example, for all its progress, China's per capita income is still $6,546, compared to $40,208 in the United States. China's gross domestic product barely reaches $9 trillion, whereas allowing for the recent volatility of exchange rates, U.S. GDP exceeds $14 trillion.

Because China's economic development is export driven, the world recession caused 23 million Chinese workers to be laid off as Chinese exports dropped by 15-18 percent, says Stephen Green, chief economist at the Sun Trust Bank in Shanghai. By the end of 2009, however, 98 percent of those had found other work, as the Chinese economy bounced back quicker than Western economies, boosted by a 4 trillion renminbi ($586 billion) stimulus package. (The U.S. economic stimulus was $874 billion.)

But the lesson to Beijing was that China can't export itself to growth. Though exports have picked up, the Chinese have turned their attention to trying to develop a domestic market. For example, to stimulate sales of domestic appliances in rural areas, the government offered 13 percent rebates to farmers who buy refrigerators, TV sets and even mobile phones. In 2009, Beijing also spent $755 million to push car sales, cutting the purchase tax from around 15 percent to 5 percent. The result was a record 770,000 sales in March alone, a 27 percent jump over the previous month. Banks had instructions to increase mortgage lending, but the government reined them in again when they started granting loans for third homes.[35]

Though officials in China say 250 million Chinese were lifted out of poverty between 1980 and 2005, about 70 percent of China's population of 1.3 billion still lives in rural areas, often in villages with few paved roads and frequent water and power shortages. An ambitious and costly urbanization program is trying to shift people to the cities.

State-controlled media limit reports about unrest, but "bottom-up pressures for change in China are intense, spontaneous and multifaceted," according to a report by Ying Ma, a visiting fellow at the Hoover Institution at Stanford University. "Every day, Chinese leaders worry about the challenge to regime stability, but they have responded by continuing to exert brutal and sophisticated top-down control."[36]

"Riots take place in China every day," Ying says. The Chinese authorities reported 10,000 protests throughout the country in 1994, and 87,000 in 2005. Mobile phones and the Internet have given protesters and activists effective new weapons, which the regime is battling tooth and nail. Using the new technology the Chinese people clamor for the government to address their grievances on the local level in increasing numbers: 10 million petitions in 2004 jumped to 30 million the following year.[37]

BACKGROUND

Presidential Challenges

Shortly after Mao Zedong's death in 1976, Chinese leaders took a hard look at their country and didn't like what they saw. China was just emerging from the Cultural Revolution, a decade of mob-led extremism started by Mao himself that had kept the country in chaos. China was desperately poor, deliberately isolated from the world economy and aloof from or opposed to nearly every international institution, including — until 1971 — the United Nations. Under Deng Xiaoping, China's leaders reversed course and embraced globalization.

Since then successive U.S. presidents have wrestled with the challenge of how to deal with China's rapid rise. The Clinton administration fashioned a policy of "constructive engagement," calling for close bilateral economic and political cooperation, at the same time urging democratization and human rights.

"Seeking to isolate China is clearly unthinkable," President Bill Clinton declared in July 1998, defending his approach. "We would succeed instead in isolating ourselves and our own policy."[38]

The George W. Bush administration used the catchphrase "responsible stakeholder," pressing China to become a responsible member of the international community and to embrace democracy. Prior to President Obama's November China trip, Deputy Secretary of State James B. Steinberg mapped out a policy of "strategic reassurance" towards Beijing, and the phrase — as intended — has stuck.

CHRONOLOGY

1970s-1980s *After Mao's death Deng institutes sweeping reforms, including relations with the United States.*

1972 President Richard M. Nixon makes historic trip to China, meets Mao Zedong and signs Shanghai Joint Communiqué declaring Taiwan part of mainland China.

1975 President Gerald R. Ford visits China, meets the ailing Mao, who dies the next year.

1978 Deng Xiaoping emerges as new leader, launches economic and social reforms.

1979 U.S. and China establish diplomatic relations. . . . Congress passes Taiwan Relations Act pledging to continue to supply Taiwan with weapons. . . . Deng visits United States.

1982 In joint U.S.-Chinese communiqué, United States pledges to gradually reduce arms sales to Taiwan.

1984 President Ronald Reagan visits China and meets Deng, who says that Taiwan remains a crucial problem in bilateral relations.

1989 President George H. W. Bush visits Beijing, invites dissidents to dinner. . . . People's Liberation Army crushes student-led pro-democracy demonstration in Beijing's Tiananmen Square, killing hundreds of protesters. . . . White House National Security Adviser Brent Scowcroft holds secret meeting in Beijing with Chinese leaders following the Tiananmen Square massacre.

1990s-2000s *China's economy welcomes Western investors; U.S.-China relations continue to warm.*

1992 Reversing a decade of U.S. policy, President George H. W. Bush decides to sell Taiwan F-16 combat planes, infuriating the Chinese.

1993 Newly elected President Bill Clinton establishes policy of "constructive engagement" with China, meets President Jiang Zemin in Seattle.

1996 China tests missiles off Taiwan to discourage vote for separatist Lee Teng-hui in the presidential election;

U.S. sends two aircraft carrier battle groups to area to support Taiwan.

1997 Britain hands Hong Kong back to China after 156 years. . . . Clinton is first U.S. president to visit China in a decade; criticizes Tiananmen massacre but strengthens U.S. commitment not to support Taiwan independence.

2000 U.S. Senate passes Permanent Normal Trade Relations bill (PNTR) giving China the same low-tariff access to the American market as other trading partners.

2001 China seizes U.S. spy plane after midair collision with Chinese fighter, hands over 24 American crewmembers after President George W. Bush apologizes for the Chinese pilot's death. . . . Bush makes first trip to China. . . . China joins World Trade Organization.

2002 Bush makes second visit to China to mark the 30th anniversary of Nixon's historic trip. . . . Future leader Hu Jintao visits White House for talks. . . . President Jiang Zemin visits Bush at his Texas ranch; they agree to cooperate on crisis following North Korea's announcement that it has nuclear weapons.

2003 With U.S. participation, Beijing hosts six-party talks on a unified approach to North Korea's nuclear weapons program.

2006 China's Great Firewall, or Golden Shield, Internet censorship system goes into service.

2008 China closes down Twitter, YouTube to block discussion on 20th anniversary of Tiananmen massacre.

2009 President Obama visits Shanghai and Beijing, makes no headway in persuading Chinese to raise value of their currency or to back sanctions against Iran.

2010 President Hu attends summit on nuclear security in Washington, despite tense U.S.-China relations over Iran sanctions, currency issues and imminent American weapons sale to Taiwan. . . . Expo 2010 opens in Shanghai. . . . Annual "strategic dialogue" between U.S. and China set for late May. . . . U.S. and China to attend G20 summit in Seoul, South Korea, in late June.

"Just as we are prepared to accept China's arrival as a prosperous and successful power," Steinberg explained, the Chinese must "reassure the rest of the world that its development and growing global role will not come at the expense of the security and well-being of others."[39]

Whatever the label, the fundamental underpinning of American policy toward China has been economic engagement. In 2000, for example, Congress granted China permanent normal trade relations (PNTR) with the United States. In 2001, the United States backed China's entry into the World Trade Organization, thus placing the Chinese under international business rules, which was reassuring for would-be foreign investors.

All Business

In his inaugural address last year, Obama echoed Clinton's 1997 statement that communist China stood "on the wrong side of history." The conventional wisdom about China was that the market forces unleashed by global trade and investment would inevitably give more people a stake in the economy and open up China politically, leading to the creation of political parties and more democracy and respect for human rights.

Only it hasn't happened. In China, the party's far from over. China calls its authoritarian capitalism a "socialist market system," and the ruling Chinese Communist Party (CPC) appears more entrenched than ever — helped by a large, efficient and pervasive police organization.

In 2009, the party celebrated its 60th anniversary, and the state-controlled media took care to trumpet the regime's economic and political achievements.

Yet how much is left of communist ideology is open to question: As the author discovered during a reporting trip to China last November, the huge portrait of Mao still looks out over Tiananmen Square, and Marxist theory is still taught at the party school for senior officials. But the old party slogans praising the proletariat class and condemning capitalism have disappeared from the walls and factories.

The party has opened membership to entrepreneurs and business people, and the state-held shares of the country's 1,300 companies, many of which are listed on the Beijing stock exchange, are publicly traded.

Challenged to explain exactly how Marxism-Leninism fits into the "socialist market system," Chinese officials quote Deng Xiaoping's famous observation that it doesn't matter whether the cat is black or white as long as it kills the mouse.

Officials today will even quote Confucius without first cautiously looking over their shoulder. The great Chinese sage has had his ups and downs. In the Cultural Revolution he was reviled as an imperial lackey because of his position as adviser to the emperor.

But Confucius has been rehabilitated as a symbol of China's glorious past. The Chinese have set up hundreds of Confucius institutes worldwide, including 25 in the United States. The institutes promote Chinese language and culture, just as the Goethe institutes promote German culture, and the Dante Alighieri institutes do the same for Italy.

Even so, "China did not take a missionary approach to world affairs, seeking to spread an ideology or a system of government," writes Robert D. Kaplan, a senior fellow at the Center for a New American Security. "Moral progress in international affairs is an American goal, not a Chinese one. China's actions abroad are propelled by its need to secure energy, metals and strategic materials in order to support the living standards of its immense population."

In Kaplan's view, Beijing "cares little about the type of regime with which it is engaged. It requires stability, not virtue as the West conceives it."[40]

As early as 2005, when China for the first time was included in the annual economic survey of the Organization for Economic Cooperation and Development (OECD), it noted, "Well over half of China's GDP is produced by privately controlled enterprises."[41] But while the trend has continued, communications, transport, infrastructure, banking and energy remain under tight state supervision.

In late November 2009, Xu Kuangdi, a senior adviser to the Chinese Communist Party, told this reporter and other visiting U.S. journalists that it would be dangerous to hold free elections because China was "not ready," and some demagogue might win by promising to take the money from the new rich and give it to the poor! "The ultimate goal is common prosperity," he said, "but we have to let a group of people get rich first."

In 2003, looking for places to put its growing export revenue, China began buying U.S. Treasury bills on a large scale. By 2005, China had acquired $243 billion worth of the U.S. debt, second only to Japan. In 2006, China overtook Japan when its holdings climbed to $618 billion.

Is China Less Welcoming to U.S. Investors?

As Chinese know-how grows, opportunities diminish for foreigners.

It's one of the ironies of the U.S. trade deficit with China that a sizable portion of the goods exported to America are made by Chinese workers for U.S. firms. Earlier this year, the state-run Xinhua news agency reported that of the 200 top exporting firms last year, 153 were "foreign funded firms" — up from 141 in 2008.[1]

It's estimated that at least a third of those companies are U.S.-owned. For example, Shanghai alone has about 3,600 American expatriate business executives — although it was around 4,000 before the 2008 economic downturn. Chongqinq, China's largest city, with a population of 32 million, lists 41 foreign firms operating there, including Lear, Du Pont, Delphi Packard and Pepsi. General Motors, the largest auto maker in China, expects to sell 3 million vehicles in the Asian market by 2015 from its Chinese plants. In 2009, the 665,000 foreign firms in China accounted for 28 percent of the nation's industrial output, 56 percent of its exports and 45 million of its workers. In the first quarter of this year, foreign investment rose 12.1 percent, to $9.4 billion, according to *Business Week*.[2]

Even so, Google's recent difficulties with hackers in China may be an indication that as the Chinese economy matures the investment climate may no longer be as welcoming as it once was. One American executive doing business in Beijing says industrial espionage is rife and that the Chinese are experts at copying products. A foreign firm has at most a two-year window to establish itself on the Chinese market before it is challenged by an emerging local competitor.

As Chinese industrial know-how grows, the opportunities for foreign investors continue to diminish, according to business executives in Shanghai and Beijing. Recently, the Chinese authorities issued a directive encouraging government agencies to buy Chinese goods.

In a country where the state is still a major customer, this is a disturbing measure. But investors remain attracted by China, argues writer Zachary Karabell, author of the 2009 book Superfusion: *How China and America Became One Economy and Why the World's Prosperity Depends on It*. Says Karabell, "There's really nowhere else to go where you have 10 percent growth, 300-600 million emerging middle class Chinese who want to buy stuff and an environment where the rule of law is increasingly at least adequate in enforcement of contracts and getting your investments out of the country."

Google quit China after its servers were hacked, adds Karabell, partly because it wasn't doing very well in the Chinese market, and because it could afford not to do business with China.

The continued uncertain global environment has focused the Chinese government's attention on generating a domestic consumer market, so far with mixed results. Parting older-generation Chinese with their money means reversing a culture of saving, but the younger generations

In 2009, possibly fearing that the global recession would undermine the dollar, China sold some $34 billion of its Treasuries — but was soon back on a buying spree. By February 2010, China held a whopping $877.5 billion in Treasuries.[42] Meanwhile, a well-heeled middle class has emerged in China. Cars create traffic jams in Chinese cities, and the once ubiquitous bicycles are now kept by many Chinese for week-end country excursions.

In Beijing, a five-star hotel is flanked by two glass-fronted dealerships, one for Maseratis, the other for Lamborghinis. Four years ago, the China branch of HSBC Bank launched a credit card: It now boasts 11 million cardholders, said D.G. "Dicky" Yip, of the Bank of Communications in Shanghai last November.

China's new rich have acquired a taste for art as well as luxury cars. First it was contemporary art by artists who a decade earlier had been suppressed or even jailed because of their avant garde works. More recently, classic traditional paintings and Chinese calligraphy have been sold at auction for millions of RMB. In a crowded auction hall in Beijing filled with Chinese bidders in November, a scroll painting by the Ming Dynasty landscape master Wu Bin sold for the equivalent of $24.7 million to a Chinese bidder.

are avid shoppers. In the modern high rise that houses the Standard Chartered Bank in Shanghai — one of the thousands that crowd the city's skyline — Stephen Green, head of research, says older Chinese stubbornly stick to the "rainy day" syndrome — but "anyone born after 1980 behaves like an American."

In the past decade, for example, Starbucks has opened more than 350 coffee shops in China, where it is flourishing at the same time its U.S. business has been hammered by recession. Starbucks' success is puzzling because the Chinese really don't drink coffee; China produces about 30,000 tons of beans a year but exports most of it.

Caren Li, Starbucks' spokeswoman at the company's downtown Chinese headquarters in Shanghai, says Green Tea Frappuccino is a predictably steady seller, but "we're promoting a coffee culture, offering the Chinese more choices besides tea." Even so, it's not really about coffee: The coffee houses with the round green logo have become trendy meeting venues (there's even one in Beijing's Forbidden City), the chic place to be seen.

In 2009, a former Starbucks executive in China, Eden Woon, launched Toys R Us in China (locally called Toy LiFung), and today the American retailer has 15 stores in the country. China may be the world's leading toy manufacturer, but its citizens buy mainly for very young children. "There's no toy culture in China because parents think toys distract children from their studies," Woon says over breakfast in a bustling hotel restaurant offering acres of dishes ranging from American pancakes and waffles to wonton soup. So Woon launched a campaign in this nation of overachievers with the message: "Toys are an important part of growing up."

Chinese flock to the 350 Starbucks coffee shops in China, including this one in Shanghai, but customers come for tea, not coffee, and because Starbucks is considered cool.

Mary Kay Inc., the Texas-based home-sales cosmetics firm, began operating in China in 1995. Headquartered in Shanghai, it marshals about 200,000 independent beauty "consultants," thanks to a skin-care line tailored to the local market, including a four-week "whitening cream" treatment that sells for the equivalent of $120.

— *Roland Flamini*

[1] Xinhua news agency, http://news.xinhuanet.com/english2010/business/2010-04/20/c_13260044.htm.

[2] "Foreign Investment in China Jumped in First Quarter," Business Week/Bloomberg, April 14, 2010, www.businessweek.com/news/2010 04-14/foreign-investment-in-china-jumps-in-first-quarter-update1.html.

The bad news for the government has been the widening gap between the urban prosperous and the rural impoverished. China's poor are a restive majority running into the hundreds of millions. In 2008, the average income of a rural worker was $690, compared to a city average of $2,290 — and higher in Shanghai and Beijing.[43] But the annual salary of a chief executive in China is around $100,000, a fraction of corporate salaries in the United States but still astronomical in Chinese terms.

To make matters worse for the poor, the government has been slow to reform a social system that cuts off the medical and other benefits of China's millions of internal migrant workers once they quit their hometowns. As things now stand many immigrants are left to fend for themselves — even when they find employment.

The social system also needs to catch up with the aging Chinese population, which is getting older faster than in the United States. The problem is exacerbated by a relatively high life expectancy — about 73 — versus 77 in the United States. By 2040 demographers say that each Chinese worker will be forced to support two parents and four grandparents.

'Harmonizing' the Internet in China

China's love affair with the Net is increasing along with censorship.

When a website is censored in China, the screen usually doesn't reveal that the government has blocked it. Instead, either a fake error message appears or an announcement about the site being unavailable, with an invitation to "Please try again."

By now, most of China's estimated 384 million "netizens" (nearly a quarter of the world's Internet users) are not taken in: They know the site has been "harmonized."[1]

In China, Internet censorship is often ironically called "harmonizing" because "harmony" — the absence of public dissent — is a key phrase in the government's propaganda. So as China's love affair with the Internet increases so does the Communist regime's censorship effort intensify — possibly because there is so much more material online for the government to worry about.

"China's blocking of overseas websites — including Facebook, Twitter and thousands of other sites is more extensive and technically more sophisticated than ever," Rebecca MacKinnon, a Hong Kong-based university journalism professor and China Internet expert, tells me via e-mail from Princeton's Center for Information Technology Policy, where she is currently a visiting fellow. "Controls over domestic content have also been tightening."

The Chinese authorities use a filtering system nicknamed The Great Firewall of China, but officially referred to as Golden Shield, to scan Internet content for specific key words and then block, or try to block, Web pages in which such words are used.

A list of blacklisted terms compiled by ConceptDoppler, a tool developed for the purpose by the universities of California, Davis, and New Mexico includes triggers such as "eighty-nine" and "June 4", the year and date of the Tiananmen Square protests, "massacre," "political dissident," "Voice of America," "Playboy magazine" and "Xinjiang independence" — a reference to the restive, predominantly Muslim province in northwestern China. Any one of these terms sends a series of three reset commands to both the source and the destination, effectively breaking the connection, says Jed Crandall, a professor of computer science at the University of New Mexico and one of the developers of ConceptDoppler, in an e-mail message.

A more recent addition to the list is "Charter 08," a lengthy manifesto calling on the Communist regime to relinquish its monopoly of power and introduce democratic reforms. Originally, Charter 08 was signed by 300 intellectuals and activists. After the document appeared briefly on the Internet — and before Chinese censors banned it — some 10,000 other signatures were added.

U.S. computer giants like Google entered the market knowing that they would have to comply with the regime's policy and exercise content censorship. Ultimately, Google found the controls too constricting to live with and earlier this year shifted its operations to less restrictive Hong Kong, at the same time complaining of Chinese hacking into the e-mail accounts of human rights activists and U.S. corporations.

Other U.S. Internet companies still operating in China, including Microsoft and Yahoo!, now face even tougher censorship restrictions. A new law, adopted on April 29 and set to take effect Oct. 1, requires them to stop the transmission of "state secrets" over the Internet, if they "discover" them — effectively requiring them to act as police informers.[2]

Some analysts maintain that while flowers were placed outside Google's Beijing office by users sorry to see it go, the impact of Google's departure is limited because the majority of China's netizens prefer to use homegrown Internet servers that exercise self-censorship rather than jeopardize their access.

Besides, the analysts point out, even with the constraints that grow daily the Internet has given Chinese citizens an unprecedented voice in the country's affairs.

"We should measure protest in China not by protests on the streets or availability of news on protests, but by the involvement of the Chinese citizens in policy decisions," says Yasheng Huang, a China expert at MIT's Sloan School.

An 'Edgy' Game

With the economic boom unfolding against a background of frequent unrest, "The No. 1 challenge for China is to maintain domestic stability and at the same time sustainable economic development," says Yang Jiemian, director of the Shanghai Institute of International Studies.

"By the latter yardstick, China had made huge progress, thanks largely to the Internet."[3]

In recent years, Internet-based campaigns have pressured the Chinese government to release political prisoners, launch investigations into scandals, such as kidnapping boys for slave labor in mines, and convict corrupt officials.[4] China's version of Facebook, called Douban, and YouTube, called YouKu, as well as thousands of Internet bulletin boards teem with debate on current events.

Still, the censorship is not well-defined, and some well-known dissident bloggers don't know when they have crossed the line until there is a knock at the door.

But mainly, it works by suggestion: "Many Internet users only have access to public computers at Internet cafes or universities, and just the existence of censorship might cause them to avoid topics they know they're not supposed to access, changing their online behavior," says Crandall.

The government maintains that censorship is partly a security measure and partly a responsibility to protect the public from what it sees as the negative side of the Internet's rapid growth.

Qian Xiaoqian, vice minister at the Chinese State Council information office, whose functions include deciding what gets blocked, says that while the government intervenes when a site is seen as plotting to overthrow the state, on another level it is also responding to public worry about the addictive nature of the Net.

"There is a discussion going on in this country about the potential negative influences of the Internet," Qian said last December over cups of tea, invariably served to visitors to any Chinese office. "Chinese parents are worried about the pornography; but not just the pornography." The government blames "Internet addiction" for youthful alienation.

A recently published survey by the Chinese National People's Congress found that 10 percent of Chinese youth were addicted to the Internet, Qian says. Many Chinese parents are sending their children to "boot camp" to cure them of "internetitis" — a solution which the government first encouraged but later seemed to back away from, warning against too much brutality in rehab methods.[5]

Critics of Chinese Internet censorship, including MacKinnon, say the regime uses such arguments to justify tightening control over the Net.

Mounting concerns over security and censorship by the government led Google to leave mainland China in March and relocate in Hong Kong.

Bloomberg/Getty Images/Doug Kanter

But Qian claims "the Chinese government assumes a very important responsibility in managing the Internet. America is a mature society. At this stage Chinese society is still not — and besides, different people have different interpretations of freedom."

For those who prefer the Internet censor-free, the United States is leading the effort to produce circumvention software that connects to blocked websites via proxy computers outside the country. Programs like Psiphon, Tor and the Global Internet Freedom Consortium have been increasingly successful at breaching the wall.[6]

— *Roland Flamini*

[1] David Talbot, "China's Internet Paradox," *MIT Technology Review*, May/June 2010, www.technologyreview.com/web/25032/page1/.

[2] Mike Elgan, "New Chinese law may force Microsoft, Yahoo, to follow Google," *IT World*, April 29, 2010, www.itworld.com/internet/106191/new-chinese-law-may-force-microsoft-yahoo-follow-google-out, and Jonathan Ansfield, "Amendment Tightens Law on State Secrets in China," *The New York Times*, April 30, 2010, p. A9.

[3] Quoted in Talbot, *op. cit.*

[4] *Ibid.*

[5] The information is from a Chinese television news "magazine" show, with a translation provided to the author.

[6] For example, www.FreeGate.com, the Freedom Consortium's software developed by a group of Chinese expatriates in the United States.

The Internet, which has gone from 620,000 users in China in 1997 to 370 million users today — more people than the entire U.S. population — has become a forum for online dissent. The authorities crack down on the deluge of cyber-dissent using a (patchy at best) online censorship, ironically known as the Great Firewall of China — which also tries to block pornographic sites. (*See sidebar, p. 340.*) Persistent blogging about subjects

More than 150 nations and 50 international organizations have registered for the Shanghai World Expo, and 70 million visitors are anticipated, making the six-month-long world's fair the largest ever. The Expo's theme — "Better City — Better Life" — is intended to showcase Shanghai as the next great world city in the 21st century.

deemed subversive can lead to imprisonment. (There are 20 million bloggers in China.) For example, Chinese writer Liu Xiaobo was jailed for 11 years on Dec. 25 after co-drafting and posting "Charter '09," a lengthy manifesto calling on the government to introduce democratic reforms.

The regime's biggest nightmare remains large-scale unemployment. To keep it at the current 4 percent level China needs to ensure continued growth generating 24 million new jobs every year.[44] Hence the need to buttress its current dependence on exports by boosting consumer demand at home. But the Chinese are not only great savers but also traditionally have an aversion to being in debt. For example, no doubt to the chagrin of HSBC officials, 80 percent of the bank's credit card holders avoid interest charges by paying their whole bill every month — compared to the national U.S. average of 20 percent.

Commenting on the government's combination of a market economy and tight control, Halper at Cambridge University says, "This is an edgy game, and things could go seriously wrong. Just trying to control the Internet is really tough work. The glue that holds the whole thing together is a ferociously powerful security service."

CURRENT SITUATION
Tense Beginning

This is a period of waiting for the other shoe to drop in U.S.-China relations following a tense first quarter of 2010.

There is unresolved business on the currency front, on Iran sanctions, on the issue of U.S. weapons sales to Taiwan and on the broader question of how the two countries should engage in the future.

The Obama administration has put a lot of effort into trying to convince the Chinese government that it is in both sides' interest to move toward what Obama calls "a more market-oriented exchange rate" for the renminbi. Following a meeting between President Obama and President Hu Jintao in Washington in April, during the Nuclear Security Summit, it seemed clear that the Chinese had not budged on revaluing their currency. Any change would not come from U.S. pressure, Hu said.[45]

In New York, the five permanent members of the U.N. Security Council are working on an Iran-sanctions resolution. "The Chinese were very clear they share our concern about the Iranian nuclear program," said Bader at the National Security Council.[46] Still, the Chinese government has not said that it will vote for a U.N. resolution and still insists publicly that diplomacy and negotiation are the way to go.

Cooperation on climate control seems at a stalemate after Hu told the December Copenhagen summit that China's own emissions control program would not be subject to U.N. supervision. For its part, the United States rejected a Chinese request that developing countries should be compensated for cutting carbon emissions.

Yu Qintgou, the official responsible for climate change at China's Ministry of Foreign Affairs, explained the familiar Chinese position in an interview in Beijing on Dec. 1. Simply put, Yu said, the world's climate change problem was not the making of China or India but of the developed countries. The United States and the other industrialized nations should "acknowledge their historic responsibility" as emitters of greenhouse gases and not put so great a burden on the emerging nations that it would set back their development, he said.

AT ISSUE

Is today's China a communist country?

YES
Xu Kuangdi
President, Chinese Academy of Engineering in Beijing, former Shanghai mayor

Written for *CQ Researcher*, May 2010

The Chinese Communist Party (CPC) has never done things by the book. In the early days, some party members, following the lead of the Soviet Union, launched the workers' movement in the cities. But the party shifted its focus to the rural areas where government control was relatively weak. We mobilized the peasants; we developed land reform.

Today, we don't do things according to what Karl Marx wrote or Vladimir Lenin said 80 years ago. We're doing things to advance the development of productive forces, and we are doing things to serve the interests of the vast majority of people.

Marx is still widely respected by the party. He is a great mind and a very great thinker on the development of civilization. His theories on capitalism inspired us on how to overcome the current financial crisis. But Marx lived 100 years ago; he couldn't predict how science and technology would develop. That is why our new ideology is to keep pace with the times. That doesn't mean we have forgotten Marx. Marxism is still our long-term goal.

The CPC is committed to building a society in which property and well-being can be enjoyed by all, a society of harmony between rich and poor. Today, we have a problem of a widening gap between rich and poor, which we are trying our best to narrow. But it will not be solved by dividing the property of the rich among the poor.

Our previous lessons showed us that the division of property is not the answer. Nor is Western democracy the answer. If we introduced Western democracy, we may have turbulence in the society.

A Western friend told me that he would only go to church three times in his lifetime. The first time is to be baptized, the second for his marriage and the third for his funeral. It doesn't follow that he doesn't have God in his heart. It's the same for us with Communism.

To live up to our beliefs we sometimes have to take different paths. As [former CPC leader] Deng Xiaoping has put it: The ultimate goal is common prosperity, but we have to let some people get rich first.

NO
Stefan Halper
Director, Atlantic Studies Program, Cambridge University'
Author, The Beijing Consensus: How China's Authoritarian Model Will Dominate the Twenty-First Century

Written for *CQ Researcher*, April 2010

There's a wonderful comment by the legendary U.S. diplomat and Russia expert George F. Kennan, who said, "Let's not ask what communism has done to Russia, but rather what Russia has done to communism." Much the same didactic is applicable to today's China.

Mao and Stalin would be spinning in their graves if they saw what was happening in China in the name of communism. China has shed any remnants of Marxist ideology, even to the point of directly addressing the question of who owns the land, a serious point of contention in the recent People's Congress. It is now accepted that land can be privately owned and houses built on it.

China is not expansionist, it does not seek to undermine the Western system: instead, its market-authoritarian system provides an example for the world beyond the West where growing numbers of leaders admire China, see China as a Third World nation at the pinnacle of world power and wish to emulate China's progress.

So while China may continue to call itself communist, it certainly isn't communism as we know it, but more of a form of state capitalism; the role of state is market authoritarian, not Marxist-Leninism. A Marxist economy is the polar opposite of the dynamic market economy China is developing today.

The Chinese leadership is highly practical, opportunistic and focused on economic growth and stability. The only remnants of communism are the single party rule of the party, a general embrace of socialist principles and the various structures that the party employs to govern the country: a politburo, a people's congress and a central committee.

Of course, it still calls itself communist, but it's just as much a corporatist state, even a form of fascism in its classical, Mussolini-type form, which is to say a process that coordinates the interest of the state and large corporations. Put another way, the business of China is business.

AFP/Getty Images/Liu Jin

China spends more than 4 percent of its gross domestic product (GDP) on its military, about the same ratio as the United States. The country's rising military spending, including the beefing up of key naval bases near Taiwan, has caused concern in Washington.

The latest tension had its origins in November, when Obama's Chinese hosts insisted on a low-key visit that minimized his contact with the public.

"It's a mystery," David Shamburgh, a professor of Chinese studies at Georgetown University, told *The Wall Street Journal* during the presidential visit. "[Obama is] a populist politician, but he's not getting any interaction with Chinese people."[47] It's not such a mystery, perhaps, when one considers Obama's popularity worldwide, in contrast to a Chinese leadership with limited contact with its own people.

Indeed, on the morning following Obama's arrival in Shanghai, the city's government-controlled English-language paper carried a large front-page photo of Hu with the prime minister of Canada, who was in China at the time. A one-column photo of Obama appeared below the fold. In a country where much importance is attached to not losing face, such signals matter.

The tension had escalated two months later when Obama made two moves calculated to anger the Chinese. First, in February the president received Tibet's exiled spiritual leader, the Dalai Lama, after Beijing had expressly asked him not to do so.

The meeting drew a protest from Beijing even though the White House kept the visit private and carefully avoided showing pictures of Obama and the Dalai Lama together.

In a second affront, Obama approved a long-delayed $6.4 billion weapons sale to Taiwan, which China continues to threaten with hundreds of missiles while at the same time insisting that it wants a peaceful solution to the island's claims of independence. The package includes 114 Patriot missiles worth $2.2 billion, and 60 Blackhawk helicopters worth $3.1 billion.

Beijing promptly ratcheted up its rhetoric, and U.S.-Chinese relations took "a nosedive," *The Washington Post* said.[48] A senior Chinese Defense Ministry official, Huang Xueping, said China was resolved to punish the United States if the weapons were delivered and that the U.S. could expect even greater consequences if Washington added advanced F-16 jet fighters to the sale.[49]

The Chinese went still further. Beijing threatened to sanction U.S. firms involved in the deal. And then it showed off its military prowess by successfully testing — without warning — an advanced missile interception system. The timing also seemed a further demonstration of Beijing's ire. "The people who tied the knot should untie the knot," said Chinese Foreign Ministry spokesman Qin Gang.[50]

Commentators attributed China's new tough and uncompromising attitude to more than one factor. They said China's seemingly quick recovery from the global financial crisis while the West continues to struggle has vindicated the Chinese development model in Chinese eyes and the weakness of the less-disciplined Western approach.

A second explanation, though, was the jostling for position in the leadership in advance of the 2012 Communist Party Congress, an event that spurs aspiring candidates to display their nationalist credentials. Behind the united front China's leadership shows to the world, deep divisions exist between the hard-line "realists" and those who favor openness in China's international dealings — and the hard-liners currently have the upper hand. According to another explanation, the regime's aggressiveness toward the outside world stems from the government's desire to find a distraction from socioeconomic problems at home.

After all, this is the Year of the Tiger — always turbulent and often unpredictable.[51]

OUTLOOK

The Taiwan Question

It remains to be seen how the Chinese will react, if or when the United States begins delivery of the weapons sold to Taiwan.

Analysts say the recently proposed (but not finalized) additional sale of F-16s would raise the level of China's objections even further. Although the original weapons deal drew protests, it had initially been negotiated by the Bush administration and was well-known to the Chinese. But Jean-Pierre Cabestan, a professor of international studies at Hong Kong Baptist University, predicts that "if an F-16 sale moves forward, we can expect another wave of difficulties between the U.S. and China."

The outlook is hard to forecast with any accuracy because of the ongoing cooperation-competition dance between China and the U.S. For example, despite its protests over Taiwan, Beijing at the same time is committed to working with Washington and other governments in securing vital sea lanes and enforcing regional stability. Early in 2010, China agreed to take a lead role in anti-piracy patrols off Somalia. Chinese navy units had not strayed outside Chinese waters for centuries, but today 80 percent of China's oil imports are shipped through the narrow Straits of Malacca that connect the Indian Ocean and the South China Sea.

There is no indication that China would actually support sanctions against Iran. In the past, China had signed on to three previous U.N. sanctions resolutions — and the Chinese eventually delayed and weakened every one of them, said Iran expert Flynt Leverett, a senior fellow at the centrist New America Foundation think tank.[52]

Also casting a shadow over the next few months is the thorny question of China's undervalued renminbi. Foreign-policy issues are rarely prominent in U.S. elections, but at a time of high unemployment and economic uncertainty, some analysts believe China's currency seems set to become a thorny question in November's mid-term elections, possibly creating anti-Chinese public sentiment.

Given the upcoming elections, some analysts say a slight currency revaluation designed to take the dispute out of the campaign is in the offing. But, says Glaser at the Center for Strategic and International Studies, "The

> *Despite its protests over Taiwan, Beijing at the same time is committed to working with Washington and other governments in securing vital sea lanes and enforcing regional stability.*

Chinese are not going to revalue their currency because we tell them to. They will choose their own time."

One reason: Chinese leaders cannot afford seeming to act in response to pressure from the "foreign devils" (*qwai lo*) — which to the Chinese is just about everybody including the United States — without serious loss of face in the eyes of their own people.

The United States has a risky card of sorts to play in the shape of the annual U.S. Treasury analysis (mandated by the 1988 Omnibus Trade and Competitiveness Act) of the currencies of foreign countries to determine whether they are manipulating the currency to gain unfair trade advantage. To Congress' exasperation, the Treasury has so far not labeled China a "currency manipulator."

If and when it does, New York's Sen. Schumer has a draft bill waiting that would impose stiff penalties on countries that manipulate their currencies, including possible tariffs. "China's currency manipulation would be unacceptable even in good economic times," Schumer said in a recent statement. "At a time of 10 percent unemployment, we simply will not stand for it."

There is an obvious political edge to Schumer's bill: The senator is up for re-election. But others also feel the time has come to confront the Chinese. The Obama administration "needs to draw a line in the sand, and say to the Chinese: 'You're exporting unemployment by undervaluing your currency by 20 percent to 40 percent,' " says Cambridge University's Halper. If the Chinese don't revalue, "we should impose similar tariffs."

It was out of consideration for Hu's visit in April that Treasury Secretary Timothy Geithner postponed publication of the Treasury report, which is normally released on April 15. No new date has been announced, but analysts say the delay is strategic, giving the Chinese more time for further reflection.

Two important dates are coming up for possible further discussion — the U.S.-China yearly "strategic dialogue" in late May, and the broader forum of the G20 summit in Seoul, South Korea, in late June.

The Chinese, however, are focused on another event they hope will boost their prestige, much as the 2008 Summer Olympics had done: The Shanghai Expo 2010, which the city expects will attract over 70 million visitors. Its theme reflects China's hopes and aspirations — "Better city, better life."

NOTES

1. "Clinton in China," BBC Special Report, July 3, 1998, http://news.bbc.co.uk/2/hi/special_report/1998/06/98/clinton_in_china/118430.stm. Also Lin Kim, "Sino-American Relations: a new stage?" *New Zealand International Review*, Vol. 23, 1998, www.questia.com/googleScholar.qst;jsessionid=LY2JTpnRvl29qyD1ByfHwVQxJtmVQQ7bcyJ6RW47LJJnw6WmnYwg!555708061!-1331918248?docId=5001372599.

2. "China's economy grew 11.9 pct y/y in Q1 — sources," *The Guardian*, April 14, 2010. www.guardian.co.uk/business/feedarticle/9031081.

3. U.S. Census Bureau, www.census.gov/foreign-trade/balance/c5700.html#2010.

4. Howard Schneider, "U.S. sets tariff of up to 90 percent on imports of Chinese oilfield pipes," *The Washington Post*, April 10, 2010.

5. Wang Yanlin and Jin Jing, "Trade dispute heats up while Obama visit nears," *ShanghaiDaily.com*, Nov. 7, 2009, www.shanghaidaily.com/sp/article/2009/200911/20091107/article_418781.htm.

6. Schneider, *op. cit.*

7. "China, India, Japan Iran's Top Partners in Crude Oil Trade," Moinews.com, April 14, 2010, www.mojnews.com/en/Miscellaneous/ViewContents.aspx?Contract=cms_Contents_I_News&r=485205.

8. For background see Alan Greenblatt, "Attacking Piracy," *CQ Global Researcher*, August 2009, pp. 205-232.

9. "China Must Protect Intellectual Property," *Korea Herald*, April 22, 2010, www.koreaherald.co.kr/national/Detail.jsp?newsMLId=20100422000363.

10. White House transcript, Nov. 9. 2009, www.whitehouse.gov/the-press-office/briefing-conference-call-presidents-trip-asia.

11. "Commentary: China, U.S. sail in one boat amid global issues," Xinhua news service, Nov. 16, 2009; http://news.xinhuanet.com/english/2009-11/16/content_12463881.htm.

12. Martin Walker, "Walker's World: Haiku Herman's G2," United Press International, Dec 7, 2009, www.spacewar.com/reports/Walkers_World_Haiku_Hermans_G2_999.html.

13. U.S.-China Joint Statement, U.S. Embassy, Beijing, http://beijing.usembassy-china.org.cn/111709.html.

14. "Hu presents 5-point proposal for boosting China-U.S. ties," Xinhua, April 13, 2010, http://english.cctv.com/20100413/102277.shtml.

15. Kaiser Kuo, "The Intertwining of Sino-American Cooperation and Competition," China Geeks Translation and Analysis of Modern China, February 2010, http://chinageeks.org/2010/02/the-intertwining-of-sino-american-competition-and-cooperation/.

16. Edwin Chen and Rob Delaney, "Hu Tells Obama China Will Follow Its Own Path on Yuan," Bloomberg, April 13, 2010, www.bloomberg.com/apps/news?pid=20601070&sid=a07psM9uKD6g.

17. "China-U.S. agreement sends warning to Iran," *The National*, April 13, 2010, www.thenational.ae/apps/pbcs.dll/article?AID=/20100413/FOREIGN/704139996/1014.

18. "Obama's Asia Visit," editorial, *Korea Times*, Nov. 10, 2009, www.koreatimes.co.kr/www/news/opinon/2010/04/202_55210.html.

19. Thomas Lunn, *et al.*, China's Foreign Aid Activities in Africa, Latin America, and Southeast Asia, Feb. 25, 2009, www.fas.org/sgp/crs/row/R40361.pdf. Report is based largely on research by New York University's Robert F. Wagner Graduate School of Public Service.

20. *Ibid.*

21. Jad Mouawad, "China's Growth Shifts the Geopolitics of Oil," *The New York Times*, March 19,

2010, www.nytimes.com/2010/03/20/business/energy-environment/20saudi.html.

22. Willy Lam, "Beijing Seeks Paradigm Shift in Geopolitics, "The Jamestown Foundation, March 5, 2010, www.jamestown.org/programs/chinabrief/single/?tx_ttnews%5Btt_news%5D=36120&tx_ttnews%5BbackPid%5D=25&cHash=a9b9a1117e.

23. "Facing up to China," *The Economist*, Feb. 4, 2010, www.economist.com/PrinterFriendly.cfm?story_id=15452821.

24. Nicholas D. Kristof, "China, Concubines, and Google," *The New York Times*, March 31, 2010, www.nytimes.com/2010/04/01/opinion/01kristof.html.

25. Drew Thompson, "Think Again: China's Military," *Foreign Policy*, March/April 2010, www.foreignpolicy.com/articles/2010/02/22/think_again_chinas_military.

26. "Annual Report to Congress: Military Power of the People's Republic of China, 2009," Department of Defense, www.defense.gov/pubs/pdfs/China_Military_Power_Report_2009.pdf.

27. "Pentagon issues annual report on China's military power," Xinhuanet, March 26, 2009, www.news.xinhuanet.com/english/2009-08/26/content_11079173.htm.

28. Pentagon report to Congress, *op. cit.*

29. Dennis Blair, "Annual Threat Assessment of the U.S. Intelligence Community for the Senate Select Committee on Intelligence," February 2010, www.dni.gov/testimonies/20100202_testimony.pdf.

30. Cecilia Kang, "Hillary Clinton calls for Web freedom, demands China investigate Google attack," *The Washington Post*, Jan. 22, 2010, www.washingtonpost.com/wp-dyn/content/article/2010/01/21/AR2010012101699.html.

31. John Pomfret, "China's Commerce Minister: U.S. has most to lose in a trade war," *The Washington Post*, March 22, 2010, www.washingtonpost.com/wp-dyn/content/article/2010/03/21/AR2010032101111.html.

32. Rowan Callick, "The China Model," *The American*, November/December 2007, www.american.com/archive/2007/november-december-magazine-contents/the-china-model.

33. Lunn, *et al.*, *op. cit.*

34. Thomas P.M. Barnett, "The New Rules: Why China Will Not Bury America," *World Politics Review*, Feb. 1, 2010, www.worldpoliticsreview.com/articles/5031/the-new-rules-why-china-will-not-bury-america.

35. Wieland Wagne, "How China is battling global economic crisis," *San Francisco Sentinel*, May 23, 2009, www.sanfranciscosentinel.com/?p=28287.

36. Ma Ying, "China's Stubborn Anti-Democracy," Hoover Institution Policy Review, February/March 2007, www.hoover.org/publications/policyreview/5513661.html.

37. *Ibid.*

38. Brian Knowlton, "Citing 'Constructive Engagement,' He Acts to Counter Critics in Congress: Clinton Widens Defense of China Visit," *The New York Times*, July 12, 1998, www.nytimes.com/1998/06/12/news/12iht-prexy.t.html?pagewanted=1.

39. Evan Osnos, "Despatches from Evan Osnos: Strategic Reassurance," *The New Yorker Online*, Oct 6, 2009, www.newyorker.com/online/blogs/evanosnos/2009/10/strategic-reassurance.html.

40. Robert D. Kaplan, "The Geography of Chinese Power," *Foreign Affairs*, May/June 2010.

41. "China could become World's largest exporter by 2010," Organization for Economic Cooperation and Development, Sept. 16, 2005, www.oecd.org/document/29/0,3343,en_2649_201185_35363023_1_1_1_1,00.html.

42. U.S. Department of Treasury, www.ustreas.gov/tic/mfh.txt.

43. http://news.bbc.co.uk/2/hi/asia-pacific/7833779.stm.

44. Li Beodong, head of China's delegation to the United Nations in Geneva, official transcript of speech in 2009.

45. The Associated Press, "China's Hu rebuffs Obama on yuan," *Minneapolis Star Tribune*, April 13, 2010, www.startribune.com/business/90728804.html.

46. Transcript of White House press briefing, April 12, 2010, www.whitehouse.gov/the-press-office/press-briefing-jeff-bader-nsc-senior-director-asian-affairs.

47. Ian Johnson and Jonathan Wiseman, "Beijing limits Obama's exposure," *The Wall Street Journal* Online, Nov. 17, 2009, http://online.wsj.com/article/SB125835068967050099.html.

48. John Pomfret and Jon Cohen, "Many Americans see U.S. influence waning as that of China grows," *The Washington Post*, Feb. 25, 2010, p. A11.

49. Andrew Jacobs, "China Warns U.S. Against Selling F-16s to Taiwan,"

50. *Ibid.*

51. David Shambaugh, "The Year China Showed its Claws," *Financial Times*, Feb. 16, 2010, www.ft.com/cms/s/0/7503a600-1b30-11df-953f-00144feab49a.html.

52. Corey Flintoff, "Will China Help Sanction Iran's Nuke Program?" NPR, April 14, 2010, www.npr.org/templates/story/story.php?storyId=125991589&ft=1&f=1004.

BIBLIOGRAPHY

Books

Halper, Stefan, *The Beijing Consensus,* **Basic Books, 2010.**
A Cambridge University professor analyzes the economic and strategic sides of U.S.-China relations.

Jacques, Martin, *When China Rules the World: The Rise of the Middle Kingdom and the End of the Western World,* **Penguin, 2010.**
A British commentator predicts that history is about to restore China to its ancient position of global power.

Karabell, Zachary, *Superfusion: How China and America Became One Economy and Why the World's Prosperity Depends on It,* **Simon & Schuster, 2009.**
An economist and historian writes that despite an increasingly less hospitable business environment, foreign investors keep flocking to China.

Mann, James, *The China Fantasy: How Our Leaders Explain Away Chinese Repression,* **Viking, 2007.**
A veteran China reporter files a passionate complaint that U.S. elites are misleading the American public to boost trade with a hostile regime.

Shirk, Susan, *China: Fragile Superpower: How China's Internal Politics Could Derail Its Peaceful Rise,* **Oxford University Press, 2007.**
A former top State Department official says understanding the fears that drive China's leadership is essential to managing the U.S.-China relationship without military confrontation.

Tyler, Patrick, *A Great Wall: Six Presidents and China,* **Public Affairs, 1999.**
An investigative reporter describes the struggles of six presidential administrations in shaping a sustainable China policy.

Articles

Mufson, Stephen, and John Pomfret, "There's a New Red Scare, but is China Really So Scary?" *The Washington Post,* **Feb. 28, 2010, www.washingtonpost.com/wp-dyn/content/article/2010/02/26/AR2010022602601.html.**
Two *Post* correspondents argue that America's reading of China is an insight into America's collective psyche.

Talbot, David, "China's Internet Paradox," *MIT Technology Review,* **May-June 2010, www.technologyreview.com/web/25032/.**
China's Internet usage is not as restricted as the regime would wish despite intense censorship efforts.

Wong, Edward, "Chinese Military to Extend its Naval Power," *The New York Times,* **April 23, 2010, www.nytimes.com/2010/04/24/world/asia/24navy.html.**
The Chinese military is building a deepwater navy to protect its oil tankers.

Xue, Litai, and Jiang Wenran, "Debate Sino-U.S. Ties," *China Daily,* **April 20, 2010, www.chinadaily.net/opinion/2010-04/26/content_9772895_2.htm.**
Two U.S.-based Chinese scholars debate the state of the U.S.-China relationship.

Ying, Ma, "China's Stubborn Anti-Democracy," *Hoover Institution Policy Review*, February-March 2007, www.hoover.org/publications/policyreview/5513661.html.
An American Enterprise Institute fellow examines why China's economic development hasn't led to democratization.

Reports and Studies

"Annual Report to Congress: Military Power of the People's Republic of China — 2009," Office of the Secretary of Defense, 2009, www.defense.gov/pubs/pdfs/China_Military_Power_Report_2009.pdf.
The Pentagon's annual assessment of the People's Liberation Army invariably draws criticism from Beijing.

Godement, Francois, *et al.*, "No Rush to Marriage: China's Response to the G2," China Analysis, European Council on Foreign Relations and the Asia Center of the Sciences Po, June 2009, ecfr.3cdn.net/d40ce525f765f638c4_bfm6ivg3l.pdf.

An East Asian historian and analyst says that while Europeans worry about an emerging U.S.-Chinese global duopoly, the Chinese are still examining their options.

Green, Michael J., "U.S.-China Relations Under President Obama," July 14-15, 2009, Brookings Institution, iir.nccu.edu.tw/attachments/news/modify/Green.pdf.
A scholar at the centrist think tank examines whether the administration's cooperative China policy will work.

Huang, Ping, *et al.*, "China-U.S. Relations Tending Towards Maturity," Institute of American Studies, Chinese Academy of Social Sciences, June 2009, ias.cass.cn/en/show_project_ls.asp?id=1012.
Four analysts offer a Chinese perspective on relations between the United States and their country.

Lunn, Thomas, "Human Rights in China: Trends and Policy Implications," Congressional Research Service, Jan. 25, 2010, www.fas.org/sgp/crs/row/RL34729.pdf.
The nonpartisan research agency offers the most current periodic report to Congress on human rights in China.

For More Information

American Enterprise Institute, 1150 17th St., N.W., Washington, DC 20036; (202) 862-5800; www.aei.org. A nonpartisan think tank dedicated to research and education on government, politics, economics and social welfare.

Brookings Institution, 1775 Massachusetts Ave., N.W., Washington, DC 20036; (202) 797-6000; www.brookings .edu. Non-profit public policy institution working for a more cooperative international system.

Center for a New American Security, 1301 Pennsylvania Ave., N.W., Suite 403, Washington, DC 20004; (202) 457-9400; www.snas.org. An independent, nonpartisan think tank established in 2007 dedicated to developing strong, pragmatic and principled national security and defense policies that promote and protect American interests and values.

Center for Strategic and International Studies, 1800 K St., N.W., Washington, DC 20006; (202) 887-0200; www .csis.org. A nonpartisan think tank that provides strategic insights and policy solutions to decision-makers in government, international institutions, the private sector and civil society.

Center for U.S.-China Relations, Tsinghua University, Beijing, China 100084; (86-10) 62794360; www.chinausa .org.cn. First research institute specializing in U.S.-China relations established by a Chinese institute of higher education.

China Institute, 125 E. 65th St., New York, NY 10065; (212) 744-8181; www.chinainstitute.org. Promoting a better understanding of China through programs in education, culture and business.

China Institute of International Studies, 3 Toutiao, Tai-jichang, Beijing, China 100005; (86-10) 85119547; www

.ciis.org.cn. Think tank and research institution arm of the Chinese Ministry of Foreign Affairs.

China-United States Exchange Foundation, 15/f Shun Ho Tower, 24-30 Ice House Street, Hong Kong; (852) 25232083; www.cusf.hk. Fostering dialogue between Chinese and U.S. individuals from the media, academic, think tank and business environments.

Confucius Institute, 0134 Holzapfel Hall, University of Maryland, College Park, MD 20742; (301) 405-0213; www .international.umd.edu/cim. One of more than 60 Chinese cultural institutes established on U.S. campuses by the Chinese government, offering language courses and cultural programs.

National Security Council, www.whitehouse.gov/administra tion/eop/nsc. The NSC is the president's principal forum for considering national security and foreign policy matters with his senior national security advisors and Cabinet officials.

Nottingham University China Policy Institute, International House, Jubilee Campus, Nottingham NG8 1B8, England, United Kingdom; (44-115) 8467769; www.not tingham.ac.uk/cpi. Think tank aimed at expanding knowledge and understanding of contemporary China.

Shanghai Institute for International Studies, 195-15 Tianlin Rd., Shanghai, China 200233; (86-21) 54614900; www.siis.org.cn. Research organization focusing on international politics, economy, security strategy and China's international relations.

U.S.-China Policy Foundation, 316 Pennsylvania Ave., S.E., Suites 201-203, Washington, DC 20003; (202) 547-8615; www.uscpf.org. Works to broaden awareness of China and U.S.-China relations within the Washington policy community.

15

Afghanistan Dilemma

Thomas J. Billitteri

An Afghan security officer guards two tons of burning heroin, opium and hashish near Kabul, Afghanistan's capital, on March 18, 2009. Nearly eight years after U.S.-led forces first entered Afghanistan, many challenges still confront the U.S., Afghan and coalition forces seeking to stabilize the country: fanatical Taliban and al Qaeda fighters, rampant police corruption, shortages of Afghan troops and a multibillion-dollar opium economy that supports the insurgents.

From *CQ Researcher*,
August 7, 2009.

On the outskirts of Now Zad, a Taliban stronghold in southern Afghanistan's violent Helmand Province, the past, present and future of the war in Afghanistan came together this summer.

The past: After the U.S.-led invasion of Afghanistan in 2001, Now Zad and its surrounding poppy fields and stout compounds were largely tranquil, thanks in part to the clinics and wells that Western money helped to build in the area. But three years ago, when the war in Iraq intensified and the Bush administration shifted attention from Afghanistan to Iraq, insurgents moved in, driving out most of Now Zad's 35,000 residents and foreign aid workers.

The present: This summer U.S. Marines engaged in withering firefights with Taliban militants dug in on the northern fringes of the town and in nearby fields and orchards.

The future: The situation in Now Zad and the surrounding war-torn region of southern Afghanistan is a microcosm of what confronts the Obama administration as it tries to smash the Taliban, defang al Qaeda and stabilize governance in Afghanistan. "In many ways," wrote an Associated Press reporter following the fighting, Now Zad "symbolizes what went wrong in Afghanistan and the enormous challenges facing the United States." [1]

Nearly eight years after U.S.-led forces first entered Afghanistan to pursue al Qaeda and its Taliban allies in the wake of the Sept. 11, 2001, terrorist attacks, the country remains in chaos, and President Barack Obama faces what many consider his biggest foreign-policy challenge: bringing stability and security to Afghanistan and denying Islamist militants a permanent foothold there and in neighboring nuclear-armed Pakistan.

351

An Unstable Nation in a Volatile Neighborhood

Almost as large as Texas, Afghanistan faces Texas-size problems, including desperate poverty, an economy dominated by illicit drugs and an unstable central government beset by Taliban militants. Afghanistan's instability is compounded by longstanding tensions between neighboring Pakistan and India, both armed with nuclear weapons. Many Western experts also say Pakistan has failed, despite promises, to rein in Taliban and other Islamist extremists.

The challenge is heightened by the war's growing casualty figures. July was the deadliest month in Afghanistan for U.S. soldiers since the 2001 invasion began, with 43 killed.[2] Twenty-two British troops also died last month, including eight in a 24-hour period. In nearly eight years of war in Afghanistan, 767 U.S. troops have died there, along with 520 coalition forces, according to the Web site iCasualties.org. Thousands of Afghan civilians also have died.

The Afghanistan-Pakistan conflict —"Af-Pak" in diplomatic parlance — poses a witch's brew of challenges: fanatical Taliban and al Qaeda fighters, rampant corruption within Afghanistan's homegrown police force and other institutions, not enough Afghan National Army forces to help with the fighting and a multibillion-dollar opium economy that supplies revenue to the insurgents.

But those problems pale in comparison with what foreign-policy experts call the ultimate nightmare: Pakistan's nuclear weapons falling into the hands of jihadists and terrorists, a scenario that has become more credible this summer as suicide bombers and Taliban fighters have stepped up attacks in Pakistani cities and rural areas,

using Pakistan's lawless western border region as a sanctuary.[3]

"The fact that Pakistan has nuclear weapons and the question of the security of those weapons presses very hard on the minds of American defense planners and on the mind of the president," says Bruce Riedel, who led a 60-day strategic policy review of Afghanistan and Pakistan for the Obama administration. "If you didn't have that angle," adds Riedel, who has since returned to his post as a Brookings Institution senior fellow, "I think this would all be notched down one level of concern."

Pakistan is important to the Afghan conflict for reasons that go beyond its nuclear arsenal. Pakistan has been a breeding ground for much of the radical ideology that has taken root in Afghanistan. A failure of governance in Afghanistan would leave a void that Islamist militants on either side of the border could wind up filling, further destabilizing the entire region.

In March Obama announced what he called a "comprehensive, new strategy" for Afghanistan and Pakistan that rests on a "clear and focused goal" for the region: "to disrupt, dismantle and defeat al Qaeda in Pakistan and Afghanistan, and to prevent their return to either country in the future."[4]

Key to the strategy is winning over the local Afghan population by protecting it from insurgent violence and improving governance, security and economic development.[5]

The effort includes new troop deployments — a total of 21,000 additional U.S. soldiers to fight the insurgency in Afghanistan and train Afghan security forces, plus other strategic resources. By year's end, U.S. troop levels are expected to reach about 68,000. NATO countries and other allies currently are supplying another 32,000 or so, though many are engaged in development and relief work but not offensive combat operations.[6]

An immediate goal is to heighten security in Afghanistan in the run-up to a high-profile presidential election on

Aug. 20. None of Afghan President Hamid Karzai's main challengers are expected to beat him flat out, *The Washington Post* noted, but some observers said other candidates could "do well enough as a group to force a second round of polling, partly because of recent blunders by Karzai and partly because many Afghans are looking for alternative leadership at a time of sustained insurgent violence, economic stagnation and political drift." [7]

Observers say Obama's approach to the Af-Pak conflict represents a middle path between counterterrorism and counterinsurgency — protecting civilians, relying on them for information on the enemy and providing aid to build up a country's social and physical infrastructure and democratic institutions. [8]

Among the most notable features of the new approach is a vow among military officials — beginning with Gen. Stanley A. McChrystal, the newly appointed commander of U.S. and NATO forces in Afghanistan — to avoid civilian casualties. McChrystal pledged to follow a "holistic" approach in which protecting civilians takes precedence over killing militants. [9]

"I expect stiff fighting ahead," McChrystal told the Senate Armed Services Committee at his confirmation hearing. But "the measure of effectiveness will not be the number of enemy killed," he added, "it will be the number of Afghans shielded from violence." [10]

The United Nations said that 1,013 civilians died in the first six months of 2009, up from 818 during the same period last year. The U.N. said 310 deaths were attributed to pro-government forces, with about two-thirds caused by U.S. air strikes. [11]

As part of his strategy, Obama called for a "dramatic" increase in the number of agricultural specialists, educators, engineers and lawyers dispatched to "help the Afghan government serve its people and develop an economy that isn't dominated by illicit drugs." He also

Gates Warns About Civilian Deaths

The number of civilians killed in Afghanistan more than doubled from 2006 to 2008, but based on the toll for the first six months of 2009, the rate may be somewhat lower in 2009 (graph at left). In 2008 nearly half of the civilian deaths were caused by executions or suicide and IED (improvised explosive device) attacks by the Taliban and other anti-government groups (graph at right). Concern over civilian deaths prompted Defense Secretary Robert Gates to call such casualties "one of our greatest strategic vulnerabilities."

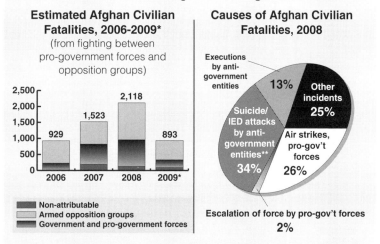

* Through June; the total is 1,013, according to the U.N.
** Includes Taliban and other insurgents
Source: "Afghan Index: Tracking Variables of Reconstruction and Security in Post-9/11 Afghanistan," Brookings Institution, July 15, 2009

supports economic-development aid to Pakistan, including legislation to provide $1.5 billion annually over the next five years. But Obama's approach on Pakistan also reflects long-held Western concerns that the Pakistani government has been at best negligent — and perhaps downright obstructionist — in bringing Taliban and other Islamist extremists to heel. Pakistan, whose situation is complicated by long-standing tensions with nearby India, will get no free pass in exchange for the aid, Obama vowed. "We will not, and cannot, provide a blank check," he said, because Pakistan had shown "years of mixed results" in rooting out terrorism. [12]

As Obama goes after the insurgency, his Af-Pak policy is under the microscope here at home.

Some have demanded that the administration describe its plans for ending military operations in Afghanistan.

Opium Trade Funds Taliban, Official Corruption

"It's clear that drug money is paying for the Taliban's operational costs."

In the crowded Afghan capital of Kabul, opulent marble homes sit behind guard houses and razor wire. "Most are owned by Afghan officials or people connected to them, men who make a few hundred dollars a month as government employees but are driven around in small convoys of armored SUVs that cost tens of thousands of dollars," reporter Tom Lasseter noted recently. "[M]any of the houses were built with profits harvested from opium poppy fields in the southern provinces of Helmand and Kandahar." [1]

The so-called "poppy palaces" are outward signs of a cancer eating Afghanistan to its core: illicit drugs and narcoterrorism, aided by official corruption.

According to the United Nations Office on Drugs and Crime, Afghanistan grows more than 90 percent of the world's opium, which is used to produce heroin and morphine. [2] Total opium production for 2008 was estimated at 7,700 metric tons, more than double the 2002 level. [3]

In her new book, *Seeds of Terror: How Heroin Is Bankrolling the Taliban and Al Qaeda*, journalist Gretchen Peters says militant groups are raising hundreds of millions of dollars a year from the opium trade.

"It's clear that drug money is paying for the Taliban's operational costs within Afghanistan," she told *Time* magazine. "That means that every time a U.S. soldier is killed in an IED attack or a shootout with militants, drug money helped pay for that bomb or paid the militants who placed it. . . . The Taliban have now thrown off their old masters and are a full-fledged criminal force on both sides of the [Afghan-Pakistan] border." [4]

The biggest challenge to curbing the drug trade, Peters said, is corruption. "As much money as the insurgents are earning off the drug trade, corrupt officials in Afghanistan and Pakistan are earning even more," she said. "It's going to be very complex for the U.S. and for the international community, for NATO, to find reliable and trustworthy partners to work with. I don't think that it is widely understood how high up the corruption goes within the Pakistani government, particularly within their military and intelligence forces."

In recent weeks, the Obama administration has shifted U.S. drug policy in Afghanistan from trying to eradicate poppy fields to seizing drugs and related supplies and helping farmers grow alternative crops. [5]

"The Western policies against the opium crop, the poppy crop, have been a failure," Richard C. Holbrooke, the administration's special representative for Afghanistan and Pakistan, said. "They did not result in any damage to the Taliban, but they put farmers out of work and they alienated people and drove people into the arms of the Taliban." [6]

The Bush administration had advocated intense efforts to eradicate poppy fields, but some experts have said the approach is counterproductive.

"The United States should de-emphasize opium eradication efforts," Air Force Lt. Col. John A. Glaze wrote in a 2007 report for the U.S. Army War College. It recommended a multi-pronged strategy including higher troop levels, more economic aid for Afghanistan, pursuit of drug lords and corrupt officials and development of alternative

A measure proposed by Rep. Jim McGovern, D-Mass., requiring a report from the Obama administration by the end of the year on its exit strategy, drew significant support from Democrats but was defeated in the House this summer amid heavy Republican opposition.

And some critics question the validity of Obama's rationale for the fighting in Afghanistan, particularly the assumption that if the Taliban were victorious they would invite al Qaeda to return to Afghanistan and use it as a base for its global jihad. John Mueller, a political science professor at Ohio State University and author of *Overblown: How Politicians and the Terrorism Industry Inflate National Security Threats, and Why We Believe*

Them, contends that al Qaeda does not need Afghanistan as a base. The 2001 terrorist attacks were orchestrated mostly from Hamburg, Germany, he points out.

What's more, he argues, "distinct tensions" exist between al Qaeda and the Taliban. Even if the Taliban were to prevail in Afghanistan, he says, "they would not particularly want al Qaeda back." Nor, he says, is it clear that al Qaeda would again view Afghanistan as a safe haven. [13]

But administration officials disagree. The Taliban are "the frontrunners for al Qaeda," said Richard Holbrooke, Obama's special envoy to Pakistan and Afghanistan. "If they succeed in Afghanistan, without any shadow of a

livelihoods for Afghans, plus exploration of the possibility of participating in the market for legal opiates used for morphine and other medicines.

"U.S.-backed eradication efforts have been ineffective and have resulted in turning Afghans against U.S. and NATO forces . . . ," Glaze wrote. "While the process of eradication lends itself well to the use of flashy metrics such as 'acres eradicated,' eradication without provision for long-term alternative livelihoods is devastating Afghan's poor farmers without addressing root causes."[7]

Brookings Institution scholar Vanda Felbab-Brown, an expert on Afghanistan's opium-poppy economy, says rural development, not poppy eradication, is the best way to attack the drug economy. "Any massive eradication right now . . . , we would lose Afghanistan," she says. "In the absence of resources available to farmers, any eradication would just prompt massive destabilization and invite the Taliban in."

Felbab-Brown says the development of new crops is key, but that such crops must be "high-labor-intensive, high-value crops" that offer more than subsistence income.

"People don't have to become rich, but they cannot continue existing in excruciating poverty. Many people will be willing and motivated to switch to a legal crop," she says, but "it needs to offer some chance of advancement."

Vegetable, fruit and horticultural crops are better options, Felbab-Brown says. Wheat, on the other hand, "has no traction" because the prices are low, people in vast parts of the country don't have enough land to make the crop pay, and wheat is much less labor-intensive than poppy growing, affording fewer opportunities for employment, she says.

For rural development to offer an alternative to illicit poppy production, it must include not only access to land,

legal microcredit and other features, but security for Afghan farmers, Felbab-Brown stresses.

"The lack of security in many ways is the key structural driver of illicit crop cultivation, because the risks of cultivating legal crops in insecure settings are just tremendous," she says.

Rural development, for example, "needs to involve roads, and not just their physical presence but also security on the roads," Felbab-Brown says. Roads are now insecure due to both the insurgents and the Afghan National Police.

"In much of the south, travel on the road is three times as expensive as travel in the north because of the number of bribes that one needs to pay at check stops. For many people, simply to take crops from Laskar Gah to Kandahar, by the time they pay the bribes that they need to pay, they will have lost all profit."

[1] Tom Lasseter, "Western Military Looked Other Way as the Afghan Drug Trade Boomed," *Charlotte Observer*, May 10, 2009, p. 13A.

[2] "World Drug Report 2009 Highlights Links Between Drugs and Crime," United Nations Office on Drugs and Crime, June 2009, www.unodc.org/unodc/en/press/releases/2009/june/world-drug-report-2009-highlights-links-between-drugs-and-crime.html.

[3] "World Drug Report 2009," United Nations Office on Drugs and Crime, www.unodc.org/documents/wdr/WDR_2009/WDR2009_eng_web.pdf.

[4] Bobby Ghosh, "Q&A: Fighting the New Narcoterrorism Syndicates," *Time*, July 17, 2009, www.time.com/time/nation/article/0,8599,1910935,00.html.

[5] Rachel Donadio, "New Course for Antidrug Efforts in Afghanistan," *The New York Times*, June 28, 2009, www.nytimes.com/2009/06/28/world/asia/28holbrooke.html?scp=1&sq=holbrooke+drug%20policy+afghanistan+rome&st=cse.

[6] Quoted in *ibid.*

[7] John A. Glaze, "Opium and Afghanistan: Reassessing U.S. Counternarcotics Strategy," U.S. Army War College, www.strategicstudiesinstitute.army.mil/Pubs/Display.Cfm?pubID=804.

doubt al Qaeda would move back into Afghanistan, set up a larger presence, recruit more people and pursue its objectives against the United States even more aggressively."[14]

As the war in Afghanistan continues, here are some of the questions people are asking:

Is the Obama administration pursuing the right course in Afghanistan?

Early in July, thousands of U.S. Marines began a massive assault in Afghanistan's Helmand River valley, the biggest American offensive of the Obama presidency and a key test of his new strategy in the region.

The operation included 4,000 troops from the 2nd Marine Expeditionary Brigade, who poured into the area in helicopters and armored vehicles. The Marines have run into stiff opposition, but the ultimate goal remains intact: protect local Afghans from insurgent violence and strengthen Afghanistan's legal, judicial and security institutions.

"Our focus must be on getting this [Afghan] government back up on its feet," Brig. Gen. Lawrence D. Nicholson, commander of the brigade, told his officers.[15]

But the mission is fraught with huge risks and challenges, and skepticism about it runs deep, even among some of Obama's fellow Democrats.

Social Conditions Worsened in Many Areas

Living conditions deteriorated between 2007 and 2008 in areas such as education, water quality and availability of electricity, according to surveys of Afghan citizens.

Condition of Infrastructure in Localities, 2007 and 2008

	Very/Quite Good (%) 2007	2008	Quite/Very Bad (%) 2007	2008
Availability of clean drinking water	63%	62%	36%	38%
Availability of water for irrigation	59	47	40	49
Availability of jobs	30	21	69	78
Supply of electricity	31	25	68	74
Security situation	66	No data	33	No data
Availability of medical care	56	49	44	50
Availability of education for children	72	70	28	29
Freedom of movement	72	No data	28	No data

Source: "Afghan Index: Tracking Variables of Reconstruction and Security in Post-9/11 Afghanistan," Brookings Institution, July 15, 2009

In May, House Appropriations Chairman David Obey, D-Wis., suggested that if the White House doesn't demonstrate progress by next year, funding for the war could slow. Asked if he could see Congress halting funding completely, Obey said, "If it becomes a fool's errand, I would hope so," according to *The Hill* newspaper. The success or failure of the Afghan policy is not in the hands of the president or Congress, Obey said, but "in the hands of the practicing politicians in Pakistan and Afghanistan. And I'm dubious about those hands." [16]

Much of the American public is similarly dubious. A June *New York Times*-CBS News poll found that 55 percent of respondents believed the war in Afghanistan was going somewhat or very badly for the United States, an increase of two points since April. Only 2 percent said the war was going "very well." [17]

Critics question the prospect of success in a country long divided by ethnic rivalries, a resistance to central governance and rampant graft that ranges from demands for petty bribes to drug corruption in high levels of government. [18]

"To pacify the place in the absence of reconciliation of the main tribes,* you'd need a very large national army" — one that would have to be financially subsidized by outside powers, says Stephen Walt, a professor of international affairs at Harvard University's Kennedy School of Government. Such an army "would have to be drawn from all these groups and imbued with central loyalty to the state. And there's never been a strong central state. Politics [in Afghanistan is defined by] factional alignments." And, he adds, the challenge is "compounded by levels of corruption and lack of institutions."

"We're sort of trying to impart a Western model of how the Afghan state should be created — with a central government, ministries, defense and so on. That's not the way Afghanistan has been run for centuries. The idea that we know how to do that, especially in the short term," Walt says, is "far-fetched."

Malou Innocent, a foreign-policy analyst at the conservative Cato Institute think tank, says America faces the prospect of an "ambiguous victory" because it is caught amid long-simmering tensions between Pakistan and India, a dynamic, she argues, that the Obama administration has failed to adequately take into account.

Pakistan has long feared an alliance between Afghanistan and India. To hedge its bets, Pakistan aids the insurgency in Afghanistan by providing shelter to the Taliban and other militants, Innocent says. At the same time, she says, Pakistan has accused India of funneling weapons through Afghanistan to separatists in Pakistan's unstable Balochistan province. [19] The ongoing India-Pakistan dispute over Kashmir also remains a cause of friction in the region.

"The regional dynamics are too intractable," Innocent says. "The countries in the region have an incentive to foment and maintain Afghanistan's instability. So we should be looking to get out of Afghanistan within a reasonable time frame — say at least in the next five years."

Innocent sees a U.S. role in training Afghanistan's own security forces and says covert operations against specific insurgent targets could make sense. But the Taliban threat centered along the Afghanistan-Pakistan

---

* The main ethnic groups are the Pashtun (42%), Tajik (27%), Hazara (9%), Uzbek (9%), Aimak (4%), Turkmen (3%) and Baloch (2%).

border cannot be definitively eradicated, she argues. "We can contain the militancy" and weaken it, she says, "but we can't believe we can have a victory with a capital V."

But Peter Bergen, a counterterrorism analyst and senior fellow at the New America Foundation, is more sanguine about the war's prospects in Afghanistan. In a *Washington Monthly* article, he challenged those who say Afghanistan is an unconquerable and ungovernable "graveyard of empires" where foreign armies have come to ignominious ends.

One telling fact, in Bergen's view, is that "the Afghan people themselves, the center of gravity in a counterinsurgency, are rooting for us to win." He cited BBC/ABC polling data indicating that 58 percent of Afghans named the Taliban — viewed favorably by only 7 percent of Afghans — as the biggest threat to their country, while only 8 percent named the United States.

"[T]he growing skepticism about Obama's chances for success in Afghanistan is largely based on deep misreadings of both the country's history and the views of its people, which are often compounded by facile comparisons to the United States' misadventures of past decades in Southeast Asia and the Middle East," wrote Bergen. "Afghanistan will not be Obama's Vietnam, nor will it be his Iraq. Rather, the renewed and better-resourced American effort in Afghanistan will, in time, produce a relatively stable and prosperous Central Asian state." [20]

Stephen Biddle, a senior fellow at the Council on Foreign Relations, a think tank in New York City, said victory in Afghanistan is possible but only if steps are taken to strengthen Afghanistan's governance. "I do think it's possible to succeed," Biddle said in late July after spending a month as part of a group helping McChrystal formulate a strategic assessment report on the war, due this month. But, he added, "there are two very different requirements for success.

"One is providing security, [and] the other is providing enough of an improvement in Afghan governance to

Afghanistan Ranks Low in Developing World

Afghanistan ranked as the second-weakest state in the developing world, after Somalia, in 2008, according to the Brookings Institution* (left). It consistently ranks near the bottom among countries rated for corruption by Transparency International (right).

Afghanistan's Rank					
Index of State Weakness in Developing World, 2008			Corruption Perceptions Index		
Rank	Country	Overall Score	Year	Rank	No. of Countries Surveyed
1	Somalia	0.52	2008	176	180
2	Afghanistan	1.65	2007	172	180
3	Dem. Rep. Congo	1.67	2006	No data	163
4	Iraq	3.11	2005	117	159
5	Burundi	3.21			

* Brookings surveyed 141 nations, allocating a score of 0-10 points for each of four categories: economic, political, security and social welfare. Benin had the median score, 6.36; the Slovak Republic was the least weak, with a score of 9.41.

Source: "Afghan Index: Tracking Variables of Reconstruction and Security in Post-9/11 Afghanistan," Brookings Institution, July 15, 2009

enable the country to function without us. We can keep the patient on life support by providing security assistance indefinitely, but if you don't get an improvement in governance, you'll never be able to take the patient off the ventilator. Of those two challenges, providing security we know how to do. It's expensive, it's hard, it takes a long time, but if we invest the resources there's a substantial probability that we can provide security through our assistance. Governance improvement is a more uncertain undertaking. There are a lot of things we can do that we have not yet done to improve governance, but ultimately the more uncertain of the two requirements is the governance part." [21]

Another member of McChrystal's strategic assessment group, Anthony Cordesman, a scholar with the Center for Strategic and International Studies, also believes the war is winnable, but that the United States and its allies must "act quickly and decisively" in a number of ways, including "giving the Afghan government the necessary legitimacy and capacity" at national, regional and local levels, reducing official corruption and "creating a level of actual governance that can ensure security and stability." [22]

CHRONOLOGY

1838-1930s *Afghanistan gains independence, but ethnic and religious conflicts persist.*

1838-42; 1878 Afghan forces defeat Britain in two wars, but Britain retains control of Afghanistan's foreign affairs under 1879 treaty.

1893 British draw Afghan-Pakistan border, split Pashtun ethnic group.

1919 Afghanistan gains independence after Third Anglo-Afghan War.

1934 Diplomatic relations between United States and Afghanistan established.

1950s-1980s *Political chaos wracks Afghanistan during Cold War.*

1950s-1960s Soviets and Americans funnel aid to Afghanistan.

1953 Gen. Mohammed Daoud becomes prime minister, seeks aid from Soviets, institutes reforms.

1964 New constitution establishes constitutional monarchy.

1973 Daoud overthrows king, is killed in Marxist coup in 1978.

1979-1989 Civil war rages between communist-backed government and U.S.-backed Mujahedeen. Soviets withdraw in 1989, 10 years after they invaded.

1990-2001 *Taliban emerges amid postwar chaos; al Qaeda forges ties with Afghan militants.*

1992 Burhanuddin Rabbani, an ethnic Tajik, rises to power, declares Afghanistan an Islamic state.

1994 Taliban emerges; the militant Islamist group is mainly Pashtun.

1996 Taliban gains control of Kabul.

1996 Taliban leader Mullah Omar invites al Qaeda leader Osama bin Laden to live with him in Kandahar.

1997 Osama bin Laden declares war on U.S. in interview with CNN.

2001 U.S. and coalition forces invade Afghanistan on Oct. 7 after Sept. 11 terrorist attacks; Taliban retreats.

2002-Present *U.S.-led invasion of Iraq shifts focus off Afghanistan; Taliban resurges.*

2002 Hamid Karzai elected head of Afghan Transitional Authority; International Security Assistance Force deployed in Kabul; international donors pledge $4.5 billion for reconstruction.

2003 U.S.-led invasion of Iraq begins, leading to charges Bush administration shifted focus and resources away from Afghanistan; commission drafts new Afghan constitution.

2004 Draft constitution approved; Karzai elected president; Pakistani nuclear scientist A. Q. Khan admits international nuclear-weapons trading; President Pervez Musharraf pardons him.

2005 Afghanistan holds its first parliamentary elections in some three decades.

2006 NATO takes over Afghan security; donors pledge $10.5 billion more.

2007 Musharraf and Karzai agree to coordinate efforts to fight Taliban, al Qaeda; allied troops kill Taliban leader Mullah Dadullah.

2008 More than 50 die in suicide bombing of Indian Embassy in Kabul in July. . . . More than 160 die in November terror attacks in Mumbai, India; India accuses Pakistani militants of carrying out the attacks; in July 2009 a young Pakistani admits to taking part in the attacks as a soldier for Lashkar-e-Taiba, a Pakistan-based Islamic group.

2009 Obama announces new strategy "to disrupt, dismantle and defeat al Qaeda in Pakistan and Afghanistan"; Gen. Stanley McChrystal replaces Gen. David McKiernan as top U.S. commander in Afghanistan; Marines attack Taliban in southern Helmand Province; July is bloodiest month for U.S. and foreign troops in Afghanistan, with 43 Americans killed. . . . Concern grows over security surrounding Aug. 20 presidential election.

Are troop levels in Afghanistan adequate?

When the Marine assault in Helmand Province got under way this summer, only about 400 effective Afghan fighters had joined the American force of nearly 4,000, according to *The New York Times*, citing information from Gen. Nicholson. [23]

Commanders expressed concern that not enough homegrown forces were available to fight the insurgency and build ties with the local population. Gen. Nicholson said, "I'm not going to sugarcoat it. The fact of the matter is, we don't have enough Afghan forces. And I'd like more." [24] Capt. Brian Huysman, a Marine company commander, said the lack of Afghan forces "is absolutely our Achilles' heel." [25]

"We've seen a shift over the past few years to put a lot more resources, including money and attention, toward building Afghan national security forces, army and police forces," Seth Jones, a political scientist at the RAND Corporation, told the "NewsHour" on PBS. "I think the problem that we're running into on the ground in Afghanistan, though: There are not enough Afghan national security forces and coalition forces to do what Gen. McChrystal and others want, and that is to protect the local population." [26]

Worries about the size of the Afghan force have been accompanied by concerns over whether U.S. forces are adequate to overcome the Taliban threat and secure local areas long enough to ensure security and build governance capabilities.

According to a report this summer by veteran *Washington Post* reporter Bob Woodward, National Security Adviser James L. Jones told U.S. commanders in Afghanistan the Obama administration wants to keep troop levels steady for now. Gen. Nicholson, though, told Jones that he was "a little light," suggesting he could use more troops, and that "we don't have enough force to go everywhere," Woodward reported. [27]

"The question of the force level for Afghanistan . . . is not settled and will probably be hotly debated over the next year," Woodward wrote. "One senior military officer said privately that the United States would have to deploy a force of more than 100,000 to execute the counterinsurgency strategy of holding areas and towns after clearing out the Taliban insurgents. That is at least 32,000 more than the 68,000 currently authorized." [28]

Adm. Mike Mullen, chairman of the Joint Chiefs of Staff, said on CBS News' "Face the Nation" on July 5

that in southern Afghanistan, where the toughest fighting is expected, "we have enough forces now not just to clear an area but to hold it so we can build after. And that's really the strategy." He noted that Gen. McChrystal was due to produce his 60-day assessment of the war this summer, adding "we're all committed to getting this right and resourcing it properly." [29]

But senior military officials told *The Washington Post* later that week that McChrystal had concluded Afghan security forces must be greatly expanded if the war is to be won. According to officials, the *Post* said, "such an expansion would require spending billions more than the $7.5 billion the administration has budgeted annually to build up the Afghan army and police over the next several years, and the likely deployment of thousands more U.S. troops as trainers and advisers." [30]

As combat has intensified this spring and summer and more troops entered the war zone, commanders focused on one of the most pernicious threats to the U.S.-led counterinsurgency strategy: the potential for civilian casualties, which can undermine efforts to build trust and cooperation with the local population. Concern over civilian deaths rose sharply in May, when a high-profile U.S. air strike in western Farah province killed at least 26 civilians, according to American investigators. [31] This spring commanders instituted strict new combat rules aimed at minimizing civilian deaths, and Defense Secretary Robert M. Gates has called such casualties "one of our greatest strategic vulnerabilities." [32]

While some fear that the deployment of more troops to Afghanistan could heighten civilian casualties, others say the opposite is true.

"In fact, the presence of more boots on the ground is likely to *reduce* civilian casualties, because historically it has been the over-reliance on American air strikes — as a result of too few ground forces — which has been the key cause of civilian deaths," wrote Bergen of the New America Foundation. [33]

Should the United States negotiate with the Taliban?

In early March, shortly before announcing his new strategy for Afghanistan and Pakistan, *The New York Times* reported that Obama, in an interview aboard Air Force One, "opened the door to a reconciliation process in which the American military would reach out to moderate elements of the Taliban." [34]

The Many Faces of the Taliban

Adherents include violent warlords and Islamist extremists.

When President Barack Obama announced his administration's new Afghanistan strategy in March, he declared that if the Afghan government were to fall to the Taliban, the country would "again be a base for terrorists who want to kill as many of our people as they possibly can."[1]

But defining "the Taliban" is tricky. Far from a monolithic organization, the Taliban is a many-headed hydra, and a shadowy one at that. It is a mélange of insurgents and militants, ranging from high-profile Islamist extremists and violent warlords to local villagers fighting for cash or glory. Western military strategists hope to kill or capture the most fanatical elements of the Taliban while persuading others to abandon their arms and work within Afghanistan's political system.

"You have a whole spectrum of bad guys that sort of get lumped into this catch-all term of Taliban . . . because they're launching bullets at us," a senior Defense official told *The Boston Globe*. "There are many of the groups that can probably be peeled off."

The Defense official quoted by *The Globe* was among "hundreds of intelligence operatives and analysts" in the United States and abroad involved in a broad study of tribes tied to the Taliban, the newspaper said. The aim is to figure out whether diplomatic or economic efforts can persuade some to break away, according to the paper. The examination "is expected to culminate later this year in a detailed, highly classified analysis of the different factions of the Taliban and other groups," *The Globe* said.[2]

Many experts break down the Taliban into four main groups:

• **The Early Taliban** — Insurgents emerged under Mullah Omar and other leaders during the civil war that wracked Afghanistan in the mid-1990s, following the end of the Soviet occupation of the country. Early members were a mix of fighters who battled the Soviets in the 1980s and Pashtuns who attended religious schools in Pakistan, where they were aided by the Pakistani Inter-Services Intelligence agency.[3]

• **The Pakistani Taliban** emerged under a separate organizational structure in 2002, when Pakistani forces entered the country's tribal region in the northwest to pursue Islamist militants.[4]

"At the time of the U.S.-led military campaign in Afghanistan in late 2001, allies and sympathizers of the Taliban in Pakistan were not identified as 'Taliban' themselves," wrote Hassan Abbas, a research fellow at Harvard's Belfer Center for Science and International Affairs. "That reality is now a distant memory. Today, Pakistan's indigenous Taliban are an effective fighting force and are engaging the Pakistani military on one side and NATO forces on the other."[5]

• **Hizb-e-Islami** — Formed by the brutal warlord Gulbuddin Hekmatyar, the group is "a prominent ally under the Taliban umbrella," says *Christian Science Monitor* journalist Anand Gopal.[6]

Hizb-e-Islami ("Islamic Party") was allied with the United States and Pakistan during the decade-long Soviet war, Gopal wrote, but after the 2001 U.S. invasion of Afghanistan a segment led by Hekmatyar joined the insurgency. *The New York Times* has described Hekmatyar as having "a record of extreme brutality."[7]

Hizb-e-Islami fighters have for years "had a reputation for being more educated and worldly than their Taliban

In broaching the idea of negotiating with the Taliban, the president cited successes in Iraq in separating moderate insurgents from the more extreme factions of al Qaeda. Still, he was cautious about reconciliation prospects in Afghanistan.

"The situation in Afghanistan is, if anything, more complex" than the one in Iraq, he said. "You have a less governed region, a history of fierce independence among tribes. Those tribes are multiple and sometimes operate at cross-purposes, and so figuring all that out is going to be much more of a challenge."[35]

Nevertheless, the notion of seeking some sort of reconciliation with elements of the Afghan Taliban has received fresh attention recently.

counterparts, who are often illiterate farmers," Gopal wrote last year. In the 1970s, Hekmatyar studied engineering at Kabul University, "where he made a name for himself by hurling acid in the faces of unveiled women."[8]

Today the group has a "strong presence in the provinces near Kabul and in Pashtun pockets in the country's north and northeast," Gopal wrote. In 2008 Hizb-e-Islami participated in an assassination attempt on President Hamid Karzai and was behind a 2008 ambush that killed 10 NATO soldiers, according to Gopal.

"Its guerrillas fight under the Taliban banner, although independently and with a separate command structure," Gopal wrote. "Like the Taliban, its leaders see their task as restoring Afghan sovereignty as well as establishing an Islamic state in Afghanistan."

- **The Haqqani network** — Some of the most notorious terrorist actions in recent months have been linked to the network, including the kidnapping of a *New York Times* reporter and the abduction of a U.S. soldier. Haqqani is "not traditional Taliban, they're more strongly associated with al Qaeda," said Haroun Mir, director of Afghanistan's Center for Research and Policy Studies in Kabul. [9]

Thought to control major parts of eastern Afghanistan, the network in recent years "has emerged . . . as a powerful antagonist to U.S. efforts to stabilize that country and root out insurgent havens in the lawless tribal areas of Pakistan," according to *The Washington Post*. [10]

The network is controlled by Jalaluddin Haqqani and his son, Sirajuddin, the *Post* said. Analysts call the son a "terrorist mastermind," according to *The Christian Science Monitor*. [11]

New York Times reporter David Rohde, who was abducted in Logar Province in Afghanistan and taken across the Pakistani border to North Waziristan, was held by the Haqqani network until he escaped in June after seven months in captivity. [12]

The network also is suspected of the suicide bombing of the Indian Embassy in Kabul in July 2008 that left more than 50 dead, *The Post* said. [13]

According to Gopal, "The Haqqanis command the lion's share of foreign fighters operating in [Afghanistan] and tend to be even more extreme than their Taliban counterparts. Unlike most of the Taliban and Hizb-e-Islami, elements of the Haqqani network cooperate closely with al Qaeda." [14]

[1] "Remarks by the President on a New Strategy for Afghanistan and Pakistan," The White House, March 27, 2009, www.whitehouse.gov.

[2] Bryan Bender, "U.S. probes divisions within Taliban," *The Boston Globe*, May 24, 2009, p. 1.

[3] See Eben Kaplan and Greg Bruno, "The Taliban in Afghanistan," Council on Foreign Relations, July 2, 2008, www.cfr.org/publication/10551/taliban_in_afghanistan.html.

[4] *Ibid.*

[5] Hassan Abbas, "A Profile of Tehrik-i-Taliban Pakistan," *CTC Sentinel*, Vol. 1, Issue 2, pp. 1-4, www.ctc.usma.edu/sentinel/CTCSentinel-Vol1Iss2.pdf.

[6] Anand Gopal, "Briefing: Who Are the Taliban?" *The Christian Science Monitor*, April 16, 2009, http://anandgopal.com/briefing-who-are-the-taliban/.

[7] Dexter Filkins, "Taliban said to be in talks with intermediaries about peace; U.S. withdrawal is called a focus," *The New York Times,* May 21, 2009, p. 4.

[8] Anand Gopal, "Who Are the Taliban?" *The Nation*, Dec. 22, 2008, www.thenation.com/doc/20081222/gopal.

[9] Quoted in Issam Ahmed, "Captured U.S. soldier in Taliban video: Held by Haqqani network?" *The Christian Science Monitor*, Global News blog, July 19, 2009, http://features.csmonitor.com/globalnews/2009/07/19/captured-us-soldier-in-taliban-video-held-by-haqqani-network/.

[10] Keith B. Richburg, "Reporters Escape Taliban Captors," *The Washington Post*, June 21, 2009, p. A1.

[11] Ahmed, *op. cit.*

[12] *Ibid.*

[13] Richburg, *op. cit.*

[14] Gopal, *The Nation, op. cit.*

Opponents of the idea argue that it could project an image of weakness and embolden the insurgency and that Taliban leaders cannot be trusted to uphold any deals they may make.

But proponents argue the Taliban is not a unified bloc, but rather an amalgam that includes those who joined the insurgency out of frustration at the lack of security in their villages or because they were forcibly drafted, among other reasons. (*See sidebar, p. 360.*)

"If you look at a security map of Afghanistan between, say, 2003 and today, you have this creep of the insurgency sort of moving up from the south and east into other parts of the country," J. Alexander Thier, senior rule of law adviser with the United States Institute of Peace. That trend, he says, suggests many local communities and commanders that may have once supported the Afghan government have turned neutral or are actively supporting the Taliban. "There's real room in there to deal with their grievances and concerns about security and justice and the rule of law so as to change that tide."

Thier says he's not talking about seeking a "grand bargain" with the Taliban leadership now ensconced in Pakistan. "If what you're envisioning is [Afghan President] Karzai and [Taliban leader] Mullah Omar sitting on the deck of an aircraft carrier signing an armistice, I don't think that's feasible or realistic," he says. What is feasible are "micro level" negotiations.

"There is an enormous opportunity to work on what I would call mid- and low-level insurgents who, for a variety of reasons, were likely not engaged in the insurgency just a few years ago and were either pro-government or at least neutral. And I think they can and should be brought back to that position."

In an article this summer in *Foreign Affairs*, Fotini Christia, an assistant professor of political science at MIT, and Michael Semple, former deputy to the European Union special representative to Afghanistan, wrote that while "sending more troops is necessary to tip the balance of power against the insurgents, the move will have a lasting impact only if it is accompanied by a political 'surge,' a committed effort to persuade large groups of Taliban fighters to put down their arms and give up the fight."[36]

For reconciliation to work, say Fotini and Semple, Afghans first must feel secure. "The situation on the ground will need to be stabilized, and the Taliban must be reminded that they have no prospect of winning their current military campaign," they wrote. "If the Afghan government offers reconciliation as its carrot, it must also present force as its stick — hence the importance of sending more U.S. troops to Afghanistan, but also, in the long term, the importance of building up Afghanistan's own security forces. Reconciliation needs to be viewed as part of a larger military-political strategy to defeat the insurgency."

Some favor waiting to begin negotiation efforts, while others say they should occur simultaneously with the military campaign. Riedel of Brookings says he sees reason to believe that "a fair number" of Taliban foot soldiers and local commanders are not deeply dedicated to the core extremist cause as espoused by leaders such as Omar. Many rank and file Taliban may be "in this for one reason or another" — perhaps because "their tribe is aligned with the Taliban for local reasons, they're getting paid by the Taliban to do this better than they could be paid by anyone else, or simply because if you're a 17-year-old Pashtun male in Kandahar, fighting is kind of how you get your right of passage," Riedel says.

If the momentum changes on the battlefield "and it's a lot more dangerous to support the Taliban," Riedel continues, "my sense . . . is that these people will either defect or simply go home — they just won't fight."

Still, he says, it's not yet time to begin negotiations. First must come intelligence networks and greater political savvy in each district and province to capitalize on any Taliban inclinations to bend, he argues. "That is primarily an Afghan job, because they're the only people who are going to know the ins and outs of this. That's one of the things the new [U.S.] command arrangement needs to focus on the most. I don't think we're there. This requires really intense local information."

Yet, while the hour for negotiating may not be ripe, "the time is now to do the homework to do that," Riedel says, in order to develop "fine-grained knowledge of what's going on."

But Rajan Menon, a professor of international relations at Lehigh University, says "not coupling" the military campaign against the Taliban "with an olive branch is probably not effective."

Because huge challenges face the military operation — from the threat of civilian casualties to the weakness of the country's central government — the prospect of a long and costly war looms, he says. To avoid that, Menon says, the military effort should be occurring simultaneously with one aimed at encouraging "pragmatic" elements of the Taliban to buy into a process in which they "have to sell [their] ideas in the political marketplace."

The Taliban pragmatists, he says, would be offered a choice: either a long, open-ended war with heavy insurgent casualties or the opportunity to enter the political process as a group seeking victory through the ballot box.

"The question is, can you fracture the [insurgency] movement by laying down terms that are pretty stringent and test their will," Menon says. Nobody knows if the arms-and-olive branch approach would work, he says, but "you lose nothing by trying."

BACKGROUND

'Graveyard of Empires'

Afghanistan has long been known as the "crossroads of Central Asia," an apt name given the long list of outsiders who have ventured across its borders. It also is known as the "graveyard of empires," reflecting the difficulty faced by would-be conquerors of its remote terrain and disparate peoples.

The list is long. It includes the Persian king Darius I in the 6th century B.C. and the Macedonian conqueror Alexander the Great in 328 B.C., followed by the Scythians, White Huns, Turks, Arabs (who brought Islam in the 7th century A.D.), and the Mongol warrior Genghis Khan in 1219 A.D. [37]

Afghanistan's more recent history is a story of struggle against foreign domination, internal wrangling between reformists and traditionalists, coups, assassinations and war.

Modern Afghanistan began to take shape in the late 19th century, after a bitter fight for influence in Central Asia between the burgeoning British Empire and czarist Russia in what is known as "the Great Game." The contest led to Anglo-Afghan wars in 1839 and 1878. In the first, Afghan warriors forced the British into a deadly retreat from Kabul. The Afghans also had the upper hand over the British in the second war, which resulted in a treaty guaranteeing internal autonomy to Afghanistan while the British had control of its foreign affairs.

In 1880 Amir Abdur Rahman rose to the throne, reigning until 1901. Known as the "Iron Amir," he sought to institute reforms and weaken Pashtun resistance to centralized power but used methods, later emulated by the Taliban, to bring Uzbeks, Hazaras and Tajiks under Kabul's authority. [38] During his reign, Britain drew the so-called Durand Line separating Afghanistan from what was then India and later became Pakistan.

Rahman's son succeeded him but was assassinated in 1919. Under his successor, Amanullah — Rahman's grandson — Afghanistan gained full independence as a result of the Third Anglo War. Amanullah brought reforms that included ties with other countries and coeducational schools. But the moves alienated traditionalists, and Amanullah was forced to abdicate in 1929. His successor and cousin, Nadir Shah, was assassinated in 1933.

His death led to the 40-year reign of Crown Prince Mohammad Zahir Shah, Nadir Shah's son, who assumed power at 19.

Chaos and War

Under Zahir, Afghanistan sought to liberalize its political system. But the effort collapsed in the 1970s, and the country became a battleground between communist-backed leftists and a U.S.-backed Islamist resistance movement.

Afghanistan had tilted toward the Soviets in the Cold War era of the 1950s, partly because of U.S. ties to Pakistan, a country created by the partition of India in 1947. Afghan leaders wanted independence or at least autonomy for the Pashtun-dominated areas beyond the Durand Line.

Border tensions led Kabul to seek help from the Soviets, who responded with development loans and other aid in 1950. The United States sought to counter the Soviet

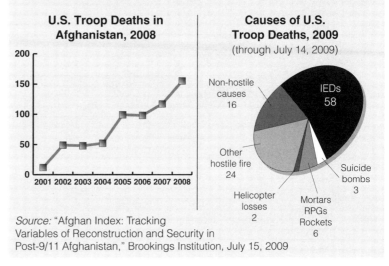

U.S. Troop Deaths Rose Steadily

U.S. troop fatalities have risen steadily since the United States entered Afghanistan in 2001 (graph at left). So far this year, IEDs (improvised explosive devices) caused slightly more than half the deaths (right).

U.S. Troop Deaths in Afghanistan, 2008

2001 2002 2003 2004 2005 2006 2007 2008

Causes of U.S. Troop Deaths, 2009
(through July 14, 2009)

Non-hostile causes 16

IEDs 58

Other hostile fire 24

Suicide bombs 3

Helicopter losses 2

Mortars RPGs Rockets 6

Source: "Afghan Index: Tracking Variables of Reconstruction and Security in Post-9/11 Afghanistan," Brookings Institution, July 15, 2009

Afghan President Hamid Karzai may face a runoff after the presidential election on Aug. 20, partly because many Afghans are looking for alternative leadership in the face of sustained insurgent violence, economic stagnation and political drift.

Union's influence, and in the 1960s both countries were helping to build up Afghanistan's infrastructure.

Between 1956 and 1978, according to Pakistani journalist Ahmed Rashid, Afghanistan received some $533 million in economic aid from the United States and $2.5 billion in both economic and military aid from the Soviets.[39]

In the 1960s Zahir introduced a constitutional monarchy and pressed for political freedoms that included new rights for women in voting, schooling and employment. "These changes, in a deeply traditional Islamic society, were not popular with everyone," the *Times* noted in a 2007 obituary of Zahir. "But his years were characterized by a rare long period of peace. This tranquility is recalled now with immense nostalgia. On the other hand, peace was not accompanied by prosperity, and the king was faulted for not developing the economy."[40]

Zahir's "experiment in democracy" did not lead to many lasting reforms, but "it permitted the growth of unofficial extremist parties on both the left and the right," including the communist People's Democratic Party of Afghanistan that was ideologically aligned with the Soviets, the U.S. State Department noted. The party split into rival groups in 1967 in a rift that "reflected ethnic, class and ideological divisions within Afghan society."[41]

In 1973 Zahir was ousted while in Europe for medical treatment. His cousin, former Prime Minister Sardar Mohammad Daoud Khan, whom Zahir had forced out in the 1960s, seized power in a bloodless coup. Daoud tried to institute reforms, but political unrest persisted.

He aligned closely with the Soviets, but his efforts to build his own political party and forge some links with the United States alienated communist radicals. In 1978, the People's Democratic Party overthrew Daoud, killing him and most of his family.

Soviet Invasion

More upheaval followed. The new leader, Nur Mohammad Taraki, imposed Marxist reforms that angered Islamic traditionalists and ethnic leaders, sparking revolts. Taraki was ousted and killed, and his successor, Hafizullah Amin, who resisted Soviet pressure to moderate his policies, was himself executed in 1979 by the Soviets.

Shortly before Amin's killing, the Soviets mounted a massive invasion of Afghanistan, starting a decade-long war that would permanently alter Afghanistan's profile in world affairs. In Amin's place, the Soviets installed Babrak Karmal. With Soviet military aid, he tried to impose authority throughout Afghanistan but ran into stiff opposition, especially in rural regions. An Islamist resistance movement called the Mujahedeen began receiving weapons and training from the United States and other countries in 1984, and soon the Soviet invasion was on the ropes.

In 1986 Karmal was replaced by Muhammad Najibullah, former head of the Afghan secret police, but the war continued to sour for the Soviets, who also were dealing with powerful political opposition at home. In 1988 Moscow signed agreements, along with the United States, Pakistan and Afghanistan, calling for an end to foreign intervention in Afghanistan. The Soviets withdrew early the following year, and in 1991 the USSR collapsed.

The Soviet invasion affirmed the idea of Afghanistan as a "graveyard" for invaders. Between 1979 and the Soviet withdrawal in 1989, some 14,500 Soviets died.[42] For the Afghan people, however, the war was a bloodbath that all but destroyed the economy and educational system and uprooted much of the population. The U.S. State Department estimates a million died.[43] Some estimates are higher.

Yet the end of the Soviet invasion brought no peace, but rather more chaos. After the Soviets departed, President George H. W. Bush withdrew support from Afghanistan, setting the stage for the conflict engulfing Afghanistan today. "Having won the Cold War," journalist Rashid wrote, "Washington had no further interest in Afghanistan or the region. This left a critical power vacuum for which the United States would pay an enormously high price a decade later." [44]

When the Soviet Union collapsed and the United States disengaged from Afghanistan, they left a country "that had become a cockpit for regional competition, a shattered state with no functioning security forces or civilian political process, a highly mobilized and armed population increasingly dependent on international organizations and cash for livelihood (including through the drug trade), and a multiplicity of armed groups linked transnationally to both state and non-state patrons," wrote Barnett Rubin, director of studies at the Center on International Cooperation at New York University, where he directs a program on Afghan reconstruction. [45]

The Mujahedeen were not a party to the accord leading to Soviet withdrawal, and through the early 1990s they continued fighting the Najibullah regime. In 1992 his government fell, and Burhanuddin Rabbani, an ethnic Tajik, became president. He declared Afghanistan an "Islamic state" but failed to ensure order.

By 1994 Afghanistan "was fast disintegrating," Rashid wrote. "Warlord fiefdoms ruled vast swathes of countryside. President Rabbani . . . governed only Kabul and the northeast of the country, while the west, centered on Herat, was under the control of warlord Ismael Khan. Six provinces in the north were ruled by the Uzbek general Rashid Dostum, and central Afghanistan was in the hands of the Hazaras. In the Pashtun south and east there was even greater fragmentation. . . . Warlords seized people's homes and farms for no reason, raped their daughters, abused and robbed the population and taxed travelers at will. Instead of refugees returning to Afghanistan, more began to leave the south for Pakistan." [46]

In 1994 a militant Islamist group — known as the Taliban and made up mainly of Pashtuns — sprang up in the south to oppose Rabbani. Their rise stemmed directly from the chaos wracking Afghanistan, Rashid wrote. "Frustrated young men who had fought against the Soviets and then returned to madrassas in Pakistan to resume their religious studies or to their villages in Afghanistan gathered around their elders demanding action." [47]

The Taliban took over Kabul in 1996, and by the early 2000s Rabbani's anti-Taliban Northern Alliance was limited to a slice of northern territory. "The Taliban instituted a repressive version of sharia law that outlawed music,

banned women from working or going to school and prohibited freedom of the press," wrote Jones, the RAND political scientist. "While it was a detestable regime that committed gross human rights violations, the Taliban succeeded in establishing law and order throughout most of the country." [48]

At the same time, the Taliban was forging links to al Qaeda. In 1996 Taliban leader Mullah Omar invited Osama bin Laden to stay with him in Kandahar, and even though "the CIA already considered bin Laden a threat . . ., he was left alone to ingratiate himself with Omar by providing money, fighters and ideological advice to the Taliban," Rashid wrote. "Bin Laden gathered the Arabs left behind in Afghanistan and Pakistan from the war against the Soviets, enlisted more militants from Arab countries, and established a new global terrorist infrastructure." [49]

The al Qaeda threat reached full force with the Sept. 11, 2001, attacks on the United States. In October President George W. Bush responded with a military assault called Operation Enduring Freedom. The Taliban promptly collapsed, and its leadership, along with that of al Qaeda, fled, in the view of many analysts, to Pakistan.

Yet still more trouble was to follow.

A Weakening Government

"The collapse of the Taliban government . . . created a condition of emerging anarchy," Jones wrote. In late 2001 a United Nations-sponsored conference in Bonn, Germany, laid down a process to rebuild Afghanistan's political system. With the Bonn agreement, "on paper, Afghanistan looked like it had a central government," Jones wrote. But "in practice . . ., Afghanistan had a fragile government that became weaker over time." [50]

The new government couldn't provide essential services, especially in rural areas, and a 2005 World Bank study found that "the urban elite" were the main beneficiaries of help, Jones wrote. [51] Meanwhile, the Afghan government had various problems, including the inability to provide security outside of Kabul, in large measure due to "the inability of the U.S. government to build competent Afghan security forces, especially the police." [52]

American force levels were low, too, with "the number of U.S. troops per capita in Afghanistan . . . significantly less than in almost every state-building effort since World War II," Jones wrote. [53] Moreover, the United States gave "significant assistance to local warlords, further undermining governance and weakening the ability of the Afghan state to establish law and order."[54]

The Taliban rebounded, aided by what critics have called a lack of focus by the Bush administration after its decision to invade Iraq in 2003. In Afghanistan, reconstruction and security issues were left unattended, critics say, leaving an opening for the Taliban — along with criminals, warlords, drug traffickers and others — to assert brutal control. Afghan opium production soared, al Qaeda sanctuaries in the border region of Pakistan festered and once again the region threatened to unleash a new wave of global terrorism.

The threat came not only from Afghanistan, but Pakistan, too.

In an article last year on the emboldened Taliban and al Qaeda forces in the Pakistani border region, celebrated *New York Times* war correspondent Dexter Filkins noted that Islamist militants continued to be backed by Pakistani military and intelligence services. Then, in 1994, came Pakistan's "most fateful move," he wrote. Concerned about the mayhem that swept through Afghanistan after the Soviet withdrawal, Pakistani Prime Minister Benazir Bhutto and her administration intervened on behalf of the Taliban, Filkins wrote.

"We created the Taliban," Bhutto's interior minister, Nasrullah Babar, told Filkins. "Mrs. Bhutto had a vision: that through a peaceful Afghanistan, Pakistan could extend its influence into the resource-rich territories of Central Asia." Her dream didn't materialize — the Taliban's conquest of Afghanistan fell short, and Bhutto was assassinated in late 2007. But as Filkins noted, the Taliban training camps, sometimes supported by Pakistani intelligence officials, "were beacons to Islamic militants from around the world."[55]

Concerns persist about Pakistan's intentions and security capabilities. In recent weeks, as militants threatened Islamabad and other Pakistani cities, Pakistan has gone after insurgents in the Swat Valley and elsewhere. But Pakistani officials also have criticized U.S. attacks on insurgent strongholds using unmanned drone planes.

The big question, as posed by Filkins and others, is whether Pakistan is willing — or able — to control the radical forces within its border region. "This was not supposed to be a major worry," Filkins wrote, noting that after the Sept. 11 attacks Pakistani President Pervez Musharraf backed the United States, helped find al Qaeda

suspects, attacked militants in Pakistan's remote tribal areas and vowed to fight terrorism — all in return for $10 billion in U.S. aid since 2001.

But Pakistani military and civilian leaders have survived by playing a "double game," Filkins wrote, promising the United States they were cracking down on militants, and sometimes doing so, while also allowing, and even helping, the same militants.

One reason for the "double game" is Pakistan's long-standing tension with India, especially over the disputed border region of Kashmir. "You can't address Pakistan without dealing with India," says Riedel, the Brookings scholar.

Some experts say Pakistan views its support of the Taliban as a hedge against an India-friendly government coming to power in Afghanistan.

"The Pakistanis have convinced themselves that India's objective is a friendly Afghanistan that can pose a second front against Pakistan," says Riedel. "They see the Afghan Taliban, in particular, as a very useful asset. It keeps Afghanistan from becoming an Indian client state, and their conviction is that . . . it's only a matter of time" until the United States leaves Afghanistan. The Pakistanis believe that "if they wait it out, their client will be the dominant power at least in southern and eastern Afghanistan."

The Cato Institute's Innocent says the Obama administration has made a "profound strategic miscalculation" by not recognizing how much Pakistani leaders fear a non-Pashtun, India-leaning government assuming power in Kabul.

India has used its influence in Afghanistan, she says, to funnel weapons to a separatist movement in southwest Pakistan's sprawling Baluchistan region — a movement that some say could pose an existential threat to Pakistan. That, in turn, has given Pakistan an incentive to keep Afghanistan from growing closer to India.

Says Innocent, "This rivalry between [Pakistan and India] is the biggest impediment to stabilizing Afghanistan."

CURRENT SITUATION
Measurable Metrics

In the weeks leading up to this summer's Helmand River operation, Defense Secretary Gates expressed optimism

Should the president announce an Afghanistan exit strategy?

YES
Malou Innocent
Foreign Policy Analyst
Cato Institute

Written for *CQ Researcher*, July 2009

No strategic, political or economic gains could outweigh the costs of America maintaining an indefinite military presence in Afghanistan. Washington can continue to disrupt terrorist havens by monitoring the region with unmanned aerial vehicles, retaining advisers for training Afghan forces and using covert operatives against specific targets.

Many policy makers and prominent opinion leaders are pushing for a large-scale, long-term military presence in Afghanistan. But none of their rationales for such a heavy presence withstands close scrutiny.

Al Qaeda poses a manageable security problem, not an existential threat to America. Washington's response, with an open-ended mission in Afghanistan, is both unnecessary and unsustainable.

Policy makers also tend to conflate al Qaeda with indigenous Pashtun-dominated militias, such as the Taliban. America's security, however, will not necessarily be at risk even if an oppressive regime takes over a contiguous fraction of Afghan territory.

Additionally, the argument that America has a moral obligation to prevent the reemergence of reprehensible groups like the Taliban seems instead a justification for the perpetuation of American empire. After all, America never made a substantive policy shift toward or against the Taliban's misogynistic, oppressive and militant Islamic regime when it controlled Afghanistan in the 1990s. Thus, the present moral outrage against the group can be interpreted as opportunistic.

Some policy makers claim the war is worth waging because terrorists flourish in failed states. But that cannot account for terrorists who thrive in states with the sovereignty to reject external interference. That is one reason why militants find sanctuary in Pakistan. In fact, attempts to stabilize Afghanistan destabilize Pakistan. Amassing troops in Afghanistan feeds the perception of a foreign occupation, spawning more terrorist recruits for Pakistani militias and thus placing undue stress on an already-weakened, nuclear-armed nation.

It's also important to recognize that Afghanistan's land-locked position in Central Asia will forever render it vulnerable to meddling from surrounding states. This factor will make sealing the country's borders from terrorists impossible.

Finally, Americans should not fear appearing "weak" after withdrawal. The United States accounts for almost half of the world's military spending, wields one of the planet's largest nuclear arsenals and can project its power around the globe. Remaining in Afghanistan is more likely to weaken the United States militarily and economically than would withdrawal.

NO
Ilan Berman
Vice President for Policy
American Foreign Policy Council

Written for *CQ Researcher*, July 2009

It has been called the "graveyard of empires," a place that for thousands of years has stymied invading armies. Today, Afghanistan remains one of the West's most vexing international security conundrums — and a pressing foreign policy challenge for the Obama administration.

Indeed, for almost as long as Obama has been in office, critics have counseled the new U.S. president to set a date certain for an American exit from Afghanistan. To his credit, Mr. Obama has done no such thing. To the contrary, through the "Af-Pak" strategy unveiled in March, the White House has effectively doubled down on the American investment in Afghanistan's security. It has done so for two principal reasons.

The first has to do with Afghanistan's importance to the overall struggle against radical Islam. In the years before Sept. 11, Afghanistan became an incubator of international terrorism. And the sinister synergy created there between al Qaeda and the ruling Taliban movement was directly responsible for the most devastating terrorist attack in American history. Preventing a repeat occurrence remains an overriding priority, which is why Washington has committed to propping up the fragile government of Afghan President Hamid Karzai with the troops and training necessary to hold its ground.

The second is an understanding that Afghanistan is essentially a derivative problem. Much of the instability that exists there today is a function of radicalism nurtured next door, in Pakistan. The Taliban, after all, was an invention of Pakistan's Inter-Services Intelligence back in the mid-1990s, and Islamabad's intelligence czars (as well as their military counterparts) remain heavily invested in its future. Today, the Taliban poses perhaps a greater threat to Pakistan's own stability than to that of Afghanistan. But a retraction of U.S. and allied forces from the latter is sure to create a political vacuum that Islamic radicals will be all too eager to exploit.

These realities have defined the Obama administration's approach. Unlike previous foreign powers that have gotten involved in Afghanistan, the United States today is interested simply in what the military calls "area denial." The goal is not to conquer and claim, but to deny the Taliban the necessary breathing room to regroup and re-entrench.

Setting a firm date for an American withdrawal would fundamentally undermine that objective. It would also serve to provide regional radicals with far greater certainty that the U.S. investment in Afghanistan's stability is both limited and reversible.

about the war in Afghanistan, but acknowledged that the American public's patience with its progress could be limited.

"I think what the people in the United States want to see is the momentum shifting to see that the strategies that we're following are working," he said on CBS' "60 Minutes." "And that's why I've said in nine months to a year, we need to evaluate how we're doing." [56]

Part of that evaluation will be done through "metrics," statistical measurements on everything from civilian casualties to the strength of the Afghan National Army. The approach is part of the Obama strategy.

"Going forward, we will not blindly stay the course," Obama said, but rather "we will set clear metrics to measure progress and hold ourselves accountable. We'll consistently assess our efforts to train Afghan security forces and our progress in combating insurgents. We will measure the growth of Afghanistan's economy and its illicit narcotics production. And we will review whether we are using the right tools and tactics to make progress towards accomplishing our goals." [57]

One measure attracting rising attention in recent weeks is that of troop levels. Michael E. O'Hanlon, a senior fellow at Brookings, wrote this summer in the *Washington Examiner* that "for all its virtues," the Obama administration's Afghan strategy "may still lowball requirements for the Afghanistan mission to succeed."

"The administration's decisions in March to increase U.S. troop numbers to 68,000 (making for about 100,000 foreign troops in all), and Afghan army and police to about 215,000 will leave combined coalition forces at only half the levels in Iraq during the surge," O'Hanlon wrote, "and Afghanistan is slightly larger and more populous."

O'Hanlon cautioned against closing the door on adding more troops and pointed to "troubling signs that the Obama administration may be digging in against any future troop requirements." While "we may or may not have enough forces in Afghanistan" to accomplish the mission's full range of goals, he concluded, "let's not close off the conversation until we learn a little bit more." [58]

NATO's Cold Shoulder

Among the thorniest of the troop-level issues is the role of NATO forces in Afghanistan. As of June, countries participating in the NATO-led International Security

Assistance Forces (ISAF), a mission mandated by the U.N. under the 2001 Bonn agreement, have committed about 32,000 troops to Afghanistan, not counting those from the United States, according to the Brookings Institution. The top three were the United Kingdom, which had committed 8,300 troops, Germany (3,380) and Canada (2,830). Several countries, including the U.K. and Germany, were expected to send a small number of additional troops to provide security for the Aug. 20 election.

The Obama administration has been largely unsuccessful in prodding European nations to send more troops to Afghanistan. In April, in what the online edition of the *Times* of London billed as a "charm offensive" by Obama on his "debut international tour," leaders on the European continent "turned their backs" on the president, with British Prime Minister Gordon Brown "the only one to offer substantial help." Brown offered to send several hundred extra troops to provide election security, the *Times* noted, "but even that fell short of the thousands of combat troops that the U.S. was hoping to [gain] from the prime minister." [59]

Nonetheless, Obama has mustered some recent support for his Afghan policy. In late July Spain's prime minister, José Luís Rodriguez Zapatero, said his country was willing to increase its force on long-term deployment to Afghanistan, *The New York Times* reported. [60]

Early this month, NATO approved a reorganized command structure for Afghanistan, agreeing to set up a New Intermediate Joint Headquarters in Kabul under U.S. Lt. General David M. Rodriquez, who will manage the war on a day-to-day basis and report to McChrystal. NATO made the move at the first meeting of its governing body, the North Atlantic Council, under new NATO Secretary General Anders Fogh Rasmussen, former Danish prime minister. [61] Rasmussen, in his first comments as secretary general, called on the United Nations and European Union to help defeat the Taliban. "NATO will do its part, but it cannot do it alone," he said. "This needs to be an international effort, both military and civilian." [62]

The effectiveness of having more NATO troops in Afghanistan has been a matter of debate. At a forum in June, Brookings scholar Jeremy Shapiro, recently back from a visit to southern Afghanistan, suggested U.S. commanders have had little faith in the NATO command structure.

"Each of the main countries there is really running its own provincial war," Shapiro said. "The overall problem is that there really is no unity of command in Afghanistan so we're unable . . . to prioritize and to shift resources to deal with the most important problems. . . . It's related to the fact that for every NATO force in Afghanistan including the Americans, there are two chains of command, one up through the NATO commander who is an American, and one to the national capital, and in case of conflict, the national capital command always takes priority.

"The result is that each of the lead countries in the south, the Canadians in Kandahar, the British in Helmand, the Dutch in Uruzgan, are focused on their own priorities, on improving specific indicators in their piece of the war in their own province or district without a great deal of attention to the impact of that measure on the overall fight."

In impoverished Uruzgan Province, for example, the Dutch are doing "impressive things" with development efforts, but Uruzgan "is to a large degree serving as a sanctuary for insurgents to rest and refit and plan and to engage in the struggle in Kandahar and Helmand" province, Shapiro said.

The Canadians and British "would argue . . . that the priority for Afghanistan is not Uruzgan, it is Kandahar and Helmand and [if] the development of Uruzgan comes at the cost of strengthening the insurgency in other provinces, it's perhaps not the best use of resources."

Shapiro said he believes that as the number of U.S. troops has increased, especially in southern Afghanistan, "the focus for the U.S. military command is on . . . assigning roles to coalition partners that don't require intense coordination. . . . What that presages is an Americanization of the war, including in the south." By next year, Shapiro said, NATO will remain in command, "but I would be very dubious that we'll be truly fighting a NATO war at that point."[63]

Americanizing the War

Such predictions of an Americanized war are at odds with the administration's perception of the Afghan mission. Obama told *Sky News*, a British news outlet, that British contributions to the war effort are "critical" and that "this is not an American mission. The mission in Afghanistan is one that the Europeans have as much if not more of a stake in what we do. . . . The likelihood of a terrorist attack in London is at least as high, if not higher, than it is in the United States."[64]

Any further Americanization of the war will doubtlessly fuel scrutiny of the Afghan strategy in Congress and bolster demands for the Obama administration to set forth an exit strategy.

This summer, the U.S. House of Representatives strongly rejected an amendment calling on the defense secretary to submit a report no later than Dec. 31 outlining an exit strategy for U.S. forces in Afghanistan.

"Every military mission has a beginning, a middle, a time of transition and an end," said Rep. McGovern, the Massachusetts Democrat who sponsored the measure. "But I have yet to see that vision articulated in any document, speech or briefing. We're not asking for an immediate withdrawal. We're sure not talking about cutting or running or retreating, just a plan. If there is no military solution for Afghanistan, then please just tell us how we will know when our military contribution to the political solution has ended."[65]

But "focusing on an exit versus a strategy is irresponsible and fails to recognize that our efforts in Afghanistan are vital to preventing future terrorist attacks on the American people and our allies," argued Rep. Howard McKeon, R-Calif.[66]

The amendment's defeat did nothing to allay scrutiny of the war. Sen. John F. Kerry, D-Mass., chairman of the Senate Foreign Relations Committee, told *GlobalPost*, an online international-news site, that he planned to hold oversight hearings on U.S. involvement in Afghanistan.[67]

"End of summer, early fall," Kerry said, "we are going to take a hard look at Afghanistan."

OUTLOOK

More Violence

Military strategists say the Afghan war is likely to get more violent in coming months as U.S. and NATO forces battle the insurgency.

One immediate concern is whether the Taliban will make good on threats to disrupt this month's presidential election. While additional troops are being deployed to guard against attacks, officials have said ensuring the security of all 28,000 polling places is impossible.[68]

Meanwhile, tensions are likely to remain between those calling for a strict timetable for de-escalating the war and those arguing in favor of staying the course.

"I certainly do not think it would be a wise idea to impose a timeline on ourselves," says Riedel of Brookings, although he points to "political realities" that include the idea "that some measure of improvement in the security situation on the ground needs to be apparent over the course of the next 18 to 24 months."

Riedel expresses confidence that will occur. Once all scheduled troop deployments are in place, he says, "it's reasonable to expect that you can see some impact from [those deployments] in 18 to 24 months. Not victory, not the surrender of [Taliban leader] Mullah Omar, but some measurable decline in the pace of Taliban activity, some increase in the number of districts and provinces which are regarded as safe enough for [non-governmental organizations] to work in."

Beyond demands for on-the-ground progress in Afghanistan, the Obama administration faces other pressures as it struggles to get a grip on the Afghanistan and Pakistan region. One is helping U.S. allies maintain support for the war. In Britain, Prime Minister Brown has faced an uproar over growing British casualties that critics say stem from an underfunded defense budget that led to inadequate troop levels and equipment. [69] At home, as the financial crisis, health-care reform and other issues put pressure on the federal budget, Obama is likely to face opposition in Congress over additional war funding.

And Obama also is under pressure to address incendiary issues left over from the Bush administration. In July, a *New York Times* report detailed how the Bush administration repeatedly sought to discourage an investigation of charges that forces under U.S.-backed warlord Gen. Abdul Rashid Dostum massacred hundreds or even thousands of Taliban prisoners of war during the 2001 invasion of Afghanistan. [70]

In an editorial, the *Times* said Obama has directed aides to study the issue and that the administration is pressing Afghan President Karzai not to return Dostum to power. But, it added, Obama "needs to order a full investigation into the massacre." [71]

In the long run, one of the biggest challenges facing the Obama administration is its effort to instill sound governance in a country saturated with graft.

Afghanistan's corruption "reveals the magnitude of the task," says Walt, the Harvard international affairs professor. "Fixing corrupt public institutions is really hard once a pattern of behavior has been established, where money is flowing in non-regular ways. It's very difficult for outsiders to re-engineer those social and political practices, even if we were committed to staying five or 10 years."

Walt says he hopes he's wrong — "that the injection of the right kind of American power will create space for some kind of political reconciliation." But he's not optimistic. "I believe several years from now, [Afghanistan] will look like a sinkhole."

NOTES

1. Chris Brummitt, "Afghan firefight shows challenge for U.S. troops," The Associated Press, June 21, 2009, http://news.yahoo.com/s/ap/20090621/ap_on_re_as/as_afghan_taking_on_the_taliban.

2. Laura King, "6 U.S. troops killed in Afghanistan," *Los Angeles Times*, Aug. 3, 2009, www.latimes.com/news/nationworld/world/la-fg-afghan-deaths3-2009aug03,0,3594308.story.

3. For background, see Robert Kiener, "Crisis in Pakistan," *CQ Global Researcher*, December 2008, pp. 321-348, and Roland Flamini, "Afghanistan on the Brink," *CQ Global Researcher*, June 2007, pp. 125-150.

4. "Remarks by the President on a New Strategy for Afghanistan and Pakistan," White House, March 27, 2009, www.whitehouse.gov.

5. See www.boston.com/news/nation/washington/articles/2009/07/23/obama_victory_not_right_word_for_afghanistan/.

6. For background, see Roland Flamini, "Future of NATO," *CQ Global Researcher*, January 2009, pp. 1-26.

7. Pamela Constable, "For Karzai, Stumbles On Road To Election," *The Washington Post*, July 13, 2009, www.washingtonpost.com/wp-dyn/content/article/2009/07/12/AR2009071202426.html.

8. See, for example, Fred Kaplan, "Counterinsur gen-terrorism," *Slate*, March 27, 2009, www.slate.com/id/2214726/.

9. Ann Scott Tyson, "New Approach to Afghanistan Likely," *The Washington Post*, June 3, 2009, www

.washingtonpost.com/wp-dyn/content/article/2009/06/02/AR2009060203828.html.

10. *Ibid.*

11. Sharon Otterman, "Civilian death toll rises in Afghanistan," *The New York Times*, Aug. 1, 2009, www.nytimes.com/2009/08/01/world/asia/01afghan.html?scp=1&sq=civilian%20death%20toll%20rises&st=cse.

12. White House, *op. cit.*

13. See also John Mueller, "How Dangerous Are the Taliban?" *foreignaffairs.com*, April 15, 2009, www.foreignaffairs.com/articles/64932/john-mueller/how-dangerous-are-the-taliban.

14. Matthew Kaminski, "Holbrooke of South Asia," *The Wall Street Journal*, April 11, 2009.

15. Quoted in Rajiv Chandrasekaran, "Marines Deploy on Major Mission," *The Washington Post*, July 2, 2009, www.washingtonpost.com/wp-dyn/content/article/2009/07/01/AR2009070103202.html.

16. Jared Allen and Roxana Tiron, "Obey warns Afghanistan funding may slow unless significant progress made," *The Hill*, May 4, 2009, http://thehill.com/leading-the-news/obey-warns-afghanistan-funding-may-slow-unless-significant-progress-made-2009-05-04.html.

17. *The New York Times*/CBS News Poll, June 12-16, 2009, http://graphics8.nytimes.com/packages/images/nytint/docs/latest-new-york-times-cbs-news-poll/original.pdf.

18. See Dexter Filkins, "Afghan corruption: Everything for Sale," *The New York Times*, Jan. 2, 2009, www.nytimes.com/2009/01/02/world/asia/02iht-corrupt.1.19050534html?scp=2&sq=everything%20for%20sale&st=cse.

19. See Malou Innocent, "Obama's Mumbai problem," *The Guardian*, Jan. 27, 2009, www.guardian.co.uk/commentisfree/cifamerica/2009/jan/27/obama-india-pakistan-relations.

20. Peter Bergen, "Winning the Good War," *Washington Monthly*, July/August 2009, www.washington-monthly.com/features/2009/0907.bergen.html#Byline.

21. Greg Bruno, "U.S. Needs a Stronger Commitment to Improving Afghan Governance," Council on Foreign Relations, July 30, 2009, www.cfr.org/publication/19936/us_needs_a_stronger_commitment_to_improving_afghan_governance.html?breadcrumb=%2Fpublication%2Fpublication_list%3Ftype%3Dinterview.

22. Anthony H. Cordesman, "The Afghanistan Campaign: Can We Win?" Center for Strategic and International Studies, July 22, 2009. Cordesman expands on his ideas in a paper available at http://csis.org/files/publication/090722_CanWeAchieveMission.pdf.

23. Richard A. Oppel Jr., "Allied Officers Concerned by Lack of Afghan Forces," *The New York Times*, July 8, 2009, www.nytimes.com/2009/07/08/world/asia/08afghan.html?ref=world.

24. Quoted in Associated Press, "Marines: More Afghan Soldiers Needed in Helmand," CBS News, July 8, 2009, www.cbsnews.com/stories/2009/07/08/ap/politics/main5145174.shtml.

25. Quoted in Oppel, *op. cit.*

26. Transcript, "Death Toll Mounts as Coalition Forces Confront Taliban," "The NewsHour with Jim Lehrer," PBS, July 15, 2009, www.pbs.org/newshour/bb/military/july-dec09/afghancas_07-15.html.

27. Bob Woodward, "Key in Afghanistan: Economy, Not Military," *The Washington Post*, July 1, 2009, www.washingtonpost.com/wp-dyn/content/article/2009/06/30/AR2009063002811.html.

28. *Ibid.*

29. "Face the Nation," CBS News, July 5, 2009.

30. Greg Jaffe and Karen De Young, "U.S. General Sees Afghan Army, Police Insufficient," *The Washington Post*, July 11, 2009, www.washingtonpost.com/wp-dyn/content/article/2009/07/10/AR2009071002975.html.

31. Greg Jaffe, "U.S. Troops Erred in Airstrikes on Civilians," *The Washington Post*, June 20, 2009, www.washingtonpost.com/wp-dyn/content/article/2009/06/19/AR2009061903359.html.

32. Quoted in Robert Burns, "Analysis: reducing Afghan civilian deaths key goal," The Associated Press, June 13, 2009, www.google.com/hostednews/ap/article/eqM5hyNJNBigtMGe2M12B2s3w6OCoAbQD98Q2VP80.

33. Bergen, *op. cit.*

34. Helene Cooper and Sheryl Gay Stolberg, "Obama Ponders Outreach to Elements of Taliban," *The New York Times*, March 8, 2009, www.nytimes.com/2009/03/08/us/politics/08obama.html?scp=1&sq=obama%20ponders%20outreach%20to%20elements%20of%20taliban&st=cse.

35. Quoted in *ibid.*

36. Fotini Christia and Michael Semple, "Flipping the Taliban: How to Win in Afghanistan," *Foreign Affairs*, July/August 2009, p. 34, www.foreignaffairs.com/articles/65151/fotini-christia-and-michael-semple/flipping-the-taliban. Co-author Semple, who has significant background in holding dialogues with the Taliban, was expelled from Afghanistan in 2007 by the Karzai government amid accusations he and another diplomat held unauthorized talks with the Taliban.

37. See, "Background Note: Afghanistan," U.S. Department of State, November 2008, www.state.gov/r/pa/ei/bgn/5380.htm; also, *Grolier Encyclopedia of Knowledge*, Vol. 1, 1991. See also Kenneth Jost, "Rebuilding Afghanistan," *CQ Researcher*, Dec. 21, 2001, pp. 1041-1064.

38. Ahmed Rashid, *Descent into Chaos* (2008), p. 8.

39. *Ibid.*

40. Barry Bearak, "Mohammad Zahir Shah, Last Afghan King, Dies at 92," *The New York Times*, July 24, 2007, www.nytimes.com/2007/07/24/world/asia/24shah.html.

41. U.S. State Department, *op. cit.*

42. *Ibid.*

43. *Ibid.*

44. Rashid, *op. cit.*, p. 11.

45. Barnett R. Rubin, "The Transformation of the Afghan State," in J. Alexander Thier, ed., *The Future of Afghanistan* (2009), p. 15.

46. Rashid, *op. cit.*, pp. 12-13.

47. *Ibid.*, p. 13.

48. Seth G. Jones, "The Rise of Afghanistan's Insurgency," *International Security*, Vol. 32, No. 4, spring 2008, p. 19.

49. Rashid, *op. cit.*, p. 15.

50. Jones, *op. cit.*, p. 20.

51. *Ibid.* The reference to "the urban elite" comes from "Afghanistan: State Building, Sustaining Growth, and Reducing Poverty," World Bank Report No. 29551-AF, 2005, p. xxvi.

52. *Ibid.*, pp. 20, 22.

53. *Ibid.*, p. 24.

54. *Ibid.*, p. 25.

55. Dexter Filkins, "Right at the Edge," *The New York Times*, Sept. 7, 2008, www.nytimes.com/2008/09/07/magazine/07pakistan-t.html.

56. "Bob Gates, America's Secretary of War," "60 Minutes," May 17, 2009, www.cbsnews.com/stories/2009/05/14/60minutes/main5014588.shtml.

57. White House, *op. cit.*

58. Michael O'Hanlon, "We Might still Need More Troops In Afghanistan," *Washington Examiner*, July 7, 2009, www.washingtonexaminer.com/politics/50044002.html.

59. Michael Evans and David Charter, "Barack Obama fails to win NATO troops he wants for Afghanistan," *Timesonline*, April 4, 2009, www.timesonline.co.uk/tol/news/world/us_and_americas/article6032342.ece.

60. Victoria Burnett and Rachel Donadio, "Spain Is Open to Bolstering Forces in Afghanistan," *The New York Times*, July 30, 2009, www.nytimes.com/2009/07/30/world/europe/30zapatero.html?ref=world.

61. Steven Erlanger, "NATO Reorganizes Afghan Command Structure," *The New York Times*, Aug. 4, 2009, www.nytimes.com/2009/08/05/world/05nato.html.

62. Thomas Harding, "New NATO head calls for 'international effort' in Afghanistan," *Telegraph*, Aug. 3, 2009, www.telegraph.co.uk/news/worldnews/asia/afghanistan/5967377/New-Nato-head-calls-for-international-effort-in-Afghanistan.html.

63. "Afghanistan and Pakistan: A Status Report," Brookings Institution, June 8, 2009, www.brookings.edu/~/media/Files/events/2009/0608_afghanistan_pakistan/20090608_afghanistan_pakistan.pdf.

64. "Taliban pushed back, long way to go: Obama," Reuters, July 12, 2009, www.reuters.com/article/topNews/idUSTRE56A2Q420090712?feedType=RSS&feedName=topNews&rpc=22&sp=true.

65. Quoted in Dan Robinson, "U.S. Lawmakers Reject Amendment Calling for an Exit Strategy from Afghanistan," VOA News, June 26, 2009, www.voanews.com/english/2009-06-26-voa1.cfm.

66. Quoted in *ibid.*

67. John Aloysius Farrell, "Kerry: 'We are going to take a hard look at Afghanistan,' " *GlobalPost*, updated July 10, 2009, www.globalpost.com.

68. Pamela Constable, "Karzai's Challengers Face Daunting Odds," *The Washington Post*, July 6, 2009, p. 7A.

69. John F. Burns, "Criticism of Afghan War Is on the Rise in Britain," *The New York Times*, July 12, 2009, www.nytimes.com/2009/07/12/world/europe/12britain.html?scp=1&sq=criticism%20of%20afghan%20war%20is%20on%20the%20rise&st=cse.

70. James Risen, "U.S. Inaction Seen After Taliban P.O.W.'s Died," *The New York Times*, July 11, 2009, www.nytimes.com/2009/07/11/world/asia/11afghan.html?scp=1&sq=U.S.%20Inaction%20Seen%20After%20Taliban&st=cse.

71. "The Truth About Dasht-i-Leili," *The New York Times*, July 14, 2009, www.nytimes.com/2009/07/14/opinion/14tue2html?scp=5&sq=U.S.%20Inaction%20Seen%20After%20Taliban&st=cse.

BIBLIOGRAPHY

Books

Coll, Steve, *Ghost Wars*, Penguin Press, 2004.
The former *Washington Post* managing editor, now president of the New America Foundation think tank, traces the CIA's involvement in Afghanistan since the Soviet invasion in the 1970s.

Kilcullen, David, *The Accidental Guerrilla*, Oxford University Press, 2009.
A former Australian Army officer and counterterrorism adviser argues that strategists have tended to conflate small insurgencies and broader terror movements.

Peters, Gretchen, *Seeds of Terror*, Thomas Dunne Books, 2009.
A journalist examines the role of Afghanistan's illegal narcotics industry in fueling the activities of the Taliban and al Qaeda.

Rashid, Ahmed, *Descent into Chaos*, Viking, 2008.
A Pakistani journalist argues that "the U.S.-led war on terrorism has left in its wake a far more unstable world than existed on" Sept. 11, 2001.

Wright, Lawrence, *The Looming Tower*, Knopf, 2006.
In a Pulitzer Prize-winning volume that remains a must-read for students of the wars in Afghanistan and Iraq, a *New Yorker* staff writer charts the spread of Islamic fundamentalism and emergence of al Qaeda that gave rise to the Sept. 11 attacks.

Articles

Bergen, Peter, "Winning the Good War," *Washington Monthly*, July/August 2009, www.washingtonmonthly.com/features/2009/0907.bergen.html.
A senior fellow at the New America Foundation argues that skepticism about the Obama administration's chances of victory in Afghanistan are based on a misreading of that nation's history and people.

Christia, Fotini, and Michael Semple, "Flipping the Taliban," *Foreign Affairs*, July/August 2009.
A political scientist (Christia) and a specialist on Afghanistan and Pakistan who has talked with the Taliban argue that while more troops are necessary, "the move will have a lasting impact only if it is accompanied by a political 'surge' " aimed at persuading large groups of Taliban fighters to lay down arms.

Hogan, Michael, "Milt Bearden: Afghanistan Is 'Obama's War,' " *Vanityfair.com*, Feb. 5, 2009, www.vanityfair.com/online/politics/2009/02/milt-bearden-afghanistan-is-obamas-war.html.
Bearden, the former CIA field officer in Afghanistan when U.S. covert action helped expel the Soviet Union, says in this Q&A that "the only thing that is absolutely certain about this war is that it's going to be Obama's war, just as Iraq will be Bush's war."

Jones, Seth G., "The Rise of Afghanistan's Insurgency," *International Security*, Vol. 32, No. 4, spring 2008, http://belfercenter.ksg.harvard.edu/files/IS3204_pp007-040_Jones.pdf.
A RAND Corporation political scientist analyzes the reasons a violent insurgency began to develop in Afghanistan earlier this decade.

Mueller, John, "How Dangerous Are the Taliban?" *Foreignaffairs.com*, April 15, 2009, www.foreignaffairs.com/articles/64932/john-mueller/how-dangerous-are-the-taliban.
An Ohio State University political science professor questions whether the Taliban and al Qaeda are a big enough menace to the United States to make a long war in Afghanistan worth the cost.

Riedel, Bruce, "Comparing the U.S. and Soviet Experiences in Afghanistan," *CTC Sentinel*, Combating Terrorism Center, May 2009, www.brookings.edu/~/media/Files/rc/articles/2009/05_afghanistan_riedel/05_afghanistan_riedel.pdf.
A Brookings Institution scholar and former senior adviser to President Barack Obama examines the "fundamental differences" between the Soviet and U.S. experiences in the region.

Rosenberg, Matthew, and Zahid Hussain, "Pakistan Taps Tribes' Anger with Taliban," *The Wall Street Journal*, June 6-7, 2009, p. A14.
Pakistani anger at the Taliban in tribal regions bordering Afghanistan is growing, and Pakistan's military leaders hope to capitalize on that anger as they mount a grueling campaign against insurgents in North and South Waziristan.

Reports and Studies

Campbell, Jason, Michael O'Hanlon and Jeremy Shapiro, "Assessing Counterinsurgency and Stabilization Missions," Brookings Institution, Policy Paper No. 14, May 2009, www.brookings.edu/~/media/Files/rc/papers/2009/05_counterinsurgency_ohanlon/05_counterinsurgency_ohanlon.pdf.
Brookings scholars examine the status of change in Afghanistan and Iraq and explain why "2009 is expected by many to be a pivotal year in Afghanistan."

Tellis, Ashley J., "Reconciling With the Taliban?" Carnegie Endowment for International Peace, 2009, www.carnegieendowment.org/files/reconciling_with_taliban.pdf.
Efforts at reconciliation today would undermine American credibility and jeopardize the success of the U.S.-led mission in Afghanistan, argues a senior associate at the endowment.

For More Information

American Foreign Policy Council, 509 C St., N.E., Washington, DC 20002; (202) 543-1006; www.afpc.org. Provides analysis on foreign-policy issues.

Brookings Institution, 1775 Massachusetts Ave., N.W., Washington, DC 20036; (202) 797-6000; www.brookings.edu. Liberal-oriented think tank that provides research, data and other resources on security and political conditions in Afghanistan and Pakistan and global counterterrorism.

Cato Institute, 1000 Massachusetts Ave., N.W., Washington, DC 20001; (202) 842-0200; www.cato.org. Libertarian-oriented think tank that provides analysis on U.S. policy toward Afghanistan and Pakistan.

RAND Corp., 1776 Main St., Santa Monica, CA 90401; (310) 393-0411; www.rand.org. Research organization that studies domestic and international policy issues.

United Nations Office on Drugs and Crime, U.N. Headquarters, DC1 Building, Room 613, One United Nations Plaza, New York, NY 10017; (212) 963-5698; www.unodc.org. Helps member states fight illicit drugs, crime and terrorism; compiles data on opium poppy production.

United States Institute of Peace, 1200 17th St., N.W., Washington, DC 20036; (202) 457-1700; www.usip.org. Provides analysis, training and other resources to prevent and end conflicts.

16

Health-Care Reform

Marcia Clemmitt

House Speaker Nancy Pelosi, D-Calif., greets 11-year-old Brian McCann during a news conference on health care in September 2009, months before she helped engineer passage of the landmark health reform law. The sweeping new law enables people with preexisting medical conditions, like Brian, to get affordable insurance.

AP Photo/Matt Slocum

From *CQ Researcher*, June 11, 2010.

E nactment of the most far-reaching health-care law in at least four decades pumped emotions to a fever pitch among opponents and supporters alike.

"Today, after almost a century of trying; today, after over a year of debate; today, after all the votes have been tallied — health insurance reform becomes law in the United States of America. Today," President Barack Obama proclaimed at the March 23 White House signing ceremony.[1]

With equal passion, Republicans unanimously rejected the landmark Patient Protection and Affordable Health Care Act, refusing to award it even a single vote.

The law "is an historic betrayal of the clear will of the American people," scolded Republican National Committee Chairman Michael Steele. Referring to the new requirement that all Americans carry health-insurance coverage, he said the law represented "an historic loss of liberty."[2]

The landmark law will extend coverage to about 32 million of the nation's 45 million uninsured people by:

- Expanding Medicaid;
- Providing subsidies to help low- and middle-income families buy insurance;
- Creating regulated insurance markets where people without employer-sponsored insurance can buy subsidized coverage; and
- Using Medicare's economic clout to cut health care costs.

Health Reforms Opposed in Majority of States

State lawmakers in at least 39 states have introduced legislation to limit, alter or oppose aspects of the health-reform plan. The measures largely seek to make or keep health insurance optional and allow people to purchase any type of coverage they choose. Such legislation passed and is in effect in three states — Idaho, Utah and Virginia — and legislation passed in Oklahoma and Georgia is ready for approval by the governors. The bills did not pass in 21 states.

State Legislation Opposing Certain Health Reforms, 2009-2010

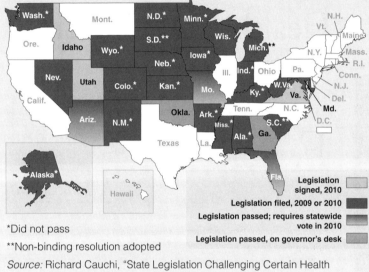

*Did not pass

**Non-binding resolution adopted

Source: Richard Cauchi, "State Legislation Challenging Certain Health Reforms, 2010," National Conference of State Legislatures, May 2010

sections contain provisions designed to essentially reengineer health care to favor efficient, effective treatments and preventive medicine over expensive but relatively ineffective services, she says. This is "urgent for a variety of reasons," including the fact that the high cost of health care is the main reason people are uninsured, says Feder.

The law launches a variety of "institutions and experiments" that policymakers hope can eventually slow the huge annual increases in health-care costs, says Michael E. Chernew, a professor of health policy at Harvard Medical School. Some are simple payment cuts to health-care players like private "Medicare Advantage" plans that most health-care economists agree have long been overpaid, he says.

But the law also will launch numerous demonstration projects aimed at developing ways to pay doctors, hospitals and other providers for delivering good health outcomes efficiently rather than continuing the current system, which mostly pays for services whether they are successful and necessary or not, Chernew explains.

"We can't be sure the [cost-cutting] things in the law will work, and critics can argue that they are not pursued aggressively enough or quickly enough," says Chernew. "Nevertheless, we have to do them, and from a pure cost-curve standpoint, [the law's framers] did whatever they could possibly do, what is politically possible."

The law also has some "pro-competitive" elements to encourage private insurers to emphasize cost and quality control as well, Chernew says. The "insurance exchanges" that will be set up in states to help people without employer coverage buy insurance "are very pro-competition" since they get insurers to compete against each other for individuals' business, Chernew says.

"It's very easy for those not in power to argue that those in power haven't done enough," Chernew says, but

While supporters tout the law's multifaceted approach to access and cost problems, conservatives argue the federal government has no right to require individuals to purchase insurance or states to participate in coverage-expansion programs. At least 20 state attorneys general and several private groups are suing to stop the law.

The law has two main facets — expanding health coverage and developing cost-control measures, says Judith Feder, a professor of public policy at Georgetown University and former staff director of the 1990 U.S. Bipartisan Commission on Comprehensive Health Care, which called for universal health coverage.

For the first time in history, the law "establishes access to affordable health care as a national responsibility," with "the great bulk of the dollars coming from taxpayers" to fund the coverage expansion, says Feder. The cost-cutting

those in power "can only do what is politically possible" in a system where health-care providers and insurers hold enormous influence.

Ultimately, Chernew acknowledges, "the law could turn out to be a disaster" because, when the results are in from cost-cutting experiments, "the solution [to rising costs] may require tough choices" to impose cost-trimming measures that doctors and patients won't like.

If that happens "and we end up not having the political will" to impose the changes, the federal budget deficit will soar because, under the law, the nation has committed itself to "a new entitlement program" — subsidizing health coverage for most low- and middle-income Americans, Chernew says.

The law takes some good steps but also leaves a few important things undone, says Mark McClellan, a former chief of Medicare and Medicaid under President George W. Bush and now director of the Engelberg Center for Health Care Reform at the centrist Brookings Institution think tank. For example, McClellan says the law's tax on high-cost employer-provided health insurance with rich benefit packages is a good way to raise money for coverage, but the tax should kick in sooner.

"It got pushed back to 2018," after complaints about unfairness, he says. But he argues that it is fair to end the tax-favored status of the most benefit-rich coverage, in favor of spending those dollars to help lower-income people gain coverage. Currently, "we pay about $250 billion a year for those employer subsidies, and most of that goes to higher-income people," he says.

One set of conservative-backed cost-trimming provisions that didn't make it into the law are so-called "consumer-side" incentives for people to take steps on their own to reduce health spending, McClellan says. For example, private insurers are implementing "wellness

Wealthy to Pay Higher Medicare Tax

Before passage of the health-care plan, middle-income families paid a higher Medicare tax than wealthy families. Under the plan, middle-income families will continue to pay a 2.9 percent tax but the tax on couples making $10 million annually would nearly triple.

Medicare Tax Under Health Reform

Middle-income family
Couple making $10 million annually

Source: Chuck Marr, "Changes in Medicare Tax on High-Income People Represent Sound Additions to Health Reform," Center on Budget and Policy Priorities, March 2010

plans" to give consumers financial incentives to take common-sense steps like stopping smoking or losing weight, which should save health-system dollars down the line, he says.

Limits on lawsuits against health-care providers also should have been included, says McClellan. Such reforms can trim 2-3 percent annually from medical spending, and while that amount may seem minimal, "it could add to the other reforms" and increase the law's cumulative cost-cutting effect, he says.

The new law also has its critics among proponents of guaranteed, universal access to health care.

"The law does not solve the problem," says Steffie Woolhandler, an associate professor of medicine at Harvard and longtime advocate of national, single-payer health care.

"If the bill works as planned, there will still be 23 million uninsured people in 2019, of whom about a quarter will be illegal immigrants," she says. Furthermore, many who get insurance under the bill will end up underinsured, she added, partly because about 16 million of the newly insured will be enrolled in Medicaid, which most doctors don't accept because of its lower payments. "They can go to the emergency room (ER), but they'll have trouble getting primary care for conditions like high blood pressure" and the like, where early treatment could keep ER-type health emergencies from happening, she says.

Many who buy insurance in the law's new exchanges also "will get woefully inadequate coverage," since the insurance available there "will cover only 60 percent" of medical costs, says Woolhandler.

"Because the law was sold largely on the basis of cost containment, the critics are able to fire at it by saying, 'It won't save as much money as you say,' " says Arthur L.

Health Reforms That Begin This Year

A few programs expand coverage for the neediest.

Most Americans won't see many effects of the health-care reform law this year. However, the law does launch a few programs that start expanding coverage for some of the neediest people and some who are easier to cover.[1]

High-risk pool — Many people with preexisting medical conditions can't get affordable insurance under current laws. To help close that gap, this year a temporary "high-risk pool" will begin offering price-capped coverage to people with pre-existing illnesses. In 2014 the new law will require insurers to take all comers.

Young adult coverage — Young adults are one of the largest uninsured groups. Beginning this year, for the first time, young adults up to age 26 can get coverage under their parents' health insurance.

Benefit limits — In the past, patients with serious illnesses were likely to lose their insurance coverage when they ran into a lifetime limit on the dollar value of their coverage. Beginning this year, the law bans lifetime dollar limits on coverage and also bans insurers from canceling a patient's insurance policy for any reason except fraud by the patient. Also beginning this year, children may not be refused health insurance because of preexisting medical conditions.

Medicaid expansion — For the first time, states may offer Medicaid coverage to all poor people, not just to mothers and their young children or the disabled.

Business tax credit — Small businesses whose workers' annual wage is under $50,000 get tax credits if they provide health insurance.

Regulating insurance premiums — Insurers must report the proportion of premium dollars they spend on actual medical services, and the federal government will establish a process for judging whether annual premium increases are justified.

— Marcia Clemmitt

---

[1] See "Focus on Health Reform: Summary of New Health Reform Law," The Henry J. Kaiser Family Foundation, March 26, 2010, and "Timeline for Health Care Reform Implementation: System and Delivery Reform Provisions," The Commonwealth Fund, April 1, 2010.

Caplan, a professor of bioethics at the University of Pennsylvania. "If, instead, you had had the discussion of whether there is a right to health care, critics would have to explicitly make their arguments for why health care is not a right," bringing out into the open the real issue, which the country must face sooner or later, he says.

"Only critics looking for some way to derail reform give a hoot about details" like individual mandates or tax provisions, Caplan said. "No nation on Earth has ever reformed its health care system by asking the public to wallow around in the details of health reform." Instead, nations including Canada, Britain, Singapore, Taiwan, Germany and Australia "secured agreement that health care is a right and then, and only then, moved on to figure out how to guarantee that right to all citizens," he said.[3]

As health reform is implemented amid protests in Washington and the states, here are some of the questions being debated:

Is the new health-care reform law a good idea?

The new law's supporters say it puts in place most of the mechanisms for coverage expansion and cost control that are politically possible in the complex, private-sector-dominated American health system, but many conservative critics have called for the law's partial rollback or repeal. They argue that increased government involvement in health care can only damage the job market, interfere with individual freedom and worsen cost problems. Critics on the left, meanwhile, say there was little point in enacting provisions that will only temporarily lower the number of uninsured Americans without creating a permanent solution.

The bill's so-called "individual mandate," requiring everyone to purchase insurance, is unconstitutional, said Sen. Orrin Hatch, R-Utah.

The purpose of insurance is to spread costs across the population — with people paying in even in years

Health Reforms That Begin in 2011 and Beyond

Changes spread costs, reduce spending increases.

The health-reform law contains hundreds of provisions designed to expand insurance coverage, spread the tax burden of paying for the new coverage fairly and eventually tame steep annual increases in spending while improving care. Most of the provisions will be phased in over the next eight years. [1]

2011

Long-term care — People may enroll in an insurance plan to fund future long-term care needs, including services that can help them stay in their own homes.

Drug company fees — Annual fees paid by large pharmaceutical manufacturers will help pay for expanding health coverage.

Hospital-acquired illnesses — Medicare won't pay hospitals to care for infections caused by a patient's hospital stay.

OTC drugs — To raise money, the law bans paying for over-the-counter drugs from tax-favored accounts like flexible spending accounts unless a doctor has prescribed the drugs.

2012

Paying health-care providers — To hold down rising medical costs and improve care, Medicare will begin paying doctors and hospitals less when patients develop preventable illnesses and study other potential incentives to get medical providers to work together to deliver care more efficiently.

2013

Standardize insurance operations — To save money and set the stage for the new health-insurance exchanges that launch in 2014, health-insurance eligibility, enrollment and claims procedures will be standardized nationwide.

Higher Medicare taxes — To raise money to expand insurance coverage, individuals with adjusted gross incomes over $200,000 ($250,000 for couples who file jointly) will pay higher Medicare taxes.

2014

Individual mandate — U.S. citizens and legal residents must carry health coverage or pay a tax penalty.

Employer contributions —To help pay for coverage expansion, employers with more than 50 workers must either offer health coverage or pay a per-worker fee.

Insurance exchanges — State-based regulated markets will help individuals and small businesses buy health coverage that is tax-subsidized on a sliding scale for people earning up to 400 percent of the federal poverty level. The federal government will establish a minimum benefit package for health coverage.

Medicaid expansion — The federal government will pay to expand Medicaid to all non-elderly Americans earning up to 133 percent of the federal poverty level.

Insurance rules — Insurance companies will no longer be able to refuse new coverage or coverage renewal to anyone, regardless of preexisting conditions or other factors. To keep insurance affordable for all, older and sicker people can't be charged more than three times what the average person in the community pays for coverage. Annual dollar limits on benefits are banned.

Insurer fees — Insurance companies will pay fees based on their size.

2018

Benefit tax — To raise funds, tax breaks will end for health plans with annual premiums exceeding $10,000 for an individual (or $27,500 for a family). Such so-called Cadillac plans benefit only richer Americans and are believed to be inefficient.

— Marcia Clemmitt

---

[1] See "Focus on Health Reform: Summary of New Health Reform Law," The Henry J. Kaiser Family Foundation, March 26, 2010, and "Timeline for Health Care Reform Implementation: System and Delivery Reform Provisions," The Commonwealth Fund, April 1, 2010.

when they don't use much health care. Those payments serve as a buffer against times when they are sick and use services — and if people wait until they become ill to sign up for insurance, insurers are unable to spread costs in this way.

For this reason, an individual mandate has been part of some Republican coverage-expansion proposals over the years, as well as the 1993 proposal by President Bill Clinton.

Hatch raised no objection to the individual mandates in the Clinton plan, "but . . . 17 years later . . . I looked at it and, constitutionally, I came to the conclusion . . . that this would be the first time in history that the federal government requires you to buy something you don't want," he said. "If we allow the federal government to tell us what we can or can't buy, then our liberties are gone."[4]

"Forcing employers to offer health insurance . . . will cost America jobs and revenue, and inhibit small businesses from growing," according to the small-business lobbying group National Federation of Independent Businesses. "It's a bad idea any time but is particularly destructive in the current economic environment."[5]

By requiring employers to pay a penalty if they don't offer workers substantial health-insurance coverage, the law "creates an incentive for employers to avoid hiring workers from low-income families, hurting those who need jobs the most," said Kathryn Nix, a research assistant at the conservative Heritage Foundation. (Low-income workers are the least likely to receive employer-based health insurance because its cost is more than most employers are willing to shoulder as an added cost of employing a worker.)[6]

Tax increases to pay for expanding coverage will damage the economy, Nix continued. For example, the law raises some taxes on investment income, a move that "will discourage investment in the U.S. economy . . . reducing the potential for economic growth."

"Families with incomes greater than $250,000 will pay a higher Medicare payroll tax — up to 2.35 percent, plus a new 3.8 percent tax on interest and dividend income. With this stroke, Democrats have managed to punish both work and the savings of American families," wrote Sally C. Pipes, chief executive officer of the free-market-oriented Pacific Research Institute in San Francisco.[7]

Increasing government involvement in health care will likely drive some doctors out of Medicare and perhaps out of practice altogether, said Robert E. Moffit, director of health policy studies at Heritage. Having public and private insurers pay for health care rather than allowing individuals to pay directly out of their own pockets for it "already [compromises] the independence and integrity of the medical profession," and the new law "will reinforce the worst of these features," because "physicians will be subject to more government regulation and oversight," said Moffit.[8]

Some critics on the left also see more harm than good in the reforms.

The law "hurts many more people than it helps," wrote blogger Jane Hamsher of the liberal website Firedoglake. "A middle-class family of four making $66,370 will be forced to pay $5,243 per year for insurance," an amount that will leave many without enough discretionary income to cover other bills, she said.[9]

But reform supporters counter that expanding coverage is worth the law's cost and that its provisions are not unconstitutional.

"There is a long line of [Supreme Court] cases holding that Congress has broad power to enact laws that substantially affect prices, marketplaces and commercial transactions," including cases decided by the current conservative-dominated court, wrote Ian Millhiser, a policy analyst at the liberal Center for American Progress. "A law requiring all Americans to hold health insurance does all of these things," so its constitutionality is not in question, he said. The 2005 case *Gonzales v. Raich*, for example, "establishes that Congress can regulate even tiny insurance providers who serve only a handful of local residents because such local activity substantially affects a multistate market," said Millhiser.[10]

"The Supreme Court decades ago held that the business of insurance fell within Congress' regulatory authority under the Commerce Clause," wrote Simon Lazarus, public policy counsel to the National Senior Citizens Law Center.[11]

The court noted that "perhaps no modern commercial enterprise directly affects so many persons in all walks of life as does the insurance business," said Lazarus. Consequently, the 1944 finding "could hardly be more consonant with Congress' identical case for expanding federal regulation of health insurance in 2009," including the "individual mandate" to buy coverage, since "many independent experts, studies and analyses concur" that without such a requirement "overall health reform will be unsustainable," he said.[12]

The law is "an enormously positive step to expand access and put in tools" to begin driving down costs, says Jacob Hacker, a Yale University professor of political science who was the chief architect of a proposal — eventually dumped from the legislation — to include a public, government-run health insurance plan to compete against private insurers. "I was a very strong advocate of the bill even after the public-plan option was off the table," he says.

Supporters argue that by making it easier for people to get non-job-based health coverage and beginning to trim costs, the law will actual improve businesses' ability to create jobs. Inability to find affordable health coverage under current law "is one of the major reasons why small businesses close their doors and corporations ship jobs overseas," said Obama.[13]

By establishing a system in which fewer people experience breaks in insurance coverage, the law will improve health and trim some costs, according to Mathematica Policy Research, a consulting firm in Princeton, N.J. Studies show that "adults with continuous insurance coverage are healthier and at lower risk for premature death than those who are uninsured or whose coverage is intermittent," the firm reported in April.[14]

"Continuous coverage also can reduce administrative costs," Mathematica said. For example, "guaranteed eligibility for Medicaid and the Children's Health Insurance Program for six or 12 months can lower states' administrative costs by reducing the frequent movement (called 'churning')" of people in and out of the programs," drastically cutting paperwork and staff time.[15]

Will people with insurance lose out under the new law?

Critics say the new law will change things for the worse for people who have either public or private insurance

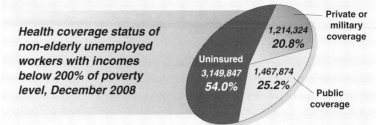

Half of Unemployed Workers Are Uninsured

Out of nearly 6 million unemployed workers with incomes below 200 percent of the poverty level, more than 50 percent are uninsured. The new law will allow unemployed people and others without job-sponsored coverage to buy tax-subsidized insurance.

Health coverage status of non-elderly unemployed workers with incomes below 200% of poverty level, December 2008

Private or military coverage
1,214,324
20.8%

Uninsured
3,149,847
54.0%

1,467,874
25.2%
Public coverage

Source: Claire McAndrew, "Unemployed and Uninsured in America," Families USA, February 2009

today. Reform supporters argue, however, that while the law will change how many people get coverage and care, it will ultimately provide better options for everyone.

Many provisions that raise revenue to pay for coverage expansion will leave insured Americans worse off, said John Berlau, director of the Center for Investors and Entrepreneurs at the free-market think tank Competitive Enterprise Institute. For example, a provision to raise tax money to fund the law's coverage expansion will ban using pre-tax dollars from a flexible-spending account or health-savings account to buy over-the-counter drugs unless a doctor has prescribed them, creating "an effective tax increase of up to 40 percent on these items," said Berlau.[16]

About 7 million Medicare enrollees will lose the more generous benefits they now receive from "Medicare Advantage" private health insurers that serve the Medicare program, said Grace-Marie Turner, president of the Galen Institute, a free-market think tank in Alexandria, Va. Payments to those insurers will be cut under the law, based on recommendations by many economists that Medicare has long overpaid the plans. But the resulting pullout of the plans from Medicare will be a significant hardship for the Medicare enrollees who've come to rely on the richer benefits Medicare Advantage plans provide, compared to traditional Medicare, Turner said.[17]

Before the law was enacted, the United States already faced a shortage of primary-care doctors and, with an estimated 32 million newly insured people by 2019 under the law, primary-care physicians will be stretched even thinner, according to *Kaiser Health News.*[18]

If Congress actually implements Medicare payment cuts named in the law, "15 percent of hospitals and other care facilities that rely on Medicare reimbursements would become unprofitable, meaning that they might drop Medicare patients," limiting "the availability of care for millions of seniors," the *Columbus* [Ohio] *Dispatch* editorialized.[19]

But health-reform supporters say that, contrary to critics' warnings, the law, on balance, will make it easier for virtually everyone to maintain continuous access to health insurance and care.

Rather than losing money, hospitals actually "come out winners" under the law, so access won't become a greater problem, said Maggie Mahar, a fellow at the liberal Century Foundation.[20]

Hospitals got in on early negotiations for the law and negotiated some payment rate cuts that they found acceptable, said Urban Institute senior fellow Robert Berenson. Now "hospitals are off-limits until 2020" from pay cuts proposed by the new board established by the law to make sure that Medicare hits its spending targets, Berenson said.[21]

Moreover, hospital payment cuts "will be offset by the fact that hospitals will be seeing an influx of paying patients" as more people gain insurance, Mahar said.[22]

And Medicare cuts will actually benefit enrollees, some analysts argue. Cutting payments for ineffective care such as hospital readmissions, for example, will not only make Medicare more economically sustainable over the long haul but help eliminate hospital stays that amount to unnecessary "hardship for the patient," said a report published by the liberal-leaning Commonwealth Fund in Manhattan.[23]

The law will help insured people avoid unwarranted insurance-premium rate increases by requiring annual review of premium increases in a public process that will, for the first time, require public input, not just explanations of their charges by the insurance company, according to the liberal consumer group Families USA. Before the law went into effect, many states had "no process for obtaining consumer input in the rate-review process," so state officials heard "only the insurers' side of the story"

and often were unaware that the proposed rates were unaffordable.[24]

Changes brought about by the law "do not pose a risk to the public," says Georgetown University's Feder. "What insured people are currently at risk of is higher costs" that will force them out of their coverage, either because they lose a job, become self-employed or an employer stops offering it, she says. Under the new law, "if there's an employment change, now for the first time they'll have a real option," she says.

In another boon for patients, "beginning this year, if you become seriously ill, insurers won't be able to drop your coverage on the grounds that you forgot some detail of your medical history when you applied for insurance," as they could in the past, said Mahar. From now on, insurers "will be able to rescind your policy only if they can prove fraud, or that you intentionally set out to deceive them. This won't be easy."[25]

Will health care reform make care more affordable?

Supporters of the new law say its tax-funded subsidies will help low-income people afford health coverage and that health-provider payment initiatives will slow out-of-control health spending. But skeptics say that the law's affordability provisions are all unproven.

Using incentives and accountability, the new law tries to nudge doctors, hospitals and other health-care providers toward eliminating unnecessary illness and treatment, said David Kendall, a senior fellow at Third Way, a center-left advocacy group in Washington. For example, "the current system . . . lets doctors who cause infections through improper hand-washing send [insurers] more bills to treat" infections that patients may get as a result, Kendall explained. The new law institutes cost-saving provisions such as requiring hospitals to "effectively put a warranty on their care by limiting the payments they get from Medicare if a patient is readmitted" too soon or in circumstances that suggest his or her earlier care was ineffective or harmful.[26]

If such an outcomes-based payment system — often referred to as a "bundled" payment system — can be developed "that providers can live with, we'll be in a much better place" than we are today when it comes to holding down costs, says Harvard Medical School's Chernew. Whether the law is making inroads should begin to become evident in about five years, he says.

Other proposed provider-payment measures "include just about everything we know" about cost control, making it a best effort at implementing cost savings on the provider side, says McClellan, the former Medicare and Medicaid chief under George W. Bush.

The "history of previous legislation is auspicious," because earlier laws that cut health-care provider payments have almost always had a bigger cost-cutting effect than analysts first predicted, said Peter Orszag, director of the White House Office of Management and Budget.[27]

In academic analyses of health-system reorganization plans that stamp out inefficient care — as the law aims to do — "the estimates of possible efficiency savings range up to 30 percent or more of medical spending," said Harvard University professor of economics David M. Cutler. Because previous analyses have underestimated the cost-saving effects of such measures, there's a good chance that "costs will fall more rapidly than expected," Cutler said.[28]

Nevertheless, even some analysts who see significant good in the law have doubts about its ability to make health care affordable.

"I suspect that the legislation is going to be more successful at coverage goals than at cost-containment goals," says Katherine Baicker, a professor of health economics at the Harvard School of Public Health. "You can throw money" at patients and providers and increase individuals' access to health care, "but we simply don't yet know how" to slow health-care cost growth, even though scholars do have ideas about what may work, she says.

Also unknown is "whether Congress will have the political will" to enforce cost-cutting measures that the law's demonstration projects find to be effective, says Baicker. Health-care providers always fight such changes because they affect income, and that means "all these things could easily be left to wither on the vine," she says. "While the demos may be promising, there is no built-in mechanism in the law to give them teeth."

For example, the law sets up a program for testing the "comparative effectiveness" of health treatments — with the goal of spending health-care dollars only for what works best, notes a report by Medicare's actuary. Requiring Medicare to base payments on comparative-effectiveness findings would reap "substantial savings," says the actuary's office. However, the law does not

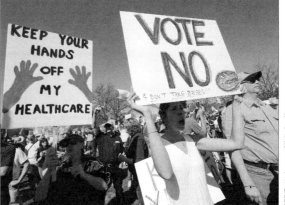

Supporters of the Tea Party movement demonstrate against the health care bill at the Capitol on March 20, 2010, just before a cliffhanger vote on the sweeping legislation the next day. Critics say the plan will cost too much and give the government too much control over Americans' health decisions.

authorize establishment of a federal board "with authority over payment and coverage policies" to force Medicare and other programs to stop paying for less effective treatments, said the actuary. Instead, the legislation only requires dissemination of the research as a recommendation for payment changes. Because of lawmakers' reluctance to impose tough changes, therefore, a program that could save a lot of money will result only in "small savings," and even those will "take many years to develop," the report predicts.[29]

"If there were an FDA [Food and Drug Administration] of cost containment, none of these measures would be considered safe and effective," quipped Mark Pauly, a professor of health-care systems, business and public policy at the University of Pennsylvania's Wharton School. Nevertheless, a few provisions, such as reducing rates of hospital readmission by letting nurses counsel patients about staying healthy and requiring hospitals to take stringent steps to ward off hospital-acquired infections, likely will save money, Pauly conceded.[30]

But some conservative critics say the law's cost-cutting initiatives simply cannot work.

"You cannot control costs unless someone does the controlling. And there is nothing in the legislation that would free either patients or doctors to do that job," said John Goodman, president of the National Center for

Policy Analysis, a free-market think tank in Dallas. Goodman is among conservatives who argue that the entire system of third-party insurance — not just public programs like Medicare — shields patients too much from the high cost of health care. Therefore, he argues that since the new law preserves an insurance system, it cannot succeed at cost control. Goodman argues that health costs will only be controlled when patients must fully confront the cost of the care they seek, so that they will bargain hard to force their medical providers "to use their intelligence, creativity and innovative ability to seek efficiencies the way people do in other markets."[31]

Furthermore, several provisions in the law "are sure to increase health-insurance premiums in the short term," says the Galen Institute's Turner. A ban on health insurers placing a lifetime or annual limit on the benefits an individual receives will raise premiums for all policy-holders, she said.[32]

Meanwhile, liberal opponents say the law lacks the most powerful known means of holding down costs. For example, allowing Americans to buy prescription drugs from Canada "could have saved American consumers roughly $100 billion," but that didn't make it into the bill because drug manufacturers strenuously object to the practice, wrote liberal blogger Jon Walker. Creating a centralized federal government authority to negotiate payments with health-care providers would also lower payment rates, and requiring insurance-benefit packages to be standardized would reduce administrative costs and allow for better comparison shopping. But neither of those common-sense measures is in the new law either, Walker said.[33]

BACKGROUND

Exceptional America

Virtually all other industrialized countries have concluded that health care is a right that nations owe their people and have created taxpayer-funded public or combination public-private systems to provide it. By contrast, the U.S. Congress has never seriously debated establishing a universal right to care.[34]

"We had a little of this conversation after the Civil War," resulting in a basic guarantee of health care as a right for veterans, says University of Pennsylvania ethicist

Caplan. Other nations have gone much farther, however. For example, after World War II, Britain explicitly discussed whether health care should be guaranteed as a right and decided that "it was part of what the nation owed to a people who had lived through the blitz" — Nazi Germany's sustained seven-month bombing of Britain during the early years of World War II, he says.

"Canada had the conversation and concluded that" a guaranteed right to health care "is part of what would bind [the geographically vast country] together as a nation," says Caplan.

"We're the only county that finds it quite this difficult to discuss" whether health care should be a right, in part because of historical struggles to harmonize a racially and ethnically diverse society, Caplan says. It's easier for a smaller, homogeneous nation to discuss using taxpayer dollars to offer health care to all, he says.

As a result, health insurance in America developed as a purely private enterprise in the first half of the 20th century. At first, there was limited concern about paying for coverage. Gradually, however, as care grew more expensive, employers began offering hospitalization insurance as a benefit for workers.

By the 1940s, large unionized companies dominated the American economy, and many used health-insurance benefits as a bargaining chip in labor negotiations. Employer-sponsored health plans successfully spread out health-care costs among large pools of workers and, by doing so, allowed each individual to pay relatively low and consistent premiums, even in years when they had accidents or illnesses. Furthermore, since the sickest people are unlikely to be employed, private insurance companies prospered in an insurance market almost entirely made up of employer-sponsored coverage.

Hybrid Solutions

Beginning as early as the 1940s, however, some lawmakers grew troubled by the realization that vulnerable populations — such as the elderly and the disabled — did not have workplace-based coverage. Many of these people couldn't afford individual policies, which in most states insurers could price according to the individual's own health risk.

Members of Congress made unsuccessful attempts to launch discussion of health coverage for all in 1943, 1945, 1947, 1949 and 1957, and Presidents Franklin D. Roosevelt,

1880s-1930s *As the cost and effectiveness of health care increase, industrialized countries mull universal access, and Americans worry about affording health care.*

1883 Germany creates first universal health-care system.

1929 School system in Dallas, Texas, launches first prepaid hospital insurance plan for employees.

1932 Committee on the Cost of Medical Care details Americans' growing difficulties in paying for care.

1935 Attempts fail to include health coverage in the Social Security Act.

1940s-1980s *Employer-sponsored insurance becomes the dominant form of U.S. health coverage. Congress enacts Medicare and Medicaid to fill coverage gaps for the elderly, the disabled and poor mothers with children.*

1943 Wagner-Murray-Dingell bill for compulsory national health insurance is introduced in Congress. . . . National War Labor Board declares employer contributions to insurance are income-tax free, opening the way for companies to use health insurance packages to attract workers.

1946 United Kingdom launches fully nationalized universal coverage system — National Health Service.

1960 U.S. health spending totals $28 billion, or 5.2 percent of gross domestic product (GDP).

1965 President Lyndon B. Johnson signs Medicare and Medicaid into law.

1971 President Richard M. Nixon places wage and price controls on medical services.

1980 Health spending tops $255 billion, or 9.1 percent of GDP.

1990s-2009 *Rising health costs force some Americans to drop coverage, prompting Congress to enact a public insurance program for children in working families.*

1993 President Bill Clinton and first lady Hillary Clinton propose sweeping health-system reforms. Insurance industry launches opposition campaign.

1994 Senate abandons the Clinton health plan without debate.

1997 President Clinton signs State Children's Health Insurance Program (SCHIP) to provide coverage for children in working families.

2000 Health spending totals $1.4 trillion, or 13.8 percent of GDP.

2002 Congress enacts Health Care Tax Credit for those who lose their jobs to foreign competition.

2006 Massachusetts enacts mandatory, universal health-coverage program.

2009 Massachusetts officials consider implementing "payment bundling" — paying doctors and hospitals a flat fee upfront to cover patients — to control cost growth in their universal-coverage plan. . . . Congress votes to expand SCHIP program. . . . President Obama and congressional Democrats slowly push coverage-expansion plans through Congress in the face of heated opposition; bill passes Senate on Dec. 24.

2010s *Implementation begins of the most wide-ranging health-reform legislation in U.S. history.*

2010 Health reform clears Congress on March 21; President Obama signs legislation intended to cover about 32 million uninsured people and re-engineer the health-care payment system to trim costs; the law's main provisions take effect in 2014. . . . The 2009 federal SCHIP expansion falters as state budgets suffer from recession. . . . Connecticut becomes first state to sign up for the 2010 reform law's option to immediately extend Medicaid coverage to poor adults outside the traditional Medicaid categories of disabled people and mothers and their young children. . . . At least 20 state attorneys general sue the federal government to stop the health-care law.

2014 Main provisions of the 2010 health law are slated to begin, including a requirement for all Americans to buy health insurance.

States Will Be Ground Zero for Many Changes

"A lot is resting on the shoulders of the states."

Public-policy experts agree that the states will play a crucial role in implementing the new health-care reforms, but they aren't all sure the states are up to the task.

"A lot is resting on the shoulders of the states" for the success of health-care reform, says Stan Dorn, a senior research associate at the Washington-based Urban Institute, a centrist think tank.

"This federalism aspect of the law is one of the biggest worries" in some respects "because reliance on states leads to enormous variation" in a program, which likely will leave some residents of the country with low benefits and little protection under the new law, says Georgetown University professor of public policy Judith Feder. Some analysts tout states as "laboratories of democracy," where innovative ideas are often pioneered and tested, but Feder argues that studies show that most states rarely innovate. "Federalism is overrated," she says.

Yale University professor of political science Jacob Hacker says ultimate success will heavily depend on the states and federal government working together. "To me, one of the biggest challenges of implementation is that the law creates dual authority in many areas," he says. "Hopefully, good partnerships will develop." Specifically, Hacker explains, the federal government will be funding subsidies for people without employer-based coverage to buy insurance in new markets, called exchanges, but the states are charged with setting up and running the exchanges.

Most of the money to fund actual new insurance coverage under Medicaid and in the new exchanges will come from the federal government, which should prove a boon to states in some respects, since it's state and local authorities who often see the consequences as uninsured people develop severe medical problems. States will end up bearing a large share of administrative expenses for the programs, however.

"The states that do the least now" to provide Medicaid coverage "will get the most money from the expansion" of Medicaid to a new group of eligible people — everyone with incomes under 133 percent of the federal poverty level, says Judith Solomon, a senior fellow at the left-leaning Center on Budget and Policy Priorities.

States generally will benefit from the Medicaid expansion because currently "very, very large numbers of the low-income people" who will become eligible for the mostly federally funded Medicaid expansion "are currently in some state-funded programs," such as mental-health programs, Solomon says.

State officials who are fretting about the cost of the new programs tend to "assume that 100 percent" of eligible people will participate, "but we've never seen any such number" in previous programs, so it's unlikely to happen this time either, says Solomon.

"That's not to say that there won't be some expenses" for states, Solomon says. Just as in the current Medicaid program, states will pick up half the administrative costs for the new, much larger Medicaid population — beginning in 2014 — while the federal government will pay for the other 50 percent of the administration.

"I'm worried about the administration side, where there's only a 50 percent federal match," says Dorn. "No state person will want to brag about hiring more state employees" since all state governments are constrained by legal requirements to balance their budgets annually, he says.

Nevertheless, when it comes to getting high numbers of eligible people enrolled, intensive outreach is crucial, plus having as many as possible automatically enrolled based on information government agencies already possess, rather than requiring them to fill out application forms, Dorn says. That makes administrative "resources the greatest implementation question."

Unless they opt out of the responsibility, states also are supposed to set up and manage the health-insurance exchanges that in 2014 are slated to begin selling coverage to people without employer-sponsored health insurance.

"But if I were a state legislator or governor, the last thing I would want to do would be to run an exchange," says Dorn. "The federal money [to administer the exchanges] runs from 2014 to Jan. 1, 2015," and after that "each exchange must raise its own money by charging fees" to insurers or health-care providers, Dorn explains. All of these players "will want services the exchanges provide but won't want to pay." That will give states a difficult balancing act: raising money while also tightly regulating the health-care market, Dorn says.

If many states are leery, "the feds might end up doing it all, which might not be a bad outcome," he says, although it's not what the law anticipates.

— *Marcia Clemmitt*

Harry S. Truman, Richard D. Nixon and Clinton all proposed guaranteed universal coverage.

Ultimately, however, Congress backed off even debating such proposals because of strong opposition from big employers, insurers and health-care providers — who feared that increased government involvement in health care would mean less autonomy in practice and lower pay. Even organized labor opposed the discussions, largely because it liked bargaining for good health-care benefits.

But the growing size of the population without coverage eventually forced Congress to act. To supplement the private health-insurance system, which left many people behind, Congress launched two large public insurance programs in 1965, effectively creating a right — or "entitlement" — to health care for two specific groups of Americans. The Medicare program covers the elderly, while Medicaid covers poor mothers with young children and some poor and seriously disabled people.

Congress expanded public coverage one more time to reach another population that was increasingly priced out of employer-sponsored coverage. The State Children's Health Insurance Program (SCHIP), launched in 1997, covers children in low- and middle-income working families.

History, then, leaves the United States with a hybrid system — about half public and half private. While the arrangement matches the policy preferences of many Americans, who tend to be political centrists, it poses a complex challenge for lawmakers faced with high rates of uninsurance and fast-rising costs.

When Nixon and Democratic Presidents Jimmy Carter, in the 1970s, and Clinton, in the 1990s, proposed health-care overhauls intended to help provide affordable care for all Americans, all three plans were complicated by their attempts to leave both public and private coverage intact. Further, because of their hybrid nature, all invited harsh criticism both from conservative Republicans, who oppose taxpayer-financed, government-regulated health care, and from liberal Democrats, who often argue that private health-insurance markets simply don't work and ought to be replaced by all-public coverage.

The Clinton Plan

In 1993 and 1994, when Bill and Hillary Clinton, now Secretary of State, proposed their health-care overhaul plan, Congress came as close as it ever has to debating a full-fledged health overhaul. The times seemed to favor action. When the Clintons' Health Security Act was proposed, up to two-thirds of Americans told pollsters they favored tax-financed national health insurance.

The Clinton proposal attempted to thread the needle of the hybrid U.S. system by maintaining large public-coverage programs while creating new, tightly regulated private-insurance markets where people could buy coverage that was tax subsidized for low-income people. In an attempt to hold onto the private business dollars that had long financed health care in the United States for workers, the plan would have required all employers to contribute to the cost.

But the proposal's complexity helped make the plan an easy target for political opponents and businesses and health-care insurers and providers who feared its complicated rules and high costs. Less than a year after the proposal was announced, Congress informed the White House that it had no plans to move the plan forward.

"The failure of the Clinton health plan . . . vividly demonstrates . . . that most Americans — even the underinsured and the soon-to-be-uninsured, the potentially uninsurable and the one-illness-from-bankruptcy — can be scared into fearing that changing America's inadequate public-private patchwork means higher costs and lower quality," Yale's Hacker wrote. "This is the legacy of an insurance structure that lulls many into believing they are secure when they are not, that hides vast costs in quiet deductions from workers' pay, [and] that leaves government paying the tab for the most vulnerable and the least well," he said. "It is the very failings of our insurance system that make dealing with those failings so devilishly hard."[35]

But many conservatives continue to argue that too-strict government regulation of health care along with insurance and public programs like Medicare are the culprits that have hopelessly damaged the health-care market and made effective overhaul difficult.

"The problems in American health care have not been caused by a failure in the health care market, but mainly by distortions imposed on the market," such as "federal tax subsidies and programs that have created a third-party payment system," said Rep. Paul Ryan, R-Wis. The key to a successful overhaul is to convert to an all-private system, by means such as creating "a standard Medicare

Reforms Face Many Hurdles

"The war to make health-care reform an enduring success has just begun."

As the health-reform law is implemented, the number of things that can go wrong is as big as the health-care system is complicated. Besides the fact that not only states but also doctors and hospitals may balk at the new provisions, future Congresses must ante up continued funding to administer the law, never a certain outcome.

The law's coverage-expansion portions "are so state-based that the states can stymie a lot," says Judith Solomon, a senior fellow at the left-leaning Center on Budget and Policy Priorities. "There can be a great deal of stalling" on getting some initiatives like a large Medicaid expansion up and running. The law also will largely rely on increased state regulation of health insurers, which could lead to large variations" around the country in how tightly insurers are held to consumer-friendly standards.

Furthermore, "Medicaid rolls in some states will expand by 50 percent or more" beginning in 2014, and "it is unclear whether these states will be able to find enough providers who are willing to accept the anticipated payment rates," wrote Henry J. Aaron, a senior fellow at the centrist Brookings Institution think tank, and Robert D. Reischauer, president of the centrist Urban Institute. Will states "raise provider payment rates, curtail Medicaid benefits (as states are legally authorized to do), or simply let patients fail to find doctors who are willing to provide them with care?" they ask.[1]

One of the balancing acts that face lawmakers seeking to expand coverage in the employer-based U.S. system is keeping enough employer money in the game to avoid overwhelming taxpayers with new costs. Accordingly, the law was developed in hopes of limiting incentives for employers to drop workers' coverage.

But already "there are some troubling signs that employers will back off coverage because of the existence of the exchanges," where workers can buy insurance — using tax-funded subsidies — if their employers don't offer it, says Yale University professor of political science Jacob Hacker. If that happens on a large scale, "for society as a whole it might be a better thing and more fair, because having employers as the basis for coverage distorts labor markets" because the fear of losing health insurance often traps people in jobs or careers they don't want, Hacker says. "Nevertheless, it's not a direction that most people want to go in."

Federal agencies must transform the law's rather general language into specific rules, and some observers say that might produce rules that are unworkable. Moreover, there's evidence that the agencies are already falling behind in the process.

"They're not going to meet their deadlines, so they should push the whole thing back," says Joseph Antos, a scholar at the free-market American Enterprise Institute think tank and a former assistant director of the

[cash] payment to be used for the purchase of private health coverage," he said.[36]

Massachusetts Plan

Over the years, many states have attempted to enact systemwide reforms on their own, frustrated by the federal government's reluctance even to discuss universal health care. The pioneers of sweeping reform included Tennessee, Oregon, Washington, Vermont and Minnesota.

Those states generally attempted to expand public coverage for the poorest residents and provide some form of tax-funded subsidies to help other low- to middle-income and sick people purchase coverage in more tightly regulated private insurance markets. But while the programs

have increased coverage, at least temporarily, all have eventually foundered as costs continued rising while taxpayer willingness to fund coverage for sick or lower-income people waned.

Massachusetts first began expanding coverage to all its citizens in 1988 and enacted its latest plan in 2006. The law shifted Medicaid funding to provide more subsidies to individuals to get insurance; placed requirements to buy or help pay for coverage on both employers and individuals; and set up a statewide regulated insurance market — known as an insurance "Connector" — which state officials hoped would force insurers to compete for enrollees based on quality and price of benefits.[37]

Reactions to Massachusetts' latest initiative are mixed.

Congressional Budget Office. "It's going to take more than the three years" the law has set aside to get the massive coverage-expansion program up and running.

Already there's evidence that agencies like the Centers for Medicare and Medicaid Services (CMS) are overwhelmed, Antos says. Neither CMS nor the Department of Health and Human Services (HHS) "is an insurance company" or has much experience in insurance, a serious lack since a massive insurance expansion is a central portion of the law, and Congress has relied on the agencies to flesh out virtually all the details, Antos says. HHS Secretary Kathleen Sebelius is a former Kansas insurance commissioner, "but she admitted that she doesn't have any particular influence in health-care reform."

Drafters of the law made little use of the expertise of the insurance industry and insurance analysts and regulators, "so there will be mistakes" in implementation, charges Antos. "It was done without consultation with the many, many experts, and HHS looks as if it's not going to ask experts now."

But Hacker says it's "too soon to be that critical of the implementation." The critical judgments will be made in the next year or so, when it will be possible to begin judging whether implementation will be smooth, he says. And while rules for how much premium revenue must fund health care "are inevitably going to be contentious, I don't believe it'll preclude insurers from participating," says Hacker. "The fact is that insurers were supportive of these things because they want the revenue" that will accompany expanded, subsidized coverage.

Nevertheless, "there's such a long time before the law goes fully into effect that critics can paint it any way they want," making it very easy for opponents to turn the public against the law, says Hacker. "The best thing advocates could do for themselves is not to trumpet their achievements but to make clear that the law is a first step."

In another setback to implementation, Senate Republicans are blocking the nomination of physician Donald Berwick, a professor of health policy and management at the Harvard School of Public Health, to head CMS. Conservatives say that Berwick's work with Britain's National Health Service is a sign he would use government to destroy American physicians' independence. Supporters argue that, to advance the health-reform law's cost-cutting initiatives, CMS must have a leader dedicated to emphasizing effectiveness and efficiency in U.S. medical practice.[2]

"The war to make health-care reform an enduring success has just begun" and "will require administrative determination and imagination and as much political resolve as was needed to pass the legislation," Aaron and Reischauer warn.[3]

— *Marcia Clemmitt*

---

[1] Henry J. Aaron and Robert D. Reischauer, "The War Isn't Over," *The New England Journal of Medicine online*, March 24, 2010, www.nejm .org.

[2] For background, see Linda Bergthold, "Who Is Don Berwick and Why Do the Republicans Want to Kill His Nomination," *Huffington Post blog*, June 1, 2010, www.huffingtonpost.com/linda-bergthold/ who-is-don-berwick-and-wh_b_596859.html.

[3] Aaron and Reischauer, *op. cit.*

Costs are the big challenge, and it's not yet clear how state attempts to change the medical culture to favor efficiency over excess services and high price tags are working, says Chernew, of Harvard Medical School. "Some say that the culture in the state is changing, but others say we're on the verge of collapse."

People using the Connector to buy insurance "have had lots of different choices of health plans, and there's been good consumer service and information," says the Urban Institute's Dorn.

Furthermore, "they've been good at negotiating for low premiums" with insurers, he says. For example, Massachusetts has several extremely expensive hospital systems, which have had enormous clout in winning high payment from insurers over the years because patients want access to them, Dorn explains. But the Connector set up price competition by establishing a low-cost coverage option that didn't include the big-name systems, and consumers concerned with price, such as young people earning lower wages, have signed up for it, he says.

The state also has rewarded health insurers who keep premiums low by enrolling the most "default" enrollees — people who don't seek out the health coverage on their own — with the insurer who quotes the lowest premium. Default enrollees are often the healthiest, cheapest-to-cover people, thus helping that insurer hold down costs by having an extra helping of healthy people in their pool, Dorn says.

Advocates of single-payer systems, however, say Massachusetts' attempt at health-care expansion is doomed, just like earlier attempts. "Unfortunately, competition in health insurance involves a race to the bottom," said Harvard Medical School's Woolhandler. "Insurers compete by not paying for care: by denying payment and shifting costs onto patients or other payers."[38]

CURRENT SITUATION

Democrats in Power

With Democrats holding not only the White House but also substantial majorities in both the House and the Senate for the first time in three decades, advocates of health-care reform hoped that the 111th Congress — whose term runs from 2009 through 2010 — would finally be the one to debate a health-care overhaul for the entire population.

In his first address to a joint session of Congress, on Feb. 24, 2009, newly inaugurated President Barack Obama declared that "we must . . . address the crushing cost of health care" and thus "can no longer afford to put health-care reform on hold." High-cost health care "now causes a bankruptcy in America every thirty seconds. . . . In the last eight years, [health-insurance] premiums have grown four times faster than wages. And in each of these years, 1 million more Americans have lost their health insurance."[39]

Furthermore, he said, "already, we have done more to advance the cause of health-care reform in the last 30 days than we have in the last decade." For example, "when it was days old, this Congress passed a law to provide and protect health insurance for 11 million American children whose parents work full time" by using a cigarette tax to expand funding for the public-sector SCHIP program that covers children in working families, he said.[40]

"I suffer no illusions that this will be an easy process," said Obama. "But I . . . know that nearly a century after Teddy Roosevelt first called for reform, the cost of our health care has weighed down our economy and the conscience of our nation long enough. . . . Health-care reform cannot wait, it must not wait, and it will not wait another year."[41]

In the House, the legislation waited nearly 10 months, passing on a 220-215 vote on Saturday evening, Nov. 7,

2009, with one Republican voting in favor and 39 Democrats opposed.[42]

In the Senate, however, where the minority party wields much more power, debate dragged on into spring 2010, with the measure all but given up for dead on several occasions. Republican senators repeatedly threatened to filibuster — hold the floor without allowing the health-care legislation to come to a vote — forcing Senate leaders to muster 60-vote majorities five times to move the bill forward.

On Dec. 24, 2009, by a 60-39 margin, Senate Democrats finally passed their version of the legislation with no Republican votes. The Senate and House bills varied considerably, however, and, in such a case, both houses of Congress must — one way or another — pass identical bills before they can become law.

Thus, the cliffhanger continued for an additional three months as Democrats struggled to piece together a reform package that could win all the needed conservative Democratic votes in the Senate while retaining liberal support in the House. In addition, by 2010, Democrats' previous 60-vote, filibuster-stymieing Senate majority was reduced to 59 votes, as Sen. Scott Brown, R-Mass., was seated as the elected replacement of the late Sen. Edward M. Kennedy, D-Mass. — longtime ardent champion of health-care reform — who died of brain cancer on Aug. 26, 2009.

Ultimately, using several parliamentary maneuvers, Senate Majority Leader Harry Reid, D-Nev., and Speaker of the House Nancy Pelosi, D-Calif., engineered passage of a bill acceptable to Democrats in both houses. On March 21, the House passed the Senate's version of the bill. Then, under a process called "reconciliation," first the Senate and then the House passed a package of changes to the Senate legislation to make it acceptable to the generally more liberal House Democratic majority. Reconciliation bills — which are permitted to include only provisions that relate to the federal budget — may not be filibustered and thus require only a 51-vote majority in the Senate to pass.[43]

"Part of Obama's frustration" over health care "is that he thought that in the end some Republicans would approve" the legislation, "which is not as radical as the overhaul that Nixon proposed" in the early 1970s, says Bryan D. Jones, a professor of congressional studies at the University of Texas, in Austin.

Does Health Reform Create Winners and Losers?

More affordable coverage for sicker people will boost costs for healthier people.

Critics charge that the health-care reform plan makes some Americans winners and others losers. Some liberal critics charge that, by relying on private insurance for much of the tax-subsidized coverage expansion, Congress will essentially just direct more taxpayer dollars into the already bloated coffers of the insurance industry.

Other analysts aren't so sure, however.

Many of the people who will enroll in tax-subsidized coverage will not have had consistent insurance coverage for several years, and as a result often have developed significant health needs that will drive their spending up, said Maggie Mahar, a fellow at the liberal, New York City-based Century Foundation.[1]

According to recent analyses, around 11 percent of uninsured people are in "fair" or "poor" health, compared to only 5 percent of privately insured people who report poor health. Unlike in the past, "under the new reform law, insurance companies will not be able to charge these new customers more than they charge others in their community," said Mahar. This means that insurers are unlikely to reap a big windfall from the tax-funded subsidies, she argued.[2]

The same legislative provision that Mahar cites as making coverage more affordable for sicker people will cause health premiums to rise for younger, healthier people, however — an example of the way the law creates some winners and losers in the attempt to get more people covered, noted Trudy Lieberman, a longtime health-care journalist who is a contributing editor to the *Columbia Journalism Review.*[3]

"This is not national health insurance we're talking about, where everyone, no matter how old or young, is treated equally," Lieberman wrote. "We are talking about a private insurance market where companies have to make money to stay in business" and where one key way of making money in the past has been for companies to simply avoid insuring the sickest people so that healthier people can pay lower premiums.

Under the new law, however, insurance companies will be "required to take sick people who will file large claims" and also will be banned from charging them the extremely high premiums that they are liable for in the individual insurance market today, she said. Instead, older or sicker

people will be on the hook for premiums that are "no more than three times what [insurers] charge a younger person," and as a result premiums for younger, healthier people will rise by an estimated 15 to 17 percent. Insurers "have to make up the revenue shortfall somehow, and they'll do it by increasing the premiums for younger people. It's a balancing act Congress has permitted," she wrote. However, for young adults earning $43,000 per year or less, some of the premium increase will be offset by a federal tax credit.

In another financial balancing act, lawmakers had to determine whether to offer larger taxpayer-funded subsidies to a smaller population of people — with lower incomes — or spread out the subsidies to a larger population. More subsidies might make the law more politically popular but also would require making subsidies for the lowest-income people smaller than they might have been otherwise. Some analysts fear that lawmakers came down on the wrong side of that question.

"One big worry that I have is affordability," says Stan Dorn, a senior research associate at the Urban Institute think tank. In the 2006 coverage expansion launched in Massachusetts, the state provided "much bigger subsidies" and "much more extensive coverage" to people with incomes up to 300 percent of the federal poverty level — the group most in danger of being priced out of coverage, says Dorn. (In 2009, for example, a family of four earning about $66,000 had an income 300 percent of the poverty level.)

But the federal law took a different tack, offering smaller subsidies for every income group — including the lowest — in order to provide some level of subsidy for people with incomes up to 400 percent of the poverty level, he says. "It would have been better to concentrate more on the people up to 300 percent of the poverty level rather than spread the subsidies so far."

— Marcia Clemmitt

[1] Maggie Mahar, "Myths & Facts About HealthCare Reform: Who Wins & Who Loses?" *Healthbeat* blog, April 6, 2010, www.healthbeat-blog.com.

[2] *Ibid.*

[3] Trudy Lieberman, "The White House vs. the Associated Press," *Columbia Journalism Review online*, April 7, 2010, www.cjr.org.

Will the health-care reform law harm the federal budget?

YES
Grace-Marie Turner
President, Galen Institute

Written for *CQ Researcher*, May 2010

President Obama's health overhaul law will have a devastating impact on the federal budget, both because of what it does and what it fails to do.

It does increase federal health spending, creates expensive open-ended entitlements and uses budget gimmicks to hide the true costs of the massive expansion of federal spending.

And it fails to lower health costs, bend the cost curve down or provide real solutions to the trillions of dollars in red ink facing existing entitlement programs, especially Medicare and Medicaid.

Nonetheless, to win passage of the health law, supporters insisted the law would be fiscally responsible and would reduce the deficit. Not a chance.

The Congressional Budget Office (CBO) recently said the law will cost $115 billion more than originally estimated, pushing the total cost above $1 trillion. But this underestimates the true costs by hundreds of billions — if not trillions of dollars — due to the law's deception and budget gimmicks.

Part of the true cost was concealed by delaying expensive subsidies until 2014 while starting many of the tax hikes and Medicare cuts much earlier. Further, the law is purportedly paid for with $569 billion in tax increases and $528 billion in cuts to Medicare. But these Medicare cuts are highly suspect given Congress' history of pushing them off to keep doctor payments level — and keep physicians in the Medicare program. Keeping payments just at current rates will cost $276 billion over 10 years, according to the CBO.

When these and other costs are included, the more accurate price tag for ObamaCare is $2.5 trillion over a decade.

Rather than helping contain escalating health spending, as promised, ObamaCare pushes it higher. Medicare's chief actuary, Rick Foster, says federal health spending will rise by $311 billion by 2019 thanks to the law.

And this estimate doesn't include tens of millions more people who could lose their health insurance at work. The law threatens employers with big fines and subjects them to unpredictable health insurance cost increases; many are considering dropping coverage. If they do, millions more workers would be dumped onto health exchanges where they'll be subsidized by taxpayers. If this happens, federal spending will explode.

Gimmicks, new entitlements and unrealistic assumptions are just some of the many ingredients in ObamaCare that will have a crippling impact on the federal budget. We simply can't afford this law.

NO
Paul N. Van de Water
Senior Fellow, Center on Budget and Policy Priorities

Written for *CQ Researcher*, May 2010

The Congressional Budget Office (CBO) estimates that the new health reform law will reduce deficits by $143 billion over the first decade (2010-2019) and by about one-half of 1 percent of gross domestic product, or about $1.3 trillion, over the second decade (2020-2029).

The law will extend coverage to over 30 million uninsured Americans and provide important consumer protections to tens of millions of insured Americans whose coverage may have critical gaps. It will more than pay for these improvements by making specific reductions in Medicare, Medicaid and other programs and by increasing tax revenues (such as by raising the Medicare tax on high-income people).

Despite CBO's finding that the law will reduce deficits, some people have argued that it will actually increase deficits, claiming that CBO's cost estimate includes savings that won't occur, omits costs that should be included, or both. Those claims don't withstand scrutiny (see "Health Reform Will Reduce the Deficit," www.cbpp.org/files/3-25-10health.pdf).

For example, some claim that the law's Medicare savings are unrealistic because Congress never lets Medicare reductions take effect. History shows this is untrue. Over the past 20 years Congress has enacted four pieces of legislation that include significant Medicare savings; virtually all of the savings in three of them (the 1990, 1993 and 2005 budget reconciliation bills) took effect, as did nearly four-fifths of the savings in the fourth piece of legislation (the Balanced Budget Act of 1997).

Some contend that the health-reform law should include the cost of permanently fixing Medicare's sustainable growth rate (SGR) formula for setting physician payments. The poorly designed formula turned out to require much larger cuts in physician payments than Congress intended when it enacted SGR, so Congress has regularly acted in recent years to prevent the full SGR cuts from taking effect. But the SGR cost is in no way a result of health reform — the government will incur this cost regardless of health reform, not because of it.

Because rising health-care costs represent the single largest cause of the federal government's long-term budget problems, fundamental health reform is key to their solution. Experts agree that slowing the growth of health-care costs will require an ongoing process of testing, experimentation and rapid implementation of what is found to work. The health-reform law begins that process. It starts to transform a system that delivers ever more services into one that provides effective, high-value health care.

The new law is "a much more conservative policy than was considered in the past," says the Urban Institute's Dorn. For example, in the Clinton plan, "we were going to leave behind our employer-based coverage, and there would have been a uniform benefit standard" for all health insurance. The Clinton proposal also included "explicit regulation of insurance premiums" to prevent them from rising too high and largely dictated what insurance benefit packages could contain, says Dorn. "This bill doesn't have any of that."

In fact, many Democrats liken the bill to the 2006 Massachusetts plan, passed by a Democrat-dominated legislature and signed into law by then-Gov. Mitt Romney, a Republican.

"A lot of commentators have said . . . this is sort of similar to the bill that Mitt Romney . . . passed in Massachusetts," said Obama.[44]

Many conservatives, including Romney, heatedly deny that the Massachusetts plan has much in common with the 2010 federal law, however.

"We don't like . . . the intrusion of the federal government on the rights of states" in the federal law, which requires states to participate in health-coverage expansions, nor the taxes the law will raise to pay for coverage, said Romney.[45]

Implementing the Law

Perhaps the biggest difference the law will make for most people is that, beginning in 2014, it will provide a new, regulated insurance marketplace. People who cannot get employer-sponsored coverage can shop for health insurance at the so-called state exchanges. The law also will provide many people with subsidies to help pay for that coverage.[46]

Also in 2014, people with incomes up to 133 percent of the federal poverty level can get Medicaid coverage, paid for mostly by the federal government. Currently, only certain groups of people, mainly poor mothers and their young children and some severely disabled poor people, are eligible for Medicaid.

Health insurers will face a very different set of rules and expectations in the new system, says Georgetown University's Feder. Today U.S. health insurers compete for profits largely based on "risk selection" — trying to be the insurer whose benefit packages attract the healthiest people, because money that doesn't go to medical care can

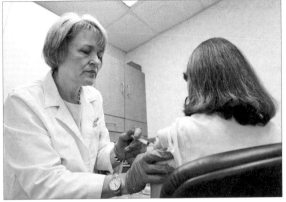

Bloomberg via Getty Images/Steve Hockstein

Nurse practitioner Kathryn Quinn administers a flu shot at a clinic in a CVS store in Wyckoff, N.J. Proponents of the health-reform law say using nurse practitioners for more tasks often performed by physicians will help keep health-care costs down.

go to profits. While the law "doesn't stamp out risk selection, it sure as hell treads on it," she continues, mainly because, ultimately, it will require insurers to take all comers and will also require that a certain minimum percentage of premiums go towards medical care, she explains.

Many of the law's provisions aimed at cost containment involve "putting new [health-care-delivery and payment] arrangements in place and getting providers into them," says Feder. Under the new arrangements, providers like doctors and hospitals "would retain earnings if they're efficient and deliver high-quality care rather than delivering a high volume of care," as occurs under current systems, she says.

"It's going to take a lot of money and new resources for Medicare to implement and implement quickly" the law's many new programs, says former Medicare and Medicaid chief McClellan. "It normally takes seven to 10 years" for a good idea to actually become part of the Medicare program. "But we don't have that kind of time."

Furthermore, there's the fear that, as in the past when Medicare has proven that certain techniques for saving money worked, Congress may block nationwide rollout of the methods, because of providers who worry they'll lose money, McClellan says.

"The risk is not that the bill is repealed but that pieces of it" won't be supported by future Congresses, says

Robert Blendon, a professor of health policy at the Harvard School of Public Health. For example, a Republican Congress that opposes taxes may cut funding for federal subsidies that are required to help people afford insurance, he says.

Meanwhile, congressional Democrats are mulling additional changes they say may be needed to improve the health-care system for patients, such as tightening government oversight of health-insurance premium price increases.[47]

Fighting the Law

Conservatives continue to argue that the law involves government too much in health care.

"The new law requires all Americans to purchase health insurance or pay a penalty . . . an unprecedented extension of congressional power," wrote the Heritage Foundation's Nix. Furthermore, she said, "the health-care overhaul . . . diminishes the federalist system upon which the U.S. was founded, which grants certain powers to the states in order to limit those of the federal government." The law requires that states expand their Medicaid programs, whether or not they want to, and also includes new federal regulations on health insurers, which have been largely state regulated, Nix said.[48]

One of the most prominent initiatives to halt the law is a lawsuit now backed by 20 states and the National Federation of Independent Business.

"After all the political deals were made, small businesses were left with a law that does little to address costs and instead is filled with new mandates, taxes and paperwork requirements that increase the cost of doing business," said Karen Harned, head of the federation's legal office.[49]

The Obama administration has already filed a brief in federal district court in Detroit in one of the earliest lawsuits against the law. The suit was filed by the Thomas More Law Center, a conservative legal group in Ann Arbor, which argues that the law's individual mandate to buy health insurance violates constitutionally protected freedoms.

The administration argues that decisions to opt out of health insurance are more than personal choices but have consequences for the entire country — thus making them suitable targets of federal lawmaking. The administration's brief argues that when uninsured people get sick, people who have been paying insurance, as well as taxpayers, pick up the bill for their care. Thus, "individual decisions to forgo insurance coverage, in the aggregate, substantially affect interstate commerce by shifting costs to health-care providers and the public," making them a fair target for federal legislation under the Commerce Clause.[50]

Ironically, former Gov. Romney — who signed Massachusetts' health-reform law — is among opponents who've called most loudly for stopping the new federal law. Rather than seeking judicial repeal, however, Romney this spring urged voters to support Republican candidates to win back a congressional majority in November. Then "we can clamp down on this bill . . . by not funding it," he said.[51]

OUTLOOK
Dealing with Rationing

Supporters argue that as people learn more about the new law, most will back it. However, expanding taxpayers' responsibility to help provide health coverage for most Americans will ultimately require wrestling with the toughest question: As costs rise, how should taxpayer-supported health benefits be limited — or rationed?

"As people come to understand the basic approach" of the new law, "they'll like most of it," says the Urban Institute's Dorn. Many already support "providing more help for people who can't afford insurance, requiring employers to help and setting up new rules that help people buy" insurance in a more transparent, regulated marketplace, he says.

"Once the law is implemented, people won't have to worry that, 'Oh, if I get laid off, I'll lose coverage for my asthmatic daughter' " because they will be able to buy subsidized coverage elsewhere, he says.

But single-payer advocate Woolhandler of Harvard says the new law will only temporarily slow momentum for much larger reform "because we didn't really solve anything. The cost curve was absolutely not fixed" by the legislation, "so a lot of middle-class people" will eventually find their coverage threatened again. "Very quickly people are going to see that nothing is solved."

With a program in place to ensure basic health coverage to most Americans, the next debate will be about "rationing" care, says Baicker of the Harvard

School of Public Health. As the number of available health services — and their price tags — increases, "public programs, at least, almost certainly won't be able to pay for anything that has any benefit at all," but, eventually, "will need to have a higher threshold" — paying only for things that have a certain level of benefit — to avoid having health costs squeeze out all other government spending, she says.

Merely broaching the conversation — let alone reaching conclusions about what care to fund — will be extremely difficult, Baicker says.

Currently, our system rations care by pricing some people out of care altogether, except for emergencies treated in the emergency room, says University of Pennsylvania ethicist Caplan.

Because lawmakers "avoided any discussion of rationing" in the recent debate, the public is running around with the delusion that we don't ration now," Caplan says. "But the discussion we need to have should start now, because the public will need many years to accept" the notion of health spending limits, he says.

NOTES

1. Quoted in Scott Wilson, "With a Signature, Obama Seals His Health-care Victory," *The Washington Post*, March 24, 2010, p. A1.

2. Steven Thomma and David Lightman, "Obama Signs Health-care Bill, but GOP Protests Continue," McClatchy Newspapers/*Miami Herald*, March 23, 2010, www.miamiherald.com/2010/03/23/1543254/obama-signs-health-care-legislation.html.

3. Arthur L. Caplan, "Right to Reform," *The Journal of Clinical Investigation*, October 2009, p. 2862, www.jci.org.

4. Quoted in Michael Sweeney, "Hatch Attacks Individual Mandate He Previously Supported," *TPM LiveWire*, *Talking Points Memo* blog, March 26, 2010, http://tpmlivewire.talkingpointsmemo.com.

5. Quoted in "Health Care Reform: Not Ready to Be Discharged Yet," *Knowledge at Wharton* newsletter, March 31, 2010, http://knowledge.wharton.upenn.edu/article.cfm?articleid=2457.

6. Kathryn Nix, "Top 10 Disasters of Obamacare," Web Memo, The Heritage Foundation, March 30, 2010, www.heritage.org.

7. Sally C. Pipes, "Obamacare Wins: Now the Pain Begins," *New York Post*, March 22, 2010, www.nypost.com.

8. Robert E. Moffit, *Obamacare: Impact on Doctors*, WebMemo No. 2895, The Heritage Foundation, May 11, 2010, www.heritage.org.

9. Jane Hamsher, "Fact Sheet: The Truth About the Health Care Bill," *Firedoglake* blog, March 19, 2010, http://fdlaction.firedoglake.com.

10. Ian Millhiser, "If at First You Don't Succeed, Hope for Activist Judges," Center for American Progress website, March 23, 2010, www.americanprogress.org; for background, see *Gonzales v. Raich*, 545 U.S. 1 (2005), www.law.cornell.edu/supct/html/03-1454.ZS.html.

11. Simon Lazarus, "Mandatory Health Insurance: Is It Constitutional?" Issue Brief, American Constitution Society, December 2009, www.acslaw.org/node/15654; for background, see *United States v. Southeastern Underwriters Association*, 322 U.S. 533 (1944), http://supreme.justia.com/us/322/533/.

12. *Ibid.*

13. "President Barack Obama State of the Union Address, Feb. 24, 2009," About.com: US Politics website, http://uspolitics.about.com/od/speeches/l/bl_feb2009_obama_SOTU.htm.

14. Jill Bernstein, Deborah Chollet and Stephanie Peterson, "How Does Insurance Coverage Improve Health Outcomes?" Issue Brief, Mathematica Policy Research, April 2010, www.mathematica-mpr.com.

15. *Ibid.*

16. John Berlau, "Health Care: Fix Middle-Class 'Medicine Cabinet Tax' in Reconciliation," Competitive Enterprise Institute, March 23, 2010, www.cei.org.

17. Grace-Marie Turner, "Foster's Report Validates Fears," *National Journal Expert Blogs*, May 3, 2010, http://healthcare.nationaljournal.com.

18. Quoted in "True or False? Top Seven Health Care Fears," msnbc.com/*Kaiser Health News*, April 2, 2010, www.msnbc.com.

19. "Flaws of Health-care Overhaul Grow More Apparent Every Day," *Columbus* [Ohio] *Dispatch*, April 29, 2010.

20. Maggie Mahar, "Myths & Facts About HealthCare Reform: The Impact on Hospitals, and Patients Who Need Hospital Care — Part 3," *Healthbeat* blog, April 21, 2010, www.healthbeatblog.com.

21. Quoted in *ibid*.

22. Mahar, *op. cit*.

23. Stuart Guterman, Karen Davis, and Kristof Stremikis, "How Health Reform Legislation Will Affect Medicare Beneficiaries," The Commonwealth Fund, March 2010, www.cmwf.org.

24. "Rate Review: Holding Health Plans Accountable for Your Premium Dollars," Families USA Issue Brief, April 2010, www.familiesusa.org.

25. Maggie Mahar, "Myths & Facts About HealthCare Reform: Who Wins and Who Loses?" *Healthbeat* blog, April 6, 2010, www.healthbeatblog.com.

26. David B. Kendall, "A Foundation for Cost Control," *National Journal* blogs, March 22, 2010, http://healthcare.nationaljournal.com.

27. "In Search of a Fiscal Cure," *Newsweek*, May 10, 2010, p. 12.

28. David M. Cutler, "Time to Prove the Skeptics Wrong on Health Reform," Center for American Progress, April 23 ,2010, www.americanprogress.org.

29. Richard S. Foster, "Estimated Financial Effects of the 'Patient Protection and Affordable Care Act' as Amended," Office of the Actuary, Centers for Medicare and Medicaid Services, April 22, 2010.

30. Quoted in "Health Care Reform: Not Ready to Be Discharged Yet," *op. cit.*

31. John Goodman, "The Most Important Feature of ObamaCare Is Something No One Is Talking About," John Goodman's blog, March 29, 2010, www.john-goodman-blog.com.

32. Testimony before Senate Committee on Health, Education, Labor and Pensions, April 20, 2010.

33. Jon Walker, "Former Obama Aide David Cutler Ignores Proven Cost Control ideas to Inflate Grade on President's Health Care Plan," *Firedoglake* blog, March 10, 2010, http://fdlaction.firedoglake.com.

34. For background, see the following *CQ Researcher* reports by Marcia Clemmitt, "Rising Health Costs," April 7, 2006, pp. 289-312; "Universal Coverage," March 30, 2007, pp. 265-288; and "Health Care Reform," Aug. 28, 2009, pp. 693-716.

35. Jacob S. Hacker, "Yes We Can? The New Push for American Health Security," *Politics & Society*, March 2009, p. 14.

36. Paul Ryan, "A Roadmap for America's Future: Description of the Legislation," House Budget Committee Republican website, www.roadmap.republicans.budget.house.gov.

37. For background, see John E. McDonough, Brian Rosman, Fawn Phelps and Melissa Shannon, "The Third Wave of Massachusetts Health Care Access Reform," *Health Affairs online*, Sept. 14, 2006, http://content.healthaffairs.org/cgi/content/full/25/6/w420.

38. Testimony before House Energy and Commerce Subcommittee on Health, June 24, 2009, www.pnhp.org/news/2009/june/testimony_of_steffie.php.

39. "President Barack Obama State of the Union Address, Feb. 24, 2009," About.com: US Politics website, http://uspolitics.about.com/od/speeches/l/bl_feb2009_obama_SOTU.htm.

40. For background see Ceci Connolly, "Senate Passes Health Insurance Bill for Children," *The Washington Post*, Jan. 30, 2009, p. A1, www.washingtonpost.com/wp-dyn/content/article/2009/01/29/AR2009012900325.html.

41. "President Barack Obama State of the Union Address, Feb. 24, 2009," *op. cit.*

42. For background see "House Passes Health Care Reform Bill," CNN.com, Nov. 8, 2009, www.cnn.com/2009/POLITICS/11/07/health.care.

43. For background see Timothy Noah, "Health Reform: An Online Guide," *Slate*, April 12, 2010, www.slate.com.

44. Quoted in Eric Kleefeld, "Romney Spokesman: 'Romney Plan' Is Not Like Obama's Health Care Reform, Despite What Obama Says," *Talking Points Memo* blog, March 31, 2010, http://tpmdc.talking-pointsmemo.com.

45. Quoted in Andrew Romano, "Mitt Romney on RomneyCare," *Newsweek online*, April 19, 2010, www.newsweek.com.

46. For background see "Side-by-Side Comparisons of Major Health Care Reform Proposals," Focus on Health Reform website, Kaiser Family Foundation, April 8, 2010, www.kff.org/healthreform/sidebyside.cfm.

47. For background see "Senate Democrats Seek Legislation to Regulate Insurer Rate Hikes," *Kaiser Health News* website, April 21, 2010, www.kaiser-healthnews.org/daily-reports/2010/april/21/insurers.aspx?referrer=search.

48. Nix, *op. cit.*

49. Quoted in Tom Brown, "States Joined in Suit Against Healthcare Reform," Reuters, May 14, 2010, www.reuters.com.

50. Quoted in Ricardo Alonso-Zaldivar, "U.S. Files First Defense of Health Care Law in Court," The Associated Press, May 12, 2010, http://news.yahoo.com/s/ap/20100512/ap_on_bi_ge/us_health_care_challenge.

51. Quoted in Jonathan Chait, "Could Republicans Repeal Health Care Reform?" *The New Republic online*, March 19, 2010, www.tnr.com.

BIBLIOGRAPHY

Books

Grater, David, *The Cure: How Capitalism Can Save American Health Care*, Encounter Books, 2008.
A psychiatrist who has practiced in the United States and Canada makes the conservative case for reforming the health care system by ending government regulation and third-party payment through insurance and instead having consumers pay directly for care.

Hacker, Jacob S., ed., *Health at Risk: America's Ailing System — and How to Heal It*, Columbia University Press, 2008.
A Yale University professor of political science who was chief architect of the proposal — eventually abandoned by Congress — to include a public, government-run insurance plan to compete with private insurers, assembles essays by health-policy scholars on topics including the state of health-care quality.

Reid, T. R., *The Healing of America: A Global Quest for Better, Cheaper, and Fairer Health Care*, Penguin Press, 2009.
A former foreign affairs correspondent for *The Washington Post* reports his impressions of a round-the-world tour to explore health care systems.

Articles

Cohn, Jonathan, "How They Did It," *The New Republic*, June 10, 2010, www.tnr.com, p. 14.
In the early days of his administration, President Obama switched from opposition to support of an individual mandate to buy insurance.

Meyer, Harris, "Group Health's Move to the Medical Home: For Doctors, It's Often a Hard Journey," *Health Affairs*, May 2010, p. 844.
At a private health plan that's trying to reengineer medical practice to favor primary and preventive care, as the new health-reform law seeks to do nationally, many physicians balk at the change.

Milligan, Susan, "GOP Targets Nominee to Run Health Agency," *Boston Globe*, May 13, 2010, www.boston.com, p. 1.
In a move that could hamper implementation of the health-reform law, congressional Republicans have been blocking President Obama's nomination of Donald Berwick, a Massachusetts pediatrician, to head the Centers for Medicare and Medicaid Services, on the grounds that Berwick believes that cost controls and pay-for-performance are required.

Ostrom, Carol M., "Health-care Law Will Alter High-Risk Pool, but Just How Hasn't Been Worked Out," *Seattle Times*, April 18, 2010, p. A1.
Under the new health-care reform law, states and the federal government starting this summer will set up temporary programs to help people with serious illnesses obtain affordable coverage. In 2014, private insurers will be required to enroll people regardless of health status. Currently, 35 states already have such programs, and enrollees in those programs worry that Congress' legislative language may lock them out of the federal plan even though they might get more affordable coverage there.

Reichard, John, "After the Win, No Time to Lose," *CQ Weekly*, April 5, 2010, p. 814.
Federal health agencies face unprecedented challenges in developing rules for the huge, multifaceted health-reform law and making its multiple, complex programs work.

Reports and Studies

Butler, Stuart M., "Evolving Beyond Traditional Employer-Sponsored Health Insurance," The Hamilton Project, Brookings Institution, May 2007, www.brookings.edu/papers/2007/05healthcare_butler.aspx.
A health-policy scholar from the conservative Heritage Foundation, a Washington think tank, explains the legal, regulatory and business changes he believes would be required to create a stable health-insurance system based on conservative principles, as the current employer-based system crumbles.

Cauchy, Richard, "State Legislation Challenging Certain Health Reforms, 2010," National Conference of State Legislatures, May 2010, www.ncsl.org.
States and the federal government share a complex set of responsibilities for regulating health insurance and health care in the United States, which has often set some states at odds with the federal government. As federal health-reform legislation slowly moved through Congress over the past year, at least 39 state legislatures have proposed bills to limit, change or oppose certain federal actions on health care.

Lazarus, Simon, "Mandatory Health Insurance: Is It Constitutional?" American Constitution Society, December 2009, www.acslaw.org/node/15654.
A lawyer for the National Senior Citizens Law Center argues that contested provisions in the recently passed health-reform law, including the individual requirement to buy health insurance, are constitutional, based on longtime legal precedent.

For More Information

Alliance for Health Reform, 1444 I St., N.W., Suite 910, Washington, DC 20005-6573; (202) 789-2300; www.all-health.org. Nonpartisan group providing information on all facets of health coverage and access, including transcripts and videos of Capitol Hill briefings from experts with a wide spectrum of views on reform.

The Commonwealth Fund, One East 75th St., NY, NY 10021; (212) 606-3800; www.commonwealthfund.org. Private foundation that supports research on and advocates for universal access to affordable, high-quality health care.

The Heritage Foundation, 214 Massachusetts Ave., N.E., Washington, DC 20002-4999; (202) 546-4400; www.heritage.org. Public-policy think tank provides analysis of health reform and health care from a conservative viewpoint.

John Goodman's Health Policy Blog, National Center for Policy Analysis, 12770 Coit Rd., Suite 800, Dallas, TX 75251-1339; (972) 386-6272; www.john-goodman-blog.com. Conservative analyst who advocates for free-market policies provides daily commentary on health care and health reform.

Kaiser Health News, www.kaiserhealthnews.org. Foundation-funded, editorially independent nonprofit news group provides information on current events affecting health care.

National Conferences of State Legislatures, 444 North Capitol St., N.W., Suite 515, Washington, DC 20001; (202) 624-5400; www.ncsl.org. Nongovernmental group that tracks proposed state legislation related to health-care reform.

National Journal Expert Blogs: Health Care, http://healthcare.nationaljournal.com. Reporters from the political magazine and a wide variety of health-care experts and analysts provide commentary.

The White House Blog: Health Care, www.whitehouse.gov/blog/issues/Health-Care. Obama administration officials comment on implementation of the new law.